W9-ABW-750

NADINE COHODAS

STROM THURMOND

and the Politics of Southern Change

SIMON & SCHUSTER
New York London Toronto Sydney Tokyo Singapore

Simon & Schuster
Simon & Schuster Building
Rockefeller Center
1230 Avenue of the Americas
New York, New York 10020

Designed by Carla Weise/Levavi & Levavi
Manufactured in the United States of America

10 9 8 7 6 5 4 3 2 1

Library of Congress Cataloging-in-Publication Data
Cohodas, Nadine.
Strom Thurmond and the politics of Southern change / Nadine Cohodas.
p. cm.
Includes bibliographical references and index.
1. Thurmond, Strom, 1902- . 2. South Carolina—Politics and government—1865–1950. 3. South Carolina—Politics and government—1951- 4. South Carolina—Race relations. 5. Civil rights movements—South Carolina—History—20th century. 6. Southern States—Politics and government—1865–1950. 7. Southern States—Politics and government—1951- 8. Southern States—Race relations. 9. Civil rights movements—Southern States—History—20th century. 10. Legislators—United States—Biography. 11. United States. Congress. Senate—Biography. I. Title.
E748.T58C64 1993
975.7'04—dc20 92-32417
CIP

ISBN: 0-671-68935-5

To my mother and in memory of my father

Contents

	Preface	9
CHAPTER	1. Standing with the People	11
CHAPTER	2. The Legacy of Pitchfork Ben *1870–1928*	18
CHAPTER	3. On the Move *1929–1937*	37
CHAPTER	4. Insulation Against the Turmoil *1938–1946*	53
CHAPTER	5. Making Choices *1947*	93
CHAPTER	6. Irreversible Course *January 1948–June 1948*	126
CHAPTER	7. Candidate by Default *July 1948–December 1948*	154
CHAPTER	8. In the Shadow of the Court *1949–1953*	194
CHAPTER	9. The Year of Precedents *1954*	239
CHAPTER	10. Resistance and Resolve *1955–1960*	268
CHAPTER	11. Breakthrough *1961–1964*	315
CHAPTER	12. The Center Cannot Hold *1965–1970*	363

CHAPTER 13. Readjustment 414
1971–1979

CHAPTER 14. Back over the Rubicon: A Man Redeemed, a Life Remembered 454
1980–1992

Abbreviations Used in Source Notes 499
Notes 501
Bibliography 547
Acknowledgments 554
Index 557
Picture Credits 575

Preface

I FIRST LAID eyes on Strom Thurmond in the summer of 1979, when I went to cover a Senate Judiciary Committee meeting for Congressional Quarterly. All I knew about the senator from South Carolina—by then nearly seventy-seven years old—was that he was an "old seg," as a crusty southern newspaper editor called him, that he'd been in the Senate twenty-five years, and that at a rather advanced age he had married a very young woman and had four children.

By the end of 1982, after Thurmond had been chairman of the committee for two years, I was sure his career would make a great story having less to do with his personal vigor than his political durability. My conviction only deepened as I covered him over the next seven years, four of them while he was still chairman of the committee and another three while he was the committee's senior Republican.

The violence in Los Angeles in May of 1992 is a reminder that opening up our political institutions to minorities is not the same as providing some measure of equal opportunity to everyone. But making government more reflective of our pluralistic society is nonetheless an important step and one that required significant adjustment for politicians like Thurmond—white men from the South—who had once held all the power.

There were many moments between the summer of 1979 and March of 1989, when I started work on this book, that showed how this "old seg" had crossed the racial divide. One from 1988 served as both inspiration to me and an illustration of the story and the politician behind it.

In the summer of 1988, Congress had finally passed new fair-housing legislation. The original 1968 law, which Thurmond and every other Deep South senator opposed, was short on enforcement tools. The new proposal allowed the federal government to penalize those who discriminate in the sale or rental of housing. Twenty years removed from the initial fair-housing fight, Thurmond was now willing to support this new version. As he headed into the Senate for the final vote on the revisions, he saw Althea Simmons, the NAACP's chief Washington lobbyist, standing in an anteroom. He immediately went over to her, put his hand on her shoulder, and smiled as he told her, "I'm gonna vote with you."

Washington, D.C.
September 1992

1.
STANDING WITH THE PEOPLE

ON JUNE 18, 1982, a typically warm day in Washington, D.C., Strom Thurmond, the senior senator from South Carolina, officially left the Old South and arrived in the New.

The trip that afternoon was only a quarter-mile, but the journey had taken thirty-four years.

The senator had been to the floor of the United States Senate ten thousand times before to listen, to speak, and to vote, and as he made his way from his office in the stately Russell Building to the Capitol, nothing on the surface seemed out of the ordinary.

But when he entered the Senate chamber shortly before two and answered the roll call on passage of the 1982 Voting Rights Act, Thurmond made his own personal history. It was the first time in his long career that he had ever supported a civil rights bill, legislation that confirmed the federal government's role in protecting the freedom and opportunities bequeathed to all Americans by the United States Constitution. Thirty-four years earlier, on July 17, 1948, Thurmond had temporarily left the Democratic Party over civil rights to challenge Harry Truman for the presidency. On September 16, 1964, he left for good to help Barry

Goldwater's presidential campaign as the South's most prominent Republican. The party had been anathema to the region's voters for nearly a century, a reaction to the Civil War and its aftermath that put the South in the hands of the Democrats. But Thurmond cleared away the underbrush of history so that other white southerners could follow him into a Republican Party that was now more appealing to them. All across the South over the next twenty-five years, Republicans were elected governors, to state legislatures, and to Congress.

Though he had never been the chief strategist nor the most astute tactician for the white southern cause, Thurmond was its most energetic, vocal, and consistent defender. Alone among his contemporaries in the region, he had survived not only to see southern society transformed but to remain a participant in its political life for more than sixty years. In his long career, Thurmond played a central role in two developments of great significance to his region and the nation—the revolution in race relations, seen most clearly in the new political role of blacks; and the realignment of the two major parties in the South. The senator fought against the upheaval in the racial order, and it was that very conflict that made him the premier southern Republican.

To examine the sweep of Thurmond's public life is to explore the power of race to shape politics, to see first the unquestioned acceptance of segregation, then the fierce resistance to any challenge to "custom and tradition," that deceptively benign euphemism, and finally to witness the accommodations that were required when southern blacks stepped forward to claim their place in southern political life.

What made that change possible was the power of laws to shape behavior if not, initially, beliefs, to alter old routines of daily living in a hundred small ways and with them long-held expectations about how society is ordered.

The Civil War had ended just thirty-seven years before Thurmond was born. His grandfather had been a Confederate soldier. He walked back to his home in Edgefield County from Appomattox after losing his horse in battle. The story was as real to young Strom as if it had happened to him.

Senator Thurmond shared the fierce pride most white southerners felt about "the War Between the States," as they called it, and in every civil rights bill he saw deliberate punishment of his homeland. He fought each one, and he threw his rhetorical might against every Supreme Court decision protecting minorities from discrimination. In 1957 he talked for more than a day on the Senate floor against a modest civil rights bill because he didn't like the jury trial provisions. In 1964 he objected to government mandates that opened up restaurants, hotels, movie theaters, and parks to both races. In 1965 he railed against the Voting Rights Act, not, he said, because he didn't want blacks to vote but because he didn't want the federal government telling states how to run their registration and election procedures. He ignored language from state constitutions that had purposefully kept black citizens from the ballot box.

Thurmond had no patience for the brazen college students who sat down at whites-only lunch counters in southern cities, no sympathy for the freedom riders who were beaten up in Anniston, Birmingham, and Montgomery, and none for the young marchers gassed on the Edmund Pettus Bridge in Selma. They were "outside agitators" who had tried to stir up trouble, and they had found it.

But they had also made the senator an involuntary participant in the civil rights movement. As long as he chose to stay in public life, he had to adjust to public laws, and none was more important than the Voting Rights Act of 1965 that gave the franchise back to the black community. Thurmond loved to say he was "standing with the people," and from 1928, when he won his first political contest, until 1965, the people who counted were white. By June 18, 1982, he had redefined "the people" to embrace black Carolinians as well.

Race during these turbulent years was a deceptive element in southern politics, for it masked real philosophical differences among the region's public officials. Thurmond was a genuine conservative who disdained federal government solutions to problems he believed were state and local. The cure from Washington was always worse than the disease. Senator Olin D. Johnston, Thurmond's colleague from South Carolina, Senators Lister Hill and John Sparkman of Alabama, J. William Fulbright of Arkansas, even Mississippi's "pert little monster," the vitriolic Senator Theodore Bilbo, were more moderate in their overall ideology. They believed in federal power and took pride in the programs they helped create.

But race wiped out these distinctions. When the time came to consider antilynching laws, the poll tax, public accommodations, voting rights, and equal opportunity, otherwise diverse legislators came down on the side of discrimination in order to survive.

There were, however, degrees of difference even in this racial unity. While other senators voted with what they perceived to be the prevailing white interests, Thurmond stoked the fires of resistance in countless speeches, press releases, and reports to his constituents, and this is what set him apart. He was a cheerleader for segregation, even if the cheers he led were not always couched in racial terms but in the antiseptic rhetoric of states' rights.

To his advantage, Thurmond operated at a safe distance from the front lines of change. At the height of the movement, he was a step removed from the mayors, police chiefs, sheriffs, and governors who ordered police dogs, fire hoses, and state troopers to move against the civil rights demonstrators. Because of 1948, because of the 1957 filibuster, because of the resistance of the sixties, Thurmond did become a symbol of white intransigence, but the distance he was afforded as a federal rather than state legislator saved him from confrontations that might later have come back to haunt him.

Ike Williams has known the senator for two decades, first as head of the South Carolina NAACP and then as a private consultant in Columbia. He found it ironic that his office was in the Strom Thurmond Pavilion, one of many installations that bear Thurmond's name as an expression of thanks for the federal money that has flowed into the state through the senator's hands. Williams never believed Thurmond operated from racial animus, though the effect of his actions was the same as if he had. "I never thought Strom Thurmond actually hated black people," Williams said. "He just never really needed them."

After 1965 he did, and it is a tribute to Thurmond's skill that with his record, he had survived to cast a vote in 1982 on the law that had transformed his world. His energy and instinct, his appreciation for the importance of contact with "the people" made him so resilient. After Thurmond was elected governor in 1946—his first statewide victory—*The Timmonsville Times* said he had "proven that shaking hands with a farmer in Red Creek and a lawyer in Charleston is still the best down-to-earth pay-off politics possible in South Carolina." Forty years later, Thurmond was still plying his trade the same way, and the most dubious of visitors to South Carolina, northern liberals old enough to remember the sixties, came away awed after watching him work crowds of whites and blacks gathered in town squares around the state. An instant after greeting a resident, he could recall the individual's parents or some piece of family history that made the brief political encounter personal. The senator's ability to feel the pulse of his constituency was unsurpassed, often to the surprise of younger aides who believed they could teach their much older boss a thing or two.

In 1957, Harry Dent, later Richard Nixon's special assistant, was one of Thurmond's senior aides. He had long disdained the senator's habit of jotting sympathy notes to people he didn't know. One such letter was written to a couple whose son had been killed in a farm accident near Aiken, where Thurmond now lived.

When Dent saw the letter, he decided to tell the senator how empty and crass such gestures looked and to put a stop to the practice. He went into Thurmond's personal office, a copy of the letter in his hand, made his speech, and then for emphasis crumpled the letter up and threw it in a nearby wastebasket. The senator listened politely, nodding in agreement as Dent said, "Let's don't do that any more." Dent thought he had made his point.

Several weeks later Dent was eating breakfast at a restaurant in Aiken when three local men stopped in to say hello to him and his companion, another Thurmond aide. One of them swore he would never forget the senator for the rest of his life. About six weeks earlier, the man explained, his little boy had been killed by a hay baler. A few days later a letter of condolence had come from the senator. "I know that it probably was just a political letter," he said. "In fact, Mr. Dent . . . it was probably your letter. But I'll tell you something," the man continued, tears welling in his eyes. "The senator had to sign that letter, and in his busy day up there in Washington, D.C., when he signed that letter, he had to stop just that long to think about my little boy."

A chastened Dent drew in a long breath and thought to himself, "Good grief, here I'm the one trying to tell a master politician what to do."

Twenty-six years later—in September 1983—Mark Goodin, the senator's aggressive young press secretary, learned a similar lesson from Thurmond at the annual Southern 500 stock car race in Darlington County. Thurmond was asked to speak before the race started. A few days earlier, Soviet pilots had shot down a Korean airliner that had drifted into Soviet airspace, and Congressman Larry McDonald of Georgia was among those who had died in the incident.

Before heading to the microphones, Thurmond asked Goodin

if he should say anything about the KAL downing. Goodin told him it was not appropriate. The senator nodded and went on his way to the podium to address the crowd that had jammed the stands and the infield. "It's great to be here at the granddaddy of all stock car races," the senator began. "And it's great to live here in the United States of America." He paused for just a second. "And I'll tell you one thing about the greatness of this country. In America, we don't shoot down civilian airliners."

Fifty thousand people sprang to their feet in a thunderous roar that went on for five minutes.

"I hated to go against you," Thurmond told Goodin when he came back to the press area. "But after a while in this business, you kinda get a feelin' for these things."

The senator's "feelin' for these things" had helped him withstand the enormous change in the South that had felled other politicians. As Thurmond's constituency turned from all white to white and black, he used good works at home rather than advocacy in Washington to cement his relationship with the new black voters. Shortly after Mississippi Republican Thad Cochran arrived in the Senate (he was one of Thurmond's political descendants), Thurmond explained to the younger man how he could vote against federal government programs drafted to help minorities but not lose black support at home. "Your black friends will be with you," he told Cochran, "if you be sure to help them with their projects."

Some occasions brought forth a more personal touch. Althea Simmons was head of the NAACP's Washington bureau from 1979 until her death in September 1990. A woman of great presence, she had gone straight from Howard University law school into the NAACP's field operation in the South. She had argued with voter registrars in Mississippi, stood up to white lawmen in Alabama, and for her own protection learned to change rental cars every few days so that the Ku Klux Klan would not know where she was. She had lobbied Thurmond dozens of times, and while all the meetings were cordial, she rarely came away with what she wanted, his support. During one of these sessions in his office Simmons had deliberately taken a seat near the back because she had to leave early to catch a plane. When she got up as unobtrusively as possible and headed for the door, Thurmond stopped the discussion and asked where she was going. She explained that she had to make a flight. The senator picked up his phone, called one of his drivers to take her to the airport, and instructed him to make sure the plane didn't leave without her.

Thurmond probably would have done the same for a white lobbyist. That he did so for one who was black had particular meaning because of all that had come before.

The senator's long journey ended in the light of reconciliation. It began in the shadows of conflict driven by fear.

2.
THE LEGACY OF PITCHFORK BEN

1870–1928

LONG BEFORE STROM Thurmond became one of Edgefield's famous sons, this verdant swath of land in South Carolina's western quadrant was home to many of the state's most provocative characters. James Bonham and William B. Travis, defenders of the Alamo, were Edgefield men. So was Pierce Mason Butler, who commanded South Carolina troops in the Mexican War, and Andrew P. Butler, the U.S. senator who spent his career defending slavery. Senator Charles Sumner of Massachusetts once skewered Butler for being a "Don Quixote" devoted to "the harlot slavery." Two days after that speech, on May 22, 1856, United States Congressman Preston S. Brooks—another Edgefield man and Butler's nephew—marched into the Senate chamber and beat Sumner into unconsciousness with a heavy cane. (It took Sumner three years to recover.)

When the schism between North and South grew irredeemably wide, still another Edgefield man, Governor Francis B. Pickens, led South Carolina out of the Union. It was December 20, 1860, and South Carolina was the first southern state to secede.

Alongside this passion and pride of homeland was Edgefield's quieter side, nurtured by successful white lawyers and by ambitious planters who made the most of the area's adaptable soils. They encouraged good manners and respected education. Young people could learn English literature and Latin in Edgefield's schools. Many with the means and inclination attended established northern colleges.

Edgefield was founded in 1785 when a larger district that included virtually all of the northwestern part of the state was divided into smaller areas. The district became a county in 1868 and was reduced to its current size in 1917.

The town of Edgefield was the political center of the county and appropriately became the site of the redbrick courthouse built imposingly on top of a ridge that sloped between two creeks. The building's wide stairway descended into the town square, which from earliest days was the gathering place for commerce and conversation. A water trough for horses ran through the center of the plaza to accommodate out-of-town visitors, and in bad weather it was not unusual to see buggies mired in mud up to their axles.

Although Edgefield was not the district's commercial center, there was plenty of business activity in the village. A March 1851 account in *The Edgefield Advertiser* noted that along with four preachers, the town had twelve lawyers, four doctors, one dentist, four teachers, over a dozen shops, three churches, one restaurant, and one printing press.

When war against the North began, Edgefield's men marched off to defend their homes and their way of life from this same town square.

It was a defense that failed. The war destroyed the economic underpinning of antebellum society, the plantation, and its aftermath brought new indignities to the white southerners. The hated Reconstruction, forced upon the region by Republicans in Washington and by northern carpetbaggers bent on helping the freed slaves, had reordered society, giving to blacks the social and political perquisites that once belonged only to whites. It was two Edgefield men, Matthew C. Butler and Martin W. Gray, who showed the rest of the state that routine politics would not be enough to retake power in postwar Edgefield, where the six hundred black voters outnumbered the four hundred whites. Intimidation, harassment, even violence would be required.

The theory made sense to one of Edgefield's young, hardworking farmers, Benjamin Ryan Tillman, whose family had migrated to the area before the Revolution, fought on the side of the fledgling country, and then received land grants that enabled them to become major landowners. Ben Tillman was only seventeen when the Civil War broke out. Though age was no bar to fighting, a serious illness that had cost him his left eye prevented him from serving with the Confederates. But he identified with the cause, and growing up in a slave-owning family, he accepted as given the master-servant relationship that defined the two races.

A brief period of forced equality with blacks followed the war, but white resentment only grew. At twenty-six, Tillman happily joined forty-four other white Edgefield men to form the Sweetwater Sabre Club, a private militia created to drive blacks out of the electorate. Similar organizations had already cropped up in other states—the White League in Louisiana, the White Line in Mississippi, the White Man's Party in Alabama. By the summer of 1876 the Sweetwater Club had already driven black militiamen, the supposed protectors of their community, out of much of Edgefield, but there was still a company of black soldiers in the town of Hamburg, near the Georgia border, that had to be dealt with.

In the warm days of July, club members devised a plan after two young whites were charged with disrupting one of the soldiers' regular drills. The men were to stand trial in Hamburg, and the Sweetwater Club, spoiling for a fight, assembled near the local court during the proceeding. Sensing trouble, the judge postponed the trial, but not to be denied their confrontation, the Sweetwater men tracked the black militiamen to the town armory, where they had made temporary quarters. The white fighters told the sequestered soldiers to lay down their arms, but they refused.

By nightfall, as word of the standoff spread, a mob of white men from nearby Augusta, Georgia, joined club members, and the shooting began. One white man was killed; many of the black soldiers fled in terror, and two were killed in the escape. But the mob did not stop there. Five blacks from among the captured militiamen were selected for execution and led off to their deaths. Tillman loaned his pistol for the killings.

He gloried in the violence of that bloody night, enshrined in South Carolina history as "the Hamburg Riot." He dismissed critics in the Republican-leaning northern papers and ignored calls to prosecute those responsible for the killings. Instead, he and his brother George organized a procession of white men to literally wave a bloody shirt in defiance of their detractors. Tillman personally delivered yards of homespun material to the white women of Edgefield, who made garments for forty men. Wild berries smudged on the rough material created the effect of blood. Tillman then created a gigantic black effigy marked with bullet holes and affixed two slogans: "Awake, arise or be forever fallen," and "None but the guilty need fear."

Wearing their crudely stained shirts and holding high the grisly effigy, the marchers produced the desired effect. Whites cheered the procession; blacks cowered in their homes. "We had in truth waved the bloody shirt in the face of the Yankee bull and dared him to do his worst," Tillman recalled.

If the Red Shirt campaign first brought Tillman to prominence, the farmers' revolt of the 1880s cemented his place in the state's history. A critical moment for the rising politician was his August 1885 speech to the joint session of the State Grange and the State Agricultural and Mechanical Society at Bennettsville. There was an air of expectation when the conventioneers heard that Ben Tillman was going to speak and "say something out of the ordinary," and an overflow crowd jammed the courthouse to await his remarks.

Most of the other speakers had been polished, even elegant, with their well-tailored suits and long hair. Tillman, with his serviceable clothes, swarthy complexion, and flashing single eye was a mixture of the plain and the uncouth. He started slowly in his high rasping voice and apologized to his listeners for his hesitancy. But the longer he talked, the better he got, laying out a gloomy picture of agriculture's decline and pointing a finger directly at the government and the city-dwelling financiers.

The people, he charged, "have been hoodwinked by demagogues and lawyers in the pay of finance."

The farmers in the courthouse went wild. Almost every sentence brought thunderous applause. The organizations' officers sat in stony silence, insulted and angered by Tillman's harsh words.

It didn't matter that Tillman was unable to pass the resolutions he had proposed setting forth new farm programs. His challenge to the status quo had made a profound impression that would be his stepping-stone into state politics.

By this time, Tillman's enemies had derisively dubbed him the "Agricultural Moses." He accepted their title. "The pent-up indignation of the farmers has found a voice through me," he declared. "I should be a coward to refuse to lead."

For the moment, he disdained political office for himself, contending that "I commenced this fight pure and honest and 'only a farmer.' I will end it as I began." But by 1890 Tillman had seen two protégés fail to capture the governorship. Now he decided to run himself.

Tillman secured the Democratic nomination without opposition, though disaffected Democrats ran a third-party candidate, Alexander C. Haskell. He accused Tillman of going outside regular party procedures to get the nomination and of "falsely charging the state government with dishonesty, corruption and perjury." Tillman beat him by better than a four-to-one margin.

When the throngs gathered in Columbia December 4 to see him take the oath of office, Tillman triumphantly told the crowd, "Democracy, the rule of the people, has won a victory unparalleled in its magnitude and importance." But it was Democracy as Ben Tillman defined it. "The whites have absolute control of state government, and we intend at any and all hazards to retain it," he told the crowd. "The intelligent exercise of the right to suffrage . . . is as yet beyond the capacity of the vast majority of colored men."

Tillman became even more rabid on the subject of race after his reelection as governor in 1892. An opponent of lynching during his first administration, he turned 180 degrees in his second. "There is only one crime that warrants lynching," he said, "and governor as I am, I would lead a mob to lynch the negro who ravishes a white woman." The change in tone apparently sent a message to the populace. During Tillman's first administration, there had been five lynchings. In his second, there were thirteen.

When his term was up, Tillman was elected to the United States Senate, the expected progression for an ambitious man, and it was during this campaign that he earned the sobriquet "Pitchfork Ben." He had promised that when he got to Washington he would use a pitchfork to prod President Cleveland—"an old bag of beef—in his old fat ribs." But it was by directing the writing of a new state constitution that Tillman made the deepest imprint on the state's political life.

The existing constitution had been drafted in 1868 during Reconstruction, and by embodying such progressive principles as education for all and political representation according to population regardless of race, it bore a resemblance to those of northern states.

Tillman unveiled his proposal at a constitutional convention in October of 1895. The first part provided that until January 1, 1898, any male South Carolinian could vote if he had lived in the state for two years, in his county for one year, and in the voting precinct for four months; he had to have paid his poll tax six months before the election, "understood" the constitution, and not been found guilty of any one of a specified list of crimes. The list—thievery, adultery, arson, wife beating, housebreaking, and attempted rape—was drawn deliberately to include those crimes perceived to be most commonly committed by blacks. The crimes of murder and fighting, which white men were thought disposed to commit as well, were conspicuously absent from the list. The residency and poll tax requirements would be especially hard on poor blacks who frequently moved around in search of work. Finally, the administration of the "understanding clause" was left to white election officials. (Twenty-five years after this provision went into effect, several black women in Columbia—almost all college graduates—were denied the right to register. Election officials said they had not passed the educational requirement.)

Tillman's constitution also forbade any mixing of blacks and whites in schools, and local officials were not required to divide funds equally between the two school systems.

Confronted with the flagrant attempt to eliminate their race from politics, the black delegates to the convention tried every rhetorical device to reverse the tide. One newspaper commentator reported that the men had made their arguments "as fully and as eloquently as they could be presented." But their entreaties fell on deaf ears, and Tillman's disfranchising provisions carried the day. On December 4, 1895, the convention adjourned, and by virtue of a special provision, the constitution went into effect the following New Year's without a referendum by the voters.

The black convention delegates who had fought so eloquently but unsuccessfully against Tillman's plan warned that whites would be remorseful over their retreat from democracy. They couldn't have been more wrong. White Carolina took to black disfranchisement as though it were a fundamental law of nature.

Tillman's work had not gone unnoticed among other white southern leaders. In Mississippi, James Kimble Vardaman, a lawyer, newspaper editor, and sometime Democratic gubernatorial candidate from Greenwood, had read about the upstart farmer and found "a virtility [*sic*] and widespread honesty about the old fellow's speech which all honest men admire." By the turn of the century he would rival Tillman as one of the South's most rabid white supremacists.

For a decade, Vardaman had wanted to be governor and had failed twice. But in the fall of 1901 President Theodore Roosevelt gave him another chance by inviting Booker T. Washington to dine at the White House. Vardaman seized the opportunity to play the protector, whipping crowds to a frenzy when he talked about the "coon-flavored miscegenationist" in the White House and said he didn't care "if the walls of the ancient edifice should become so saturated with the effluvia from the rancid carcasses that a chinch bug would have to crawl upon the dome to avoid asphyxiation."

Where other politicians made speeches, Vardaman staged events. Dressed in white from suit to boots, his sturdy face and his wavy, shoulder-length dark hair set off with a wide-brimmed black Stetson, he made grand entrances to Mississippi towns astride a lumber wagon drawn by teams of white oxen. More than once, the "White Chief," as he was known, was welcomed with booming cannons and brass bands.

When he wasn't exhorting crowds in person, Vardaman was doing it in writing as editor of *The Commonwealth,* an eight-page paper published in Greenwood that made Roosevelt a regular foil. After learning that Washington—"the saddle-colored philosopher of Tuskegee," he called him—had dined at the White House, Vardaman said the president "had no more decency than to take a d——d nigger bastard into his home, introduce him to his family and entertain him on terms of absolute social equality."

When Roosevelt came to the Mississippi Delta for a hunting trip, Vardaman ran this ad: "WANTED, sixteen big, fat, mellow, rancid 'coons' to sleep with Roosevelt when he comes to go bear hunting. . . ."

By November of 1902, Vardaman had found an issue that would catapult him into the governor's mansion—getting rid of Minnie M. Cox, the black postmaster of Indianola, a small Delta town about thirty miles from Greenwood.

Mrs. Cox was an educated, dignified woman who had been appointed by President Benjamin Harrison in 1893 after no white Republican had qualified for the position. Over the years she had been reappointed and promoted, and the federal postal inspector in the state, Charles Fitzgerald, had praised her for running her office "in the most satisfactory manner." But her relationship with white Indianola, which had always been friendly, deteriorated by the spring of 1902. What apparently fueled the discord was Roosevelt's intention to reorganize the Republican Party in the South. Some Mississippians thought the president would allow white Democrats to replace black officeholders because there were so few Republicans available. Suddenly, Fitzgerald reported to his superiors in Washington, the community discovered that "they had an obvious nigger postmaster, a fact it took them 10 years to find out."

Vardaman saw political gold in the fracas and went to Indianola to mine the turmoil. Stamping furiously up and down the podiums, his long hair flying loose and his resonant voice rising to a fever pitch, he taunted residents with the specter of "negro domination" and chided them for "tolerating a negro wench" in the post office.

This, followed by warnings in *The Commonwealth* that permitting "niggers" to hold office "only serves to excite race antagonism, which in turn brings death, destruction and demoralization upon the poor negro," was too much for Mrs. Cox. She resigned as postmaster in January 1903 and fled to Birmingham, Alabama. Local citizens boasted that if she returned to Indianola "she would get her neck broken inside of two hours."

Roosevelt retaliated by closing the Indianola post office, and white Mississippi was outraged. The Indianola affair was fresh in people's minds when Vardaman announced his candidacy for governor later in the year. He made it the centerpiece of his white supremacy campaign and even promised that as governor of Mississippi he would repeal the Fourteenth and Fifteenth Amendments to the U.S. Constitution, the Civil War amendments, which gave blacks full citizenship rights.

He publicly condoned lynching for "the negro fiend," and said to constant applause that he "would lead the mob to string the brute up, and I haven't much respect for the white man who wouldn't." Black education was a waste, he said, because a black was "a lazy, lying, lustful animal which no conceivable amount of training can transform into a tolerable citizen." Besides, too much education would simply ruin a good field hand. Playing on fears of black domination—Mississippi was 59 percent black—Vardaman said that if Roosevelt's policies of social and political equality continued, "we would have to kill more negroes in the next twelve months in Mississippi than we have had to kill in the last twenty years."

Vardaman was rewarded for his race-baiting campaign with easy election to the governor's mansion.

It was a South molded by Ben Tillman and James Vardaman that welcomed James Strom Thurmond into the world and the town of Edgefield on December 5, 1902. That same year marked the end of the political careers of the state's remaining black elected officials. Both were defeated in their bids to remain in office, and no other black would hold an elected state position for another sixty-eight years. In that very month, Minnie Cox was run out of Indianola, Mississippi.

Young Strom (his parents never used "James") was born in the family's large three-story home near the Edgefield town square. He was the second child of John William Thurmond, a prosperous lawyer, farmer, and community leader, and Eleanor Gertrude Strom. Strom's older brother, Bill—John William—had been born barely two years earlier. Over the next seven years, four other Thurmonds would arrive: Gertrude, Allen George, and the twins, Mary and Martha.

Turn-of-the-century Edgefield bustled. Stores with a thriving trade surrounded the square, reflecting the changed order brought about by the destruction of the plantation-based economy after the Civil War. Now former slave families and the sharecropping white farmers worked small parcels of land and had to shop for their own supplies. Fires in 1881, 1883, and 1892 had burned most of the town. When the merchants and landlords rebuilt their stores, they gave the square a certain architectural harmony. One of the buildings just a stone's throw from the courthouse was the small, two-room law office of J. William Thurmond.

When Strom was four and Bill was six, the family moved to a larger house not far from the courthouse, where J. William and his wife owned about six acres of land and where the boys could learn about farming. This was J. William's first concern. "Let them plow," he declared. After that, other lessons followed. "Stint them until they know the value of money" was his philosophy.

"Encourage them until they have a religious creed. Teach them to rely on themselves. Let them mingle with others to learn human nature and . . . know more about [their professions] than do their competitors."

Even before Strom was old enough to understand his father's demanding credo, he seemed to be possessed of an innate drive. By the time he was two he could ride ponies, horses, goats, even a bull and could outrun his older brother, Bill. After Allen George was born and old enough to compete, Strom could best him as well. There was never a doubt that Strom would succeed in life. The only question was where all this drive would be channeled. The answers lay in a combination of place—Edgefield County and its vigorous political tradition—and people: Ben Tillman, who had fostered the white-controlled society of Thurmond's youth, and J. William, who gave to his son his own personal values and professional interests.

The Thurmond home was an ideal place for a growing family. There was plenty of room for the children to play and for J. William to host regular midday dinners for politicians and lawyers who came through town. It was not unusual for congressmen, judges, or a governor or two to drop by, and Mrs. Thurmond frequently had to peer down Penn Street to see how many people were following Thurmond home. Feeding the guests was never a problem because the Thurmonds had a ready supply of food and plenty of hired help around the house—cook, housekeeper, yardman, and driver. If more people showed up than were expected, the cook was simply sent to the smokehouse to cut down another ham.

These dinners were all that an ambitious young boy could ask for. Politics was discussed at every meal, and if the company seemed slow to start, the precocious Strom would ask questions himself. The only drawback was hunger pangs. The children were not allowed to eat until the guests had finished, and sometimes that meant waiting through three seatings of adults. Bill Thurmond often joked that he didn't know chickens had more than backs and wings until he was an adult.

The political atmosphere on Penn Street was just one influence J. William brought to his family. His philosophy of achievement and determination was leavened with a faith in education, shared by Eleanor, and with generosity toward those in his ambit. He kept an eye out for acquaintances, white and black, who had hit on hard times, buying them a sack of sugar or flour to tide them over, sending his sons to deliver vegetables from the family plot, or, in some instances, dispatching the cook for a few days' work. When he visited the tenant farmers, he always brought presents for their children. Every fall, Thurmond had a barrel of apples shipped in from Maryland, which he passed out to his Edgefield neighbors. In his childrens' eyes, he "couldn't stand to think that anybody was hungry."

Between them, J. William and Eleanor Thurmond owned hundreds of acres of land outside of Edgefield, and in addition to letting their sons work in the fields, they, like other landowners, rented out property to sharecroppers. Thurmond kept a running account for them at the all-purpose store on the town square so they could get what they needed and not have to settle up until the end of each year. The Thurmonds looked after their extended family as well, letting nieces and nephews stay at the Penn Street house while they went to school in Edgefield.

When Strom and Bill were youngsters they went to Miss Mary Butler's private school, where Strom won most of the school's spelling contests. The boys switched to the public schools when the other children came along and private education proved too expensive. But J. William spent extra money to correct Bill's stuttering problem, and when Bill seemed to be having difficulty in high school, J. William sent him to a military academy. (Apparently it worked. Bill went to the University of South Carolina, later becoming a doctor and a faculty member at the University of Georgia medical school.)

Like any youngster, Strom could be a tease. He and Allen George used to chase Mary around the house with their mother's fur boa, threatening that the stuffed head would bite her. And when his twin sisters teased him about having to milk the cows, he wasn't above turning a teat in their direction, sending a stream of milk in their faces. He also had a gentler side. He taught his sisters to dance and swim and made a point of carrying Gertrude's books to school for her in bad weather.

Though Ben Tillman was not a relative, he was a symbolic part of the Thurmond family. J. William, himself a state legislator, did legal and political work for Tillman, serving for a time as Pitchfork Ben's campaign manager. Just what drew J. William to Tillman was not entirely clear; Thurmond seemed to be many things Tillman was not: a well-established, prosperous lawyer, an educated man—in short, the kind of person Tillman sought to remove from power. But there was a strong regional tie between the Edgefield men, and Tillman appealed to those who felt isolated by an incumbent regime in Columbia interested less in the farmer and more in industrial growth. (Tillman later rewarded Thurmond for his loyalty by getting him named U.S. attorney in a new South Carolina federal district. The job was made difficult by the fact that Thurmond had killed a man in 1897 in an argument over Tillman's politics. Thurmond claimed it was self-defense and, though he regretted the "unfortunate occurrence," he felt "perfectly justified before God and man" over what he had done.)

To black Carolinians who read of Tillman's race-baiting speeches at political gatherings, to fellow United States senators who shuddered at his tirades on the Senate floor, Tillman may have been the most vicious sort of demagogue. But to the Thurmond children, Pitchfork Ben was like a kindly, if sometimes curmudgeonly, uncle. During their regular visits to his farm, the children were always tickled to see the gold, five-pronged pitchfork Tillman prominently displayed in the parlor, and because Tillman often wore an eyepatch over his injured eye, he reminded Allen George of a pirate.

The first time Strom was taken to the farm—he was just six years old—Tillman made an impression that the boy never forgot. "Now when you get there, you go up and put out your hand and shake hands with him," J. William told his son.

"Senator, this is Strom Thurmond," the boy said, dutifully extending his hand as his father had requested.

"What in hell do you want?" came the brusque reply.

"I want to shake hands with you."

"Why in hell won't you shake, then?" said Tillman, taking firm hold of the boy's hand and showing him what he meant. It was Strom's first lesson in the political art of meeting people, and more than eighty years later Thurmond was still shaking hands as though Tillman were giving him instructions about a good grip.

He had taught the boy in more indirect ways, too. Strom lived in a society whose customs were dictated by Tillman's ideology, and as he looked around him, young Thurmond could see that anyone who did anything important had white skin, while those with dark skin were in servile positions. Black women might tend the Thurmonds' wounds and cook their food, and black and white boys might work together in the fields, but at day's end the Thurmonds and their servants went their separate ways. During the school year there was complete separation of the races—decreed by Tillman's constitution and given the imprimatur of the Supreme Court in the landmark *Plessy v. Ferguson* case, the 1896 ruling that gave legal sanction to "separate but equal" facilities for the races.

Black and white lives may have been separate, but they weren't equal. In the thirty years since the end of Reconstruction, Edgefield blacks, like those in other parts of the state, had suffered reversals. Stripped of their political power, they were forced into the lowest-paying jobs, if they could find them at all.

With no political power and diminished economic power came lower social status. The "Jim Crow" laws had segregated virtually every facet of life in the state, consigning blacks to inferior facilities. Railway coaches were segregated in 1898, steamboats and ferries in 1904. The year before, Columbia, fifty miles east of Edgefield, had segregated its streetcars. In 1906, Columbia's National Loan and Exchange Bank segregated its elevators even though it was not required by law. There had been complaints that blacks had crowded themselves into cars with white female employees of the building.

With Jim Crow in place, many in the South thought that the race question had been settled for good. Certainly in the Thurmond household race was not a pivotal issue. Whites had their place and blacks theirs, and no one contested the social order; this was a time not to rock the boat but to reap the benefits of the occasionally violent labors of Tillman and Vardaman. So while politics was central to life on Penn Street, it was not the overt politics of race. The subject came up in the context of political campaigns, not in and of itself.

Thurmond's first sustained exposure to the rhetoric of race came during the 1912 gubernatorial race, when he was only nine years old. What thrilled the boy was the energy of the candidates' debates, not the substance of their remarks. Incumbent governor Cole Blease, who—without Tillman's blessing—claimed to be his political heir, was running for reelection. He shared with Tillman a gift for the stump speech but took the race-baiting rhetoric a step further, openly condoning lynching. His bigotry was of the basest sort. "You can take a Negro," Blease insisted, "a tub of the hottest water you can get him into, and use all the soap you can use . . . and in five minutes he will smell just as offensive as he did before you washed him."

Blease had no real legislative program, but that didn't seem to matter to the populace. What they liked about "Coley," as he was known, was his personality and his viewpoint. He looked at life as the common man did and gave the people what they valued more than any legislation: recognition and respect.

Blease's opponent was Supreme Court Justice Ira B. Jones, a dignified, intelligent man whose political skills were no match for the governor. Where Blease was by turns colorful, acerbic, and aggressive, Jones was stiff, tentative, and defensive. During the campaign, Tillman lamented that the justice was "absolutely a child in Blease's hands."

Although Jones also believed in white supremacy, he expressed his views with much less virulence. He suffered dearly for it. "You people who want social equality vote for Jones," Blease shouted during one speech. "You men who have nigger children vote for Jones. You who have a nigger wife in your back yard vote for Jones." Jones defended himself only by citing his record of state service and by insisting that he did not favor racial equality.

Finding the justice by far the better of the two candidates, J. William served as Jones's campaign manager. He took his son with him to a few of the campaign meetings, and when the boy heard the two candidates go at each other at one debate, the young Thurmond made a silent vow that one day he, too, would be governor.

Blease, knowing that his emphasis on lynching was a sure tactic, stuck with his rhetoric and easily won the election.

The ugly emotional appeal of lynching was a perplexing issue for educated people like the Thurmonds. They didn't condone lynching, certainly, but they didn't raise a sustained voice against it, either. They regarded it as a part of the times and sought to keep it distant from their lives. At bottom, however, lynching was simply the most extreme expression of a social caste system that was as inherent a part of their beliefs as was reverence for the family. It was difficult to escape the issue, for Vardaman, Tillman, and Blease had demonstrated so well how racial hostility, wrapped around the ideal of the pure, defenseless southern woman, could be harnessed into a potent political force.

When news of a lynching reached the Thurmond household, Strom was given the usual explanation: a black man had raped a white girl, and her white protectors, he remembers being told, believed they "had to take drastic action to let them know they weren't going to stand for it." While young Strom's understanding of the rape-lynch cycle conformed to generally accepted belief, there were in fact many lynchings that took place for other reasons—murder, arson, robbery, assault and battery, and simply frightening a woman.

Black Carolina was all but powerless to protect itself from the excesses of a white-controlled world. Conditions frustrated even men like Richard Carroll, a Baptist minister from Columbia who preached self-help for his brethren and was considered by white society to be, as one of them put it, "one of the noblemen of his race." Despite the amicable relations he enjoyed with whites, Carroll resented the fact that "conscientious and responsible blacks like himself" were subject to the caprice of whites.

By 1915 some of South Carolina's blacks tried to organize politically. A group of Columbia residents who were able to meet the state's requirements for voting founded the Capital City Civic League, organizing it for the purpose of "contesting and contending for our every Constitutional Right, privilege and immunity in a quiet, legal and peaceful manner." That same year the group made overtures to the NAACP, the fledgling organization founded by W. E. B. Du Bois, and by February 1917 the Columbia branch of the NAACP was formed. It continued the effort for more black participation in voting but also worked on getting playgrounds for black children, roads paved, and blacks hired as policemen.

While the new organization may have caused ripples in Columbia, there was no evidence that this activity touched the Thurmonds' lives in Edgefield. Strom, nearly fifteen years old, was getting ready to finish high school (it ended at tenth grade) and head to Clemson College. The biggest event in his life was the arrival of the first family car, which he learned to drive immediately. No license was necessary, and one drove at one's peril. The car could be dangerous even at a dead stop, as Strom found out. One cold morning when he was trying to start it, the engine crank kicked back and cracked a bone in his arm, sending him sprawling to the ground in pain.

While he knew his way around a farm by the time he was a teenager, Strom also had an instinct for business. When World War I broke out, one of the Thurmond neighbors, Albert Covar, had to leave his crops in the field. Strom bought Covar's land with six hundred dollars he had saved, and after the harvest he made a nice profit.

In the fall of 1918, just before he turned sixteen, Strom started college at Clemson. (By coincidence, Tillman, the man responsible for building the school, died that summer following a cerebral hemorrhage just before his seventy-second birthday.) Strom was all determination and drive at Clemson. He didn't just study agriculture but found plenty of time for an array of extracurricular activities. He was a member of the track team, the championship cross-country team, the baseball, basketball, and football teams, and the debate club; he was president of the campus literary society and a member of the senior dancing club. Though not a natural athlete, he worked hard at sports, particularly track. During vacations at home he prompted surprised looks from neighbors not used to seeing young men running down the street in shorts. He trained even more rigorously at Clemson, sometimes running the seventeen miles between the college and Anderson, a small town due south.

His picture in the 1923 yearbook, *Taps,* shows a handsome young man with close-cropped hair, light, penetrating eyes, and just the hint of a smile. The inscription underneath includes an aphorism apparently of Strom's choosing: "One cannot always be a hero, but one can always be a man."

The comments that follow, charting his growth and his impact at Clemson, credit "this handsome young man" as a "ladies' man of the 'first water' who provoked "so many extra heartbeats among the fairer sex."

The entry concludes with a wish that was to come true many times over. "May success ever be yours, Strom, old boy."

On his first Sunday back in town after graduation, Strom went to church and took an unobtrusive seat in the back row. The next Sunday he was teaching the men's Bible class, although he didn't know the Scriptures half as well as his father. "That was Strom all over," said one bemused friend. "He has tremendous push and drive."

Not yet twenty-one, Thurmond landed a job teaching farm techniques to students in the schools of nearby McCormick. He also acquired a Harley Davidson motorcycle and, something of a daredevil, sped over the red-clay roads from Edgefield to McCormick, occasionally hands off the handlebars.

Thurmond taught only white students, and in much better circumstances than his black counterparts. Despite the doctrine of separate but equal, obvious disparities existed between the black and white systems, the result of a decades-old debate on just how much education blacks should have. One school of thought, represented by Blease and Vardaman, believed it was futile and even detrimental to educate blacks. "Instead of making an educated negro," Blease contended, "you are ruining a good plow hand and making a half-trained fool."

The more benign view conceded that blacks were entitled to some education, but there was indifference about its quality. The main goal was to teach skills that would keep the "good plow hand," not to create independent thinkers who might challenge whites in the upper echelons of society.

The chasm between the two systems was made clear in official state education reports. William K. Tate, rural elementary school supervisor, found that by 1915, years of neglect had left Negro school buildings "miserable beyond all description." They lacked comfort, equipment, proper lighting, and sanitation. "Most of the teachers are absolutely untrained," he said, and added that often the county superintendent did not even know where the black schools were.

The annual per-pupil expenditures painted a similarly dramatic picture. In 1910, the average expenditure for white students was $10.80. It rose to $14.94 by 1914. During the same period, the average expenditure for black children dropped from $2.00 to $1.86.

By 1920, expenditures for black students were up to $3.04 per pupil, but at the same time, money spent on white students had risen to $26.08 per pupil. In 1920, black public schools spent a total of $427.30 on libraries and $5,431.85 on furniture and apparatus. White schools spent $18,068.04 on libraries and $161,988.85 on equipment.

None of this concerned Thurmond—at least not yet. But within ten years his political career would require him to confront more directly the effects of "custom and tradition" on education.

As soon as Thurmond started teaching at McCormick High School, he branched out beyond the classroom, becoming the basketball and football coach. When some in the community questioned the value of athletics, Thurmond, earnest as he could be, was quick to defend sports for teaching that determination breeds success. Football, he said, promotes "clean living, self-restraint and a good physique. The habit of quick thinking, correct decisions and alertness of action is thereby trained, for the game requires the player to work his head." He even found something good to say about prizefighting, that it teaches how to avoid "nervous strain."

With illiteracy rates still high among both black and white populations in 1924, local leaders were always interested in ways to get basic skills to more people. When the McCormick American Legion auxiliary pledged its own resources, Thurmond responded with a letter to the editor of the *McCormick Messenger.* "I shall be glad to teach any white adults who have had poor opportunities for an education the fundamental principles, even the alphabet itself," he wrote, "and will do this any time, night or day, when not engaged in my duties at the high school, without remuneration." His casual reference to race reflected both the segregated society of the time and his unquestioning acceptance of it.

The social order was made equally clear at a benefit that year for the McCormick boys' basketball team: a play called *The Coontown Aristocrats.* The names of the characters, some of them played by members of Thurmond's basketball team, were takeoffs on racial stereotypes: Mrs. Gawge Washington Jones, Moses Abraham Highbrow, Sampson Ulysses Beanpod. Many of the song titles were in the slang of illiterate blacks: "Carve Dat Chicken" and "Dese Bones Gwine Rise Again." There was no concern among McCormick's teachers and students that the satire might be offensive, and Thurmond thought enough of the event that he saved the program for his personal scrapbook.

While stories about his teams' victories and defeats kept Thurmond's name in the papers, he found additional ways to keep his name before the public both in McCormick and back home in Edgefield. He wrote articles on growing vegetables, on the proper selection and care of fruit for a home orchard, and on the best way to poison the dread boll weevil—dusting rather than "syrup mixtures."

After a year in McCormick, Thurmond accepted an offer to teach in Edgefield and to be the high school football coach. He quickly earned a reputation as both a dedicated instructor and a tough coach. Not wanting to be idle during the summer, he taught boys at a rural farm school that provided instruction in English, civics, health, and arithmetic as well as agriculture. After a one-day visit to the program in August of 1927, the editor of *The Augusta Herald* wrote an article full of superlatives. Under a headline citing Summerland's "zealous instructors," the editor noted the general enthusiasm of students and teachers for their tasks, then concluded by thanking Thurmond for his "kindly, solicitous attention." He had discovered the special touch that thousands of others would come to know.

By 1928, Thurmond decided he was ready to begin the journey he had promised himself sixteen years earlier, during the Blease-Jones debate. With five years of teaching and coaching under his belt and a reputation for competence to go with it, he challenged the incumbent county school superintendent, W. W. Fuller, who it turned out was a distant in-law. Thurmond balked at running against a family member, but only temporarily; ambition wiped out any hesitancy.

His decision to run was made easier because the white community seemed dissatisfied with the way the schools had been run. Some residents thought Fuller spent too much time hunting and not enough time on education matters.

Although Thurmond had an experienced politician in the family, he didn't ask for his father's help. He ran a low-key campaign typical of the day—introducing himself to people and repeating his general theme of providing better schools. He called for new courses in character, health, and for a program of free health examinations from local doctors and dentists for white and black schoolchildren.

The August 29 primary election was the only race that mattered, and the vote did not start off well. The first returns to come in were from the towns of Edgefield and Johnston, and Fuller was ahead, prompting J. William to wonder aloud if he should have worked on his son's campaign. But as the evening wore on and the rural vote came in, the picture changed. Thurmond carried these areas by a large majority and won the nomination—guaranteeing his election—by a handsome 1,312–802 margin. It was the Summerland farm program that made the difference, he later said, for it had allowed him to "make a lot of friends out there with the country people."

Thurmond took office as county superintendent July 1, 1929, five months shy of his twenty-seventh birthday. The politician was on his way.

3.
ON THE MOVE

1929–1937

NO STATE GAVE Franklin D. Roosevelt more support in his first presidential election than South Carolina. He won 98 percent of the vote. Fewer than 2,000 Carolinians cast their ballots for Herbert Hoover, and in one county the tally was an embarrassing 5 for Hoover and 3,103 for Roosevelt.

More than anything else, Roosevelt had inspired hope in Carolinians that he could lift the state out of the ravages of the Depression. Over 20 percent of the population was on relief, twice the national average. Life for black Carolinians in 1932 was especially grim, particularly in rural areas, where the unpainted shacks that served as home often lacked windowpanes, electric lights, or proper sanitary facilities. Some were without wells and outhouses. Midwives delivered most of the babies, and medical care was all but nonexistent. Despite Red Cross efforts to help feed and clothe the poorest, in southeastern Beaufort County two blacks died of starvation that year.

By 1932 state government was drained of funds to cope with poverty and unemployment. Much of the burden shifted to the counties, which were likewise ill-equipped to handle the devastation. South Carolina was the birthplace of John C. Calhoun, whose nullification doctrine a century earlier asserted the authority of a state to defy the federal government by refusing to enforce its directives. But even in this cradle of states' rights, Carolinians understood that national solutions were required to bring the country and South Carolina back.

Roosevelt was willing to be aggressive, arguing that the federal government could appropriately involve itself locally for the benefit of the citizenry. To a young man like Thurmond, who was already planning another run for political office, this bold promise of action was appealing. He raised money for Roosevelt, supported his nomination at the Democratic Party convention, even went to Washington to attend his inauguration. It would be another fifteen years before he would rise up against the burgeoning federal government that was Roosevelt's legacy.

In addition to the presidential election, South Carolina in 1932 was in the midst of a contest for the United States Senate that was a throwback to the earlier days of overt racial appeals. Cole Blease, by now sixty-two, had won a Senate seat in 1924 but was defeated for reelection. He tried to return to the Senate in 1932 by challenging a colorful fixture of South Carolina politics, Ellison D. ("Cotton Ed") Smith, a minister's son and cotton farmer from the central part of the state, who had been in office since 1908.

Smith was South Carolina's answer to James Vardaman, showing a flare for theater on the stump that would keep him in office longer than any state politician who came before him. During one small-town gathering in his first campaign, Smith rode to the courthouse standing atop five bales of hay set in a wagon drawn by two garlanded mules. One old cotton farmer stood behind him on the wagon, exuding gratitude, while another knelt at his feet, kissing his shoes in appreciation for the high price of cotton. As a brass band played "Dixie," Smith twirled his mustache and smiled at every burst of applause. When the wagon stopped in the center of the square, Smith caressed the white cotton boll in his lapel and promised loudly enough for all to hear, "My sweetheart, my sweetheart, others may forget you but you will always be my sweetheart."

Cotton earned the endearment for many years. Each time Smith had to stand for reelection, the cotton market was on the rise, giving him the edge against all opponents. But in 1932 his luck ran out as prices plunged. Unable to claim credit for high cotton prices, Smith turned to the old standby of white supremacy, promising that he, better than anyone else—including Blease—would keep blacks in their place, even if it took a lynching or two. Legend has it that the most effective speech Smith delivered in the 1932 race was so base that it was never printed. For years it was referred to in the hill country simply as "The Speech"—a stark description of the rape of a white woman by "a big burly black brute" that was punctuated by shrieks and groans at the appropriate moments.

Blease forced a runoff election, but Smith beat him by the sizable margin of thirty-five thousand votes.

That was also the year Thurmond first ran for a state office. Despite the political climate, however, the man whose name would one day be synonymous with segregation did not resort to Smith's brand of race-baiting. His hallmark was a doggedness and drive that would take him out of Edgefield, to the state capitol in Columbia, and eventually to Washington, where he would eclipse Cotton Ed's record of longevity. To get there required a thoughtful plan for advancement begun several years before.

In 1929, while settling in as Edgefield's superintendent of education, Thurmond began to study law with his father. He had thought about going to medical school as his two brothers had done and had even applied for admission, but he really wanted a political career and reasoned that practicing law was the better preparation.

State bar regulations did not require attendance at law school. Applicants simply prepared themselves for the bar exam however they wished. The younger Thurmond didn't think there was any better lawyer or teacher than J. William, who had a thriving practice and a well-stocked law library and was working on his own book of important legal cases. Strom began his studies at night in J. William's office across from the courthouse.

During the day Thurmond concentrated on his education duties. He made good on his campaign promises, instituting new courses on health, character, and forestry and persuading the county's doctors and dentists to examine the schoolchildren, white and black. Black children in some of the outlying schools were not tested, but that was because of difficulties in working out the arrangements; these one-room schools did not always keep a regular schedule. Although segregation was strict, the barriers broke down when it came to health; white doctors would examine black schoolchildren.

When Thurmond took office, he found an $18,000 debt in the school system and set about trying to improve the system's financial condition. He ended up cutting expenses by $33,000 over his three-and-a-half-year term, and school taxes subsequently were reduced in twenty of twenty-eight districts in the county. Although the stock market crash of 1929 and the onset of the Depression that followed caused other school systems to falter—Charleston couldn't pay its bills in cash, and other systems were two months behind in meeting their obligations—Edgefield did not miss a payday, earning Thurmond praise in the press.

With his school duties now under control, Thurmond turned more assiduously to his law studies with his father. Law school normally is a three-year curriculum, but young Thurmond was a man in a hurry. He wanted to finish in eighteen months so he could get started practicing. To make his workday more efficient, he moved his superintendent's office from the courthouse to J. William's law office.

J. William's program was a combination of theory and actual practice. He had his son read cases in various areas of the law, but he also let him draw up property deeds, mortgage documents, and complaints for lawsuits. A few months into his studies, Thurmond got even more experience than he bargained for when J. William fell ill with heart problems and asked his son to handle a complex inheritance argument in state Supreme Court. The main question was whether the illegitimate siblings of a dead man, Olin Johnson, were his sole heirs or whether Johnson's legitimate brothers and sisters, born after Johnson's parents had married, had a right to inherit under state law. J. William represented the illegitimate brothers and sisters.

The justices agreed to let Strom stand in for his father and, legal briefs in hand, the young man went to Columbia and won the case, convincing the justices to reverse a lower court.

It was an unusual start to a legal career. Lawyers don't generally begin with a Supreme Court argument, particularly when they're not yet licensed to practice. But Thurmond's courtroom apprenticeship was not over yet. He handled two other cases in J. William's stead before he was officially admitted to practice, both of them trials. His affinity for the courtroom was apparent: By the time he was officially admitted to practice December 13, 1930, he had compiled a perfect 3–0 record. Thurmond liked to brag that he had tied with a Harvard law school graduate for the best bar exam score that year.

Officially licensed to practice now, Thurmond remained as school superintendent, and within a month—January 1931—he received some additional public duties in Edgefield he hoped would add luster to his career. The news reached him in Columbia, where he happened to be working, via telegram from J. William: YOU UNANIMOUSLY ELECTED ATTORNEY FOR TOWN. IMPORTANT MATTERS FOR YOUR ATTENTION. COME TODAY. . . . (The next year he was also elected attorney for the town of Johnston.)

Between his school responsibilities and his public and private legal duties, Thurmond had plenty to do, but his thirst for politics wasn't quenched. By 1932 he had his eye trained on the next move up the political ladder. On May 11, he announced that he would be a candidate for the South Carolina Senate.

While Cotton Ed was going to ride the race issue back into the U.S. Senate, Thurmond had no need to address it directly. There was no challenge in South Carolina to "custom and tradition" and therefore no need to prove who was segregation's best defender. There was also nothing in Thurmond's background that would have made him a virulent and vocal racist. He was from a refined and educated family.

On the other hand, like so many other successful whites, Thurmond accepted the world as he saw it, untroubled by the obvious disparities between the lives of whites and blacks, inequities that raised the question of whether South Carolina belonged to its black residents, too. They were, after all, barred from the beautiful state parks and beaches, even though those areas were supported by public funds. In the towns and cities, blacks had little or no opportunity to use the libraries, playgrounds, or other recreational facilities. Even the policemen who patrolled black neighborhoods were white, and these neighborhoods did not look like the white areas of town. Streets in the black sections were left unpaved and unlit by the white city councilmen, and only at white schools were there traffic lights or policemen to protect children at street crossings.

But in his campaign for the state Senate, none of this was discussed. Thurmond wanted to talk about the issues important to the county's white voters: a better education system, lower taxes, more fiscal restraint in Columbia. He found himself with an unlikely primary opponent: B. R. Tillman, as he was known, son of Pitchfork Ben. The development surprised Thurmond, for he had had dinner with Tillman before announcing his own plans and thought Tillman was not going to run. Shortly after their meeting, however, B. R. reversed course and became a candidate.

Having retained his athletic build since Clemson days, Thurmond cut a neat figure on the stump. He always wore suits and carried himself with the erect military bearing he had learned as a college cadet. He remembered Ben Tillman's advice on handshaking and made each person feel he meant it when he said, "Nice to see you." His speaking style was serviceable if not riveting. What came through was energy and a sense of purpose occasionally punctuated by a dash of wit.

The candidate presented a wide-ranging, even progressive platform that emphasized educational reforms. He favored extending the school year for whites from seven months to nine months (black children had no guaranteed term), and suggested revising the method of financing schools so that farmers were not so heavily taxed. He called instead for raising revenues by taxing income, inheritance, and intangibles. He wanted to streamline the state agriculture department, abolish the state bank examiner's office, and do away with the state game warden system.

With bank failure threatening, Thurmond favored a new law to protect deposits, and because of the state's economic condition he wanted to eliminate, at least temporarily, free tuition and scholarships for college students. Instead he supported student loans that could be repaid at a low rate of interest. Finally, he called for shorter legislative sessions, promised to oppose any extra pay for legislators, and, in fact, vowed to cut legislators' salaries.

Tillman had a similar program, but he failed to mount a serious challenge. He carried his father's name but little of his clout. Thurmond won the August primary, the only race that counted, by a whopping 2,350–538 margin.

Before taking office in Columbia as Edgefield's senator, Thurmond gave up his county school duties. His January 10, 1933, letter of resignation was typical of his earnest, confident, slightly self-serving style. His twin duties, he said, were to Edgefield's children and its taxpayers, but because it was impossible to please everybody, and to get the best results for the least money, "I took the responsibility and did what I thought was right and best for the county and the schools."

Thurmond arrived in Columbia eager to start his legislative career, but the flu forced him to spend his first week in bed. Although he had to be sworn in seven days after the other senators, he was not about to let his freshmen colleagues get the jump on him. From his sickbed he wrote a letter to *The State*, one of the capital's newspapers, outlining his ideas for the legislative session. Fiscal restraint was the priority item. "We should make up our minds to cut appropriations; for our people are simply not able to pay high taxes," he said. Savings could be made in the state education system because it was "top heavy" with personnel. Counties should be given major responsibility for running their school systems, and the legislature's involvement should be reduced. More state revenues could be raised by increasing the license tag tax on heavy trucks, allowing a reduction in the tag tax for family automobiles.

When he finally took his seat in the Senate, Thurmond followed up on his campaign promise and promptly introduced a resolution to cut legislators' pay from four hundred dollars a session to two hundred. He devoted his first speech to the subject, and not surprisingly it struck a nerve with more senior members. They came to the Senate floor to give the freshman a piece of their mind. Thurmond did not hesitate to respond in kind.

"Are you willing to cut the governor and judges fifty percent along with us?" asked Senator H. Kemper Cooke of Horry County, interrupting Thurmond's address.

"I'll answer your foolish questions when I get through," he retorted.

Another senator told Thurmond he wanted "the amount I was promised" and put in a resolution exempting himself from the proposed pay cut. A third accused Thurmond of playing "cheap politics" and wasting three or four weeks on the pay resolution when the Senate could be passing necessary spending bills.

But Thurmond insisted that cutting pay would "create confidence of the people in the general assembly." A man was "worth the service he can render to his state and nation," and that, Thurmond said in all seriousness, could not be paid for in money.

The resolution was defeated when senators voted to postpone it indefinitely, a more subtle way of killing it than a flat-out rejection. Thurmond, however, returned two hundred dollars to the state treasury.

The pay issue aside, Thurmond's first year was typical of most freshman years, a combination of learning the system and tending to parochial concerns. He introduced twenty-seven bills and saw nine of them pass, but they were not major pieces of legislation. Five were designed to help Edgefield County—measures like establishing an elected cotton weigher for the town of Johnston, abolishing the county tax collector, and creating a new election precinct.

Another bill that passed classified eggs so that buyers would know which were farm grown in South Carolina and which had been shipped to the state from elsewhere. The legislation was temporarily tied up by an unrelated fight over a tax exemption for the Ku Klux Klan.

Senator James H. Hammond of Richland County said that the Klan, which owned property in Columbia, was deserving of the exemption because it was a charitable institution. Others argued that if the Klan got an exemption, so should other property-owning organizations, like the Knights of Columbus and the Ancient Free Masons. Amendments were introduced exempting them, too. Lost in the debate was any discussion of the Klan's penchant for violence. Opponents voted against the bill, which passed 14–12, out of pique that their own exemption amendments had been rejected. Thurmond was not recorded as voting.

One unsuccessful bill that Thurmond introduced reflected his apparent willingness to cater to constituent requests even if he didn't necessarily agree with them. The measure would have restricted the low-level jobs of "attachés, helpers, porters and servants" in the state office buildings to white individuals. It was killed on a procedural vote shortly after it was introduced. Its swift death, he maintained later, was evidence that "I never pushed it." He introduced the legislation, he said, as "a sop" to some white constituents.

He also introduced bills, as he had promised during the campaign, to abolish the state bank examiner's office and to reorganize the agriculture department. But these proposals went nowhere.

In Thurmond's second year, 1934, seven of his ten bills passed (the most important gave citizens a refund on their motor vehicle licenses). More important, he continued to solidify friendships that would help him in a more activist third year.

Signs of a progressive politician became apparent at the start of the 1935 session, though they were tinged with a conservative streak that would later define Thurmond's political profile. Thurmond turned his attention to the state's education system, introducing bills to extend the school term, to pay higher teachers' salaries, to provide for the rental of schoolbooks, and to allow the use of beer taxes for school expenditures.

Although only the textbook rental bill passed as a separate measure, the legislature did pass an overall school measure that raised teachers' salaries and extended the school term. Thurmond was a major player in the effort, handling critical negotiations for the Senate when he and colleagues met with House members to iron out their differences. By the time the session was over, he had carved out a niche for himself as an expert on education, and he joined a handful of key legislators and teachers to watch Governor Olin D. Johnston sign the measure.

Thurmond introduced another education bill late in the session, but this one had nothing to do with funding. It was a loyalty oath for public school teachers, requiring them to swear allegiance to the national and state constitutions. Failure to take the oath could subject a teacher to a hundred-dollar fine or thirty days in jail, and violation of the oath could bring a five-thousand-dollar fine.

Thurmond drafted the bill after learning that a University of North Carolina professor, visiting South Carolina students in Columbia, had advocated student demonstrations against war and against bearing arms unless the United States were invaded. He called the professor's remarks "outrageous." Thurmond maintained that the bill was "not aimed at teachers as a class," who he said were "at least 99 percent true Americans," but he maintained it "would eliminate any who may not be what they seem and would require foreign exchange professors to abide by American ideals." The bill, he added, "is against Pacifism, Communism, Socialism and all the isms except Americanism."

The bill did not go unnoticed nor unprotested. Two days after *The State* wrote about it on the front page, a letter writer called the legislation "part of a widespread effort throughout our beloved nation to limit freedom of speech." Teachers' "academic and civil freedom must be preserved," the writer said, "or the very foundations of our American liberties will be threatened."

The bill died in committee shortly after it was introduced, but it reflected Thurmond's suspicions about those who challenged

American values as he perceived them—suspicions that would continue throughout his career.

In the last year of his first term, 1936, Thurmond's efforts to improve South Carolina schools brought him commendation from the state teachers, whose journal, *South Carolina Education,* called him "a constant worker for education" because he played such a large role in helping to get the 1935 school bill through a "stormy" legislative session. By now Thurmond had shown he was a competent and serious legislator who could wield influence on issues he cared about. His style of persuasion was based on personal attention to colleagues' needs rather than on political threats. He was neither a Senate leader nor a power broker nor part of any faction. As his later career would illustrate even more sharply, he was a man who worked on his own. Given what lay ahead, his legislative achievements would turn out to be less important than the friendships he made with politicians from across the state. These relationships were to smooth his passage on to higher office.

Thurmond ran unopposed for reelection to his second term, and the ugly racial winds that swirled around that year's presidential politics did not directly touch him. The conflicts between an aggressive federal government and an established racial order in the South were becoming more apparent, as were the tensions between northern and southern Democrats. The latter charged that their northern colleagues were paying too much attention to blacks, and once again Cotton Ed was at the center of the turmoil. As a senior state politician he was a delegate to the national Democratic convention in Philadelphia. On the second day of the session, June 24, Cotton Ed was in his seat waiting for the program to begin when a South Carolina newspaperman found him and whispered that "a nigger is fixing to open the session with a prayer."

"Great God Almighty," the senator shouted, jumping to his feet to round up a few friends and bolt out of the convention hall. Near the door he stopped to look back at the platform, just to make sure the reporter had told him the truth. At first the poor lighting made it hard to see who was there, and for a moment Cotton Ed wondered whether the reporter was simply trying to get a good story. Just then the platform lights went on, and the senator got his answer. "By God," he exclaimed, "he's black as melted midnight! Get outa my way. This mongrel meeting ain't no place for a white man."

The following day he elaborated for *The State* on why political equality could not be accepted in the South: "Political equality means social equality and social equality means intermarriage and that means mongrelizing of the American race."

Blasting fellow Democrats, the senator charged that the "doors of the white man's party have been thrown open to snare the Negro vote in the North."

Cotton Ed did come back for the June 25 session, but by that evening he was angry all over again when Arthur W. Mitchell, the only black member of Congress, appeared on the podium to make an address. "This is another dose. I have had enough," he groused. "This time I am leaving the convention to stay gone."

Cotton Ed's declaration that the doors of the Democratic Party had been thrown open to blacks was overstatement. In South Carolina, the doors remained firmly shut in the elections that mattered, the primary contests for the many state and local positions that came open every two years. But blacks who managed to meet the strict election requirements could vote for president in November, and registrars took note of how many were rushing to sign up to vote for FDR. "They say Roosevelt saved them from starvation, gave them aid when they were in distress," reported one registrar in Charleston. "Now they were going to vote for him." This was the beginning of a political realignment in black America from the party of Lincoln to the party of FDR, predating by a dozen years the start of a contrary realignment in the white community.

Four other Carolinians had walked out of the convention with Smith, but not Thurmond; his disaffection with the party had not yet reached the breaking point. He continued to support Smith despite the senator's harsh racial appeals.

Eleven months before Philadelphia, Smith had used his "old school eloquence," as *Newsweek* called it, in a filibuster against a federal antilynching law because he believed it would change custom and tradition. "Nothing to us is more dear than the purity and sanctity of our womanhood," he preached to the Senate, "and, so help us God, no one shall violate it without paying the just penalty which should be inflicted upon the beast who invades the sanctity of our womanhood. . . . The virtue of a woman is a thing which should not be displayed in courts when the criminal is known."

Language like that was not Thurmond's style. It was a fact he would later use as a shield against the charge of racism, reminding accusers that "I never said a word against black people." But loyalty to party outweighed any discomfort he had with Smith's race-baiting. And like almost all other whites, he found nothing improper about denying full citizenship rights to blacks, particularly when they, themselves, seemed to accept their inferior status.

Although the NAACP by this time had grown beyond Columbia to include chapters in Charleston and Greenville, the organization made no attempt to end segregation or to become a part of the state's political life. Instead, the chapters were satisfied with occasional efforts to get fair play for blacks under the white man's rule.

Traveling around the state in 1932, Robert W. Bagnall, the NAACP's director of branches, was disappointed by the lack of racial activism. While Bagnall did not find "the tenseness and fear which in the past hung over white and black," he did find among blacks "a complacency and satisfaction which [I] was puzzled to explain in view of the circumstances." The state's blacks "have suffered a social hell so long that they have become adjusted to it and are hardly aware of it," he said. Instead of activism, there was "a timorousness which reminded me of a child which has been maltreated. . . . Afraid to do the most ordinary things, [they] have developed a defense mechanism by assuring themselves that these things—voting, etc.—are unimportant. . . .

"The only hope for the Negro in the South to obtain opportunity," the prescient Bagnall observed, "is to develop the technique of power—political and economic power—to be organized and used in his own behalf."

The fulfillment of Bagnall's hope for black political power was better than two decades off, and when it came, the world as Thurmond knew it would shake to the core. For the moment, though, the two races coexisted in relative, if unequal, peace.

Now in his second term in Columbia, Thurmond turned his attention in 1937 to getting electricity to more rural areas. Toward that end, he pushed through legislation that created statewide soil conservation programs, a prerequisite to construction of a federally funded dam to generate the needed power.

He also worked on a spending bill authorizing several colleges to construct new buildings. The allocation of funds was another illustration of the prevailing racial climate. The Colored Normal Industrial, Agricultural and Mechanical College was given authority to spend $55,000 for a new dormitory, a decent sum to be sure. But it was a fraction of the $150,000 given to The Citadel, the $302,500 given to the University of South Carolina, the $330,000 for Winthrop, a college for women, and the $160,000 given to Clemson. Granted some of these white schools might have had larger enrollments than the black school, but that, too, was a reflection of the secondary status given to black education.

During that session, Thurmond's colleagues rewarded him for his work on education by giving him a seat on the Winthrop Board of Trustees. (The college later named a building after him.)

The one oddity in Thurmond's otherwise methodical career was his personal life. Most men thirty-four years old had already married and were raising a family. But Thurmond remained single. His standard line was that he was too busy concentrating on his career. Still handsome and fit, however, he enjoyed his reputation as a ladies' man and encouraged it with jokes about the good times he had when the nurses came to lobby in Columbia.

The young senator's personal life had changed in one important respect, though. In June of 1934, J. William had died. His death had an impact on his community as well as his family: All of Edgefield's businesses closed during the hour of his funeral. Although all of the Thurmond children were close to their father, J. William's death was a special blow to Strom, who had followed in his professional and political footsteps. He had so thoroughly absorbed the elder Thurmond's philosophy of duty and service that he would eclipse J. William's own considerable accomplishments by the time he was fifty.

By the time J. William died, Strom had built a reputation of his own as an astute lawyer and had plenty of business. The clients he accepted and the way he handled their cases showed a man with a pragmatic instinct. He liked to try cases—it was the "romance of the courtroom," he said—but he always looked hard to settle a dispute rather than push litigation.

Thurmond's easy personal relationship with black Carolina was evident in his law practice. He willingly represented black clients—in fact his first clients, the heirs of Olin Johnson, were black. He treated their cases diligently, willing to help them find their way through a legal system controlled by whites. Sometimes he departed from the custom of the time to address black women as "Madam" and black men as "Mr.," titles of courtesy generally reserved for whites.

Although as a teacher in McCormick, Thurmond had offered his after-hours reading classes for whites only, he did make efforts on behalf of black schools when he was Edgefield's attorney. The county was home to a black high school and junior college, Bettis Academy, located in a rural area near the border with Aiken County. By the mid-thirties, the school was badly in need of repair, and the president sought Thurmond's help in getting government money for the school.

Thurmond agreed to write two letters, both of them illustrating his attentive, if patronizing, attitude. Noting first that he was familiar with Bettis Academy from his days as superintendent of Edgefield schools, Thurmond's letter to a state education official praised the academy for "performing a great work in training young colored people of this section of the State, and preparing them to go out and render helpful service to the unfortunate mass of colored people in the rural districts." He pointed out that "Bettis Academy needs more buildings, classrooms and dormitories, as the present buildings are entirely inadequate and since the school is growing yearly." While the people of Edgefield were willing to help, Thurmond added, "the colored people are very poor . . . and the white people are in only moderate circumstances, having been hard hit by the boll weevil, unfavorable seasons and other reverses for which they are not responsible."

The second letter, written to the head of the state Works Progress Administration, asked the agency to allow modifications in procedures so that previously approved construction could begin. This letter, too, was polite and filled with praise.

But a month later, by contrast, Thurmond was pressing the federal government to speed up funding for several white school projects in the county. Nine black schools were also on the list—Thurmond described them as "in terrible shape"—but they were listed behind three white schools and renovations to the Edgefield jail. The jail was "a disgrace," Thurmond said, because the inadequate space required a mixing of the races. As such, the problem "deserves the utmost attention from WPA officials."

Thurmond also tried to turn a Civilian Conservation Corps camp in Edgefield from a black camp to one for whites. He and M. H. Mims, the state representative for Edgefield, wrote their congressman, John C. Taylor, asking for the change. "We are anxious that the Civilian Conservation Corps Camp located in this County be composed of white rather than negro personnel," they said, "and kindly request that you take this matter up with the Federal Government immediately and have the change made."

With such a busy and diverse practice—everything from handling personal injury cases to evaluating potential Edgefield jurors for out-of-town lawyers—Thurmond needed to be well organized to keep up with his legal and legislative duties. While the legislature was in session, he left work for his secretary that would keep her busy from Tuesday morning, when he left, until Friday, when he returned. He prided himself on prompt responses to clients' requests: it was not unusual for them to see a next-day reply, and he rarely turned away business.

Thurmond's strategy had been correct: being a lawyer was good preparation for a political career. Just as his legislative work in Columbia brought him statewide political contacts, his law practice in Edgefield expanded his network with ordinary citizens. He cultivated them with the same care he gave a potential vote on a bill. He wrote countless letters of recommendation for individuals seeking jobs, sent get-well messages to the sick, and was scrupulous about sending sympathy cards. While the sentiments expressed were no doubt genuine, the hope was that the recipients would remember Strom Thurmond when he came calling for their vote.

Like any lawyer, however, Thurmond sometimes had to write less-friendly letters. When one client was extremely late in paying $258 for help in a criminal case, Thurmond sent a stern reminder. "As you know you had a very hard case and the Electric Chair was waiting for you," Thurmond wrote. True to form, though, Thurmond turned to more flattering cajolery. "I saved your life and I feel certain that you know this is true, and further feel that you have appreciation about you and that you will want to pay me for saving your life. . . . You can certainly pay $20 per month on the note until it is paid for."

Such problems, endemic as they are to attorneys, did not diminish Thurmond's enjoyment of practicing law. His appetite for politics, however, had been irrevocably whetted by his success in Columbia, and he kept his antennae out for the next opportunity to move ahead. In the summer of 1937 he saw his chance to wed the "romance of the courtroom" with politics.

4.
INSULATION AGAINST THE TURMOIL

1938–1946

THURMOND'S ANNOUNCEMENT August 10, 1937, that he was running for a state judgeship caught his fellow legislators by surprise; they had thought he aspired to the governor's mansion, not the courthouse. Thurmond did want to be governor, but he saw the judgeship—vacant because of the death of incumbent C. J. Ramage—as another stepping-stone. As a state senator and a lawyer, Thurmond had significantly widened his political contacts, but he knew his sphere was still limited. As a trial judge, his rotating court assignments would take him around the entire state. He would meet local politicians and community leaders everywhere he went. Free publicity would be his for the asking. When he delivered his grand jury instructions at the opening of each term, the newspapers would be there. When he presided over an important case, reporters would record his remarks. At lunchtime and in the evenings after court, he could walk around town meeting and greeting people with a ready-made entrée.

There was a less obvious benefit to going on the bench that would become apparent only in hindsight. This new job would take Thurmond out of active politicking and keep him away from the discontent that was growing over the race question. Granted he might preside over cases involving clashes between blacks and whites, but in contrast to the free-for-all that often occurs in political debate, these legal conflicts would be in the more orderly judicial arena.

When World War II broke out and Thurmond volunteered for service, his overseas duty would take him far away from the racial tensions that were continuing to escalate in South Carolina. The black community was beginning to organize, tired of its second-class status and encouraged by Roosevelt's aggressive leadership from Washington. The hostile reaction among the state's white political leaders was predictable and would come to a head when the Supreme Court, in a prelude to the potent role it would play in the next decade, spoke out on the important issue of voting.

The South Carolina that awaited Thurmond after the war would be different from the one he had left, but these changes would neither deter nor distract him from his quest for higher political office.

Thurmond's decision to run for judge was easy. Getting elected would be harder. To this day South Carolina is only one of two states where the legislature elects the state judges. (Virginia is the other.) The process gives an obvious advantage to sitting legislators. But Thurmond knew he might face opposition from the well-connected George Bell Timmerman, a prominent lawyer who was chairman of the state highway commission, had been a state prosecutor for sixteen years, and was several years older than the thirty-four-year-old Thurmond.

Thurmond decided that if Timmerman entered the race, he would bow out. So he visited Timmerman and asked for a prompt decision because of the entreaties he said he was getting in Edgefield to run for Ramage's seat.

After more than a week with no answer despite a personal request through a friend, Thurmond felt he couldn't wait anymore, and on August 10, 1937, he made his announcement. Two days later Timmerman announced, too, and on the same day wrote to apologize for being "so circumstanced that I could not reach an earlier decision, but in keeping with my promise I am letting you know my decision."

Finding himself facing the veteran politician, Thurmond didn't flinch. But he knew that to thwart a Timmerman candidacy he would have to work the legislature from top to bottom and lock up commitments as early as possible. It would mean a constant effort—letter writing, phone calls, and personal visits all over the state—but Thurmond was confident of his own energy and of the help he would get from the friends he had already made in his political career.

Even before he knew Timmerman would be in the race, Thurmond had contacted the state's legislative powerhouses, House Speaker Solomon Blatt and Senator Edgar Brown, both of Barnwell County, and asked for commitments of support. When events proved that they were both Timmerman men, Thurmond settled on a strategy to have them stay neutral.

Shortly after a conversation with Thurmond August 10, the speaker wrote that he had forgotten he'd already promised an unnamed friend (it was Timmerman) that he would support him if he ran. But Blatt told Thurmond that "I am grateful to you for the many kind things that you have done for me and want to support you."

Four days later, Thurmond wrote back to Blatt, suggesting that if it was indeed Timmerman the speaker was pledged to, he should take no part in the campaign because he knew both men. Two days later Blatt answered, confirming his support for Timmerman but not acknowledging Thurmond's request to stay neutral. Instead, he closed with appreciation "for the many fine things that you have always done for me and I regret very much that both you and George Bell are in the race at this time. I want you to know that I have the very highest regards for you."

Unperturbed that he couldn't get Blatt's commitment, Thurmond brazenly asked the speaker to help get the support of a mutual acquaintance, Representative Calhoun Thomas of Beaufort. "I consider you and Calhoun two of my close friends in the House," he wrote, "and if both of you cannot support me it would certainly be the part of fair play if one of you would support me."

Blatt promised to talk to Thomas and contact Thurmond again. "I am in hopes that the matter can be adjusted to the satisfaction of all parties concerned," Blatt said.

On August 28, Thurmond sent a final letter to Blatt—his third—to nail down a promise to abstain from working for Timmerman. The candidate said he had been told by two friends that the speaker would stay out of the race, and "I appreciate this consideration by you."

Thurmond followed the same strategy with Senate leader

Brown. On August 17, Brown wrote Thurmond telling him that he was supporting Timmerman. "I regret very much that you are in this race," Brown said. "I thought your ambition ran in another direction."

On August 23, Thurmond acknowledged receipt of Brown's letter and reminded him of his promise in a phone call that "you would take no part in the race other than vote since it was between two close friends of yours. Everything looks exceedingly bright and I feel that I shall be elected," a confident Thurmond closed.

The entreaties to Blatt and Brown were just one piece of Thurmond's strategy. He still had the rest of the legislature to lobby, and while Timmerman might be doing the same thing, Thurmond was determined to "leave no stone unturned," as he told one friend, in his search for votes. He started with identical letters to two friends, Joseph H. Bryson of Greenville and G. W. Freeman, Jr., of Bennettsville, who had urged him to seek Ramage's position. Telling both of them that he had received encouragement to run "from all over the state," he gave the men their marching orders: "I wish you would please . . . contact as many members of the General Assembly as you know and try to get commitments from them to me if you can. If you cannot get written commitments . . . then say as many nice things as you can about me (even though it hurts your conscience) and encourage them as much as possible to vote for me."

The day he announced he also set in motion a letter-writing effort to the entire General Assembly. The letter, signed by T. B. Greneker, a close friend and former state senator from Edgefield, was typed by Thurmond's secretary.

In his ringing endorsement Greneker described the candidate as "one of the leading lawyers in this section of the State. It goes without my saying that Senator Thurmond is qualified in every manner to fill the office of Judge. He is studious, energetic, able and a man of fine judgment. He is a gentleman of unimpeachable character and integrity and stands for high principles. He would be fair in his dealings with litigants and his decisions would be unbiased and would represent what he thought was right."

Five days after the Greneker letter was mailed out, Thurmond started to work his connections directly. In one letter to a probate judge Thurmond said he had never expected a vacancy to arise so early but claimed "it has been an ambition of mine to become

Judge." Then came the sales pitch: "You have lots of friends throughout the State and can be of tremendous assistance to me in this race. I am wondering if you would please see the members of the House from your County in my behalf." Thurmond asked the judge to report back promptly on the results of his meetings.

Thurmond was not even shy about asking for help long-distance from nonpolitical acquaintances. He asked a friend who had moved to Florida if she would "get your Mother and Father to speak to members of the General Assembly from your county on my behalf. I should certainly appreciate their doing so."

By the third week of his campaign, Thurmond was receiving written commitments from fellow legislators. Quince Britt from northwestern York County sent him just the kind of letter he hoped for. "I expect to vote for you for judge, and shall be glad to help you in any way that I can," he wrote. "I shall contact some of my friends in the House in your behalf and hope that your election will be a landslide. You are authorized to show this letter to any of the members of the General Assembly."

But letters and phone calls were not enough. Thurmond made personal appeals to nail down his votes, beginning an ambitious four-month swing around the state at the end of August to sell himself. Always wearing suits to "show a little dignity," Thurmond made these trips alone, crisscrossing the state in his four-door Chevrolet. (He liked four-door cars, he said, because "if you have a wreck and your front doors are banged up and you can't get out, you've got two more chances.")

Even his thank-you notes to the people who put him up were filled with politicking. He closed one by listing four local men he needed and asking his host's help in contacting them, followed by yet another sunny appraisal of his race: "Everything appears bright and I am very much encouraged over the outlook."

A month into his statewide canvas, Thurmond felt the campaign was going splendidly. He told Bryson that "I have about two-thirds of the Senate pledged to me and about one-half of the House or a few over." To his friend W. P. Baskin, an up-and-coming Democratic Party activist, he wrote that "Everything is looking fine," but that "it will not do to leave any stone unturned." He asked Baskin to visit four legislators still on the fence, adding that he was "anxious for my friends to keep their eyes and ears open and to keep working on the matter until the roll is called."

The main argument Timmerman forces were using against Thurmond's candidacy was that he was too young for the job. "Of course, this contention amounts to nothing," Thurmond wrote to one friend, citing two other judges who had been elected when they were younger than he was. He also argued that a man of thirty-five, which he would be by election time, "is as mature and has generally had as much experience as a man a few years ago at 50 or 55." He argued that because of his varied law practice, he was as experienced "at the Bar as the average lawyer 55 or 60 years old" and that his willingness to make the ultimate sacrifice, money—because "my practice is more lucrative than the Judgeship salary"—showed he belonged on the bench.

Thurmond kept up the travel and letter writing—he sent more than one hundred letters through the fall and winter. Not wanting to miss any opportunity, he even added a campaign note to his thank-you for birthday greetings he received from a friend in Orangeburg: "If you will say a word to the members of the Legislative Delegation from Orangeburg County in my behalf I should appreciate it very much." As an afterthought, Thurmond reminded his friend that "to be most effective, it should appear to the members that the matter arose entirely with you, so please keep this confidential."

By the time the state legislature gathered in Columbia early in the new year to make their decision, Thurmond felt he had done all he could. On January 13, the day of the vote, he got up as usual around 7:00 A.M. in his room at the Columbia Hotel (he shared it with Representative M. H. Mims at $1.75 a night), put on his Sunday suit, the better of his two outfits, and walked a few blocks to the Capital Cafe for his regular breakfast: fruit, cereal, and milk. After going over his vote totals in his Senate office one last time, he joined fellow senators to walk across the wood-paneled rotunda for the joint session in the larger House chamber. While other senators took seats with the House members, Thurmond found a place in the gallery, wanting to avoid any appearance of last-minute lobbying.

The House gallery was packed in expectation of a close tally between Thurmond and Timmerman, the race for another judicial vacancy, and the elections of insurance and public service commissioners.

Thurmond took out a pad of paper and prepared to write down the votes as the roll was called. His name was put in nomination by his Edgefield colleague, Mims. After Mims finished recounting Thurmond's qualifications, the legislators waited to hear the nominating speech for George Bell Timmerman. None was forthcoming. Bewildered looks passed across the room as the silence continued. Finally, Senator Brown—a Timmerman supporter—made a motion to close the nominations and elect Thurmond by acclamation.

The motion prevailed instantly and applause filled the hall. After Thurmond and the other new judge, L. D. Lide, were called to the rostrum and formally congratulated by the General Assembly, Thurmond thanked his colleagues for the "high honor" and promised that "I shall try to make a fair, reasonable and impartial judge."

And what of George Bell Timmerman? After the vote, theories flew around the capital about why he wasn't nominated. Up until the last minute the expectation was that his name would be put forward, and his supporters had been buttonholing legislators the evening before the critical session. Nearly everyone—except, perhaps, for Thurmond—predicted a close vote. Timmerman never offered any explanation for his sudden withdrawal. The predominant speculation was that he had made too many enemies as a result of bitter disputes between the highway commission and the governor and that he could see the handwriting on the wall.

Thurmond later agreed that the handwriting had been on the wall, but he contended it was in his own script. "We had him beat two-to-one," Thurmond would insist. "He saw he was defeated."

Thurmond's victory garnered front-page headlines and comment all over the state, particularly from those who had predicted the opposite result. After analyzing the contest, *The Anderson Independent* concluded that if it wasn't quite David versus Goliath, Thurmond had won "a political upset of major proportions, which stunned even those who usually feel that they know what is going to happen."

Blatt, whom Thurmond had lobbied so assiduously but who never quite joined his camp, made certain to send the new judge his good wishes. "I want to offer my congratulations upon your election. . . . I have always been a great admirer of yours and am appreciative of your friendship. . . . I know that you will make an able judge."

The tenacity and thoroughness Thurmond showed in this election were to be repeated in many more over the next half-century.

Men half his age, unable to keep up with him, would marvel at his energy. What lay behind the doggedness was a simple commitment: "When I go after a thing, I go after it to win."

Thurmond and Lide were sworn into office January 20, 1938, at the Supreme Court. After Chief Justice John G. Stabler administered the oath of office, the two judges received their robes. Thurmond gave his sister, Gertrude, the honor of placing his on his shoulders.

In going from lawyer to judge, Thurmond had moved up one rung in a legal system that was whites only. Although judges and lawyers spoke about equal justice for all, the words were not the reality in this segregated society that kept nearly half the population—43 percent—in inferior status. (By 1920, South Carolina had become majority white, the prospect of greater opportunity in the North having spurred black migration out of the state.) The courtrooms, the jails, the chain gangs, the work farms, and the penitentiary were places filled by blacks but ruled over by whites, and the law seemed to be their instrument of power.

When Thurmond sought the judgeship in 1937, blacks made up more than half of all criminal defendants and nearly 60 percent of the state prison population. More blacks than whites were poor, and as a result they often had a difficult time in court. Judges were not required to appoint attorneys for the indigent. Except for defendants facing the electric chair, police weren't required to issue warnings about individuals' rights, and there were few procedural rules a defendant could use to check the power of the state.

The legal assistance blacks did obtain from whites was not always of the highest caliber. Modjeska Simkins, a Columbia businesswoman and black activist, had been upset enough about one case in 1931 that she single-handedly began a campaign to get better representation for five men charged with murder. In a letter to *The State* Simkins called the trial a farce. The main witness, she pointed out, was a man whose grasp of reality was in doubt.

The trial "was had in a community fired by foregone conclusions; the counsel for the defense were afraid to, or for some reason did not, offer a reasonable defense," she wrote. "The trial was rushed through in such a manner that it could easily be termed a pseudo or legalized lynching."

The defense lawyer's closing statement could have been made by the prosecutor. He called his clients' alleged act "one of the worst, boldest, most brazen and heinous killings I have known. They have killed a friend of mine, widowed his wife." With a straight face he then asked the jurors for full deliberation of the case and to think of his clients as though their skins were not black.

The State eventually published a moderate editorial that wondered in print whether justice was done at the trial. The question was moot the very next day when the five men were executed.

Although Simkins and many other blacks may have considered the trial a legalized lynching, one positive development by the time Thurmond went on the bench was that actual lynchings had all but disappeared in South Carolina. Race, however, was still a ubiquitous if silent factor that controlled the lives of black Carolinians.

Thurmond began his judicial duties February 21, 1938, in Laurens, a small town about thirty miles south of Greenville. He was given a formal welcome by lawyers and town leaders. The local newspaper chronicled these events and provided a summary of his remarks to the grand jury—he urged them to monitor all institutions in the county, with special care given to the new mandatory school attendance law he had helped enact. Almost as an afterthought, one article noted that Thurmond "passed life sentences on two Negroes . . . as his initial act here shortly after court got under way." (The men had been convicted of killing another man.)

In Thurmond's first week he disposed of twenty-nine cases that were a typical mix for the criminal courts: several housebreakings, a larceny case, an assault with intent to kill, and a few violations of the liquor laws.

By the end of the year it was clear that Thurmond had correctly judged the visibility his new position could give him, and he made the most of his opportunities in and out of the courtroom. While his official remarks to grand juries were an opportunity to share his thoughts on a wide variety of issues, he also made himself available for speeches to civic and church groups and at least one family reunion. These events were duly recorded by the newspapers.

His address to the Charleston Lions Club in December 1938 was reminiscent of speeches he had given as a legislator a few years earlier. He decried the rising crime rate, which he said now cost the United States $15 million—400 percent more, he told the men, than was being spent on education. The reasons for the high crime rate were corrupt politicians and a "breakdown of parental responsibility in this country." The xenophobic streak that had surfaced in the loyalty-oath bill also reappeared. "Foreigners frequently come to this country only for the protection they can get from our government—ready to give nothing in return." Under no circumstances, he cautioned, should the government allow wholesale immigration into the United States.

Six months into their first year on the bench, Lide and Thurmond had exchanged letters about how the work was going. After telling Thurmond he had heard "good reports everywhere concerning the services you are rendering" and praising J. William's lawbook as "the most valuable book I have," Lide asked for Thurmond's views on sentencing criminal defendants when state law gave the judge wide latitude. Lide described this task as "the one that gives me the most concern."

In his reply, Thurmond also expressed concern about setting sentences. He said he focused on details, "taking into consideration the past record of the defendant, his demeanor, his schooling, his reputation, his family background and other points to try to arrive at a sentence that would be fair and just." In one case involving a guilty plea, he asked so many questions that the prosecutor thought he was actually going to try the defendant. "I made up my mind that the aim of every Court should be to render justice," Thurmond concluded, "and although I believe in proper procedure [I] would sacrifice technicalities of form to arrive at justice."

South Carolina's regimented society, like the South as a whole, made that difficult. It was not necessarily a matter of conscious, overt discrimination, but rather a failure to recognize that in a system that kept nearly half the population subjugated, inequalities were inevitable. All a judge should have had to do was look at the juries that sat in judgment of the defendants—all white, all male. But the appropriateness of excluding blacks and women from service didn't register, nor did the notion that the "custom" of racial segregation might skew the equal justice Thurmond sought.

By 1938 the political waters around the judge were churning, although he was safely on shore in his judicial robes. The growing pressure from the North to change the racial status quo had prompted great resistance from southern politicians, and the introduction that year of a new federal antilynching bill had brought the conflict to a head in the Senate. Debate on the subject helped focus attention on a relatively new southern senator, Theodore ("The Man"—his self-proclaimed nickname) Bilbo, a Democrat from Mississippi whose trademark was his diamond-studded horseshoe tie tack.

Sixty-four years old, physically diminutive—"a pert little monster," to one of his detractors—Bilbo was a taut combination of energy and shrewdness. A protégé of James Vardaman, he held the same white supremacist ideas as the White Chief, though he presented them with slightly less verve. He had been a state senator, a lieutenant governor, and had served two terms as governor before his first election to the Senate in 1934. He seemed to lead a charmed political life. He had twice been charged with violating the law, winning an acquittal on one charge and serving ten days in jail for the other. But after throwing himself on the mercy of the voters, he had twice been elected to higher office. "Glib and shameless, with that sort of cunning common to criminals that passes for intelligence," said one of his longtime critics, Mississippi writer William Alexander Percy. "The people loved him." Just how much was revealed in the 1930 census, when more than two hundred children proudly announced that their first name was Bilbo.

Early in his political career, Bilbo was not the first to make race an issue, but if the matter arose he left no doubt about his views. "Let us treat the negro fairly," Bilbo said. "Give him justice; teach him that the white man is his real friend; let him know and understand once and for all that he belongs to an inferior race and that social and political equality will never be tolerated in the South."

He was particularly incensed by the threat of racial integration. "The moment the white people of the South cease to maintain separateness in social community life . . . between the two races, that moment," Bilbo warned, "they begin the ruinous march toward amalgamation with the negro race with all its deplorable consequences." As a United States senator he proposed legislation to deport twelve million blacks to Africa and wrote an entire book on the evils of race mixing. "God created the whites. I know not who created the blacks," he said by way of explanation for his proposal. "Surely the devil created the mongrels."

When the antilynching bill was debated in the Senate in 1938, Bilbo, along with other southern senators, protested that the measure was a violation of the rights of the states to manage law enforcement matters. Their opposition, they insisted, was not because they condoned lynching or mob rule. Bilbo was convinced that black pressure groups were behind the legislation and that senators were pushing it to placate the "mulattoes, the quadroon, the octaroon, and all the rest of the mongrel breed yelling for the passage [of] . . . this law."

The bill did not seek to punish the lynchers; it punished local law officers who failed to protect a prisoner from a mob. No such legislation was necessary, Bilbo maintained, because the "ministers of the Christian churches, the good women of the South, the good men of the South, have for years been striving to build up a wholesome and controlling sentiment against lynching."

A sustained Southern filibuster prevented the bill from coming to a vote when the Senate failed twice to cut off debate.

Although the legislation would not become law that year, the threat of a repeat performance in another Congress made it an election issue in the U.S. Senate race under way in South Carolina. Once again Cotton Ed was up for reelection, once again the declining cotton market had deprived Smith of the political sweetheart he had wooed so successfully in earlier campaigns, and so once again he made race a main feature.

"You don't find Senator Smith trying to ride into the Senate on a cotton bale these days," one of his opponents, Governor Johnston, pointedly noted. "He's trying to ride in on a poor nigger."

Smith had two other opponents besides Johnston—state senator Brown and the Roosevelt administration, whom Smith had been bucking since FDR became president. White House operatives were hoping he would be defeated. Unlike Bilbo, a staunch supporter of most of FDR's programs (which earned him the moniker "redneck liberal"), Smith continued to object to most of the New Deal and tried to make the administration the whipping boy for the low price of cotton.

The major plank of Smith's platform, however, was white supremacy, and through the summer campaign preceding the

August primary he portrayed the New Deal as a veiled attack on southern traditions. He warned Carolinians that they were "facing the worst situation since the horrid days of Reconstruction." He published pamphlets decrying the antilynching bill and in hushed tones told citizens where they could find pictures of prominent New Dealers associating with blacks.

Cotton Ed admitted to audiences that in the early days of the campaign, he had been advised to soft-pedal the white supremacy theme because it was a worn-out tactic and might cause unnecessary hostility in Washington. The candidate had tried to act on this advice, he claimed, and had spent hours preparing and rehearsing a speech to make it "high-toned and learned," but he had failed. His retelling of the attempted transformation, with its reference to the walkout at the 1936 Philadelphia Democratic convention, provided an awesome display of the man's ability to entertain: "Oh, I was going to make it highbrow if there ever was a highbrow speech," Smith would begin. "I got way up there in the clouds and began it. I started off on the Plains of Runnymede, got down through the Battle of Kings Mountain and was headed for the Civil War via the cussed protective tariff, with a lot about the immortal John C. Calhoun.

"I felt somebody down in front was watching me," Smith continued. "Of a sudden I looked down and there on the front seat was an old farmer with a torn black hat on his head and tobacco juice running down both sides of his mouth. I hesitated for a moment and looked at him. When I did," Smith would explain, "he growled: 'Aw, hell, Ed, tell us about Philadelphy.' After that I came on down and I never did get up on that high plane. I know what the people of South Carolina are interested in. White supremacy, that time-honored tradition, can no more be blotted out of the hearts of South Carolinians than can the scars which Sherman's artillery left on the State House at Columbia. And, please, God, I'm tellin' about it."

With the enduring themes of support for Roosevelt and white supremacy, the 1938 contest reflected the Democrats' growing intraparty struggle. Though not supportive of every White House idea, Johnston and Brown thought there was much more good than bad in Roosevelt. Johnston proudly declared himself a "100 percent New Dealer" and accused Smith of disloyalty to the Democrats and endangering the party. Calling Smith, by now seventy-five years old, the "sleeping senator," he took dead aim at what was held to be Smith's strong constituency by accusing him of being out of town when important farm legislation was before Congress.

Brown, who had come within five thousand votes of beating Smith in 1926, also cast his lot with FDR, declaring "I'm a New Dealer. I'm a Roosevelt New Dealer. Roosevelt is a big-hearted, Christian man who wants to do the best thing for the people of this country," Brown said, adding that Cotton Ed's white supremacy tactics were irrelevant to political reality. "I am not worried about the racial question," he explained. "That was settled in the days of the Red Shirts. We are all anti-Nigger in the black belt. . . . I wouldn't make a political issue out of walking out while a Nigger was praying," Brown added, a snide reference to "Philadelphy."

Smith retorted with harsh jabs of his own, calling Brown "Bacon Brown" because he was promising to "bring home the bacon from Washington if elected." He referred to Johnston as "Brother Oleander," for no other reason than that the crowds liked it, and he charged that "Brother Oleander tries pitifully to imitate my actions and voice. But he can't imitate my brains—because he ain't got any."

The ugly rhetoric of the primary campaign did not go unnoticed in the black community. An irate Simkins wrote a letter to *The State* chastising the politicians for using racial slurs to avoid debating more serious issues. "Why should those unnecessary, hackneyed, and nauseating statements concerning 'white supremacy,' 'keeping Negroes in their places' and so on be used as smoke screens in an effort to anesthetize the thinking white citizen, or to arouse the highly emotional and therefore unthinking white man? . . . Why won't they discuss issues and plans vital to the welfare of South Carolina?" All that blacks wanted, she said, were the rights guaranteed to other citizens.

Even before all the returns from the August 30 primary were in, Smith's victory was assured. For many white Carolinians, the honeymoon with Roosevelt was just about over, eclipsed by their fears that an increasingly intrusive federal government would infringe upon their cherished customs. Upon hearing the news of Smith's victory, about two hundred Smith supporters dressed in red shirts traveled from Orangeburg to Columbia (about fifty miles) to celebrate what they considered another Red Shirt victory.

There was no evidence that Thurmond participated in the

campaign on behalf of any of the candidates. Judges customarily refrained from political campaigns, apart from their own races for the bench. It was a fortunate tradition for Thurmond because, although he gave his vote to Smith, he avoided going on record with the kind of hyperbole that generally accompanies endorsements.

Thurmond was reelected without challenge in 1940 to a full four-year term on the bench. Earlier in the year he had presided over his first case to result in an execution. J. C. Hann, a white twenty-seven-year-old alcoholic millworker, was charged with slitting his ex-girlfriend's throat with a razor. He pleaded insanity, but the jury did not accept his story, convicted him of murder, and did not recommend mercy. The death sentence was automatic. Hann appealed, contending that Thurmond had erred in his instructions to the jury on the insanity defense, but the state Supreme Court upheld the verdict. "The presiding judge went into the whole matter fully and carefully," the justices said, "stating the law as favorably to the defendant as established principles would warrant, charging [the jury with] all requests presented by defendant's counsel." Hann was subsequently executed.

Three more death penalty cases followed. In one of them, the defendant received a new trial after the Supreme Court said Thurmond had not correctly explained the law on self-defense. The black defendant was convicted a second time of killing a white man and was subsequently executed.

The death penalty trial Thurmond handled in the coastal town of Georgetown was the most complicated, and because of the appeal that was filed, it required Thurmond to set out in the record the reasons for important procedural decisions he made. As expected, Thurmond demonstrated a working knowledge of the case and the relevant law, but he also proved himself to be a trustworthy caretaker of the "custom and tradition" that had so far served him so well.

George Thomas was arrested in Georgetown on December 14, 1940, after a woman reported being raped by a black man as she walked home about 10:00 P.M. As news of Thomas's arrest spread, white men armed with rifles and shotguns gathered at the jail and demanded that Sheriff H. B. Bruorton turn over Thomas. Bruorton refused, but in a short time the crowd had swelled to a mob of about three hundred angry armed men. To stall for time, the sheriff handed over a black prisoner—not Thomas—and the crowd took him to be identified by the white woman. When she was unable to do so, they drove her to the jail and kept her there while ten more prisoners—none of them Thomas—were paraded in front of her one by one. She was unable to identify any of them. Meanwhile, national guardsmen had been stationed around the jail and a machine gun was mounted on a second-story balcony. While the sheriff continued to stall, he somehow arranged a face-to-face meeting between Thomas and the woman, who identified him as her attacker.

Thomas was taken out of the jail under cover and driven halfway across the state to the penitentiary in Columbia. At least one carload of men was reported in pursuit, forcing the officers to pick their way along back roads to avoid a confrontation.

White vigilantes roamed through Georgetown and assaulted blacks they found walking in the streets. This activity continued for the next several days, and most of the black community went into hiding until the National Guard could restore order. Later in the week an editorial in the *Georgetown Times* explained away the jailhouse violence as "regrettable but . . . due to pent-up, heated passions" and hinted that a lynching would have been preferable. "If the situation had ended Sunday, it would have been much better for all concerned."

The state Supreme Court scheduled a special session of criminal court and assigned Thurmond to try Thomas. Trial was set for the last week of January 1941, six weeks after Thomas's arrest and the violence that followed. A week before the trial, Sheriff Bruorton asked the governor to mobilize another National Guard unit in Georgetown "for the duration of the term of court." A unit was already scheduled to be stationed at the armory for unrelated reasons, so guard officials decided that more troops were not necessary. The governor, however, did send several state police officers to help keep order, and he had a personal representative on hand for the trial who had the authority to call out the local unit of guardsmen if necessary.

Joseph Murray, Thomas's NAACP-appointed attorney, arrived in Georgetown just before the proceedings and reported to Thurmond that his own life had been threatened. He had written Thurmond with a similar message in mid-January and also suggested that he and the judge ride over to Georgetown together, which suggests a chumminess between lawyer and judge that by today's standards would be considered inappropriate. (Ultimately, Murray and Thurmond arrived in Georgetown separately because of a conflict in their schedules.)

To convince Thurmond that the threats against his client were real, Murray told Thurmond that he had wanted to bring Thomas back to Georgetown for a preliminary hearing but was warned against it by the magistrate and Sheriff Bruorton. They told him there "was and is a high probability of the negro I represent being lynched should he be carried back there. . . . I have also heard from reliable sources that I will also be in danger should I go there to defend this negro but I am not so apprehensive of any danger unless I am shot in the back."

When the trial opened, Murray moved for a change of venue, contending that Thomas could not get a fair trial in Georgetown's charged atmosphere. He told Thurmond again of the threat on his life and filed an affidavit detailing the events following Thomas's arrest. He also said that he had tried and failed to get help from local counsel in picking a jury.

In rebuttal, solicitor J. Reuben Long presented five local lawyers who testified that they had not been consulted about helping Murray; each of them said they would not have refused such employment if properly compensated. A local newspaper reporter testified that there had been strong public sentiment against Thomas at the time of the crime, but that this ill feeling had all but subsided by the time the trial started. He called the court term one of the quietest he had seen in years.

Cebrun Moss, on detail from the governor's office, testified that he and other officers sent over to Georgetown had visited drugstores and hotels and had walked around the streets and had heard nothing in the way of threats or comments that suggested Thomas could not get a fair trial.

Thurmond denied Murray's motion, and the trial proceeded. Despite a decision that local tensions were not high, several policemen remained on duty at the courthouse, and all traffic was barred from passing by while court was in session.

Thurmond's opening comment for the jury selection was a candid appraisal of the racial status quo: "George Thomas is a negro, so it will be unnecessary to inquire as to [any family] relationship to him, since all jurors at this term of court appear to be white."

When the victim testified, she identified the defendant and said he had stopped her to ask the time as she was walking home from work. She became frightened and started to run, but he ran after her, caught her, and dragged her to a nearby vacant lot, where he assaulted her.

Asked by defense lawyer Murray why she didn't scream, she replied that Thomas had first choked her, then threatened to kill her if she did.

On the second day of the trial, Thomas testified that he was not near the victim's home when the attack occurred. His wife, his son, and his sister-in-law said that on the night of the attack he had come home at 7:15 P.M. in an intoxicated condition, eaten his dinner, and fallen asleep at the kitchen table. He stayed there, they said, until 10:45 P.M. and then went to bed until the next morning. Seven other witnesses corroborated Thomas's whereabouts.

White prosecution rebuttal witnesses contradicted Thomas's story, and a state patrolman corroborated earlier testimony that grass and burrs had been found in the front of Thomas's underwear.

The jury deliberated for about an hour and returned a verdict of guilty with no recommendation of mercy. The verdict carried an automatic death sentence, which Thurmond imposed the next morning.

Murray moved for a new trial, contending that Thomas had not received a fair trial because of the atmosphere around Georgetown. Thurmond denied the request and later issued an order to this effect that explained why he had refused to throw out the verdict. He had "never seen a trial conducted in a fairer, more impartial manner," he wrote, "all the attendants at the Court being perfectly peaceable, quiet and orderly and no disorder or even suggestion of disorder of any kind appearing in or around the Court House or elsewhere that came to the attention of the court."

The order made no mention of the vigilantes' attacks and the lynching attempt after Thomas was arrested. Thurmond said Thomas had been taken to the penitentiary "along with other prisoners . . . due to the congested condition at the county jail."

The presence of national guardsmen a few blocks from the courthouse had no connection "directly or indirectly" with the trial. Thurmond said the guard had been "called out by the Government for the purpose of induction into service and were stationed several blocks away." There were "only such officers seen in and around the Court House as was [*sic*] actually necessary to carry on the usual normal Court business." His report conflicted with newspaper reports of police officers guarding the courthouse and of traffic being blocked from the area.

Thurmond stated that only "a few people attended the court," while news accounts described the courthouse as packed.

As further evidence that "these sex cases tried at that term of Court did not arouse undue public feeling against these defendants," Thurmond pointed out that another black man, Isaac Gibson, later was tried for allegedly raping a white woman and that the jury came back with a recommendation of mercy. (Thurmond sentenced Gibson to forty years in prison but pointedly told him the only reason it wasn't longer was that state law didn't allow it.)

Thurmond's report apparently was persuasive. The high court said he had been justified in refusing to move the trial out of Georgetown, and on February 20, 1942, Thomas was executed.

Given the documentary evidence—Murray's letter to Thurmond and his sworn affidavit, news reports of the vigilante attacks and potential lynching—Thurmond's refusal to move the trial is difficult to understand. Rather than err on the side of caution to make sure Thomas got a fair hearing in the white community, he filtered the information through the only lens he knew, that of a prosperous white man, and he apparently chose to rely on the prosecution witnesses who promised that Georgetown's white citizenry could render an unbiased verdict. Having done so, he had to justify his action to the Supreme Court, even if it meant describing an atmosphere that was at odds with documents and contemporaneous reporting by the local newspaper. As important, there was nothing in his life up to that moment that would have led him to question the inequality of segregation, so perhaps he believed George Thomas was getting the hearing he deserved.

In Thurmond's view, he never presided over what Modjeska Simkins would call a "pseudo or legalized lynching" and never condoned an actual one. On at least one occasion he had spoken out against it. In January 1940, Thurmond was holding court in Greenville. Before starting the term, he had received a letter from local attorney Stephen Nettles asking him to "say something about the Klan" when he addressed the grand jury. (Blacks had been trying to stage a voter-registration drive, and the Klan was waging a war of intimidation against them just short of overt violence.) "Unless this business is stopped shortly," Nettles wrote, "we are going to have serious trouble right here in Greenville, and when it comes I think the blame will rest largely on our sheriff, who appears to be utterly indifferent about the matter." Nettles said he was confident that "local public sentiment is strongly against the illegal action of the Klan . . . and if you will put the influence of your office behind it I believe the result which all good citizens desire will be realized."

Five days later, in remarks to the grand jury, Thurmond condemned the activities of the "masked riders" as "the most abominable type of lawlessness." He pointed out that they violated a state law against going out masked and forcibly taking a person from his home to threaten or assault him. "I am not in sympathy with any such doings," Thurmond said. "Anyone convicted [of violating the law] need expect no mercy at my hands."

The chance to make public pronouncements, of course, was part of what had brought Thurmond to the bench, and he particularly enjoyed opportunities to expound upon the traditionalist philosophy of duty, service, and rectitude he had absorbed from his father and had refined on his own as a teacher, legislator, and judge. "Religious training is most important in preventing crime," Thurmond told one student who wrote to ask him about the criminal justice system. "I have never had a regular Sunday School attendant or a person who I concluded was a good church member come before me for a crime. I have had only one Boy Scout to come before me, and no Girl Scout."

In an observation that seems to describe his own life as well, Thurmond told the student that "I thoroughly agree with an article I read some time back that heredity determines a person's drive, ability, energy and certain other personal qualities, but that the environment greatly determines conduct."

Although murder cases obviously fell into a different category, Thurmond said he was "a great believer in reclaiming offenders of the law, and [I] go a long way to try to accomplish this, especially with first offenders, and with young offenders."

His activities on the bench seemed to bear this out. After a year in office, Thurmond expressed concern about the lack of options in sentencing young men between the ages of seventeen and twenty-five. "When we send a young man to the chain gang or penitentiary, we don't know whether he will come out a better citizen or a criminal,'' he said. ''I fear that in most cases he comes out a criminal.'' Thurmond thought the state should build detention homes for these youths, and he tried a few creative sentencing efforts of his own.

One of these—suggesting to two young boys who had received stolen bicycle parts that he would suspend their sentences if they enlisted in the army, secured a position with the Civilian Conservation Corps, or obtained jobs with ''reliable people''—didn't set well with the army. A recruiting officer wrote to remind the judge that ''Only men of good character are accepted by the army and they have to prove their character.'' He asked Thurmond to strike any reference to the army from the court record ''in order that our citizens may know that the security of their liberty and their 'pursuit of happiness' does not depend upon an army composed of the derelicts of society but upon a fine, upstanding body of soldiers.''

Thurmond used his reply to the recruiter to point out that ''young boys of tender years . . . can be led into the path of rectitude if placed in the proper environment''—a criminal justice policy once again based on his traditionalist philosophy.

By 1941, Judge Thurmond already was well known around the state. But late in the year he got even more publicity when he was dubbed a hero for stepping into the middle of a fracas between two old-line Edgefield families, the Timmermans and the Logues.

On a November Sunday morning, the county sheriff and his deputy had gone to the Logue home to arrest Sue Logue and her brother-in-law, George, for hiring the hit man who had killed Davis Timmerman. Timmerman and the Logue family had been feuding for years. When the officers arrived, they were allowed entry and then were ambushed by George Logue and Fred Dorn, a sharecropper who worked for him. The sheriff was killed instantly. Though fatally wounded, the deputy pulled out his gun and shot Dorn before staggering outside. He was picked up by a passing motorist and taken to the nearby Augusta, Georgia, hospital, where he died a short time later.

Word of the shootout spread through Edgefield; Thurmond learned of the fight as the morning service ended at the Baptist church. He was concerned about further violence, so he immediately drove the ten miles to the Logue home.

By the time he arrived, a crowd of local citizens armed with rifles and shotguns already had gathered. Thurmond determined he had to do something to prevent more bloodshed. He didn't know who was in the house and whether they were armed. But to show that he had no weapon, he took off his jacket, unbuttoned his vest, and turned his pockets inside out. He walked up to the house alone. A voice behind the door asked what he wanted. Thurmond identified himself and asked to talk to Sue and George Logue. The voice said George was not home and that Sue was not feeling well. Thurmond insisted on speaking to the woman and finally was told to go to the back door. There he found himself facing a Logue family friend with a shotgun aimed straight at him. Thurmond managed to talk his way into the house and learned that George had, indeed, left the house and that Dorn's body had been removed. He persuaded Sue to surrender and leave the house, assuring her of safe passage through the hostile crowd outside.

He made good on his promise, and over the next few days South Carolina papers were full of stories about Thurmond's heroism, complete with pictures of the grim-faced judge escorting Sue Logue out of her blood-spattered house.

The publicity only enhanced Thurmond's reputation for grit and determination and made him more of a political celebrity.

Nonetheless, five months later Thurmond voluntarily gave up his judicial position to enter the army for service in World War II. On April 17, 1942, he reported for active duty as a captain at Governor's Island in New York. As a state judge, and one who was nearly forty years old at that, he was exempt from service, but he wanted to serve and to serve in combat. His past military experience, including four years of training at Clemson and then regular attendance at officers' training schools, enabled him to report directly for active duty.

The political world that Thurmond left behind was changing, and as he headed for New York, neither he nor anyone else could know how significant those changes were going to be or how they would alter the political atmosphere he would return to four years later. Just as the judgeship had kept him out of racial politics, the army would insulate him from him the turmoil brought on by a restive black community emboldened by an important Supreme Court ruling and a growing number of northern white allies.

Well before Thurmond left there were small signs of change in black Carolina, a reflection of the more visible stirrings under way in the North. The early thirties had been a quiet period, to the frustration of such northern activists as the NAACP's Bagnall and acclaimed black writer Langston Hughes, who wrote in the NAACP magazine *The Crisis* that Southern black colleges were "doing their best to produce spineless Uncle Toms." Another writer, J. Edward Arbor, also writing in *The Crisis,* blamed the churches and the black press. "Southern blacks," he charged, were "hog-tied by the fundamentalist do-nothing colored churches," a "preachocracy," he called it, that only advised humility and patience. The black papers were nothing but "cheaply printed prayer books" that offered "praise of those who exploit them."

While several civil rights organizations existed, their political strength was negligible, although the groups were well intentioned. The South Carolina Council of the Association of Southern Women for the Prevention of Lynching, for example, was a group of white women who sought pledges from law enforcement officials that they would work to stop lynchings. Another group, the Charleston Interracial Committee, was primarily known for one annual event, an integrated public meeting on "Race Relations Sunday" that took place during the week of Lincoln's birthday. The event alternated each year between the largest white church and the largest black church, with a black speaker featured in the white church and a white speaker featured in the black church. The white members were almost uniformly members of Charleston's aristocracy, and its leader, the elderly Clelia McGowan, worked on the premise that while whites should listen to blacks, blacks had not yet "come of age" and needed her to speak on their behalf. In 1931, the committee succeeded in establishing a branch of the public library for blacks, but no black was placed on the county library board. Mrs. McGowan, who was secretary of the board, believed they were represented through her presence.

By 1934 there were four chapters of the NAACP, in Charleston, Columbia, Darlington, and Greenville. Within three years NAACP branches had sprung up at two black schools, Allen University and Benedict College. By 1939 the NAACP had grown to eight state branches, including a new chapter in Cheraw, in the northeast corner of the state. Levi S. Byrd headed this operation, and in October he was the moving force to create an umbrella organization that would unify the state branches for more effective action. By the end of the year, the mood of the black leaders was captured in a manifesto issued by the Cheraw branch:

> To be set aside as a subject group by social prejudice and government sanction; subject to the dominance of all and any who might assume authority to command, is to be robbed of the same native rights which others demand and for which they barter their lives. . . . What the Negro needs is INTEGRATION, instead of SEGREGATION. These conditions are exact opposites. They are to each other as plus is to minus. The one affirms, the other denies. All the blessings of life, liberty, and happiness are possible in integration, while in segregation lurk all the forces destructive of these values.
>
> Reason and right deny us nothing. When these prevail, all will be well.

The ferment in South Carolina was symptomatic of movement further north, where congressional allies of the budding civil rights activists were making their moves to enact new antidiscrimination laws. Although the antilynching bill of 1938 had failed, its supporters were not deterred from pushing other legislation intended to bring blacks full citizenship rights. In response, southerners shouted "states' rights," a battle cry they would raise for another thirty years.

The next civil rights initiative was the anti–poll tax effort. By 1940, most states, except for several deep southern states—among them South Carolina—had eliminated the tax. From 1942 to 1946 a number of proposals were introduced in the House and Senate to eliminate the tax from the remaining states, but none was successful.

As the poll tax fight was going on, another effort was under way on the employment front. Pressured by blacks, the Roosevelt administration began efforts to assure fair employment practices in hiring and promoting members of minority groups. With A. Philip Randolph, head of the Brotherhood of Sleeping Car Porters, in the lead, blacks complained of not being employed in wartime industries in proportion to their numbers in the total population. Early in 1941, Randolph's threat to stage a massive protest strike in Washington brought action. On June 25 Roosevelt issued an executive order directing recipients of federal wartime contracts to refrain from discrimination in employment on the basis of race, education, color, or ancestry. The order established a five-man

Committee on Fair Employment Practices to resolve allegations of discrimination. Another executive order, in 1943, strengthened the agency by giving it a larger budget and allowing it to expand activities through regional offices.

The war effort also forced American leaders to confront more directly the manner in which the country's majority treated its largest minority. It smacked of hypocrisy, after all, for the United States to identify with democracy the world over and to proclaim itself the leader of the free world while condoning rank discrimination against blacks at home.

Because the fair employment committee was authorized through Roosevelt's wartime powers, it would not survive the war unless Congress created a permanent agency. One bill to establish a Fair Employment Practice Commission (FEPC) was introduced in the House in 1942, but a concerted drive did not get under way until 1943, when the National Council for a Permanent FEPC was created. A three-year struggle failed to produce results, however, and legislation to protect the agency was finally put to rest early in 1946, when the Senate failed to end a filibuster against the measure.

Condemning the filibuster, Simkins collected signatures for a telegram that was sent to Bilbo, his junior colleague from Mississippi, James O. Eastland, and the other southern senators. "IT IS NOT ONLY TIME TO SING AMERICA," the telegram said, "BUT IT'S A TIME TO LIVE IT AND LOVE IT."

Simkins's letter of thanks to those who supported the wire was evidence of the new, more aggressive mood in South Carolina's black community. Blacks, she said, "have shown that we can throw ourselves like a rising wind and a mighty wall against the forces of fascism—and Nazism—if you please, right here in our back yards."

While blacks were trying to organize in the South and their allies were pushing reform in Congress, a case was working its way from Texas to the Supreme Court that would give civil rights activists an important boost in the area of voting rights. In 1943 the justices had agreed to hear a Texas case, *Smith v. Allwright,* which would determine the legality of keeping blacks from voting in primary elections.

In another case eight years earlier, the court had ruled that a political party was a private association and could set whatever membership rules it wanted. With the *Smith* case, the justices decided to reexamine that premise, and on April 3, 1944, an eight-to-one majority reversed the previous ruling.

The court said that primary elections in Texas were conducted by the Democratic Party under state statutory authority. As a result, the party, when it was following these statutory prescriptions, became "an agency of the state" and therefore the same rules concerning discrimination and restriction of the right to vote that applied to the general election could be applied to the primary. The "organic law" of the country, the court said, "grants to all citizens a right to participate in the choice of elected officials without restriction by any state because of race."

Black America and its northern white allies hailed the decision as a major step forward. Governor Ellis B. Arnall of Georgia, perhaps the South's most moderate politician, declared the white primary dead. He defied the state's conservatives when he refused to call a special legislative session to seek ways to circumvent the ruling. "The Supreme Court of the United States says that everyone—Jews, Catholics, Baptists, Negroes—is allowed to vote, and so long as I am governor the opinion of the court will be carried out." But most southern politicians looked for ways to preserve the status quo, and nowhere was the search more vigorous than in South Carolina. Ben Tillman seemed to rule from the grave.

When the Supreme Court first decided to hear the *Smith* case, South Carolina politicians knew they could be vulnerable. A 1938 law gave the state convention of any political party or association the right to determine who could vote in any state, county, or municipal primary election—another barrier to black participation in elections to go along with the proscriptions Tillman had written into the state constitution in 1895.

To insulate those elections from being considered state activities, the legislature in April of 1943 passed a measure repealing state primary laws, to take effect in June of 1944, in time for the next year's election cycle. The repeal, however, dealt only with primaries for state offices and did not address primaries for local positions. Another session of the legislature would be needed to go the final step.

The *Smith* decision was just the latest outrage for conservative Carolinians. Many were ready to leave the Democratic Party before the high court pronouncement. William Watts Ball, the influential editor of *The News and Courier* in Charleston, typified their concerns. "If whites stick to the Roosevelt Democratic

Party," he said, "they will have to accept the Negroes into their own party in South Carolina. That is why I have cut loose from the National Roosevelt Democrats and am supporting an independent National Party in South Carolina."

By March of 1944, sixty white Carolinians had formed the Southern Democratic Party. The group's initial manifesto was an attack on the federal judiciary tinged with anger at national Democratic leaders. "We believe in the courts as arbiters among those who seek justice according to recognized principles of law," the statement said, "instead of courts appointed to clothe with judicial sanctions the dreams, theories and fantacies [*sic*] of undisciplined minds."

On February 29, 1944, the state House had adopted a resolution demanding that "henceforth the damned agitators of the North leave the South alone." "We indignantly and vehemently denounce the intentions of all organizations seeking the amalgamation of the white and negro races by co-mingling of the races . . . ," the signers said. They reaffirmed their "belief in and . . . allegiance to established white supremacy as now prevailing in the South," and pledged "our lives and our sacred honor to maintaining it whatever the cost, in war and peace." Cotton Ed sent a congratulatory telegram from Washington, telling his state colleagues that "we are damned tired of these butterfly preachers who do not know conditions in the South."

The black community was understandably outraged. "Your resolution . . . is astonishing to the Negroes of South Carolina," black leaders said in a letter to John D. Long, the legislator who had introduced the resolution. "Negroes throughout South Carolina disclaim any idea of amalgamation of whites and Negroes." They pointed out that it was white men who "took advantage of Negro women for immoral purposes"; but for that, "all Negroes for the most part would have been black." They insisted that the goal of the black community is simply "full justice in the courts of South Carolina."

The letter was signed by two leaders of the South Carolina Citizens Committee, Inc., an organization created when white leaders had begun to harass the NAACP by first insisting the group needed a state charter and then threatening to refuse that charter. The Citizens Committee, a state corporation with a parallel membership and board of directors, began to do much of the work that the NAACP did.

It was against this backdrop that the Supreme Court's bombshell exploded, sending South Carolina's white leaders scrambling for a way out. Ball's *News and Courier* suggested returning to the convention method of selecting nominees, abandoning the primary altogether. "To retain [the primary] and admit 300,000 Negro men and women to vote in it would make South Carolina uninhabitable by decent white people," said a front-page editorial.

Predictably, Cotton Ed was fuming. "The recent ruling is the answer to the question of why eight years ago I walked out of the so-called Democratic Convention in Philadelphia," he said, "why I made white supremacy a major issue in my last campaign; why I was willing to be called a reactionary by the Democrats of the north, and yes, even by my own countrymen."

His South Carolina colleague in Washington, Senator Burnet R. Maybank, blamed "agitators" for upsetting the customs of segregation. "We know what is best for the white people and the colored people," he declared. "We are going to treat the Negro fairly, but in so doing we do not intend for him to take over our election system or attend our schools." State Representative Long, sounding like Tillman, threatened: "We'll fight him at the precinct meeting, we'll fight him at the county convention, we'll fight him at the enrollment books, and by God, we'll fight him at the polls if I have to bite the dust as did my ancestors!"

For the first two days Governor Johnston was silent, asserting that he was "not alarmed." But within a week, sensing the agitation around him, he declared himself ready and willing to call a special session of the General Assembly in South Carolina to "keep our white Democratic primaries pure."

On April 15 the legislature reconvened, and addressing a hushed chamber, an emotional Johnston reminded the men that following the Civil War, "where you now sit, there sat a majority of Negroes. What kind of government did they give South Carolina when they were in power?" he asked. "The records will bear me out that fraud, corruption, immorality and graft existed during that regime that has never been paralleled in the history of our state. They left a stench in the nostrils of the people of South Carolina that will exist for generations to come."

The way to protect the state, the governor said, was to repeal all primary laws. The legislators took him at his word. By April 20, 150 bills had been passed to remove state control over the primaries.

Virtually all of white Carolina approved of the special session, though writer James McBride Dabbs was a lonely voice of dissent. "I am utterly ashamed of the state of South Carolina for its recent action," he wrote in a letter to *The State*. "It was a graceless, mannerless thing to do. At this moment in history when South Carolina soldiers are fighting all over the world to protect democracy, South Carolina announces to the world that her government intends to protect the doctrine of white supremacy."

The day after the legislature convened, the presidents and administrators of the state's black colleges met and adopted a resolution deploring the special session for "accentuating the tension between the races at a time when sane and rational thinking is more necessary than ever before." And in Columbia, more than one hundred black doctors and dentists jointly condemned Johnston's decision "at a time when all soldiers, white and black, are giving their blood and lives" in the war effort.

These strong words were ignored as the rapid-fire repeals were passed. *Newsweek*, with its customary panache, called the legislature "Killbillies."

Three months later Johnston knew how effective the Killbillies' work had been. With help from South Carolina voters in the July primary, he ended Cotton Ed's thirty-six years in the Senate and was heading to Washington to take the veteran's seat. No blacks were able to vote in that primary.

By the time the Democratic National Convention met in Chicago in midsummer, southern frustration with Roosevelt had become palpable. The president had decided to drop Henry Wallace as his running mate and was under some pressure to pick a southerner to fill the spot. Although South Carolina's James F. Byrnes, a former senator and Roosevelt confidant, was reportedly under strong consideration, FDR chose Missouri senator Harry Truman (a man whose life would later intersect with Thurmond's in the most profound way). In the platform fight, a white supremacy plank was voted down. Eighty-nine dissident delegates nominated Harry Byrd of Virginia to express their displeasure with the president, and some even considered forming a third party.

Despite conservatives' unhappiness with Roosevelt, South Carolina's old Democratic guard, led by state Senate leader Brown, remained loyal, and FDR won 87.6 percent of the state vote in November. At the same time, Carolinians approved an amendment to the state constitution deleting all references to the conduct of primaries. It was the final step to get out from under *Smith v. Allwright.*

Although blacks had been shut out of the July primary, there had been one significant development in black political circles. In May, the Progressive Democratic Party had formed so that blacks, with support from a handful of liberal whites, could select delegates to the state Democratic convention, put forth an agenda, and recruit candidates. By the middle of the month the group had organized in thirty-five of the forty-six counties, and the party had put forward Osceola McKaine to challenge Johnston for the Senate. McKaine got only 4,500 votes, but the symbolism was important. The party wanted to demonstrate to the black community that one of its own could run for office.

For its part, the NAACP was quietly preparing a different strategy, using law students to research methods of attacking the new electoral scheme in court. It would be two years before these efforts would bear fruit. In the meantime, the organization successfully backed a lawsuit challenging pay differentials between black and white schoolteachers.

Despite Thurmond's keen intuition for politics, he had no firsthand knowledge of this growing ferment in the black community back home and hence no real appreciation of how it could erupt into a direct assault on custom and tradition. His military service was keeping him completely absorbed. Thurmond had entered the army as a captain but was a lieutenant colonel by the time of the D day offensive. After an initial stint in New York, where he did legal work for army intelligence, he was sent to England in October of 1943 and then on D day landed in France with the Eighty-second Airborne. He was wounded when the glider carrying him crashed into a field behind German lines.

Thurmond's wartime activities were regularly reported in South Carolina newspapers. In December, *The State* featured a front-page picture of him receiving the Bronze Star from the commanding general of the First United States Army, the kind of publicity that could only help an aspiring politician. Even some of his letters home found their way into the papers. Thanking a friend for congratulating him on his promotion, Thurmond hinted at the pressure he was under: "My, my I have been through a lot since then." After the D day landing, he went on, "I fought as a combat officer for some days . . . before returning to Army Hdq—

had so many narrow escapes that it is a miracle to me that any of us landed by glider are still alive."

Thurmond left the army October 15, 1945, and promptly resumed his judicial duties. (He had been reelected in absentia, and without opposition, in 1944.) But the promise he had made to himself to one day be governor was never far from his mind, and he wasted little time getting in position for the election the following year. He went out on the lecture circuit, speaking to service clubs about his war experiences and keeping his name in the newspapers. Wherever he went he heard encouraging words: friends wanted him to run for governor.

By early May of 1946, Thurmond had made his final decision. On the fifteenth he officially resigned from the bench and announced he was a candidate for governor. His resignation, he said in his speech, was "to avoid any possibility that the judiciary of our state might, to the slightest extent, be involved in political discussion."

He touted his qualifications—twenty-three years of public service as a schoolteacher, county superintendent of education, state senator, circuit judge, and soldier—but most important, "We need change in South Carolina, a big change. The people are demanding it."

As Thurmond knew from his own experience in the state Senate, the South Carolina legislature was all-powerful. While the governor could veto legislation, appoint individuals to state offices, and grant pardons, he did not have significant authority over budget matters. He was only one member of a three-man commission that developed state spending policy; the other two were the chairmen of the Senate Finance Committee and the House Ways and Means Committee. He also had no direct control over the state highway commission or the public service commission, both elected by the legislature.

Thurmond promised to be an activist chief executive to make sure that the functions of that office would not be "usurped or controlled by others." A notorious issue during the Blease administration had been the number of pardons, paroles, and sentence commutations he granted—more than seventeen hundred in his four years in office. Sometimes he had justified his decisions by his mood: "I felt so good when I came downtown this morning that I decided to grant three pardons," he explained after one instance of executive generosity.

Thurmond promised there would be none of that during his administration. "I know from my years of service on the bench the high esteem in which our people hold the courts . . . and I will not use the power of executive clemency to undo their judgments," he said.

The emotional heart of Thurmond's speech was a breathless recitation of goals for South Carolina's future. The postwar world offered the state "unlimited possibilities" to exploit its natural resources. Industry and business could be encouraged to locate within its borders; better transportation and marketing methods would increase the income of the state's farmers, and, through trade and commerce with the rest of the nation and in world markets, South Carolina could raise its economic level and "capitalize on our finest crop, our young people as they come of age, so that they can stay here and contribute to the future prosperity and welfare of South Carolina, and will not be forced to go elsewhere to find the opportunities in life to which they are justly entitled."

Follow this plan, Thurmond promised, and "we can quickly modernize and expand our public school and college facilities," guaranteeing teachers the compensation they deserve and "the future which their profession should enjoy." He predicted expanded programs of public health and public welfare, stressing assistance to the aged, the blind, and dependent children.

"We dare not, we must not, fail to meet the challenge of the future," he concluded. "We need a progressive outlook, a progressive program and a progressive leadership. We must face the future with confidence and with enthusiasm."

Thurmond's challenge in this election was not that he faced one formidable foe but that he faced so many. By the time the filing period was over, eleven men had declared for the office, a result of the basic localism of South Carolina politics. Unlike other states, where party machines or the cult of personality—a Long in Louisiana, a Talmadge in Georgia—dictated politics, South Carolina was a kind of free-for-all: each candidate started with his solid home base and hoped to build on that with support from surrounding areas. Localism encouraged loyalty to individuals, and by the time Thurmond was ensconced in the United States Senate, he would make it work in his favor. He could roam the state free and clear without running into an established organization seeking to perpetuate its existence by backing its own candidate. And as a master of personal politics, he would turn South Carolina into one big neighborhood.

If there was any clear division in South Carolina politics, it was the cleavage that Ben Tillman so successfully exploited decades earlier when he rallied the "Upcountry" farmers of the western part of the state against the "Lowcountry" aristocrats centered in Charleston. But given the underlying localism, this division simply meant there would be several candidates from each group, and it was up to the voters in the first primary to winnow the choices for the second.

The ten candidates who joined Thurmond in the gubernatorial campaign were incumbent governor Ransome J. Williams; Dr. James McLeod, a conservative physician from Florence; A. J. Beattie, at sixty the oldest candidate and the state comptroller general in the early 1930s; Dr. Carl Epps, whose main platform was prohibition; Del O'Neal, a former Hollywood stuntman and sometime stock car driver who backed liquor by the drink; Representative John D. Long of Union County, who had cosponsored the white supremacy resolution in 1944; Marcus A. Stone, a lumberman from Florence who ran on a platform of five freedoms: "freedom to work, freedom to drink, freedom to do business, freedom to farm and freedom from taxation": A. L. Wood, who told voters Christ was the answer to drinking problems; Roger W. Scott, who was also a candidate for state representative; and former congressman John C. Taylor of Anderson.

The tradition in South Carolina, going back to the days of Tillman, was for all candidates for statewide office to travel from county to county and present themselves in a mass to the citizenry. Often these meetings went on for hours and took on the air of a carnival, with packs of voters cheering on their candidates and quasiprofessional hecklers trying to make life miserable for the other fellow. Tillman had called this hands-on politicking "the purest form of democracy in America," and apparently South Carolinians agreed. Certainly Thurmond felt these outings were tailor-made for him. He used every available moment, including lunch breaks (he ate a sandwich on the run), to shake hands and solicit votes.

The large number of candidates for the 1946 campaign made the county-by-county trek a political marathon. With five candidates running for lieutenant governor as well, that meant sixteen candidates just for the executive branch, plus several for other offices. Speeches were limited to twelve minutes per candidate, but that still meant more than three hours of talking—and the candidates were going to do this twice a day until the August primary.

The road show opened June 11 at Winnsboro, a town thirty-five miles north of Columbia. About 250 people gathered in the town auditorium for their first look at the field and to hear how the candidates would sell themselves. Roger Scott was the most pointed, lambasting Thurmond and three other hopefuls as "political acrobats" who were just using the governorship as a springboard to higher office and who "don't know what they are talking about" when they claim to have an agenda for the future.

Thurmond came up with what was, in essence, a conspiracy theory of the status quo. He claimed that the "Barnwell ring," a group of legislators led by Brown and Blatt, was running the state for its own ends, not the good of the people. It is a "matter of common knowledge that the government of South Carolina is under domination of a small ring of cunning, conniving men," Thurmond declared. "It is said that their influence extends even into the governor's office. . . . We have government of the ring, by the ring and for the ring."

Thurmond was hardly the first Carolinian to talk about the "Barnwell ring," but he was the first to make it work so well as a political tactic. The notion of "the ring" stemmed from the unusual concentration of political influence in the hands of a few men from tiny Barnwell County, in the state's southwest corner. In fact, members of "the ring" frequently and sometimes bitterly disagreed with one another on important political matters, but there was a certain cohesion to the group. They were successful men—bankers, lawyers, planters, and others with a significant stake in the established order, and as legislators they generally adhered to a conservative policy, yielding at the fringes when the demands for change were loud enough. Usually that manifested itself in increased state spending and higher taxes.

Political commentators initially didn't think much of Thurmond's effort to make the Barnwell ring a campaign tactic. One called it a "somewhat synthetic issue," and another pointed out that Edgefield had been a kind of ring itself, because of its politically active residents.

Thurmond kept on, however. On June 19 he told the small crowd in Conway, due east of Columbia, that "the leading henchmen and go-betweens of the Barnwell ring" had begun to raise money to beat him. "I gladly accept the challenge of opposition from that crowd," Thurmond said, adding a further charge that "the money that gang raises is not coming from the good people of the state."

On the morning of a hot and muggy June 25, the campaigners reached Barnwell, where two hundred people crowded into the small county courthouse for what promised to be a "stomp down good meeting." What made it all the more interesting was that the objects of Thurmond's attacks, Brown and Blatt, would be on hand. As county Democratic chairman, Brown presided, inviting all candidates to speak freely—though within the bounds of respectability. The closest he came to acknowledging Thurmond's attacks was to comment that South Carolina had a friendly spirit and good government despite newspaper reports indicating otherwise.

When Thurmond took the floor to a mixture of applause and heckling, he asserted, with his customary force and seriousness, "I am the candidate who has attacked the Barnwell ring on the stump and I will attack it today. . . . So long as this ring and its henchmen dominate South Carolina you won't get the reforms the people want. When I get through telling what I know about the ring," he promised, "the eyes of the people of South Carolina will be opened."

Stone, the lumberman from Florence, who had been defending the alleged ring, accepted Thurmond's new offer to debate anyone on the ring issue. Thurmond immediately called for the debate to be held in Spartanburg on the night of July 10, following appearances by the group in the northern counties of Union and Cherokee.

The debate never happened. On July 3, Stone announced he was withdrawing at the request of Brown and Blatt. Simultaneously he released letters he had received from the two men, each calling into question the sincerity of Thurmond's attack on the ring. Thurmond, they declared pointedly, had sought their support before he formally entered the governor's race—a possibility that hardly seems farfetched given that the two men were powerful state officials and that Thurmond had assiduously sought their backing when he was running for circuit judge in 1937.

Brown's letter pointed out that Thurmond had served "a term

or two with me in the Senate and was ever high in his praise of my leadership." Moreover, Thurmond had even praised Barnwell County's fine management and said it "was due to the superb leadership of our delegation." Brown claimed it was for reasons of health that he had declined to support Thurmond—or anyone else—which at the time Thurmond had understood. "I thanked him. He thanked me. We parted in various attestations of friendship. . . .

"I believe Strom was at the time sincere," Brown concluded. "The people must now judge for themselves why his overnight change of heart."

In Blatt's version, Thurmond had come to his home in January to ask for his support in the gubernatorial campaign but had been told that "my boy had just got out of the service, and I was so thankful to have him back home that I had given no consideration to the race for governor.

"In the course of the conversation," according to Blatt, "Mr. Thurmond praised my services to the state, said that I had made a fair and impartial presiding officer, and told me that if I would give him my support he would . . . give a member of my family employment in the governor's office. . . .

"It is passing strange," Blatt continued, "that, although I was a member of the Barnwell County delegation in January of this year, Mr. Thurmond praised me then and earnestly solicited my support."

Thurmond called the letters "a lot of baloney." The Barnwell delegation didn't want a debate, he insisted, "because they are scared of what I'll say." Thurmond issued his own letter to Stone denying that he had sought backing from Brown or Blatt. He dismissed the quid pro quo of a job offer as a lighthearted response to a joke. He would continue to denounce the Barnwell men, Thurmond insisted. "Their efforts to exert a stranglehold on free speech in South Carolina will have no effect whatsoever upon me or the right-thinking, honest and courageous people of our state. Their stranglehold on South Carolina will be broken."

The bickering continued with a final exchange of letters filled with contradictory versions of the conversations between Thurmond and the Barnwell legislators. Brown's concluding slap observed that "this campaign is not without some reward. It has at least accomplished the removal of Mr. Thurmond from the bench of South Carolina. It is far better to have him blatherskiting over the state in a political campaign even though he occasionally stabs a friend in the back than to have his politically ambitious body wrapped in a judicial robe sitting on the bench where justice is supposed to be administered."

Blatt's reply was a blunt challenge: "If Mr. Thurmond knows of one dishonorable act that I have ever done in public office, it is his duty now to tell it, and this can be done just as easily during the campaign meetings as in a joint debate with Mr. Stone or anyone else."

Instead, Thurmond sought to use the canceled debate to his advantage, continuing to blast Blatt and Brown as "scheming, conniving, selfish men." In a flurry of patriotism he wove his war record into the ring issue by mentioning "scheming, conniving, selfish men" who had gained power in Germany, Japan, and Italy and by comparing the Barnwell crowd to these "gangs." "I was willing to risk my life to stamp out such gangs in Europe," Thurmond said. "I intend to devote my future to wiping out the stench and stain with which the Barnwell ring has smeared the Government of South Carolina for, lo, these many years."

It is difficult to know where the truth lay in the charges and countercharges about "the ring" and its control of the state. There is no question about the considerable influence and power wielded by the Barnwell legislators, but there is no evidence that they were venal, dishonest men who violated state laws with impunity. While Thurmond could raise legitimate questions about the concentration of power in the hands of a few, he seems to have painted the ring as a much more nefarious force than it actually was. What is more significant than the actual truth is what the episode reveals about Thurmond, the politician. At minimum it shows once again his great determination for the task at hand, his ability to concentrate on today and tomorrow and not worry about what happened yesterday. His entreaties to Brown and Blatt when he was running for judge and the details revealed in their bitter exchange of letters show that, even with a politician's rhetorical discount applied, professional relationships did exist among the men. So it is plausible that he sought their support for the governor's race. It is a mark of Thurmond's single-mindedness, thick skin, and short memory that he could turn on them if that's what it took to blunt their political clout.

By the end of July, the gubernatorial campaign had slowed down. The ring issue had been interesting for a while, and it had kept Thurmond's name before the public. But there were other factors he could use to his great advantage: his commendable legislative, judicial, and military service. As important were Thurmond's personal traits—his drive and determination coupled with a maturing political instinct that helped him gauge the voters' mood. The achievement of a goal he had set for himself thirty-four years earlier was within his grasp, and he was not going to let it slip away.

Despite the racial tensions brought on by the civil rights initiatives of the previous two years, the campaign was generally devoid of racial demagoguery. Part of the reason was that there had been no direct challenge yet to white Carolina's ruling elite. Thurmond made only one comment on the subject: "I will never favor mixing the races in schools, in churches, theaters, restaurants and elsewhere. I will never sign a bill to mix the races."

As one political reporter observed, states' rights and white supremacy had become "so much a part of the thinking of South Carolina that little controversy has been aroused." The observation implicitly ignored more than 40 percent of the population. The thinking described was only white Carolina's.

When the results of the August 12 primary came, Thurmond was the top vote-getter, followed by Dr. McLeod. This set up a runoff between the two, with the second primary—the election that would make either one governor—set for September 3.

In the intervening time, McLeod sought to paint Thurmond as the candidate of the CIO. He claimed that a union leader had said so, and he was shocked that Thurmond had not denied it.

Backing of the labor group was hardly a blessing. In conservative South Carolina it could be as devastating as being thought soft on race. Thurmond denied the charge and leveled one of his own, arguing that McLeod was not a loyal Democrat because he had voted for Harry Byrd for president in 1944. Thurmond, by contrast, was an FDR man all the way, describing the president at one campaign stop as the world's greatest leader. Serving overseas, Thurmond had not been a firsthand observer of the discontent many white Carolinians had felt about Roosevelt. There is more than a little irony, given the not-too-distant future, in Thurmond's assailing a fellow Democrat for deserting the party.

Thurmond's solid record of achievement served him well, and compared to McLeod he was considered the more moderate candidate. *The Herald* of Spartanburg gave him a ringing endorsement in its August 31 edition, headlining its editorial THURMOND FOR A PROGRESSIVE SOUTH CAROLINA.

Thurmond won the September 3 vote easily, beating McLeod by more than 35,000 votes. In just a few more months, the dream of the nine-year-old boy would come true.

In the meantime, however, Thurmond was going to get some rest. He was tired and thin—he had lost nearly fifteen pounds—after a campaign that not only had impressed voters with his energy but had also worn out some of his campaign aides. He had recruited a group of young war veterans to serve as drivers, but he found he had to change them every week because the men could not keep up with his fast-paced treks around the state.

The last day of the campaign was typical. The night before the September 3 vote, Thurmond made a radio address in Columbia. He got up Tuesday expecting to go over to Edgefield to vote and then return to Columbia to await the returns. But he got word that Charleston was "in bad shape." Although he did not expect to carry the county, Thurmond didn't want to lose it by too much. So he summoned that week's driver, raced the fifty miles west to his precinct in Edgefield to vote, then turned around and headed east across the state to make a last appeal to Charleston voters. On the way, he also heard that a county official south of Columbia was thinking of voting for McLeod, so he met with the man on the way back in an effort to turn him around. He didn't get back to his headquarters in Columbia until late at night and wasn't able to make his victory speech until nearly 11:00 P.M.

Thurmond called his election "a triumph of good government" and said his administration would "encourage teamwork between all factions of all the people."

Whether or not white Carolina noticed, there were unmistakable clues during the primary vote that a sea change was under way in the state's definition of "all the people." Despite the Democratic Party's best efforts, ten blacks had managed to vote in Spartanburg during the first primary. Another seven had tried in Columbia and Anderson but had been turned away. A short article in *The State* reported that in the second primary three blacks had voted in Spartanburg.

One of the blacks who had been turned away August 12 in Columbia was George Elmore. Thurmond was unaware of what had happened at the polling place, but the governor-elect was going to hear much more about Elmore in the coming year. The period of insulation was over. Within weeks Thurmond would be back in the political fray full-time.

5.
MAKING CHOICES

1947

THE CRISP WIND that swept through Columbia the day of Thurmond's inauguration seemed to be the perfect metaphor for a man who had campaigned as the breath of fresh air to blow away the "Barnwell ring." Now it was time for the independent spirit of Edgefield.

While this year started a new era in Thurmond's political life and a productive period for most of South Carolina, 1947 was also a significant demarcation for the entire South. It was the beginning of a shift in political power that ultimately would end unilateral control by white men and would realign loyalties within and between the two major parties. The black community's surge for equal rights was only in its nascent stages, but already this new assertiveness was affecting southern white leaders. At home they looked secure, but their grip on the levers of power in Washington had slipped perceptibly. They could no longer dictate events and were thrust into the position of reacting. All-out confrontation would come the next year.

For them it was a time for making choices: whether to resist the pressure for change or to jettison the past and join the march to the future. Steeped in a 150-year tradition of racial separation, precious few took the latter course. Those who did paid dearly.

It was also a time that tested philosophies, matching the narrow ideology of states' rights against the personal and political aspirations of black America. Legal and political challenges by black leaders and their northern supporters were going to push the white South into a corner, and the region's political leaders would come out fighting on behalf of the amorphous "state." They clung to the Tenth Amendment to the Constitution, finding solace and solutions to every political problem in the provision's declaration that all powers not delegated to the United States and those the charter did not prohibit for state use belonged to the states or the people. In short, the states were paramount, and an all-powerful central government that might impose its will from Washington was not only suspect but, when social custom was at stake, a violation of the Constitution as they viewed it.

To the emerging civil rights community, however, portraying the struggle as a battle over the allocation of political power missed the much larger point. To black citizens the issue was human dignity—the right to vote, the right to a decent education, the right to full participation in American life. From their perspective, the recalcitrant states had abdicated their right to leadership.

Though not yet visible, the disparate elements that would force the confrontation were already gathering as Thurmond readied himself to assume power in Columbia. In another part of the city, George Elmore, denied the chance to vote the previous August, already had told NAACP lawyers that he was willing to be a plaintiff in a lawsuit challenging the white primary. The litigation was only one piece of a larger legal and political strategy that was taking shape in the black community.

In Washington, the special committee President Truman had appointed to investigate civil rights nationwide was working on a report whose publication would set off a chain of events that ultimately would engulf the new governor.

And 114 miles east of Columbia, in Charleston, federal District Judge J. Waties Waring, a product of the same traditions that had molded Thurmond, had already started his journey away from the customs that bound white Carolinians together. The results of his transformation would rock the power structure.

Waring and Thurmond were neither personal friends nor had

they worked together as colleagues, but their intersecting careers would sharply demonstrate how two men who seemed on the surface to have so much in common could use the power of their offices so differently. One would break down barriers; the other would defend them with all of his energy.

One man was a judge with lifetime tenure, the other a politician dependent on the electorate's approval. While that distinction surely freed Waring to take a different course, the real difference between him and Thurmond rested in each man's philosophy about law and society—specifically whether that philosophy could comfortably embrace change when it clashed with "custom and tradition." Thurmond would experience his own transformation, but it was going to take another quarter-century.

Thoughts of political conflict were far away as Thurmond and his proud family and supporters gathered in Columbia January 21 for the inaugural festivities. Three days before the ceremony, Thurmond had announced that the inaugural ball would be open to the public and held at the statehouse for the first time in decades. No special invitation would be required. In keeping with the populist theme of his campaign, Thurmond "wanted the people to feel the capitol belonged to the people." The event originally had been scheduled for a downtown hotel, but planners changed their minds after they realized how many Carolinians were going to turn out.

Thurmond woke up at his customary early hour that morning and put on a new suit he had bought for the occasion. He showed no signs of nervousness, just impatience to get going. His mother and his sister Gertrude, whom he had selected to serve as his hostess in the mansion, were already with him. Other family members were making their way separately to Columbia. The ten-car caravan bearing the inaugural party was escorted to the capitol grounds by army units, state guardsmen, and cadets from The Citadel, Clemson, and the University of South Carolina. There the party entered the statehouse and moments later emerged onto the platform, where, below, a shivering crowd estimated at five thousand awaited them.

Thurmond and his mother stepped forward for the oath. Although he had put back some of the weight he had lost during the nonstop campaign, he still cut a trim, athletic figure. The biggest change was a balding pate that only accentuated his high forehead and strong jaw. With Eleanor Thurmond looking on, Strom faced Supreme Court Chief Justice D. Gordon Baker, raised his right hand, and swore to "preserve, protect and defend" the constitutions of South Carolina and the United States. Then he settled into his fifteen-thousand-word inaugural address.

Thurmond decided not to read the entire address (the full text became part of the official record), which was notable as much for its length and breadth as for its ideas. Most of them were Thurmond's, but the speech was drafted by Robert McC. Figg, a well-respected lawyer from Charleston whom Thurmond had known for more than a decade, and Walter Brown, a businessman friend from Spartanburg who was active in party politics. They functioned like data processors for Thurmond, weaving together the ideas he gave them from notes he had stuffed into his suit pockets for later perusal. There was no soaring rhetoric in the address, just the sturdy prose of determination.

Before detailing his agenda, Thurmond paid homage to South Carolina's past, with the particular attention one might expect a southern politician to pay to "the War Between the States." South Carolina had helped this country become "a haven for those who were oppressed," he told the crowd, and after "that unfortunate conflict" the state had "carried her cross, and by superhuman struggle we maintained our civilization and helped our nation win two world wars."

Thurmond reminded his listeners that "our people are tired of ring rule," but hastening to salve old wounds, he insisted that he had "no feeling against any person or group of persons who may have differed with me last summer." Thurmond then settled into his agenda for the future.

The priority item was reorganizing state government to streamline the more than one hundred agencies that had sprung up over the last fifty years. "No one will argue or seriously deny that efficient public administration will thus be promoted," he said.

He called for revisions in the Constitution of 1895—the one Ben Tillman had written—because "it is puzzling to laymen, legislators and courts alike." He also called for abolition of the poll tax because it could be a hindrance to voting, and for secret ballots in the general elections. (While ballots by political party were standard in states' primary elections, South Carolinians also had to cast their votes by party in the general elections in November.)

Thurmond's proposals in the area of labor and education could be considered progressive. He wanted South Carolina to join other states by adding an occupational disease law to the workers' compensation statutes, and he wanted to require that textile and other plants maintain temperature and humidity levels conducive to their employees' health.

While Thurmond praised the progress that had been made in public education, he said it fell "far short of what must be done in the future." He recommended establishing kindergartens and nursery schools and making greater use of "modern media" for instruction, such as audio-visual aids and radios. He called for more school libraries, noting that only 39 percent of the schools had any libraries at all.

Finally, he told the audience that "more attention should be given to Negro education. The low standing of South Carolina educationally is due primarily to the high rate of illiteracy and lack of education among our Negroes. If we provide better educational facilities for them, not only will much be accomplished in human values, but we shall raise our per capita income as well as the educational standing of the State." Thurmond was not calling for an end to segregation, but he was willing to concede that the "equal" part of "separate but equal" needed improvement.

The governor also called for "equal rights for women in every respect. More women should serve on boards, commissions, and other positions of importance in the State Government," he said. "I favor equal pay for equal work for women. I recommend that women be permitted to serve on juries in this State as the presence of women in the courtroom and in the jury room would be a wholesome influence. . . .

"We dare not falter; we must succeed," Thurmond said in closing, "and we will succeed if we approach the task as a determined and united people."

Reaction to the new governor's speech was generally favorable. Several newspapers noted that, if nothing else, the scope of the address set it apart from any inaugural remarks in recent memory. "The new chief executive had something to say on practically every phase of our state government," said *The State.* "It was an earnest message, earnestly delivered." What was evident "not only from the tone of his remarks, but from his past record," the paper added, was his "determination not easily stymied."

The "people's" inaugural ball was a smashing success. South Carolinians jammed the statehouse to shake hands with the new governor—now in formal evening attire—to meet his family, and to dance until one in the morning.

Thurmond hadn't waited for his inauguration to begin the work of his regime. Not long after his election, he tried to mend fences with Edgar Brown after his attacks on him during the campaign, and he also began to exert influence in the House, where happily for him there was going to be a leadership change. Solomon Blatt, the other leader of "the ring," had announced that he would not seek another term as speaker, and Thurmond was determined to influence the selection of Blatt's successor.

Because the General Assembly had more statutory power than the governor—one political reporter pointedly remarked that about all the power and authority Thurmond had was to prevent "the entrance of Asiatic cholera into South Carolina"—the choice of a new speaker was particularly important. Thurmond wanted to make sure he had someone in the job he could work with and who supported his basic goals. Not long after the August 1946 primary, Representative Thomas Pope of Newberry, who had just returned from the war, announced that he wanted to be speaker, and by the fall he had about forty commitments of support. Within a month, Representative Bruce Littlejohn of Spartanburg, another returning veteran, announced that he, too, was seeking the position. Littlejohn had been a strong supporter of Thurmond during the 1938 fight for circuit judge against George Bell Timmerman. More recently, Littlejohn had played a critical role for Thurmond in the second gubernatorial primary, so the new governor felt a certain debt to him.

Although he had no particular animus toward Pope, Thurmond worked on Littlejohn's behalf, lobbying the only way he knew how—member by member with phone calls and personal visits. His message was straightforward: "If I'm gonna make South Carolina a good governor, I've got to have a speaker who's gonna cooperate with me. Littlejohn will do that, and I'm not too sure how well Pope will."

Thurmond's intervention was not out of the ordinary—Olin Johnston had intervened, albeit unsuccessfully, in the 1937 speaker's race—but it still raised eyebrows among the state's political observers. Reminding readers that Thurmond had campaigned against "ring rule," *The Timmonsville Times* wondered whether a double standard wasn't at work. If the "interference of the Chief Executive in the election of a House Speaker isn't an effort to build up his own group into power, exactly what is it?" the *Times* asked. And whether he got his way or not, more than one paper warned, resentment might ensue, resulting in a loss of "harmonious legislative enactments."

Thurmond paid no attention to the press warnings, and his lobbying campaign paid off. Littlejohn beat Pope, 67–50. Later, the Spartanburg Democrat freely admitted that "except for Thurmond I probably would not have been elected speaker." In one stroke, the new governor had established himself as an aggressive leader and, with Littlejohn in power, had improved his chances of getting his legislative agenda through the House.

Less than a month into his term, Thurmond was confronted with the most brutal racially inspired murder in the state in fourteen years. Willie Earle, a Greenville black, had been arrested February 16 and charged with stabbing a white taxi driver, Thomas W. Brown. The next day, thirty-five gun-toting white men forcibly took Earle from the Pickens County jail, beat him beyond recognition, and then shot him dead. Earle's body was so badly mutilated that he had to be identified by two dirty one-dollar bills in his pocket.

As soon as he heard the grisly news, Thurmond condemned the violence: "The case of Willie Earle is not only regrettable, but is a blot on the state of South Carolina." He ordered the head of the state law enforcement office to use "every facility at his disposal until this case has been completely solved." He said he spoke for "the people of this state" in declaring mob rule an offense against "decency, law and the democratic way of living."

By the first of March, thirty-one men—most of them taxi drivers—had been arrested. Thurmond promptly issued a statement commending the officers who helped apprehend them. "To my knowledge," he said, "this is the first case of this nature which has resulted in the apprehension of all those suspected of participation in the crime."

The story was not to have the satisfying outcome that many South Carolinians hoped for. But for the moment, Thurmond reaped the benefits of his decisive action south and north, principally in the form of increased respect from his admirers.

Recapping the story after the arrests were made, *The New York Times* praised the governor but predicted he had "earned the enmity of the purveyors of race hatred" and would probably lose votes in future elections.

There was a limit, however, to what was acceptable comment from the North. When the American Civil Liberties Union sent a hundred dollars to its local affiliate to help bring Earle's killers to justice, R. B. Herbert, a member of the state chapter, wrote back to say thanks-but-no-thanks. "In this case Governor Thurmond has acted with unhesitating vigor in trying to uphold the law and the officers have responded in a fine way. What we want to do is to encourage respect for law and order and in my opinion it really does not help for outside interests to be brought in, no matter how well intentioned."

Typical of the torrent of letters that came to the governor's office was one from C. Lamar Black, who lived north of Columbia in York and who wrote to tell Thurmond that his "prompt and aggressive action . . . has been a source of gratification to those of us who supported you in the campaign. . . . We feel confident that the principle of 'Due Process of law' has in the Governor of South Carolina an able champion, and we are very grateful."

Osceola McKaine, the black Progressive Democrat who had run for the U.S. Senate against Olin Johnston, wrote in words of praise from Belgium, where he now lived. "The immediate and principal reason for writing this letter," McKaine said, "is to commend you for your very courageous action in the lynching of Willie Earle. It has been a very long time since a Governor of South Carolina has shown by his *actions* [emphasis his] that he would really fight for even-handed justice for all of the citizens of our State regardless of their race, religion or resources."

Given the choices Thurmond would make in the coming months, McKaine's concluding wishes were overly optimistic: "Governor Thurmond, you have already done our State and America a great service; and you have given new hopes to the decent white citizens and to the Negro population of South Carolina and of the Southland. It is your sacred duty to continue this service, to keep these hopes high and to carry them higher. It is in your power to make South Carolina an example of democracy in action which other States will be happy to follow."

A similarly optimistic assessment came from essayist James McBride Dabbs, who told Thurmond, "I am under the strong impression that the majority of people in South Carolina are ready for a progressive government; we are being held back by a reactionary political machine, and by the resistance of a few bitter-enders, who cannot recognize the trend of the times. We who look to the future are proud to follow your leadership."

While Dabbs may have correctly identified South Carolinians' wish for "progressive government," definitions of "progressive" differed. Political and legal activities already were under way in the black community that would test just how much change the white establishment would accept.

The Progressive Democratic Party had continued to work since the party's formation in 1944, and chairman John H. McCray was constantly traveling around the state urging blacks to get more involved in the political process. As important, legal strategies for expanding the black franchise and black educational opportunities were crystallizing and were soon to become apparent to the white community.

McCray was an articulate young man who had been valedictorian of his high school class in Charleston and a graduate of Talladega College in Alabama. By 1947 he was the editor of *The Lighthouse and Informer,* a black newspaper published in Columbia. His speeches on behalf of the Progressive Democrats were an extension of his newspaper work.

One of McCray's more pointed presentations was on January 25 (four days after Thurmond's inaugural speech) to a group of black women in Charleston. "The burning, most important vital question in the South today is whether or not the South's ten million Negroes are to be admitted into first-class citizenship," McCray said. "So urgent and general is this issue that within the past two years, the people of the South have become divided over it."

Sixty years after Reconstruction, McCray said, southern blacks were just beginning to realize that "the one difference between them and other southerners" was the power that comes from voting "for or against men who run the government." When blacks studied the political and social differences between the two races, he went on, they "made some remarkable discoveries."

They discovered, for example, that because blacks didn't vote, South Carolina in 1945 spent ninety dollars on each white child but only thirty-three dollars on each black child; they learned that less than 6 percent of all funds for higher education were spent on blacks even though they made up more than 44 percent of the population; and daily blacks saw "little colored boys and girls trekking several miles to and from school . . . while little white boys and girls whizzed by on modern, up-to-date buses."

All this and more, McCray said, was because blacks could not walk into the polls on election day and vote the politicians responsible out of office.

Six weeks later, in a speech in Orangeburg to the students of all-black Claflin College, McCray continued his plea for political participation, urging the young men to "concentrate on one main objective: The Ballot. The ballot holds the answer to 99 percent of our present worries. It will establish equal opportunity to learn; it will remove the head-whipping police officers; it will enact such laws as may be necessary to destroy lynching mobs, the poll tax restriction and it will make both sides of the railroad track livable and with the same amount of paving and street lighting." He called it a disgrace that "while the first thing this country demanded in defeated Europe and Asia was a free democratic election, . . . right here in our State are 815,000 men and women who cannot vote in the primary, which for fifty years has been the only meaningful election in the State."

With the NAACP's help, George Elmore was trying to change that. A chunky, fair-skinned black—light enough to pass for white—Elmore had been serving as the secretary of the Progressive Party's Richland County affiliate when he was denied the right to vote in the August 1946 primary. Five months later, when he first agreed to be the plaintiff in the suit challenging the white primary, he was a taxi driver who had not been doing particularly well. His lack of a steady job turned out to be a bonus, however. Fearing reprisals, the NAACP had been trying to find a plaintiff who didn't owe his or her job to the white community. Modjeska Simkins and her husband, by this time very active in the NAACP, stepped in to help, giving Elmore a job managing one of their businesses.

Well before Thurmond's inauguration, the NAACP had been looking for a legal theory to invalidate the exclusion of blacks from primary voting. Law students at Columbia University had already written a lengthy memorandum on possible avenues of attack, and Thurgood Marshall, the NAACP's special counsel, and his staff were studying the recommendations and seeking advice from other lawyers, including the United States Justice Department.

At the same time, McCray was gently urging the NAACP to get involved in South Carolina. In a January 18 letter to Oliver W. Harrington, the NAACP's director of publications in New York, McCray painted a sobering picture of possible southern developments. Although Ellis Arnall, when he was governor of Georgia, had insisted that his state follow the dictates of the *Smith v. Allwright* decision, which ended the white primary in Texas, McCray feared that Arnall's likely successor, Herman Talmadge, would attempt to follow South Carolina and curtail black voting. Several other southern states, McCray wrote, "are awaiting the Georgia move as a signal for their own repeals [of primary-election laws] and schemes for preventing Negroes from participating in primaries."

Within four days, McCray's letter was answered—not by Harrington but by Marshall. "To make a long story short," the lawyer said, "we are not ready for legal action in South Carolina. . . . It is a terrifically tough job," Marshall added. "We consider the matter important enough to drop everything and get this case started. . . ."

Marshall made good on his word in three weeks. On February 21, the case of *Elmore v. Rice* was filed in Columbia. (Rice was Clay Rice, one of the election managers of the Ninth Ward in Richland County. There were fifty-nine other named defendants, including John I. Rice, chairman of the Richland County Democratic Party, and the members of the county party's executive committee.)

The complaint charged that Elmore and "other qualified Negro electors" presented themselves on August 12, 1946, to the regular polling place of the Ninth Ward requesting ballots and permission to vote but that the defendants, following the instructions of John I. Rice, had refused allegedly because of the plaintiffs' race or color.

Elmore's lawyers asked for five thousand dollars in damages, a judgment declaring that the party's policy was unconstitutional, and an order permanently barring the party from denying qualified blacks the right to vote in primary elections because of their color.

Although the NAACP put out a press release about the case, the filing of the lawsuit had little impact in South Carolina. The next day *The State* ran a medium-length story on page 10, a straightforward presentation of the complaint's allegations with only one peculiar twist. In explaining that Elmore claimed he had been denied the right to vote in the primary, the word "right" was in quotation marks. This "right" was still an open question in white minds.

The Elmore litigation was one of two race-based cases to land on South Carolina's federal court docket that year—another sign that the state's black leaders were determined to challenge the racial status quo. As important, the timing of the lawsuits would turn out to be a remarkable boon to the NAACP lawyers because of the judge who ended up handling both matters. The other was brought against the University of South Carolina by John Wrighten, a young black man from Edisto Island, just off the coast south of Charleston.

The eighth of nine children, Wrighten came from a hardworking family whose industriousness had enabled the children to get an education. He had attended the Avery Institute, a school run for black students by the American Missionary Association, and had been a member of the NAACP youth chapter as a teenager. By the standards of the day, this made him a militant. Personal experiences had only deepened Wrighten's commitment to the black cause. State law officers had failed to prosecute the men who killed his brother-in-law, a headstrong black who had refused to work for whites, and as a youngster, Wrighten had been stung by the prevailing racial double standard: when he worked as a cabin boy at a tourist court, he saw white men use the cabins for trysts with black women.

World War II interrupted Wrighten's schooling, but after returning from the service he finished at Avery, then decided he wanted to attend college—but not at the school for blacks. In 1943 he boldly applied for admission to the all-white College of Charleston. Officials told him they would rule on his application by October, but Wrighten backed off, deciding instead to enroll at the Colored Normal Industrial, Agricultural and Mechanical College of South Carolina at Orangeburg, commonly known as State College.

After a year in Orangeburg, Wrighten, this time with thirty-two other blacks, again tried to gain admission to the College of

Charleston. But under pressure from local black leaders who feared problems for Avery Institute and renewed racial tensions in the city, the students withdrew their applications.

Wrighten returned to Orangeburg, but in June of 1946, before his graduation, he decided to push the boundaries once again. He applied for admission to the all-white law school at the University of South Carolina in Columbia. Wrighten's application was immediately rejected because he was black, but this time the young man refused to back down. He contacted Harold Boulware, a black Columbia attorney who had been working with NAACP lawyers in New York on a variety of matters, and now the state NAACP was ready to file a lawsuit on Wrighten's behalf.

Like the Elmore case, Wrighten's lawsuit was filed in Richland County, and in the normal course of events the case should have been heard by George Bell Timmerman, the roving federal judge who generally handled cases in the central part of the state—the same Timmerman whom Thurmond had bested for a state judgeship in 1938 and whose son, George Bell junior, was now Thurmond's lieutenant governor. Timmerman was one of three federal judges in South Carolina. One judge, C. Cecil Wyche, presided over cases in the western part of the state, and J. Waties Waring was responsible for the eastern section.

For some years prior to his appointment to the federal bench, Timmerman had been a member of the Board of Trustees of the University of South Carolina. Even though he had resigned to take the judgeship, he believed that it was inappropriate for him to try a case so directly involving the university. So Timmerman asked Waring if he would handle the Wrighten lawsuit.

Waring not only agreed to take the school case but, noticing that there was another discrimination lawsuit on Timmerman's docket—George Elmore's white primary challenge—he suggested that he handle that one, too, because of the similarity of the issues. Waring had already ruled on two other cases involving racial discrimination, and his interest in this subject was growing.

None of the parties knew it at the time, but this private agreement between the two judges would turn out to have extraordinary consequences. Like Thurmond, Timmerman and Waring were products of their time and place: decent, even cordial in their personal relationships with individual blacks but as imbued with the notion of white supremacy as any other South Carolinian of the ruling class. There was, however, one important difference.

Timmerman and Thurmond were satisfied with the status quo. J. Waties Waring was not, and presiding over these new civil rights cases would only hasten his growing belief that something was wrong with "custom and tradition."

Waring was born July 27, 1880, in a Charleston that was trying to recover from the devastation of the Civil War. Like other white young men of the time, he and his schoolmates were absorbed by a sense of tradition, joking that they were raised on "rice and recollections."

Waring wanted to be a lawyer, but because of his family's finances, law school was out of the question. He studied for free in the law firm of a family friend and two years later passed the bar exam without problem. Waring quickly became active in politics, interested more in the contacts that might help his law practice than in eventual elective office. Following tradition in the state, he was a Democrat, which won him, among other appointments, the job of Charleston's corporation counsel, or city attorney.

Waring held that job until he was appointed to the federal bench. While representing the city, he handled his share of racial matters, but he had no interest in upsetting the applecart. Nothing he did betrayed southern tradition nor his colleagues' trust that he would handle matters to their liking. "Most of the Negroes I knew were ex-slaves and you loved them, were good to them," he later explained. "We didn't give them any rights, but they never asked for any rights, and I didn't question it."

Waring was comfortable enough with the status quo that he could be an unapologetic supporter of Cotton Ed Smith, serving as his Charleston campaign manager and a close political adviser. Later he would concede that Smith was "a good deal of a demagogue," but in 1938 Waring had no trouble helping him in the bitterly fought election.

That same year Waring also played an important role in Burnet R. Maybank's successful run for governor, and in 1942 Maybank in turn supported Waring for the judgeship with Smith's acquiescence. Though many Carolinians would later rue the day he became a federal judge, Charleston welcomed Waring's appointment. The city council sent him a congratulatory letter, and *The News and Courier* said he was "a man of excellent character" and called his appointment "too long delayed."

Waring, by now sixty-one, looked every bit the role, with his angular face, aquiline nose, and slightly graying hair. The black robe, combined with a patrician bearing, only added to the judicial aura.

By the time he heard the *Wrighten* and *Elmore* cases in June of 1947, Waring had already begun to move away from "custom and tradition." Part of the change was visible in his personal life. In 1945 he had shocked Charleston society by divorcing his wife of thirty years to marry a twice-divorced northerner, Elizabeth Avery Mills Hoffman. Waring's divorce and remarriage—which elicited an abundance of snide comments—was an obvious break with the past. Less obvious was the incremental conversion of a white supremacist mind-set.

The discrimination cases on the federal court docket were to be the catalysts for Waring's change. He later described them as "the basis of my racial experience." The first such case involved teacher pay.

Late in 1943, the NAACP filed a lawsuit on behalf of black teachers in Charleston, who were paid substantially lower salaries than their white counterparts. When Thurgood Marshall came down from New York to help Boulware try the case, he thought of Waring as "just another southern jurist who would give me the usual legal head-whipping before I went along to the Circuit Court of Appeals." But to his happy surprise, he found Waring to be so fair a judge that it turned out to be "the only case I ever tried with my mouth hanging open half the time."

Waring had made his position clear to Charleston officials that "the Fourteenth Amendment was still in the Constitution" and that it still prevailed for all citizens in his court. Before the formal hearing on the case was over, the school board's attorney asked to suspend the proceedings. The board agreed to a consent decree requiring equal salaries for black and white teachers.

Waring's second teacher pay case involved a challenge to racially discriminatory pay schedules in Richland County. While the case was argued chiefly on technicalities, Waring's ruling made it clear that technicalities should not stand in the way of equity.

Waring had to confront a more dramatic racial case the next year when he was asked by Timmerman to try a lawsuit involving the alleged beating of a black serviceman, twenty-seven-year-old Isaac Woodward, Jr., by a white sheriff, Lynwood Shull. Woodward had been left totally blind by the assault. (Timmerman was from Shull's hometown of Batesburg and felt he could not try a case involving an acquaintance.)

Woodward, who had been discharged from the army August 12, 1946, had boarded a bus in Augusta that same night and was heading toward Winnsboro, where his wife lived. At Batesburg he was taken off the bus by police for allegedly being drunk and raucus and was arrested after an altercation with law officers. Woodward pleaded guilty the next morning to public drunkenness and disorderly conduct and was fined fifty dollars. He had only forty-four dollars, so the mayor, who had tried the case in city court, took that amount and suspended the rest of the fine. With his eyes red and swollen from the previous night's encounter, Woodward was admitted later that day to a veterans' hospital in Columbia. He was released three months later a blind man.

By late summer, Woodward's plight had become a cause célèbre in the black papers, with civil rights groups charging that Shull had gouged Woodward's eyes with a blackjack. In mid-August some twenty thousand people gathered at a benefit rally in New York in support of the soldier. The day before the event, Shull told inquiring reporters in South Carolina that indeed he had hit Woodward with his blackjack, but only because the soldier had become unruly. "I hit him across the front of the head after he attempted to take away my blackjack. I grabbed it away from him and cracked him across the head."

After Woodward told his story to the Justice Department, federal officials, concerned that a grand jury would never indict Shull, instead instructed U.S. Attorney Claude Sapp to file an "information," or affidavit, charging Shull with violating a Reconstruction-era law that made it a crime for individuals to act "under color of any law, statute or ordinance, regulation or custom" to interfere with a person's rights "secured or protected" by the United States Constitution.

The information specifically charged Shull with, among other things, violating Woodward's "right to be secure in his person and to be immune from illegal assault and battery; the right and privilege not to be beaten and tortured by persons exercising the authority to arrest."

At the trial, Woodward and Shull offered their very disparate accounts of what had happened. Woodward said Shull had simply started beating him, and Shull claimed self-defense because Woodward tried to grab his blackjack and was "advancing on me." Three character witnesses—including, to the chagrin of the black community, one black minister—said Shull was a man of decent character and reputation. The government did not put on any witnesses who could corroborate Woodward's version of events.

By this time Waring had no illusions about the racial dynamics of the case. He reminded jurors that they should "put aside prejudice and give due justice. . . . You are trying only one police officer," he told them, not southern racial traditions or "black against white."

But Shull's attorneys were not to be deterred. One asserted that Woodward belonged to "an inferior race" and that his "vulgar" talk in alleged exchanges with Shull was "not the talk of a sober South Carolina Negro. . . . If Lynwood Shull is convicted today," the lawyer warned, "you will be saying to the public officers of South Carolina that you no longer want your home, your wife, and your children protected." Shull's other lawyer drew on the emotional symbol of the Civil War, telling jurors that if a verdict for Shull and against the government "means that South Carolina'll have to secede again, then let's secede."

Waring had little doubt what the verdict would be, but he was determined that the proceedings would have "a little more atmosphere of respectability." After the jury retired to deliberate, he told the bailiff he was going out for a twenty-minute walk. When the bailiff protested that "the jury ain't going to stay for twenty minutes," Waring retorted, "They're going to stay out twenty minutes because they can't come in until I come back."

The jury was ready when Waring returned. The verdict, as expected, was acquittal. *The State* praised the outcome, warning that the "intercession" of the federal government in the case could only lead to a renewal of the argument over states' rights. "It is therefore an unwholesome influence against unity in the Union, and something to be studiously avoided whenever possible."

Waring had no comment on the verdict, but the entire incident had a profound effect on him and on his northern-born wife, who considered it her "baptism in racial prejudice." She began reading everything she could find about southern race relations and forced her husband into more pointed discussions on the subject than he had ever had before. It was a distressing period of reexamination for Waring, calling even more sharply into question the "custom and tradition" he had accepted for so long.

Gradually his internal evolution began to manifest itself in the courtroom. He ended the practice of race-coding juror lists—in the past, the letter *C* had been placed by the names of blacks. He also made sure that there was integration in jury seating. The judge had noticed that juries might start out integrated, but after a recess blacks would almost always file into the jury box last and take seats at the end of the panel. To prevent this, Waring told his court clerks to assign seats to the jurors and instructed them to keep those seats during the entire proceedings.

The judge also took a step toward integration outside the courtroom. During a lunch break, a black juror threatened to call Waring because he was being forced to eat in a restaurant kitchen. The deputy reluctantly added two extra chairs at the white jurors' table, and when the judge learned about the incident he told the chief marshal to make sure that from then on jurors always ate together. If whites complained, Waring instructed the marshal to explain that the separation of jurors in a pending case was a violation of the law. Some restaurant owners complained, but no one put up a huge fuss. "After all," Waring later observed, "a judge has got a good deal of power. When he does these things, there isn't anybody can tell him he can't do it."

The observation goes to the heart of the practical difference between a judge and a politician. They serve different masters and perform different functions. A judge answers to the law in deciding disputes between individuals in conflict. For Waring that meant confrontation with the everyday aspects of "custom and tradition"—discrimination.

But if a judge answers to the law, politicians answer to the people, and their success is determined in large part by how accurately they understand and reflect what their constituents want. On the issue of race, constituents had clearly decided opinions. To head too far in a different direction would mean defeat. "Anybody who had a chance to be elected," Thurmond would say late in his career, "had to stand with the thinking of his people, or couldn't vary too far from it." Although Thurmond had also been a judge and had dealt with his share of black litigants, the issue of discrimination had never been joined in his courtroom. Even handling the Willie Earle lynching was different. The case involved a black victim and white perpetrators, but the incident was really about lawlessness—an easier issue to grapple with than the more complex matters of social order and change.

The *Elmore* case was going to force these very matters to the forefront. But before the lawyers could present their arguments to Judge Waring late in the spring, the Earle case reappeared.

On May 12, 1947, the trial of the thirty-one men arrested for the lynching of Willie Earle opened in Judge J. Robert Martin's courtroom. Before the proceedings, twenty-six of the defendants had made statements to federal and state law enforcement officers admitting their presence at the lynching. Some even identified who had fired the shotgun blasts that killed Earle.

After one day of jury examination, a panel of white men was seated to hear the evidence. Over the objection of defense lawyers, who claimed the defendants' statements were coerced, the prosecutors—including a state attorney sent at Thurmond's request—presented the incriminating information to the jury. It took the state six days to lay out its case, after which the defense made a surprise move. The lawyers declined to put on any evidence. In part they believed they could argue that there was a reasonable doubt about the defendants' guilt, but more important, the attorneys were banking on their gut feeling that whites would not convict other whites of killing a black.

They turned out to be right. After seven hours of deliberation, the jurors—textile workers, a mechanic, a salesman, and a divinity student—acquitted the twenty-eight men still on trial. (Judge Martin had dismissed charges against three of the defendants.)

The judge was so distressed that he turned his back on the jury, grabbed his panama hat, and stormed out of the courtroom without thanking the jurors for their service. Above the tumult, one of the defense lawyers shouted, "I think this is a perfect example of proving that the Department of Justice . . . and other people up North should keep their mouths out of the South's business."

The press reaction suggested that not everyone in the region agreed. The next day *The Atlanta Journal* said of the remark, "What an insult to decency and intelligence! What an answer to those who argue for the enactment of a federal antilynching statute." While praising South Carolina for at least bringing the men into court, the editorial called the verdict a "farcical end" that compounded the felony by putting "the most vital link in the processes of justice—the jury itself—on a level with the mob."

The Greenville News said the trial had "given a new and

stronger emphasis to South Carolina's determination to uphold the principles of justice and law." Though the state had failed to "secure the evidence requisite to any conviction, the trial stands out as a landmark of a state's earnest and deep-seated purpose to tolerate no flouting of the established processes of justice."

Thurmond tried to take a positive tack in responding to the angry letters he received after the verdict. "I took a very firm stand on the matter," he wrote one citizen, "and I think great good was accomplished by having the accused arrested and tried even though the jury acquitted them. I believe that position will assist in the future in preventing lynchings."

Just as the brouhaha of the Earle case was winding down, the two race discrimination cases—*Wrighten* and *Elmore*—were moving into their next phase. Waring had set hearings in both cases for June. Although Wrighten's lawsuit was heard second, it proved to be the less dramatic of the two, focusing on one aspect of higher education—law school. Elmore's lawsuit, on the other hand, went to the heart of white political power—voting.

The NAACP was basing Wrighten's claim for admission to the University of South Carolina law school on a 1938 Supreme Court decision, *Missouri ex rel. Gaines v. Canada.* In that case, the justices said that states must provide a law school for blacks "substantially equal" to the one that exists for whites or allow the black students to attend the white law school. South Carolina had no law school for blacks, and Wrighten's lawyers demanded that the state either establish one or let Wrighten go to the university.

South Carolina officials were hardly happy with either option. Ben Tillman's constitution was still in force, and Article IX prescribed that "no child of either race shall ever be permitted to attend a school provided for children of the other race." In the official view, "child" was broad enough to encompass South Carolinians in their early twenties who wanted to go to law school. To meet the dictates of *Gaines,* they might have to spend more money on black education.

At the June 5 hearing on Wrighten's complaint, Robert L. Carter, one of the NAACP lawyers, argued that because there was no law school for blacks comparable to the one at the university, and because Wrighten was qualified to enter law school, he should be admitted to the whites-only school.

Assistant Attorney General T. C. Callison retorted that Congress and the federal courts had recognized "the right of segregation when segregation does not discriminate." He pointed out that South Carolina had passed laws in 1945 and 1946 authorizing a new law school for blacks at State College in Orangeburg and that money had been appropriated in 1947 after Wrighten's suit was filed. It would have been "ridiculous" to spend money before then, Callison said, because there had never been a law school applicant.

"The state is not discriminating because of color," Callison argued. "It's doing everything it can to be prepared when Wrighten decides he wants to go to the Orangeburg school. . . . It doesn't take a big law school, a big law library to give a good law education," he continued. "Some of the best lawyers and judges in this state never saw the inside of a law school."

James H. Price, the university's attorney, told Waring that the new law school would be ready by mid-September, and he expressed some annoyance at the litigation. "We want the Negroes to be educated," he added. "But if they'll just leave us alone, we'll work these things out with friendship and love between the two races."

Thurgood Marshall had the last word for Wrighten, discounting claims that the school would be ready in a few months. "Why, the board of trustees hasn't even approved it yet," he said, pointing out that there was no building, no law faculty and no law library. Carter and Marshall contended that Wrighten deserved to be admitted immediately to the university because the new law school was not a reality.

On July 12, Waring turned down the NAACP's argument, saying it was "only fair and just, in view of all the circumstances," to give the state until September to open the Orangeburg school. If the school was open by then, he added, and Wrighten could enter a law school "satisfactorily staffed, equipped and . . . on a substantial parity in all respects with the services furnished at the University Law School," then his demands would have been met.

On the other hand, Waring said, if these conditions were not met "completely and fully, then the plaintiff will be entitled to entrance at the Law School of the university." The third alternative, Waring said, was that the state provide no law school education to either whites or blacks.

State College opened a law school in September with a dean

and three faculty members but no law building or library. Wrighten refused to attend.

By mid-1948 the state had appropriated $200,000 for a building and $30,000 for library acquisitions, but only eight students were enrolled in the law program and only four of them were law students. After further legal proceedings, Waring issued an order in July 1948 declaring that it was "almost impossible to intellectually compare" this school with the university's law school, which had 342 students enrolled in the 1947–48 academic year. He was somewhat bemused that the state would spend so much money for eight black students just "to prevent the meeting of whites and Negroes in classrooms." He determined, however, that such decisions were up to the legislature and that the state had complied with his order and the Supreme Court's ruling in *Gaines*.

By the fall of 1949 a two-story law school building had been completed. Wrighten enrolled, graduated in 1952, and after three failures passed the state bar examination on the fourth go-round.

The *Wrighten* litigation ruffled few feathers in the state. Although it had threatened a direct attack on higher education, the case ended up as another ratification of separate but equal. George Elmore's suit, on the other hand, was about politics and power, and there were few if any living politicians who could remember the last time a significant number of blacks voted in an election that mattered.

Interest in the case was high among white political leaders beyond South Carolina as well, particularly in Georgia, where there were nascent moves once again to restrict black suffrage. In the midst of his unsuccessful fight to replace his deceased father as governor, Herman Talmadge had written South Carolina Democratic Chairman William P. Baskin (Thurmond's strong ally in the 1938 judicial election) seeking information about the *Elmore* lawsuit. On May 16 Baskin answered his letter, laying out the theories the state intended to rely on in answering Elmore's contentions.

Referring to the 1944 legislature's repeal of all primary laws, Baskin said that the 1946 election had been "conducted by our voluntary association without any statutory or constitutional provisions authorizing the primaries or in any manner regulating or punishing fraud in connection therewith. We are satisfied that under the [Supreme Court] decisions we should win the suit and preserve for South Carolina its white primary." Baskin closed with

the "hope that Georgia will soon join South Carolina in so adjusting its laws as to insure White supremacy."

But Marshall and Boulware had framed their arguments around a 1941 election fraud case from Louisiana, *United States v. Classic,* where the high court had presented alternative criteria for determining whether a primary was an integral part of the electoral structure and thus covered under the constitutional protections for voting. The inquiry, the court said, was not limited to whether there was a particular state law governing the primary. There could also be inquiry into whether the primary "effectively controls the choice" of the voter. Where that occurs, the justices said, "the right of the elector to have his ballot counted at the primary is . . . protected" by the Constitution. The NAACP lawyers contended that this was the situation in South Carolina, citing statistics to prove that the primary was the only vote that mattered: since 1875 the winner of every congressional Democratic primary had been elected in November.

The party's attorneys argued for a strict interpretation of the high court's earlier primary decisions. In every case the primary at issue had in fact been regulated by state law. In the *Elmore* case, by contrast, the primary was not part of the "statutory process of election." As a result, "there is no Constitutional right to vote in such primary."

The hearing on Elmore's challenge took most of June 3 and 4. During the first day, University of South Carolina law professor Charles B. Elliott contended that according to Elmore's argument, "state inaction [concerning the conduct of the primary] is the equivalent of state action. If the court grants this to be correct," Elliott claimed, "it will emasculate the Tenth Amendment"—again the states' rights defense. The party's lawyers argued that because no law governed the primaries, membership in the state Democratic Party was like membership in a sewing circle, church, or country club. But Marshall, focusing on the Supreme Court's two-pronged inquiry in the *Classic* case, contended that it made "no difference whether state primary laws were repealed" because the party was still "exercising a governmental function." News of the proceedings was given front-page treatment in *The State.*

During closing arguments the next day, Christie Benet, one of the Democrats' lawyers, asked what was to prevent a communist "from forcing himself into the party and primary."

"When a Negro stands for his rights," Marshall retorted, "he is not a communist. . . . Where I come from," he added, "Democrats are welcome whether they are white, black, green or yellow."

Although neither side called the party chairman, Waring decided he wanted to hear from him. In his answers to the judge, Baskin made no effort to hide the fact that the state's goal was to restrict black voter participation.

After the hearing, Waring gave each side ten days to submit briefs. Barely a month later—July 12, 1947, the same day as the *Wrighten* ruling—the judge hurled his judicial thunderbolt. He sided with the NAACP and told the state's white leaders in no uncertain terms that from now on blacks could register and vote in the primaries.

In his decision, Waring first traced the history of electoral politics in South Carolina, observing that during Reconstruction, when a flood of newly freed blacks were given the right to vote, some restrictions "to prevent a deluge of untrained, unlettered and unprepared citizens from taking over control of the state government" might have been necessary. Several generations had passed since then, and the law had "modernized the matter of suffrage in these United States."

Noting that South Carolina was the only state still holding a white primary—blacks could vote in Texas, Louisiana, and "even in Georgia"—Waring added caustically, "I cannot see where the skies will fall if South Carolina is put in the same class with these and other states.

"It is time," Waring said in his final jab, "for South Carolina to rejoin the Union. . . . Racial distinctions cannot exist in the machinery that selects the offices and lawmakers of the United States; and all citizens of this State and Country are entitled to cast a free and untrammelled ballot in our elections."

Waring had made his choice, and the decision would cost him. It was only a matter of time until he and his wife, Elizabeth, harassed and ostracized, severed relations with Charleston's white community and moved north to New York. He had been prepared for repercussions beforehand, telling Elizabeth, "We may have to pay a pretty heavy penalty."

Predictably, Waring's ruling was banner-headline news across the state. Democratic officials, who would shortly decide to appeal the ruling, had no immediate comment. Black leaders, though, were understandably elated. McCray called a special convention of the Progressive Democrats to plan the party's course of action, and James M. Hinton, head of the state NAACP, called on the Democratic Party to make "provisions immediately to include all qualified Negro voters" on the party's rolls. But he was not optimistic. "Yet to be seen and hurdled are a number of assorted schemes and devices we expect to be employed by the vanquished upholders of white supremacy," he said.

Editorial comment was surprisingly muted in several of the state's papers. Commentators seemed to be stung more by Waring's rhetoric than by his decision. *The Evening Post* of Charleston bristled at the notion that it was "time for South Carolina to rejoin the Union." "It would have been edifying," the *Post* said, "had Judge Waring informed them how long South Carolina has been out of the Union." As for Waring's challenge that it was "time to fall in step with other States and to adopt the American way of conducting elections," the *Post* asked, "Isn't it time for the federal courts, lower and higher, to adopt the American way, by respecting the compact under which certain rights were reserved to the States and the people?" Considering what was to come, it was a prescient query.

More restrained observations came from *The Sumter Daily Item*. "For our part, we cannot get wildly excited over Judge Waring's decision," the paper said. Pointing out that Waring was an "able jurist" and also came from an "old Charleston family, so [he] cannot be accused of a 'Yankee tinge,' " the paper believed he had "laid aside sectional prejudices and decided the case on what he believed to be sound law." Predicting Waring's decision would be upheld in higher courts, the *Daily Item* suggested that the state "make the best of it. We don't believe South Carolina is going to the dogs, just because Negroes are allowed to vote in our primaries, in spite of the doleful forebodings of professional politicians."

The paper was not referring to Thurmond but to Senator Maybank, who had lambasted the decision as "clearly wrong" and insisted the state would appeal the matter all the way to the Supreme Court. Senator Johnston was somewhat less outspoken. He simply said he was confident the decision would be reversed.

The News and Courier, still under the direction of the conservative William Watts Ball, was more strident. If Waring's decision was upheld, the paper said, there was "nothing left for South

Carolina but to abandon completely the name of the Democratic Party" and establish "an exclusive white man's political club under a new title."

Thurmond declined to speak about the ruling. He was in Salt Lake City addressing other governors about military preparedness. He could have used the prestige of his office to force Baskin and other party leaders to accept Waring's decision and end the matter. But that would have violated Thurmond's own rule—getting too far away from "the thinking of the people." Instead he took the middle ground. He did not have the courage of Ellis Arnall, who told Georgians after the 1944 *Smith* decision that blacks were going to vote in the primary, but neither did he exhibit the defiance of Olin Johnston, who had encouraged white supremacists to resist the *Smith* ruling at whatever cost. Waring's choice had been one of bold action: he had, in his own words, "dared to raise the iron curtain that has surrounded the state for so many years." Thurmond's choice was one of studied inaction, though that would change early in the next year.

In the wake of Waring's decision, political activity in the black community continued to escalate throughout the summer. In Columbia, McCray and Hinton already were thinking about sending rump delegates to the 1948 Democratic convention. East of the capital, blacks in the impoverished rural communities of Clarendon County petitioned the state for more school bus transportation for their children, beginning a process that would turn into a direct assault on separate but equal.

This growing activity in the black community did not go unnoticed in white political circles. Wayne Freeman, the *Greenville News* reporter in Columbia, was prompted to write that "South Carolina negroes are becoming increasingly active in what appears to be an (at least loosely) organized effort to obtain 'the constitutional rights' they claim are denied them and to halt what they term discrimination against their race."

Freeman described a meeting during the first week of August in which a group of blacks met with Thurmond to talk about improving conditions at the John G. Richards Industrial Training School for Negro Boys. The delegation, which included McCray and Hinton, specifically asked for more training in trades instead of agriculture, the construction of a laundry to make it easier for the boys to have clean clothes, and better clothing for attendance at religious services. After the meeting Thurmond told reporters he saw considerable merit in the proposals and asked the State Industrial School Board to study the recommendations, a signal that the black leaders had gotten the governor's attention even if there was no concrete promise of action.

If 1947 was a year of political choices for white Carolinians, for Thurmond it was also a time of personal ones. At forty-four he was still a bachelor, armed with his standard retort that he was too busy with his career to find a wife. He relished his bachelor status, though; news photos of the period show him crowning beauty queens and attending balls with attractive young women on either arm. In one striking picture, Thurmond is crowning nineteen-year-old Jean Griffin, "a lovely ash-blonde from Spartanburg," as Miss South Carolina. The accompanying story explains that Thurmond took full advantage of his duties. After crowning Griffin, "Governor Thurmond remarked, 'She walks well, she looks good. Let's see how she kisses.' With that the governor firmly emplanted a kiss."

Thurmond's reputation had preceded him. "I wasn't too surprised," Griffin reported. "I'd heard he might do that."

By the middle of 1947, however, the governor decided he had found the right woman, a young southern belle with just enough dash to make life interesting.

He first saw Jean Crouch in the fall of 1941, when he was a judge and she was a high school student in Elko, a small town in Barnwell County. They met briefly when she and her class came to watch a session of court. In their short conversation at the courthouse, Thurmond told Jean that she had pretty eyes.

Four years later, Thurmond, by then governor-elect, was reminded of Jean's pretty eyes when he stopped by her father's office—Horace Crouch was superintendent of education in Barnwell and a longtime party activist—and saw her picture on Crouch's wall. The face looked familiar. Told it was Crouch's daughter, Thurmond immediately asked if she might be interested in working in the governor's office when she finished college at Winthrop. Crouch told Thurmond to ask her himself when she came to the capital for a meeting of the South Carolina Education Association. Thurmond did seek her out and made his offer.

Several weeks later, Thurmond, apparently smitten, wrote Jean a postcard from the Southern Governors Conference in

Miami, Florida, and then he came up with a ploy to see her again, this time during the inauguration. Trying not to be too transparent, he suggested to Winthrop president Henry R. Sims that a delegation of young women from the school—say, the class president (Jean), the student government president, and perhaps two or three others—be allowed to attend the ceremony.

While Jean and the new governor didn't spend time together that day, she returned to Columbia in February with other Winthrop students and visited the governor's mansion. Thurmond heard she was nearby and invited her to have lunch with him and his sister. She accepted, even though she had already eaten. The budding though circumspect romance continued the next month when Thurmond invited Jean to the American Legion horse races in Columbia, but he specifically told her to "bring along a friend, a girl friend."

As governor, Thurmond had more perquisites at his command than the ordinary suitor: he named Jean queen of the 1947 Azalea Festival. When he crowned her, he took special pleasure in bestowing the customary kiss.

Thurmond renewed his offer of a job in Columbia, but on the advice of an aide eager to avoid any appearance of impropriety, he suggested a position in one of the state agencies rather than his office. Nonetheless, Jean retorted, "What are you hunting, a secretary or a playmate?"

Thurmond ignored the sharp reply and simply told her to "come on down. We'll expect you."

After thinking it over, Jean told him she would rather work in the governor's office. Thurmond was chagrined, assuming that meant she didn't want the kind of relationship he did. After all, he didn't think he could court her right in his office. Nor did she give him much encouragement when he came to Winthrop in June to deliver the commencement address. Jean didn't even look at him as he held out her diploma. Later in the day, however, she warmed up, agreeing to ride back to Elko in the governor's car.

Jean came to her new job in Columbia on the first of July, and a short time later she and another secretary accompanied Thurmond to the Salt Lake City meeting of governors. By early fall their romance was an open secret, and by that time Jean had finally explained to Thurmond why she had decided to work in his office: "I knew if I got tucked away, I'd never see you."

Friends privately dubbed the couple "the plowboy from Edgefield and the milkmaid from Elko."

Part of Thurmond's routine now was to arrange his schedule so that at the end of the day he could accompany Jean home to her apartment near the capitol. His excuse was that it might be unsafe for her to walk the few blocks by herself. The two would also go to events together. One newspaper photo at the beginning of the football season showed Thurmond, dressed in a sports coat, slacks, and a cowboy hat, sitting in his special box at the Furman–South Carolina football game next to Jean, dressed in a snappy white jacket with a diagonal stripe and a dark skirt. The article gave a hint that something serious was in the wind when it noted that Jean had been a member of his secretarial staff "until her recent resignation."

What occasioned that resignation was an understanding between the two that their relationship was serious enough to talk about marriage. On September 9, before the two had reached any formal decision, Jean wrote her parents about her romance. "We've thought about it," she told them. "We know what we want. He'll always be good and kind to me, so we're going to do what will make us happy for always. Please don't think for a minute that I'm swept off my feet 'cause I know what I'm getting into. He's Governor now, but that will last only 3 years," she continued, not fully realizing her intended's political ambition. "Marriage will last a lifetime."

Then Jean addressed the obvious. "I realize the difference in our ages and we've talked about it"—Jean was then only twenty-one and Thurmond forty-four—"but both agree it will make very little difference. . . . This is what I want and will make me *completely* happy."

Four days later Thurmond took care of the formalities. He called Jean into his office and asked her to take a letter. "Darling Jean," he began, "you have proved to be a most efficient and capable secretary, and the high caliber of your work has impressed me very much. It is with a deep sense of regret that I will have to inform you that your service will be discontinued as of the last day of this month.

"I have been giving a great deal of thought to your new assignment and have concluded that you can serve humanity best, perform duties that will be more worthwhile to the State, and most especially make the Governor happier, in the new duties which I desire you to undertake."

Telling her that she would be missed in the office, Thurmond added, "I must confess I love you dearly and want you for my own.

I didn't realize that a girl could attach herself so to a man and could entwine herself around his heartstrings as you have done. It seems to have been no special effort heretofore to fight off love, but in your case, I have made a complete failure in the attempt and frankly admit that your charms have won me—heart and soul."

"Yours in love," he closed, "J. Strom Thurmond."

Later that day Jean sent back a reply. "My dearest Strom, Yes! My love always, Jean."

The age difference may not have bothered Jean, and to hear Thurmond tell it, he wasn't concerned either. "I'd rather marry one twenty years younger than twenty years older," he later joked. But the disparity evoked plenty of comment, not all of it favorable. One constituent sent the governor a cartoon showing a man seated at the breakfast table while his obviously young wife jumped rope with the waffle-iron cord. "Are you sure you didn't fib to me about your age when we got married?" the caption read.

Thurmond sent back a deadpan reply: "This acknowledges receipt of the cartoon which you sent about getting married, and concerning the age matter. I think this is an interesting cartoon and wish to thank you for sending it."

One anonymous citizen was highly critical. "You have made the worst political blunder in the world by not . . . selecting a wife more in keeping with common sense and sanity than you have," the writer said two weeks after the engagement was announced. "Ninety percent of the people of the State think you are acting very foolish indeed. Of course the young girl knows no better and is sacrificing her life for a little notoriety which will soon end."

Still fit and trim in middle age, Thurmond was determined to show people he was not too old for Jean. The day before the November 7 wedding, the governor posed for *Life* magazine dressed in tennis shorts and standing on his head. The caption was pointed: "VIRILE GOVERNOR demonstrates his prowess in the mansion yard day before wedding."

(The *Life* picture was not the first time Thurmond had turned himself upside down for photographers. Just after he was elected governor, Thurmond, on vacation at a Georgia beach, did a handstand on the sand wearing only his shorts, "just to show he can," the caption said.)

The private family wedding was short—eleven minutes—and formal. The bride wore a long white gown with a veil. The groom wore a morning coat. Afterward, photographers from the state newspapers were allowed in to photograph the festivities. Splashed across the front pages were the bride and groom reenacting the postceremony kiss.

Three weeks later, after their wedding trip, the newlyweds held a reception that drew five thousand people to the mansion. After ninety minutes the couple had to take a break so that Jean could massage a cramp in her right hand. Thurmond could shake hands for hours, but the new Mrs. Thurmond was a novice, getting her first taste of what was in store for a politician's wife.

Thurmond hadn't let his personal life distract him from government business. He had kept his distance from the race discrimination cases in Judge Waring's court, concentrating instead on his legislative program. Already he had been able to raise teachers' salaries to their highest level and had signed legislation increasing funding for education overall, creating a state system of trade schools, and providing more money for state parks and for the elderly, dependent children, and individuals with physical or mental handicaps. He continued to push for other reforms, particularly the overall reorganization of the government he had promised in his inaugural address.

Thurmond also kept an eye on the national scene, and unlike some of his more conservative brethren in the state Democratic Party, he remained comfortable with President Truman. On October 2, Thurmond had gone to Louisville, Kentucky, to participate in a panel discussion that was broadcast over the radio. As part of the presentation he gave a short address called "Let's Look at '48." Focusing almost exclusively on international matters—the victory in World War II, Truman's stand at Potsdam, his fight to restore world commerce—it was a ringing endorsement of the president.

"We who believe in a liberal political philosophy," Thurmond said, "in the importance of human rights as well as property rights, in the preservation and strengthening of the economic and social gains brought about by the efforts of the Democratic Party . . . will vote for the election of Harry Truman and the restoration of Congress to the control of the Democratic Party, and I believe we will win."

There is more than a little irony in this encomium to Truman, given the events that would unfold in the next few months. The seeds of Thurmond's change of heart were sown later in the month when the president's committee on civil rights released its lengthy report "To Secure These Rights," a title taken from the Declaration of Independence: ". . . that [all Men] are endowed by their Creator with certain inalienable Rights, that among these are Life, Liberty, and the Pursuit of Happiness—That to secure these Rights, Governments are instituted among Men." (Administration wags thought of the panel as Noah's Ark because it was made up of two blacks, two women, two Catholics, two Jews, two businessmen, two southerners, two labor leaders, and two college presidents.)

The report, divided into four parts, described the state of civil rights in the country, chronicled the history of civil rights problems in America, described the current situation, laid out the government's role in protecting and preserving civil rights, and made recommendations for action. While the report surveyed problems all over the United States, the committee said that "many of the most sensational and serious violations of civil rights have taken place in the South. There are understandable historical reasons for this. Among the most obvious is the fact that the great proportion of our largest, most visible minority group—the Negroes—live in the South."

The report examined violence perpetrated against minorities, barriers to their participation in the political process, and the denial of equal opportunity in employment, education, housing, and public accommodations such as parks, beaches, and playgrounds. The committee made a strong case for federal government responsibility to enforce civil rights, declaring that it was sound policy "to use the idealism and prestige of our whole people to check the wayward tendencies of a part of them." As important, a denial of civil rights in one part of the United States has international implications. After a lynching, the report said, "the world looks to the American national government for both an explanation of how such a shocking event can occur in a civilized country and remedial action to prevent its recurrence. Similarly, interference with the right of a qualified citizen to vote locally cannot remain a local problem. An American diplomat cannot forcefully argue for free elections in foreign lands without meeting the challenge that in many sections of America qualified voters do not have free access to the polls."

Among other things, the committee called for a reorganization and strengthening of the civil rights section of the Justice Department, a federal antilynching law, a federal law to bar discrimination based on race or color in voting in state or federal primaries, a federal fair employment practices act, and an end to the poll tax.

The report did not set off any great reaction. It was more like a stick of dynamite waiting to explode when President Truman, following up on its recommendations, lit the fuse three and a half months later. For the time being, "To Secure These Rights" lay dormant.

When Thurmond delivered his end-of-the-year address to the state, he looked forward to the next year with optimism, reeling off a list of twelve items that he wanted the legislature to take up in the coming months.

But other matters were going to distract him in 1948, and as a fitting omen for the future, on December 30, 1947, the U.S. Court of Appeals for the Fourth Circuit unanimously upheld Judge Waring's decision in George Elmore's voting case.

"The disfranchised can never speak with the same force as those who are able to vote," the opinion said, adding that "no election machinery can be upheld if its purpose or effect is to deny to the Negro, on account of his race or color, any effective voice in the government of his country or the state or community wherein he lives." In South Carolina, the opinion concluded, "the denial to the Negro of the right to participate in the primary denies him all effective voice in the government of his country. There can be no question that such denial amounts to a denial of the constitutional rights of the Negro."

Asked for his reaction, Governor Thurmond offered a terse no-comment.

6.
IRREVERSIBLE COURSE

January 1948–June 1948

ON JANUARY 19, 1948, Fielding Wright stepped to the podium of a Jackson, Mississippi, stage and used the occasion of his first inaugural address as governor to warn Mississippians that troubled times lay ahead. So troubling, he said, that loyal Democrats like himself might be forced into drastic action because the national party was ready to assault "our institutions and our way of life."

"As a lifelong Democrat, as a descendant of Democrats, as governor of the most Democratic state, I would regret to see the day come when Mississippi or the South should break with the Democratic Party in a national election. But vital principles and eternal truths transcend party lines," Wright declared. "We must make our leaders fully realize we mean precisely what we say and we must, if necessary, implement our words with positive action. We warn them now to take heed."

Few outside Mississippi paid much attention to Wright's defiant speech. But within a month it would be clear that he had correctly gauged southern sentiment, even if some of his fellow politicians weren't ready to follow him out of the party. Southern discontent, however, was only one corner of the landscape at the start of this presidential year. Henry Wallace, Roosevelt's former vice-president, was openly talking about a third-party challenge to President Truman from the left, urging sweeping civil rights legislation to end segregation.

Standing in the middle, Truman knew he had to find a strategy that would keep defections both by liberals and conservatives to a minimum. Because of Wallace's apparent strength, Truman felt pressure to move in his direction and take his chances that regardless of what he did, the South would remain loyal. The civil rights committee's report, "To Secure These Rights," had lain dormant since October, but used effectively, the administration could make it a potent political tool with which to push legislation. Uneasy southern politicians who had never felt completely comfortable with Truman could only wait and watch.

In South Carolina, white Democrats faced a special problem. Blacks would be voting in the August primary unless the Supreme Court reversed Judge Waring and the Fourth Circuit, and the specter of even more political agitation in the black community was ever present.

The previous year had been the prologue, when a careful politician could avoid getting sucked into the roiling waters of race. But this presidential year would be the climax. No longer able to avoid the storm, Thurmond would put himself on an irreversible course. The progressive streak that had surfaced in the legislator and freshman governor would take second place to his fidelity to "custom and tradition," and a public persona would be established that was going to mark him for the rest of his career. Decades after the battle of 1948 was over, Thurmond would still wonder why his political ideology, pegged as it was to the literal text of the Tenth Amendment, had played so poorly against the broader notion of social justice.

Until 1948, states' rights ideology had played no role in Thurmond's career because the primacy of South Carolina had not been challenged directly. He assumed, as did other political descendants of Calhoun, that the federal government would be kept in check. Though he believed in certain principles—hard work, honesty, duty—he didn't operate from political theory but from an instinct that told him when to move and where. Like other successful politicians, he knew that "timing is everything," and if there were unintended consequences from some of his actions, well, he would handle them as they came along.

For twenty years Thurmond had focused almost exclusively

on the duties of the offices he held. But when northern politicians in Washington threatened to unravel the southern way of life, his emphasis shifted. Week by week events drew him onto the national stage, and with deepening fervor he embraced states' rights as a defense against change. His rhetoric hardened into all-out resistance.

By the end of the year, Waties Waring would become a hero to black America and a traitor to tradition-bound white Carolinians. Thurmond would be the embodiment of the segregationist cause.

The year started out routinely in Columbia. Pleased with the successes of his first year in office, Thurmond used his January 14 address to the General Assembly to praise the legislators for their cooperation and to applaud the progress they had made together. But he told the men he expected much more from them over the next few months.

The speech had a progressive ring to it. And on the surface it was, like the inaugural address, the wish list of a forward-looking politician. Tucked into the remarks, however, were subtle and probably unintentional clues to the confrontation that lay ahead. In discussing the reorganization of state government, Thurmond included a brief passage about the limited powers of Congress versus the broad powers of the states, and in expressing his pride in the previous year's education reforms, he revealed a lack of appreciation for the continuing gulf between opportunities for blacks and whites. Thurmond correctly noted that black schools had gotten more aid in 1947 than ever before, but the larger issue of fundamental inequality between the separate school systems escaped him.

Thurmond was not yet inclined to challenge the Truman administration, but the report of the president's civil rights committee had not gone unnoticed in the General Assembly. Even if Truman had not immediately turned the recommendations of "To Secure These Rights" into legislative proposals, the South Carolinians wanted to have their views on record. In a letter to state Democratic chairman Baskin, forty-eight members denounced the national Democratic Party for "advocating ideas flagrantly repugnant to the South" and suggested it was time to "reconsider our position in the national party."

Four days after the legislators sent their missive to Baskin,

President Truman raised the stakes. He had promised in his annual address to Congress January 7 that within a matter of weeks he would present a comprehensive civil rights program to the country. It was a move calculated to blunt the expected Wallace candidacy and shore up Truman's support in parts of the country considered crucial to victory in November. His special counsel and senior political strategist, Clark Clifford, had given the president a pointed memorandum in November 1947—"The Politics of 1948"—predicting a three-party presidential race: Truman, Wallace, and Governor Thomas E. Dewey of New York for the Republicans. The contest, he said, would be decided by the black urban vote in California, Illinois, New York, and Ohio.

Much of his memo would prove to be on target, but he made one significant miscalculation. In urging moves to counter the expected Wallace candidacy, Clifford said, "It is inconceivable that any policy initiated by the Truman administration no matter how 'liberal' could so alienate the South in the next year that it would revolt. As always, the South can be considered safely Democratic. And in forming national policy can be safely ignored."

Following up on Clifford's advice, Truman delivered his civil rights message to a joint session of Congress February 2. "The protection of civil rights is the duty of every government which derives its powers from the consent of the people," the president said. Declaring that the federal government had a "clear duty" to see that constitutional guarantees were not denied or abridged "anywhere in our union," Truman insisted that the government's duty could be fulfilled "only if the Congress enacts modern, comprehensive civil rights laws, adequate to the needs of the day, and demonstrating our continuing faith in the free way of life."

The president called for abolition of the poll tax as a prerequisite for voting, enactment of a federal antilynching law, creation of a permanent Federal Employment Practices Commission, and new measures to ban discrimination in interstate transportation facilities.

Although the speech incorporated fewer than a third of the committee's recommendations, reaction throughout the South was swift and virulent—much more so than the Truman administration had anticipated. Barely twenty-four hours after Truman finished speaking, the Ku Klux Klan set the tone in Swainsboro, Georgia, where two hundred men dressed in sheets paraded to the courthouse and burned a cross on the courthouse lawn. It was a gesture repeated in other small towns in the South.

The rhetoric in the South and on Capitol Hill was the figurative equivalent of the cross burnings. "This proves that organized mongrel minorities control the Government," charged Mississippi's Senator Eastland. Echoing the debate from previous years, Eastland contended that the proposed new laws were unnecessary. Blacks and whites "live together in contentment," he said. "Both races know and respect each other . . . the Negro receives a square deal. Both races recognize that the society of the South is built upon segregation." Georgia congressman Gene Cox said Truman's program "sounds like the program of the Communist Party."

"Distasteful, unthinkable, and ridiculous," was how Arkansas governor Ben Laney described the president's ideas. Laney said he wasn't sure what the South could do, but "I am ready to help even to extreme measures."

The entire South Carolina congressional delegation—Senators Maybank and Johnston and the six representatives—likewise denounced the program, as did a number of state politicians. Within days, the Jasper County Executive Committee voted to withdraw from the national party.

Publicly, Thurmond had no immediate comment after the speech, but that did not mean a lack of attention to the subject. Within four days the southern governors would meet in Florida, and there would be plenty of time to discuss matters then. In fact, the governors were already being beseeched by their constituents to take up Truman's program at their session.

Southern newspapers lambasted the proposals. Mississippi's response, as in previous civil rights debates, was the harshest. The Jackson *Clarion Ledger* called them "a vicious and unconstitutional program" that was "blatantly and malodorously another cold-blooded and treacherous offer by the national leaders to swap destruction of the South for the votes of the communist and radical groups that properly belong with Henry Wallace and for the votes of Negroes who may hold the balance of power in a few states."

The Columbia *State* was more restrained, conceding that "it does seem that Mr. Truman is going out of his way to evoke protests from the South as to his policies. But viewing the matter dispassionately and not as a defense, we ask the question: Has he suggested anything that wasn't proposed by Mr. Roosevelt and Eleanor?"

On February 6 in Washington, the day the governors were gathering in Wakulla Springs, Florida, a number of southern senators drew their line in the sand. Allen J. Ellender of Louisiana vowed that the civil rights bills would "never see daylight" if supporters tried to bring them to the Senate floor. And Richard Russell of Georgia, the most prominent southern senator, joined the fray by accusing the president of planning an American-style "Gestapo" to eradicate segregation in the South. The potential revolt of the South, Russell said, "is more serious than any I have seen in my lifetime."

The same day there was another piece of bad news for white Carolinians. The Fourth Circuit denied a request for a rehearing of the *Elmore* case. The Supreme Court was now the only thing standing between blacks and the upcoming August primary.

The governors who gathered in Wakulla Springs, a small town just south of Tallahassee, were all worried about the challenge from Washington, though they were not of a single mind on how to respond. So great was their concern that they scuttled their agenda and closed their meeting to the press in order to develop a response to Truman in private.

The most rabid participant was Mississippi's Wright, who had announced before leaving home that a week after the conference his state would "mobilize for an all-out fight," one he was sure would "spread like wildfire and sweep before it all those who today stand as enemies to our institutions and our way of life." Wright's proposal to the governors called for all "true Democrats" to meet on March 1 to consider forming a new party.

Other governors, however, were not ready for such a bold move. Alabama's James E. Folsom was willing to challenge Truman on civil rights, but he believed the national convention, set for July in Philadelphia, was the better forum. While Governor M. E. Thompson of Georgia found the president's proposals "unnecessary and unwise," he said they would not, by themselves, prompt him to "join any movement directly or indirectly that would cut the feet from under the Democratic Party and its leaders, and thereby deprive the South of its greatest strength."

Tennessee's James N. McCord joined Millard F. Caldwell, the host governor, in rejecting a separatist movement. Caldwell opposed any action that could conceivably help a Republican get elected.

The two main options before the governors were Wright's call for immediate and dramatic action and Folsom's suggestion of a five-month delay. Neither seemed attractive to the group.

Enter Thurmond with a middle-of-the-road proposal—a "cooling-off" period during which a committee of the governors would evaluate the impact of the civil rights proposals on the South, meet with national Democratic Party officials to clarify the measures and express their strong reservations, and finally report back at another session of the governors' conference. The governors endorsed his ideas with one modification. Thurmond originally had proposed a sixty-day waiting period but at Wright's insistence the time was cut to forty days.

Thurmond had gone to the meeting well prepared. Brown, his businessman friend from Spartanburg, had told him that if he wanted to make his mark, he had better have something to offer when the debate on civil rights got going. So Brown and Figg helped him prepare the resolution ahead of time, and he ultimately prevailed over Wright. In the process he established himself as a new voice for the white South.

While Thurmond's proposal was more moderate than Wright's, the accompanying rhetoric was not. It sounded like the eruption of a festering wound. Even if Thurmond had not written every word of it himself, it was clear that in this, his first direct political confrontation over race, he was ready to sound the cry of battle. From this point on there was no turning back.

"The people of the States represented by the members of this Conference here have been shocked by the spectacle of the political parties of this country engaging in competitive bidding for the votes of small pressure groups by attacking the traditions, customs and institutions of the section in which we live," Thurmond's motion began.

Recalling the struggle to recover economically from the Civil War, Thurmond reminded his listeners that "economic underprivilege in the South has known no color line." Only through "the solution of our economic problems," he insisted, would racial problems disappear.

It was the political leaders of the country, he charged, who would not let them continue with their task. "Their political attacks are calculated only to hamper our efforts and actually militate against the welfare of the very people whom they assert they are trying to help."

The motion took the president's proposals one by one, criticizing the antilynching bill, the anti–poll tax proposal, and the FEPC as ill-considered and unnecessary at best, dangerous at worst to southern society. The result would be a breakdown of laws "which knowledge and experience of many years have proven to be essential to the protection of the racial integrity and purity of the white and the negro races alike."

As if to underscore the error of Clark Clifford's political analysis, the motion added: "We are expected to stand idle and let all of this happen, for the sole purpose of enticing an infinitesimal minority of organized pressure blocs to vote for one or another candidate for the Presidency. It is thought that we have no redress. This assumption ignores the electoral college set up in the Constitution of the United States."

Belief in the electoral college as the South's best hope for power had surfaced a year earlier in a book, *Whither Solid South,* written by Alabama lawyer Charles Wallace Collins and promoted by Senator Eastland and Governor Wright. Collins first argued for a coalition of southerners with northern and western conservatives. But if such a coalition never materialized, then, Collins suggested, the South could set up its own party to exert influence. He pointed out that the states of the Old Confederacy—South Carolina, Mississippi, Florida, Alabama, Georgia, Louisiana, Texas, Arkansas, North Carolina, Virginia, and Tennessee—had 127 votes in the electoral college, which was sufficient to hold the balance of power as long as there were two competing and reasonably equal political parties in the North. With no clear winner in the electoral college, the presidential election would be decided in the House of Representatives, and there the South could have enormous bargaining power. "A Northern deadlock," Collins wrote, "could lead to the election of a Southern president."

Thurmond's motion concluded with a pledge by the governors to act with "dignity and self-respect and restraint. We should refuse to be stampeded or to indulge in idle oratory. We must consider the matter calmly and deliberately to the end that by joint and common action and decision we may demand and obtain for our people the consideration and respect to which they are entitled."

The next day Thurmond was named to head a special committee that would attempt to gain concessions from the national Democratic leadership.

The South Carolina NAACP, which earlier had been optimistic

about progressive leadership from Thurmond, called the resolution a "keen disappointment."

Over the next two weeks, Mississippi and South Carolina continued their public displays of opposition to Truman. On February 12, as Fielding Wright had promised, four thousand Mississippi Democrats met in Jackson to lay the groundwork for a nationwide revolt against the national party. In what was as much essay as reportage, *The Clarion Ledger*'s Gene Wirth wrote: "White Mississippians, blood of the Confederacy and of true Jeffersonian Democracy, overflowed onto two streets from Jackson's city auditorium Thursday to express and to act upon their sentiments against proposed anti-southern legislation.

"This 'voice' of the people, united as one voice, represented men and women from all sections of the state and from all walks of life. It was their meeting and they liked it. They spoke and they were heard. It was truly a Democratic meeting."

After the ritual singing of "Dixie," the group adopted a resolution calling for a conference in the spring "of all true white Jeffersonian Democrats."

One note of caution came from the state's junior United States senator, John Stennis, who had been elected the previous November after Senator Bilbo's death. Stennis urged the crowd to reconsider their revolt and pledged to work "toward getting our rights recognized and protected by the Democratic Party." But this group was in no mood for caution.

Four days later, Governor Wright announced that the states' rights movement had prompted so much response that it was necessary to open a headquarters in Jackson. On February 22, representatives of nine other southern states came to Jackson to draw up battle plans for blocking the civil rights legislation and for furthering the states' rights cause. After this public session, a small group of the southerners met behind closed doors and pledged $61,500 to spread the word about the movement in Mississippi and elsewhere.

White South Carolina Democrats put their disaffection with the national party on record February 12 when the state House of Representatives unanimously adopted a resolution condemning Truman's civil rights proposals as "un-American." One week later they made their feelings known to the nation with a very public snub.

President Truman was to be the featured speaker February 19

at the annual Jefferson-Jackson Day Dinner in Washington, D.C. A few days beforehand, Johnston's wife, Gladys, a vice-chairman of the event, called Senator J. Howard McGrath of Rhode Island, chairman of the Democratic National Committee. She wanted assurances that no member of the Johnston entourage would be seated next to a black person.

When McGrath failed to provide such a guarantee, the South Carolinians, including the Thurmonds, refused to attend even though more than one thousand dollars had been paid for tickets. Because Mrs. Johnston was expected to play a role in the event, the Johnston table was located close to the speaker's rostrum. To keep the prized—and highly visible—table empty, Governor Johnston hired a former heavyweight boxer to attend the dinner and prevent anyone from using South Carolina's space.

Johnston's boycott garnered the national press attention he had hoped for, and his office was flooded with congratulatory letters, telegrams, and phone calls. (One letter addressed to Mrs. Johnston bragged that "applications for Ku Klux Klan membership are booming and there's a healthy increase in the manufacture of Red Shirts in South Carolina.")

The day after the dinner, southern congressmen banded together to announce their unified opposition to the Truman proposals. Three days later, February 23, Thurmond and his committee had their meeting with Chairman McGrath. In advance, the governors had prepared several leading questions designed to force concessions from the national party leader. Typical was the first one: "Do you as Chairman of the Democratic National Committee, deny that the proposed anti–poll tax law, the proposed antilynching law, the proposed FEPC law, and Federal laws dealing with the separation of races . . . would be unconstitutional invasions of the field of government belonging to the states under the Bill of Rights in the Constitution of the United States?"

McGrath replied that he did not believe the proposals were unconstitutional. In response to other questions, he refused to agree to block the proposals or to promise to put a states' rights plank in the Democratic Party platform.

The southerners emerged from the session virtually empty-handed. *The New York Times* noted in its front-page coverage that McGrath "would not yield on a single point as they fired question after question at him." After huddling in private, the governors' committee issued a statement warning that the South did not stand alone but would be joined by "Democrats everywhere who are opposed to a centralized government invading the rights of people and the rights of the respective states." The Democratic Party, they said, "will soon realize that the South is no longer 'in the bag.' "

The committee set forth a five-part plan designed to solidify southern influence by using state party machinery to select delegates to the Philadelphia convention and the electoral college who would support their cause. Critical to a restoration of southern power, the governors said, was a return to the "two-thirds" rule, requiring that a presidential nominee get two-thirds of the convention delegates' votes rather than a simple majority. Roosevelt had engineered the move to majority rule in 1936 in order to dilute the South's power.

A week after the McGrath meeting, the South Carolina Democratic Executive Committee officially joined the growing southern revolt by adopting a resolution opposing the nomination and election of Truman. "We express in no uncertain terms our resentment at the deliberate and contemptuous betrayal of the Democrats of the South by the national party leadership," the resolution said.

Thurmond made a brief appearance at that meeting, condemning the civil rights legislation as "an invasion of the right of self-government. . . . The president has gone too far," Thurmond declared, adding that "as far as I am concerned, I am through with him."

On March 4 in Washington, Stennis, who had counseled caution in Jackson, used his maiden speech in the Senate to blast the president. He called Truman's program a "political fraud" and a "brazen effort to capture the vote of the misguided and misled rank-and-file Negro in the 1948 elections." The next day, in Columbia, *The State* gave the speech front-page treatment.

Back in Jackson, Mississippi party officials continued to organize. The "Peoples' Committee of Loyal States' Rights Jeffersonian Democrats" was established. Its motto was "Let's give the government back to the people," and Governor Wright was designated honorary chairman.

The southerners' dissension was news in the North as well as the South. In an article that was only slightly catty, *The New Republic* noted that the unhappiness in Dixie was apparently serious. "In past election years," the magazine observed March 8,

"Southerners have usually been content with headlines proclaiming their 'revolt,' followed by a brief period of pouting, before they quietly voted the straight ticket again on election day. This time the 'revolt' has started months before the convention time, and its leaders are not political unknowns, but the Democratic state organization leaders themselves."

The time between Wakulla Springs and the governors' self-imposed deadline was a dispiriting one. Their concerns were falling on deaf ears at national party headquarters, and at home the white citizenry was alarmed by the threat to segregation that would come with federal intrusion. Forty years later, the political calculations that moved Thurmond to act remained fresh in his mind: "The southern states all had laws on racial questions. . . . The reason I took the position I did was, one, that was the law of South Carolina, the law of my state, next it was the custom of my state, and next it was the thinking of the people I represented."

Absent from the equation were two significant elements—an appreciation of the inequities that were driving the civil rights legislation, and an accurate reading of the consequences for his own political career. It seemed impossible that any of Truman's civil rights proposals might actually be enacted, let alone later ones that would be even stronger. For a pragmatic politician who believed that "timing is everything," all that counted was a correct analysis of the present and the willingness to seize the initiative.

On March 13, the governors reconvened in Washington, D.C., to receive the Thurmond committee's report. Rather than serving as a "cooling-off period," the forty days since Wakulla Springs seemed to have turned up the temperature. The report was a plan for battle. "The Committee has reached the unavoidable conclusion that . . . the proposed [civil rights] program, and the precedents which will be created therefrom, would constitute a total departure from the fundamental principles upon which the government of the United States was founded," the governors said.

Taking Truman's proposals one by one, the report cited flaws and dangers in each of them, followed by what was fast becoming the standard refrain about protecting "racial integrity and purity of both the White and Negro races alike" and for preserving the peace. There was also a veiled warning of possible violence. The "sudden interference with the laws dealing with the separation of the races would do great injury to the very people intended to be benefitted," the report said.

Finally, the report said Truman's proposal was a "betrayal of the rank and file of the Democrats of this country, because so many of the proposals are openly and deliberately directed against our traditions, customs and institutions."

Complete unanimity among the southern governors was impossible, reflecting the enormous pull of Democratic loyalty and a natural fear of charting a radical and unknown course. But the report was adopted, and buoyed by the session, Thurmond returned to South Carolina more deeply entrenched in the philosophy of states' rights and speaking with more stridency.

Attacking the desegregation proposals in "To Secure These Rights," Thurmond told one rally, "A little more practical help on economic lines and a little less fallacious racial theory would accomplish a great deal more for the improvement of the level of life and opportunity of all our people of whatever race." As an example he cited the effort to save Meharry Medical College in Nashville, a school for blacks, which had fallen on hard times; critics saw the effort as an attempt to avoid integration. "Observe how the President's committee insults the people of the South in this statement of their report: 'It is sound policy to use the idealism and prestige of our whole people to check the wayward tendencies of a part of them.'

"*They* have the idealism and prestige; *we* in the South are the wayward," Thurmond said with obvious bitterness. "It was regarded as *so* wayward for the southern governors to help save Meharry Medical College for the education of Negro doctors to serve their people."

Calling the proposals Truman's attempt to "stab us in the back" with federal laws "as detrimental to the South as those proposed in the Reconstruction period by the Republican Party," the governor repeated his call for southerners to "stand together in the Electoral College" and throw the presidential election into the House. "On principle, we can do nothing else and still remain true to our heritage. No fight was ever won by staying out of it. Our cause is right and just. We shall honor ourselves by pressing it to the end."

Not all southern politicians were ready to answer such a call. Incumbent senators and congressmen feared the loss of seniority on Capitol Hill and of patronage back home. On March 23 Senators Russell of Georgia, Maybank of South Carolina, Lister Hill of Alabama, and Clyde R. Hoey of North Carolina obtained airtime from the Mutual Broadcasting System to address Truman's civil rights program. While they attacked the proposals themselves—Russell feared the "disastrous loss of personal liberties which marks the centralized police state"—they stopped short of calling for outright revolt.

In Alabama, the state's premier politicians—Senators Hill and Sparkman and Governor Folsom—were counseling patience and calm. But despite their advice Alabama was joining Mississippi and South Carolina as a stronghold of rebellion. Although Alabama's three leading politicians did not favor a revolt, they were about to be outmaneuvered by skilled politicians able to capitalize on good organization and on the emotionalism that always surrounded race.

Former governor Frank Dixon, an ardent and polished white supremacist, had remained influential in state politics because of support from important financial interests. Even before Truman's civil rights speech, he and the equally conservative state Democratic chairman, Gessner T. McCorvey, had engineered a resolution by the state party warning the national party not to attack segregation. Although they had won this early round, Alabama Democrats were hardly unified. By the early spring there were three factions—a liberal group (by comparison to others) promoting Folsom as a favorite son; the rebels who opposed Truman and his civil rights program, led by McCorvey and Dixon; and the party loyalists, led by Senators Hill and Sparkman and the state's seven U.S. representatives.

When party members gathered April 5 at the Jefferson Davis Hotel in Montgomery, state chairman McCorvey roused the crowd when he declared his loyalty to the Democratic Party of Alabama. "Nobody in this room is going to bolt the party to which they belong," he declared—and that party was the *state* party. Alabama Democrats would "affiliate" with the national Democrats, he added, but only if the party would not try to "ram down the throats of the South" the Truman civil rights measures. He added that the Alabama Democrats already had filed an emblem with the secretary of state: a rooster with the words WHITE SUPREMACY over its head and FOR THE RIGHT under its feet.

Despite cheers for McCorvey, there were enough detractors at the session to postpone delegate selection for the convention and the electoral college. By the May 4 vote, however, potential delegates would have to tell the party chairman whether they would pledge to walk out of the Philadelphia convention if a civil rights plank was included in the platform.

For the next three weeks the state's papers were full of stories about which delegates would pledge to walk out and which would stay. Editorial opinion was diverse. Ads paid for by rebel Democrats decried Truman's civil rights program in bold letters. "Defeat Truman's Civil Rights Program—Safeguard Segregation—What 'Civil Rights' Means to You," the ads began. Then they listed the parade of horribles that would result: "abolishment" of segregation in all public schools, colleges and church schools; "abolishment" of segregation in restaurants, hotels, streetcars, buses, barbershops, beauty shops, and swimming pools; and "compulsory upgrading of Negro employees to positions of supervision over whites in the same racial ratio."

In a story on the upcoming Alabama vote—the first balloting to test the strength of the southern revolt—*New York Times* reporter John N. Popham offered a cogent analysis of what he called "the usual paradoxical political picture in the South." Noting that both Sparkman and Hill were recognized nationally as liberal legislators, he pointed out that they opposed Truman's civil rights program "to insure voting strength in their local area."

The May 4 vote was inconclusive enough to require a runoff June 1. The results were largely a victory for the rebels. All presidential electors would oppose any candidate supporting the civil rights proposals, and fourteen of the twenty-six delegates to the convention were pledged to walk out. That the conservatives had done so well was unusual given that the state's traditional political powerhouses—the governor and two senators—were not so bent on revolt.

In neighboring Georgia, the leading politicians also opposed outright defection, even though they, too, denounced Truman's proposals. The forces advocating rebellion were not as organized as they were in Alabama. Moreover, Georgians were still preoccupied with a looming fight between M. E. Thompson and Herman Talmadge about succeeding the late governor-elect Gene Talmadge. By virtue of a state Supreme Court ruling, Thompson was serving as governor. But the younger Talmadge was challenging him.

Former governor E. D. Rivers was a voice for unity when he

reminded Democratic colleagues that the party "has led our country to victory in two world wars. This party rescued us from the misery of depression. This party is keeping us at the peak of employment and earnings. This party is sponsoring the only possible plan for world peace. These are the things closest to the hearts of our people, without which the pros and cons of civil rights would not be worth debating." But while Rivers was preaching unity, Georgia was nonetheless represented at all meetings about the southern revolt.

The next one was set for May 10 in Jackson. But before Carolina Democrats headed west for the session, they had to deal with another important development in state politics. The party had taken the *Elmore* case to the U.S. Supreme Court, and on April 19, Thurgood Marshall received a telegram with the best possible message: PETITION FOR CERTIORARI AGAINST ELMORE DENIED TODAY. The high court had refused to review the Fourth Circuit decision. So its ruling and Judge Waring's underlying decision stood. Blacks could vote in South Carolina's Democratic primaries, at least in theory.

The NAACP's Hinton issued an immediate statement. "It is the wish of all Negroes that the South Carolina Democratic Party will bow in obedience to the courts, and will as good citizens, good sports who have abiding faith in our judicial system, now welcome Negroes into the Democratic primaries. They could do no less and Negroes expect no more."

Governor Thurmond, who had avoided commenting at all when Waring first issued his decision, waited two days to respond to the Supreme Court's refusal. His brief statement was angry but controlled. "I was shocked by the action of the United States Supreme Court in refusing even to hear the Democrats of South Carolina in the primary case. Every American citizen has lost a part of his fundamental rights by this decision, and is less a free man than he was before," Thurmond said, "because it denies to our people their constitutional freedom of peaceful assembly."

If the governor was ungracious in his response, at least he did not counsel defiance. That would be left to the party apparatus, which would pull one or two more gimmicks from its sleeve before the August primary.

Editorial comment in the state capital after the Supreme Court decision was mild and somewhat critical of Thurmond. The tone of the editorials suggested that, at least with respect to voting, many white Carolinians were willing to reach a hand across racial lines. In "sober consideration," *The Columbia Record* asked, "have the Negroes won anything by the Supreme Court decision to which they were not entitled?" Questions of justice aside, the paper said that black enfranchisement would bolster the chance for a true two-party system, which it believed was the only way for South Carolina to have "influence in national affairs commensurate with its population." In little more than a decade, Thurmond himself would prove the truth of that observation.

Several days later, *The State* tweaked Thurmond more sharply. An editorial entitled "No Cause for Shock" speculated that Thurmond had spoken after two days only because he "felt called upon to." Though reassuring its readers and the governor that it was "no more in favor of federal interference in the affairs of the individual states than is Governor Thurmond or anyone else," the paper added that it did not consider the decision "a matter of vital importance" but rather "a matter of course. And we believe that the thinking white citizens of South Carolina view it in the same perspective."

South Carolina Democrats were not scheduled to meet until mid-May to address the *Elmore* problem and pick delegates for the Philadelphia convention. In the meantime, Thurmond headed for Jackson, where the Mississippians had asked him to give the keynote address at the convention of States' Rights Democrats. He was an understandable choice, having shown leadership at Wakulla Springs and an angry tenacity later in Washington in the disappointing session with McGrath. The fact that Thurmond was from South Carolina and not Mississippi was another plus, helping to make the session look less like a local meeting and more like a southern gathering.

By this time, the potential bolters had been given a new moniker—one they disliked but that nonetheless was going to stick—the "Dixiecrats." (Credit for the name is given to William Weismer, telegraph editor of *The Charlotte* (N.C.) *News,* who couldn't squeeze "States' Rights Democrats" into a headline.) When the word first appeared in *The Birmingham News,* former governor Dixon protested, contending that the movement was returning to "the original concepts of the founding fathers of our nation and the Democratic Party."

As the site of the most militant opposition to Truman's civil rights proposals, Mississippi was the appropriate place for the May

10 session, all the more so given that its governor had sounded a note of defiance nearly three weeks before Truman's provocative civil rights address. He was in high gear by the time "true Democrats" were making their way to Jackson for the May 10 session. To help set the stage for the event, Wright picked the unusual hour of 7:30 A.M., Sunday, May 9, for a radio address pitched primarily to the state's black population.

The governor's speech was by turns soothing, patronizing, and mildly threatening. Wright said he wanted to correct the "maliciously false and dangerous representation" that those who opposed the civil rights proposals were hostile to blacks while those who favored them were their friends. "The stirring up of prejudices is unfortunate for both races in the South," Wright added, "but more particularly for yours. . . . It would be better for you to place your trust in the innate, uncoerced sense of justice of the white people with whom you live, moving through the slow but sure and steady processes of time, than to depend upon any artificial programs of compulsion and force, as now proposed by insincere, distant people who do not know you and who cannot conceivably have your real interests at heart."

Then came the warning. "The decision is yours," the governor said. "If you cast your lot with those who are your friends . . . you will reap the benefits. If you prefer to follow the leadership of the other element, I am sorry—but you will find that you will be much happier in some other state than Mississippi. . . . If any of you have become so deluded as to want to enter our hotels and cafés, enjoy social equality with the whites, then kindness and true sympathy requires me to advise you to make your home in some state other than Mississippi."

The states' righters, Wright concluded, "are sincerely desirous of preventing chaos and confusion striking at your families and your neighbors. . . . Our campaign of opposition [to Truman] will be conducted with dignity and determination. And throughout your individual rights and liberties shall be respected and safeguarded, not by the Federal Government, but by your duly constituted local and state authorities."

The speech caused barely a ripple. *The Clarion Ledger*, which had printed excerpts of Wright's remarks on the day of the address, carried no reaction from either white or black Mississippians afterward.

On May 10, fifteen hundred delegates, including some from

the border states of Kentucky, Missouri, Oklahoma, and West Virginia, and perhaps two thousand spectators gathered at the city auditorium for their meeting. Shortly before their arrival they had gotten another piece of disconcerting news from the North. On May 3, the Supreme Court had ruled 6–0 that covenants to bar blacks or other racial minorities from owning property were legally unenforceable—one more indication that the South was alone in the fight to preserve "custom and tradition."

As the delegates made their way into town, they had been greeted by Confederate flags posted along the main roads. Banners reading "Welcome States' Rights Democrats" hung over the Jackson Municipal Auditorium doors. Once inside, the Texas delegation gave a rousing version of "The Eyes of Texas Are Upon You." The entire crowd sang a chorus of "Dixie," and after a string of introductions, it was finally Thurmond's turn to give the keynote address. He had brought Figg and Brown to Jackson with him, where both men had closeted themselves in a hotel room to give the governor the barnburner he wanted. Thurmond, meanwhile, was at the governor's mansion with Jean, where they, along with Governor Laney of Arkansas and his wife, were guests of Governor Wright. Wright had said a few days earlier that if southerners didn't win concessions from the national leadership, he would back Thurmond or Senator Walter George of Georgia to run for president.

The speech was the strongest Thurmond had made to date, an unapologetic call to arms filled with doses of history, political theory, and legislative analysis.

"We have gathered here today because the American system of free constitutional government is in danger," the governor began. "We are here because we have been betrayed in the house of our fathers, and we are determined that those who committed this betrayal shall not go unpunished."

Venting anew anger at the South's treatment, Thurmond said that when the campaign was over, "leaders in both political parties will realize we no longer intend to be a doormat on which Presidential candidates may wipe their political shoes every time they want to appeal to minority groups in doubtful states."

Recalling the evils of the Civil War, Thurmond reminded his listeners how much the South had "suffered from vicious propaganda. No effort was spared to make it appear that we fought to perpetuate human slavery, and thereby obscure the fundamental constitutional and economic issues which brought on that unhappy conflict."

And today, he charged, in an effort to pass the civil rights measures, "the American people are being propagandized to believe that Southerners have been mistreating the Negroes in our midst, and that we are unfit for local self-government. . . . We hear not a word of the tremendous efforts which have been made through the years to give both races in the South the opportunity to improve and progress," Thurmond lamented. "We hear not a word of recognition of the progress which the Negro has made since slavery days as a result of the efforts of the Southern people"—all without help from northern "emancipators."

As was the custom by now, Thurmond went through Truman's proposals one by one and gave the standard criticisms of the "force bills," as he called them, though with his accent it came out "foce." The anti–poll tax bill was foolish because "we all know that the poll tax does not burden the right to vote. It is a minor revenue measure yielding comparatively little money." He noted that he had advocated repeal in South Carolina. While only seven states had a poll tax, the federal proposal was hardly harmless, Thurmond insisted. "If Congress can use this law to establish the power to deal with the right of the American people to vote, it can establish a form of federal suffrage. It can exercise control over the ballot boxes of the nation."

The antilynching bill was unconstitutional because "the federal government does not have the constitutional right to deal with crimes occurring within the states. . . . All the states have laws against murder," Thurmond said. "Many have specific laws against lynching, which is a cowardly form of murder. This proposed law is unnecessary because enlightened public opinion has virtually stamped out this crime."

The FEPC law would create a new bureaucracy that could "harass and interfere" with business and with labor unions. "Every man's private business would almost be made a public one," he insisted. He could be ordered to hire employees he didn't want and could be brought into court for violations but not given a jury trial. "The mind of man can hardly conceive of more duress and apprehension than this would produce."

Thurmond repeated the standard refrain that separation of the races was "necessary to maintain the public peace and order. . . . We know that [the laws] are essential to the protection of the racial integrity and purity of the white and Negro races alike." And he repeated his call for "a little more help along practical economic lines and a little less fallacious racial theory."

The foolishness of the desegregation proposals was evident from the country's experience with Prohibition, Thurmond claimed. "If the Federal government could not stop people from drinking, then how can a Federal law force people to break off social customs and traditions as old as civilization itself?

"These big-city machine bosses and their puppets in office, as well as those who think everything can be done by law from Washington, should once and for all realize that on the question of social intermingling of the races our people draw the line. No decent and self-respecting Negro would ask for a law to force people to accept him where he is not wanted," Thurmond declared. "They themselves do not want social intermingling. They are entitled to equality of opportunity, and they will get it through our efforts. But all the laws of Washington and all the bayonets of the army," said Thurmond in a line he would repeat in the months ahead, "cannot force the Negro into our homes, our schools, our churches, and our places of recreation."

Reminding these "true Democrats" of the source of all this trouble, Thurmond said he hoped the president would decide not to run. But since Truman was apparently going to force his nomination, the future course was clear. "So far as I am concerned the die is cast and the Rubicon is crossed," Thurmond declared. "As the governor of a sovereign state, I do not intend that the rights of my people shall be sacrified on the block of blind party loyalty."

He urged conference members to go back to their states and make sure that the delegates to the national convention had the freedom to oppose any nominee who supported the "so-called Federal Civil Rights program." It would send a message to the party that "the South's electoral votes are no longer 'in the bag.' . . .

"Party bosses and ward heelers" who have "kidnapped the Democratic Party and deserted its principles may force Truman's nomination," the governor thundered, but—and this was Bob Figg's favorite line—"Harry S. Truman has never been elected President of the United States and he never will be."

The Texas delegation rose in unison and hollered its approval.

"I know in my heart what the Southerners who have gone before us would do in the crisis which faces us," Thurmond concluded. "Let us remain true to the trust which they handed to our care, and carry on to final victory."

In a matter of seven months, Thurmond had gone from a little-known governor to a voluble crusader for states' rights. He hadn't planned his political career this way, but provoked by Truman and encouraged by his fellow white southerners, he had been drawn step by step ever more deeply into a movement that was, at bottom, designed to preserve segregation.

Where other southerners came to the cause out of genuine racial animus, Thurmond embraced it primarily as a philosophy of political power whose racial effects were secondary. He recognized the need to improve the lives of black southerners, but he was comfortable promoting only change that fit within "custom and tradition" and that was dictated by the white establishment.

The Tenth Amendment had become the centerpiece of his ideology, and for the rest of his political career the primacy of the states would frame every discussion about government. In 1948, however, this philosophy served to protect white southern power and helped to perpetuate white supremacy.

Although Thurmond presented himself in Jackson as a soldier in the service of states' rights, his address was much more than a sterile debate on constitutional interpretation, and from this point on his detractors would define him as a segregationist standard-bearer and little more.

Not surprisingly, Thurmond's speech brought wild cheers and foot stomping. He was interrupted for applause thirty-one times in forty-five minutes, and when the address was over, dozens of delegates swarmed up the aisle to shake his hand.

The rest of the proceedings were much less energetic. The extreme heat coupled with the delayed lunch hour caused the once-enthusiastic crowd to dwindle considerably. By the time the delegates were ready to adopt resolutions for action, attendance had shrunk to 150 spectators and about 500 delegates.

The resolutions included a statement of principles that generally tracked Thurmond's speech. The delegates also ratified a plan of action that included support for a states' rights plank in the Democratic Party platform and opposition to any civil rights language.

The plan further called for a July 17 meeting in Birmingham if southern delegates either were not admitted to the convention or were unable to fulfill their goals. This proved to be too much for the Georgians, who felt they could never bolt the Democratic Party nor do anything that might help the establishment of a third party. During one closed-door meeting, Chairman James S. Peters told the other southerners that in Georgia, "the Democratic Party is like a religion."

Concerned about the charge that they were in open revolt, the states' righters sought to cover themselves with the same rhetoric they had put into the new house organ, *The States' Righter.* "In no sense can this action be described as bolting the party, forming a new party nor as the holding of a rump convention," they declared in a final resolution. "The national party organization is merely an association of the various state party organizations and the plan of action outlined herein serves to return the party to the people and to the principles on which it was founded."

In this case, however, action spoke louder than words.

By the time South Carolina Democrats gathered at Township Auditorium in Columbia May 19 for their convention, dissatisfaction with the president was at its high point. The keynote speaker delivered a stemwinder, exhorting the crowd to "fight to the last ditch" to "defeat those who would lynch the South."

Despite an intraparty squabble with the Olin Johnston faction (there was speculation that Thurmond would challenge him for the Senate in 1950), Thurmond controlled the convention. Party rules were a big help. Each county was given twice as many votes as it had members in the General Assembly. As a result, the influence of politicians with large black populations was increased because so many of their residents—the black citizens—couldn't vote. These black-belt politicians, concerned about the threat to their way of life, were among Truman's most hostile critics and Thurmond's most vigorous supporters, and they found in their governor a protector of the status quo. The majority of those eventually designated as delegates to Philadelphia were pledged to Thurmond's cause.

The delegates would not go to Philadelphia with a free hand, however. The convention instructed them to refrain from voting for Truman or for any other candidate who supported Truman's civil rights program. And on the first ballot, the delegates were told to vote for Thurmond as a favorite son candidate, the first time since 1877 that the state was prepared to take a stand against a Democratic nominee.

In an editorial the day after the convention, *The State* said approvingly that the "first step was taken . . . to take South Carolina out of the regular Democratic bag for the first time since the Reconstruction era."

Party leaders had one more piece of unfinished business before they left Columbia. Given the Supreme Court's refusal to review the *Elmore* decision, the prospect of black voters in the August primary loomed large. Democratic officials wanted to find a way to limit black participation, and after a heated executive session behind closed doors, the party leaders decided to adopt an oath every Democrat had to take. It was a transparent effort to keep blacks from the polls.

The key part of the oath required Democrats to swear that they "understand, believe in and will support the principles of the Democratic Party of South Carolina" and to state their belief in and support for the social, religious, and educational separation of the races. In addition, each Democrat was required to "solemnly swear that I believe in the principles of states' rights, and that I am opposed to and will work against the FEPC law and other federal laws relating to employment within the states."

Adoption of the oath would turn out to be a miscalculation. It provoked the black community into filing another lawsuit, and it became a catalyst that allowed disaffection within the party to rise to the surface. Moderate white Democrats who believed the state party had gone too far would finally decide to go public.

But the first to be heard from were the Progressive Democrats, who met one week after the regular party's convention. On May 26 more than 250 delegates gathered in an auditorium at the state capital, welcomed by signs and placards declaring "Down with half-citizenship—We want full citizenship"; "We're for Truman, not Thurmond"; "Special privileges for none—South Carolina for everybody." Although most of the delegates were from Charleston and Columbia, there was representation from twenty-six of South Carolina's forty-six counties. Two whites were at the session—the Reverend Robert Ayers, secretary of the Baptist Student Union of South Carolina, and the Reverend John Isom of Spartanburg.

The session opened with a rewritten version of "Give Me That Old Time Religion" called "That Old Democratic Spirit." It included a verse praising the party "good enough for Jefferson, Jackson, and Truman" but "not good enough for J. Strom Thurmond."

In his keynote speech, the group's executive secretary, Arthur Clement, Jr., assailed Thurmond. While he was on the bench, in the army, and running for governor, Clement asserted, "Thurmond was a perfect gentleman. Then he got elected and became a member of the office-holding industry. Then all hell broke loose in all of its diabolical fury. All of the training, the culture, the proud and civilized restraint that should mark any gentleman irrespective of his race evaporated like the morning dew." The governor who was supposed to bring South Carolina "wise statesmanship" instead turned into "another wailing rabble-rouser, a whirling regional school fanatic, a states' rights slave with a handful of followers in South Carolina and Mississippi."

At Clement's urging, the Progressive Democrats agreed to send a twenty-eight-member delegation to the Democratic National Convention. It would be headed by John McCray and would include Clement, Hinton, and George Elmore. They were pledged to support Truman.

In addition to demonstrating their loyalty to the president, the Progressives' decision to send delegates to Philadelphia was a good tactical move. The group knew it had almost no chance of being seated over the regular party delegation, but if the anti-Trumanites walked out, then there would be another delegation of Democrats available to be seated.

(Ironically, the evening of the Progressives' convention Thurmond made a statewide radio address on the accomplishments of the 1948 General Assembly. Symptomatic of his unquestioned acceptance of separate but equal was Thurmond's discussion of black educational opportunities. He said there were "adequate" facilities that existed through the college level for blacks, though he conceded the need for new professional schools to serve them. His observation ignored the continuing disparity in per-pupil spending for whites and blacks, and he was unaware that right then in nearby Clarendon County, a school discrimination case was under way that would turn into a direct assault on segregation.)

Ten days after the state convention, the onerous party oath was still a major topic of discussion in the state. The criticism intensified to such a point that three of the Democrats' leading attorneys, Irving Belser, Charles Elliot, and Christie Benet, publicly said they had had nothing to do with drafting it. *The Columbia Record* declared that "only a member of the Nazi party in Germany could take the oath and mean it."

The public disapproval was intense enough for Chairman Baskin to call the executive committee back into session May 28 to reconsider the subject. A number of members from the northwestern part of the state wanted to scrap the oath entirely, but the committee decided only to modify it "to remove any possible objection on the grounds of religion." The new oath no longer required a voter to "understand" the principles of the state party, nor did he have to profess belief in the "religious" separation of the races, only in social and educational environments. The party also struck the section that required party members to work against the FEPC.

The revised oath still generated protests, and at least one party official, Richland County chairman John Rice, feared that the national committee would not seat the Carolina delegation because of such narrow instructions from the state party. He also feared another lawsuit if blacks were kept from voting in the primary.

By this time, white Carolinians unhappy with the regular party had already formed a loose-knit organization. A report of the fledgling party first surfaced in *The Greenville News*. The conveners initially declined to identify themselves and described the organization as a "grass-roots movement."

On June 2 the group went public when it released a letter inviting citizens from across the state to a "leadership" meeting in Columbia. In response to questions about why the group was forming, spokesman Gadsden E. Shand, a Columbia businessman, said that "defiance of orders of the United States Supreme Court by any individual or organization represents a threat against law and order and cannot be ignored." The organization did not endorse Truman's civil rights program, Shand added, but it would support the nominees of the national party.

On June 8 about one hundred individuals, half of them women (in contrast to the male-dominated regular Democrats), gathered to form what would later be known as the Citizens Democratic Party. No experienced politicians were part of the group, but they were some of the most racially liberal whites in the state. Among them was James McBride Dabbs, chairman of the South Carolina division of the biracial Southern Regional Council, who had written Thurmond such an optimistic letter after the Willie Earle incident.

After considerable discussion about how to respond to the regular Democrats, the group named a subcommittee to meet with Chairman Baskin and present a five-point ultimatum: Recall the state convention and require adherence to the Supreme Court white primary decisions; repudiate the voting oath; send delegates to Philadelphia with no instructions except for an order *not* to walk out; agree to support the national party in the general election; and open future state executive committee meetings to the public. The group further decided that if the state party did not respond within ten days, a second meeting would be held to select a separate delegation to challenge the regular party in Philadelphia.

The day before the meeting there had been a small milestone in South Carolina. Eight blacks had signed a state Democratic enrollment book at Bennettsville despite the state party's rule limiting party membership to whites.

Within a week, six county chairmen, led by Richland's John Rice, were openly defying Baskin. They publicly stated that blacks would be permitted to sign party enrollment books and could vote without having to affirm the oath. The counties represented about one-fourth of the state's population.

On June 17, the special committee of Citizens Democrats met with Baskin to ask for another convention so that delegates could reconsider their actions. Although Baskin listened politely, he refused. The next day the executive committee held another closed-door meeting and declined to change party rules.

On June 29, the Citizens Democrats reconvened, and although they claimed not to be creating a new party, their actions suggested otherwise. The nearly eighty people who attended agreed to send twenty delegates to Philadelphia. Among the more interesting features of this move was the decision to include delegates who had not attended either meeting. Among these were two prominent black Carolinians—E. H. McClenney, president of Voorhees College in Denmark (about an hour south of Columbia), and M. F. Whittaker, president of State College at Orangeburg.

Although he could have weighed in with the power of his office, Thurmond had remained silent during the brouhaha over the oath. But in late June he wrote Baskin about the problem. The issues he raised were more procedural than substantive. In the letter, which was made public June 26, Thurmond said he was concerned because several counties were administering the party rules as they wished instead of following party procedure. Because of the confusion, the governor said, many white Democrats were failing to enroll in the party and would be unable to vote in the primary.

He called on Baskin to reconvene the party convention after the Philadelphia session so that differences could be ironed out. "The party belongs to the people who make it up," Thurmond wrote. "The responsibility of straightening out the existing situation is too heavy to expect the executive committee to bear it alone." Thurmond added that he did not want to "second-guess" the committee because he had not participated actively in the events that had led up to the trouble. Other pressing business—the fight against "the encroachment on the sovereignty of the states of the Union under the guise of the so-called civil rights"—had preoccupied him. "Not having been able to help in the task," the governor said, "I certainly do not want to appear to assume the attitude of now saying what should or should not have been done."

Baskin made no immediate reply. He simply acknowledged receipt of the letter.

Before the disparate delegations left for Philadelphia, there was one more development important to the regular Democrats. On July 8, David Brown, a black from coastal Beaufort County, filed a lawsuit with the NAACP's help to prevent the regular party from using the oath. Judge Waring took the case, and the same day he issued a temporary restraining order to bar the party from discriminating against black Carolinians. He set the case for hearing right in the middle of the Democratic convention.

As Thurmond headed for Philadelphia, he was the titular head of a fractious group of Democrats. Although many white southerners were not yet ready to follow him, Thurmond had, by his own admission, crossed the Rubicon. He was about to find out what life was like on the other side.

7.
CANDIDATE BY DEFAULT

July 1948–December 1948

BY THE TIME Democrats arrived in Philadelphia the second week of July, a buoyant group of Republicans had just left the city. They were jubilant over the nomination of Governor Dewey and his running mate, Governor Earl Warren of California, and confident they would prevail over their fragmented opponents. The arrival of the Democrats was a different scene entirely. No bands welcomed the delegates to hotel lobbies; no hordes of excited conventioneers hustled toward elevators to get to their rooms at the Bellevue-Stratford, convention headquarters. Business was so slow that hotel managers, usually besieged by last-minute requests for accommodations, were taking calls for cancellations. Cab drivers complained they had no passengers.

The apparent inevitability of Truman's nomination and his eventual defeat had put party activists in a dispirited mood. The growing threat of a southern revolt only exacerbated the malaise. "The Democrats act as though they had accepted an invitation to a funeral," the Associated Press appropriately observed in a preconvention report. And one political analyst described the atmosphere as one of "sodden gloom."

General Eisenhower loomed as the party's savior; perhaps he could provide southerners with a candidate not wedded to civil rights while giving the liberal wing a chance for new, more aggressive leadership. Such was the hope of big-city party leaders who feared that Truman would take their local tickets down to defeat.

Carrying South Carolina's twenty convention votes with him, Thurmond supported the Eisenhower alternative and was ready to release his delegates to the general if it appeared he would be nominated. The governor went a step further. Instead of going directly to Philadelphia, he and Jean took the train to New York July 8 for a private meeting with Eisenhower, now president of Columbia University, to encourage him to run.

Eisenhower received the couple cordially, listened to Thurmond's entreaty, thanked him for coming, and politely said no. He told Thurmond, as he had indicated to others, that he couldn't run unless *both* parties nominated him. Thurmond could only smile at the naive proposal. War hero or not, Thurmond later reflected, "politics just doesn't work that way."

At a news conference after his meeting, the governor appealed to Truman to withdraw from consideration and "cooperate in nominating a ticket which will enable the Democratic Party to win." Without naming an alternative, Thurmond reminded reporters that South Carolina would not support Truman, explaining, "We believe in civil rights down there but not a federal invasion of states' rights."

Over the next week, Thurmond would play only a secondary role in the Democrats' convention drama and in the more parochial sideshow that was about to unfold in Judge Waring's courtroom in Charleston. But by the end of the month, the forty-five-year-old governor would take center stage for the South when the promised revolt, which had gathered steam in Philadelphia, finally became a reality.

That it was Thurmond who ascended to lead the charge, and not some better-known southerner, was an outgrowth of the deep schism in the region about how best to handle the growing fervor for black civil rights. Should there be open revolt against the Democratic Party? Or was it better to stay within the party structure and try to influence policy? More prominent southerners were uncomfortable with a direct challenge to the national Democrats, particularly one that had such a racial tinge to it. Many leaders, even if they weren't ready for an end to segregation, felt the South risked hindering the economic progress made in the painful decades after the Civil War by making the South an inhospitable place for investment. They, too, were troubled by events in Washington, and even if they hadn't yet developed the right response, they were convinced the Dixiecrat strategy was the wrong one. They wanted to look forward to a prospering, thriving South, not backward to the plantation mentality of the antebellum era. These staunch Democrats also worried, despite the bolters' assurances to the contrary, that another party vying for Democratic voters—Wallace was already running as a Progressive—would play right into a Dewey victory.

The reluctance of the first-tier southerners to make the fight would make more difficult what already was an uphill battle. Instead of nationally known politicians championing the cause, the states' righters would end up uniting behind a relative newcomer whose mettle was untested. That Thurmond was willing to step forward is further evidence of his ambition and his confidence. He could seize an opportunity without worry about the future consequences of his decision.

The campaign would also highlight the continuing divergence between the careers of Thurmond and Judge Waring. While the governor, with ever more vigor, was defending "custom and tradition" on the national political stage, the judge was holding court in a new voting rights suit to turn some of that custom on its head. Their separate paths continued to be a vivid illustration of how differently power could be exercised in response to the black community's demands.

The Democratic convention was the catalyst for the tumult that engulfed the last six months of 1948. Every day, from the preconvention maneuvering to the applause after Truman's late-night acceptance speech, held some new drama that spelled bad news for the states' righters. The daily setbacks only strengthened their resolve to go their own way.

Even before the convention opened, some important unfinished business with national implications was taken care of. On July 9 Eisenhower sent a telegram to Florida senator Claude Pepper, one of his biggest boosters, urging that he not put his name before the convention. "No matter under what terms, conditions or premises a proposal might be couched, I would refuse to accept the nomination," the general warned. A reluctant Pepper gave up the effort.

Although Truman's nomination was now a virtual certainty, the southerners were not ready to give up their opposition. Over the next four days there would be a flurry of activity to develop some kind of protest. But the false starts, missteps, and competing agendas among the region's delegates telegraphed the problems that lay ahead for the states' rights movement.

On July 10, representatives of seven southern states gathered to put together a strategy and found they didn't have an opposition candidate. All they could do was concentrate on keeping a strong civil rights plank out of the platform. Meanwhile, Senator Johnston, South Carolina's national committee member, had toyed with the idea of trying to force the committee to ask Truman to withdraw, but he declined to go forward, even when offered the chance by a confident Chairman McGrath, who was in fact prepared to kill any such proposal.

The New York Times's William S. White, who had been following the disgruntled southern delegates, reported the next day that the outlook was bleak for the regional protest. The "most experienced and realistic among the Southerners already gathered here were prepared to say in private that there was now 'nowhere to go except Truman,' " he wrote.

The evening of July 11 almost four hundred delegates from twelve southern states gathered at the Ben Franklin Hotel to continue their opposition effort, but after a day-long search the group still had no candidate. They did agree to fight for a states' rights plank in the platform. Governor Laney, who chaired the meeting, also threatened a walkout by some of the southerners if Truman were nominated.

Thurmond spoke up at that session, trying to rouse the audience in the best fist-pounding tradition. "We have been betrayed, and the guilty should not go unpunished," he declared. He called on the southerners to "stand together, fight together, and if necessary, go down together. . . . We should place principle above party even if it means a political defeat."

While the southern papers portrayed the meeting as another step in the region's rebellion, the *Times*'s White provided a more hard-nosed analysis. The southerners, he reported in a front-page story, "collapsed utterly tonight as an effective force in the Democratic National Convention" because the delegates were unable to find an alternative candidate "even to stand symbolically against Mr. Truman in the convention."

The Atlanta Constitution, unintentionally no doubt, seconded the *Times*'s analysis with a story on how Georgia was hunting for a candidate to put up against President Truman, who "they concede will win the nomination."

By the next day, July 12, there was a discernible move among southerners to back Laney, but this, too, would go awry.

At a state caucus that day, Thurmond released his delegates to the Arkansas governor, explaining to South Carolinians that Laney's term as governor was expiring and he could thus devote plenty of time to the campaign. "I have told the people of South Carolina that I am fighting for a principle and that I wanted nothing out of it for myself," Thurmond said. Along with Arkansas, Mississippi had also joined up behind Laney, who was known as "Business Ben" because of his financial success in the state.

After a stormy evening meeting, the Texas delegation also agreed to give token backing to Laney but only on a first ballot and "so long as his candidacy [is] in the framework of the Democratic Party." The Texans' ambivalence reflected an uneasiness with the revolt that was to persist over the next four months. On the one hand, Texas Democrats were totally opposed to Truman's civil rights program. But on the other, nearly one hundred years of Democratic loyalty militated against outright rebellion. The delegation initially had declined to back Laney because he had promised to oppose Truman in the November election. But before making any final decision, the Texans had recessed their caucus until they could hear from Laney in person.

At about eight-thirty that night the governor finally stood before a hot, crowded room full of delegates to make his pitch. "Where is the courage of Texas?" Laney cried, his voice rising. "The time has come when some of you had better stand on your feet and say what you think. If I am to have a creditable vote in the convention—and I am trying to save a situation, a party and a country—we need Texas," the largest southern delegation and therefore extremely important for any effective protest. He pointed out that the head of the delegation, Governor Beauford Jester, had participated in earlier discussions that called for a meeting of States Rights' Democrats in Birmingham after the Philadelphia session.

Conceding that the Texans had put him "on the spot," Laney

declared what he claimed were his firm intentions: "For my part I want nothing from the Democratic Party if I have got to compromise principle. . . . I shall use every measure that is legal and proper in this fight. I am going to go through with it. Millions of southerners are going through with it. I am going to do it whether you vote for me or not."

Despite his fervent plea to the Texans, Laney, too, would ultimately get cold feet and be a major disappointment to the Dixiecrats. But for twenty-four hours he was the South's best hope.

In what presaged even harsher criticism to come, Ralph McGill, the provocative editor of *The Atlanta Constitution,* used his editorial-page column the next day, July 13, to disparage Laney and the states' righters, whom he called "the scheming, divided little men from Mississippi, South Carolina and Arkansas." Laney, McGill wrote, seemed to be "drooling" for the chance to be the presidential candidate, "or so it seemed as he bounced about here, repeating his speeches for television and anyone else who wanted to register his deathless revelations for posterity."

In McGill's view, the better tactic was to keep the fight within the Democratic Party and unite behind Senator Russell as a symbolic protest candidate.

From his vantage point as editor of the *Constitution,* McGill would play an important, if indirect, role in the presidential race. His trenchant observations would not only describe the political climate in 1948 but also influence it. He would remain an important southern voice over the next twenty years, in the words of one admirer the region's "homebred conscience."

The second official day of the convention, July 13, was an important one for South Carolina. It was time for the three groups claiming to represent the state to have their say before the Credentials Committee. The party regulars, led by Thurmond, were being challenged by the Progressive Democrats, the organization created by black Carolinians, and by the Citizens Democrats, the more moderate whites. While the protests mirrored regional divisions among the state's white powers, they also were concrete evidence of the black leaders' focus on the ballot. Black Carolinians were tired of being on the sidelines. Now they were petitioning to become legitimate participants in the only electoral game that mattered, Democratic Party politics, and the debate before the

Credentials Committee illustrated the difficult road to recognition.

On July 10, a special panel of the Democratic National Committee had held a preconvention session to consider the Progressive Democrats' protest. The basis of their opposition to the regular organization was that blacks had not participated in the precinct meetings at which delegates were chosen for the county and state conventions. Senator Johnston, who represented the official state delegation, which was pledged to Thurmond, claimed surprise at the protest. "That is the first I heard of it," he said.

After Chairman McGrath explained the circumstances, he asked if anyone representing the Progressive Democrats was in the room. There was no answer.

"If they are not here, I would like to see it disposed of right now," Johnston told McGrath.

"Is Mr. John McCray present?" McGrath asked, calling for the group's leader. When McGrath heard no response, he authorized Johnston to go ahead and speak on behalf of the state party.

Johnston quickly moved for the seating of the regular delegation, noting that "We did have meetings in each precinct and in the counties and . . . we have been recognized all along." He gave no answer to the Progressives' charge of discrimination.

National committeeman Frank McHale of Indiana pointed out that the Progressive Democrats "could not substantiate" the allegations of bias, and he concluded that "we would have no grounds to recommend anything other than the approval and sitting of the regular delegation because of the authentic certification of officers."

Although McCray was scheduled to be in Philadelphia on July 10—a reporter for *The State* had found the hotel he was staying at—he had not been told of the time of the committee meeting. Newsmen were unable to reach him until well after the proceeding.

The following day an unhappy McCray announced that he would appeal the special panel's decision to the Credentials Committee. A hearing on the matter was scheduled for July 13. At the same time, the committee planned to hear a challenge from the Citizens Democrats, who also had filed their protest papers July 11.

At the July 13 session the Credentials Committee, which included Senator Johnston, heard the Citizens Democrats first. L. A.

Fletcher, the group's chairman, made the opening presentation, telling the panel that there were two reasons for the protest. First, Fletcher said, the regular delegates had been elected at an all-white convention in a state that was between 40 and 42 percent black. "And yet," he asserted, "there was not a Negro vote or a Negro representative, I believe, at the convention." Fletcher's second reason was the "thought-control, fascistic oath" the party had adopted. In addition to swearing to support racial segregation, the Democrats "further make me swear, in order to be able to vote, that I believe in other things that are contrary to the basic document, the Constitution of the United States of America."

When one of the committee members asked Fletcher to state succinctly the issue behind his challenge, he replied, "The issue is that groups in South Carolina have been deprived of the privilege of exercising the free, unhampered right to vote."

How many delegates did Fletcher want? "Whatever we are permitted to seat."

David Baker, a young attorney from Columbia, charged that the oath had "disenfranchised all . . . of the intelligent people of South Carolina." The effect, he contended, was that the regular Democratic Party "has bolted the party itself and [so] we are the Democratic Party."

The Progressive Democrats' pitch, made by executive secretary Arthur Clement, Jr., rested on the method the state party had used to elect its national convention delegates: at a party meeting rather than through a primary. To participate it was necessary to be enrolled in party books as a member, and blacks were denied enrollment even when they sought to join.

Clement told the Credentials Committee that the Progressive Democrats wanted proportional representation at Philadelphia—eight of South Carolina's twenty seats, reflecting the percentage of blacks in the state population.

To underscore the disparity between black and white voters, McCray told the committee that even when primaries were held, blacks faced discrimination because they had to meet more stringent requirements than whites. This, he pointed out, was contrary to Judge Waring's rulings.

When McCray finished, Thurmond got up to rebut the challengers on behalf of the regular party. The governor began with a dry recitation of the various rules and regulations the party had followed in selecting its delegates. Then he became more emotional, even threatening. "Madam Chairman and members of this committee, I simply wish to say that no state in the Union has been truer to the Democratic Party than has South Carolina. We have polled the largest vote for years and years for the Democratic Party of any state in the nation." Pointing out that the current delegation included the governor, both United States senators, many mayors, "and other prominent people in the state," Thurmond maintained that "the regularly elected delegates here . . . constitute the regular Democratic Party of South Carolina."

Fletcher's claim that the Citizens Democrats represented churches, civic groups, and labor organizations was "merely poppycock." Referring specifically to the assertion of church involvement, the governor said, "The biggest denomination in South Carolina is the Baptists. I am a Baptist. They have taken no action in this matter."

Next came an attack on the challengers' claims to represent a considerable population. "As one speaker told you here, they had seventy or eighty delegates at a convention. There are nearly two million people in South Carolina," Thurmond pointed out. "We had more people in one precinct meeting than they had at either of their state conventions."

Did he oppose the Progressive Democrats' request for proportional representation? Of course, Thurmond declared. So great was the opposition that Thurmond threatened a walkout by the entire delegation if the Progressive Democrats' demand was met.

Were precinct clubs open to membership or participation by Negroes? asked committee member George Vaughan, the black assistant attorney general from Missouri. Thurmond gave an evasive answer.

"I want you to answer your question," Vaughan persisted.

"I will answer you nothing," the governor snapped.

Immediately Arthur Clement rose to his feet to ask Thurmond a question, but he already had left, prompting Clement to toss off his own barb: "He is the governor of my state, to my regret."

Senator Johnston took up where Thurmond had left off. He explained to the committee the "peculiar situation" in South Carolina, where there were no laws regulating parties—a deregulation that had in fact been put into effect specifically to block Supreme Court–ordered enfranchisement for blacks. "We went through this same process after the laws were marked off the statute books that we did before the laws were marked off. We had our precinct meetings, our county meetings, and our state meetings," Johnston went on, inadvertently underscoring Judge Waring's point in the *Elmore* case—that, laws or no laws, the Democratic Party still ruled the state.

Addressing himself to the Progressive Democrats' request for proportional representation, Johnston wondered whether it was appropriate for the committee "to pass upon civil rights. . . . Shall we say to my friend from New Mexico that the Indians in his state shall have representation at the national convention in proper pro rata share that they have in their states?" he asked. "Or shall we say that the Italians in New York shall have a certain representation before this committee?"

McCray tried to counter Johnston's testimony. He reminded the committee that state Democrats had lost the *Elmore* case. "We would like to have this committee know," McCray added, "that if it hadn't been for Senator Johnston, South Carolina would never have lost its primary laws to begin with." It was Johnston who, as governor, had engineered the special legislative session at which the deregulation dodge was put into effect. "It is not surprising at all . . . ," McCray told the committee, "[to] all of us who come up here from South Carolina, to hear somebody say they will walk out. They have walked out of the Democratic Party."

When one committee member asked McCray why his group had not filed a protest when the regular Democrats were selected at the precinct level, his answer revealed his exasperation. "The point we are trying to emphasize here," McCray said, "is that we could not belong to the club or precinct, so how could we file a case, sir, when we could not get in?"

Victories over delegations of established party leaders are never easy, and the South Carolina challenges were no exception. When the five hours of arguments and discussion were over, the committee eventually voted 24 to 3 to seat the regular party delegates. (Vaughan, joined by Charles Misner of Michigan and H. H. Humphrey of South Dakota, voted "no.")

Later that day the Mississippi delegation also had to defend itself against efforts to take away the state party's seats, though in this case the challenge came from more moderate Democrats who backed the president. Some Credentials Committee members contended that the delegation was disloyal because of its outspoken opposition to Truman. But during the evening session of the full convention, the floor decided not to go along with the committee's recommended punishment. The decision was made on a controversial voice vote, but an antisouthern move was evident when several states fought for the chance to announce that they had voted against Mississippi. Finally, Senator Alben Barkley of Kentucky, the presiding officer, who would end up as Truman's running mate, announced that twelve states and the District of Columbia had asked that the record show they opposed Mississippi. Their votes totaled 503, only 115 short of the required majority to unseat the state delegation.

While the southerners' opposition to any civil rights plank in the platform was clear, less visible—but equally concerted—were efforts by the liberal wing to *strengthen* the party platform over its 1944 incarnation. In March—while the southerners were fighting with McGrath and preparing for their Jackson meeting—the Americans for Democratic Action (ADA) had started its campaign by sending a letter to party leaders urging that the convention adopt a strong civil rights plank.

While Truman had resisted pressure to backtrack on civil rights, he also had no wish to further inflame the southerners. Democratic leaders tried to placate both the North and the South by amending the 1944 plank superficially for the convention. A new introductory sentence was inserted—"The Democratic Party commits itself to continuing to eradicate all racial, religious and economic discrimination"—and there were two slight wording changes. Although the plank specified the party's belief that "racial and religious minorities have the right to live, develop and vote equally with all citizens and share the rights that are guaranteed by the Constitution," it still recommended only that "Congress should exert its full constitutional powers to protect those rights."

Hubert Humphrey, the vibrant young mayor of Minneapolis, was one of four ADA members named to the 108-person Platform Committee. He also sat on the small Drafting Committee, where he had fought unsuccessfully for stronger language in what he and his allies considered a bland statement. Of particular concern was the intentional ambiguity in its reference to the "full constitutional powers" of Congress. While the encouragement of Congress to act might be comforting to the activists, the states' righters could just as easily argue that the Tenth Amendment prevented Congress from doing very much at all.

After failing to win stronger language in the drafting sessions, Andrew J. Biemiller, another ADA member of the Platform Committee, promised to continue the fight on the convention floor by offering a minority plank on civil rights.

Once the July 13 evening session was over, delegates supporting a stronger civil rights plank gathered at a nearby clubhouse the ADA had rented to plan their strategy for the next day. Biemiller and Washington, D.C., lawyer Joseph L. Rauh already had prepared an amendment to the majority's proposal that read: "We call upon Congress to support our President in guaranteeing these basic and fundamental rights: (1) the right of full and equal political participation, (2) the right to equal opportunity of employment, (3) the right of security of person, and (4) the right of equal treatment in the service and defense of our nation." This paragraph was intended as a substitute for the troublesome sentence about Congress's "full constitutional powers."

Although Humphrey had been active in the committee fights, during the all-night session he was ambivalent about being the point man on the convention floor. Only thirty-seven years old, he already was the dominant political personality among Minnesota Democrats. He had been warned by Truman operatives that he risked his career by pushing so hard on civil rights. "You'll be splitting the party wide open if you do this," said one White House loyalist. But equally intense pressure was coming from Humphrey's ADA colleagues, who were counting on his speaking talents to dominate the debate and at least give them a chance on the convention floor. At one point, Humphrey asked his father, a convention delegate from South Dakota, for advice, but the senior Humphrey only offered platitudes. "Do what you think is right," he told his son, "but try not to do anything that will hurt the party."

About five in the morning Eugenie Anderson, another Minnesotan, proposed adding one more sentence to precede the litany of civil rights guarantees: "We highly commend President Harry Truman for his courageous stand on the issue of civil rights."

"That's it," Humphrey said when he heard the new language, "I'll do it," apparently satisfied that he could push hard for civil rights and still keep some link to Truman.

The fight was to prove more complicated than anticipated.

Even before the conventioneers gathered for the July 14 afternoon session, three other minority reports had surfaced on civil rights, all of them originating from the South: one from Texas, another from Tennessee, and a third from Mississippi. The betting was that none of the minority planks could prevail, least of all the plank of the liberal "kids," as the ADA delegates were called by the more seasoned northern power brokers. But during the day the big-city delegations began to find the liberal plank more attractive, recognizing the issue as one that could galvanize their voters in an otherwise gloomy political season. By the start of the afternoon session, Biemiller, Humphrey, and their newfound allies thought they had a chance.

The southern amendments were presented first, each one prefaced with conciliatory reassurances that they were being offered not to "defy the Democratic Party or drive a wedge between people of different thought in this party," as one presenter said, but "in an effort to restore . . . harmony among the members of the Democratic Party." And each southern amendment was to serve only as the party's reaffirmation of its "adherence to the fundamental principle of States' Rights."

The presenter from Tennessee, however, issued a warning. The party could not win without the South, he said, and "if we are defeated, then I say to you that you are witnessing here today the dissolution of the Democratic Party in the South."

Humphrey, too, began in a conciliatory tone, as he introduced the ADA's plank. "I realize that there are here today friends and colleagues of mine, many of them who feel just as deeply and keenly as I do about this issue, and who are yet in complete disagreement with me." But Humphrey was determined to stay his course. "There will be no hedging," he promised, "and there will be no watering down, if you please, of the instruments and the principles of the civil rights program. My friends," he continued, "to those who say that we are rushing this issue of civil rights, I say to them, we are one hundred seventy-two years too late. To those who say that this civil rights program is an infringement on States' Rights, I say this, that the time has arrived in America for the Democratic Party to get out of the shadows of States' Rights and to walk forthrightly into the bright sunshine of human rights."

Applause rocked the convention hall. With Illinois and California in the lead, delegates flowed into the aisles, where they cheered and paraded for ten minutes even though there was no music to spur them on.

All three southern proposals were handily rejected. Now it was time for a vote on the civil rights plank. But there was so much confusion that a delegate from Florida first asked presiding officer Sam Rayburn of Texas to clarify that it was indeed the proposal that Humphrey had supported.

When the roll was finally completed, the ADA's minority plank had prevailed on a vote of 651½ to 582½.

A mixture of cheers and boos filled the hall, and even though Handy Ellis, chairman of the Alabama delegation, stood waving his state's banner to get recognition, Rayburn refused to give him a nod. Instead, he called for adoption of the full platform by voice vote and then recognized Representative John W. McCormack of Massachusetts, who moved for a ninety-minute recess.

Eugene ("Bull") Connor, one of Alabama's more boisterous delegates, kept shouting in vain for recognition to announce that Alabama was walking out.

When the convention reconvened, Ellis was finally recognized by the chair and announced that Alabama's presidential electors had been instructed "never to cast their vote for a Republican, never to cast their vote for Harry Truman, and never to cast their vote for any candidate with a civil rights program such as adopted by this convention." Half of the delegation had also been pledged to walk out in the event a civil rights plank was included. "We bid you good-bye," he said, and thirteen Alabamans got up from their seats and marched up the center aisle to the door. They were joined by the entire twenty-three-member Mississippi delegation.

Some of the other southerners cheered, but most of them sat downcast in their seats.

Although at least one member of the South Carolina delegation wanted to walk out, the delegation had caucused during the recess and voted to stay. Before the caucus ended, Thurmond had talked by phone with Laney, who told him he was withdrawing as a presidential candidate and releasing all his delegates because he didn't want to run on the party platform. "I don't want to run under that platform, either," Thurmond told his own delegates.

Some of them still wanted to vote for him, but he told them to vote instead for Senator Russell, who had decided to let his name be placed in nomination as a protest against Truman.

Considered the boy wonder of Georgia politics, Richard Russell was a natural focal point for southerners. He had been elected to the state House at twenty-three and had become speaker at the age of twenty-nine. At thirty-three he became Georgia's youngest governor, and by 1933, when he was only thirty-five, he was the youngest man serving in the U.S. Senate. To be certain that he never would lose a battle over procedure, Russell had made a point, upon first arriving at the Capitol, to receive special tutoring from the Senate parliamentarian, and to remain alert to the smallest detail he pored over every day's *Congressional Record* line by line.

By 1948, Russell had been a power in Washington for a decade, having risen to prominence shortly after he led his first filibuster—against an antilynching bill—in 1935. Though he was a staunch opponent of federal civil rights proposals, he approached the matter with a more patrician attitude than some, holding himself above the race-baiting tactics of an earlier generation.

After heading the 1935 filibuster, Russell became the leader of the southern bloc every time a civil rights bill came up. The Georgian had also worked his way up the seniority ladder, and by the time Democrats gathered in Philadelphia he was one step away from the chairmanship of the Armed Services Committee—a powerful inducement against too vigorous a revolt against his party colleagues.

As the meeting of States Rights' Democrats in Jackson had made clear, Georgians as a whole were not ready to march out of the Democratic Party. So when Charles Bloch, the vice-chairman of his delegation, rose to nominate Russell, he first told the convention that "we delegates from Georgia are not bolters. . . . We sit over there, seventy-two strong, and we shall be sitting there when this convention shall adjourn."

Thurmond had the honor of seconding the nomination, the first time he ever addressed his entire party. He had already prepared a speech for Laney, and the sentiments, which focused less on the man than on Thurmond's ideology, were broad enough that the governor could simply scratch out "Laney," write in "Russell," and go right ahead. "We believe that state sovereignty is a principle which transcends parties and personalities and cannot be surrendered under any circumstances," Thurmond said, adding that "those principles of government upon which we wage our fight, those principles of government cannot be bartered away and they will not be bartered away."

When hecklers booed him, Thurmond retorted, "It is medicine you don't want to hear, isn't it?"

Turning to Russell, Thurmond said he "has done everything to preserve the state. He stands as a shining beacon to those who believe in constitutional government and who want to see our American way of life preserved."

It was no surprise when Truman was nominated on the first ballot, getting 947½ votes to Russell's 263. The Georgian received the votes of all the southern delegations except for 13 from North Carolina for Truman, 1 from Florida for Indiana's Paul McNutt, and those of the absent Mississippi delegation. (Although half of the Alabama delegation had walked out, the group was still able to cast its full 26 votes for Russell.) There was a moment of small drama when the roll call reached Mississippi. As the state's name was called, there was prolonged silence. Finally, a barely audible voice said, "Mississippi is gone home."

In his postconvention wrap-up the *Constitution*'s McGill reminded readers soberly that "It is important that the South know it had no friends here [at the convention]. It is important for the South to realize that the thinking of the Nation differs from their thinking. . . . It will be a great mistake," McGill warned, "if our writers and our politicians do not let the people know it, and more important, know it for their own thinking and speaking and planning for the South. Opposition is not enough."

As South Carolina's dispirited delegates made their way home from Philadelphia, state chairman Baskin and eighty-six other Democratic Party officials named in David Brown's July 8 complaint were on their way to Judge Waring's courtroom. Baskin and a few other delegates had even had to leave Philadelphia just as the convention began when Waring sent them a wire: a request to continue the ban on the party's controversial oath and its treatment of black voters was scheduled to be heard July 16, and Waring would not postpone it.

Three northern counties were immediately dismissed from the lawsuit because they had ignored party directives and had continued to enroll blacks. Greenville, Pickens, and Laurens counties had the state's smallest black populations and were less concerned about potential black voting power than were counties with a large black census.

Waring's comments in dismissing the three counties left no doubt about where he stood: "I feel quite ashamed that there are only three counties in this state that recognize not only the meaning of the decision made by me [in the *Elmore* case] . . . but much further the supreme law of the land as true Americans."

Thurgood Marshall had returned to South Carolina to represent Brown; the Democratic Party was represented by Sidney Tison and Thurmond confidant Figg, although Tison handled the actual courtroom work.

Marshall called just two witnesses, David Brown and Chairman Baskin. Marshall asked Brown to describe briefly the events surrounding his enrollment in the Democratic Party and his later purge from the party rolls. (On June 26, black citizens in Beaufort County had been notified to show cause before the county Democratic executive committee why their names should not be stricken from the enrollment books. On July 2, after Brown and others testified before the committee, the names of all blacks enrolled on the books had been purged.)

Brown testified that one official had talked about how whites treated "the colored race good," but shortly after the officials spoke, Brown said, the names of all blacks were purged from the county rolls.

State officials were contending that Brown was affiliated with the Progressive Democrats and that he therefore had no right to participate in the primary of the Democratic Party. Questioned by Marshall, Brown said he was not a member of the Progressive Democrats, didn't know that they had sent delegations to the 1944 and 1948 Democratic conventions, and had always voted a straight Democratic ticket in the general elections.

Tison's harsh questioning caused Brown to modify his story; the witness admitted that he had attended Progressive Democratic Party meetings at a Beaufort church and had made contributions to the party.

Marshall then called Baskin to the stand and asked him to describe the modifications the party had made to the oath. (The word "religious" had been dropped from the requirement of adherence to "the social, religious and educational separation of the races," and "understand" had been struck from the requirement that Democrats "understand, believe in and . . . support the principles" stated in the oath.) The significance of these deletions was unclear, and Waring was intrigued enough to interrogate Baskin himself. Their exchange turned the courtroom into surrealistic theater.

"Why did you strike out the word 'understand'?" Waring

asked. Should a man swear to something he doesn't understand? he wondered. Is it "objectionable to swear to something he understands?"

"No, sir," Baskin replied.

"Mr. Baskin," Waring continued, "just tell me what it means. I'm interested in the mentality of these changes and of the committee—how did the committee figure out such a thing?"

Baskin said he couldn't remember exactly but that someone had suggested that the word "understand" was "surplus."

"It was surplus for a person to understand what he swears to, is that your opinion, too?" Waring asked.

"No, sir. No, sir," Baskin quickly replied.

But the judge persisted. "You don't think it's material for a man to say whether he understands an oath or not. . . . It's all right for a man to say 'I believe' without understanding—you think that's a wholly immaterial matter, don't you?"

"Judge," Baskin interjected, "I don't quite agree."

"But you are going to make people generally swear to what they believe without understanding?" the judge persisted.

"No, sir," Baskin said, "it was not that intention."

"Well," said an exasperated Waring, "leave it as it is."

When Baskin finished, Marshall rested the plaintiff's case.

Tison said the defense had no witnesses to call, but an obviously unsympathetic Waring challenged Tison to argue the defendants' position himself. "It would interest me immensely," Waring said, "if the authors . . . would go on the stand and tell me how their minds worked in evolving these things. If they don't care to do that, I'd be glad to hear your argument."

"I don't think I could explain to Your Honor satisfactorily," Tison said.

"No, sir," Waring replied, "I don't think so."

Tison assured the judge that the Democrats would follow any order Waring issued, but in an apparent dig at Waring's failure in the *Elmore* decision specifically to ban racial bars to party membership, Tison told the judge to write an order clearly enough so that "he who runs may read it."

Waring bristled and took the bait, insisting that the white primary decision had "distinctly" forbidden discrimination in both voting and party enrollment. Party officials should have understood this, not only "as a matter of law but as a matter of common sense." This couldn't have been ignorance, he was sure—not "in a body of several hundred men who are practiced politicians and have been running the Democratic Party in this state for many years. . . . And, therefore, it must have been deliberate, and an attempt to evade the spirit of the opinion."

His only recourse, Waring said, was to issue an order so clear, as Tison put it, that "he who runs may read it." The order, with a full opinion to follow, would grant Brown's request for a preliminary injunction and would require that enrollment in the party and participation in its primaries be open "to all parties, irrespective of race, color, creed or condition. I'd better put all those things in there, though we are discussing only race here," Waring added, "because the next time they may exclude some of the Jews or Roman Catholics, or say somebody else can't come in—maybe they'll have a religious test."

The next primary was scheduled for August 10, and the judge ordered the enrollment books open through July 31. In a spirited tongue-lashing he promised the Democrats and the people of South Carolina a written opinion making clear that "the time has come when racial discrimination in political affairs has got to stop." No court had any business, he took pains to point out, interfering in "social or family contacts . . . but American citizens have got to be treated [with] equality when it comes to electing public officials."

Criticizing the oath as "absurd," Waring praised the county officials who "put their feet on the ground and stood up in public and said, 'We are Americans; we are going to obey the law.' Now the rest of the state is going to obey the law."

Waring seemed to sense that his decision and his provocative rhetoric might have personal repercussions. "Now gentlemen, you've put the burden on me, and I'm going to do it," he asserted. "It isn't a popular thing to do. I don't care about popularity; I'm going to do my duty." He finished with a warning that anyone who disobeyed his order could be found in contempt of court and could face a fine and imprisonment.

As promised, Waring's July 20 formal opinion generally followed his comments in the courtroom, although in somewhat more restrained form. He specifically rejected the defendants' argument that Brown and others with some relationship to the Progressive Democrats could not join the regular Democrats. "It is not shown that the so-called Progressive Democratic Party was adverse to the Democratic Party but it appears to be a group who

. . . had joined together . . . to get into the Democratic Party." There was no reason, Waring continued, "why one should be debarred from joining an organization because he had joined some other organization for the sole reason of attempting to get in the first-named one."

Waring minced no words in his conclusion. The Democratic Party, he said, "is not a private party or club and is subject to the laws of the United States," which meant it was specifically prohibited "from making any discrimination on account of race, color or creed in allowing enrollment, membership and full participation in its organization and in the election." Once and for all the party must be made to understand—"and that is the purpose of this opinion—that they will be required to obey and carry out the orders of this court, not only in the technical respects but in the true spirit and meaning of the same."

Waring's ruling, like the *Elmore* decision before it, drew mixed editorial response. The conservative *News and Courier*, by now even more disenchanted with Charleston's native son, went so far as to publish a front-page editorial telling the Democrats, as its headline boldly stated, HOW TO STOP THE CLUB ENROLLING blacks. Pointing out how expensive the enrollment process was, it suggested that the party organizations in each county close their offices and refuse to hire enrollment clerks, who, the editorial added, should not have to work for nothing. "Will any federal court give orders to the treasurer of a society or party about how he shall spend its money?"

Reaction in other places was more favorable. *The Greenville News* considered the ruling "complete vindication of the course followed by Greenville and the two counties that had defied the party's primary rules." The *Florence Morning News* called the decision "bitter medicine" but the kind the state party had asked for because of a "long series of actions antagonistic to, not to say defiant of, previous court decisions."

Such benign comment was the minority view, however. Waring's prediction of personal repercussions came true as resentment against Waring intensified. He and his wife started to get crank calls day and night accusing him of being a "nigger lover." White Charlestonians shunned the couple on the streets, and their friends in white society dwindled rapidly.

As Waring was using his position on the bench to break new ground, Thurmond was on his way to Birmingham to defend the old.

Events in Philadelphia had made it clear that the South was far from unanimous about the wisdom of another conference of States' Rights Democrats. "Only the thoughtless ones will be rushing off to Birmingham and the proposed rump convention there," McGill wrote in a postconvention story. There was nothing wrong with states' rights, he said. In fact, it was an old Democratic Party plank based on the fear of a centralized government. "But what we had here [in Philadelphia] as the loudest voice of the South were the wild and reckless and usually ridiculous statements by the Mississippians and some from Alabama, South Carolina and Louisiana. They made no sense. The convention crowds laughed at them. They were often so preposterous as to embarrass even their own members. They hurt the South."

Although *The State* in Columbia was less harsh in its postconvention editorial, the paper counseled caution to those who would split from the party. "Concerted Southern action cannot be counted upon," they were reminded, because "there is strong sentiment to fight the fight within the party; that is to hold onto what we have and use it as we will."

But no amount of editorial finger wagging could dampen the states' righters' spirits. In contrast to the gloom of Philadelphia, Birmingham was full of enthusiasm and excitement. All through the day July 16, delegates and interested onlookers streamed into the city, talking excitedly about their hopes and plans for protecting the South. At headquarters in the Tutwiler Hotel, a publicity man had been hired to welcome members of the media and answer their questions. The Birmingham Chamber of Commerce provided soft drinks and sandwiches for them. In the hotel lobby, badges were available to any true believers in states' rights. Although the city itself was not decorated, Municipal Auditorium, which had been provided free of charge, was. To embellish their argument that the States' Rights Democrats were a national movement, conference organizers had deliberately decorated the hall with an American theme, not Dixie. Instead of the Confederate battle flag, the flags of the forty-eight states were hung along with the Stars and Stripes.

As six thousand delegates jammed into the auditorium for the opening session of the July 17 meeting, none of them knew what would happen later in the day or who their standard-bearers would be. The list of prominent individuals who were *not* there was much longer than those who were. In fact, Mississippi senators Eastland and Stennis were the only national politicians who came. Other southern senators stayed away. Virginia was represented by four college students from the state university and a young woman who had stopped off on a cross-country tour. Tennessee was also represented by college students; Kentucky's banner was carried by an Alabaman who had once lived in the state. North Carolina was even further removed. A native Alabaman, seeing the state's banner standing unattended, grabbed it and joined the crowd. "Somebody's got to carry it," the volunteer said.

Governor Laney was in town, but, uneasy about the entire event, he remained closeted in his hotel and never came to the auditorium.

Thurmond had not planned to be in Birmingham either and had gone home to Columbia from Philadelphia. He was scheduled to review South Carolina National Guard troops at Camp Stewart, Georgia, on the morning of July 17. But shortly after returning from Philadelphia, he got a call from states' righters urging him to come to their meeting. The governor decided that he could rearrange his schedule, and he announced the afternoon of July 16 that he would join the states' righters after all. He quickly honored his Georgia commitment and then flew into Birmingham in time for the afternoon session July 17.

Thurmond had just gotten downtown when he was approached by Frank Dixon, former governor of Alabama, and Fielding Wright about running for president. He was not their first choice—in fact, the day before there had been speculation that he would be somebody's vice-presidential running mate. But by the morning of July 17, Ben Laney had turned down the offer of the nomination. So had Dixon, even though Alabamans had pleaded with him to run. If Fielding Wright wanted to be the presidential candidate, he apparently didn't have enough support to carry the day.

So an informal committee of leaders had settled on the determined and ambitious governor from South Carolina. Although he was the second choice of some, the third of others, and on top of it a second-tier southern politician, he still had plenty to offer the states' righters: he had been a leader at Wakulla Springs, a loyal prosecutor confronting Chairman McGrath, an inspiring keynoter in Jackson, and a soldier for the cause in Philadelphia.

Time was running short before the afternoon session; Dixon and Wright told Thurmond he had about an hour to make up his mind. For a man with such an intuitive feel for politics, sixty minutes were plenty.

The biggest negatives, as Thurmond thought through the proposition, were the repercussions for his career in a region that still prided itself on loyalty to the Democratic Party. The Civil War and Reconstruction were not just memories to the white South but symbols of deep pain inflicted by the Republicans. If Thurmond could be blamed for giving the White House back to a GOP that seemed no better than Truman, then his last day in the governor's mansion could be his last day as a politician. But weighed against this possibility was the chance to stand up for principles he firmly believed in. Described and presented in forceful terms, he felt sure they could strike a response in anyone South or North who had ever felt put upon by government. And if the message was heard by sufficient numbers, then Thurmond could deny either major candidate a victory and force the election into the House as the original states' rights theorists had contemplated. Beyond these broad political considerations, there was also the plain fact that a run for the presidency, no matter how it turned out, would give Thurmond more national exposure. He had no doubt that he could hold his own in competition with more well known politicians.

If "timing is everything" in politics, then perhaps this was the time for Thurmond to move. He said yes, and Wright agreed to be the vice-presidential nominee.

Word quickly spread to the auditorium, which was filling to capacity for the afternoon session. The Confederate flag was now much in evidence, as demonstrators waved the Stars and Bars while they marched around the hall in prenomination demonstrations. One young man held high the portrait of Robert E. Lee as he wove his way through the aisles. After seventy-nine-year-old Beulah Waller of Byron, Georgia, performed a spontaneous jig on stage, the crowd went wild, so much so that the presiding officer had to have the band play "The Star Spangled Banner" to restore order—a bit of irony, given that the Birmingham meeting was a rebellion.

Alabama states' righter Horace Wilkinson presented a statement of principles that had been drafted by a resolutions committee. The statement declared opposition to the "totalitarian, centralized bureaucratic government and the police state called for" by the Democratic and Republican platforms. It also declared: "We stand for the segregation of the races and the racial integrity of each race; the constitutional right to choose one's associates, to accept private employment without governmental interference, and to earn one's living in any lawful way. We oppose the elimination of segregation, the repeal of miscegenation statutes. . . ."

Thurmond finally came to the podium to thunderous cheers. While he didn't speak completely off the cuff, he did not have a formally prepared speech. Instead he used notes on pieces of paper that he would stuff in his pocket after finishing each page.

Birmingham was Thurmond at his most combative. Asserting that Truman may have forced himself on the Democratic Party, he told the crowd that the president was not going to force himself on the nation.

"I want to tell you," Thurmond continued, "that the progress of the Negro race has not been due to these so-called emancipators"—this word was spit out with unmistakable venom—"but to the kindness of the good southern people. . . . I want to tell you," he went on, jabbing his right index finger at the crowd, "that there's not enough troops in the army to force the southern people to break down segregation and admit the Negro race into our theaters, into our swimming pools, into our homes, and into our churches." The crowd roared its approval.

Four decades later, the film footage that remained from the Birmingham convention would be a revelation to Strom Thurmond's aides. One top assistant remembers chills running down his spine when he watched the speech. "I couldn't believe I was working for the same man," he said. Another wordlessly shook his head.

But that was the difference between the politics of the eighties and the politics of 1948. When the "troops in the army" excerpt was read back to Thurmond forty-one years after the event, it was initially met with incredulity. Convinced that the excerpt was accurate, Thurmond said quietly, "If I had to run that race again, some of the wording I used would not be used. I would word it differently." The observation seemed to be more about semantics than substance, for in his long career, Thurmond has never conceded that pressure from Washington was required to make the white South yield to the insistent demands of the black community. Nor has he ever wavered in his belief that the Constitution severely limits the powers of the federal government.

Thurmond had intended that sentence to signify the South's abhorrence of a forced change in "custom and tradition." It was not supposed to be a battle cry for white supremacy. In fact, after the speech he sought to distance himself from such avowed white supremacists as Gerald L. K. Smith, telling reporters, "We do not invite and we do not need the support of Gerald L. K. Smith or any other rabble-rousers who use race prejudice and class hatred to inflame the emotions of the people."

The Washington D.C. *Evening Star* was willing to take him at his word, observing that Thurmond's "record as a progressive advocate for a better deal for the Negro in the South entitles him to a respectful hearing" when he says he is waging the fight "as a matter of principle resting on states' rights and not as a champion of white supremacy."

But Thurmond's attempt to focus solely on the intellectual notion of states' rights was blunted by the very statement of principles he had promised to uphold and his own words tying states' rights to the South's right to preserve segregation. As practiced, it was not separate but equal, but white supremacy.

Before leaving Birmingham for South Carolina, Thurmond professed surprise at the turn of events, telling reporters, "I came here to say a few words and found myself recommended for President." There was an element of truth to his flippant observation. He had not intended to come to Birmingham and did so only after a special request. That Figg and Brown, who had gone with him to Wakulla Springs and then Jackson, were not with him in Birmingham attests to the spontaneous nature of the developments in Alabama.

The governor returned to Columbia July 18 as the head of only one faction of southerners. Reflecting the deep ambivalence in the region, the statement Governor Laney had finally issued could hardly have cheered conference organizers. "Whatever is done must be done through and by the official Democratic organization in each respective state," he said. He would not support any rump organizations. While he agreed with opposition to the Democratic Party platform, "the spirit of obstinacy and revenge is not the spirit of the Southland."

Laney's suggestion to work through the "official Democratic

organization'' was going to be a tall order; the States' Rights Democrats had just picked their own presidential ticket to challenge Truman and Barkley. If they were still going be "official" Democrats, in each state they would have to win out over those party members still siding with Truman and get Thurmond's name on the ballot instead. If they could not, then the states' righters would be considered third-party insurgents.

Prominent southern editors already considered the Birmingham group to be rebels, and the dim view they took of the movement would remain during the campaign. Their constant criticism would hamper the Dixiecrats' efforts to pick up support. McGill, writing in the *Constitution,* maintained that "solving the South's problem isn't a matter for sideshow drums at Birmingham." It was going to take planning, he said, to create an opposition party in the South "down to the precinct level. This morning, as we look to see where we are," he concluded, "we can see 'we ain't really any place at all.' "

Virginius Dabney of the *Richmond Times-Dispatch* pronounced himself pleased that "Virginia took no official part in yesterday's Claghornesque goings-on at Birmingham," a reference to the buffoonish southern caricature, Senator Claghorn, made famous on the Fred Allen radio show. The participants, Dabney said, were "persons with whom a self-respecting group of Southerners could scarcely afford to be associated." All in all, Dabney concluded, Birmingham was "a show of Confederate flag-waving and futile posturing." A few days later he called the Dixiecrats' conference "bogus genuflections in Birmingham at the shrine of Robert E. Lee."

Jonathan Daniels, the unsympathetic editor of *The News and Observer* in Raleigh, was equally harsh. The only result of the rebellion, Daniels said, "would be the destruction of the Democratic Party and the election of Dewey."

In a separate story, staff writer Robert E. Williams fleshed out the prevailing wisdom—given its greatest play in South Carolina—that Thurmond was using his candidacy to bolster a challenge to Johnston in the 1950 Senate race. Thurmond has repeatedly denied that this was a major motivation for his Dixiecrat campaign. While he was interested in going to the United States Senate, he maintained that his decision to challenge Johnston didn't come until much later—after he finished his last two years as governor.

Some of Thurmond's closest political allies, who had not accompanied him to Birmingham, believed his presidential run would hurt his career, and they were chagrined when they learned he had taken up the bolters' cause. (Bob Figg, who nonetheless played an important role in the states' rights campaign, insisted years later that if he had been with Thurmond in Birmingham he would have done all he could to keep him off the ticket.)

Even some Alabama papers threw cold water on the bolters' conference. *The Montgomery Advertiser* criticized the racist atmosphere of the event, arguing that the South needed support from the rest of the country but was not going to get it "by shouting 'nigger.' . . . We cannot win friends by hoarse blasphemies and the appearance of unreasoning obstinacy."

In his post-Birmingham column, McGill joined the critics. With prescience he observed that the "true Southerner will see that, despite the hypocrisy and the infuriating smugness of the North, we cannot longer oppose civil rights. It is true that they are pushed cynically by the big-city machine for votes. But, the fact remains that under the Constitution, all citizens have a right to vote and to the protection of the law. We cannot defend a moral wrong. The [Philadelphia] convention showed," McGill said, "that every State outside the South was against us."

The News and Courier of Charleston took an opposite tack. In a front-page editorial, "Thurmond for President," the paper said, "In casting their eight electoral votes for Strom Thurmond, South Carolinians need not feel they are throwing away their ballots nor espousing another lost cause. On the contrary, they not only can follow their principles but can establish in the eyes of the nation a new measure of Southern independence."

Thurmond thanked the paper's editor for the boost, which he found "particularly gratifying since it came at a time when it could accomplish the most."

The Columbia *State* came down somewhere in the middle of the critics and supporters. After congratulating Thurmond and praising his leadership in the states' rights movement, the paper said that "a program for Southern protest would rest on firmer ground if it came from a Southwide meeting preceded by county and state conventions, to get the will of the people."

The leaders of the movement agreed and already had planned for a more official convention in Houston August 11, where Thurmond and Wright could be formally nominated.

Although the presidential campaign wouldn't begin in earnest until August, the jockeying for position between the Republicans and Democrats started July 27 in Washington. Truman had called Congress back to town for a special session, saying he wanted action on the civil rights proposals and several other initiatives, including new, low-cost housing, an increase in the minimum wage, and an anti-inflation tax. Angry Republicans, who controlled both chambers, accused the president of playing politics by summoning them for what they called a "rump session." Senator Russell, the leader of twenty senators from the South, swore he would "fight to the limit" against the civil rights proposals.

The first measure considered was the anti–poll tax legislation. As promised, the southerners staged a filibuster and blocked any Senate action. After a five-day stalemate, Republican leaders took the bill off the floor. Routine committee hearings were held on some Truman initiatives, and Congress did approve a scaled-down housing bill as well as a $65 million loan for construction of the United Nations building. But the special session adjourned August 7 with little of Truman's agenda accomplished, and the lawmakers returned home to tend to their own reelections.

For the States' Rights Democrats, now headquartered at the Heidelberg Hotel in Jackson, important technical matters came before any actual campaigning—getting on the ballots of the southern states, and if possible through the regular Democratic Party machinery as Laney had urged. Running in the predominantly one-party South without the Democratic Party endorsement was, as one political observer put it, "suicidal. The Democratic Party label was the key to victory." The biggest problems—and ultimately the biggest disappointments—were going to be in North Carolina, Texas, and Georgia.

North Carolina leaders, loyal to the national party, had been lukewarm toward the states' rights movement from the beginning. Governor R. Gregg Cherry had backed away from the southern governors' rebellion in February and March, and after the Philadelphia convention the state's top elected officials quickly endorsed Truman. Because of a dispute with the state election board over the filing of the Dixiecrats' petition for recognition, it ultimately took a lawsuit to get Thurmond and Wright on the North Carolina ballot at all.

By late August there was some good news. Four states—Alabama, Louisiana, Mississippi, and South Carolina—had chosen presidential electors pledged to Thurmond and Wright. And they would be listed on the ballots as representing the Democratic Party. (Truman's name did get on the ballot in three of the states, but he was kept off completely in Alabama.)

Texas would be difficult to win because the party structure was dominated by Truman loyalists. The state delegation's performance in Philadelphia had demonstrated that Texans were willing to go only so far in their rebellion, and Governor Jester had muted his public criticism of the president—a fact that had brought Jester public criticism from the states' righters. They took out a full-page newspaper ad in *The Dallas Morning News* August 5 reminding readers that in March he had signed a "solemn agreement with other Southern Governors" to oppose the "so-called civil rights program" and to see to it that their state's electoral votes were withheld from nominees who supported the program. "If he agreed that Texas electoral college votes should not be cast for Truman on March 13, why is he for Truman now?" the ad asked.

Early in August, the party's executive committee delivered a disappointing blow to the states' righters, handily rejecting their request for a statewide referendum on whether the Texas Democratic electors should be pledged to Thurmond or Truman. In mid-September, Truman forces officially prevailed, throwing their support to the president and relegating Thurmond to the role of third-party insurgent.

More disappointment came from Georgia, where the Dixiecrats were hoping to capitalize on Herman Talmadge's victory over Governor Thompson in the September 8 primary. Talmadge was the more conservative of the two, and as the son of the race-baiting Gene Talmadge, he seemed a sure bet to support the states' righters. But Talmadge threw cold water on that hope when he announced that it was the duty of the state Democratic executive committee to determine which presidential candidate would receive support.

Governor Thompson (in office until just after the November election) called the legislature back into session in an effort to clarify the alternatives for the state's voters. "I insist that the people of Georgia should have the right to vote for anybody they want to vote for," he said. As a result, separate slates of electors were put forward by the Truman and Thurmond backers, but it was still the Truman supporters who ran under the Democratic Party label. As in Texas, the states' righters were considered a third party.

Personally, it didn't matter to Thurmond what label he ran on. His mission was to send the states' rights message, and once again he would demonstrate that there was no more energetic messenger anywhere.

Immediately after Birmingham, Thurmond had resigned from the Democratic National Committee, and from then until the November 2 election he would be in perpetual motion throughout the South (there were only a few trips north).

After twenty years in state and local politics, Thurmond was most comfortable with the personal style of campaigning that took him to courthouse steps in town after town, where he would make four or five speeches a day, sometimes in two different states. Not everyone in the campaign thought this strategy was a plus. Judge Merritt Gibson of Texas, who had overall responsibility for the campaign, complained that Thurmond wanted to speak at every little "pigtrail" and wished he would conserve his time and energy for events with larger crowds.

But the States' Rights Democrats had neither the money nor the sophisticated organization of the Truman and Dewey campaigns. Thurmond had to rely on the small number of campaign workers in Jackson to do whatever long-distance advance work they could to roust out the crowds. It was rare that he traveled with a press assistant to beat the drums.

Despite the limited organization, from August through the first week in November southern papers routinely carried pictures of Thurmond stepping out of cars and airplanes on his way to the next campaign stop, usually accompanied by Jean, who often traveled with him. (Northern reporters apparently had trouble understanding Thurmond's accent. *Time* reported that he called Jean "Sugar," but the couple's correspondence shows that his pet name for his wife was "Sugie.")

Jean provided a glimpse of their lives in a letter she scribbled to her family about the events of August 25 in Arkansas. The day started early—a 2:00 A.M. call from newsmen who wanted an appointment later in the day. Then:

> Breakfast—again with photographers! Officials from Marianna came to hotel to drive us 60 miles to Marianna. The plane trip (from South Carolina) was perfectly safe compared to that 85 mile per hr. trip between two patrol cars to Marianna. Did not stop in town, but were

> driven on out 7 miles on winding *dusty* road to the Bedco Creek Lake. . . . Shake hands with each of the many persons waiting on the porch of hotel for us. . . . Strom was whisked away to press conference and lunch with men.

Thurmond's first campaign foray was to Cherryville, North Carolina, to speak at the annual Watermelon Festival. There he unveiled a basic stump speech that was to vary little throughout the campaign: a bit of local color tailored for each campaign stop, followed by criticism of his rivals and the civil rights proposals, and finally a reaffirmation of the states' rights cause.

In Cherryville, the South Carolinian told residents he felt "close to the people of North Carolina" because the two populations "are like one people—their traditions are the same, their customs are the same, and they think and act alike." He accused the political leaders in Washington of being part of a "cheap political scramble to gain the votes of minorities" and described them as being "mad with the lust for power."

Truman's proposals, he said, were "a program so full of narcotics that the American people are in danger of being lulled to sleep by it. They have named this program 'civil rights.' "

While he didn't return to his "troops in the army" bravado of Birmingham, Thurmond nonetheless spoke threateningly about segregation. "If the segregation program of the president is enforced," he said, "the results of civil strife may be horrible beyond imagination. Lawlessness will be rampant. Chaos will prevail. Our streets will be unsafe. And there will be the greatest breakdown of law enforcement in the history of the nation." The next part he underlined in his script for emphasis: "Let us also tell them, that in the South, the intermingling of the races in our homes, in our schools, and in our theaters is impractical and impossible." (The last three words were underlined twice.)

The sameness of the speeches that followed Cherryville prompted Allan M. Trout of the Louisville *Courier-Journal* to note in the fall that Thurmond seemed to be conducting "a field filibuster" instead of a presidential race. "Ordinarily you would expect a candidate for President to discuss the issues of domestic and foreign policy," Trout wrote, "what he would like to do for labor, agriculture and business. . . . But Thurmond's harp has only five strings, and the only tune he plucks is 'The Civil Rights Blues.' " (The five strings were the hated civil rights proposals.)

The official opening of the states' rights effort was the August 11 convention in Houston, where Thurmond and Wright formally accepted nominations as president and vice-president of the States' Rights Democrats. When Alabama's Frank Dixon introduced Thurmond, reminding the audience that Edgefield had also been the home of two Alamo heroes, William B. Travis and James Bonham, the crowd erupted into loud cheers. The band struck up "Deep in the Heart of Texas," segued into "The Eyes of Texas," and concluded with the ubiquitous "Dixie"—all before Thurmond had uttered a word.

Thurmond actually gave two speeches that night, one at the convention with a sprinkling of local observations about Texas, and a second that was broadcast over the radio. But the two addresses were basically the same—another broadside against the Democrats for deserting principle and championing the "misnamed civil rights program, which inevitably leads to a police state. . . ."

As he would throughout the remainder of his career, Thurmond rebuked those who criticized the South for its racial policies, implying that there was hypocrisy in their judgments. "Even in states where there are anti-segregation laws, the people voluntarily establish segregation; otherwise, there would be no Harlem in New York City, no Chinatown in San Francisco, no South Side in Chicago," he asserted.

Contending that there were "millions of Americans who subscribe to the principles we are fighting for," Thurmond called on states' rights supporters "to make their voices heard on behalf of the Dixiecrat ticket."

Radio commentators, underscoring the states' righters' uphill fight in Texas, took pains to note after the speech that the most prominent politician in the crowd was the mayor of Houston. State senators and representatives, members of the congressional delegation, and the governor were nowhere to be seen.

A month later Thurmond returned to Texas and gave his most racially pointed speech. Most of the address was the standard business about the evils of centralized government and the pitfalls of Truman's proposals. But when he got to the FEPC law, Thurmond took a turn. Discussing the right of the American worker to "choose to work in a place where he is with his kind of people," Thurmond contended that if the proposal were enacted, workers would find "that at the counters, desks or benches they will be forced to work, side by side, with all types of people of all races; that in the lunchrooms, rest rooms, recreation rooms, they will be compelled by law to mingle with persons and races which all their lives they have, by free choice, avoided in social and business intercourse."

To sharpen his point, he offered his audience an example. "Suppose you work for a company or belong to a union which is by law forbidden to make any kind of so-called racial discrimination. . . . Think about the situation which would exist," he suggested, "when the annual office party is held, or the union sponsors a dance. There the races must also be mingled or else the sponsors face fines or jail sentences."

This passage, which was not repeated in later Thurmond speeches, was, in addition to being a scare tactic, a dynamic illustration of the threat most white southerners felt to their cherished "custom and tradition." It wasn't so much that blacks and whites would be in the same room. After all countless southern white children had been raised with affection by black women and then as adults chauffeured around by loyal black men. What was so disturbing about this FEPC proposal was that blacks and whites might now come together on a new footing, as peers.

Why Thurmond lapsed into this kind of rhetoric is unclear. Perhaps he was trying to rally his supporters. That he left the rhetoric out of future speeches suggests a discomfort with such an aggressive campaign pitch. In an address the very next day to Texas states' righters, Thurmond took a calmer approach. "This is no fight against the Negro race," he said. "We have worked out a way of life, in difficult circumstances, between the two races. The Negro race has progressed farther in three score years than any race in history. It has progressed because it has had the sympathetic help of the Southern white people of good will." But he couldn't resist issuing a warning. Destroy that good will, "and chaos will result."

Analyzing Thurmond's campaign swing through Kentucky a few weeks later, John Ed Pearce, another perceptive *Courier-Journal* writer, acidly described the candidate's approach to race. "States' Rights is the issue only insofar as it concerns the right of States to solve—or refuse to solve—their race problems," Pearce wrote. "The real issue is one word, and that word is never spoken. It is one thought, and that thought is never expressed. The issue is Nigger. . . . Mr. Thurmond, of course, never says the words; he's not the type. And it is comical to listen as he tiptoes around the issue, like an old-fashioned father trying to explain sex to his son without saying the words."

Thurmond "is not the classic race-hater," Pearce observed in his insightful conclusion. "He is a man deeply troubled by threat of social change that would destroy a way of life to which he is accustomed, and raise into a position of legal equality a people he has been reared to regard as inferior. He is torn, as the majority of Southerners are, between a desire to be a decent Christian man, and an inner insistence on a racial system that is, in itself, un-Christian."

Years later, Thurmond's shield against charges of bigotry would be the claim that he "never said a word against black people," that he never said the word that was on so many people's lips. He didn't have to. The central issue in 1948 was not the particular rhetoric but the ideas and philosophy the language represented. The absence of the word "nigger" may have provided a more refined messenger, but it did not obscure the message. By the time the 1948 presidential campaign had faded into history, what would count was the symbolism of what Thurmond had done—standing for the segregationist South.

Thurmond received some national attention October 11 when *Time* magazine put him on the cover, headlined, THE DIXIECRATS' J. STROM THURMOND—IS THE ISSUE BLACK AND WHITE? In a snappy three-page story, *Time* gave its readers a brief history of his traditions (there was a cartoon of Pitchfork Ben), a capsule summary of his political philosophy ("the dialectics of states' rights"), and a glimpse into his personal life. This portion was illustrated with a picture of the famous prenuptial headstand.

Two weeks later *Newsweek* also gave the Dixiecrats three pages, including discussion of an embarrassing but revealing episode. In July Thurmond had sent a routine letter to William H. Hastie, governor of the Virgin Islands, inviting him to visit Columbia. Thurmond hadn't realized that Hastie, a former federal judge and former dean of Howard University law school, was black. Thurmond had conveyed his "earnest hope" that Hastie and his family would visit Columbia and "be our guests at the Mansion."

Hastie declined the invitation but expressed appreciation for the offer, telling Thurmond he and his family would be welcome at the Government House in the Virgin Islands. When the exchange of letters was publicized in early October, Thurmond provided a charmless explanation: "I would not have written him if I knew he was a Negro," he said. "Of course, it would have been ridiculous to invite him."

The October publicity didn't help the Dixiecrats draw voters, as was evident in Virginia. Although Thurmond barnstormed through the state that month, even spending the night with Governor William M. Tuck, the governor declined to say outright that he was supporting Thurmond. Meanwhile, the state attorney general, J. Lindsay Almond, endorsed Truman and urged Virginians to remain in the party. Three of the state's gubernatorial candidates also backed the president.

Reflecting on the Dixiecrat campaign twenty years after the race, Tuck explained why so many prominent politicians refused to gamble on the Thurmond-Wright ticket: "What's the sense of jumping out of a fourth-story window if it isn't going to save somebody's life?"

During the last week of the campaign, Thurmond made a rare foray out of the South, delivering a speech in Boston October 30 and then returning to Columbia two days later to give a final radio broadcast. In that speech, he credited Truman's civil rights speech nine months earlier—"the most astounding presidential message in political history"—for the birth of the states' rights movement. After hearing the president's proposal, backed up by the national party's "vicious civil rights plank," it was clear that "the people of the South had to fight. If we had not, we would have forfeited any claim to the nation's respect. We would have entered into a state of political bondage which would have made our section of no consequence in the affairs of the country."

The states' righters, he maintained, had "paved the way for the reorganization of the Democratic Party and its rededication to the principle that the states shall govern their own internal affairs." Thurmond was not proved right on his latter point, but over the next fifteen years the country's major political parties definitely realigned. He, himself, would be one of the main catalysts for the shift.

The Thurmonds went over to the Edgefield courthouse to vote and then returned to Columbia to wait for the polls to close. Twenty-two-year-old Jean had the privilege of casting her first vote ever for her husband.

The most striking development as the returns poured in November 2 was Truman's upset win over Dewey; predictions had been nearly universal that the president would lose. The States' Rights Democrats placed third in the popular vote, garnering only 2.5 percent of the 47.3 million votes cast. Truman won with 51 percent to Dewey's 46.5 percent. The Dixiecrats were a distant third in electoral votes. They got 39 to Truman's 333 and Dewey's 189. (Originally, the Dixiecrats had won 38 electoral votes, but when the electoral college convened, one elector from Tennessee bolted, raising the total to 39.)

Thurmond and Wright carried just four states—Alabama, Louisiana, Mississippi, and South Carolina. Henry Wallace carried none and received no electoral votes.

When the surprised pundits wrote that Truman, amazingly, had won the presidency not only without New York, Pennsylvania, and Michigan but also without the South, Ralph McGill was quick to respond. In a telegram, the irritated Atlanta editor reminded CBS newsman Eric Sevareid of those who had supported the Democratic Party and "successfully and earnestly fought the fraudulent and hypocritical Dixiecrat movement." The revolt, he pointed out, was confined to just four states. "From our viewpoint . . . Mr. Truman could not have won without Georgia, Florida, Tennessee, Virginia, North Carolina, and other Southern states [Arkansas and Kentucky] which voted for him."

To Thurmond, his four states were a watershed. "That's where we did the greatest service, to pull four states away from the national Democratic Party and show the sky wouldn't fall," he said later. "Ever since then the South has been independent." Even after running in eight more elections, Thurmond would maintain that 1948 was the most important because in his mind it set the South on its own course.

Although Thurmond argued over and over that the states' rights campaign was not about race, analyses of the election results undercut that contention. The lion's share of the Dixiecrats' votes came from whites who lived close to large numbers of blacks in the nation's black belt. To these white voters, apparently, the Thurmond-Wright ticket was the best hope for preserving their interests and their way of life. Thurmond received 87.2 percent of the vote in Mississippi, the state with the largest black population; 72 percent in his home state, with the second-largest black population; just under 50 percent in Louisiana, which had the next largest black population; and 79.8 percent in Alabama, whose black population was just one percent lower than Louisiana's. In Texas, where Thurmond received only 9.3 percent of the vote, he ran strongest in counties with large black populations.

Thurmond also tried to portray the states' righters as a national movement, but the voters didn't see it that way. (A contributing factor no doubt was the campaign's concentration on the South.) Of the total vote garnered by Thurmond and Wright, 98.8 percent came from eleven southern states. They received votes in only nine states outside the South, and their biggest success in those states was the border state of Kentucky, where they attracted a slight 1.3 percent of the total.

Reflecting on the campaign years later, Thurmond sought to explain why the states' rights message didn't play better in the South. With more ruefulness than anger, Thurmond lamented the fact that the major papers were hostile to their effort. "That's the reason Cherry in North Carolina went the other way," he said, blaming *News and Observer* editor Jonathan Daniels's scathing attacks on the Dixiecrats. "If we'd had a good strong paper in each state, we'd have carried those probably. . . . Since we didn't have the leaders, we didn't have the news media, and didn't have TV . . . I couldn't reach the people."

Not that Thurmond didn't try. J. Melville Broughton, who was running for the U.S. Senate in North Carolina, wrote one newspaper editor that Thurmond had called him and "did his best to argue me into showing some interest in their cause." Broughton told Thurmond he "did not feel that in North Carolina there was any substantial sentiment in favor of the movement." He added that "so far as my observation had gone, the Democratic press of the State is almost solidly against this movement."

Thurmond also blamed adverse press coverage for the lack of support from Herman Talmadge in Georgia, who "didn't come through like I thought he would." Thurmond said that the governor-elect had told him "the newspapers in Georgia were so strong the other way."

In Thurmond's mind, the principal reason the newspapers failed to support his candidacy was "tradition. The whole South had been Democratic for over a hundred years, and even in the news media, they felt they wouldn't dare to come out any other way."

Part of Thurmond's analysis was correct. In the pretelevision age, newspapers both shaped and reflected public opinion, and lack of support from three prominent southern dailies—*The Atlanta Constitution, The News and Observer* in Raleigh, and the *Richmond Times-Dispatch*—was a factor any public official had to consider. But Thurmond was too facile in his emphasis on Democratic loyalty as the reason for his lack of endorsements. The party tradition was certainly strong—indeed, the states' righters tried to cast themselves as "true" Democrats—but this just pointed up the differences in how party tradition was defined. The McGills, Danielses, and Dabneys were uncomfortable with the racial cast of the states' rights pitch and concerned that the movement was really a splinter party that would hurt regional interests.

In one of his columns, "The Dixiecrat Mind," McGill gave voice to these feelings. "The Dixiecrat type of mind, and the Dixiecrat type of politics . . . will set the South back thirty years or more," McGill asserted. The South, he acknowledged, was "up against great social, political and even more important, we are up against great economic changes." But solutions would require "the best in us. . . . We have already seen how our loudest Klaghorns [he spelled the caricature differently than Dabney] have prejudiced our case and hurt us at the convention—making it impossible for the Northern friends of States' Rights to join with Georgia and others who sought them orderly and with dignity. Therefore," he concluded, "we must despise those who prostitute the Confederate flag and the song 'Dixie' to their own uses."

The day after the election, Thurmond sent the customary congratulatory telegram to Truman. "The American people have spoken at the ballot box and you are entitled to the united support of a united people," Thurmond said. "You can rest assured that as governor of South Carolina I shall cooperate with you and your administration in every constitutional endeavor looking toward the progress of our people and a lasting peace."

The telegram was an artful one. The governor pledged his support for "every constitutional endeavor," leaving himself room to criticize and rebel over those initiatives he believed would violate his cherished Tenth Amendment.

He also took time out to write *News and Courier* editor Ball "to express my sincere appreciation for the fine cooperation and splendid service you rendered during our fight for States' Rights.

. . . Although we did not win the presidency," he said, "we have shown the political leaders of this Nation that the South can be independent. With courage, persistence and determination our cause will ultimately win."

The 1948 presidential campaign was a personal *tour de force* that displayed to the nation Thurmond's energy, determination, and willingness to dedicate himself fiercely to a principle. Nonetheless it was a mixed blessing politically. The short-term benefit was broader name recognition that could boost him to higher office. But over the longer term, the states' rights campaign became an identifying factor as fixed as the color of his eyes. While a link to the movement did nothing to hinder his ability to win South Carolina elections—it doubtless brought him votes years after the fact—it cast a shadow over every other aspect of his career.

There was never a second thought about making the fight, never a waver from the insistence that the issue was the Constitution, not race. But decades after the event, some wistfulness would intrude as that shadow passed over his memories of the campaign. "Some of them got in their mind that I was just a racist," Thurmond said. "Well, honestly in my heart, I've never been a racist."

Although the presidential election was over, there was still some unfinished electoral business in South Carolina.

As a result of Judge Waring's injunction in July about thirty-five thousand blacks had voted in the August 10 primary—the first time since Reconstruction that blacks had voted in sizable numbers. The total, though, was well shy of the several hundred thousand blacks who could have voted.

Primary day had been a special moment for Waring, who had spent it driving around Charleston with his wife, Elizabeth, stopping at polling places with large black enrollments. Two days later, after a two-hour conference with Waring, Thurgood Marshall and Harold Boulware told reporters that no substantive violations of the judge's order had been observed.

Shortly after the primary, Charleston writer Rowena W. Tobias astutely observed in *The New Republic* that Waring's July ruling was of tremendous import. "The last citadel of 'white-only' voting has been breached by federal fiat," she wrote, "a far more significant fact in changing the pattern of Southern politics than all the shenanigans of Thurmond, Wright, Laney and company."

Waring's July order had been only a temporary injunction. On November 23, he heard arguments on Brown's plea to make that order permanent. Three days later the judge issued another order in Brown's favor. Once again Waring's opinion was direct and harsh. He said it was "an absurdity" to argue, as the Democrats had done, that their new party oath and accompanying rules had conformed to the earlier *Elmore* decision. Under these rules, he said, "a Negro could never attend any meeting, could never have any vote in the election of the officials in charge of the party affairs, could never have a vote or even a voice in the adoption of rules, platforms or any part whatsoever in the government of the party. . . . The proposed oath," Waring added, "cannot be said to have any purpose other than the exclusion of Negro voters.

"It is quite apparent," the judge concluded, "that the defendants set out to continue a form of racial discrimination in the conduct of primary elections in this state. This is illegal and must be stopped."

Waring finished the year viewed as a traitor by much of white Carolina, while Thurmond, preparing to resume his gubernatorial duties, was a hero. Over the next four years, the diverging paths of these two public officials would be instructive, a microcosm of the South's festering tensions over civil rights and an illustration of the respective roles of politics and law.

8. IN THE SHADOW OF THE COURT

1949–1953

MANNING, SOUTH CAROLINA, the seat of Clarendon County, is a town steeped in the state's official history. Named for nineteenth-century governor Richard I. Manning, the town has been home to four other governors, all of them related, including Manning's son and his grandson.

In 1950 this was still "an old country town with old country ways," as a tour book had described Manning a decade earlier. Large, neat houses and tourist homes with wide, well-kept lawns lined Brooks Street, the main thoroughfare, providing a kind of promenade to the courthouse at the center of town. A single block below the courthouse accommodated most of the little stores and shops that served its two thousand residents.

This was white Clarendon County, and it bore no resemblance to the impoverished Clarendon that lay out in the country beyond the manicured lawns. Home for the majority black population was likely to be a rudimentary shack with few amenities. Running water and indoor plumbing were virtually nonexistent. The luckier blacks who lived in town could have running water if, at their own expense, they tapped into the city water line. Not one street in the black section of Manning was paved.

Clarendon is less than sixty miles east of Columbia, but as the fifties dawned, it could have been in a different world. The growth and modernization that were slowly coming to the Palmetto State had thus far eluded the county, certainly its black citizens. The mainstay of the economy was still farming, and most of that was cotton or grain. The majority of the farmers were black tenants who did not own their land and who worked out lease arrangements with their often absentee white landlords. The relationship mirrored the political arrangement. Blacks made up 71 percent of the population yet felt powerless to press the minority white power structure for change.

In 1950 the official count of the federal government showed 4,590 black households in Clarendon, with an average annual income of less than $1,000 for two-thirds of them. The median age in the county was eighteen, the youngest of any county in South Carolina. That meant that Clarendon had a large group of black school-age children. Few of them, however, attended school beyond fourth grade, and fifteen years earlier, when the last reliable survey was taken, 35 percent of all Clarendon blacks older than ten were illiterate.

So it is not surprising that the black community's first challenge to Clarendon's white rule came over education, when Levi Pearson sued the county in July of 1947 because it refused to provide a single bus to ferry his children and other black youngsters to their ramshackle schools. His lawsuit, as well as cases from four other jurisdictions, would grow into an all-out assault on segregation that was going to turn the Supreme Court into the pivotal force in the civil rights movement. Despite the politicians' stump speeches and stadium rallies, for the moment it was the federal judiciary that would define the course of racial progress; politicians could only react. But like their forebears in the days of Tillman, Vardaman, Blease, and Ed Smith, candidates for office continued to find race a powerful tool. The central theme, though not always overtly stated, was who best could preserve segregation. In less elegant parlance, the issue, as white politicians joked, was: Whoever could yell "Nigger" the loudest would win.

South Carolina at the beginning of this new decade epitomized the escalating war of racial politics—an increasingly assertive black community inciting correspondingly hostile whites. As the Clarendon lawsuit moved forward, the state would also witness one of the most bitter contests for the United States Senate. Two other states, North Carolina and Florida, had similarly ugly senatorial contests in 1950—each of them shaped by race. Delaware, Kansas, Virginia, and the District of Columbia were struggling with their own desegregation lawsuits that would eventually come to the Supreme Court. But in South Carolina the lawsuit and the Senate race were going on at the same time, the first adding fire to the second.

The Senate contest pitted Thurmond, the outgoing governor, against incumbent senator Olin Johnston, the former governor, and while other issues divided the two candidates, race proved to be the critical factor when the votes were counted. Normally not a man to second-guess himself, Thurmond would later express regret about this campaign. The second thoughts, however, were largely over tactics, not substance, for it was an article of faith that painting the other fellow as soft on segregation was good politics.

Because it was the first election in which South Carolina blacks could vote in any numbers, the campaign exposed the raw edge of racial politics even more than the 1948 election. With some justification, Thurmond believed he had done more for black Carolina than any previous governor, and he could reel off the numerous kindnesses he had shown blacks over the years. But never before had Thurmond, the politician, told "white Democrats of South Carolina, the challenge is up to you . . . it is your time to stand up and be counted for South Carolina Democracy"—his code for the right to segregate. Never before had he charged that the NAACP was a menacing group of "bloc voters" who were bent on taking over the state.

These were signs of the continuing transition in southern politics that had forced white candidates to choose sides. In theory their options were the same ones that had faced the region a few years earlier: to fight for segregation or to accept change and, with it, the legitimacy of black America's quest for equality. But now that court decisions were putting their social order in imminent danger, the choice was obvious, and southern politicians railed against the judiciary with familiar rhetoric, unembarrassed about their flagrant appeals for white votes.

Judge Waring had made a clear choice in 1947 and again in 1948 when he bucked convention and made sure blacks could vote in South Carolina primaries. With the Clarendon lawsuit sitting in his court, the judge was now going to have the opportunity to make an even more important choice, ruling on the constitutionality of segregation itself. His decision would surprise no one, and when the Clarendon proceedings were over, Waring would leave the federal bench and South Carolina for retirement in New York, beloved by blacks, a pariah to whites.

Thurmond's choices would bring unaccustomed defeat in 1950, giving him an involuntary hiatus from frontline politics. His stint in the private sector would turn out to be financially lucrative but short.

Politics rather than contentious litigation was still the first order of business when Thurmond returned to his duties as governor after the 1948 race. His third annual address to the General Assembly was an optimistic presentation that saw progress at "every turn and on every side." In the previous year, he boasted, the General Assembly had passed "the most progressive and constructive school legislation in the history of the state," including money for a survey of the entire public school system.

In light of the ferment already under way in Clarendon County over unequal school systems for blacks and whites, it was ironic that the governor, who acknowledged the desperate need for improvements in education, would insist, "It is economic means, and not the will to do the job, which we lack." He admitted that South Carolina ranked "forty-fourth among the forty-eight states of the nation in school expenditures per pupil," but he did not mention that South Carolina still spent twice as much for white students as it did for blacks. In his own way, though, Thurmond was cognizant of the needs of the black community. "The productive potential of our colored people is perhaps our largest undeveloped economic resource as a State . . . ," he said. "Education is the means whereby we can most quickly equip our colored citizens to make their maximum contribution to the State's total economy, to the great advantage of both races." Thurmond proposed higher teachers' salaries to attract good instructors, improved transportation for children, and money for building new schools, "especially those so badly needed for colored children."

The message was encouraging, but reality was another thing. White Carolina was not going to spend substantially more money on schools for blacks until determined Clarendon parents took the state into federal court.

The governor saved for last discussion of his favorite subject, states' rights. But while he warned against "concentration of governmental power on the banks of the Potomac"—he called it "as dangerous to human liberty as it was on the banks of the Tiber in Italy or on the banks of the Rhine in Germany"—he now also cautioned the General Assembly not to "neglect our correlative responsibilities." The tone was gentler and less defiant than his posture during the presidential campaign.

Thurmond's commitment to states' rights was primarily philosophical now. When activists met February 7, 1949, in Birmingham to form the National States' Rights Bureau, with Governor Laney presiding, Thurmond chose not to attend, sending a representative instead. He also told an inquiring Alabama newspaper editor that in his view, the states' rights cause was a movement, not a separate national party. But Thurmond did take a hard line against any compromise between the states' rights faction of the South Carolina Democratic Party and the pro-Truman wing, presaging the confrontation that would erupt later when the Democratic National Committee considered which South Carolina Democrats would be accepted on the panel.

For the most part, though, these broader political concerns were in the background during 1949, and Thurmond could focus on more parochial matters. In the spring, he made speeches to two different black groups that reflected the generally benign but limited view of most white politicians who had to grapple with the escalating racial tensions. Addressing the all-black Palmetto State Teachers Association, Thurmond urged the two races to "work together in harmony." He touted the progress that had been made since he became governor, in particular the trade schools that had been established during his administration for whites and blacks. "Anyone who has studied the operation of these schools is amazed at the short time in which an unskilled person may learn a good trade which will support him all his life," he said. He also noted that his proposal for an industrial school for black girls was pending in the legislature.

Speaking a few weeks later at a fund-raising dinner for a new black hospital in Sumter, Thurmond again talked of harmony between the two races but made clear that it must be within the context of "existing laws and traditions"—a euphemism for segregation. The speech was perhaps the most complete statement of his views on race at that time.

Opportunities for the southern black "are greater today than ever before," he said. "His scale of living is climbing steadily." Returning to a theme from the presidential campaign that would reappear over the next decade, Thurmond blamed "outside agitators" for breeding dissent by "violently distort[ing] facts to serve their selfish ends. . . . They have played a dishonest game with the truth. They are stirring up the fears of colored men and white men alike and trying to put them one against the other.

"Race fear is a terrible thing," he continued. "It gives rise to race prejudice and race hatred, and these bring violence and death. . . . Those who seek to exploit race prejudices for their own ends do not really serve the colored race."

As he would do with greater intensity later in his career, Thurmond drew a link between racial conflict and communism, charging, "There are also those who have sought to use racial agitation" to spread "its pernicious doctrines"—a ploy he said the "agents of the Kremlin have thrived on" in other countries. "But they have failed in the South." He complimented his all-black audience because "our colored people . . . have abiding belief and faith in the American way of life."

He reiterated his support for eliminating the poll tax and said he expected voters to approve the change at the next general election. He repeated his pledge to come down hard on any who engage in mob violence, but he refused to back away from his support of states' rights and his opposition to the civil rights proposals that had been at the center of the 1948 race. As Fielding Wright had done the year before, Thurmond contended that the principle of states' rights "is of equal importance to every American, whatever his race, color, creed or national origin."

After reciting gains the black community had achieved in business, vocational training, and education, Thurmond contended that "In South Carolina, and in the South as a whole, racial relations have steadily improved. They will improve even more rapidly as our economic conditions improve," he promised, telling the audience that a better life for blacks would be achieved.

In his *Lighthouse and Informer* column after the Sumter speech, John McCray gave Thurmond a mediocre review at best, chiding him for failing to grasp the dissatisfactions and strivings of the black community and for placing the blame on "outside agitators" when white Carolina was the catalyst for unrest. "The governor missed an excellent chance to win the race's confidence," McCray said. He conceded that Thurmond had "dotted the speech with poignant points on the needs of the state in health and education. . . . But he practically nullified these by making them components to the general theme of 'outsiders meddling,' . . . an obvious attempt to deflect Negro interest from an effective 'fight for your rights' position. There stood the governor of all the people of South Carolina," McCray went on, "telling one group that it shouldn't show initiative for rights and opportunities; that it should turn its back on the only people who have brought relief, people he castigated as meddlers and agitators. . . . If southern Negroes appear susceptible to agitation"—and that was a dubious proposition, McCray said—"the real fault lies in white leaders in government" who won't use their power to help them. "The modus operandi is for the southern officeholder or aspirant to toss many bricks at Negro heads. The more he is able to toss, the greater his stature among white voters."

In late April Thurmond made a progressive but controversial move when he decided to put a woman—the first—on the South Carolina Industrial Commission, created in 1935 to administer the workers' compensation laws. The governor selected Faith Clayton, who worked at the Employment Security Commission, as part of a larger plan to reform the Commission's procedures for awarding compensation. But terming Thurmond's proposal a "sellout," labor demanded a bona fide labor representative. (The law creating the commission specified membership of a neutral chairman, two representatives from labor, and two from industry.) The governor went ahead and sent Clayton's name to the Senate in early May, touching off a filibuster that would delay her confirmation until 1950.

Early in June, Thurmond made another controversial appointment when he named a black Charleston physician, Dr. T. C. McFall, to the Hospital Advisory Council, created by the legislature in 1947 to help the state administer some $10 million in federal funds for hospital construction. It was the first time a black had been appointed to a state agency in at least four decades. McFall had been recommended by Charleston physicians. The appointment would be revisited in the harshest way in the coming U.S. Senate race.

Although the 1950 elections were a year away, speculation about the Democratic Party lineup had already begun by midsummer. "The names of J. Strom Thurmond as a candidate for the U.S. Senate, and of former Secretary of State James F. Byrnes for the governorship are being mentioned with increasing frequency today as campaign time nears in South Carolina's general election," observed one story in *The Greenville Piedmont.* Though neither man had any comment on the speculation, the paper insisted "it is a foregone conclusion among most observers that Thurmond will tilt his potent lance against veteran U.S. Senator Olin D. Johnston." His opponents, the paper reported, believed that the 1948 presidential run was the governor "firing his first shot" in the Senate race. Moreover, "every act" since he became governor was toward this end, particularly his stalled attempt to put Faith Clayton on the industrial commission and his appointment of Dr. McFall. These, opponents said, "were political moves pure and simple."

In February of 1950 nationally syndicated columnist Drew Pearson fueled a new round of political speculation when he reported in a column that Thurmond would not run against Johnston for the Senate seat. On February 12 an angry Thurmond declared that Pearson "would know nothing about any decision I have made on any subject at any time," and promised that he would make a statement about his plans after the legislature finished the 1950 session. "When I am ready to make a statement as to my political plans, I will make it directly to the people of South Carolina," the governor said.

Although nothing was official, political observers took this to mean that Thurmond would be a candidate. The rest of his statement was a taste of what was to come in the primary race. He said Johnston's reelection bid would give South Carolinians "a chance to choose between the candidates who are following the President and those who are willing to stand up and be counted in opposition to his un-American, Communistic and anti-Southern programs."

A few months earlier Thurmond had pounded the national party after one of his supporters from 1948 was refused a seat as South Carolina's representative on the Democratic National Committee. Even though the state would have no representation on the panel, Thurmond counseled against compromise with national leaders and insisted his state had been abandoned, not vice versa: "We are not the ones who left the Democratic Party."

Shortly after this blowup, President Truman said he was willing to let bygones be bygones if the bolters would accept the 1948 platform, civil rights plank included. Thurmond rejected the offer. "It must be obvious now to all Southern Democrats that the ties which have bound the South to the Democratic Party in the past have been cut," Thurmond said. Truman "boldly proclaimed that only those Democrats who declare allegiance to the civil rights programs will be recognized in the National Democratic Party. He makes this statement," he continued, "with the full knowledge that the overwhelming majority of the Democrats of the South are opposed to the civil rights program. . . ."

A breach had now developed between Thurmond and the national party that would never completely heal, and it was only a matter of time before he would go down his own political path.

There had been still another slap from the national party when Thurmond and Wright were not invited to a southern meeting in Raleigh in January 1950. Jonathan Daniels, the editor of *The News and Observer* and a strong Truman supporter, had left the two governors off the invitation list because he considered them members of a different political party than the Democrats meeting in the North Carolina capital. Thurmond let the snub pass without comment.

Elizabeth Waring had also given Thurmond a chance to point up the difference between South Carolina Democrats and the rest of the party. In comments on a radio show, Waring, who was a native northerner, said, among other things, that she favored interracial marriages "if that's what they [the couple] want."

Thurmond attributed part of Waring's answer to her northern background, suggesting that "she does not understand or appreciate our problems." But there was more. It was "quite apparent," the governor said, that "she is following the Truman line and speaks for the Trumanites in South Carolina." Noting his long-standing opposition to Truman's civil rights proposals, Thurmond added that he had "sought to warn the people as to the dangers of the Truman program and what it would ultimately lead to. Thus far, the president and his followers have gone no further than demanding abrogation of our state laws providing for the separation of the races. Now they are becoming so bold as to advocate abrogation of the laws against inter-marriage."

By the spring of 1950, speculation was mounting that Thurmond would challenge Johnston, and as a warm-up for the expected contest, the governor blasted Truman April 13 for sanctioning a Justice Department action on civil rights. The NAACP, with Justice's support, had challenged segregation in railroad dining cars. "I am glad President Truman has finally admitted that the goal his administration has been working for all along is to abolish separation of the races," Thurmond said, adding that it undercut the "Truman apologists" in the South who insisted that the administration did not favor an end to segregation. If the administration persuades the Supreme Court "to declare that we cannot separate the races in the South, the most serious situation since the days of carpetbag government will confront the Southern states," Thurmond asserted.

Sixteen days later, on April 29, Thurmond announced his candidacy for Olin Johnston's Senate seat. Although accused by his enemies of playing politics by appointing a black to a prominent state position, in his speech Thurmond did not sound like a candidate going after what would be the largest black primary vote since Reconstruction.

Halfway through his announcement, Thurmond charged that "every outside influence that hates and seeks to destroy our way of life in South Carolina will attempt . . . to dominate this election." Citing the NAACP by name, he charged that it "and other bloc organizations have been encouraged by the rulings of a turncoat federal judge [a snide reference to Waties Waring] who has forced into our primary thousands of voters who do not believe in the principles of the Democratic Party of South Carolina.

"Their emissaries," he claimed, "have already invaded our state to line up support for candidates of their choice, and they have even grown so bold as to publicly announce the candidates that they have marked for defeat." He, of course, because of the fight he made for states' rights, would have to "depend on the support of the good people of this state who take orders only from their heart and conscience. The time has come," he challenged the white electorate, "when our people must take sides and stand up and be counted if we are going to retain home rule, block the trend toward socialism, and preserve our way of life."

Thurmond had come out swinging with a calculated choice to forgo the support of black organizations. It was better politics to aim his pitch to "the good people of South Carolina," by implication the whites, and to ignore the "bad" people, blacks and their few white allies who openly challenged the status quo.

The paradox was that Thurmond was far from unmindful of

the inequities that blacks suffered. By comparison to governors before him, his own record was exemplary, though his proposed solutions were limited by "custom and tradition" and were always on white Carolina's terms. His immediate and strong response to the Willie Earle lynching, which had prompted such praise from the black community; his continued, successful efforts to get more money for black schools; his support for ending the poll tax; his appointment of McFall to the hospital commission—all evidenced his awareness of the problems and his willingness to make efforts to improve the lot of black Carolina. But it was still unthinkable that the two races could mingle freely in all facets of life, and there was far more political capital in exploiting the fear of change than in presenting himself as a moderate.

Johnston was no different from Thurmond—or any other southern white politician—on this issue. He was, after all, the governor who had called the legislature back into session in 1944 to preserve the white primary. Because of how Thurmond was now using race, it was the height of irony that Johnston was in a position to reap the benefits of two lawsuits—*Elmore* and *Brown*—prompted by his very action.

Although Thurmond and Johnston had similar styles—both loved hands-on campaigning, both had a penchant for bombast on the stump—and although they each defended segregation with a vengeance, their origins were quite different. Where Thurmond was born into a comfortable, even privileged home in Edgefield, Johnston grew up in the impoverished hamlet of Honea Path in the northern part of the state. The elder Johnston was a tenant farmer, and the family home was typical of the time—unpainted, no finished ceiling, no bathroom, and water that came from a dug well. The son's ascent in South Carolina politics was a story of tenacity, drive, and discipline.

From the time he was eleven until he was seventeen, young Johnston had finished only about eleven months of school, squeezing that in between work on the family farm and in the textile mills. Later on he often referred to himself, not untruthfully, as "a cotton mill boy." When Johnston turned eighteen, he enrolled in the Textile Industrial Institute of Spartanburg because the school allowed one week of work for one week of schooling. In just over a year, from March 1914 to June 1915, he received the equivalent of a high school diploma. When he sought to go on to college, however, he was refused admission at Furman University and Clemson because they did not recognize the textile institute as an accredited preparatory school.

With help from a friend, he was able to get an appointment with the president of Wofford College in Spartanburg, who told Johnston that while he did not meet the standards to enter the school, he could attend as a special student to take freshman work and high school courses at the same time. Johnston worked his way through two years at Wofford with an assortment of other odd jobs; during the Christmas vacations he worked in the textile mills.

Rejected by the U.S. Marines in 1917 because of flat feet and color blindness, Johnston was undeterred. He organized a company of engineers for the army, and by the summer he was in an army training camp at the fairgrounds in Columbia. By the fall, after working on two military camps in the state, Johnston and his company were sent to France, where he served for almost two years.

Following his discharge, Johnston finished up at Wofford and then earned a law degree at the University of South Carolina, supporting himself there by running the law school library. Even before graduating, though, Johnston, now twenty-six, won his first political race. At the urging of friends back home in Anderson County, he ran successfully for the state House and outpolled his nearest opponent by more than 1,600 votes.

Two more successful elections sent him to the House to represent Spartanburg, where he had moved to open a law practice after getting married. He established himself as a leader in the chamber, but in 1930, when he tried his first statewide race, he was defeated for governor—though only by 960 votes. Four years later, using a promise to reform the state highway system, Johnston was elected, beating former governor Cole Blease in a second primary by nearly 32,000 votes.

The most spectacular incident of his term was the forcible occupation of the state highway department to fulfill his promise to break the hold of the state "highway ring." After failing with more conventional methods, Johnston called out the National Guard to prevent the current commissioner from entering his office, declared the department to be in a state of insurrection, and installed his own man. He later lost a court battle on the issue as well as a legislative fight to get control of department, but this defeat was offset by passage of the workers' compensation law and creation of the South Carolina Industrial Commission that Thurmond later tried to reform.

Not content to stop at the governor's mansion, Johnston ran for the Senate in 1938 against Cotton Ed Smith but came up short. He ran again in 1941 to fill the unexpired Senate term of James F. Byrnes, who had been appointed to the Supreme Court by Roosevelt. But this time he lost to Maybank, Judge Waring's old friend.

Johnston showed he still had statewide appeal, however, by winning the governorship again in 1942. It was two years later that he called the legislature back into session "to maintain white supremacy in our Democratic primaries in South Carolina" by repealing all of the state's primary election laws. A month after the legislature complied, Johnston announced for the third time that he was running for the Senate, once again challenging Cotton Ed. This time he beat Smith, now seventy-nine, convincingly.

It was clear from his career that Johnston took no backseat to Thurmond in terms of ambition, energy, and determination.

The 1950 Senate campaign, with its traditional county-by-county candidates' meetings, formally opened May 23; it would wind up in Columbia before the July 11 primary. Before each meeting, aides canvassed each town, trying to stir up interest in their man and assure a friendly crowd at the courthouse, where the meetings generally took place. Jean Thurmond played an active role and brought to her husband's attention Harry Dent, a bright, energetic college student who would become one of Thurmond's most influential advisers and would help him carve out a special niche in national politics. Dent accompanied Jean as she went up and down the streets looking for votes for her husband. He also was given a new Plymouth outfitted with a loudspeaker on top and a turntable in the front seat so that he could play music and then exhort the citizens to "Vote for Strom Thurmond, a man of courage."

Johnston was not without his family resources, either. His wife, Gladys, helped manage his campaign. His daughters, aged ten and twelve, carried handmade signs asking the audience to "Vote for My Daddy," and they could be counted on to assemble a contingent of their friends with signs on the senator's behalf. One such family touch provoked a revealing outburst from Thurmond.

As Johnston sat on the platform waiting to speak, Sallie Johnston and her friends took some flowers to the senator as he waited his turn. Johnston leaned over and kissed his daughter on the cheek, prompting Thurmond to jump up, send his speech flying about, and holler, "There he goes kissin' young women . . . he'll do anything."

With the exception of his attacks on the "Barnwell ring," Thurmond had always campaigned for office on his own credentials and ideas. But now that he was up against an established politician in a head-on contest, his close friend Walter Brown had advised him to go after Johnston directly to blunt the incumbent's appeal. The strategy sounded plausible, and so Thurmond went against his own rule of thumb: instead of concentrating on what he could offer South Carolina, Thurmond tore into Johnston at every opportunity, painting him as a "Trumanite" who would break down segregation and charging that he had run a "pardon racket" for prisoners during his years as governor.

At the first candidates' meeting in Lexington, just outside of Columbia, Thurmond's new strategy was evident. "I do not intend to engage in personalities," he said, "but I am not going to hesitate to show the people of South Carolina where my opponent has been weighed in the balance of South Carolina democracy and found wanting."

The governor blasted Johnston for being a disloyal Democrat, charging that he had "connived and played along with Trumanites" who tried to take over the state party in 1948. Johnston retorted that he had "talked more than any other man I know of" against Truman's nomination and had "begged" General Eisenhower to run for president. When Thurmond charged that Johnston had "repudiated his oath . . . when he supported and raised money for Harry Truman," Johnston declined at this early juncture to reply. "I don't have to take up time talking about someone else because I have plenty of other things to talk about," Johnston said. "I think the high office of United States senator is above personalities."

On May 25, Thurmond sharpened the rhetoric on party loyalty, taunting that Johnston "wobbles in and wobbles out so much it is hard to keep up with him. First he is against Truman. Then he is for Truman," Thurmond said. "Now he is against him when the Democrats of South Carolina begin blowing on his neck."

Eleven days later, the single voice of the Supreme Court drowned out the campaign rhetoric and signaled the course of the future on racial issues. In three unanimous rulings June 5, the justices dealt severe blows to segregation. While the court did not overturn *Plessy v. Ferguson,* the separate-but-equal decision, the justices showed they were becoming much more reluctant to find equality in separateness. In one case, *Sweatt v. Texas,* the court said that the all-white University of Texas must admit Heman Marion Sweatt to its law school instead of forcing him to attend a new law school for blacks. The court said the new law school did not have the same educational opportunities as the university and thus denied Sweatt equal protection guaranteed by the Fourteenth Amendment to the Constitution.

In the second case, *McLaurin v. Oklahoma State Regents,* the court said that the University of Oklahoma could not make G. W. McLaurin, a black graduate student, sit apart from whites at the law school and be separated from his classmates while studying in the library and eating in the school cafeteria. The unanimous court said these restrictions "impair his ability to study, engage in discussions and exchange views with other students, and . . . to learn his profession." The Fourteenth Amendment, the court said, "precludes differences in treatment by the state based on race."

In the third case, *Henderson v. U.S.,* the case that had riled Thurmond earlier in the year, the court ruled that segregation in railroad dining cars, where the few tables set aside for blacks were cordoned off, violated the Interstate Commerce Act regulating railroads. The justices said that the "curtains, partitions and signs" amounted to an artificial classification based on race for black and white passengers holding identical tickets.

The June 5 decisions prompted predictable, if somewhat different, responses from Thurmond and Johnston. Each talked about how to preserve the old order, and if either of them sensed privately that, like it or not, a new day was coming, it was not apparent in their words. Thurmond declared that as long as he was governor there would be no breakdown in segregation in South Carolina. He said the decisions "once again demonstrate the wisdom of opposing further concentration of power in the federal government in Washington." He charged Johnston with "a share of responsibility for the Truman program to break down segregation" and claimed that the senator's "failure as a real spokesman for South Carolina democracy"—that is, the state's right to practice segregation—". . . contributed to what the Supreme Court did yesterday."

While Thurmond opposed federal aid to education, Johnston said the court rulings demonstrated the *need* for federal help for schools. He regretted the decisions, he said, but added, "Because of the financial condition in South Carolina, we cannot provide equal school facilities for the two races. In order to have segregation we must have federal aid to education under state control." Unlike Thurmond, he was not worried about the strings that might be attached to money from Washington.

Thurmond sought to get some political dividends from the generalized anger at the courts, and at Judge Waring in particular. If elected, he pledged to advocate legislation that would give citizens "relief . . . from any federal judge who destroys his usefulness and brings his court into disrespect by engaging in the villification and abuse of the very people over whom he is called to preside." Thurmond promised he would seek to bypass the cumbersome impeachment process that required formal charges by the House of Representatives and then trial in the Senate. It was not necessary to rely on such a lengthy procedure, the candidate said, "to get action against a federal judge in this state who practices social equality, mixing of the races, [and] stirs up racial discord which unless stopped may lead to insurrection."

He also took a slap at Johnston for not knowing the status of a pending move against Waring. "Now just think of that," Thurmond bellowed during one stump speech. "A United States senator who has represented South Carolina in the Senate six years having to come to South Carolina and ask the people here at home what happened to the Waring impeachment resolution."

By the second week in June there was already a sign that Thurmond's aggressive style might not be working. At one campaign meeting, he accused Johnston, a lifelong nondrinker, of toasting Senator McGrath, the former Democratic National Committee chairman who had become attorney general. And he insisted that Johnston supported the breakdown of segregation. The headline on a story in *The Anderson Independent* told readers what the paper thought of this tactic: THURMOND FIRES HIS MUD GUN AT JOHNSTON. A two-word kicker above the headline said in small capital letters: STILL RANTING.

Speaking in the northern counties of Chester and York, Thurmond focused on the pardon issue, making his accusations in a stinging speech June 8. "Starting in April 1937 and going on as long as he was governor," Thurmond charged, "my opponent went on an unconstitutional, unbridled and unbelievable pardon and parole spree." During his two terms, Thurmond continued, Johnston "sprung the penitentiary doors and turned back on the communities of this state 3,221 criminals. . . . It was easier to get out of the penitentiary than it was to get in." When hecklers told Thurmond to "quit that mudslinging," Thurmond shouted, "I know some of you fellows back there are henchmen of his [Johnston] but I'm going to give you some medicine." (Later in the campaign, when Thurmond was once again heckled, the governor told his supporters to "let 'em heckle. Don't forget, when they heckle Strom Thurmond, they heckle a man who dropped out of the skies on D day in Normandy.")

At another stop, in Oconee County, over in the far west corner of the state, Thurmond confronted Johnston on the speakers' platform and read off a list of convicts who had been pardoned, including twelve who had been convicted of murder. Jabbing his finger at Johnston like an angry prosecutor, he asked after each one, "Did you pardon him? Did you pardon him?"

For a while Johnston ignored Thurmond's attacks and disdained returning them in kind, maintaining that after "seven campaigns over the state," the people "know Olin Johnston and will vote for me on my merits and not the demerits of somebody else." But by late June, Johnston saw the need to strike back and challenged Thurmond's account of his pardon record.

Accusing Thurmond of a "five-week-old personal attack against me," the senator claimed that his predecessors had each granted more pardons in their single terms than he did in his two administrations. He accused Thurmond of ignoring records showing that "more than 80 percent of the parolees in South Carolina made good citizens." And he wondered aloud why Thurmond, who had been a state senator during Johnston's first term, waited fifteen years to complain about pardons he could have questioned as a legislator.

To get back at Thurmond for waving a picture of the senator's alleged drink, Johnston showed audiences the *Life* magazine picture of Thurmond standing on his head the day before his wedding. "You know you can get addled when you stand on your head," Johnston told listeners.

"I may have stood on my head and taken exercises," Thurmond shot back at one debate, "but I haven't straddled the fence," a reference to Johnston's back-and-forth support of Truman.

The two candidates almost got into a fight June 26 in Newberry, a small town an hour north of Columbia, when Thurmond, as he had done before, accused Johnston of remaining "silent as a tomb" in the Senate when the armed forces were being integrated. "If that's not so, Senator, stand up and deny it," Thurmond yelled.

"That's a lie! That's a lie! That's a lie!" Johnston shouted back, tired of the continuing attack.

"I'll see you outside afterward," Thurmond retorted.

When the session was over, Thurmond waited for Johnston out front. Johnston, walking toward Thurmond, reached out his hand to shake as though nothing had happened. Thurmond grabbed it, twirled the senator around and was prevented throwing a punch only when a Johnston adviser stepped between the two politicians.

Johnston also played up his credentials as a segregationist. "I'm for segregation of the races. God started it and I believe in keeping it that way," Johnston said when the candidates spoke at Florence June 21. "I defy anyone to say that Olin Johnston didn't fight civil rights."

In truth, Thurmond's and Johnston's views—like those of most other white politicians—weren't that far apart, and given what he considered his good record of achievement on race issues, Thurmond was perplexed by black leaders' stiff opposition to him. "I have done more for the Negroes of this state than any other governor of the state has," he said at that June 21 debate. "I have doubled the appropriations for their public education, have helped establish trade schools for them and I have done other things to help them." To him this was proof that "I am not prejudiced when I speak against the breakdown of segregation."

Yet as he persisted in his attacks on Johnston, Thurmond also stepped up his attack against the NAACP, charging that it and the CIO, the well-known labor organization, "have applied their pressure in Washington for federal interference in the South Carolina Senate race."

Thurmond was correct in one respect. Leaders in South Carolina's black community had determined to throw their weight behind Johnston. Despite some of the positive things Thurmond had done for blacks, since the presidential election of 1948, he had, as Clarendon County leader Billie Fleming put it, become "more obnoxious to blacks." Through his column in *The Light-*

house and Informer, John McCray, the Progressive Democratic Party leader, urged blacks to support Johnston over Thurmond, "whose every point and line was built about the Negro and who made it clear—if it wasn't clear before—that this doctrine of states' rights is nothing but the same old kicking Negroes around."

Clearly the specter of 1948 hung over Thurmond in this campaign, for in the minds of blacks, his run for the presidency had been subterfuge for white supremacy. Johnston's beliefs may not have been much different from Thurmond's, but at least he hadn't stepped forward to lead a whites-only movement, and—albeit grudgingly—Johnston had supported Truman, civil rights program and all.

Johnston, however, was not above using Thurmond's appointment of Dr. McFall against him. "The record shows . . . ," he reminded the Florence audience June 21, "that Olin D. Johnston never did, during two terms as governor of South Carolina, appoint a Negro to serve on boards with white men and women." Accusing Thurmond of hypocrisy, he dismissed Thurmond's contention that he'd had no alternative but to accept the recommendation of the Charleston physicians. "The governor did not tell you the truth . . . ," the senator declared. "He could have called for another recommendation—and still another—until the group . . . realized he was determined not to break down segregation in South Carolina."

Instead, Johnston insisted, "Thurmond, the political demagogue who campaigns on racial prejudice and hate—in a sneak bid for the Negro votes of South Carolina—has betrayed his Dixiecrat following, has betrayed our Southern traditions, and has broken down in one stroke the official barriers of segregation in South Carolina for a sordid mess of pottage."

Late in the campaign, ads appeared with big black letters proclaiming "THURMOND APPOINTS A NEGRO!" The text repeated Johnston's charge that it was only to capture black votes that Thurmond appointed the "First Negro . . . Since Days of Carpetbaggers and Scalawags." In another ad, Johnston swore he would have "suffered my right arm to have been severed from my body before I would have signed a commission for a Negro." At a Charleston campaign gathering, Johnston expressed himself less politely on the subject. "Had I been Governor Thurmond," he declared, "I would never have appointed the nigger physician of

Charleston, Dr. T. C. McFall, to displace your beloved white physician." When the four hundred blacks in the audience hissed their dissent, Johnston yelled out angrily, "Make those niggers keep quiet."

The entire issue prompted the South Carolina Medical Association to issue a statement explaining that Dr. McFall had been recommended by Charleston members of the organization and that under state law, the governor makes appointments to the Hospital Advisory Council upon the association's recommendation. The governor, the group said, "had no choice in the matter. Therefore, any attacks directed at Governor Thurmond alleging that he made this appointment on his own are false."

Thurmond responded with his own ad, repeating verbatim relevant parts of the medical society's assurances that he'd "had no choice." Forty years later, in a different political climate, Thurmond would cite with *pride* his willingness to accept the McFall recommendation.

Not all of Thurmond's ads were so benign, and by the end of the campaign, both sides were using the newspapers to make their points in the sharpest fashion. The governor took the Johnston-McGrath picture, blew it up, and provided a half page of text excoriating the senator for supporting McGrath—the man "who engineered Truman's nomination and election" and who was pledged to end segregation. "Senator Johnston knew all of this when the above picture was made," the ad said. "Yet he voted to turn over the law enforcement branch of the government and the FBI to the man who was pledged to end segregation in the South."

Johnston's own work in the textile mills as a young man, and his later support for federal programs to aid the worker, made him a favorite in the northern areas of the state, where most of the plants were located. Thurmond tried to go after that base of support with one ad contending that Truman's program would force blacks and whites to work alongside each other in the mills. "Textile Workers—Be on the Alert," the ad said, "YOUR JOB and YOUR WAY of LIFE are THREATENED!"

Johnston responded with an ad of his own quoting a telegram from Senator Russell of Georgia. The wire praised both Johnston and Senator Maybank for opposing the civil rights measures, calling them "valiant soldiers" in the fight.

Thurmond also ran ads raising the specter of "bloc voting" as a way of stirring up white fears about the emerging black electorate. "The orders have come down telling the bloc votes to scratch Strom Thurmond," one ad began. The copy quoted what it said were directions in *The Lighthouse and Informer* for voting for Johnston, explaining that a line should be drawn through Thurmond's name and that "the line should be clear and distinct." "White Democrats of South Carolina," the ad exhorted, "the challange [*sic*] is up to you. It is your time to stand up and be counted for South Carolina Democracy."

Thurmond also sought to draw a link between his candidacy and the virulent Senate primaries that already had taken place in North Carolina and Florida. In the latter, the more conservative George Smathers had beaten incumbent Claude Pepper, an unabashed liberal, in a contest that featured harsh personal attacks. Thurmond praised Smather's May primary victory, declaring that it was "a definite victory for the cause of constitutional government and the rights of the states to handle their own internal affairs without interference from Washington or dictation from faraway minority bloc bosses. . . ."

In North Carolina, Willis Smith had won a come-from-behind victory over Frank Porter Graham, accusing Graham, among other things, of being the candidate of the NAACP. It was a campaign marred by rumors and word-of-mouth distortions that had North Carolina's most conservative elements believing that Graham, who had been a respected university president, was "a damned nigger lover."

One Thurmond ad focusing on the North Carolina race declared that "bloc voting by any group is a MENACE TO DEMOCRACY." After showing election returns from selected black precincts in Raleigh, Durham, Charlotte, and Greensboro, North Carolina—where the vote was overwhelmingly for Graham—the ad copy crowed that "When the white Democrats of North Carolina saw that the Truman forces were trying to divide them and permit this minority bloc voting . . . , 100,000 votes changed and Willis Smith won the Democratic Nomination. When the final test came, North Carolina's REAL DEMOCRATS stood firm. . . . DEMOCRATS OF SOUTH CAROLINA TAKE NO CHANCES!"

A shorter Thurmond plug was a more subtle appeal to white voters: "Don't desert your heritage. Pass it on to your children. Vote for Thurmond."

The newspaper campaign was Thurmond at his least appealing. Though he denied authorship of the ad copy and claimed he had not given prepublication approval, he did allow the ads to be used in his name more than once. Thurmond never liked to think of himself as a race-baiter, but these ads were calculated to appeal to the white community's prejudice against blacks. As the press coverage showed, the campaign did nothing to enhance his reputation; but more instructive than press comments was the news that Thurmond's aggressive, strike-first strategy hadn't worked. When the votes were counted July 11, Johnston had triumphed by 27,276 votes, 186,180 to 158,904. Most observers attributed the victory to the large majority of black votes he won.

The Lighthouse and Informer believed that to be the case. Acknowledging that there was "no accurate accounting either for the number of Negroes who were registered or [who] voted," the paper estimated that there had been 60,000 black votes and that their votes—presumed to be against Thurmond—"made the difference." *The News and Courier* agreed, noting in a postelection editorial that while "neither candidate made a play for the negro votes, the negroes apparently supplied the margin of Johnston's victory."

When William Workman, *The News and Courier*'s political correspondent, analyzed the returns of a predominantly black ward in Columbia that was home to McCray, NAACP leader James Hinton, and George Elmore, the plaintiff in the white primary suit, he found overwhelming support for Johnston—1,249 votes to 72. "I contend that the attitude of the two men as regards negroes would never have resulted in so lopsided a vote had not the word been passed by negro bigwigs to support Johnston," Workman said.

The black and white press agreed on two other issues—that many white voters had found the entire campaign distasteful and stayed away from the polls, hurting Thurmond, and that Johnston had received the black votes because, as *The News and Courier* put it, "the candidate who was closer to the Fair Deal would be their better bet, regardless of his epithets."

This described one of the fundamental differences between the two men. Johnston was a Democrat through and through. It would have been inconceivable to him to break with the party, no matter how deep his concerns about its leftward drift. His philosophy was to fight from within. Thurmond was a maverick and a rebel, willing to step outside the boundaries and challenge convention if he felt it was appropriate. He didn't worry about the later consequences.

In a column after the election, McCray said he hoped Johnston's commitment to the Democratic Party would make him "develop into a statesman, interested in the welfare of all his people," and not "go down the road as a semi-bigot of the political variety." Of one thing McCray was sure: that Johnston, with his "experience and his already having had his former attempt to throttle the Negro chastised," would make "a safer agent of the people than the cocky, verbal filth-tossing opponent who really set the pace for the lowest campaign South Carolina has seen."

Thurmond's own postmortem on the 1950 campaign dwelt on tactics. He conceded that he should not have attacked Johnston so often and so harshly—even Jean had told him it was a mistake. He erred, he said, in focusing on what he believed were the flaws in the senator's record. The better strategy would have been to play up his own abilities. Though Walter Brown was a longtime friend and adviser, Thurmond ruefully admitted years later that he was "the only one who ever lost a race for me." At the same time, he blamed himself for not using better judgment.

Though unaccustomed to defeat, Thurmond seemed unfazed by the setback—a sign of his great ability to put the past behind him and move on. The young Harry Dent, who had heard so many courthouse audiences cheer his candidate, was crushed when the returns showed that Thurmond had lost. He marveled at the governor's composure and good humor among his supporters, who had gathered at the Jefferson Hotel in Columbia. "I never look at a dead horse's rear end," Thurmond told them, deliberately avoiding a more profane anatomical term.

"I was so disappointed," Dent recalled. "He was kind of beaming as though nothing had happened."

Thurmond's philosophy of no regrets served him well then and would continue to do so for the next forty years. In his mind, there was no use in a searching personal inquiry into the past. The right direction was forward. "I always take life as it comes," he later explained. "I didn't worry over it a'tall. Of course I was disappointed I didn't get elected—anybody would be. But I made up my mind just to look to the future. No use to whimper over something you can't help. And the past is past. That speaks for itself."

Over in Clarendon County, Thurmond defeated Johnston by about 1,000 votes. Preelection statistics gathered by Democratic Party officials estimated that fewer than five hundred blacks had registered to vote. Most of them were interested in the congressional race, in which Arthur Clement, the leader of the Progressive Democrats and the first black to run in a congressional primary, had challenged veteran L. Mendel Rivers. Rivers won in a landslide but Clement did get 370 votes in Clarendon County.

The black community's lack of participation in the election did not mean total disinterest in change. Since 1947, residents had been working with increasing energy on a lawsuit against the white-controlled school system. Statistics from the state give glaring evidence of the inequality in the county: in 1948–49, for example, the state spent $148.48 on each white student but only $69.95 on each black student. In Clarendon, which served almost three times as many blacks as whites, South Carolina spent 40 percent more on the county's white schools.

Judge Waring frequently passed through Clarendon on his way from Charleston to the central part of the state and was often struck by the "awful little wooden shacks" that served as schools for the black students. They had no running water and no indoor toilets. At Scott's Branch School in Summerton, 694 students had to use rudimentary privies. One elementary school, Liberty Hill, was a frame building with a tin roof and no underpinning. Drinking water had to be brought by bucket. Teachers in these schools had up to 79 students in a single class, while the largest white class had only 31 students. The white schools "were nothing to be very enthusiastic about," Waring conceded, "but they were fairly respectable looking." Whites had a school lunch program, up-to-date instructional tools, an auditorium for activities, and free bus service; but the black students had none of these.

The wooden shacks were the best the impoverished community could do because the state had not provided money for black schools. Parents had to put them up themselves. Although South Carolina did pay teachers' salaries, in Clarendon the average salary for white teachers was two-thirds more than for blacks.

Black parents were not unmindful of the educational disadvantages their children were suffering, but in 1947 in this rural county, where virtually all black families were dependent on whites for their livelihood, one had to think carefully about raising a challenge. They decided to start small, with an effort to get bus service for blacks.

It was James Hinton, head of the state NAACP, who first lit the fire under Clarendon blacks, when he spoke in June 1947 to a summer session of students at Allen University, the black school in Columbia. In the audience was the Reverend J. A. DeLaine of Summerton, who had built a home directly across from the Scott's Branch School, where his wife taught. He heard Hinton decry the state of black education in South Carolina—a disgrace, he called it, and as sharp a symbol of the white man's oppression as any. After all, the best way to keep the black community from rising was to keep its members uneducated and unable to compete with whites for better jobs, Hinton said. Blacks in other southern states were on the move. But in South Carolina there was only silence. "No teacher or preacher in South Carolina has the courage to find a plaintiff to test the legality of the discriminatory bus-transportation practices in this state," Hinton declared.

The words were not lost on Reverend DeLaine. Within days of Hinton's challenge, he drove over to the 160-acre farm of Levi Pearson, who had three children attending the Scott's Branch School, and told the farmer what Hinton had said. Pearson thought the matter over and agreed to be the plaintiff the NAACP was looking for.

After meeting in Columbia with Harold Boulware, who had helped Thurgood Marshall with the *Elmore* and *Brown* cases, Pearson approved a petition, dated July 28, 1947, stating that he was the father of three children and asking that "school bus transportation be furnished, maintained and operated out of the public funds" in the Summerton school district. The petition was on behalf of his children and "other Negro school children similarly situated." It was submitted to the county superintendent of education and to the secretary of the state board of education. If Thurmond knew about this, there is no record of any reaction. (Many years later, he said it would have been unusual for education authorities to contact him; like many other agencies in state government, the education division was not directly under his control.)

Despite repeated letters, Pearson and Boulware heard nothing for three and a half months. Early in November, Boulware wrote the chairman of the school board requesting a hearing. When there was no response by December, Pearson and Boulware decided they would have to go to court.

On March 16, 1948, suit was filed in federal district court in nearby Florence County. Contending that Pearson's children were suffering "irreparable damage," the suit asked for a court order barring the state from using race to decide which students were given free bus service. The complaint was signed by Boulware and by Thurgood Marshall, who had reviewed the case and taken an interest in it on behalf of the national organization.

Pearson v. County Board of Education was scheduled for consideration June 9 in Charleston. But on June 8, the case was thrown out of court on a technicality. White county school officials had checked Pearson's property tax receipts and determined that he was in the wrong school district to bring the suit. It was an embarrassing setback for DeLaine and even worse for Pearson. The repercussions were immediate. He soon found that no white farmer would lend him a harvester to bring in his crop; he could only watch his oats, beans, and wheat rot in the fields. Everything would be all right, the whites told him, if he would just stop talking about buses and quit associating with the NAACP. Pearson refused, but the effort had to start all over again.

Nine months later, on March 12, 1949, he and DeLaine took a group of Clarendon blacks to Columbia for a meeting with state and national NAACP leaders, including Marshall. Though discouraged by the setback the previous year, the New York lawyer had a new strategy for the next round. This time, Clarendon residents were not going to tie a case to one plaintiff but would find a group of twenty, and this time they were not going to stop at buses. Though only asking for equal treatment in buses, this suit would be crafted to bring forth a decision on buildings, teachers, and teachers' salaries by highlighting the total inequality of the system. Anything short of an overhaul would be a violation of the Fourteenth Amendment.

In an atmosphere already charged with intimidation, finding twenty plaintiffs was a daunting task, but DeLaine, fortified by another preacher, the Reverend J. W. Seals, was determined to do it. For the next four months the two ministers held informational meetings at churches around the county, and even though a special kind of excitement flowed through the black community, it stopped short of inducing anyone to sign up as a plaintiff. Tenant farmers knew they could be thrown off their land at any time, a fear reinforced by the whites who promised that any obstreperous black could find himself "a homeless hero."

Ironically, it was an ill-considered move by white Clarendon leaders that finally pushed local blacks into action. School officials had fired the principal at Scott's Branch School in Summerton and replaced him with S. I. Benson, a black man with no college degree whose chief attribute, in the eyes of the black community, was doing the white man's bidding. Dissatisfaction with the new principal grew, intensified by a mysterious lack of accounting for one thousand dollars raised at school rallies and by the charges he levied on the students before giving them their state education certificates. Black parents complained long enough so that the white school authorities finally gave them a hearing.

The embattled principal failed to refute the charges and was fired October 1. White leaders wanted DeLaine to become the new principal, but when he declined, they appointed his wife, Mattie, as acting principal in an effort to neutralize him. It did no good. By this time, said one black farmer who prepared to join the NAACP effort, "There was a fire here that no water was gonna put out."

By November 11—eight months after Thurgood Marshall's request—Reverend DeLaine had secured the twenty names the lawyer wanted. Heading the list alphabetically—which meant the suit would bear his name—was thirty-four-year-old Harry Briggs, a navy veteran with five children who worked at a service station pumping gas, repairing tires, and greasing cars. His wife, Liza, was a chambermaid at the Summerton Hotel.

The white community did not look kindly on Briggs's move. Right before Christmas, he was let go by his boss. When Liza Briggs refused her employer's request that she urge her husband to take his name off the petition, she found herself unemployed. Many other signers suffered similar reprisals.

In January 1950, DeLaine came to the defense of his community, firing off a three-page open letter that was circulated through Summerton. "Is this the price that free men must pay in a free country for wanting their children trained as capable and respectable American citizens?" he asked. "Shouldn't officials employ the dignity, foresight and intelligence in at least the honest effort to correct outstanding evils? . . . Is it a credit for Summerton to wear the name of persecuting a segment of its citizens? Shall we suffer endless persecution just because we want our children reared in a wholesome atmosphere?"

Such harsh words could not go unnoticed in white Clarendon. DeLaine now received mail threats from people signing as "the Ku Klux Klan," he was harassed on the highway, and his wife and nieces lost their teaching jobs. Then he was named in a two-hundred-thousand-dollar slander suit brought by Benson, the principal who had been charged with abusing his office and fired. An all-white jury subsequently awarded the former principal twenty-seven hundred dollars.

Finally, in May of 1950, as the U.S. Senate race was getting under way, *Briggs v. Elliott* was filed in federal district court. The respondent, Roderick W. Elliott, was chairman of the board of the school district.

It would be several months before the lawsuit came to court. In the meantime, DeLaine had been transferred to a church in Lake City, some thirty-three miles east of Summerton, for his own safety. In September, while awaiting the first court proceeding, he wrote Elizabeth Waring—by now more outspoken in her sympathy with the black cause—that he could no longer endure "the sly reign of terror and fear." (Several months later his Summerton home would burn to the ground. Firemen called to the scene stood by and watched, explaining that the house was outside the town limits. It was, by one hundred feet.)

Judge Waring had scheduled a pretrial conference on the *Briggs* case for November 17. The court session would bring together an interesting cast of characters, not the least of which was Waring himself, who by this time had assumed pariah status in Charleston. The isolation and enmity were fueled by a provocative speech Elizabeth Waring had made earlier in the year to Charleston's black YWCA branch. Among other things, she told the audience of blacks that "you are in the springtime of your growth when great achievements are attained." Southern whites, by contrast, were "a sick, confused and decadent people . . . full of pride and complacency, introverted, morally weak and low." Reaction in the white community was predictably hostile. For the next two weeks the Warings' phone rang constantly with abusive, threatening calls, and a torrent of hate mail came to their home and the judge's office.

Governor Thurmond considered Elizabeth Waring's speech "beneath comment," but several congressmen happily offered their criticism, one of them calling her speech "typical of the remarks of the professional agitator." Although Mrs. Waring had specifically criticized the Charleston papers for their coverage of the black community, *The News and Courier* declined to print an editorial denying the charge. It did, however, suggest that "discontented blacks . . . escape to Northern cities."

On the evening of October 9, the Warings' peace was shattered when a brick crashed through their living room window, showering them with glass fragments as they played cards before bed. Crouched low to the floor, they made their way into the dining room to call the local FBI, the city police, and the judge's bailiff. Charlestonians, including the authorities, dismissed the incident as a prank. The next day, Waring issued a statement condemning the attack as "evidence of the stubborn, savage sentiment of this community" and linking it to the Dixiecrat movement, which he criticized as "the dying gasp of white supremacy and slavocracy"; he promised to continue his "fight for freedom and democracy."

Representing Clarendon blacks in the courtroom would be Thurgood Marshall, who had already won the teacher pay case and two voting rights disputes before Waring. Born in Baltimore in 1907, the son of a dining car waiter and a schoolteacher, Marshall had followed his brother to Lincoln University, a small black school in Oxford, Pennsylvania. One week into law school at Howard University, he was sure he had found what he wanted to do for the rest of his life—pursue the battle for civil rights.

Very early in his practice in Baltimore, Marshall started to do work for the local NAACP, helping to lead a picketing campaign against white merchants who refused to hire black salespeople, even though most of the customers were black. He also organized efforts to persuade Maryland congressmen to back the federal antilynching bill.

Marshall started preparing his first civil rights suit in 1933; the result was the integration of the University of Maryland law school in 1936. Two years later he was the NAACP's chief lawyer, taking over in the New York office from the highly esteemed Charles Houston, who had been Marshall's teacher at Howard. For the next fifteen years, Marshall would travel wherever there were individuals willing to take on the system—"shufflin' through Dixie" was how he put it, using the self-mocking but pointed humor that helped ease tensions in the highly charged race cases.

In 1944, the *Afro-American,* a Baltimore newspaper, wrote that the robust Marshall, with his carefully trimmed mustache, "carries himself with an inoffensive self-confidence and seems to like the life he lives. He wears and looks especially well in tweed suits."

Marshall liked to think of himself as shrewd and tough, but not reckless, especially in white man's territory. During one trip to

Mississippi—a favorite story of his—Marshall was thinking about staying overnight in a small town. "I was out there on the train platform, trying to look small," he explained, "when this cold-eyed man with a gun on his hip comes up. 'Nigguh,' he said, 'I thought you oughta know the sun ain't nevah set on a live nigguh in this town.' So, I wrapped my constitutional rights in cellophane," Marshall said, "tucked 'em in my hip pocket . . . and caught the next train out of there."

Clarendon's chief counsel, Robert Figg—Thurmond's long-time confidant—had served for more than a decade as the prosecutor for Charleston County and was considered one of the state's premier lawyers. Unlike many other attorneys, including Waring, who had "read law" under a mentor, Figg had had a formal legal education: two years at Columbia University. He also had the ability to cordon off his personal views from his professional responsibilities as he saw them. The same was true of his obligations as a friend. It was his friendship for Thurmond, which began when the two were young lawyers in the thirties, rather than any strong belief in states' rights ideology that made him one of the inner circle. If Thurmond needed to blast Truman, well, Figg would help write that speech, even though he himself had considerable regard for the president. If Johnston needed a lawyer in 1944 to help find a strategy for saving the white primary, then Figg would go to Columbia to serve the governor. "It was never political. It was personal. It never had anything to do with issues," he would say later. The same with Clarendon County, where one of the local attorneys, S. Emory Rogers, had asked him to help out. "I was a lawyer representing the Summerton schools at the behest of its lawyer," Figg said.

Although Marshall and his cocounsel, Robert Carter, wanted Waring to strike down the entire practice of separate schools for black children on constitutional grounds, *Briggs v. Elliott* was framed as a lawsuit protesting only the failure to provide bus service. The idea was to invoke equal protection—that under segregation, black schools were inferior in every respect to those maintained for white children—but to raise the claim indirectly to avoid triggering a special three-judge federal court that would be empaneled for such a broad constitutional challenge. Their reasoning was obvious—there were very few Judge Warings on the federal bench, and finding another friendly vote in the U.S. Court of Appeals for the Fourth Circuit would be nearly impossible.

By the time the parties gathered in court, Judge Waring had seen through their ploy. Whatever his sympathies, his fidelity to proper jurisprudence made him want no part of it; if constitutional principles were to be invoked, let the lawyers step up to the plate and address them directly. He suggested that the plaintiffs ask for a dismissal of *Briggs* in its current form and then "bring a brand new suit, alleging that the schools of Clarendon County . . . are segregated, and that those statutes are unconstitutional, and that'll raise the issue for all time as to whether a state can segregate by race in its schools." Both Marshall and Figg were surprised, but the NAACP lawyer agreed to the suggestion, and on December 22, 1950, the new complaint was filed. As procedure dictated, Judge John J. Parker convened a three-judge panel consisting of himself, Waring, and Judge Timmerman.

Waring could have been no more optimistic about the outcome than Marshall and Carter, but finally there would be a direct challenge to segregation, and he could play at least some role in the decision.

Although Waring generally kept a low profile before the hearing convened, he did grant a long, revealing interview to Carl Rowan, the black journalist, who was working for the *Minneapolis Morning Tribune.* Waring acknowledged that there were costs to his growing isolation from Charleston colleagues. "I admit I miss the shop talk. I miss chatting about this Supreme Court ruling or such and such a case." But the judge insisted he had no regrets. "Socially, I miss no one. I lost small brains and found larger ones. I have met southern negroes and northerners of both races whom I would not have known except for this. . . . White supremacy," he continued in a poetic and acute observation, "is a way of life. You grow up in it, and the moss gets in your eyes. You learn to rationalize away the evil and filth, and you see magnolias instead."

Clarendon County was at least forcing some of official white South Carolina to push aside the magnolias, although Clarendon leaders had refused to concede any inequalities in the schools. After he started investigating for himself, Bob Figg was quick to appreciate that the state was going to have a serious problem in the courtroom if it tried to ignore conditions in Summerton. To prepare for the case, he had gone to Clarendon to see for himself what the white and black schools looked like and had cross-examined Rogers about what defenses he might make. Years later,

Figg admitted that "the facilities were not only not equal . . . they were very embarrassingly unequal."

The lawyer returned to his Charleston office and called Governor Byrnes, who had just begun his term in January. He had a message that was decidedly different from the resistance of Clarendon officials. "This is going to be a very embarrassing situation," Figg told Byrnes. "The other side is just going to have a field day. They're going to make us look ridiculous." Figg wanted to short-circuit the plaintiffs. He told the governor that the state should admit the inequities and ask for time to make the improvements necessary to reduce the disparity between the two systems. It was the best way to avoid a frontal assault on *Plessy v. Ferguson* and separate but equal.

The governor was hardly a new face on the South Carolina political scene. His election as governor, as one young state legislator put it, was more a "crowning" than an election. He had been a senator, Supreme Court justice, and secretary of state under Roosevelt. He had hoped one day to be his running mate. All that worldly experience, however, did nothing to alter Byrnes's fidelity to the racial status quo—in Judge Waring's parlance, he still saw only magnolias.

In his January inaugural speech, Byrnes asserted that the end of segregation would "endanger the public school system in many states." A week later he told the South Carolina legislature that the "overwhelming majority of colored people" did not want "forced" integration. "The politicians in Washington and the Negro agitators in South Carolina who today seek to abolish segregation in all schools will learn that what a carpetbag government could not do in the Reconstruction period cannot be done in this period."

The governor's comments in March were even more provocative. "If the court changes what is now the law of the land, we will, if possible, live within the law, preserve the public school system, and at the same time maintain segregation. If that is not possible, reluctantly," he promised, "we will abandon the public school system." The harsh remarks did not intimidate black leaders. Shortly after Byrnes spoke, Hinton, the state NAACP president, said the organization would not give up its lawsuit. "The courts are our only recourse. Negroes will not turn back," he promised. "Whites and Negroes will have public schools in South Carolina after all of us have died and present officials either are dead or retired from public life."

Although Thurmond was now a private citizen, *Briggs* had caught his eye. Writing Figg about another matter just before the hearing, Thurmond, who called the case "the most important one to our state and the South," suggested that Figg and his team consider "defaulting" rather than pushing for a court decision. By giving in to the black plaintiffs, Thurmond said, only the Clarendon schools would be affected, while an adverse court decision would affect South Carolina and the other states in the Fourth Circuit.

In typical Thurmond fashion, the letter focused on tactics, not substance. It did not address the merits of the lawsuit, but implicit in his suggestions to Figg was the belief that segregated schools should continue.

When the parties gathered for the May 28 hearing there was a palpable sense in the black community that a new era was in the making. By the time Waring arrived at the courthouse at 9:00 A.M., an hour before the hearing was to begin, so many blacks had jammed the courthouse steps and corridors that the marshal had had to put up rope barriers to clear a passageway for the judges, lawyers, and other court personnel. Waring was deeply moved by the scene. It reminded him of a pilgrimage. "There were battered-looking automobiles parked all around the courthouse," he recalled later. "People showed a great desire [for] a little whiff of freedom. They had never known before that anybody'd stand up for them, and they came there because they believed the United States District Court was a free court, and believed in freedom and liberty."

The day before the trial, Marshall—expecting continued resistance from white school authorities—had told colleagues there would be a lengthy hearing, perhaps two weeks, so that his side could detail the gross inequities in the school system. With the help of sociologists' testimony, he also intended to illustrate the detrimental effects of segregation on the children. But Bob Figg had other ideas. Within minutes of Judge Parker's call to order, Figg rose to address the court. "If the court please," he said, "I wanted to make a statement on behalf of defendants that it is conceded that inequalities in the facilities, opportunities and curricula in the schools of this district do exist. We have found that out from investigating authorities."

Parker told Figg he could talk about this in his opening statement.

"I just thought that if we made the record clear . . . at this time, it would serve perhaps to eliminate the necessity of taking a great deal of testimony," Figg replied.

Marshall's stunned look let Figg know he had scored a hit. Marshall certainly didn't want most of his case ruled moot and his carefully planned witness presentations sabotaged. But Parker decided to let Figg go ahead and give what amounted to an opening statement ahead of the plaintiffs, who by tradition led off.

"The defendants," Figg began, "do not oppose an order finding that inequalities in respect to buildings, equipment, facilities, curricula and other aspects of the schools provided for white and colored children now exist, and enjoining any discrimination in respect thereto."

School officials were urging the court "in its discretion to give them a reasonable time to formulate a plan for ending such inequalities and for bringing about equality of educational opportunity in the schools of the districts." Figg added that he expected the judges to retain jurisdiction over the case so that the court could step in if the defendants failed to comply with "constitutional standards."

As an indication of the state's seriousness, Figg went on, the legislature, at Byrnes's request, had approved a 3 percent sales tax, the first in the state's history, whose proceeds were to be used to finance a bond issue providing up to $75 million in additional educational funds. Another $7.5 million was to be provided for the acquisition of school buses.

Figg's ploy begged the question. It did nothing to address the underlying challenge to a segregated system—indeed, the state's very efforts to upgrade the black schools were evidence of the inequity inherent in segregation. On top of it, Figg was asking the black plaintiffs to wait even longer for redress, even though they already had waited three years.

Though Marshall was obviously surprised by Figg's attempt to narrow the focus of the lawsuit, he had no intention of giving up and accepting the defendants' proposal. Figg's statement had "no bearing on this litigation at this stage," Marshall argued. "I think it is an effort to prevent the plaintiffs in this case from developing their case in the only fashion which will enable us to present a full and complete case." To prove the unconstitutionality of segregation, Marshall insisted, "we must be able to show the inequalities as they actually exist."

Sensing impatience in Judge Parker, Marshall decided against calling some of the witnesses whose testimony was meant to establish what the defendants now admitted. He did call Matthew J. Whitehead, an assistant education professor at Howard University, who had made two surveys of the school district's facilities and who spoke in detail about the condition of the black schools. Their only visual aids were run-down blackboards. There were no lunchrooms, and instead of desks the children had to use cracked tables and broken chairs. The white schools had three indoor toilets each for girls and boys. The black schools had only outdoor facilities. At Scott's Branch School, Whitehead said, there was "one seat for three hundred boys and one seat for three hundred four girls."

(Several months later *News and Courier* reporter Bryan Collier made a trip to Summerton and wrote that Whitehead had been mistaken. Though the bathroom facilities at Scott's Branch were "disreputable," he reported there were four seats each for the girls and boys in addition to four rudimentary urinals "made crudely by cracking 10-inch clay pipes in half and setting pieces upright in a concrete drain.")

Cross-examined by Figg, Whitehead refused to concede that repairs alone could sufficiently improve the black schools.

Marshall now was ready to turn from the tangible problems of segregation to the underlying constitutional question of whether separate could ever be equal. Harold J. McNally, an associate professor of education at Columbia University, told the judges that "White children as well as Negroes are being shortchanged where segregation is practiced. So far as Negroes are concerned," he said, "segregation itself implies a difference, a stigma, and relegates the segregated group more or less to second class."

Dr. Kenneth Clark, an assistant psychology professor from the City College of New York, testified about a "doll test" he had administered to many young children. When some four hundred young children had been asked to choose between brown- and white-skinned dolls, youngsters of both races, he said, had generally preferred the white doll. The same result obtained when he questioned sixteen black Clarendon children. The preference for white dolls was evidence that segregation began instilling attitudes of inferiority at a young age. He had come to the conclusion, Clark said, that "the Negro children of Clarendon County have been subjected to an obviously inferior status and have been definitely harmed, with the kind of injury that will endure as long as the situation endures."

Questioning Clark, Figg sought to trivialize the professor's testimony by pointing out that the doll test had been developed only by Clark and his wife, that no one else was present while Clark questioned the children, and that sixteen Clarendon children provided a very small sample from which to base such a large conclusion. Primarily because he was in an area he knew little about, Figg did not press Clark any further. "You don't cross-examine in a probing way if you're not sure what the answers are going to be," Figg explained later. Besides, "His numbers were small and unimposing. . . . In the courtroom, his manner was quiet and matter-of-fact. Nobody took it seriously."

That was a miscalculation. By the time the Supreme Court finally resolved *Briggs,* Clark's testimony would turn out to be a critical element in ending school segregation.

When it was time for the defense, Figg called E. R. Crow, a former county school superintendent now serving as director of the Educational Finance Commission, the agency created to supervise South Carolina's equalization efforts. Crow explained how the new revenues were going to be allotted. In response to Figg's question about the consequences of "mixed schools," Crow said, "In my opinion it would eliminate schools in most if not all of the counties."

"Would there be community acceptance or the possibility of violent emotional reaction?" Figg asked.

"There would be violent reaction, I am sure."

This piqued Marshall's interest during his cross-examination. "Do you mean to say that the white people of South Carolina would deprive their own children of an education because of this?" Marshall asked.

"I didn't say that," Crow replied. "But I don't believe the legislature would appropriate money, or that communities would levy taxes to support mixed schools."

When Crow insisted that "the elimination of segregation would bring undesirable results," Marshall pressed the witness further.

"As a matter of fact, Mr. Crow, isn't your opinion based on the fact that you have all your life believed in segregation of the races?" Marshall asked. "Isn't that the reason, the real basis of your opinion?"

"That wouldn't be all of it," Crow said.

"Is that a part of it?"

"I suppose that is part of it."

Late in the morning of May 29, only the second day of the hearing, Marshall began his closing arguments. Judge Parker had made clear he wanted to move on. Marshall started by citing the recent Supreme Court decisions, such as *Sweatt,* as evidence that the justices were now ready to hold that even when facilities were equal, segregation itself was detrimental.

"In South Carolina you have admitted inferiority of Negro schools. All your state officials are white. All your school officials are white. It is admitted. That's not just segregation," Marshall asserted. "It's exclusion from the group that runs everything. The Negro child is made to go to an inferior school; he is branded in his own mind as inferior. This sets up a roadblock in his mind which prevents his ever feeling he is equal. You can teach a child the Constitution, anthropology, and citizenship," he went on, "but he knows it isn't true."

Clarendon County "violat[es] the law every day it operates this school system," Marshall continued, unmoved by the defendants' request for more time to correct the problems. "I know of no statute that permits anyone to come into court and ask time to stop doing something which is unlawful . . . ," he said. "There is no relief for the Negro children of Clarendon County except to be permitted to attend existing and superior white schools."

Figg presented a completely different view of the dispute. He noted that the Congress that had adopted the Fourteenth Amendment, with its guarantee of equal protection, had also set up segregated schools in the District of Columbia. What's more, since the amendment's adoption, segregation had become a well-established legal doctrine, "a normal and not an abnormal procedure." Racially mixed schools had not worked during Reconstruction, Figg said, and they would not work now. While progress had been made in race relations, to force race mixing in education now would create "utter confusion." Racial problems, Figg asserted, "are not soluble by force but by the slow process of community experience."

When Parker asked Figg what kind of judicial decree he had in mind, Figg suggested "a reasonable time" to complete the state's improvement program.

Parker replied that he was "not much impressed with that," and Figg tried again.

"I think, if Your Honor please, that the decree should take into account the fact that school buildings cannot be built overnight." If there were problems, the court would retain jurisdiction and could order "immediate and proper relief."

Parker was not impressed with that answer either. He doubted the efficacy of a special court holding on to the case and in effect acting as a "wet nurse" to white authorities as they tried to upgrade the black schools. But the judge's questions, were nonetheless a signal to Waring that his colleague was not swayed by the broader arguments against segregation.

All that was left now was to wait for the decision. Predictions were not difficult. Timmerman, as Waring later reminisced, was "a rigid segregationist," while he himself was "an equally rigid anti-segregationist." And Judge Parker, in Waring's mind, was "an extremely able judge who [knew] the law and follow[ed] the law, but quite unwillingly in the southern country." It was no surprise to him when they disagreed.

As black and white Carolina awaited the three-judge panel's ruling, there was considerable discussion among South Carolina politicians about how to respond to the lawsuit. Although the $75 million bond issue had passed, some politicians tried unsuccessfully to block it, charging in state court that the bond issue should have been approved by voters in a referendum.

Influential leaders, including Byrnes and Senator Brown (Thurmond's old nemesis from the "Barnwell ring"), supported the bond issue. Brown contended that the money allowed the state to improve the schools and maintain segregation. Some politicians were even more outspoken, particularly the young speaker *pro tempore* of the House, Charleston's Ernest F. Hollings, who was just beginning his rise in state politics. The public schools were in "miserable" condition, he said in remarks to a Charleston civic club. Sixty percent of South Carolina's draftees were rejected because of illiteracy, the highest rate in the nation. "We used to be able to say, 'Thank God for Mississippi,' " he said, "but we can't say that anymore."

In Charleston County alone, he continued, there were sixty-five one- or two-room schools with no toilets and no running water. In nearby Johns Island he had seen a single-room school that tried to accommodate two classes of forty-three and forty-seven children—all taught by one teacher. "There were three little colored children in every desk, and on the walls were the U.S. and South Carolina Constitutions guaranteeing every child, white or black, equal chance. The name of that school was Promised Land. I don't think you are proud of things like that," Hollings said. "I know I am not."

If it was now apparent that something had to be done about the black schools, that something was equalization, not desegregation. The 2–1 decision handed down June 23 reflected prevailing sentiments and Judge Waring's pretrial analysis. Judge Parker wrote the majority opinion for himself and Judge Timmerman, ruling that segregation itself was not a denial of the Fourteenth Amendment's equal protection guarantees and denying the plaintiffs' request for an order requiring the defendants to admit blacks to the white schools. "We think," wrote Parker, "that segregation of the races in public schools, so long as equality of rights is preserved, is a matter of legislative policy for the several states, with which the federal courts are powerless to interfere."

Amplifying on this theme, Parker said it was "universally held: that each state shall determine for itself, subject to the observance of the fundamental rights and liberties guaranteed by the federal Constitution, how it shall exercise the police power, i.e. the power to legislate with respect to the safety, morals, health and general welfare. And in no field is this right of the several states more clearly recognized than in that of public education."

With approval, he cited *Plessy,* noting that it was "equally well settled that there is no denial of equal protection of the laws in segregating children in the schools for purposes of education, if the children of the different races are given equal facilities and opportunities." The recent Supreme Court cases that Marshall had cited did not change things because the courts, "although urged to overrule *Plessy v. Ferguson,* expressly refused to do so. . . . The other decisions were similar."

Parker's decree, published in full in *The News and Courier,* did, however, declare that the schools for "colored pupils are not substantially equal to those afforded for white pupils," and that this violated the Fourteenth Amendment. The defendants were ordered to "proceed at once" to make the schools equal and were also ordered to report to the court within six months "as to the action taken by them to carry out this order."

In a stinging dissent, Waring charged that the defendants, by their admission of inequalities in Clarendon, "have endeavored to induce this Court to avoid the primary purpose of the suit." If a case of this magnitude can be turned aside "by the mere device of admission that some buildings, blackboards, lighting fixtures and toilet facilities are unequal but that they may be remedied by the spending of a few dollars," Waring wrote, "then indeed people in the plight in which these plaintiffs are have no adequate remedy or forum in which to air their wrongs." Calling separate but equal a "false doctrine" and "patter," he wrote that "it is the duty of the Court to meet these issues simply and factually and without fear, sophistry and evasion." If the court was going to "straddle or avoid this issue" by adopting the remedy suggested by the defendants, "then I want no part of it."

What followed was a discussion of the history of the Fourteenth Amendment, a brief discourse on the "sophistry and prejudice" that attend efforts to distinguish one race from another—"Who is to decide what is the test?" Waring asked—and an indictment of the existing system. "We see the results of all this warped thinking in the . . . frightened attitude of so many of the Negroes in the southern states; and in the sadistic insistence of the 'white supremacists' in insisting that their will must be imposed irrespective of rights of other citizens."

Waring maintained that it was particularly important to seek to eradicate prejudice at an early age. "There is absolutely no reasonable explanation for racial prejudice. It is all caused by unreasoning emotional reactions and these are gained in early childhood. Let the little child's mind be poisoned by prejudice of this kind and it is practically impossible to ever remove these impressions. . . . If segregation is wrong then the place to stop it is in the first grade and not in graduate colleges."

Waring said it was apparent from expert testimony, "as it should be to any thoughtful person, irrespective of having such expert testimony, that segregation in education can never produce equality and that it is an evil that must be eradicated. This case presents the matter clearly for adjudication," and it was his conclusion "that the system of segregation in education adopted and practiced in the state of South Carolina must go and must go now.

"Segregation is per se inequality."

Lest anyone doubt the role Elizabeth Waring played in her husband's evolution, the judge dedicated one copy of the dissent to her: "To my precious Elizabeth. This could not have been done without her love and encouragement and support."

The outcome of the case was not really a surprise to either

side. From the Clarendon parents' perspective, the one advantage of the three-judge panel was that it permitted a direct appeal to the Supreme Court. It was an avenue the NAACP said it intended to take, making *Briggs v. Elliott* a building block in the piece-by-piece strategy of forcing the high court to face the entire segregation issue.

Briggs was to be Judge Waring's last major case. By January 26, 1952, he had served ten years and, given his age, was eligible for retirement at full salary. He sent letters to President Truman and Judge Parker informing them of his intention to retire on February 15. He also told Judge Parker, who had scheduled another hearing on *Briggs* for February 29, that he would no longer serve on the panel. He explained that because the issues at the hearing "are entirely under the separate but equal theory and seem to be entirely irrelevant to the basis of the case, which is the matter of whether Racial Segregation is Constitutional, I would not be willing to accept a designation to sit with you in the case or take any part in it." Parker accepted Waring's decision and assigned another judge to the panel.

On February 18, 1952, Waties and Elizabeth Waring left by train for New York "with no regrets whatever." "I have been decried and despised and hated," he told one reporter. "But I shall be satisfied if it can be said of me, as it was said of Grover Cleveland: 'We love him for the enemies he made.' "

Waring was bowing out of South Carolina public life for good. The hiatus that had begun for Thurmond thirteen months earlier would be only a temporary one. But, like his time overseas during World War II, its timing was fortuitous; he was nowhere near the Clarendon lawsuit, personally or politically. His record was there implicitly—Clarendon schools had not improved markedly during his administration. But now out of office, he could no longer be made to answer when the state was called to account.

As he turned over state affairs to Byrnes in January 1951, Thurmond's four years in office were reviewed in the white press, where the assessments were generally positive. Typical was William Workman's end-of-the-administration wrap-up in *The News and Courier.* Thurmond "has carried out most of his promises to the people of South Carolina," Workman said. Chief among them was a promise to serve out his full four-year term—something not every governor, including Johnston, had done. He cited election-law reform Thurmond had pushed through the legislature, noting that it had almost been killed by a split in the General Assembly between supporters of Thurmond and Johnston. And he listed the improved state health facilities and better teachers' salaries, which were "at an all-time high."

When Thurmond leaves the governor's mansion, Workman concluded, "he also leaves a reputation for hard work, boundless energy, unlimited ambition and complete personal honesty. He also leaves South Carolina a better state government than he found four years ago."

Similar praise came from *The State,* which credited Thurmond with "four years of tireless service." Among his achievements, the paper said, was "effective work in bringing new industries to South Carolina. . . ."

The view among black leaders was less rosy, as McCray's columns in *The Lighthouse and Informer* had shown over the years. Thurmond might have made some improvements, but from the black perspective they were too few and tinged with suspicion because of the 1948 presidential campaign and the vituperative 1950 Senate contest.

There had been much speculation about what Thurmond would do when he left Columbia. After weighing various options, he decided to move to Aiken—about fifteen miles from Edgefield—to practice law with Charles Simons and his partner, Dorsey Lybrand. Simons, a younger man Thurmond had known for more than a decade, had been a political ally during his years as governor and had managed his Senate primary campaign in Aiken County.

One reason for choosing Aiken was the atomic reactor the government had just announced it would build at the nearby Savannah River. Thurmond knew that the land condemnations to build the plant, coupled with the larger work force that would soon be present, meant a large client base for any lawyer willing to work hard.

The Aiken lawyers were delighted to have the governor join them. Lybrand and Simons quickly became Thurmond, Lybrand and Simons in deference to the new, highly visible partner, and Thurmond was given the prized corner office of their unimposing second-floor suite above a shop on one of Aiken's main streets.

To help the Thurmonds get started in their private life, friends of the couple from around the state bought them a new Cadillac sedan and gave them five hundred dollars in cash to help furnish their new home. The presentation was made by Leon Moore, former mayor of Spartanburg, who correctly suggested to the one hundred guests gathered at the mansion that Thurmond's political career probably was not over. "None of us figures we are buying oats for a dead horse," he said.

The governor's practice of law was like his approach to most other things—long on energy, determination, and instinct and short on the detail work. The bombast of his stump speeches carried over into the courtroom. His law partners were more attuned to the niceties of legal argument, but Thurmond thought they were a good mix. He liked to joke that he "taught Charlie Simons how to make money." There was probably some truth to Thurmond's jovial boast. The story in Aiken was that before the governor started to practice there, lawyers representing families in wrongful-death cases would usually seek fifty thousand to seventy-five thousand dollars in damages. "When Strom came to town," Simons later recalled, "the asking price went sky-high."

One of Thurmond's proudest achievements was getting a federally chartered savings and loan association for Aiken. Simons did the complicated legal work. Thurmond did the legwork, using his well-known personal touch to convince Aiken businessmen to ante up seventy-five thousand dollars in promised deposits the government required—this in a week's time shortly after he arrived.

With one exception, Thurmond stayed away from criminal work, but that exception was a dramatic murder case, which he accepted because he knew the defendant. Margie Prescott Kennedy, who had grown up in Edgefield, had been charged with murdering her husband, former Augusta public safety commissioner John B. Kennedy. On June 30, 1951, she had fired five bullets into him during an unusually bitter argument. Some of the shots were fired into Kennedy's back as the wounded man fled the house.

Thurmond, with the help of two Augusta lawyers he had retained, portrayed Kennedy during the trial as a longtime wife-beater who had subjected his wife to "physical brutality." When she testified, Mrs. Kennedy tearfully called her life "years of hell." The medical testimony was nothing short of incredible. A doctor who had attended the wounded man at the hospital until he died testified that Kennedy had died from "natural causes," not the multiple gunshots. Kennedy had had heart trouble, was diabetic, and had other serious ailments. "He could only have been expected to live from one to two years under his existing physical condition," the doctor explained. "The bullets were just the straw that broke the camel's back."

After only four and a half hours of deliberation, the jury—all of them men—found Mrs. Kennedy not guilty. The next day, October 18, 1951, papers in Georgia and South Carolina carried front-page pictures of a weeping Margie Kennedy embracing her smiling attorney, Strom Thurmond.

But while Thurmond's attention was now directed toward his law practice, politicians hadn't stopped paying attention to him. Starting with the Republican nominating convention the following July, he came under pressure from South Carolinians supporting General Eisenhower, the Republican presidential nominee, to work publicly on his behalf as other Democrats, including Byrnes, were doing. Thurmond resisted the many entreaties, not explaining why until a few days before the election. "I have not publicly spoken out in the campaign," he wrote Byrnes, "because . . . the forces opposing General Eisenhower would try to use my name in publicity intended to hurt him in certain sections of the North." He didn't make public his intention to vote for Eisenhower until November 2, two days before the election. *The News and Courier* deemed it worthy of a front-page story.

Within a year, as the 1954 elections drew nearer, there was renewed speculation about the former governor's political career. Two days apart, separate newspaper articles speculated on his plans. "The $64 question in South Carolina political circles at the moment is this: What will Strom Thurmond do in 1954?" wrote William Workman, this time for *The Augusta Chronicle* October 30, 1953. Would he run for the U.S. Senate? Would he run for governor? Or would he run for anything at all? Thurmond was "keeping his plans to himself at this stage of the game," Workman reported, "but his silence is stimulating rather than suppressing the political speculation surrounding his name." Worthy of note was that in recent months he had stepped up his activities in the U.S. Army Reserve and had been making speeches around the South about national defense.

On November 1, *The Atlanta Constitution* carried a story from Columbia headlined STROM THURMOND IS ENIGMA IN S.C. AS

POLITICAL POT BOILS. The reporter, S. I. Latimer, Jr., said talk of a Senate race was generally discounted in favor of speculation that Thurmond would either again seek the governorship or simply stay put in Aiken making money. "On the other hand," Latimer noted, "Thurmond is all over the state attending meetings and shaking hands," a sure sign of keeping his options open.

No decisions had to be made at this early date, but 1954 promised to be an interesting year for other reasons as well. *Briggs v. Elliott,* along with the four other cases challenging segregation, was still before the Supreme Court. On June 9, 1953, the court had deferred decisions until the next year, asking the parties to submit new briefs and reargue the cases in December. The lead case would be the one from Kansas, *Brown v. Board of Education.* A ruling was expected by the middle of 1954. From Clarendon County east to Charleston and west to Columbia, black and white Carolina had to wait and wonder about what lay ahead in the new year.

9. THE YEAR OF PRECEDENTS

1954

ONE SPRING DAY in 1954, Harry Dent, Thurmond's former aide and now a young reporter in Washington, D.C., made his usual call on Burnet Maybank, South Carolina's senior senator, to chat about home-state matters. Maybank was up for reelection in November and was a particularly good source this year for the pulsebeat in South Carolina. But during the visit the senator moved the conversation away from political gossip to the subject on everybody's mind back home, the five desegregation cases that were before the Supreme Court.

"You know," Maybank told Dent, "whenever that decision comes down, everything in the South is going to change."

Technically, the cases from South Carolina, Kansas, Virginia, Delaware, and the District of Columbia were about black and white children going to school together. But they were also a challenge to the way white and black southerners of all ages had lived together for sixty years. If the Supreme Court could force integrated schools, then all sorts of other barriers would topple that separated blacks from whites in their daily lives and that kept the badge of inferiority pinned to black America.

For the last ten years, southern politicians had done their part in the fight for "custom and tradition," stifling every piece of legislation designed to bring an end to segregation. But now the NAACP had gone to court, seeking from the judicial branch what it had not been able to win in the political arena. With the exception of Judge Waring, few of the judges in the lower federal courts presented problems for segregationists; they were products of the same white communities under challenge by the NAACP. But the justices in Washington, D.C., even some of the southerners, were something else again. Segregation had not been outlawed in the higher education cases they had already decided, but anyone who paid attention to the decisions of the previous five years knew deep down that separate but equal was close to extinction.

Neither Burnet Maybank nor anyone else could predict exactly what the Supreme Court was going to say; only that life back home would never be the same again. Nor did the senator have any way of knowing that he would not be on hand to witness the wrenching evolution. Maybank's sudden heart attack on the first of September would catch South Carolina by surprise. It would also have a direct bearing on Thurmond's career.

For the first half-century of his life, South Carolina was Thurmond's universe. But in 1954, two separate events would make Washington, D.C., the focal point of his political life. The Supreme Court's May 17 declaration that segregation in education was unconstitutional would topple one of the pillars that had supported white supremacy and would set in motion a decade of change that would remake Thurmond's world. Maybank's death and the resulting machinations of Democratic Party officials created a political opportunity that would bring Thurmond back into public life for good and propel his career to the nation's capital, where he would hold office for more than thirty-five years.

That Thurmond could turn the state party's missteps into an uphill victory for a Senate seat was further proof of his ambition and his ability to seize the moment. His vanquished opponent would be state senator Edgar Brown, the leader of the "Barnwell ring," but this time he would be more than the whipping boy of Thurmond's 1946 gubernatorial race; he was a real-life candidate. When Thurmond beat the venerable legislator, he became the first person ever to win election to the Senate by a write-in vote.

While South Carolina would remain the underlying focus of his attention—as the home state is for any congressional officeholder—from now on Thurmond would be a national politician. In Washington, he would be at a safe distance from the tumultuous local reaction to the desegregation ruling, and later he would be one step removed from the everyday decisions of mayors, police chiefs, sheriffs, and governors that were so controversial a part of the civil rights movement. But from the Senate floor he would help fuel white resistance at home to black America's escalating push for equal rights. For more than a decade after he arrived in the Senate, the nine men who worked literally across the street from the Capitol would be fodder for Thurmond's rhetorical cannon.

For the first half of 1954, the ferment over the desegregation lawsuits overshadowed electoral politics in the South. Legislators were busy developing tactics for responding should the high court decision go against them. With Governor Byrnes's encouragement, three years earlier South Carolina had led the region in devising a strategy that might forestall integrated schools. In April of 1951, a month before the Clarendon case was argued, the General Assembly had authorized a committee to research alternatives to public schools if the justices banned segregation.

In October of 1951, after the NAACP had appealed *Briggs v. Elliott* to the Supreme Court, Byrnes announced another important decision. South Carolina's side in the Clarendon case would be argued at the high court by John W. Davis, "one of the ablest constitutional lawyers in the nation," Byrnes said. It was a view shared by all who had seen the successful Wall Street lawyer, a former solicitor general, argue before the justices.

Three months later Governor Byrnes took one more step toward preserving "custom and tradition." In his January 1952 address to the legislature, he urged members to repeal the provision in the state constitution requiring South Carolina to provide "a liberal system of free public schools" for all children between the ages of six and twenty-one. The General Assembly subsequently agreed to submit the issue to state voters, and in the November election, repeal was approved by a two-to-one margin.

As the political maneuvering was going on, there were continuing legal developments in the Clarendon case. State officials, seeking to comply with Judge Parker's ruling, had filed two reports with the court showing how much the black schools had been improved. The first, filed December 21, 1951, did show demonstrable progress. Although the three-judge panel had retained jurisdiction over the case, Judge Parker declined to issue any final ruling on whether the state was now in compliance. Instead, he sent the report on to the Supreme Court to be part of the NAACP appeal. In a short opinion a few weeks later, the high court sent the case right back to South Carolina, telling Parker to continue with the case and give the justices "the benefit of the views of the District Court upon the additional facts. . . ."

Two justices, Hugo Black, the former Alabama senator who, like Waring, was turning away from "custom and tradition," and William O. Douglas, dissented. Supporting the NAACP's broader challenge to segregation, they called the progress report "wholly irrelevant to the constitutional questions presented by the appeal to this court."

On March 3, 1952, the state submitted another report to Parker's three-judge court, which now included Armistead M. Dobie of Virginia instead of the retired Waties Waring. Ten days later Judge Parker wrote that South Carolina's submissions "show beyond question that defendants have proceeded promptly and in good faith" to comply with the original ruling. Parker noted that since the statewide building program had begun, South Carolina had spent over $5.5 million for black school construction, while less than $2 million had been spent for white schools.

Brushing aside the NAACP's challenge to segregation, Parker said the court believed the law was valid and that "the inequality suffered by the plaintiffs results, not from the law, but from the way it has been administered. . . ."

The *Briggs* case was still pending at the Supreme Court, however, along with the three other state desegregation cases and the one from the District of Columbia. In the fall of 1953 there was a pivotal development, though it was completely divorced from legal research and brief writing. On September 8, sixty-three-year-old Chief Justice Fred Vinson died of a heart attack in his Washington, D.C., hotel room. The chief had hardly been buried before rumors circulated about a successor. On September 30, 1953, President Eisenhower ended the speculation by nominating Governor Earl Warren of California. He asked him to be on the job when the new term started October 5 even though he would not be formally confirmed by the Senate until March 1, 1954. Warren was not a particularly popular selection. New York *Daily News* columnist John O'Donnell wrote bluntly that "a better Chief Justice could be found among a score of top-flight jurists. After all, the charming, competent Governor—a truly honest and upright man—never sat on a bench in his life, not even for five minutes in a police court."

Warren, who had been Thomas E. Dewey's running mate in 1948, had served for thirteen years as the prosecutor in Alameda County, the third-largest county in California. Later he became the state attorney general and then governor in 1942. In Californians' view, he performed so admirably in that job that in 1946, Republicans *and* Democrats nominated him for reelection.

The one dark spot on Warren's career was his support for the forced relocation of Japanese Americans after Pearl Harbor. In provocative remarks to a gathering of governors in 1943, Warren had said, "If the Japs are released, no one will be able to tell a saboteur from any other Jap. . . . We don't want to have a second Pearl Harbor in California." Despite his later misgivings about the entire process, Warren did not publicly express his regret over the relocation until thirty-four years later, in his autobiography published posthumously in 1977.

Black America, on the other hand, had at least one piece of information about Warren to prompt optimism. In the spring of 1952, as part of its coverage before the Republican convention, the Pittsburgh *Courier,* a newspaper for the city's black community, had asked potential candidates their views on civil rights. Warren was quoted as stating, "I am for a sweeping civil rights program, beginning with a fair employment practices act. . . . I insist upon one law for all men." The nation should not fear the word "welfare," he said, adding that "We must not shrink from the known needs of social progress."

The NAACP believed its litigation strategy had given the court a chance to make "social progress." Although the cases before the court shared a common issue—the legality of segregation—each provided a different factual setting to illustrate the dimensions of discrimination.

The Kansas case, which now led the docket, had been filed February 21, 1951—just after the Clarendon lawsuit—when a group of blacks decided that the only way to shake up the white Topeka educational establishment was to take the school system to court. The case was known as *Brown v. Board of Education of Topeka,* named for Oliver Brown, who had worked several years as a welder in the Santa Fe Railroad's shops and had his union membership as protection against possible economic reprisals from the white community.

The NAACP suit was an outgrowth of activity that had begun in the late 1940s and had reached a critical point in the fall of 1950, when Topeka's white education leaders refused to listen to the requests of black parents to end the separate school systems.

On June 25 and June 26, four months after the suit was filed, the *Brown* case was heard in Topeka. On August 3, Judge Walter Huxman of the U.S. Court of Appeals for the Tenth Circuit delivered the opinion for himself and his two district court colleagues—Arthur J. Mellott and Delmas C. Hill—all of them rock-solid, respected white Kansans.

The court found "no willful, intentional or substantial discrimination" existing in the Topeka public schools. But the larger question of whether segregation itself constituted inequality was another matter, governed principally by the *Plessy* decision and one that followed it, *Gong Lum v. Rice,* a case that had relied on *Plessy* to uphold Mississippi's decision to require a Chinese child to attend a school for blacks. The judges in Topeka now had to determine whether *Plessy*'s sanction of separate but equal had been completely eroded by the Supreme Court's 1950 decisions involving the law schools at the University of Oklahoma and the University of Texas—the *McLaurin* and *Sweatt* decisions.

Huxman said the high court had made clear it was restricting itself to equal protection claims concerning segregated graduate schools. As a result, Huxman and his colleagues believed that *Plessy* and *Lum* "have not been overruled and that they presently are authority for the maintenance of a segregated school system in the lower grades."

One of the nine Findings of Fact attached to the opinion, however, provided a ray of hope for the losing side. Drawing on the testimony of social scientists, the judges said: "Segregation of white and colored children in public schools has a detrimental effect upon the colored children. The impact is greater when it has the sanction of law; for the policy of separating the races is usually interpreted as denoting the inferiority of the Negro group. A sense of inferiority affects the motivation of a child to learn." Without affecting the outcome of the case, the finding did conclude that "Segregation with the sanction of law therefore has a tendency to retard the educational and mental development of Negro children and to deprive them of some of the benefits they would receive in a racially integrated school system."

A few days after the decision, one of the NAACP lawyers correctly observed that although Judge Huxman's opinion had gone against the black plaintiffs, the decision "puts the Supreme Court on the spot, and it seems to me that it was purposely written with that end in view."

More than a decade later, Huxman would acknowledge as much, admitting that "we weren't in sympathy with the decision we rendered. If it weren't for *Plessy v. Ferguson* we surely would have found the [Kansas segregation] law unconstitutional. But there was no way around it—the Supreme Court had to overrule itself."

The NAACP was trying to give the justices ample opportunity to do so. The next challenge came in the East, in Delaware, where all the public schools, even in Wilmington, the state's most moderate city, were segregated. No black nurses worked in white hospitals; no black clerks worked in banks or retail stores. Restaurants, movie theaters, and hotels were strictly segregated. The state college for blacks was not nationally accredited, and no black had been admitted to practice law in the state until 1929, eighty-five years after the first black had been admitted to practice law in Maine. The Delaware lawyer was Louis Lorenzo Redding. He had graduated from Brown University, won a scholarship to Harvard Law School, and when he was admitted to the Delaware bar in 1929, the Wilmington newspapers took note of the fact.

Twenty-two years later, Redding and the NAACP went to court with two cases that challenged segregation in Delaware's public schools. The first came from Claymont, a suburb about nine miles north of Wilmington, where black children were barred from attending the combination grade school and high school, which sat on a pretty fourteen-acre landscaped site. Instead, they had to take a city bus to downtown Wilmington to Howard High School, located in the midst of factories, warehouses, and worn-down tenements. The trip was at least fifty minutes each way. The pupil-teacher ratio at Howard was one-third higher than at the white Claymont school, and the white school offered a variety of courses and extracurricular activities the black school did not. Ethel Belton and seven other black parents in Claymont agreed to take their dissatisfactions to court.

The other case came from Hockessin, a small rural town west of Wilmington near the Pennsylvania state line. While white students were bused to their neat, well-appointed school, black students had no public transportation to their one-room schoolhouse. It was Sarah Bulah, the mother of young Shirley, who finally decided to do something about the inequity. After writing state officials, including the governor, she received a reply explaining that "we have no transportation facilities" for Shirley Bulah's school. Mrs. Bulah went to see Louis Redding, but he told her he would help only if she would challenge the entire segregated system instead of simply trying to get transportation to the black school. She and her husband agreed.

The two cases were filed first in federal court, but the Delaware attorney general argued that because it was a state law that governed segregation, the lawsuits ought to be filed in state court. Chancery Judge Collins Jacques Seitz, who had already ordered the state university to desegregate, presided over the cases, *Belton v. Gebhart* from Claymont, and *Bulah v. Gebhart* from Hockessin, named for Ethel Belton and Sarah Bulah. (Francis B. Gebhart was the first defendant alphabetically on the state board of education.)

The cases were heard over four days in October 1951. Almost five months later, on April 1, 1952, Seitz found that there were continuing violations of the separate-but-equal doctrine. While he refused to rule that segregation was per se illegal, citing *Plessy* and *Lum,* Seitz did say that when a plaintiff had shown such violations, "he is entitled to have made available to him the state facilities which have been shown to be superior." He ordered the black students admitted to the white schools, the first time a segregated white school was required to admit black children. Thurgood Marshall told the press afterward, "This is the first real victory in our campaign to destroy segregation of American pupils in elementary and high schools."

Seitz's decision was affirmed by the Delaware Supreme Court August 28, 1952.

The Seitz ruling was an encouraging moment that helped ease the disappointment coming from Virginia. Between the time the Delaware cases were first argued and Seitz's April 1952 decision, the fourth desegregation case had been argued and decided unfavorably.

White children in Prince Edward County, a rural area about

sixty miles west of Richmond, had not gotten a real high school until the 1920s, when one was built in the county seat of Farmville. Black children did not get theirs until 1939, built with federal funds from the Public Works Administration and an allocation from a state loan pool known as the State Literary Fund. Their school was inadequate almost before it opened. Built to accommodate 180 students, 167 enrolled on its first day. The next year the school exceeded its capacity when 219 students entered. There was no gymnasium, locker rooms, cafeteria, auditorium with fixed seats, or infirmary—all things found in the white high school—and black teachers were paid substantially less than those at the white school. The one small sign of progress was the bus service the county began to provide in the early forties for black children who lived in outlying areas.

By 1947, when the high school was at twice its capacity, officials put up three temporary buildings that provided a cheap but problematic solution. The buildings were made of wood and covered with tar paper and leaked regularly. With only stoves for heat, those who sat close to them in the winter got too hot, while those far away had to wear their overcoats. The buildings looked like oversized chicken coops and quickly became known as "the shacks."

State law allowed the shacks to be used for no more than five years, giving school authorities sufficient time to consider a larger, more complete building program and a bond issue to finance it. But black parents who were dissatisfied with the shacks wanted more immediate relief. They went regularly before the white school board in 1950 and 1951 to get a firm commitment for a new black high school, but they always came away empty-handed, told that the time was not ripe for a bond issue.

Finally, on April 23, 1951, the students took matters into their own hands, declaring a strike to protest their inadequate facilities. They wrote the NAACP for help, and a few days into the protest, two NAACP lawyers arrived in Farmville for consultations. When it became clear that the students would not be dissuaded, the two lawyers, Oliver Hill and Spottswood Robinson, told them the NAACP could not help them unless they agreed to sue for an end to segregation. Furthermore, the lawyers said, there had to be support from the adult black population.

At a mass meeting May 3 in a Prince Edward church, the older generation of blacks agreed to the desegregation plan. On May 23,

1951, one month after the students had started their strike, Robinson filed a lawsuit in federal court in Richmond on behalf of 117 students who asked that Virginia's law requiring segregated schools be struck down. The first plaintiff listed was fourteen-year-old ninth-grader Dorothy E. Davis, the daughter of a Prince Edward farmer. The case became known as *Davis v. County School Board of Prince Edward County.*

The lawsuit was not heard in Richmond until February 25, 1952, nine months after it had been filed. This time the three-judge panel was headed by Armistead Dobie, Waring's replacement in the Clarendon case. His colleagues were two native Virginians who had had long careers in government practice before going on the bench, Sterling Hutcheson and Albert Vickers Bryan.

One week after the trial the judges ruled unanimously that segregation in Virginia was based "neither upon prejudice nor caprice nor upon any other measureless foundation" but had "for generations been a part of the mores of her people. To have separate schools has been their use and wont."

Maintaining separate school systems was not "social despotism," Judge Bryan wrote for the court. In fact, testimony suggested that "whatever its demerits in theory, in practice it has begotten greater opportunities for the Negro. . . . We have found no hurt or harm to either race." Instead of desegregation, the tribunal ordered Prince Edward to pursue "with due diligence and dispatch" the equalization of facilities for black students.

In the state that had been the capital of the Confederacy, the NAACP's setback, however disappointing, was hardly surprising.

The organization had already generated one other challenge to segregation, this one involving the federal law governing Washington, D.C., as segregated a community as any in the country. Although blacks in the nation's capital did better than most of their southern counterparts—the average black family in the district earned one-third more than the average for families, black *and* white, in South Carolina—the problems in the city were nonetheless enormous. Housing was in short supply, and the capital's ghetto was as bad as any slum in the United States, worse than most. Schools were old and overcrowded, many of them on double and triple sessions.

Early in 1951, about the time the Clarendon case was reaching federal court, James Nabrit, Jr., another of the NAACP's legal team, had gone into federal court on behalf of twelve-year-old

Spottswood Thomas Bolling, Jr., to challenge segregation in the Washington schools. The defendant was C. Melvin Sharpe, the president of the city's board of education.

Although facilities for black students were obviously inferior to those for whites, that fact was not an issue. Instead, Nabrit argued that the District of Columbia had the burden of showing any reasonable basis for, or public purpose in, racial restrictions in school admission.

In April 1951, a month before the Clarendon trial and the filing of the Virginia suit, U.S. District Judge Walter Bastian dismissed the case. He agreed with the school board that Nabrit had not raised a claim entitling him to any relief. No claim of unequal facilities had been raised, Bastian said, and the challenge to the constitutionality of segregation had been rejected in other cases. Nothing, therefore, was left in the lawsuit.

Taken together, the five cases gave the Supreme Court five different ways to look at segregation and its impact on students. The four state cases would eventually be consolidated for one Supreme Court decision. The fifth, from the District of Columbia, would be handled separately because it involved the federal government, not a state, but the issue of segregation was the same. All five presented Earl Warren with an enormous challenge in his opening months on the bench. He never wavered, though, in what he believed was the proper outcome. "I don't remember having any great doubts about which way it should go," he would recall twenty years after the fact. "It seemed to me a comparatively simple case. Just look at the various decisions that had been eroding *Plessy* for so many years. . . . On the merits, the natural, the logical and practically the only way the case could be decided was clear. The question was *how* the decision was to be reached."

As the court opened Monday, May 17, there was no way to know which decisions would be announced that day. Even most of the justices' law clerks were in the dark. Talk about the segregation lawsuits had been kept to a minimum for fear that discussions might become public. David Vann, a young lawyer from Alabama who was Black's clerk and lived at the justice's home in Alexandria, Virginia, knew that Warren's clerks had visited Black the previous weekend, but the justice hadn't indicated that there was anything significant about the meeting.

As he drove Black to court for the midday session, nothing in their conversation gave Vann a clue about what was to happen.

Shortly before noon, Vann poked his head into Black's office and asked if there was anything the justice needed; the clerk hadn't planned on accompanying him to the courtroom. Black waved him off, so Vann went down the hall to ask E. Barrett Prettyman, Jr., Justice Robert Jackson's clerk, to join him for lunch.

"I can't," Prettyman said. "My judge is here."

Now Vann knew something was up. Seven weeks earlier Jackson had suffered a heart attack and had been in the hospital ever since. When Vann looked in the office, he could see the justice being helped with his robe.

"I immediately said to myself, 'They're going to hand down the school case or they wouldn't bring him from the hospital,' " Vann later recalled.

Vann went down to the law clerk's dining room to round up his colleagues, but Justice Stanley Reed's clerk didn't believe him. His boss hadn't said anything, and Reed's wife, who was always on hand for important decisions, wasn't there.

But Vann had been right. Justice Tom Clark provided confirmation when he told the clerks a few minutes later, "I think you boys ought to be in the courtroom today."

The May 17 session began as all others had, with the routine admission of lawyers to the Supreme Court bar. After that, the justices in ascending order of seniority read the opinions they had to deliver. First Justice Clark read an antitrust opinion; then Douglas read a decision about the federal government's ability to collect an indemnity from an employee found guilty of negligence and another about the right of a bakery workers' union to picket retail stores.

Finally Warren declared, "I have for announcement the judgment and opinion of the court in No. 1—*Oliver Brown et al. v. Board of Education of Topeka.*"

The chief justice's opening gave no hint of what the court had decided. He first explained that the four state cases had been considered together because, although they were based on "different facts and different local conditions," a "common legal question" united them. That question was whether "minors of the Negro race" were denied the equal protection of the laws when barred from public schools under the "so-called 'separate-but-equal' doctrine announced by this court in *Plessy v. Ferguson.*"

The history of the Fourteenth Amendment, while casting some light on the issue of equal protection, was "not enough to resolve the problem with which we are faced," Warren said. At the time the amendment was written, "Education of Negroes was almost nonexistent, and practically all of the race was illiterate. In fact," the chief justice said, "any education of Negroes was forbidden by law." It was therefore not surprising that "there should be so little in the history of the Fourteenth Amendment relating to its intended effect on public education."

Warren then reviewed the cases that already had been decided under the amendment, including *Plessy* and the recent higher-education cases that had chipped away at the 1896 ruling. The question squarely facing the court now, he said, was whether *Plessy* was applicable to public education. And with black and white schools being "equalized insofar as the quality of black school buildings, curricula, teachers' pay and other 'tangible' factors," Warren said, no decision could turn only upon a consideration of these "tangibles." "We must look instead to the effect of segregation on public education.

"In approaching this problem, we cannot turn the clock back to 1868 when the Amendment was adopted, or even to 1896 when *Plessy v. Ferguson* was written. We must consider public education in the light of its full development and its present place in American life throughout the nation," Warren went on. "Today education is perhaps the most important function of state and local governments. . . . Today it is a principal instrument in awakening the child to cultural values, in preparing him for later professional training, and in helping him to adjust normally to his environment."

The crucial question, then, was this: "Does segregation of children in public schools solely on the basis of race, even though the physical facilities and other 'tangible' factors may be equal, deprive the children of the minority group of equal educational opportunities?

"We believe that it does."

Nearly two-thirds of the way through the decision, the chief justice had finally shown which way the court had gone. The question remaining was the size of the majority.

Recalling again the higher-education cases—*Sweatt v. Texas* and *McLaurin v. Board of Oklahoma State Regents*—Warren said that the considerations for equal education at the graduate level "apply with added force to children in grade and high schools. To separate them from others of similar age and qualifications solely because of their race generates a feeling of inferiority as to their status in the community that may affect their hearts and minds in a way unlikely ever to be undone." And he cited the Finding of Fact in the Kansas case that segregation had an even more severe impact "when it has the sanction of law; for the policy of separating the races is usually interpreted as denoting the inferiority of the Negro group."

Because this was directly contrary to the *Plessy* decision, Warren had to address the conflict. "Whatever may have been the extent of psychological knowledge at the time of *Plessy v. Ferguson,* this finding is amply supported by modern authority. Any language in *Plessy v. Ferguson* contrary to this finding is rejected."

As Vann listened to Warren read the rest of the decision, he tried to figure out who would dissent, but he couldn't read anything in the justices' faces.

"We conclude unanimously," the chief justice continued, departing from his prepared text, "that in the field of public education the doctrine of 'separate but equal' has no place. Separate educational facilities are inherently unequal. Therefore, we hold that the plaintiffs and others similarly situated for whom the actions have been brought are, by reason of the segregation complained of, deprived of the equal protection of the laws guaranteed by the Fourteenth Amendment."

Later in the day, when Vann saw the chief justice in the hallway, the clerk said, "You changed that opinion when you read it today."

"What do you mean?" asked a puzzled Warren.

"You added the word 'unanimously,' " Vann replied.

"I thought it was getting pretty sticky in there," the chief justice explained, alluding to the tension in the courtroom over the unanswered question.

From the beginning, Warren had seen the importance of avoiding a divided court. That he was able to declare a unanimous decision was a tribute to the political skills he had brought to his judicial duties. The last justice to fall into line was Stanley Reed of Kentucky, who was resistant to declaring an end to the custom and tradition that had been a staple of his life. Reed's law clerk, George Mickum, was present at one of Warren's final discussions with Reed and recalled that the chief told his colleague, "Stan, you're all by yourself in this now. You've got to decide whether it's really the best thing for the country."

In his memoirs published twenty-three years later, Warren said the "real credit for achieving unanimity, in my opinion, should go to the three justices who were born and reared in that part of the nation where segregation was a way of life and where everyone knew the greatest emotional opposition to the decision would be forthcoming." He cited Black of Alabama, Clark of Texas, and Reed of Kentucky. "The others of us, while enthusiastic and fervent in our desire for unanimity, were not in danger of being faced with animosity or harassment in our states because of centuries-old patterns of life."

There was still the matter of what the court would require as a remedy. The justices wanted more time and more information before going further, so they ordered the cases set for reargument on the issue later in the year. Warren's explanation of the process was a deft one. By noting the decision's "wide applicability," he signaled that the justices were not confining themselves to the specifics of the cases before them. By asking for more information and by inviting the state attorneys general to join the federal government in friend-of-the-court briefs, he showed the South that he understood the trauma desegregation would bring and that the court would give the region an opportunity to help shape the decree.

So while the decision was a symbolic landmark of the greatest importance, *Brown v. Board of Education,* by itself, did not admit a single black student to a white school.

Before leaving the courtroom that Monday, the justices also handed down the District of Columbia case, *Bolling v. Sharpe.* "Segregation in public education is not reasonably related to any proper governmental objective," Warren said, "and thus it imposes on Negro children of the District of Columbia a burden that constitutes an arbitrary deprivation of their liberty in violation of the Due Process Clause." If the Constitution prohibits the states from maintaining racially segregated schools, the chief justice concluded, "it would be unthinkable that the same Constitution would impose a lesser duty on the Federal Government."

By 1:20 P.M., less than thirty minutes after he had started, Earl Warren had declared to the country that a united Supreme Court had abolished separate but equal.

In New York City, Judge Waring felt vindicated. Although the justices had not mentioned his dissent in *Briggs v. Elliott,* Warren had come awfully close to "segregation is per se inequality" when he declared that "in the field of public education, the doctrine of 'separate but equal' has no place."

Although southern political leaders were not uniform in their reactions, it was surprising that there was any moderation at all in some of their remarks. In fact, the moderation masked an underlying resistance that would emerge later when the Supreme Court and the black community showed they were not to be deterred in the desegregation fight.

Governor Byrnes pronounced himself "shocked to learn that the court has reversed itself" on the separate-but-equal matter, but he also struck a note of caution, saying, "We must await the final decree of the Supreme Court and in the meantime, I earnestly urge all of our people, white and colored, to exercise restraint and preserve order." A similar "go slow" recommendation came from Governor Hugh White of Mississippi.

In Georgia, on the other hand, Governor Talmadge said the high court had "reduced our Constitution to a mere scrap of paper. It has blatantly ignored all law and precedent and usurped from the Congress and the people the power to amend the Constitution and from the Congress the authority to make the laws of the land."

Up in Washington, Senator Eastland issued a short statement of resistance. The South, he said, "will not abide by nor obey this legislative decision by a political court. We will take whatever steps are necessary to retain segregation in education." Senator Russell, the leader of the southern bloc, was only slightly less beligerent in his written statement, calling the court a "pliant tool of the executive branch. Ways must be found to check the tendency of the court to disregard the Constitution and the precedents of able and unbiased judges [in order] to decide cases solely on the basis of the personal predilections of some of its members as to political, economic and social questions," he said.

Senator Maybank, one of only two senators to comment on the Senate floor (the other was Republican Francis Case of South Dakota), said the "decision shocked me. In my judgment, it was a shameful political rather than a judicial decision." His colleague, Senator Johnston, blamed the Eisenhower administration for the ruling, citing in particular the appointment of Earl Warren. Now that the decision had been handed down, Johnston said, "the only thing a state can do is to work out its problem within its own individual state."

Most editorial comment in the southern papers was restrained, but the very appeals for peace and calm revealed that something of immense proportions had occurred and that more than an abstract principle was at stake. "We receive the decision with distaste and apprehension," *The News and Courier* said in a front-page editorial. "But it is too late to secede and start another war between the states. Other means must be sought to live within the laws of our country." Over in Columbia, *The State* observed, "It is stating it mildly to say that the court's decision will create many problems. The state's very best thought is needed in solving them." While surprised that the court "could ignore the powerful arguments . . . in the South Carolina case," *The State* had to acknowledge that the court had spoken. "In the meantime, this newspaper expects no excitement between the races. This is a time for calm deliberation."

Other papers echoed the call for calm. Even Jackson, Mississippi's *Clarion Ledger,* which declared that "May 17, 1954 may be recorded by future historians as a black day of tragedy for the South and for both races," boasted that Mississippians "can conduct ourselves in such fashion as to cause historians to record that we faced that tragedy and crisis with wisdom, courage, faith and determination. . . . It should not cause any panic, any violent emotional reactions or any disturbances of normal racial relations." Considering the violence about to erupt in Mississippi, *The Clarion Ledger* was sadly off the mark.

These larger papers had more readers and greater impact than South Carolina's *Florence Morning News.* But with an economy of words, this little daily faced the larger meaning of the decision head-on and in so doing identified the reason for the decade and a half of turmoil that would ensue. "The Southern and some other states are faced with the most gigantic social revolution since the days of Reconstruction," the paper said. "The court's decision cuts the foundation from under a way of life that has existed in the Southland for generations. . . ."

Continuing his law practice in Aiken, private citizen Thurmond made no public comment on the *Brown* decision. Officially he was on hiatus from political life. But the Democratic Party's behavior after Senator Maybank's fatal heart attack September 1 quickly brought him back to politics—this time for good. Once again he would demonstrate his independent—some would call it maverick—streak by building a campaign around the same theme that had inspired his states' rights presidential run: resistance to a power structure from above that was imposing its will on the citizenry. It was another harbinger of the more dramatic defection a decade later.

Maybank's death at his Flat Rock, North Carolina, summer home was completely unexpected. The politician died in his sleep shortly after midnight. Relatives said he had been feeling fine the previous day.

With the regular election barely two months away, the state Democratic Party had to act quickly to find a new nominee. On September 3, just hours after Maybank's funeral in Charleston, the executive committee hustled back to Columbia for a public nominating session at the Jefferson Hotel.

A resolution calling for a primary was proposed, but there were conflicting opinions about whether state law and party rules would permit it at such a late date. The committee killed the proposal on a 31–18 vote—a tally that was going to be much ballyhooed over the next seven weeks.

Rembert Dennis of Berkeley County then made a motion nominating state senator Edgar Brown. "I, too, as many of you, favor a primary to get a candidate," he said. But "in this emergency we do not have time for a primary under our election laws." While Dennis worried that the committee might be disfranchising voters, he pointed out that South Carolinians "can vote for anyone they like—but we here can name the choice of the Democratic Party of South Carolina for our senator." Brown was chosen without a dissenting voice.

For more than a decade the sixty-six-year-old "Bishop of Barnwell" had also been known as "Mr. Democrat," a tribute to his long and effective service to the party. Like Thurmond, Brown had studied law under a tutor, and after passing the bar in 1910 he entered private practice. But he quickly immersed himself in politics, and by virtue of holding both public and party office over the next forty years, he became what one scholar called "the most powerful man in the government of South Carolina."

The question was never whether Edgar Brown was qualified to go to the United States Senate, only the route by which he would get there. In 1954 Brown was banking on the assumption that Carolina voters shared his respect for party loyalty and its corresponding political reward. But however strong these values may have been, they were outweighed by deep resentment within the body politic of anything that diminished the people's right to participate in selecting a candidate.

The negative reaction to Brown's coronation was swift and widespread. Within hours of his selection, the move to draft Thurmond as a write-in candidate was under way, headed by Francis P. Coleman, the mayor of Mount Pleasant, a town just outside of Charleston. Calling the committee's action a disgrace, Coleman charged, "It's nothing less than a handful of men dictating to two million people."

In another of its front-page editorials—this one "People Weren't Consulted"—*The News and Courier* criticized the party's action. While conceding that Brown was an able politician, the paper said, "His mandate comes not from the people but from the politicians."

By the next day, the possibility of Thurmond as a write-in candidate was front-page news in *The State,* which noted that "a vast chorus of disapproval" had greeted Brown's nomination. Asked about his plans, Thurmond was noncommittal at this early stage, telling inquiring reporters that he didn't known anything more than what he read in the papers. Just before the committee met for its September 3 nominating session, however, Thurmond had told the Charleston paper, "Certainly I do think the people of South Carolina should have the opportunity to make the choice. . . . I think the people would strongly resent any other procedure, and they would resent it rightfully."

Four other men surfaced as potential write-in candidates, but only one of them, lumberman Marcus A. Stone, who had run for governor in 1946, pursued his campaign until the end. At the same time, Republicans sought to field a candidate to run for Maybank's seat, but the secretary of state ruled that the GOP group trying to certify a candidate had not complied with state election regulations.

Mounting dissatisfaction with Democratic Party officials became evident in newspaper editorials throughout the state. The *Florence Morning News* correctly forecast that "the action that denies the people the right to vote, coupled with the reputation of the 'Bishop of Barnwell,' is going to give unusual strength and life to any opposition movement, no matter who heads it."

William Workman, *The News and Courier*'s political writer,

also criticized the party and in effect endorsed a write-in campaign. "South Carolina voters had better sharpen their pencils—and their wits—if they want any voice in the selection of a United States Senator," he wrote. He paid tribute to Brown's political skills, but wondered why a man who was so "astute and practical" sought "to receive as a gift that which he has been unable to win as a prize."

In a slap at Brown September 6, Governor Byrnes, who had earlier said he favored a primary, named Greenville businessman Charles E. Daniel to fill the remaining four months of Maybank's term. *The News and Courier* noted that "In naming Mr. Daniel, Gov. Byrnes has ignored the fast deal whereby State Sen. Edgar Brown is being promoted to the U.S. Senate without consent of the people."

The resentment expressed in the newspapers was one way Thurmond could gauge public sentiment. The phone calls and mail were another. On September 4 he received a telegram from the coastal city of Georgetown with a message typical of the dozens of other missives he had received: "DEAR STROM, DON'T LET BROWN GET AWAY WITH THIS. WE WANT DEMOCRACY NOT TOTALITARIANISM." The same day Thurmond got a letter from Spartanburg, "from a group of your friends," asking him to "announce your candidacy at once. [W]e feel that the political ring in the lower State is trying to cram Edgar Brown down the throats of two million people which is not in keeping with Democratic Principles."

The letter continued with a suggestion that Thurmond "stress the fact that you are for States' Rights and are opposed to mixing of the races in any way."

On September 7, the day after Daniel had been named interim senator, Thurmond announced that he would be a write-in candidate unless Brown withdrew and agreed to run in a primary. In his formal statement, Thurmond charged that the state committee had engaged in "political maneuvering which began only a few hours after the death of our distinguished Senator Maybank." The committee could not transfer Maybank's nomination to any other candidate, he asserted, adding that in the absence of a special primary, "Democrats are absolutely free under the rules of the party, under their oath, and under the law to go into the general election and vote for the candidate of their choice."

Thurmond reassured Democratic voters that, if elected, he

would participate in the Senate's Democratic caucus and vote as a Democrat in organizing the Senate. "No act of mine as long as I am a member of the Senate will conflict with the principles of the Democratic Party of South Carolina as enunciated by the state convention of our party."

The News and Courier endorsed Thurmond in yet another front-page editorial, "Thurmond Is the Man," that would epitomize the strong press support he would get over the next six weeks. "Once before, when Southerners hunted for a way out of voting for a deal they resented, Strom Thurmond came forward," the paper said. "That was in 1948. He didn't have a chance of election. But he ran anyway, as a matter of principle. . . . Again a principle is at stake. It is bigger than personalities." Edgar Brown, the endorsement said, "would represent not South Carolina but 31 members of the Democratic Executive Committee."

The State withheld any endorsement, but predicted that "a spectacular fight" was in the making.

Before the campaign was over, fourteen of South Carolina's sixteen dailies would support Thurmond's write-in effort, as would seventy-three of its eighty-six weeklies—a critical factor in the outcome.

By telephone, telegram, and letter, a barrage of good wishes came to Thurmond after his announcement. One South Carolinian, who signed a postcard as "A Voting Democrat," wrote, "All I would like to say is . . . SIC'IM, STROM, SIC'IM." Another card, from "two who are waiting to *write in* your name," exclaimed, " 'Good!' For this we were hoping. Such denial of the rights of us voters as the Ex. Com. has made is most unbelievable."

Moments after his announcement became public, the new candidate fielded congratulatory phone calls at his law office in Aiken, where he sat at the phone for fourteen hours September 7. His wife, Jean, acted as a telephonic traffic cop, answering one line as she told Thurmond who was waiting on the other. "I've gotten hundreds of calls. Haven't been up from the desk since nine o'clock this morning," Thurmond told one caller. "I've heard from every county in the state. Getting calls from all groups and classes of people—the mill workers, farmers, industrialists, legislators, and county officers. They are all behind me. It's the greatest upsurge of sentiment that I have ever witnessed in my lifetime," Thurmond said, beaming.

Two days after Thurmond's announcement, Brown established the campaign theme he would lean on for the next seven weeks. Declaring that Democratic voters were "obligated" to support him, Brown said, "The people must determine whether there will be party loyalty." He deserved their loyalty because he was the "legal nominee, made so by the committee. I did not write the election law by which the committee acted."

But the negative reaction to Brown's nomination continued into a second week. Democratic committees in northern, western, and central counties held special meetings to denounce the executive panel's action, adding to the stigma that Brown was unable to shake through the rest of the campaign.

On September 13, state party chairman Neville Bennett struck back at those who were attacking him and his fellow committeemen. Critics, he contended, ignored the fact that the executive committee could not have legally held a primary. "The meeting was quiet, orderly and thoughtful. Practically the entire meeting was devoted to the consideration of the one question, 'How can this Committee provide for a legal primary?' " Legally, it couldn't, he contended—although some Democrats had argued there were ways to have the primary. Though Bennett didn't mention Thurmond by name, he noted that the very law under attack had been passed in 1950, when Thurmond was governor, with his support, and that the governor had signed it.

The committee members, Bennett said in an emotional conclusion, "are not men who will usurp or preempt the rights of the people. They are not un-American. And such charges levelled against them and the Committee wholesale are, in my opinion, libelous under the law."

Later in the campaign other committee members would speak out in their own defense. Lewis M. Clyburn of Lancaster County charged Thurmond with resorting to "deliberate falsehoods in an attempt to stir up the public's emotions so that he might ride a bandwagon to Washington." He called Thurmond's claim that only thirty-one individuals nominated Brown "a flat untruth" because the actual vote was a unanimous voice vote.

These passionate defenses had great technical and rhetorical merit, but they overlooked the all-important matter of public perception. They also misjudged the power of political tradition in South Carolina, where the legend of Pitchfork Ben Tillman—who had taken the nominating power away from party conventions and established the primary instead—was still strong. It was a point tailor-made for Thurmond, who had, after all, learned the primal lesson of politics—contact with the people—straight from Tillman. Compared with Edgar Brown, he was now the people's champion.

By the second week in September, Thurmond and Brown had set up campaign headquarters in Columbia. Newspaper stories began to appear explaining how to vote for a write-in candidate on either a voting machine or a paper ballot. And in Charleston, informal classes in write-in voting got under way.

Because this was not an official multicandidate campaign, Thurmond and Brown were not scheduled to face each other in the traditional county-by-county debates. But both made appearances September 14 in the northern town of Gaffney in what were their first remarks as rival candidates. Brown, as expected, focused on party loyalty, telling listeners, "It is known that I have unfalteringly served my state and the Democratic Party, sometimes when it was unpopular to do so, for forty years, and that the only real issue now is whether the people want a regular Democrat in the Senate or someone who runs on a write-in ticket. It is not a question of personalities," Brown insisted. "It is a question of who can do most for the state at this time." Reminding the audience of his role as a national committeeman with close ties to the "controlling conservative element" of the national party, he said that "the people should decide whether they want me or an independent in the Senate, who like Wayne Morse of Oregon would be at liberty to vote with the Republicans or Democrats at will. There cannot be two Democrats running on the same ticket in the general election," he added. "I am the official legal Democratic nominee."

Thurmond, predictably, stuck to his theme of blaming the party committee for selecting Brown. "The people of South Carolina are justifiably angered and alarmed over the fact that thirty-one men have arrogated unto themselves the precious right of naming the United States senator. They will not take it lying down," he declared. He repeated his call for a primary, but if that was not forthcoming, "the people will not be denied. They are going to demand their right to a free and democratic choice by going to the polls November 2 and writing in their votes." As Brown had done, Thurmond contended that the campaign "is one of principle not personalities," although his "principle" was not the same as Brown's.

Thurmond later asked Brown to debate him further, but the senator rejected the offer. "Let me make it perfectly clear at the outset that I have nothing to debate with my opponent," Brown said. "This is not a primary. I am not seeking nomination. I am the official nominee of the Democratic Party, I am the legal nominee of the Democratic Party. I am the only nominee of the Democratic Party."

The same day as their nondebate in Gaffney, Governor Byrnes gave an indirect boost to Thurmond, announcing that "it would be a great service to the state" if the party executive committee would "rescind the previous action and give the people the right to vote" in a primary.

Brown, Bennett, and other committee officials huddled all day September 15 at party headquarters in Columbia, but the panel eventually decided to stick by its original action.

On September 18, while Brown was figuring out how to get maximum advantage from his strong Democratic Party ties, Thurmond executed a bold gesture, pledging that if he won the write-in election he would resign from office after only two years, before the regular 1956 Democratic primary, and let South Carolina citizens choose a senator for the remaining four years of the term. In announcing his pledge, Thurmond repeated his contention that the campaign was "a fight for government by the people instead of government by a small group of committeemen. . . . I have no selfish ambition in this fight," he insisted. The resignation pledge was to "make the principle at stake crystal clear."

In his own mind, Thurmond was not ambitious—not in the sense of self-aggrandizement. It was true that he wanted to advance his political career, but not for personal gain. What others might see as "selfish ambition" to get to Washington, he saw as determination to serve his constituents.

Brown ridiculed Thurmond's resignation pledge. "I'm afraid my opponent is just resorting to another trick to pull the wool over the eyes of the voters," he said. "Don't be fooled by this 'I want a primary' talk of my wrathfully indignant opponent. He only gets worked up into wrathful indignation when he is the beneficiary of the indignation." Thurmond, Brown charged, was no more than a political opportunist who said, "Now I'm a Democrat. Now I'm a Republican. Now I'm an independent and now I'm a what-have-you."

The first week in October proved to be a turning point in the race, not because of events in South Carolina but because of comments filtering down from Washington, D.C. In September, Olin Johnston had announced his support of Brown, though not with the most enthusiastic of endorsements. All Johnston said was, "I am a Democrat, and I will support the Democratic nominee in the general elections, upholding South Carolina election laws." Now the senator inadvertently helped create an issue when he told a reporter that Thurmond would have a hard time winning a write-in campaign. "On voting day . . . one out of three people that go to the polls that day will not even know Edgar Brown and Strom Thurmond are even running. They will just mark the straight Democratic ticket."

The next day Stephen Mitchell, chairman of the Democratic National Committee, compounded Johnston's accidental slight when he told a National Press Club audience that it would be too much for South Carolina voters to write in Thurmond's name. Mitchell, who was from Illinois, told reporters, "They may have a different level of education down there, but in Illinois, if a man had his name printed on a ballot and if the people had a choice of marking an 'X' by his name or writing in the name of J. Strom Thurmond, the man with the printed name would win."

Hours after Mitchell's remarks were reported in the October 6 Columbia *State*—it was reporter Harry Dent's story—Thurmond played the moment for all it was worth, defending his state's honor against the perceived slight. "Evidently this friend and supporter of the committee candidate thinks that the people of South Carolina cannot write. He does not know how illiteracy has been reduced in our state," Thurmond said. "With relatively few exceptions our people can write their own names and they can and will write the name of Strom Thurmond" in the general election. "They will let this Chicago lawyer know that South Carolinians resent his interference in the politics of this state."

Now Thurmond could rail against two supposed enemies of "the people," the thirty-one members of the executive committee who had taken away the voters' choice, and the meddling outsider who had impugned their intelligence.

Brown had another setback that same week when four Charleston Democrats running for the legislature urged him to "step down and submit your qualifications to the people." The four took issue with Brown's definition of loyalty. "We are loyal to the democratic way of doing things, loyal to the American system of fair play, with equal opportunity for all, loyal to this nation and this State, yes, and loyal to the Democratic Party of South Carolina and its legally selected nominees. We are not loyal, however, to one such as yourself, who has been selected in an autocratic fashion without a vote of the people."

The four told Brown that "as matters now stand . . . you represent a danger to our democracy and we are unalterably opposed to your election."

Then in mid-October Brown received some more outside help he didn't need when several state newspapers published endorsements of his candidacy by Harry Truman and his aide, Major General Harry H. Vaughn, the latter speaking in particularly harsh terms about Thurmond. He said the former president had told him he could "forgive little things like rape and murder but he [could not] forgive a guy that goes back on the party."

Already sensitive to accusations that the national party was meddling in the Senate race, Brown denounced the offerings as "misleading, untrue, vicious and a clear attempt to prejudice some South Carolina voters against me as the Democratic nominee."

Thurmond, now at the helm of a well-staffed campaign team, simply persisted with his basic themes. Unlike his run for a judgeship sixteen years earlier, this campaign included supporters and county organizations who sent out letters and brochures. Some letters included sample ballots so that the recipient would know how to write in Thurmond's name. Later on, the campaign would take out full-page newspaper ads showing readers how to vote for him.

Thurmond's campaign brochures, featuring his picture and a list of public offices and accomplishments, continued to harp on the notion of voters' choice. "Write-In for the Right to Vote!" one of them declared, insisting that it was civic duty, not personal ambition, that had brought Thurmond into the race.

John West, brought in late in the game to manage Brown's campaign, considered Thurmond's write-in effort to be "100 percent expediency. Strom has never been loyal to anyone but Strom," West asserted. Brown's ads reflected this sentiment, referring to Brown as "Mr. Democrat" and warning voters to "stop, look and listen" because of the dangers of a write-in candidate. "A write-in candidate belongs to no party. He may claim to be Democrat, Republican, Independent, Socialist or what-not."

One of the more humorous Brown campaign ploys needled Thurmond for his now-famous prenuptial headstand. A campaign flier with the picture of the governor on his head was captioned: "1954—Upside Down Again!" The reverse side explained that "In the United States Senate you have to stand on your feet, not on your head." And a newspaper ad asked voters, "Who is your choice—MR. DEMOCRAT or MR. ACROBAT?"

Race hardly played a role in the campaign, even though the *Brown* decision had been announced only four months earlier. When race did emerge, it was because of Brown. In one of his campaign letters he reminded recipients that "the Democratic Party is the only party that has ever been a friend to the people of the South. In 1952 the candidate for the Republican presidency [Eisenhower] stood on the State House steps in Columbia, and among numerous promises assured South Carolina that segregation would be left up to individual states. I am sure you all know what happened."

One of Brown's newspaper ads was more direct. "SEGREGATION," it declared in two-inch-high capital letters. "Who ended it at the Charleston Navy Yard, at Ft. Jackson and other military outposts? The Republican President, Mr. Eisenhower." The ad listed instance after instance of desegregation, each time asking who was responsible. The answer was always "The Republican President, Mr. Eisenhower." Then turning to home, the ad asked, "Who ended segregation in South Carolina state appointments by naming the first Negro to a state Board since the period of the Carpetbaggers and Scalawags in Reconstruction days?" The answer: "Strom Thurmond, while Governor, did just this and is hailed by the Negro newspaper 'Lighthouse and Informer' for it."

A week before the election, Brown suffered a serious blow when Governor Byrnes announced, "I shall write in the name of Strom Thurmond." Byrnes reminded voters that he had urged the state committee to hold a primary right after Maybank died and that later he had called on Brown to resign and let a new election go forward. He had tried to stay out of the fray, he said, but when Brown's campaign literature featured his name and picture, Byrnes said he wanted to make his position clear. "If we vote for the committee candidate, we thereby approve the action of the committee in refusing to order a primary," the governor asserted. "It may encourage other committees to deny the right to elect other officials."

Stung by the governor's statement, Brown lashed out at Byrnes, charging that he "has turned his back on a lifelong and loyal friend and the party which has made him a national figure." What hurt, he said, was that "he has let his Republican influences cause him to turn his back on me after a lifetime of friendship."

Byrnes, it turned out, was willing to do more for Thurmond than just endorse him. The governor's office was visible from Brown headquarters in the Wade Hampton Hotel. One night, as campaign workers were toiling late, they could see that the governor was still working, too. The next morning, enterprising Brown supporters got hold of the governor's telephone logs and saw that he had been telephoning influential people all over the state, presumably on behalf of Thurmond. "We could just sense that he switched a lot of them," recalled West, who would become governor sixteen years later in a campaign of great symbolic importance to Thurmond. "The governor has that authority."

The write-in effort was further helped when the state attorney general ruled in late October that a write-in voter didn't have to spell Thurmond's name exactly or get it precisely on the correct line for the ballot to be counted. Attorney General T. C. Callison said it was the "intent of the voter" that should determine the legitimacy of the ballot and that such decisions were to be made by the county managers for the election.

Week by week Brown had been losing ground, but West didn't realize it until he noticed the attendance dropping at the receptions the campaign threw before each University of South Carolina football game. Early in the campaign, "everybody was coming by to greet the senator before heading on to the game," West later said. "It was just a great crowd, all the leaders, all the political bigwigs." A few weeks later at another home game, the crowd was one-third the size it had been—a signal that Brown was no longer a sure bet.

West's intuition was accurate. When the votes were counted November 2, Thurmond had won with a stunning 63.1 percent of the votes, a margin just short of 60,000. The final tally was 143,442 to 83,525. Stone received fewer than 300 votes.

Offering his "deepest gratitude publicly to my friends," a jubilant Thurmond called his victory a triumph over a "ruthless machine." He specifically praised the newspapers and radio and television stations "for the full and fair presentation of news" about the campaign. Brown countered that Thurmond supporters had been "misled" into voting for a "symbol which had been manufactured by the Republican press in the state."

Campaign manager West believed that Thurmond had simply outhustled his opponent and that the senator, who was already sixty-six, had been no match for the fifty-one-year-old Thurmond. Years after the race, Brown seemed to agree. Explaining why he had not pledged to resign after two years as Thurmond had, the legislator said, "I was sixty-six. I was riding the crest of service here, and I wasn't going to give it all up for a year or two-year term and then be out of office at sixty-eight. I couldn't have made the campaign in 1956," he conceded. "Physically, I couldn't have made the campaign. . . ."

In a postelection editorial *The State* noted that Brown's defeat was the first time since Reconstruction that a Democratic nominee for state office had been defeated. The paper had no idea then what a trend Thurmond had started.

10.
RESISTANCE AND RESOLVE

1955–1960

ON THE SURFACE, George Lee, the robust and genial minister to Belzoni, Mississippi's black community, hardly seemed the type to cause trouble. But whites in this small Delta community didn't trust him because he was financially independent and, even more disquieting, he wanted change. In the minister's mind, the best avenue was the ballot box, not the courthouse. As Thurgood Marshall and the flotilla of NAACP lawyers were mounting the legal attacks on school segregation, Reverend Lee had been preaching the gospel of voter registration at the black Baptist churches in Humphreys County. When the minister got word of the Supreme Court's decision in *Brown,* he considered it to be a good omen but not much more than that for everyday life in Belzoni. Although blacks outnumbered whites two to one, they had no political, economic, or social power. The court's proclamation aside, they were still forbidden to attend white schools, eat in white restaurants, or sit in bus seats reserved for whites. And they never would, the reverend maintained, as long as they didn't vote.

Six months before the high court decision, Lee and a friend, Gus Courts, had started a chapter of the NAACP, and by January of the new year they had thirty-two members. By the spring, they had persuaded four hundred residents to register to vote.

Belzoni's white community retaliated instantly. The potential voters were fired from their jobs, were denied credit, or they found their rent suddenly raised. The result of the intimidation was predictable. The vast majority withdrew their registration.

Reverend Lee decided to meet hostility with diplomacy, telling the white leadership at one meeting that since "all the bordering counties are permitting Negroes to pay poll taxes, register and vote without any ill effects, we feel sure that the same could happen in this county. . . . We respectfully ask that you will at this time endorse and support our efforts to become full-fledged citizens in this county." The white leadership had other ideas. Shortly after that meeting a delegation came to see the reverend and his wife to make a deal. The couple would be allowed to vote if Lee ceased his voter registration campaign. Lee said no thanks.

By the spring of 1955, Lee and Courts had persuaded ninety-two black people to register again, and the white citizenry moved from intimidation to violence. Blacks found their car windshields knocked out, and a black club was ransacked. A note was left behind warning, "This is what will happen to Negroes who try to vote."

Lee and Courts received death threats on a regular basis. In a crudely typed note to national NAACP headquarters, Courts said he had been forced to resign as president of the branch and urged officials to send any future mail "in a plain envelope and leave NAACP [off]. I have a reason for this." Although Lee tried to take precautions as the hostility intensified, his luck ran out the night of May 7, 1955. Driving toward home, he was hit with gunfire from a passing car. Half of his face was blown off, but he managed to pull himself out of the car and make his way to a cabstand. Two black drivers took Lee to a hospital, where he died not long after. The county sheriff initially refused to investigate, concluding despite overwhelming evidence to the contrary that Lee had been fatally injured in a car accident. The lead found in Lee's face, the sheriff said, was probably from fillings in his teeth, though he later backed off the transparent suggestion.

Eventually the sheriff decided that perhaps Lee had been murdered, but despite pressure from the NAACP, including letters to President Eisenhower and Attorney General Herbert Brownell, no one was ever arrested for the killing. The sheriff said Lee was probably shot by another black in an argument over a woman—a charge the black community called preposterous.

What was to have been a celebration of the first anniversary of the *Brown* decision turned into a memorial service for Lee and a declaration from the NAACP "to let the state, country and the world know that we are going to continue our Fight for Freedom."

George Lee's death was the most dramatic and vicious evidence of the anxiety that pervaded the white South after *Brown*. Three weeks after Lee was killed the justices would explain how their landmark desegregation ruling was to be implemented. Not wanting to force complex and divisive solutions overnight, the justices would urge an end to segregation in education with "all deliberate speed."

"All deliberate speed" was going to be nearly two decades, but *Brown II* (the decision's instant moniker) made real what for a year had been only a symbolic declaration. It became a clarion call that initiated an era of resistance in the white community and resolve in the black that marked a rebirth, albeit halting and difficult, of the black franchise. Though he would not be alive to see the results, Reverend Lee would be proved right in his emphasis on the ballot as a means of change. To the chagrin of white southerners, voting statistics in two presidential elections were going to make northern Republicans and Democrats realize the potential power of the black vote. The politicians would respond accordingly: with support from the North and opposition from the South to any new federal law that would facilitate black voting.

Lee's death would be followed in Mississippi by the summertime murders of two other blacks, one of them a fourteen-year-old boy. But by the end of 1955 blacks in neighboring Montgomery, Alabama, had shown the country that violence would not deter the drive for equality. On December 1, Rosa Parks, a Montgomery seamstress, was arrested after she refused to give up her seat in a segregated city bus. The arrest prompted an eleven-month boycott that ultimately resulted in desegregation of Montgomery's buses.

A few months later, in 1957, the Southern Christian Leadership Conference was formed. At the helm was an organizer of the Montgomery boycott, the Reverend Martin Luther King, Jr. By the fall, President Eisenhower would send federal troops into Little Rock to aid a troubled effort to integrate Central High School, and southerners wondered if a second forced Reconstruction was under way.

Just as blacks were plotting their strategies to end segregation, whites in every southern state were devising their own tactics to fight back. At the hub of the wheel of resistance were the benignly named "White Citizens' Councils." Not surprisingly, the first was formed in Indianola, Mississippi—the same Delta community that had gotten rid of Minnie Cox, the black postal official, a half-century earlier. Over the next three years, council movements would spring up in every southern state: at the height of their influence in late 1956, there would be over three hundred thousand members. The largest councils were in Mississippi and Alabama, each claiming about eighty thousand members. South Carolina's councils, which peaked at about thirty thousand members, were formed at the instigation of two likely promoters, S. Emory Rogers, the school board attorney for Clarendon County, and Farley Smith, the son of the infamous Cotton Ed. Rogers would eventually leave his regular professional duties to head the statewide movement.

The mainstream southern press initially took a dim view of the councils and their focus on economic reprisals against blacks. "Manicured Kluxism" was how *The Montgomery Advertiser* described their efforts to make it "difficult, if not impossible, for any negro who advocates desegregation to find and hold a job, get credit or renew a mortgage."

The councils reacted defensively to charges that they were the Klan dressed up in three-piece suits. They emphasized that they were respectable segregationists: doctors, lawyers, bankers, teachers—in short, community leaders who eschewed violence and simply wanted to protect and preserve their way of life.

Although the councils did not have a great number of prominent politicians in their ranks, the groups were not without influence. South Carolina's lieutenant governor, Ernest F. Hollings, declared that their leadership at the community level could "help to restore decency in government and maintain peace and security for all people, both white and Negro," and the General Assembly commended the organizations for efforts "to preserve and maintain proper relations between all races residing in the State."

Strongest in the counties with heavy black populations, the councils became the voice of the white community, and though their power had ebbed by the end of 1957, they were the catalyst for organized opposition to integration after *Brown*.

The White Citizens' Councils fought desegregation at the local level. In Washington, D.C., the southern members of Congress played a different role, stopping or at least diluting every piece of federal civil rights legislation that might disturb the status quo. By the very act of opposition they helped foster the climate of resistance at home. Their reaction to the black community's growing assertiveness was so visceral that no apparent thought was given to the driving force behind that assertiveness—human dignity too long denied. Instinctively, these politicians knew that this blind spot was one they had to cultivate in order to be reelected. They took shelter in the belief that "their" blacks were content. It was the outside agitators, communist inspired at that, who were stirring up trouble. In political terms, Thurmond neatly explained that officeholders like himself "were standing with the people." "The people," however, were only those who had white skin, and it was this view Reverend Lee had believed the ballot could change.

Once he got to the Senate, Thurmond wasted no time expressing himself on racial issues, though he was not the southerners' leader and never would be on tactical matters—that was Russell of Georgia. But within a year Thurmond, going his own way as he always had, would be more visible than most of his more senior colleagues. Where other southern senators might seek the comfort of the back bench while reliably "standing with the people," Thurmond needed no such cover. If by his own admission he had crossed the Rubicon six and a half years earlier in Jackson, by 1955 he had comfortably set up camp on the other side. The determination to stand for principles as he defined them and his bent for the dramatic gesture, however ill-received by colleagues or the press, would be neither curbed nor refined in the larger, more sophisticated world of Washington, D.C. The Senate would have to take Thurmond as it found him.

To give South Carolina's new senator a head start in the Capitol, interim senator Charles Daniel resigned December 24, 1954, and Thurmond was appointed in his place, giving him seniority over the other incoming first-year senators. As he promised he would do, Thurmond—despite his conflicts with the national Democrats—joined the other party members as they organized into Senate committees—an important strategic decision given that the Democrats had only a two-seat edge over the GOP, forty-nine to forty-seven. But at the opening caucus Thurmond let it be known that the party had no hold on him. Several of the other newcomers thanked the Democrats for all that the national organization had done for them, but when Thurmond got up he reminded the group that the Democratic Party hadn't helped him one bit. "They spent money against me, so I don't want any Democrat up here to think I owe 'em anything," he said, "but I hope we can work together for the good of the country."

South Carolinians had expected Thurmond to be coolly received in the Senate. In a *News and Courier* article several weeks before his arrival, an anonymous veteran senator had advised that "Strom Thurmond should be closely attentive to his duties in committee, he should give close attention to debate on the floor—but for two years he should not participate in it if he can avoid it"—advice Thurmond assiduously declined to heed.

In fact, Thurmond's first year in the Senate went more smoothly than predicted. Instead of being met with thinly veiled hostility from Democrats, he was treated warmly. He also proved very effective at taking care of South Carolina's interests. "While Johnston carries on a running attack" against the president and cabinet officials, one correspondent wrote the following September, "Thurmond often makes telephone calls to their departments and gets good results for South Carolina." It was Thurmond who would persuade the Agriculture Department to keep open a cotton classification office at Charleston after Johnston's efforts had failed, and who pressed Senator Stennis to restore appropriations for a hospital at Fort Jackson.

It had taken Thurmond about six weeks to get his Senate office organized. By mid-March he felt ready to report to his constituents on how things were going. On the seventeenth he inaugurated his newsletter, *Strom Thurmond Reports to the People*, writing that he had been given three committee assignments, Interstate and Foreign Commerce, Government Operations, and Public Works. The newsletter was put together by Harry Dent, who was now the senator's press aide. He was hired after a short interview that let the young man know how much the senator prized loyalty and commitment: "Don't you worry about Harry Dent," Thurmond told him. "You worry about Strom Thurmond, and I'll take care of Harry Dent." Both men kept their word for what would be a decades-long relationship.

Two years later the senator would make another important hire when he brought J. Fred Buzhardt, Jr., the son of one of his old law partners, to Washington as his legislative assistant. While Dent was the strategist in the office who saw politics with a broad view, Buzhardt was the more conservative ideologue who would give Thurmond's speeches a hard intellectual edge. This would be evident shortly after he joined the staff, when Thurmond was invited to address a group at Harvard University. Buzhardt wrote a speech for Thurmond chiding northern liberals for a selective reading of the Constitution that exalted individual rights and disparaged—even ignored—states' rights.

Jean Thurmond was fond of both men—she had been Dent's ally since their work during the 1950 Senate race—but she fretted about Buzhardt's near-evangelical conservatism. She made her husband promise never to make a decision with him alone. She wanted Dent on hand as a leveling agent. The young men complemented each other nicely, and together they were going to help make the senator a pivotal force in the political realignment of the South.

Although Thurmond's committees did not handle civil rights bills, this in no way deterred him from seeking to influence the legislation. And although he would closely monitor agricultural and trade matters—two issues of concern to South Carolina's farming and textile communities—it was civil rights rather than the more parochial South Carolina interests that would bring him national attention.

That Thurmond was already part of the growing debate over civil rights was evident in a skit performed in December 1954 at the Gridiron Dinner, the annual gathering of the city's most influential journalists and politicians. He was referred to in a number featuring southern governors who bemoaned the *Brown* decision in song. The biting parody, to the tune of "White Christmas," cut to the heart of the issue: "We're dreaming of a white schoolhouse / Just like the one we used to know / Before integration in education / Laid our dear traditions low."

The News and Courier bristled that in the burlesque, "the serious implications were half buried under the popular misconception of a dimly perceived event."

Although in January President Eisenhower's State of the Union address had predicted "historic progress in eliminating . . . demeaning practices based on race or color," there was hardly any civil rights activity in the Senate in 1955. The major effort was in the House, where Representative Adam Clayton Powell, Jr., the black Democrat from New York City, sought unsuccessfully to bar racial segregation in public housing, public schools, and the National Guard. Despite Eisenhower's speech, the president opposed Powell's ideas as "extraneous" matters on major legislation designed for another purpose.

At the end of May the nation's attention once again turned to the Supreme Court in anticipation of the justices' decree in the school segregation lawsuits. Although the cases had been set for argument at the end of 1954, events intervened to push the hearing back until April. Justice Jackson, who had so determinedly gotten himself to the court for the May 17, 1954, decision, suffered another heart attack in October, this one fatal. On November 8, Eisenhower nominated John Marshall Harlan, the grandson of the only justice who had dissented in *Plessy*. Unhappy southern senators delayed his confirmation for four months, until March 16, 1955. Thurmond was one of the eleven senators, nine of them from the South, who voted against him.

On April 11, 1955, the justices finally began oral arguments for *Brown II*, which ended up taking thirteen hours and twenty minutes spread over four days. Some of the most dramatic moments came in debate on the Clarendon case, where Bob Figg and S. Emory Rogers had taken over for John Davis. Rogers bluntly told the court that the decision a year earlier had created "terrific problems" in the county. Clarendon was not like the District of Columbia, he insisted. Overnight desegregation could not be foisted upon his county. Because of its large black population and the comparatively small white one, integration in Clarendon would not mean what most people had in mind. "It would actually be the sending of a few white children that we have there to the Negro schools . . ." In *Brown* the justices had explained the impossibility of turning the clock back to 1868, when the Fourteenth Amendment was adopted, or to 1896, when *Plessy* was decided. Now Rogers wanted to offer the flip side. "I do not believe that in a biracial society we can push the clock forward abruptly to 2015 or 2045," he said. Local attitudes would change slowly, and so the best way to resolve the litigation was to send the cases back to the local federal judges and give them a free hand to fashion remedies.

Rogers got into a testy exchange with the chief justice—some of the lawyers thought Rogers might be cited for contempt—when the attorney suggested that Clarendon's willingness to abide by a Supreme Court decree depended on what that decree said. That verged on heresy to Warren. "It is not a question of attitude—it is a question of conforming to the decree," Warren said with an unmistakable chill in his voice. "Is there any basis upon which we can assume that there will be an immediate attempt to comply with the decree of this Court, whatever it may be?"

Rogers said again that he thought something could be worked out with the local federal courts, but he refused to budge from his original notion that a simple court order could not undo a century of "custom and tradition" and produce integration. "I would have to tell you that right now we would not conform—we would not send our white children to the Negro schools."

Thurgood Marshall, the last to argue for the black litigants, wound up his presentation with a simple but compelling point that drew on the class distinctions in everyday southern life. Referring to the state of Virginia's claim that low academic and health standards of blacks would be detrimental to the white students, Marshall dryly observed that "it is interesting to me that the very people that would object to sending their white children to school with Negroes are eating food that has been prepared, served and almost put in their mouths by the mothers of those children, and they do it day in and day out, but they cannot have the child go to school."

On May 31, the justices finally delivered *Brown II.* Instead of writing a detailed decree themselves, they followed the advice of Rogers and others and turned the job over to the local federal courts, ordering them "to require that the defendants make a prompt and reasonable start toward full compliance with our May 17, 1954, ruling." In the short opinion (only seven paragraphs) the court said it recognized the complexities involved in the cases but also noted that "substantial steps" to end segregation in public schools had already taken place in the District of Columbia and in communities in Kansas and Delaware. The decision, therefore, was of prime importance to South Carolina and Virginia, who had held off until the court spoke.

Before reaching the infamous "all deliberate speed" passage, the justices talked of "practical flexibility" in working out local solutions, but at the same time they warned that "it should go without saying that the vitality of [the *Brown* decision's] constitutional principles cannot be allowed to yield simply because of disagreement with them." It would be clear only years later how much running room they had left to those who wanted to subvert the very purpose of their eloquent command for equality.

Reaction to the decision among white southerners was mixed. Many politicians and school officials believed they had won a victory. Governor Hugh White of Mississippi felt sure "we are a long way off from integration." But a more hostile interpretation came from Senator Eastland, who thundered from Washington that "Southern people will not be violating the Constitution or the law when they defy this monstrous decision."

And in Georgia, Governor Marvin Griffin promised that "The people of Georgia and the present administration are determined irrevocably that we are not going to mix the races in the classrooms of our schools and colleges in Georgia." *The Atlanta Constitution* struck a milder tone in its editorial, essentially praising the court for a temperate ruling. "The decision is no call to arms for demagogues and race baiters," the paper said. "It must be a bitter blow to those who were ready to ride to glory on a hate platform. It will be received with relief by the reasonable majority of both races."

Further south, in Alabama, *The Montgomery Advertiser* astutely described the next battlefront and its beleaguered warriors, the federal courts and the federal judges. No matter how leisurely a judge might wish to proceed, the paper observed, "he is nevertheless bound by a clear and unmistakable Supreme Court ruling that school segregation is illegal. Our federal judges are going to become, perhaps, the unhappiest public servants in the land, pulled one way by their sworn duty and another by the realities of the white man's passions of repugnance and defiance towards race mixing. Obedience to the Supreme Court's ruling will leave Alabama judges with the feeling of putting their people to the sword."

In Thurmond's home state there was the same mix of reaction. Predictably, *The News and Courier* discussed the matter in another of its front-page editorials, this one to announce "what the court didn't say"—that is, it had fixed no deadline for desegregation. The paper opted for a continuation of separate but equal so that "the great bulk of pupils could continue going to their respective schools exactly as in the past."

From Clarendon County came an even harsher verdict. Officials would close the public schools, both white *and* black, to avoid integration. (Officials in Prince Edward County, Virginia, went even further, voting to cut off school funds for the upcoming year because of the Supreme Court decision.)

Senator Johnston charged that the ruling was influenced by a "communist conspiracy" and joined Eastland in calling for a Senate investigation of groups and individuals identified with the alleged conspiracy. Thurmond was restrained in his criticism of the court, but the anger that would erupt from him within the year was brewing. Issuing a statement from the small South Carolina town of Great Falls, where he was addressing a high school graduating class, Thurmond said, "I am opposed to the original decision and its implementation. The failure of the court on May 17, 1954, to recognize well-established constitutional principles and legal precedents cannot at this time be offset by its recognition that local conditions differ. Today's decision did not change the decision of May 17, 1954."

Although the court had spoken, nothing further could happen until the NAACP filed petitions seeking to desegregate the white schools. Even before the first petition in South Carolina, there was agitation among whites for a more organized response to the black group, but the first White Citizens' Council wasn't formed until August 1955, after blacks filed a desegregation petition in the small town of Elloree, just west of Clarendon County. With help from *The News and Courier,* which published several articles in late summer about Mississippi's councils, the South Carolina movement spread, with new groups sprouting at the rate of more than one per week. Newspapers across the state were filled with stories about every new council that was created to defend the white way of life. By July 1, 1956, South Carolina had fifty-five of them.

The Clarendon council was formed in September 1955 to take preventive action. Two months before, the same three-judge panel that heard the Clarendon case set out its guidelines for following *Brown II.* As *The News and Courier* had done two months earlier, Judge Parker dwelt on what the justices had not said. "Nothing in the Constitution or in the decision of the Supreme Court takes away from the people the freedom to choose the school they attend," he wrote. "The Constitution in other words does not require integration. It does not forbid such segregation as occurs as the result of voluntary action. It merely forbids the use of governmental power to enforce segregation."

As one of its first acts, the Clarendon council's "Race Relations Committee" sent a warning letter to black leaders in Summerton, the town that was the focus of the lawsuit. "Should one race try to force one of its children on the school of the opposite race," the letter said, "it is the decision of the State government that both schools will cease to operate in that community. We, the Race Relations Committee, approve." The group claimed it wanted to "cooperate with you, our colored friends and neighbors, in your struggle for a higher standard of living and we are most anxious to help you in your physical welfare and character building efforts." But while the committee said it would meet with black leaders, it refused to meet with the NAACP and "anyone who signed the petition seeking integration in our schools. . . ."

Rogers denied that the council had put economic pressure on Clarendon blacks, but he conceded to a visiting northern reporter that "Some have been denied credit. I would not extend credit to a member of the NAACP. I would not rent my land to a member of the NAACP. Everybody in Summerton feels the same way. You would too if you had an organization that was trying to destroy everything you believed in."

By himself, Thurmond could not undo the two *Brown* decisions, and he could not force any of the offending justices off the high court, but he could throw up roadblocks in the Senate to judicial nominees he thought were in the mold of the current bench. When he learned that Solicitor General Simon E. Sobeloff had been nominated to the Fourth Circuit Court of Appeals, the circuit that included South Carolina, Thurmond immediately announced his opposition. Sobeloff had been credited with devising the "middle-of-the-road" approach the Supreme Court took in the desegregation decree.

While others might have considered it middle-of-the-road, Thurmond found it unacceptable. "A brief review" of Sobeloff's record, he said, "convinces me that he could not sit in impartial judgment as a member of the court which may review cases involving the constitutional rights of the States." Appointments like Sobeloff, by both Truman and Eisenhower, convinced him that states that "believe in the Constitution and states' rights can expect no comfort from either major political party."

Within two weeks, Senators Eastland and Johnston joined the opposition and blocked Sobeloff's nomination for the rest of the year. It was only a temporary victory, though. Sobeloff was confirmed a year later with no problem.

In August, evidence of the rising tensions over race came once again from Mississippi. Within a span of fifteen days, two blacks were killed. On August 13, Lamar Smith, a sixty-three-year-old farmer and World War II veteran, was gunned down on the courthouse steps of Brookhaven, in the southern part of the Delta. Smith had had the temerity to campaign against an incumbent county supervisor and had cast a vote against him in the August 2 primary. Eleven days later, while at the courthouse on business, Smith was approached by several white men who started to argue with him. One of them took out a pistol and shot Smith at close range. Although the sheriff could hear the gunshot and could see a white man spattered with blood leaving the scene, he waited eight days before arresting three men for the killing. Though there were several witnesses, no one would testify about what he had seen on the courthouse lawn; without any evidence, the grand jury declined to return an indictment. The three white men were freed. Local officials claimed that the murder was the result of a political dispute, not a racial one, but the NAACP said that Smith "had received several threats on his life if he did not slow down his political activities."

Eighteen days after Smith's murder, the bloated body of fourteen-year-old Emmett Till, a bullet in his head, one eye gouged out, and part of his skull crushed, was pulled from the Tallahatchie River. Two white men, Roy Bryant and J. W. Milam, were arrested for the murder. Young Till, visiting from Chicago and unschooled in Mississippi's ways, had dared to speak to Bryant's wife in a store, calling out, "Bye, baby," as he left.

The two men were charged with beating Till, shooting him, and then wiring a seventy-five-pound cotton gin fan to his neck before dumping him in the river.

When Till's body was returned to Chicago, his mother insisted on an open-casket funeral so that everyone could see what had happened to her son. The impact of the murder was dramatic. As Myrlie Evers, whose husband, Medgar, would also be murdered, recalled years later, "It said even a child was not safe from racism and bigotry and death." The outrage over the case prompted a huge influx of money to the NAACP, but it did little to change conditions outside or inside the courthouse.

Bryant and Milam admitted kidnapping and beating Till, but

they claimed they had left him alive. White Mississippians raised ten thousand dollars to pay their legal expenses, five local white lawyers volunteered to represent them at the September murder trial, and after barely an hour of deliberation, an all-white jury found them not guilty. In November, a county grand jury refused to indict the two on kidnapping charges.

Thurmond always condemned such acts of violence, just as he had denounced the lynching of Willie Earle eight years earlier. But he never made the connection between the society that fostered the killings and the killers themselves. It was easier to isolate this egregious conduct as an ugly aberration that could be handled in the legal system. But as so many cases had shown, including the 1947 trial in South Carolina, the local judicial systems were a reflection of the society that produced the perpetrators; they could not be counted on for justice.

By the end of 1955 all the southern states were hardening their attitude against compliance with *Brown II.* They did more than just form White Citizens' Councils; a new strategy was emerging, and with it a new vocabulary of resistance: "interposition." It was actually the rebirth of a concept Virginians had developed in 1798, urging states to "interpose" themselves to block a perceived abuse of federal power in the young democracy. Calhoun of South Carolina gave the concept added force when he came up with "nullification" to oppose a federal tariff. Now it was Virginia's turn again, through one of its county attorneys, William Old, who rediscovered interposition for use in this new conflict with the federal government. Whatever the words, the idea was rooted in the Tenth Amendment, that the states had authority under the United States Constitution to challenge the federal government.

Old had circulated a pamphlet promoting interposition in August of 1955, a month after the formation of the first White Citizens' Council. At the same time, a special "Committee of 52" in South Carolina gathered seven thousand signatures on a petition urging the legislature to "interpose the sovereignty of the state of South Carolina between the federal courts and local school officials." In November, *The Richmond News Leader* gave interposition its biggest boost with an editorial campaign. By April 1956 the legislatures in four Deep South states, Alabama,

Georgia, Mississippi, and South Carolina, along with Virginia had passed resolutions of interposition.

Observing the southern resistance from Washington, Thurmond remained convinced his own hostility to *Brown* was not only philosophically comfortable but good politics as well. On January 26, 1956, when white Carolinians gathered four thousand strong in Columbia for a pep rally of sorts against "forced integration," Thurmond joined them.

The meeting was the first gathering of the South Carolina Association of Citizens' Councils, and the featured speaker was Senator Eastland. Johnston was also on hand, as were Governor Timmerman, former governor Byrnes, and state House Speaker Solomon Blatt—as obvious a sign of respectability for the councils as any organization could want. Eastland fired up the crowd by calling the justices "nine politicians in judicial robes" and charging that their desegregation decisions were influenced by a "propaganda barrage" inspired by a "radical pro-Communist political movement." Interposition was the only way for the South to regain its power.

Thurmond was not a main speaker at the Columbia rally. His task was to introduce Eastland, and he used his brief remarks to assert that the justices were "not worthy to wear the robes of their high office."

Back in Washington, Thurmond used his first newsletter of the year to express regret that Eisenhower had endorsed a civil rights commission in his State of the Union address. It was the president's first request for civil rights legislation, and in calling for a bipartisan commission to investigate discrimination, Eisenhower said that "in some localities . . . Negro citizens are being deprived of their right to vote and likewise being subjected to unwarranted economic pressure."

Thurmond considered the commission proposal another example of overreaching from Washington. "Such a resolution shall never be passed as long as I am able to stand on the floor of the Senate," the senator said in his newsletter, underlining his promise for emphasis.

(Ultimately, Thurmond was unable to make good on his boast, but the Senate did block legislation in 1956 despite House action.)

By late February, Thurmond had a decision to make that would affect the rest of the year. As part of his write-in campaign he had promised voters to resign and run in a primary at the next election cycle, and that time was rapidly approaching. Already a number of friends and advisers were urging Thurmond to back off the promise. A delegation of business leaders even came up to Washington for a personal meeting to tell the senator that giving up his seniority was not good for the state. But Thurmond was adamant. On March 3 the senator announced that he was sticking by his campaign pledge. In a statement sent out to constituents and made part of the *Congressional Record,* Thurmond said he would resign as of April 4, the day before the filing deadline for the June 12 primary, and that he would run in the primary for the remaining four years of the term.

In his report to constituents, Thurmond added that he was resigning before the primary because "I would not want to have any advantage which might result from my holding office during this primary campaign."

The senator's decision drew warm praise from southern colleagues and salutes from Carolinians for being true to his word. Dent, who had privately hoped the senator would remain in office, was convinced years after the fact that Thurmond's willingness to resign became a critical element in his hold on the South Carolina electorate. In a single stroke he had once again proved that he was both bold and trustworthy. Dent also felt Thurmond earned the quiet respect of his colleagues by taking the risk, even those senators at odds with him politically. "None of them would have done that," Dent insisted.

While he still held his Senate seat, though, Thurmond had work to do. Since the beginning of the year he had been developing his own anti-integration initiative, a united southern attack on the original *Brown* decision. The idea interested Harry Byrd of Virginia, and early in February the two senators pressed for a meeting of the entire southern caucus. While they waited to see whether the caucus would meet, Thurmond prepared a draft declaration and sent it to the other senators.

This first proposal was restrained, considering the bombast that so often crept into Thurmond's speeches. It criticized the May 17 decision for disregarding the historical background of the Fourteenth Amendment and relying instead on "the opinions of modern-day sociologists and psychologists." Because the Constitution did not mention education and because the Tenth Amendment reserved to the states those things not specifically delegated elsewhere, his proposal argued that "public education is a matter for the States and the people to control." The draft ended with eight specific declarations criticizing the court, commending states that were resisting the decision, protesting "the usurpation of legislative power by the court," and urging approval of a resolution insisting that "equal protection is provided to all citizens where separate but equal public facilities are maintained. . . ."

Some of the senators opposed the idea of any manifesto; others, while not adamantly against it, said the declaration would do no good in the larger fight against the court decision. But when Thurmond and Byrd said they would issue a statement themselves with as many signers as they could get, Senator Walter George of Georgia, the senior southern senator, called a meeting for February 8.

After a series of editing sessions involving several different drafting committees, the final document, "Declaration of Constitutional Principles," was ready for signatures March 12. Nineteen southern senators signed what became known as the Southern Manifesto, and eighty-one members of the House signed a separate copy. The only southern senators who did not sign were Estes Kefauver and Albert Gore of Tennessee and Majority Leader Lyndon B. Johnson, whose refusal was not unexpected. Stennis conceded that Johnson "wasn't just a senator from Texas, he was a leader and had a different responsibility in that degree."

Senator George read every word of the declaration into the March 12 *Congressional Record.* Although it incorporated all of Thurmond's points, the final version had a more graceful touch and dramatic tone than his original draft. "The unwarranted decision of the Supreme Court in the public school cases is now bearing the fruit always produced when men substitute naked power for established law," the manifesto began. "The Founding Fathers gave us a Constitution of checks and balances because they realized the inescapable lesson of history that no man or group of men can be safely entrusted with unlimited power."

By signing the document, the senators were declaring the Supreme Court decision "a clear abuse of judicial power." It was, they said, the climax of "a trend in the Federal Judiciary undertaking to legislate, in derogation of the authority of Congress, and to encroach upon the reserved rights of the States and the people."

Echoing Thurmond's original draft, the manifesto pointed out that the Constitution did not mention education, then talked briefly about the Fourteenth Amendment and discussed separate but equal, a concept that "became a part of the life of the people of many of the States and confirmed their habits, customs, traditions and way of life. It is founded on elemental humanity and common sense, for parents should not be deprived by government of the right to direct the lives and education of their own children."

Although no constitutional amendment or act of Congress had been passed to change "this established legal principle almost a century old," the declaration continued, "the Supreme Court of the United States, with no legal basis for such action, undertook to exercise their naked judicial power and substituted their personal political and social ideas for the established law of the land."

By its act, the court was now responsible for "creating chaos and confusion" in the affected states, and for "destroying the amicable relations between the white and negro races that have been created through ninety years of patient effort by the good people of both races. It has planted hatred and suspicion where there has been heretofore friendship and understanding."

The final declarations, similar to those in Thurmond's first draft, were offered with "the gravest concern for the explosive and dangerous condition created by this decision and inflamed by outside meddlers. We reaffirm our reliance on the Constitution as the fundamental law of the land," the senators said. "We commend the motives of those States which have declared the intention to resist forced integration by any lawful means." They added an appeal to states and individuals "who are not directly affected by these decisions to consider the constitutional principles involved against the time when they, too, on issues vital to them, may be the victims of judicial encroachment. . . .

"In this trying period," the manifesto concluded, "as we all seek to right this wrong, we appeal to our people not to be provoked by the agitators and troublemakers invading our States and to scrupulously refrain from disorder and lawless acts."

When George finished his reading, Thurmond took the floor and later repeated his views for television cameras. The "opposing propagandists" had neglected the facts "in their zeal to persuade the world there is but one side to this matter," Thurmond said. South Carolina had tried to avoid any disruption of "the harmony" that had characterized black and white relations for generations, but outside agitators had made the task difficult. If not for the "professional racist lawyers" hired with "funds contributed by persons who were permitted to deduct the contributions from their taxes"—a reference to the NAACP—he was sure that "our people of both races in South Carolina would have continued to progress harmoniously together." As proof he noted that in Clarendon County the black school was a better facility than the white one. "Yet Negroes continue to seek admission to schools for the white race."

Thurmond insisted that he and other southerners were "free morally and legally to fight the decision. The people and the States must find ways and means of preserving segregation in the schools. Each attempt to break down segregation must be fought with every legal weapon at our disposal. . . . All of us have heard a great deal of talk about the persecution of minority groups. The white people of the South are the greatest minority in this nation," he declared. "They deserve consideration and understanding instead of the persecution of twisted propaganda."

While the Republicans sat silent, liberal Democrats felt moved to respond. Oregon's Wayne Morse was the most dramatic. Based on the arguments just presented, "you would think today Calhoun was walking and speaking on the floor of the Senate," he thundered. "I say again today that the doctrine of interposition means nothing but nullification. If the gentlemen from the South really want to take such action let them propose a constitutional amendment that will deny to the colored people of the country equality of rights under the Constitution, and see how far they will get with the American people."

A unanimous Supreme Court, made up, Morse noted, of men "with the tradition of the South in their veins, has at long last declared that all Americans are equal and that the flame of justice in America must burn as brightly in the homes of blacks as in the homes of whites."

The southerners' declaration was front-page news north and south, but it was *The New York Times* that astutely placed the event in the larger political context. William S. White, who had written so cogently about the 1948 convention in Philadelphia, considered the manifesto a break in the "three-year practical armistice on civil rights issues" that Johnson and House Speaker Sam Rayburn, also of Texas, had tried to forge with their southern colleagues and the northern moderates.

Anyone who knew Thurmond or who listened to the way he described himself—a South Carolina Democrat—should not have been surprised that he was a leader in this potentially divisive move. Being a team player had never been uppermost in his mind, and it certainly wasn't now, when "custom and tradition" was at stake.

As he had promised, Thurmond resigned from the Senate April 4 and went back home to Aiken. As many Carolinians had predicted, nobody filed to run against him in the primary.

In July, everyone's attention turned to the national party conventions. Eisenhower and Nixon were renominated, and Stevenson once again was the Democratic nominee. This time his running mate was Kefauver of Tennessee, who had been elected by the convention rather than selected personally by Stevenson. Kefauver won on the second ballot, narrowly beating out the young Democratic senator from Massachusetts, John Kennedy.

Civil rights matters were once again a focus of discussion as the Democrats decided how to respond to the two *Brown* decisions. The party platform recognized the high court decisions as law but rejected "all proposals for the use of force" in carrying them out. The convention turned aside a plank that called for legislation to assure equal voting rights and employment opportunities. Instead, the platform pledged to "continue efforts" to eliminate illegal discrimination in these areas. Thirty-seven of South Carolina's forty convention delegates, including Thurmond, voted against even this moderate platform.

(In their platform, Republicans said they accepted the *Brown* decision and expressed the belief that "true progress can be attained through intelligent study, understanding, education and good will." The party also called on "all branches of the federal government" to support the "work of the courts" in achieving equality before the law.)

The summer and fall passed uneventfully for Thurmond. He did travel to Nashville, where he was invited to address the first anniversary celebration of the Founders of Tennessee's Federation for Constitutional Government, one of the state's resistance groups that numbered among its members wealthy business executives. By this time, Thurmond had his anti–Supreme Court speech well honed, accusing the justices of "the most vicious form of federal encroachment" on the rights of the states and warning that "we are slowly being destroyed by judicial law. . . ." Zeroing in on the *Brown* decisions, Thurmond charged that the court "has, in effect, set themselves up as an almighty board of education to regulate the public school system in my state, your state, and every other state of this great Union—and we don't like it." He aimed his harshest blast at black leaders, calling them "the Red-tinted officials of the NAACP, whose nefarious record stands as proof of its unworthiness."

Eisenhower and Nixon were handily returned to the White House in November, and Thurmond, who was unopposed, had a free ride back to the Senate for four more years.

Before the 1957 session got under way, the Supreme Court spoke once again on race. The justices November 13 affirmed a lower court decision that struck down Montgomery, Alabama's ordinances requiring segregation on city buses. A month later they refused to rehear the case, ending the segregation, at least by law, and the boycott that Rosa Parks had started. With a victory in Montgomery, black civil rights leaders looked forward to 1957.

Although the Eisenhower administration had previously seemed aloof from civil rights matters, this year the president was going to be drawn more deeply into the issue. Thurmond, on the other hand, had been expressing himself on the matter since 1948 and was about to escalate his rhetoric from a constant grumble to a roar.

As George Lee had prophesied, the ballot was the catalyst for change. Movement on civil rights in 1957 was directly related to the election returns in 1956. In northern industrial cities, a substantial number of black voters were shifting away from the Democrats to the GOP, and neither party's northern wing could ignore this trend. Republicans believed they could shore up party ranks by appealing to minorities; Democrats feared that if they couldn't pass a civil rights bill now, when they controlled the House and the Senate, they would pay in the next election.

There was also striking news from the South, where Republicans had done well among urban blacks. As the memory of Franklin Roosevelt diminished and the visibility of the Russells, Thurmonds, and Eastlands increased, black defection from the Democrats rose. Three days after the election Senator Humphrey charged that Democrats "are digging their own graves by inaction in the field of civil rights."

The story of the southern black vote was a complex one, for

1

Strom Thurmond at the age of six months.

The home Strom Thurmond lived in as a child in Edgefield, South Carolina. This rambling house on Penn Street was a short distance from the town square and courthouse, the center of Edgefield life. Thurmond's father, J. William, often brought friends home for the family's midday meal. Their lively discussions around the dinner table gave young Strom his first exposure to politics.

2

3

Pitchfork Ben Tillman made his mark in South Carolina by leading a farmers' revolt against the entrenched commercial powers. A virulent white supremacist, he was the architect of the state constitution adopted in 1895 that disfranchised black Carolinians and mandated segregated schools for South Carolina children. (Tillman was almost always photographed in profile because he lost his left eye as a teenager.)

4

J. William Thurmond, Strom Thurmond's father, left, and Democratic gubernatorial candidate Ira B. Jones conferring at a candidates' meeting in Edgefield during the 1912 election. Strom attended this meeting and, entranced by the political debate, vowed that someday he would run for governor.

5

The Edgefield High School ninth-grade class, 1917–18. Thurmond is in the top row at the far right.

6

Thurmond was active in a number of extracurricular activities at Clemson College. He is second from the left (in the white shirt) in this picture of the Calhoun Literary Society, of which he was president in the 1922–23 academic year.

7

After finishing college, Thurmond taught school. During the summers he taught special classes for boys interested in farming. This session was in 1925, and Thurmond is showing the boys how to pluck a chicken.

8

Thurmond after his election in 1928 as Edgefield County superintendent of schools. During his campaign he promised to streamline the education budget, institute new courses on health, and provide free health exams for the county's children.

9

10

As a state senator from Edgefield County, Thurmond worked on a number of education issues. He played a key role in passage of an education reform bill in 1935 that raised teacher salaries and extended the school year. He was on hand, third from the left (in double-breasted suit), as Governor Olin D. Johnston signed the bill.

Thurmond volunteered for service in World War II in 1942, giving up his position as a state trial judge. He served in France, and here is driving a German tank that was captured in Normandy in June 1944.

11

Governor-elect Thurmond and his mother, Eleanor Strom Thurmond, at her Edgefield home in December 1946. Early in his administration he earned a reputation as a progressive governor, but before his term was up he would become one of the South's leading defenders of segregation.

12

The state capitol in Columbia during Thurmond's inauguration as governor on January 21, 1947.

13

14

Thurmond, who fancied himself a ladies' man, and two young women during a summer vacation in Myrtle Beach, South Carolina, in 1947. He was a few months shy of his forty-fifth birthday.

Thurmond and Jean Crouch attend a football game in Columbia on October 11, 1947. Her parents announced her engagement to Thurmond the next day.

Life magazine ran this picture of Thurmond and Jean Crouch the day before their wedding, November 6, 1947. The caption read "VIRILE GOVERNOR demonstrates his prowess in the mansion yard."

15

16

The Thurmonds after their wedding at the governor's mansion in Columbia.

17

Thurmond addressed a caucus of southern delegates in Philadelphia, Sunday evening, July 11, 1948. His anger at northern Democrats and their civil rights proposals was apparent as he told the group, "We have been betrayed, and the guilty should not go unpunished." Arkansas governor Ben Laney is seated next to Thurmond.

18

On the third day of the 1948 national convention, a group of Democrats backing a stronger civil rights plank than the one originally proposed for the party platform unveiled their proposal. Hubert H. Humphrey, an up-and-coming Democrat who was the mayor of Minneapolis, was chosen to present the new language. His stirring speech caught the attention of the delegates when he challenged them to "get out of the shadows of States' Rights and . . . into the bright sunshine of human rights." The new civil rights plank was accepted, prompting all of the Mississippi delegates and half of those from Alabama to walk out of the convention.

19

John McCray, editor of The Lighthouse and Informer, *a newspaper published in Columbia, was a leader of the Progressive Democratic Party, which had petitioned the Democratic National Committee for representation at the convention in Philadelphia.*

20

After winning two federal lawsuits brought with the help of the NAACP, black Carolinians were allowed to vote in the South Carolina Democratic Party primary in August 1948. Because there was virtually no Republican Party in the state, the primary was the only election that mattered. Black residents in Columbia are lined up here to cast their votes.

21

U.S. District Judge J. Waties Waring, left, who had ruled in favor of black litigants challenging restrictive voting practices in South Carolina, is pictured here at the start of a school desegregation case in May 1951 with two other federal judges, John J. Parker, in the middle, and George Bell Timmerman. In Briggs v. Elliott, Parker and Timmerman voted to uphold segregated schools. Waring dissented. The Supreme Court later overturned the decision on the same day it banned segregated schools in the Brown v. Board of Education case.

Vice-President Richard M. Nixon swearing in Thurmond as a United States Senator on January 5, 1955. Thirteen years later Thurmond was instrumental in Nixon's election to the White House.

22

After more than a decade of disaffection with the Democratic Party, Thurmond switched to the Republican Party in September 1964 and then campaigned for nominee Barry Goldwater. The two are seen here at a rally in Greenville, South Carolina.

23

Thurmond's closest and most influential aides in Washington were Harry S. Dent, center, and J. Fred Buzhardt, right. They helped persuade him to switch parties in 1964 and then to back Richard Nixon in 1968. Each was rewarded with an important job in the Nixon administration.

24

25

When Thurmond arrived in Miami for the 1968 Republican Party convention, he was surrounded by Nixon backers.

26

Thurmond had declared his support for Nixon in June 1968 and worked hard during the GOP convention in Miami to keep southern delegations from defecting to Ronald Reagan, who had a substantial following in the region. Here Thurmond is heading toward the convention floor with Nixon backers Representative Rogers C. B. Morton of Maryland, right, and Senator Paul Fannin of Arizona, left. Thurmond attached a personal note to his own copy of this picture, explaining that his "action during the convention was crucial in providing key support for Nixon's effort to win the nomination."

27

A month after the November 1968 election was over, Thurmond, now sixty-six, married twenty-two-year-old Nancy Moore of Aiken. They are shown here in the spring of 1971 with their first child, Nancy Moore.

28

Nearly two years before he was up for reelection in 1972, Thurmond started to court South Carolina's black community more aggressively. One of his new supporters was civil rights activist Victoria DeLee, who said she would support Thurmond because he was "getting the job done." Thurmond helped DeLee get a $70,000 federal grant for a day-care center.

29

One of Thurmond's most attractive political assets was his family, shown here near their home in Columbia in December 1977. From left, Paul, twenty months; wife Nancy; Julia, three; Thurmond; Strom junior, five; and Nancy Moore, six.

30

31

Thurmond faced his toughest opponent in 1978, Democrat Charles D. "Pug" Ravenel, a native of Charleston and graduate of Harvard, where he had been a student leader. The forty-year-old Ravenel repeatedly challenged the seventy-five-year-old Thurmond to debate during the campaign, but the senator refused to do so. Here the two candidates have a chance meeting while campaigning at a shopping center in Greenville.

To prove that he was still fit and energetic two months shy of his seventy-sixth birthday, Thurmond slid down the pole at a Columbia firehouse in October 1978. His son Strom was celebrating his sixth birthday at the station. Thurmond repeated the slide more than once to give photographers and reporters ample opportunity to record the event.

32

When Thurmond took over as chairman of the Senate Judiciary Committee in January 1981, one of the most important issues that faced the panel was renewal of the Voting Rights Act of 1965, which had transformed the southern electorate. Thurmond had opposed the original act and two extensions. To show their support for the legislation and to pressure Thurmond to back the law now, a thousand demonstrators marched into his birthplace of Edgefield on June 28, 1981.

33

Thurmond reviewing the troops at Fort Jackson, South Carolina, on October 9, 1982.

34

Throughout his entire life, Thurmond was a physical fitness buff. He continued to work out regularly at a health club through his eighties. Here he is during an evening exercise period in the winter of 1991, several weeks after his eighty-eighth birthday.

while blacks were voting in greater numbers, they still faced formidable barriers to meaningful participation. A study by the biracial Southern Regional Council had shown that black registration in the eleven states of the old Confederacy had more than doubled between 1947 and 1956, from 595,000 to just over 1,200,000. Exemplary as this improvement appeared, the council pointed out that only about 25 percent of voting-age blacks had registered compared with 60 percent of the eligible whites. Mississippi provided a particularly compelling example of black disfranchisement. In the thirteen counties with majority black populations there were 72,325 voting-age blacks yet only 3,304—a paltry 4 percent—had registered to vote.

The council reported that "killings, beatings, the dragging of Negroes from their homes in the middle of the night—these are now rare occurrences compared to previous decades." Instead there was a more refined but still effective way to keep down black voting—the literacy test. Blacks wanting to vote, the council concluded, "are more likely to be barred by a question on the Constitution than by a rope or whip."

A few months before the council's report was published, John Herbers, then a correspondent for United Press, had described how the heavy-handed efforts to bar black voters resonated outside the South. "Bars against Negro voting, against his right to participate in the functions of government, is the point outsiders always find the most shocking about the Southern way of life . . . ," he wrote in the fall of 1956. "Mississippi has been successful in selling racial segregation to some outsiders. A great many Northerners can understand why Southern whites fear things like intermarriage and social mixing. But they look at voting in a different light."

Ten years would pass before enactment of a voting rights act with enough muscle to make a difference, but 1957 would be a start.

In his State of the Union address January 10, Eisenhower called for passage of a civil rights bill with three main components: the bipartisan investigative commission he had requested the year before, a civil rights division in the Justice Department, and more authority for the attorney general to use court orders to protect civil rights. This third part of the proposal was the most volatile, a red flag to southerners concerned about court-ordered integration.

Two days after the State of the Union speech, Senator Russell challenged the president, telling him that the civil rights proposal in its "present form" would be "vigorously resisted by a resolute group of Senators." Alluding to the 1956 election returns and the political discussions they had spawned, the Georgian acknowledged the "great political pressure to pass this bill." But he pledged that "I will not compromise in the slightest degree where the constitutional rights of my state and her people are involved."

Senate Judiciary chairman Thomas C. Hennings, Jr., a Democrat from Missouri, tried to get subcommittee hearings on the president's measure, but southern Democrats, joined by some Republicans, blocked the effort. Meanwhile in the House, hearings went forward in a Judiciary subcommittee. On February 26, Thurmond, who was a one-man army of opposition, journeyed across the Capitol to deliver detailed testimony against the pending legislation.

Not only was a civil rights commission unnecessary—congressional committees could do the job, Thurmond said—but "there is no justification for an investigation in this field." Giving the attorney general broad injunctive powers would be an invitation to "meddle with private business, police elections, intervene in private lawsuits and breed litigation generally. They would keep our people in a constant state of apprehension and harassment."

Thurmond also threw a barb at the antilynching bills that still were on the agenda, using statistics from the South and the North to argue that the focus was on the wrong region of the country. At his request the Library of Congress had searched for cases classified as lynchings, and relying on reports from Tuskegee Institute in Alabama, the library had come up with only fifteen lynchings between 1946 and 1955—and not all the victims were blacks.

By contrast, FBI reports for the same years in Chicago, New York, and Washington, with a total population of fourteen million people—about two million fewer than in six southern states—showed 6,630 murders and manslaughters. "These facts speak for themselves," Thurmond said, wondering aloud why the "6,630 killings which have taken place in three cities of fourteen million people have attracted no attention" in Congress.

The senator's testimony notwithstanding, two and a half weeks later the subcommittee approved legislation embodying the president's civil rights program. The full committee sent the measure to the House April 1 after making only minor changes. The House passed it without change June 18.

Now it was time for the issue to be joined in the Senate. Stymied by the Judiciary Committee's refusal to hold hearings, two of the bill's supporters used a procedure that bypassed the panel and placed the legislation directly on the Senate calendar, where a majority could force its consideration at any time.

Well before the debate even began, Russell and Majority Leader Johnson had had a number of private visits about the legislation, each session reflecting the senators' own specific concerns. Both were consummate strategists, however, with a gift for assessing the larger political forces at play, and they dealt in the world of the possible, which was not always the preferable. Russell first and foremost wanted to protect his state and the South from an encroaching federal government that would force integration. Johnson needed to keep control of the Senate, watch his flank in Texas, and at the same time try to enhance his reputation for leadership by moving a civil rights bill he believed was inevitable—and necessary.

Publicly, Russell said only that Title III—the section that gave the attorney general broad powers—would allow "the whole might of the federal government . . . to force the commingling of white and Negro children in the state-supported schools of the South" and that he would have to vote against it. Privately, he made sure Johnson understood that the South would not accept that section under any circumstances and that he would personally lead a filibuster. Johnson would find it virtually impossible to pass a bill, and on top of that would find himself in a bind with Texans, who would see how valiantly the other southern senators had fought in defense of the region. But maybe, Russell said, they could do business if two conditions were met: elimination of Title III, and the addition of a new amendment requiring a jury trial in contempt of court cases that arose out of disobeying the federal government. Southerners wanted to avoid being at the mercy of a single judge.

Johnson was not without his own bargaining chip: a deal to preserve some of the intricate, even byzantine Senate procedures that had served the South so well. The most popular—the filibuster—could be used to stop a bill from coming to the floor and later to prevent its passage. As things stood, two-thirds of the body—sixty-four senators if all members were present—was required to cut off a filibuster. An effort by northern moderates to make it easier to shut off debate had failed in 1953, but since that time reformers had picked up seventeen new allies, not yet a majority but getting closer. Johnson admonished his regional colleagues to seek compromises and let a civil rights bill pass so that the two-thirds rule for cloture, the term for ending debate, would remain.

On July 8, William Knowland of California tried to call up the civil rights bill for the Senate's consideration, prompting eight days of talking by southerners. (Senate officials estimated there were sixty-six speeches in all.) The nonstop debate signaled their public opposition, but at the same time it was the catalyst for serious negotiations in private off the Senate floor. They had borne enough fruit in a week's time so that a compromise—as Johnson had urged—was at hand. This became clear on July 16 when the Senate finally agreed to bring the civil rights bill to the floor. The vote on this technical "motion to proceed" to the bill was 71–18. All eighteen "nay" votes came from the South.

Sandwiched between stemwinders from Hill and Talmadge, Thurmond had made a long speech July 11 arguing that the real objective of the proposal was "to force upon the South, by use of craftily designed laws, the acceptance of racial integration. Do not be deceived by the statements that the main purpose of this bill is to protect the voting rights of Negro citizens," Thurmond asserted. "The real purpose is to arm the federal courts with a vicious weapon to enforce race mixing."

Pointing the same accusatory finger he had in House committee testimony five months earlier, Thurmond told Senate colleages that "even the most biased observer who has been through the slums of [northern] cities—including the Nation's capital—has viewed scenes far worse than can be found in the South. Living conditions of a Negro family in the poorest house of the rural South are not as undesirable as the squalor of slum dwellings in the cities."

The senator ended his twenty-page peroration with a plea for moderation. "Profound human emotions are bound up in this entire matter," he said. "Traditions, customs and mores cannot be resolved by political agitation, by court fiat, or by force of law. Urgency of action will not attain the results sought by the sponsors of this legislation," he insisted. "Understanding should replace urgency in this matter."

Thurmond had finished for the day, but it was not the last time the Senate would hear from him on the civil rights bill of 1957.

Speaking at a news conference July 18, Eisenhower promised he would never use federal troops to enforce school integration, telling reporters he would never have to because "the common sense of America will never require it." Unfortunately, circumstances he had not anticipated were in the offing.

Southerners won an important victory the next week when the Senate July 24 agreed to kill the objectionable Title III. The bill now essentially limited the attorney general's authority to protecting the right to vote. But southern pressure for a jury-trial amendment still remained.

The civil rights community and the administration were vehemently opposed to any jury-trial proposal, arguing that it would render the bill completely ineffective, especially where voting rights were concerned. Roy Wilkins, who was now head of the NAACP, argued the generally accepted wisdom that no southern jury would ever convict white state officials charged with keeping blacks from the polls. There was ample evidence they wouldn't even convict when blacks had been brutally slain.

For a week, private negotiations and public posturing, including a plea from Eisenhower to keep a jury-trial amendment out of the bill, dominated Senate activities. But the compromise that was developing provided for jury trials in a host of cases beyond voting rights matters when jail time was a possibility. The southerners quickly picked up valuable support from organized labor, whose members had too many sharp memories of strikes broken by state militias on the order of a single judge.

Shortly after midnight on August 2, Johnson felt the time was right to move on the compromise amendment. When the roll call was over, the proposal had prevailed 51–42. Later in the day Eisenhower complained that the jury-trial addition had made the bill "largely ineffective."

On August 7, the Senate passed the full bill by a vote of 72–18. The only southerners who supported it were Johnson, his Texas colleague Ralph Yarborough, Tennessee's Gore and Kefauver, and George Smathers of Florida—all border state senators. Their states had smaller black populations than the Deep South and consequently less tension over racial issues. For these senators, a vote in favor of a civil rights bill did not mean the automatic end of a career.

To Thurmond, even the partially eviscerated bill was unacceptable, but it was then made even worse by a new jury-trial compromise struck in negotiations with the House. The final provision provided that in contempt cases over voting rights the defendant could request a trial by jury but only if a judge had already imposed a fine greater than three hundred dollars or of more than ninety days' imprisonment.

Thurmond wanted southerners to fight the new compromise. At a southern caucus August 24 in Russell's office, he pressed his position but to no avail. When the Senate took up the legislation shortly after the House passed it, Thurmond made a surprise move to bury the measure in the Judiciary Committee, but his motion was rejected. A testy Johnson commented that Thurmond had not even given him the courtesy of warning him ahead of time.

With the other southern senators unwilling to make an all-out assault on the bill, Thurmond decided to go his own way. At 8:45 P.M. on August 28 he went out onto the Senate floor; he began talking at 8:54 P.M. and would not finish what he had to say until 9:12 P.M. August 29—a record twenty-four hours and eighteen minutes.

The decision to make a stand was his alone. He didn't consult anyone on his staff, but early in the evening Dent thought something was up when Thurmond began gathering reading material to take to the floor. Earlier he had gone to the Senate steamroom for a long time, dehydrating himself as much as possible so that as he drank water later in his filibuster, his body would absorb it like a sponge. Leaving the chamber even for the bathroom would have meant giving up the floor.

Jean Thurmond had known her husband would not be home for dinner, but she had no idea he wouldn't make breakfast either. She cooked him a sirloin steak at their apartment, wrapped it up in tinfoil, and brought it to his office around dinnertime along with a large piece of pumpernickle bread.

Before he left for the floor, Thurmond put a handful of malted milk tablets in one pocket and throat lozenges in another. Jean went up to the third floor of the Senate, to sit in the special gallery for senators' family, where she would stay the entire night. Nearby was the NAACP's chief lobbyist, Clarence Mitchell.

"Mr. President, I rise to speak against the so-called voting rights bill, H.R. 6127," Thurmond began, standing in front of his desk at the back of the chamber. Then he read aloud the election statutes of every state in order to show why federal voting laws were unnecessary. There were about fifteen senators on the floor as he began his speech, but not long into his oratory the number dwindled.

About 1:30 A.M. Arizona Republican Barry Goldwater gave Thurmond a little relief when he asked permission to insert some material into the record. A half hour later Thurmond finished with the election laws and then turned to the right to jury trials in contempt cases. He started with an opinion by Chief Justice William Howard Taft, "a great man and a great American," Thurmond said. He discussed the opinion, lacing his reading with criticism of President Eisenhower for misstating facts about Taft's position on the issue.

During the night, Dent and another aide, concerned about Thurmond's health, tried to get their boss to quit, but the senator was insistent. Periodically, he asked Dent whether telegrams or calls had come into the office. He had been hoping that when news of his one-man stand got out, people throughout the South would rally to his side and urge their own senators to join the cause.

Shortly before 4:00 A.M. Jean Thurmond signaled to Dent, down at her husband's side, to come up to the gallery. "It's time for him to quit," she told him. "You've got to stop him."

"We've been trying," Dent replied, "and we haven't been able to do it."

At 6:30 A.M. Republican leader Knowland came into the chamber to tell Thurmond he was fighting for a lost cause. It was an ironic moment because in most respects Knowland was as conservative as Thurmond, yet here he was hounding the South Carolinian about his stalling tactics on a civil rights bill. Congress was not going to adjourn without passing a civil rights bill, Knowland said. He wondered aloud whether Thurmond was trying to impress upon the Senate the need to change the rules so that it would be easier to choke off these marathon talkfests.

"I would merely say that my purpose in making the extended address is for educational purposes—to educate the Senate and the people of the country," Thurmond replied.

By this time Thurmond's voice was just above a whisper, so low that it was nearly impossible to hear him in the galleries surrounding the chamber. But by midmorning he seemed to recover his strength and began rereading a statement he had delivered two days earlier urging that the bill be sent back to the Senate Judiciary Committee.

Shortly after 11:00 A.M. Senator Paul Douglas, a Democrat

from Illinois, came to the floor with a large pitcher of orange juice, poured a glass, and gave it to Thurmond, who drank it with gusto. Dent, realizing that too much liquid could force the senator to the rest room, quickly grabbed the pitcher and put it on the floor out of his reach. (Though Dent had wanted Thurmond to quit much earlier, by now, as a loyal aide, he was not going to sabotage the effort.)

Just before 1:00 P.M. Thurmond nearly lost the floor when he sat down while answering a question from William Langer of North Dakota. Dent frantically whispered to him to get up, which he did, and Herman Talmadge, who was presiding, apparently chose to ignore his colleague's momentary lapse.

There was another interruption in the afternoon, when Democrat William Proxmire was sworn in. Thurmond rushed into the cloakroom to get a bite of a sandwich, reminded by Dent that he needed to keep one foot in the chamber. While he kept the cloakroom door open, he went all the way inside. But Vice-President Nixon, who was presiding by this time, had been going through some papers at the rostrum and didn't notice that he could have forced Thurmond to relinquish the floor.

During the day, Thurmond had dropped in on the Declaration of Independence, the Bill of Rights, and Washington's "Farewell Address," but he read their majestic phrases in such a low monotone that they could have been so many items from a grocery list. Once, when the senator's drawl had slid into a barely audible mumble, Knowland asked him to speak up. Thurmond suggested Knowland move a little closer to the rear of the chamber, but the Californian replied that he was "well satisfied" with his seat.

By late afternoon, Dent was deeply concerned about Thurmond's health. He was approaching twenty-four hours in his filibuster and had had hardly a thing to eat. Finally, Dent went to see the Senate doctor to get his assistance in ending the marathon.

Dent went back to the floor with explicit directions from the physician: "You tell him to get off his feet or I'm going to take him off his feet."

Around 9:00 P.M. August 29, Thurmond decided to wind things down. "I should like to believe that some have been convinced by my arguments, and that my arguments have been accepted on the basis on which I intended them to be accepted—as arguments against what I am convinced is bad proposed legislation," Thurmond said. "I expect to vote against the bill," the senator added, to the laughter of his colleagues. After telling Senate officials and clerks that he was "deeply grateful for their courtesies" during his daylong effort, Thurmond announced, "I now give up the floor." He left the chamber at 9:12 P.M., having broken the previous filibuster record of twenty-two hours and twenty-six minutes set by Senator Morse three years earlier.

Dent was waiting in the cloakroom with a pail in case Thurmond needed to relieve himself in a hurry. But he brushed his aide aside and went to find his wife. Jean Thurmond greeted her husband with a kiss that was photographed by the waiting press and prominently displayed in many newspapers the next morning. She told reporters that he often got mail addressed to "Strong Thurmond" and that the previous day had proved the writers correct.

(Earlier in the year the senator had garnered press attention for a different kind of strength in adversity. In March he and Senator Frank Lausche had been flying together to Charleston when the plane developed engine trouble. Thurmond was sleeping, and when Lausche woke him to tell him about the problem, Thurmond paid no attention. Lausche repeated the news a few minutes later. This time, Thurmond opened one eye, said, "I know it," and went back to sleep. After the plane had made a safe landing, Thurmond told reporters, "There was nothing I could do about it; I wasn't flying the plane." The next day *The Washington Post* explained: "Strom Thurmond Snoozes Serenely When One of Two Motors Also Konks Out.")

After the filibuster was over, the Senate approved the final bill 60–15. This time Johnson, Yarborough, and Kefauver were the only southerners who voted for the bill. Gore was not recorded, but because of a special Senate rule he was allowed to indicate in the *Congressional Record* that he would have supported the measure. On the other side, Johnston, Ervin, and Sparkman were similarly not recorded, though they noted their opposition to the bill.)

The day after the vote Russell felt he had to offer the South an explanation of why he and other southerners did not join Thurmond's one-man campaign. Indeed, Thurmond's office had received hundreds of calls and telegrams from southerners congratulating him on his stand. Frankly, Russell said, there were not enough votes to prevent choking off a full-fledged filibuster if they had tried one. Furthermore, the strategy might have prompted the other side to scuttle the compromise and restore broader powers to the attorney general. The senators had determined that they had "nothing to gain and everything to lose" by attempting a stall. In a jab at Thurmond, Russell added, "Under the circumstances we faced, if I had undertaken a filibuster for personal aggrandizement, I would have forever reproached myself for being guilty of a form of treason against the South."

The more restrained approach brought concessions that confined the bill basically to voting rights but without effective enforcement tools. That the legislation kept "the withering hand of the federal government out of our schools and social order is to me the sweetest victory of my twenty-five years as a senator . . . ," Russell said. Without these modifications, he went on, southerners "might have gone to their death resisting federal bayonets or have wasted away in federal concentration camps seeking to keep their children in schools attended by their own kind." Southerners should be aware, he cautioned, that "they are in for difficult times.

"I can only urge our people to display the same courage, devotion and patience that enabled our forebears to survive the years of Reconstruction," Russell said. "The politically dictated persecution which may await us can eventually outrage the sense of decency inherent in the masses of the American people of today." Correct in many other judgments during his long career, Russell was 100 percent wrong on this one. The decency of Americans on which he counted would indeed come into play but not on the side he thought.

The Civil Rights Act of 1957 became law on September 9 when Eisenhower signed the bill while vacationing in Rhode Island. On the same day, Martin Luther King, convinced that legislative compromises meant blacks had to do more for themselves, called a council of preachers together in Montgomery. The clergymen officially proclaimed themselves the Southern Christian Leadership Conference.

Although black leaders and their most vocal white supporters were disappointed with the final bill—some thought it was worse than nothing—passage of the measure was symbolically important for the civil rights cause. "It's just a beginning," an enthusiastic Johnson told one group of activists. "We've shown that we can do it. We'll do it again in a couple of years."

In more personal ways, the 1957 legislation helped flesh out the political portraits of Lyndon Johnson and Strom Thurmond. The majority leader had added to his reputation as a master deal maker. He had kept the chamber from revolt, appeasing his southern flank while satisfying the northerners. With energetic ease he could talk to both sides, telling Illinois Democrat Douglas at one moment, "If we're going to have any civil rights bill at all, we've got to be reasonable about this jury-trial amendment," and whispering to Ervin a few minutes later to "be ready to take up the Nigra bill again" as soon as the pending business was finished. As significant for Johnson, he was able to put his own stamp on the legislation so that the Civil Rights Act of 1957 was not something created wholly by a Republican administration. James Reston was moved to observe in *The New York Times* that one of the prime topics of discussion in the Senate cloakroom was "how it was that Lyndon Johnson managed to get so many odd fellows together." This was just a taste of what was to come from this rangy, powerful Texan who would eventually make good on his promise to "do it again in a couple of years."

For Thurmond, the filibuster joined the states' rights campaign as a permanent part of his political identity. Thirty-five years after the fact, no one had yet broken his filibuster record, and he remembered the event in such vivid detail that it was hard to believe three decades had passed. He was adamant that the South could have filibustered successfully if Russell had gone along. He refused to concede that the Georgian's tactical compromises were necessary and remained convinced that Russell was motivated more by a desire to help Lyndon Johnson pass a civil rights bill—and thereby boost the Texan's presidential hopes—than by a wish to protect the South or the filibuster rule.

At the very least the 1957 filibuster was another example of Thurmond's energy and stamina. To supporters, his marathon performance proved yet again his dedication to his beliefs regardless of the prevailing currents. To detractors, however, the filibuster was just another grandstand maneuver that had no impact on the final outcome and only indulged Thurmond's philosophy of "seize the moment, the consequences be damned." The broader worries—provoking damaging changes to the filibuster rule or having a more draconian measure forced on the South—were of no moment. Strom Thurmond was not about long-term strategy. What was important to Thurmond was "standing with the people," and the correspondence flowing in before, during, and after the civil rights debate convinced him that he was standing with at least a vocal segment of them. The mail was so voluminous that it had to be catalogued by month and divided into in-state and out-of-state folders. After the Southern Manifesto was presented, one woman from Georgia praised Thurmond for "your courage and wisdom." "Wouldn't it be possible to remove much of the Negro population from the South?" she asked. "I sincerely wish that this might be done, and would be glad to even contribute personally to the expense of such a plan."

Typical of the laudatory mail that came in as Thurmond was preparing for his filibuster was one from a Walterboro man, who encouraged the senator in a telegram to "fight on the floor to the last ditch the dastardly attempt" to pass the bill. "We appreciate the great fight that the southern senators have made," he added. "Don't give up the fight now."

There was the occasional letter urging "a more Christian and far-seeing view of the racial problem," and Thurmond answered these by asserting that southerners treated blacks better than northerners did, and that in any event, he did not "believe it to be practicable to mix the races." Despite these letters, however, it was clear to Thurmond where "the people" stood.

The passage of the civil rights bill and the modest fireworks that accompanied it in the Senate were nothing compared to the explosion over civil rights in Arkansas. On September 3, after a federal district judge ordered Little Rock to integrate its schools immediately, Governor Orval Faubus called out the National Guard to stop nine black students from enrolling in all-white Central High School. Faubus, however, claimed that the troops were needed to "keep order" because violence and bloodshed might occur. A crowd of about five hundred whites had assembled for a sunrise protest that morning.

On September 4, nine young blacks tried to enter the school, but the guard blocked their way as an angry crowd, more militant than the previous day, jeered and shouted, "Niggers go home." It was an eerie counterpoint to the nineteen hundred white students who streamed into school to start the new year, greeting old friends after the summer break and carrying textbooks and lunch boxes as though it were just another day.

On September 20, after increasing pressure from a federal judge and a hastily arranged meeting between Faubus and a vacationing Eisenhower, the governor agreed to remove the militia from the school. On Monday morning, September 23, with the black students at last in the building, the violence Faubus had predicted finally erupted. Despite the presence of local and state police to protect the black teenagers, a belligerent and sometimes hysterical mob, one thousand strong, smashed its way into the school and forced the students to withdraw. Police got them out shortly before noon. Integration at Central High had lasted three hours and thirteen minutes.

This was too much for Eisenhower. He had pledged not to use force to integrate the schools, but now there was no denying a crisis. He couched it, however, not in terms of integration but rather in terms of an insurrection, and he told Attorney General Brownell that if it had to be, "then let's apply the best military principles to it and see that the force we send there is strong enough that it will not be challenged and will not result in any clash."

By the evening of September 24, one thousand soldiers had converged on Little Rock. School integration resumed the next morning, when the nine black students entered Central High protected by a cordon of armed soldiers who surrounded the school.

From Washington, Senator Russell, "normally mild mannered and soft-spoken," *The Atlanta Constitution* noted, lit into the administration. He accused the president of using "storm troopers to intimidate and coerce the people of the South. . . . This sort of totalitarian rule might put Negro children in white schools," he said, "but it will have a calamitous effect on race relations and the cause of national unity."

In the opinion of the Columbia *State,* "Mr. Eisenhower has let his South-hating advisers, led by Brownell, lead him into a situation that reflects no credit upon his administration. And we fear he has taken action that could worsen, instead of improve, race relations."

Had Thurmond been in the country he surely would have commented on the debacle in the harshest possible terms. But, a military reservist, he was in Europe on duty and didn't return until the initial brouhaha had subsided. Little Rock, however, remained fixed in his mind as an outrageous assault on state power. Early in 1958 new developments arose in the dispute, now magnified by the growing pressure for more civil rights legislation. This time Thurmond would have his say, venting his frustration and anger at a federal government gone out of control. With each new development his rhetoric grew harsher, a symbol of the heightened resentment and hostility in so many southern quarters over this menacing threat to segregation.

Since the previous September, the nine black students had remained at Central High, but further desegregation efforts were stymied by continued opposition from the local White Citizens' Council. On February 21 the Little Rock school board went back to federal court asking for a delay in the court-ordered integration schedule until tensions at the high school eased. Noting the event the next day, Thurmond inserted a story about the new lawsuit into the *Congressional Record.* "The folly of forced racial integration has been clearly demonstrated," he said. "The action of the federal administration in this matter was illegal and irrational."

In May, Thurmond blistered Senator Herbert Lehman, Democrat from New York, for asserting that the fight against integration in the South was hurting American foreign policy. Lehman had said that the United States was "losing the battle of Asia, Africa, and Latin America in Little Rock, Charleston, and Richmond."

Thurmond admitted that there had been violence in Little Rock, but it was "committed by U.S. Army soldiers against white Southerners and by the President of the United States against a sovereign State and against the Constitution. . . . No," Thurmond charged, "it is not in the peaceful and racially separate schools of Richmond and Charleston that students stab one another in the corridors, that teachers are assaulted by students, and thirteen-year-old girls are raped under the basement stairs by pupils. It is in the integrated school system that these things occur." Tossing a barb at Lehman, Thurmond said he was certain "it will bring a flush of shame to his cheeks and a pang of regret to his heart when he stops to realize that, instead of criticizing the South for political purposes, he could have addressed his great talents to the fearful situation which exists in the crime-ridden integrated schools of New York, a situation which brings glee to our enemies and disgust to our friends abroad."

After the Supreme Court refused September 13 to give Little Rock any more time to integrate, Thurmond bellowed that "The bias which Chief Justice Warren and other members of the Court demonstrated . . . is evidence that today's decision was made by closed minds which are more concerned with mixing the races where it is neither desired nor practical than with fostering the education of our children and preserving the Constitution."

In a speech in October he escalated his rhetoric, calling the justices "nine puppets of the NAACP." Thurmond's insult was part of a fifteen-page critique of the high court—"the greatest enemy of the American people." There was not just one troubling decision, the senator said, but "a series of opinions which place a premium on being a member of a minority group or an adherent to a Red-tinged philosophy."

Three weeks later, the senator went even further, telling a thousand southerners in Augusta that "We in the South are not about to surrender, not now or in the future." He urged the enthusiastic crowd to "declare total and unremitting war on the court's unconstitutional usurpations and unlawful arrogations of power. We shall launch the most massive campaign of all-out non-violent resistance ever witnessed on this continent . . . resistance which we pledge to keep up until the constitutional freedoms for which our ancestors struggled and died [are] secure.

"Let us make it grimly clear to the court," Thurmond urged, "that we reject both of its unacceptable alternatives: that we will maintain an adequate system of mass education for all people—either public or private—and that we will maintain it segregated."

If Thurmond had not served another day as a United States senator, he would have been remembered by many who look back on this time only as the consummate white reactionary. His reliance on states' rights would have been discounted as subterfuge for white supremacy, and his relentless opposition to civil rights would have made his estimable record as governor seem insignificant. But Thurmond was a survivor, an energetic one at that, and there were many more episodes of history that he would influence and that would influence him. Just as his staff in the 1980s were startled by the 1948 footage from Birmingham, so too did they shake their heads in wonderment at his stridency in this turbulent period.

In the new year, the senator proposed legislation for collaring the Supreme Court. Late in January he introduced a bill establishing minimum qualifications for appointees to the high court. Among other things, any nominee would have to have at least five years' experience on a federal district or appellate court or on a state trial or appellate court. Thurmond said he hoped the bill (which was never enacted) would help return the court "to its proper sphere of activity." In his Senate remarks he tore into the court once again for "the outstanding judicial blunder of all times"—the *Brown* decision—and for decisions making it more difficult to prosecute criminals and to protect against alleged subversives. The court, Thurmond said, "has thwarted efforts of both the Congress and the Executive Branch to insure the internal security of our country. It has unleashed on society self-confessed rapists, murderers and other criminals."

The new year brought one positive development for the senator. On January 19 he finally was given a seat on the Armed Services Committee. He had always believed in a strong national defense and had wanted to get onto the committee earlier, but a combination of the seniority system and Lyndon Johnson's pique at the headstrong Carolinian helped keep him off. In a story announcing the new assignment, *The Greenville News* noted that "in contrast to prior years, Thurmond cooperated with Majority Leader Lyndon B. Johnson by avoiding extended debate on proposed rules changes." With cooperation came rewards. Now Thurmond could play a role in keeping the military strong, and he would hold on to this cherished post for the rest of his career.

In February, Eisenhower sent Congress a new set of civil rights proposals. Though it would take another year for a bill to pass, the wrangling in 1959 brought to the surface the three-way split in congressional sentiment. Southerners remained stalwart in their opposition to any civil rights measures. Northerners, on the other hand, were divided: some favored the moderate legislation proposed by the administration and backed by House and Senate leaders, while stronger measures were supported by a majority of northern Democrats and about a third of the Republicans. The message for the South, however, was unmistakable. It was not whether another bill would eventually pass but what it would look like.

Among other things, the president had asked for an antimob law, making it a federal crime to interfere with a federal court order on school desegregation; an antibombing law, making it a federal crime to cross state lines to avoid prosecution for bombing a church; a proposal giving the Justice Department the right to inspect voting records and requiring preservation of the records; an extension of the Civil Rights Commission, due to expire in the fall; and provisions for the emergency schooling of children of armed forces personnel in the event the public schools they attended were closed by integration disputes.

On March 18, Thurmond went before the Senate Judiciary Committee's Constitution Subcommittee to comment on "the so-called civil rights proposals." While some were worse than others, as a whole, Thurmond said, the legislation was "punitive" and "viciously anti-Southern." Taken together, they treated the South like a "conquered province."

In April, violence once again intruded on the national scene. Mack Charles Parker, a truck driver in the southern Mississippi town of Poplarville, was arrested and charged with raping a white woman. Although Parker had been out with friends the night the woman was raped, most whites in Poplarville believed Parker was guilty. Three days before he was to stand trial, eight masked white men dragged Parker from his jail cell, beat him, shot him in the heart, and threw his body in the Pearl River. Though he wasn't found until ten days later, white Poplarville knew quickly that Parker was dead, and they knew who had done it. Yet when FBI agents investigated, no one would speak up. Fear—and a sense that the killing was justified—kept anyone from coming forward. The county prosecutor said he would refuse to prosecute anyone arrested for the crime, a promise he kept even after persistent FBI agents came up with solid evidence against the lynch mob.

The county prosecutor refused to present the FBI evidence to the state grand jury, and when the federal government sought to get an indictment under civil rights statutes, the federal grand jury likewise refused to indict. No one was ever prosecuted for the murder. One Mississippi official explained why the lynching was needed: "If we set back and waited for the government to prosecute and punish Mack Parker, it would never happen. So we did it ourselves."

To civil rights advocates, this kind of brutal episode was precisely why civil rights legislation was needed. The white South—and Thurmond was the epitome—could talk about states' rights, but the rhetoric rang hollow when there seemed to be a paucity of state responsibility.

Although Parker's lynching received nationwide attention, the outrage outside of Mississippi was not enough to power legislation in Washington. In 1959 the civil rights bills went no further than the House and Senate Judiciary Committees. The only exception was the extension of the Civil Rights Commission, which received funding through November 1961 in an unrelated appropriations bill. But before it was passed, southerners, including Thurmond, trooped to the Senate floor to denounce a report the commission had issued September 9 recommending the use of federal registrars to assure that minorities could vote. The report also recommended the withdrawal of federal aid from public and private schools that refused to integrate, and it endorsed a policy of integration in housing developed with federal funds.

Back in South Carolina, Governor Hollings, later to be considered one of the new-generation southerners, issued a statement at the end of the year explaining his "policy of 'no cooperation'" with the Civil Rights Commission. He had refused to appoint a state advisory panel to work with the commission because "we need no such advisory forum."

Moreover, "by participating in this political scheme, we extend the idea that there is a need and at the same time give substance to a commission in violation of fundamental constitutional principles. I believe the commission with its powers is unconstitutional."

Politics should have consumed Thurmond's life in 1960. He was up for reelection, this time for a full six-year term, and it was another presidential year. Southern Democrats still felt alienated from their northern counterparts, and civil rights was sure to be an issue once again in the platform. Johnson had long harbored presidential ambitions and was planning to make a run for the White House this time around, but so was the much younger Kennedy, a handsome, glib politician who had not impressed Thurmond very much.

But for Thurmond it was a personal crisis that dominated the first weeks of the year. In the spring of 1959, friends had begun to notice that Jean was more pale than usual and had lost weight. By midsummer she was feeling even more tired and had to curtail her usual schedule of escorting constituents around the Capitol three days a week. In late August she had back-to-back fainting spells, which prompted Thurmond to get medical attention for her. A day or two later she had a seizure, and within a week she was a patient at the National Institutes of Health. Doctors removed a brain tumor they believed was the cause of her problems.

Because she was so young and possessed that legendary southern charm, Jean Thurmond had been instantly popular in the Senate circle, more so than her husband. As soon as she came to town she had been the subject of newspaper articles focusing almost exclusively on her youth, her attractiveness, and her skill in handling wifely duties. They hardly suggested that she was a partner to Thurmond in ways beyond traditional homemaking. But those closest to the senator at the office knew she influenced him, not only smoothing his rough edges but giving him substantive advice. Dent and Buzhardt joked from time to time that just when they had gotten Thurmond to agree to do something, "he'd go home and sleep with Jean and come back with his mind changed."

The doctors determined that the tumor was not malignant, but Jean was still not out of the woods. In early October she was well enough to go home to Elko to recuperate. Thurmond, by now a brigadier general in the Army Reserve, left a few days later for two weeks of active duty; doctors had assured him Jean was doing as well as could be expected.

Thurmond wrote her regularly, offering in one note to resign from the Senate if that would help her recovery, but the Thurmonds were back in Washington to celebrate their twelfth wedding anniversary November 7. Jean, however, was not making the kind of progress she had hoped—Betty Dent, Harry's wife, could see this when, on one visit, Jean couldn't remember the names of the Dent children.

Toward the end of a monthlong recess back in Elko, Jean's condition deteriorated markedly, and on January 3 she was flown back to the NIH in an air force hospital plane. Surgery was performed to relieve pressure on her brain, this time from a rapidly progressing malignant tumor, but she slipped into a coma and never regained consciousness. She died at 8:35 A.M. January 6, surrounded by the senator, her parents, and a few other family members.

The entire South Carolina congressional delegation attended Jean's funeral, along with Governor Hollings and former governor Timmerman, Majority Leader Johnson and his wife, and Senators Russell, Eastland, Stennis, Talmadge, Yarborough, and John

McClellan of Arkansas. When Dent and Buzhardt heard that LBJ had come to Aiken, their first response was one of cynicism. "That rascal," Dent said, shaking his head. "He'll go that far to win the senator." He was referring to Johnson's interest in the presidency and his desire to have Thurmond's support.

After the funeral, Dent was standing beside the senator as people came through the receiving line. When Johnson came through he expressed his sympathy, telling the shaken Thurmond how much he had admired Jean. Thurmond told Johnson that he appreciated his making the trip to Aiken, and through his tears told the majority leader, "I hope you're the next president of the United States."

"Fred," said Dent, turning to Buzhardt, "he got what he came for."

The loss of Jean Thurmond manifested itself most obviously in the senator's daily routine. Now that he had nothing to go home to, he stayed in his office late at night when there really was no need for it, keeping a secretary on hand to help reorganize his desk drawers or calling in aides for a late-evening meeting. Fortunately there were still political concerns to keep him occupied—his own reelection, the presidential election, and the push for another civil rights bill.

Thurmond devoted his January 25 newsletter to criticism of the civil rights proposals that had remained on the congressional agenda. He was most distressed about the Civil Rights Commission's recommendation for federal voting registrars in the South. Five separate bills to accomplish this purpose had already been introduced. "Seldom, if ever, have legislative proposals been considered which flaunted so many constitutional provisions," he said. If any one of them passed, he insisted, it would be "the most outright defiance of the Constitution since passage of the Reconstruction Acts."

Consideration of the voting proposal began in the Senate on February 15. By the end of the month debate on the bill had blossomed into a full-fledged southern filibuster. During that time, the Senate met around the clock with only two breaks.

Addressing the legislation in his March 7 newsletter, Thurmond swore that "Regardless of what compromises may be advanced in the 'civil rights' extended debate—and they will come—the only complete victory I can count for the South, and ultimately the nation, is no bill at all. Toward this end I pledge my utmost efforts."

On March 10 a bipartisan group of liberal senators moved to cut off debate but were unable to rally a two-thirds majority. Two weeks later the House helped move things along, passing its own civil rights bill by a healthy 311–109 vote. When the House bill came over to the Senate, sponsors of the Senate measure abandoned their own legislation and instead decided to work with the House proposal. Senators gave the Judiciary Committee until midnight March 29 to revise the bill for full Senate action.

In the interim, Thurmond took time out to announce March 25 that he was running for reelection. Six days later he learned he would have token opposition in the primary from eighty-year-old R. Beverly Herbert, who had been a leader of the moderate Democratic group in 1948. Herbert said he was seeking the nomination because the southern side on civil rights needed a better voice. While Thurmond had been a good governor and was a good senator, Herbert contended, "the presentation of the Southern side of segregation and civil rights before the United States Senate and the country has been weak, lame and inadequate." He said the country needed to know "the full truth about the NAACP," particularly what he insisted was its communist backing, and that southerners had done a great deal to improve black schools. With very little campaigning, Thurmond would trounce Herbert in the primary, getting 89.5 percent of the vote.

The Senate began consideration of the civil rights bill March 30 and passed the measure a week later, April 8. The vote was 71–18. All eighteen "nay" votes once again came from the South. The only southerners who supported the measure were Johnson, Yarborough, Gore, and Kefauver.

The House passed the Senate version April 21 by another sizable margin, 288–95. Eisenhower signed it into law May 6.

The heart of the bill was the section to protect voting rights. While the final provisions were an improvement over existing law, southerners had forced through enough changes that the government, in order to enforce voting protections, would have to wend its way through a cumbersome melange of federal procedures. The most ardent civil rights advocates contended that the new law was really a southern triumph, not theirs.

To help blacks register, the attorney general first had to win a civil suit for deprivation of civil rights brought under the 1957 law. That done, he could then ask a court to hold another proceeding and make a separate finding that there had been discrimination against potential black voters in the community under challenge. If the finding was made, then any black could apply to the court for an order declaring him qualified to vote provided he met certain conditions. State officials would be notified of the order and would then be required to permit that individual to vote. Contempt of court could result from disobeying the court order.

The Civil Rights Commission had recommended a far simpler plan that would have allowed the president to designate registrars after determining that state officials had refused to register qualified black voters.

Thurgood Marshall called the new law "a fraud" that would take two or three years of a good lawyer's time to register one black. And a disgruntled Roy Wilkins complained that "A Negro has to pass through more checkpoints and more officials than he would if he were trying to get the U.S. gold reserves in Fort Knox."

Following Eisenhower's recommendations of the previous year, the final legislation also included criminal penalties for bombings and bomb threats, and for obstruction of court orders by mobs.

A week before Senate passage, Thurmond had gone to the floor for another speech, this one giving passionate voice to southerners' deep-seated feelings that they were pawns in a northern game to win black votes in the cities. A staunch defense of segregation, it was a mixture of hurt feelings, pride, history, philosophy, and psychology and was largely Buzhardt's work. Lest anyone miss the *Congressional Record* for April 1, Thurmond's office published his remarks in a twenty-five-page press release that claimed "Senator Russell and other Southern senators have described [this speech] as one of the best given in the Senate on the South's position on segregation."

The efforts to court blacks had now become so extreme, Thurmond said, that a presidential candidate not only could not be a southerner but he "must, indeed, have demonstrated forcibly his anti-South attitudes." There was not a desire for true integration of black and white, Thurmond charged, for such integration did not even exist in the North. What makes the North angry, the senator went on, "is the South's having a different *kind* of segregation from the kind the North has." Efforts to impose "so-called civil rights programs and racial integration on the South," he claimed, are based on "this powerful subconscious desire to make the South conform."

The North had not and would not be successful. The Civil War proved that. "Despite all the physical destruction and death that violence accomplished, the North," the senator insisted, "failed to destroy the South spiritually." Thurmond was the best evidence.

Thurmond also devoted his April 11 newsletter to the civil rights bill, pointedly titling this one "Not All Black." (The double entendre by 1990s standards was probably unintended, for in 1960 "black" was not a synonym for "Negro.") The report was a discussion of all the things the NAACP had been unable to get in the legislation, including the registrars proposal and the provision, excised in 1957, to give the attorney general authority to bring a wide range of civil rights suits. Another NAACP defeat, he said, was failure to get congressional endorsement of the 1954 *Brown* decision.

"This is not the end of the rejected proposals," Thurmond warned. "As long as the minority bloc votes constitute or can convince politicians they constitute the balance of power in heavily populated states, politicians will attempt legislative lynchings of the South to incur their favor. As shown by this year's Congressional fight, all is not black yet; and as long as we keep our guard up and fight vigorously, all will not be black."

Next on the agenda was the Democratic Party convention, and by the time it was over Thurmond would be one step closer to leaving his party for good. Senator Kennedy had come to Los Angeles—the first time a convention had ever been held in the California city—as the front-runner, the result of his successes in the primaries and of backing from the party's urban leaders. Johnson was still in the running, banking on holding the southern states behind him.

South Carolinians reaffirmed their support for LBJ when the delegates caucused July 11 in Los Angeles. Thurmond told the group that Johnson was "the best friend of the South among the presidential candidates." Although Hollings, now South Carolina's governor, had been reported leaning to Kennedy, he too announced his support for the Texan.

Nine men were nominated for president, but Kennedy received a clear majority on the first ballot. The next day Kennedy turned to Johnson to be his running mate in an obvious effort to court the South. LBJ had carried every Deep South state except Mississippi, which had reserved its 23 votes for its favorite son, Governor Ross Barnett.

What goodwill Kennedy may have engendered by selecting Johnson was outweighed in many southerners' minds by the platform's civil rights plank. It was the strongest the party had ever adopted, calling for establishment of a Fair Employment Practices Commission, a permanent Civil Rights Commission, and authority for the attorney general to bring lawsuits to aid desegregation. The platform also demanded that "every school district affected by the Supreme Court's school desegregation decision should submit a plan providing for at least first-step compliance by 1963, the 100th anniversary of the Emancipation Proclamation."

Senator Ervin's effort to delete the provisions on the FEPC, the Civil Rights Commission, and the attorney general's expanded authority was rejected on a voice vote. Delegates from nine southern states signed a statement repudiating the civil rights section and offered a minority report to the convention, but that too was rejected by voice vote, after an hour-long debate.

Calling the platform "so outrageous as to be ridiculous," Hollings issued a statement July 14 making clear that South Carolina's continued presence at the convention was "in no sense an approval of the platform report." The same day, *The News and Courier* made clear its distaste for the platform by calling it the "Lynching at Los Angeles." The platform "makes a mockery of the Constitution," the paper charged. "It is a bald appeal to the herded Negro voters of key Northern states."

A week after the convention, Thurmond (with rhetorical help from Buzhardt) issued a five-page attack on the party platform that was as blistering as his passionate Senate speech April 1. Calling it a strategy for divide and conquer, Thurmond said, "The document's approach is directed not at Americans and citizens as such, but at innumerable special interest groups, blocs, and minorities. To each, with the exception of fifty million Southerners, the platform dangles a juicy lure of political pap. For Southerners it offers only derision, contempt and beratement." Before he got to the civil rights section, Thurmond belittled the foreign and domestic policy sections for being misguided and even dangerous to American interests. "The so-called civil rights plank," he wrote, "is the most extreme, unconstitutional and anti-Southern ever conceived by any major political party. It is difficult to imagine how a more obnoxious and punitive approach could have been composed. Even the NAACP in all its fervor has never proposed more drastic steps."

All in all, the senator said, the platform "is a blueprint for a welfare state and an end to individual liberty and dignity in the United States of America. It is a road map for economic collapse and unconditional surrender to the forces of socialism. It is a chart for amalgamation of the races and a reduction of the individuals of which the country is formed to the lowest common denominator. It sounds the final death-knell of the Democratic Party known to our forebears and completes the transition to a party dedicated to socialism, welfare statism, conformity and centralization of power."

Strom Thurmond had been a disaffected Democrat for almost a decade. The convention marked the last leg of his journey out of the party. Over the next three months he would distance himself from the ticket, all but admitting that he was going to vote Republican.

To Ralph McGill, the aggressive editor of *The Atlanta Constitution,* Thurmond's defection from the party would be welcome. On August 9 he used his regular column to blame Thurmond and other states' righters for the South's political decline. "Since 1948, Southern political power steadily has waned. And if any accusing fingers are to be pointed, they should be directed toward the leadership in South Carolina and Alabama, which spearheaded the Dixiecrat third party."

The next day an angry Thurmond shot back, "If the South had listened to 'Rastus' McGill in 1948 and if it listens to him now, we will enter a new era of Reconstruction under the direction of the NAACP and ADA, 'Rastus' McGill and his ilk." (The liberal Americans for Democratic Action had consistently given Thurmond poor ratings for voting against almost every measure the organization had supported.)

By September the rumors were strong in South Carolina that Thurmond was going to support Republican presidential candidate Richard Nixon and his running mate, Henry Cabot Lodge. But through Harry Dent, Thurmond denied the assertions. He insisted that he was remaining uncommitted and that he had not backed Kennedy and Johnson publicly only because of their support for the party platform.

By early November the hints were stronger that Thurmond would not support the ticket. The day before the election he renewed his criticism of the Democratic platform, saying he would vote his conscience "even if this does not suit the party bosses of the National Democratic Party." If the bosses "desire to retaliate against me, then they will just have to retaliate." Thurmond told one constituent in a letter made public just prior to election day that because he had fought against most provisions in the party platform, "I do not feel that I could in good faith or in good conscience turn around now and tell my people that I think they should vote for this platform, which carries for them in the South only humiliation and harassment."

John Kennedy prevailed November 8 by a slim margin, only slightly more than 100,000 popular votes. The electoral vote margin was more comfortable, 303 to 219. Fourteen electors, apparently loyal to an outspoken southerner, voted for Thurmond for vice-president—6 from Alabama and 8 from Mississippi.

One aspect of the postelection analysis paralleled 1956. Republican Party chairman Thruston B. Morton said Nixon had been hurt because he lost a large number of black votes to Kennedy. Claude Sitton of *The New York Times,* a southerner who had recently joined the paper, observed in his day-after story that while some white southerners were alienated by Kennedy's support of Martin Luther King, most observers contended "that these losses were offset by the Negro support he picked up." Kennedy and his brother Robert, Sitton explained, had made phone calls on King's behalf after the civil rights leader had been jailed on a minor traffic offense in Atlanta.

It was at once an example of the potential might of the black vote and a clue to the southern preacher's growing ability to shape the political agenda. Thurgood Marshall had used the courts. King was using the pulpit and the streets. Both had forced the parties to respond, and Thurmond had found the Democrats' answer increasingly wanting.

A natural assumption was that the senator would switch parties, but Harry Dent laughed out loud when he heard a report after the election that Thurmond would become a Republican. "He could have run as a Republican this year, if he wanted to," Dent said, squelching the rumor. "And I'll tell you this: If he had, he would have won. But he has no plans to run as a Republican in 1966. A man would be foolish to decide now what he's going to do six years from now," Dent added.

Wisely, Dent had left his boss some running room for the future.

11.
BREAKTHROUGH

1961–1964

EVEN JOHN KENNEDY'S critics had to admire the youthful spirit of the man, standing hatless and without an overcoat to deliver his inaugural address in the twenty-two-degree chill that enveloped Washington. The short speech captured the exciting promise Kennedy's election had meant to so many young men and women like himself. And it was of them he seemed to be speaking when he declared in his distinctive Boston cadence: "Let the word go forth from this time and place, to friend and foe alike, that the torch has been passed to a new generation of Americans. . . ."

He alluded to domestic issues that January day, but Kennedy's address was really a message to the world community, a statement of America's resolve in the face of global challenges. "Let every nation know, whether it wish us well or ill, that we shall pay any price, bear any burden, meet any hardship, support any friend or oppose any foe in order to assure the survival and success of liberty," he told the assembled throng. The international focus was fitting, for while Kennedy had invoked the notion of a "new frontier" to describe this new decade, on the explosive internal issue of race there were others blazing the trail far ahead of him and for a time ahead of the country's established black leadership. On February 1, 1960, a group of well-dressed black students from North Carolina A & T College, tired of the strictures of segregation, had marched into an F. W. Woolworth store in Greensboro and demanded to be served at the all-white lunch counter.

Ten days later the protest had spread to other North Carolina cities, moved into Virginia and South Carolina, and then to Florida and Tennessee. The students' aggressiveness threw white businessmen and political leaders on the defensive and shook up the older black leaders, who had not been consulted and were initially hesitant to back such brazen tactics.

The hesitancy was not long-lived. By the time John Kennedy proclaimed the passing of the torch, the metaphor had become an apt description of the civil rights movement. No longer a collection of diffuse tactics, the movement was going to surge forward with relentless energy over the next three years until the wall of resistance in Washington was breached; by then the first civil rights law would be passed that struck with specificity and force against the discrimination in American society. The Supreme Court's *Brown* decision had been pilloried as law made by nine unelected men. But the Civil Rights Act of 1964 would be tangible evidence that the nation's elected representatives, presumably sensing the mood of the people, were now following the court into a new era.

The struggle at the beginning of this new decade at times looked like an undeclared war, with its massing of troops on both sides and its painful episodes of violence. Between 1961 and 1964 at least eighteen people would be murdered. Four of them were black schoolgirls who died when a bomb went off one Sunday morning in 1963 at Birmingham's Sixteenth Street Baptist Church.

Such reprehensible acts always had the opposite effect intended by the perpetrators. Far from deterring the civil rights activists, the brutality stiffened their resolve. It also brought them new supporters—white and black, north and south—who were outraged at the senseless violence. This in turn increased the pressure on Kennedy, who faced a dilemma that mirrored Harry Truman's fifteen years earlier: how to extend a hand on civil rights without alienating the southern flank of the party? That the question was continually asked reveals an eternal truth about politics. Even when protections for human dignity are at stake, they have to be weighed against the vote count.

Kennedy had appealed for blacks' support more visibly than Truman had, and they had come through for him in the tight race against Richard Nixon. Now they wanted results. Restive and insistent by 1963, their demands escalated in demonstration after demonstration, but it was not until Medgar Evers was shot to death in the driveway of his Jackson, Mississippi, home that the president asked Congress to give him new laws to fight discrimination.

The tragedy of Dallas prevented Kennedy from seeing the legislation through. So it was Lyndon Johnson, using his formidable political skills and poignant reminders of the slain president, who achieved passage of the 1964 Civil Rights Act. Prior to this moment southern senators, clinging to the dependable cry of states' rights, had tried to sustain a solid bloc of opposition. But even back home cracks in the wall appeared now and then when the pressure for change, enhanced at times by the hand of the federal government, was so great that resistance gave way to negotiation and moderation.

Thurmond wanted no part of compromise and accommodation. He cast himself as the defender of "constitutional government," a bulwark against the country's slide toward socialism and the anarchy of the civil rights unrest. Thurmond's "constitutional government," however, presumed an interpretation of the document that paid little attention to those who had been left out when the country's charter was first written. It was their demands for recognition that collided head-on with his ideology.

The senator's commitment to states' rights guaranteed a growing hostility to most of the new proposals streaming out of the White House in these years. Sam Stilwell, who had joined the senator's staff in March 1961 right out of the University of South Carolina law school, developed a stock answer when folks back home asked if Stilwell worked for the government. "No," he retorted. "I work against the government."

Resistance was good politics. Orval Faubus, whose popularity shot up after he defied the government in Little Rock, had proved that. So had Alabama's John Patterson, who had beaten George Wallace in the 1958 gubernatorial campaign, prompting Wallace to vow that he would never be "out-segged" again. Four years later, Wallace ascended to the governor's mansion in Montgomery, transformed into Alabama's most ardent segregationist.

Though Thurmond never ordered police dogs on marchers, turned fire hoses on children, nor stood in a schoolhouse door, his continual assaults on integration were not without effect. He helped nourish the climate of resistance that made it difficult for more moderate voices to emerge, let alone be heard. He was too much the activist to adopt the middle ground taken by a number of his southern colleagues and say as little as possible beyond voting the interests of white constituents.

By 1964 civil rights groups had pierced the national conscience and pushed their concerns to the top of the country's agenda. Thurmond's response to the social upheaval was not to change his message but to speak from a new platform. He broke through the political wall that had surrounded the South since Reconstruction, cut his Democratic ties, and joined the GOP. The bold streak that had led him to defy the odds in 1946 when he ran for governor, in 1948 when he ran for president, and in the 1954 Senate write-in campaign had surfaced once again.

Other southern leaders may have longed to follow Thurmond out of the Democratic Party, but worries about their own political fortunes kept them in the fold, and he made his journey alone. Over the next twenty-five years, younger, more polished southern Republicans would eclipse Thurmond and solidify the GOP's hold in much of the white community. But no one could erase the fact that he had been first and that, if not for him, their opportunities might not have come at all.

Well before Kennedy took office in January it was apparent to senior Democratic senators that Thurmond would be a thorn in the new administration's side. Some legislators had already broached the possibility of forcing Thurmond and Virginia's Harry Byrd out of the party because of their perceived disloyalty during the 1960 campaign. Senator Joseph Clark, a Democrat from Pennsylvania, had suggested as much in a television interview, and Thurmond fired off an indignant reply, denying that he had "fought the ticket actively" in South Carolina. All he had done was refuse to endorse the platform or ticket of either of the parties. "I have never been a party liner," he explained, "because my personal convictions mean far more to me than do committee assignments, patronage or any of the other instruments of personal political power which come through conformity to the party line. My first obligation is to my electorate . . . ," he reminded Clark, "and they have have elected me and re-elected me."

Thurmond said he would accept whatever decision the Democratic caucus made when it met January 9, "but I do not expect to be run out of the Caucus by mere emotional outbursts and tirades against my non-conformity." The caucus did not expel Thurmond or Byrd, and however bad the fit, the two remained Democrats.

During his campaign Kennedy had asked Senator Clark and Representative Emanuel Celler, the New York Democrat who headed the House Judiciary Committee, to draw up civil rights legislation, but the administration said after the bills were introduced in May that "the president does not consider it necessary at this time." Other things were on his agenda, and he didn't want to alienate southern supporters—whom he needed for other initiatives—so early in his first term. (In an unusual turn of phrase, Thurmond had called the bill a "horrendus absurdum." Dent later explained to inquiring reporters that the term had been used by the Romans to describe a "horrible absurdity.") The only measure that would pass in 1961 was an extension for the Civil Rights Commission. But despite the paucity of legislation, there was plenty of debate on civil rights, some of it in reaction to events taking place outside of Washington, all of it a prologue to the fights looming ahead.

On March 25, Thurmond made his public debut as a defender of "constitutional government," tangling with New York Republican Jacob Javits on a network television debate over desegregating public housing. Javits argued for integration.

The senator spent hours preparing for the debate, keeping Stilwell in the office until 11:00 P.M. several nights before they headed up to New York for the program. They carried with them a large map showing that New York's segregated housing patterns were more dramatic than those in southern communities, a point so prominent in Thurmond's mind that it wiped out most of the more technical, legal arguments his staff had prepared.

The nub of Thurmond's "constitutional government" argument was really the states' rights creed tailored for localities and individuals. "It is my belief that local citizens are best equipped to deal with their own needs and problems," he explained, "and it would be foolish indeed for the national government to step in and strike down the remedies which local citizens have found . . . to best satisfy their needs for housing and for their dealing with racial differences."

Javits did not deny that there was segregation in New York, but he dismissed Thurmond's argument as not germane. "I cannot see where you can get any comfort from the fact that we are not perfect," he said. Seeking to broaden the issues in the debate, he asked why New York's imperfections should be a comfort to anyone when the goal was to "bring about some compliance with the Constitution, and indeed with common morality in terms of our country."

The consensus among Thurmond's senior staff was that their boss had not done very well. No matter what Javits said, Thurmond had responded that things were worse in New York. Not only that, the senator had looked stiff and uncomfortable in front of the camera, as though he regarded it as an enemy and not an ally to carry his message.

Radio was a different matter: Thurmond was quite accustomed to using weekly broadcasts to get his views across, and civil rights still figured prominently in the scripts, the hard edge of previous years undiminished. Six days after the session with Javits, Thurmond used a two-minute radio spot to attack the new activity in the black community, disparaging the "integrationists" who were trying to force their will on the region through "their sit-in and kneel-in demonstrations and other agitations." He mocked them for claiming that a "higher law" overruled "private property rights and the liberties of others," and insisted that "they thrive on martyrdom." And as always he sneered at politicians who treated segregation as "fair game to shoot at" in order to curry minority votes or even "a call to high national office."

In May, the nation's attention shifted to Alabama, where violence once again erupted in the face of new pressure from the black community. On May 4, thirteen members of the Congress of Racial Equality—CORE, as it was known—had headed south from Washington on two buses—one a Greyhound, the other a Trailways—to integrate bus terminals along the way. An extension of the previous year's sit-ins, this was a more direct challenge to "custom and tradition." A lawsuit was an intellectual confrontation with the past, but this would have the immediacy of human contact.

By May 13, after a bloody confrontation in Rock Hill, South Carolina, near the North Carolina border, the freedom riders arrived in Atlanta. Martin Luther King, in town to greet them, saluted their courage in facing down the segregationists, but he expressed concerns about the next stop, Alabama. He confided to Simeon Booker, a reporter for *Jet* magazine accompanying the riders, that the public was in an ugly mood.

When the Greyhound rolled into Anniston, a small city due east of Birmingham, a crowd of men stood waiting armed with clubs, bricks, iron pipes, and knives. They pounded on the bus and slashed its tires, until the driver, responding to pleas from terrified passengers, revved up the engine and backed away. Anniston police escorted the bus out of town. But racing down Highway 78 behind the Greyhound were about fifty cars with perhaps two hundred men.

The effects of the tire slashing were quickly apparent, as the bus began listing from side to side. Realizing his situation, the driver pulled off the highway, turned off the engine, and fled into the countryside. Like hunting dogs attacking their quarry, the mob converged on the bus, using bricks and a heavy ax to smash the windows. Finally, someone tossed a firebomb through a hole in the back window, and other men tried to seal the door to prevent the riders from escaping the swirl of black smoke.

The arrival of Alabama state troopers firing warning shots into the air finally ended the melee. The riders were taken to the Anniston hospital. Hours later a photograph of the crippled bus, smoke billowing out of its windows, was sent out on international wires for all the world to see.

All was quiet back at the Anniston station when the Trailways bus pulled in an hour after the Greyhound had left, but the calm was short-lived. When the group refused a demand from some Anniston whites that the black freedom riders move to the back of the bus, white fists started to swing, and the blacks were dragged to the back. Custom and tradition restored, the driver reboarded the bus and took his bruised passengers out of town. Next stop Birmingham.

With the first bus disabled at the side of the road, Ku Klux Klan members, stationed at Birmingham's Greyhound terminal, had to race four blocks to the Trailways station when they learned the Trailways had arrived first. Within moments fists flew and two riders, one white, one black, were beaten to the ground. The others tried to retreat but found that the Klansmen had blocked their way.

In their fifteen minutes of violence—an apparent time agreement with city police—the mob not only had beaten the riders but had injured seven bystanders badly enough for them to be hospitalized. Reporters were attacked, including a photographer from the Birmingham *Post-Herald,* who was hit with a lead pipe, his camera smashed.

The next day, *The Birmingham News* accused the freedom riders of "moving through the South to create racial trouble and make headlines," but they had harsher words for the city's own authorities. "Where were the police?" the paper asked, singling out Police Commissioner Eugene "Bull" Connor (his nickname came from his low, booming voice) for dereliction of duty. In a front-page editorial the following day, the *News* put a measure of the blame on Governor John Patterson. Under the headline THUGS MUST NOT TAKE OVER OUR CITY, the paper accused Patterson of "announcing officially in so many words that, though he was the state's chief executive, though he had many state highway patrolmen at his command, though he had the National Guard which he could have called out, he could not guarantee protection to a group of race agitators. . . . Law is law and authorities are fully equipped by the public and at the public expense to handle disorder."

Shaken by the violence heaped upon them, the freedom riders, hearing that Patterson had refused a request from Attorney General Robert Kennedy to give them safe passage through the state, abandoned plans to continue through Alabama and flew to New Orleans May 15.

The next day another group of activists in Nashville, determined to prove that they would not be intimidated, decided to continue the freedom rides through Alabama. After four days of tense negotiations among themselves and with state and federal officials, the group left Tennessee and headed into Montgomery, the Alabama capital, arriving late on the morning of Saturday, May 20.

Moments after their arrival the riders were attacked by a dozen men wielding baseball bats, bottles, and lead pipes.

During the two-hour melee at least twenty people were beaten, and one of Kennedy's assistants at the Justice Department, John Seigenthaler, was hurt badly enough trying to rescue a young white girl, that he had to be treated at a local hospital.

By nightfall, the federal government had sent four hundred federal marshals to Montgomery to restore order. In an official statement, President Kennedy called the situation "a source of the deepest concern to me as it must be to the vast majority of the citizens of Alabama and all America." Kennedy called on Patterson and the mayors of Birmingham and Montgomery "to exercise their lawful authority to prevent any further outbreaks of violence."

Patterson retorted that he had "no sympathy for law violators whether they be agitators from outside Alabama or inside-the-state troublemakers." His allegiance was made clear when he added that while the state would do its utmost "to keep the public highways clear and to guard against all disorder, we cannot escort busloads of rabble-rousers about our state from city to city for the avowed purpose of disobeying our laws, flaunting [*sic*] customs and traditions and creating racial incidents."

When the threat of violence escalated May 21, Patterson declared martial law in Montgomery. National guardsmen, armed with bayonets and wearing their riot gear, were dispatched to protect a black church where a meeting was in progress. Eventually, a white mob had to be dispersed when it tried to push its way past federal marshals who were already there. Inside, Reverend King had to postpone his speech for two hours while the unruly whites shouted taunts from outside. To help keep the frightened parishioners calm, King and the Reverend Ralph D. Abernathy, pastor of the church, urged them to keep singing. When King finally spoke, he said the violence in Alabama meant the state had "sunk to the level of barbarity comparable to the tragic days of Hitler's Germany."

On Monday, the third day of the trouble, Robert Kennedy ordered two hundred more federal marshals into Alabama and warned that the federal government would "take whatever action necessary."

The following day, the biracial group of freedom riders decided to continue its journey into Mississippi, a prospect that alarmed the neighboring state. In short order, Governor Ross R. Barnett called on Robert Kennedy to advise "the agitators to stay out of Mississippi," adding that help from federal officials was not wanted.

On Wednesday, May 24, twenty-seven freedom riders entered Mississippi under armed military escort. The riders, who arrived in two groups, were seized and jailed in Jackson when they refused a police order to leave the bus terminal's white cafeteria. They were the first of more than three hundred freedom riders that summer who went into Mississippi and directly to jail for their "breach of the peace."

Troubled by the events in Alabama, Thurmond felt compelled to make a Senate speech on the subject May 23. Mixed into his attack on the civil rights workers, the press, and the government was the specter of communism. A nefarious outside force was at work, the speech suggested; not only the southern way of life was threatened by these activities but all of America's as well.

Although Thurmond decried the violence and urged restraint on both sides, he had little sympathy for the activists and less for their cause. "Violence plays into the hands of the agitators," he cautioned, "for the horrors created by the picture of an angry mob effectively shield from the public all the evil instigation which lies at the root of the trouble." He faulted the press for ignoring "the obvious fact . . . that this is not a one-sided issue. . . . There can be no question that the purpose of the sponsoring organization, CORE, was to create trouble at all costs, and it succeeded. It ill behooves those who conspired and cooperated in begetting the violence to exhibit such a self-righteous attitude when it occurs."

Quoting from a *News and Courier* editorial, Thurmond now added communism to the debate. "Though it was unwilling to intervene effectively in Communist Cuba," the paper said, "the U.S. Government moved armed men into Alabama despite the protest of the Governor of that State." While not accusing all CORE members of being communists or "even conscious tools of communism," the paper contended that the activists "confuse freedom, social justice and democracy with subversion and revolution. Perhaps they are only muddle-headed idealists and fiery youths in search of excitement. But they are being used to tear out the vitals of the Republic." In the midst of this turmoil, the paper warned, "our people should not fall into traps set with Red bait."

Back home in South Carolina May 27, Thurmond continued his barrage against the freedom riders, calling them "Red pawns and publicity seekers" before a receptive audience of the Veterans of Foreign Wars. Once again he cautioned against the violence, which "hurts the Southern cause and wins sympathy for the integrators." But he charged the activists with "playing directly into the hands of the communists in agitating racial disturbances in the South."

To prove his point he cited testimony from FBI director J.

Edgar Hoover before the Senate Judiciary Committee. "Communist propaganda has always been quick to seize on problems of minority groups," Hoover had said. The proof, according to Hoover, had come from the lips of Benjamin Davis himself, the national secretary of the Communist Party USA, who "told the party in March 1960 that these demonstrations were considered the next best thing to 'proletarian revolution.' "

Charges that the civil rights movement was communist inspired seemed to rise in direct proportion to the intensity of activity. The white resistance apparently could take comfort in the belief that this assault on their way of life was the result of foreign intervention. Surely it was un-American. The allure of the argument was evident in the letters southerners sent to Washington to express their displeasure with the strife all around them. The missives seemed to confirm that the politicians had struck a chord by connecting the civil rights agitation to the Red Menace.

One Georgia woman wrote asking Senator Russell to "use your influence to unmask this man Martin Luther King. He is not interested in the negro as an individual," she contended, "but is using them to further the cause of communism. It is time this man is unmasked before America."

Thurmond's concern about communist domination went back at least two decades—as a young legislator he had tried to require South Carolina teachers to take a loyalty oath. He saw the current turmoil as just one more manifestation of infiltration. While he would exploit this theme in resisting civil rights efforts over the next few years, his most aggressive anticommunist battle was in protecting the government's treatment of army officers who wanted to speak out about the alleged Red Menace. He called it "muzzling the military." His concerns were triggered by the dismissal of Brigadier General Edwin Walker, who had commanded the troops at Little Rock, because he had reportedly tried to influence how the men in his command voted in the 1960 election. According to news reports, Walker had also referred to Eleanor Roosevelt, President Truman, and former secretary of state Dean Acheson as "definitely pink," and had branded as confirmed communists Edward R. Murrow, director of the United States Information Agency, CBS news commentator Eric Sevareid, and newspaper columnist Walter Lippmann.

Embarrassed by the charges, the army relieved Walker of his command pending an investigation. Later the army said the general had been "admonished" once before for his political activities but that he had failed to heed "cautions" from his superiors.

It took seventeen speeches by Thurmond and the help of seventeen thousand telegrams to his Armed Services Committee before the panel approved an investigation into the regulations governing appropriate speech by military personnel. (The senator preferred to think of the approval as authority "to study and appraise the use of military personnel and facilities to inform military personnel and the public of the total menace which the forces of world communism pose to the free world.")

After thirty-six days of testimony over four and a half months, the subcommittee filed its report in October of 1962: no remedial action by Congress was required because problems found to exist could be corrected by executive action.

Thurmond and Senator E. L. Bartlett of Alaska declined to sign the majority report. Bartlett issued a two-page explanation briefly outlining a single disagreement with the majority. Thurmond filed a 160-page report. His chief recommendation was that the "Military Establishment should continue to use its personnel and facilities to the maximum extent to inform the public on the issues of the cold war."

Those hearings helped secure Thurmond's reputation as a leading anticommunist in the Senate, and Buzhardt, who was known to have worked closely with the senator, was kept busy by conservative activists wanting his advice and ideas. The darker side of all the attention was the pressure put on Thurmond to take over where the late Senator Joseph McCarthy had left off. Robert H. Welch, the leader of the far-right John Birch Society, made more than one entreaty to Thurmond to become a member of the organization's board, but Thurmond, with the strong approval of Dent and Buzhardt, declined to associate himself with the group.

All of this anticommunist concern dovetailed nicely with the escalation of the civil rights movement and Hoover's campaign to discredit its leaders with strategic leaks about alleged communist infiltration. "There was no question but that we were fed information," Dent recalled years later. Thurmond didn't act on the allegations that were passed on to him, but they helped deepen his suspicions about Martin Luther King and his associates, and confirmed in his mind how correct he had been all along in his opposition to the movement.

When a two-year extension of the Civil Rights Commission

came before the Senate in August of 1961, Thurmond, characteristically, was among the most vehement opponents of prolonging the commission's life. "Although the Commission was created ostensibly for the purpose of dealing exclusively in the field of voting rights, they have, as anticipated, delved into the field of housing, education and employment," Thurmond said in a broadside delivered August 29, the day before the bill was sent to the House. "They have contributed nothing to improve race relations, but have done much to deteriorate them." It would be "an act of wisdom," he said, "for the Congress to permit to die that which should never have been spawned and which grows more hideous with each day's age." But Congress kept the panel alive.

Efforts to register more black voters in the South were never far from center stage, even as the freedom riders' more dramatic tactics captured the headlines. But in the rural South registration drives were better done unobtrusively; black suffrage went to the heart of white political power.

Herbert Lee, a farmer in the southern Mississippi town of Liberty, proved to be an invaluable aide to Bob Moses, who was running a voter education project in the state for the Student Nonviolent Coordinating Committee—SNCC, or "Snick," as it was known—which had been formed by a group of black student activists committed to change. Lee drove Moses and E. W. Steptoe, the local NAACP president, around the countryside to talk to other farmers about voting. In 1961 there was only one black registered in all of Amite County. It didn't take Moses long to find out why. The first time Moses went with three blacks to register at the courthouse, he was arrested and put in jail for several days. The next time, he was beaten. Another SNCC worker received the same treatment. This was enough to dissuade Amite County blacks from even thinking about registering. Many stopped coming to NAACP meetings.

But Lee and Moses kept traveling around, and Moses sent detailed reports of his activities to John Doar, an attorney in the Justice Department. Distressed by the accounts, Doar came to Amite County in September 1961 to see for himself. The first thing he wanted was a list from the NAACP of activists whose lives were in danger. Herbert Lee's name was at the top.

Doar went to Lee's farm September 24 after his visit with the

NAACP's Steptoe. But the farmer was not at home, and Doar flew back to Washington. The next day Lee drove up to a cotton gin in Liberty with a truckload of cotton. In front of several bystanders, state representative E. H. Hurst, who had followed Lee to the cotton gin, pulled up beside him. Lee slid out the passenger's side, but Hurst, now out of his truck, ran around to confront him. Hurst later claimed that Lee had tried to attack him with a tire iron, so he hit him in the head with his pistol, which went off accidentally and killed him. A white and a black eyewitness told the same story to a coroner's jury the next day, and Lee's death was ruled a justifiable homicide. The Jackson *Clarion Ledger* dutifully reported this version of events.

Moses found the black witness to the shooting, a hardworking logger named Louis Allen, who confided that he had gone along with the story to protect himself. Coming forward would mean certain reprisal, and even if the government could protect him—a doubtful proposition—there was no guarantee Hurst would be convicted. (Three years later Allen would be shot to death as he prepared to come forward with the truth—that Hurst had shot Lee without provocation.)

Lee's death was not national news, but it reverberated throughout the civil rights community and the Justice Department—one more piece of evidence that would eventually build a compelling case for tougher voting rights protections.

Despite the marked increase in civil rights activity in 1961, President Kennedy entered his second year of office still able to withstand pressure for broad civil rights legislation. But the White House did support a constitutional amendment outlawing the poll tax, and federal legislation allowing anyone with a sixth-grade education to vote in federal elections, bypassing the traditional literacy test.

Thurmond had made his case against the literacy bill in his April 30 *Report to the People,* contending that for years "it has been a popular sport to shoot at State qualifications for voting, particularly the literacy tests which are designed to insure . . . that votes are cast intelligently." The bill died in May when supporters failed twice to break a filibuster.

The battle against the poll tax had a long congressional history. Efforts to outlaw it by federal legislation had failed five times between 1942 and 1949. In every succeeding year since then Senator Holland of Florida had instead introduced a constitutional amendment.

Although Thurmond didn't approve of a poll tax—he had campaigned successfully for its repeal in South Carolina—he opposed the constitutional amendment as another effort to infringe on states' prerogatives. Furthermore, it was unnecessary. Once ratified, he insisted, the amendment "would have no significant effect on the numbers of persons who have the opportunity to vote. . . ."

Nonetheless the amendment passed the Senate March 27, and the House approved it August 27. (It was ratified by the required thirty-eight states in 1964 and affected only the five states that still had a tax, Alabama, Arkansas, Mississippi, Texas, and Virginia.)

In September, the senator focused his resistance on Thurgood Marshall. The year before, President Kennedy had temporarily appointed him a federal appeals court judge, pending his confirmation by the Senate, a process delayed an entire year by opposition from southern Democrats. The nomination finally was uncorked after Labor Day, when the Judiciary Committee sent Marshall's name to the full Senate, over the opposition of Chairman Eastland. Three out of fifteen committee members, Sam Ervin, Olin Johnston, who had held hearings over four months on the nomination, and John McClellan, joined Eastland in voting against the civil rights lawyer.

Although Johnston spoke briefly against the nomination, it was Thurmond and Eastland, with a brief interlude by Stennis, who took most of the Senate's time airing their criticisms of Marshall.

Thurmond's critique was the most extensive, casting doubt on Marshall's credentials because "for almost the entirety of his legal profession, he has been associated with only one particular side in a limited field of litigation." If ever the Second Circuit took up a question involving integration, the senator said, "the nominee's decision . . . would be foreordained." As important, the circuit handled a variety of matters having nothing to do with race, and judges needed "a well-grounded general knowledge of every aspect of the law. Judging from the nominee's background, he, of necessity, lacks this most essential legal background."

Thurmond couldn't resist another attack on *Brown*. "Without doubt," he charged, "the NAACP and its legal branch, the Legal Defense and Educational Fund under the guidance and control of the nominee, has been responsible for the shift in the Court's reliance from the law to sociology."

And of course there was mention of communism. Relying on quotes from a six-year-old House speech by Arkansas representative E. C. Gathings, Thurmond read into the record House Un-American Activities Committee claims that at least 78 of the NAACP's 177 officers and officials in 1954 had "communist front records." It was apparent, Thurmond concluded, that "many of the people with whom he [Marshall] has been closely associated over the years have highly questionable backgrounds. This taken into consideration, along with his lack of overall legal experience, convinces me that this most important seat on the Federal bench should be filled by someone other than Mr. Thurgood Marshall."

After only four days, the full Senate approved Marshall's nomination by a vote of 54–16. All sixteen "nay" votes were cast by southerners.

The distress over Marshall's appointment was a small prelude to a much more dramatic event unfolding in Mississippi, where James Meredith, a twenty-nine-year-old black air force veteran, was seeking to enter the University of Mississippi in Oxford. During ten tense days of long-distance pressure from Washington, federal court orders from New Orleans, and proud obstinance from Governor Barnett, the country watched as Meredith tried on four separate occasions between September 20 and October 2 to register for classes in the northern Mississippi town.

On Friday, September 28, the United States Court of Appeals, sitting in New Orleans, had found Barnett in contempt and ordered him to obey the order to admit Meredith by the following Tuesday or face arrest and a fine of ten thousand dollars a day. To underscore his defiance of the federal judiciary, Barnett had declined to appear at the hearing and instead remained in Jackson with his advisers. The next evening he ventured out to the Ole Miss football game (played in the capital city), where his arrival set off a thunderous cheer. At halftime, the governor, to the shouts of "We want Ross," went to midfield to introduce the new state song, "Go Mississippi." The crowd was already revved up, but Barnett took them to a fever pitch when he waved a clenched fist in the air and declared, "I love Mississippi. I love her people. I love our customs. I respect our heritage."

It was a stunning moment. He never said "integration," "segregation," "white," or "nigra," but the governor had gotten his message across in the most indelible way and in the ideal forum. Football was a sacred rite in Mississippi, and not only were there no black players in this southern shrine, there were no black spectators either. The heavy demand for tickets in the white community precluded the usual "colored-only" section in some far-off corner of the stadium reserved for the common folk. It was entirely fitting as well that the university and its sister institution, Mississippi State, were alone among state-supported schools in the country in refusing to schedule games against schools that used black players.

Early September 30, just after midnight, President Kennedy stepped in, calling Mississippi's National Guard into federal service and sending army troops to nearby Memphis in case they were needed. The president took the actions after three late-evening phone conversations with Barnett that had left the president, according to aides, doubtful that the governor could maintain law and order in Oxford in the coming week.

The calls back and forth continued on Sunday, and Barnett, increasingly concerned about his own standing, reached a new deal with the administration. Barnett could continue to protest, but Meredith would be flown into the university that afternoon and would be allowed to register the following day, Monday, October 1.

Kennedy addressed the nation Sunday evening after making sure that Meredith was safely on campus; Barnett spoke to Mississippians, claiming that the state had been "physically overpowered" in Oxford. In short order a riot broke out and bands of students and adults, many of them from other states, roamed through the campus, lobbing rocks and bottles at marshals. Army troops did not arrive until more than five hours after the violence erupted.

By Monday, Meredith had enrolled, but it took three thousand soldiers and guardsmen and four hundred deputy United States marshals to put down the fifteen hours of rioting. To do so, the troops had to fire rifles and hurl tear-gas grenades. At least three individuals were killed, one of them a French newspaper reporter, Paul Guihard, who was found in front of a woman's dorm about ten minutes after the rioting broke out with a bullet between his shoulders.

Over the next two weeks more than twenty thousand troops were brought into Oxford—three times the town's population—to maintain calm.

The Mississippi Senate responded to the turmoil by passing a resolution expressing its "complete, entire and utter contempt for the Kennedy administration and its puppet courts." From Washington, Eastland issued a report prepared by the university inviting the Mississippi congressional delegation to come to the campus "to investigate the action of the representatives of the Department of Justice, including United States marshals and attorneys of the department, and their incompetency and unjustified action which led to and provoked this action on the campus."

While other southern senators may have been equally dismayed by the turmoil in Oxford, Thurmond went beyond his now-customary step of issuing a statement. He issued two, and made public the text of a telegram he sent to President Kennedy.

As tensions were first escalating back on September 27, Thurmond had coupled his twin passions, anticommunism and states' rights, to belittle the White House. "If the Administration would demonstrate as much determination about decontaminating Cuba of communism as it has in forcing . . . Mississippi to bow to federal usurpation of power over education, the American people could rest much easier about the forward momentum communism has attained around the world," he said. Should the administration "violate the Constitution and send troops to Mississippi," then, he suggested, the American people "should demand that the Administration at least be as brave and bold in facing up to the communists. After all," Thurmond concluded, "the enemy of America is in Cuba and elsewhere, not in Mississippi."

Three days later, when the prospect of troops in the state seemed more imminent, Thurmond had dispatched a telegram to the White House, telling the president that the thought of using force in Oxford "is most shocking and disturbing to millions of Americans, not only in Mississippi and the South, but throughout the country." It would be "unconstitutional, abominable and highly dangerous." Once again raising the specter of communism, Thurmond added, "The current situation in Mississippi illustrates clearly the dangers of usurpation of power by the National Government and also the possibilities of oppression which exist for people under the rule of a powerful central government."

The letters coming into Thurmond's office from South Carolina were evidence of the strong support for his position back home. Typical was one from a couple in Greenville, who told Thurmond, "We are thankful to God for senators like yourself and others who are for their people."

A week after the violence was over in Oxford, Thurmond went to the Senate floor to put into the *Congressional Record* five pages of newspaper and magazine editorials critical of the federal government's actions. He said he wanted his colleagues to read the items. Among the most unusual was an elegiac treatment of the subject that first appeared in *The Richmond News Leader* and was reprinted in *The News and Courier.* The rich prose could not hide the unmistakable anger.

"What is to be said, retrospectively, of the terrible crisis that saw a military heel pressed down on Oxford?" the editorial asked. "The tangled roots of race inheritance creep through dark primeval ooze. In the mind's eye, one sees the formation of a new Republic under written Constitution; one recalls the painful incubus of slavery, long years of poverty. We have seen, in our lifetimes, the growth of judicial oligarchy far removed from the governed people. And all these figure in the Mississippi story.

"Yet history, in the familiar phrase, is after all no more than the biography of men; and the immediate story is the story of fallible human beings: a President, an Attorney General, a chief marshal, a southern Governor, a Negro."

The editorial warned that in "the long haul, the lessons to be learned from Oxford go to the power of the purported law in the hands of powerful men. If the aphorism ever was doubted, it cannot be doubted now: The Constitution is what the judges say it is. And it is what the bayonet says it is, too."

The new year opened with another breach of "custom and tradition," this one in South Carolina, where Harvey Gantt, a young black man from Charleston, sought to enter Clemson, Thurmond's alma mater. The previous July he had decided to transfer from Iowa State University's architecture program, and that meant going to court to challenge South Carolina's laws against integration. Federal District Judge C. C. Wyche initially ruled against him, but a federal appeals court reversed Wyche's decision and refused to stay the effect of its ruling. Chief Justice Earl Warren also refused to issue a last-minute stay, clearing the way for Gantt's enrollment at the school.

As the case was reaching its climax, *The News and Courier*

surveyed state and congressional representatives for their views. Thurmond was alone among the congressional delegation in his willingness to take a stand. "I am opposed to Gantt's admission to Clemson," the senator said. "The admission of students is a responsibility for the trustees and any other action in connection therewith would have to be taken by the executive or the legislative branch of the State government."

The depth of discomfort was evident in the mail sent to Clemson's president, Robert C. Edwards, and confirmed that Thurmond was standing with a sizable percentage of the people. One group calling itself "Concerned Clemson Alumni," in a letter also distributed to the student body, charged that "Integration is *COMMUNISM IN ACTION* and is one of the most potent weapons being used in the Red 'cold war' to take over America." The group said that South Carolina's leaders "must stand up and exhaust every legal avenue before submitting to brute force and federal tyranny." Should they fail, the group advised, and "unconstitutional federal force finally thrust a negro student in your midst, we urge you to leave him alone; don't notice him; ostracize him and all those who associate with him. Do not resort to violence, for that is what the Commies want."

As the day of Gantt's admission drew nearer, resistance erupted in the state Senate, where a group of legislators briefly proposed closing down the school rather than admit a black student. The move fizzled, however, when key senators, albeit "with reluctance," vetoed the plan as counterproductive. Outgoing governor Ernest Hollings preached a sermon of common sense and moderation to his colleagues. "As we meet," he told them, "South Carolina is running out of courts. If and when every legal remedy has been exhausted, this General Assembly must make clear South Carolina's choice, a government of laws rather than a government of men."

The News and Courier, addressing the Gantt case January 23, approvingly quoted Thurmond's reference to the "mockery of judicial procedure" in the case. (The senator had issued a press release after the appeals court decision, charging that the judges had "substituted fiction for fact and expedience for law" and had "indicted itself as completely irresponsible.")

The paper was sure that black activists were looking not only for "token integration," but for "total mingling of the races" and warned that "resistance will grow in proportion to the force used to overcome it." Resistance, according to the editorial, was justified by natural history. "Clannishness is not necessarily evil," the paper concluded. "Family loyalty is a positive virtue. In recognizing racial differences," the editorial observed, "civilized people are only exercising selectivity which nature itself long ago installed without reference to modern sociological theories."

Vowing to avoid another Mississippi, Governor Donald S. Russell, who had just taken office, and other state officials decided on a policy of "peaceful, but reluctant compliance," as the Charleston paper put it. Gantt could come to Clemson, but the state would continue to press a full appeal to the Supreme Court. On January 23, five days before Gantt was admitted, Robert Kennedy called the governor, inquired whether Russell anticipated any trouble, and offered federal help. Russell declined, telling the attorney general that the state could handle the situation, assuring him that the administration "would not be embarrassed."

Authorities sealed off the campus January 28 as Gantt got settled in his dormitory room and enrolled for classes. *The News and Courier* ran a five-column picture of a smiling Gantt facing a crowd of news reporters, photographers, and students outside the main campus building, Tillman Hall. It had been named for Clemson's original benefactor, Pitchfork Ben Tillman, and to those at all familiar with South Carolina history, the tableau was laden with symbolism. At once it illustrated where South Carolina had been and where it was going.

Under the headline FORCED ACCOMMODATION, *The News and Courier* offered the hope on its editorial page that integration might not proceed beyond the Clemson campus. Conceding that South Carolina "now has joined the other 49 states at least in symbolic breach of the racial barrier in public education," the paper congratulated South Carolina for its "remarkably effective" resistance. "If the pace does not greatly accelerate in the next decade, no great damage will have been done by the incident at Clemson. Coping with what comes next is the problem."

It was a prescient observation, for black leaders in 1963 were developing a much more aggressive strategy of demonstrations and boycotts to end segregation and turn up the pressure for new legislation in Washington.

Thurmond was ready to stand at the barricades. To concerned white constituents who wrote him, he said that stopping civil rights legislation was "my purpose in Washington. . . . I assure you that I am doing all I can to hold the line and to reverse the trend in this direction." To one Greenville man he added, "I don't know of anyone that has fought harder to preserve separation of the races than I have."

George Wallace of Alabama, who had just taken over as governor, aimed to be just such a person. Though he and Thurmond would ultimately march to a different tune, at this moment they were in perfect harmony. Moments after being sworn in January 14 in Montgomery, the new governor told his people, "Let us rise to the call of freedom-loving blood that is in us and send our answer to the tyranny that clanks its chains upon the South. I draw the line in the dust and toss the gauntlet. . . . Segregation now . . . segregation tomorrow . . . segregation forever."

Responding to black leaders' growing irritation with his timidity, President Kennedy stepped forward with a modest legislative proposal February 28. In a written message to Congress, Kennedy asked for a stronger voting rights bill, more federal assistance for desegregating schools, and a four-year extension of the Civil Rights Commission.

Thurmond reacted swiftly and with bite. "The President's message on so-called civil rights has a strong odor of political flavoring judging by the great amount of braggadocio contained therein," he said. "No one needs their voting rights protected in South Carolina." The senator repeated his opposition to keeping the Civil Rights Commission alive and to giving it authority to provide assistance to public or private agencies. "This could well mean aid to the NAACP or other race-baiting organizations," he warned. He promised "quite a protracted battle" if the legislation surfaced in the Senate.

Throughout the spring of 1963, however, the action was in Alabama, not Washington, where King and his followers vowed to fill up the Birmingham jails to end segregation at city lunch counters, and in central Mississippi, where Bob Moses and other SNCC workers were continuing their voter registration drive.

Birmingham exploded in early May when police turned fire hoses and dogs on a group of students who were trying to march to City Hall to protest segregation. The morning of May 4, readers of *The New York Times,* among them President Kennedy, were treated to a riveting and distressing sight—a police dog given just enough leash to sink his teeth into the stomach of a Birmingham black: fourteen-year-old Walter Gadsden.

Later that morning the president told a group from the Americans for Democratic Action that it had made him "sick," and that while he lacked the authority to intervene directly, he was sending aides to mediate the crisis. Tensions eased as city leaders and civil rights activists hammered out a desegregation compromise, but rioting broke out again the morning of May 12 after two buildings in the black section of town were bombed. Later in the day the president sent troops to Alabama military bases, and that night he told the nation that the government "will do whatever must be done to preserve order, to protect the lives of its citizens and to uphold the law of the land."

This prompted Thurmond in his May 20 newsletter to lambast the "centralizers" who wanted to gather all power in Washington, and specifically the "tactic of using federal troops to force compliance with federal court orders." Accusing the administration of intimidating state and local officials in Alabama, Thurmond argued that no federal laws or court orders had been violated in Birmingham, so the president had no authority to send troops in the first place, particularly when local law enforcement officials had shown their willingness and ability to maintain law and order.

Turning to King, Thurmond wondered why he had been made "a court favorite at the White House, even to the extent of receiving presidential phone calls while in jail in Atlanta and Birmingham for creating domestic troubles. . . . The voice of public protest should be heard on this action all across this land," Thurmond concluded, "for such an action merely plants the seeds for additional dictatorial actions in all sections of the country."

Over the next two weeks, as Kennedy was working on new civil rights proposals, Thurmond used television, radio, his newsletters, and the Senate floor to blast the administration. He swore that efforts to extend the Civil Rights Commission would be met "with my most vigorous opposition," and he pilloried the administration for fostering "dictatorship over American business" by forcing integration in private as well as public life only "to appease the Negro vote bloc." It was evident, Thurmond said, that despite the government's constitutional mandate to "secure the Blessings of Liberty," this administration "places greater stress on equality than personal liberty."

The aim of the communists, Thurmond argued, was "to make everybody common or equal"; therefore, "the cry of the equalitarians is not the American creed, but rather it is the creed of Marxism and the come-on of communism." With approval, he cited Alexander Hamilton's observation 190 years earlier that "Inequality will exist as long as liberty exists. It unavoidably results from that very liberty itself. This is the choice Congress will have to make: Liberty or Equality."

"Liberty or equality" was a catchy formula, but one that defined the conflict in a facile and distorted manner. It set up an unnecessary dichotomy that portrayed efforts to bestow the benefits of citizenship on those who had been deprived as somehow devaluing the lives of those who had enjoyed the benefits for so long. As important, it ignored the complicity of southern politicians, state and national, in the problems that now faced them. If out of one eye Thurmond saw only the "Red Menace," out of the other, as Judge Waring predicted, he saw only magnolias.

Twenty-five years later, "liberty or equality," dressed up with contemporary symbols, would be used to good advantage by conservative Republicans—most notably Jesse Helms—to solidify their gains in the South.

With demonstrations already spread to hundreds of cities and the possibility of violence increasing, on June 11 Kennedy made his strongest address to date on civil rights. "We are confronted primarily with a moral issue," he said in a televised speech from the White House. "It is as old as Scriptures and as clear as the American Constitution. The heart of the question is whether all Americans are to be afforded equal rights and equal opportunities; whether we are going to treat our fellow Americans as we want to be treated." Turning Thurmond's "liberty or equality" choice on its head, the president found no conflict between the concepts. The nation, he said, "was founded on the principle that all men are created equal, and that the rights of every man are diminished when the rights of one man are threatened." Kennedy promised to have new civil rights legislation sent up to Congress within days.

Medgar Evers, the NAACP's first field secretary in Mississippi, had watched the speech with other officials and stayed in the organization's office later in the evening to discuss strategy. By the time Evers got home it was past midnight. Myrlie Evers had let her children stay up that night to greet their father, but at the instant they heard his car door slam, they also heard the unmistakable bang of gunfire.

Trained to be on the alert for such incidents, Evers's children fell to the floor. Mrs. Evers raced to the front door, turned on a light, and saw her husband, keys in his hand, crumpled and bleeding on the driveway. Hearing her screams, neighbors rushed to help get Evers to a hospital. He was dead within an hour. The bullet that had pierced his body had crashed through a front window of their home, continued through a wall, and ricocheted off the refrigerator before coming to rest on a kitchen counter.

The next morning, police found a high-powered rifle with a telescopic sight in a small clearing near Evers's house. The FBI eventually traced fingerprints on the rifle to Byron de la Beckwith, a charter member of the White Citizens' Council. Although he was tried twice for murder, de la Beckwith escaped conviction when neither jury could reach a verdict. (He was facing retrial on the charges in 1992.)

Passions in Jackson were at the breaking point when five thousand people gathered June 15 in a silent tribute to Evers. A group of younger blacks, their frustration boiling over, began marching in defiance of a court order, singing as they went. Police and fire engines moved into position on the streets and the youths began throwing rocks. Several police officers drew their pistols, and it was only the courage of John Doar, who had come to attend Evers's funeral, that defused a potential riot.

The picture of him that ran in newspapers the next day gave new meaning to the notion of interposition. Standing alone in the middle of the street, a pack of white policemen behind him cradling their billy clubs, Doar raised his hands in a gesture that asked for peace and patience. Claude Sitton, *The New York Times*'s roving southern reporter, told readers that Doar had walked out in the street "with bottles and bricks crashing around him" to plead for calm. "You're not going to win anything with bottles and bricks," he yelled above the din, as a group circled around him. Doar sought a spokesman for the black youths. A young man emerged and told the angry group, "This man is right."

"My name is John Doar. D-O-A-R," the official called out repeatedly. "I'm from the Justice Department, and anybody around here knows I stand for what is right." Other blacks then joined the effort to calm the mob, and trouble ultimately was averted.

In his eulogy to the slain activist, an angry Roy Wilkins laid the blame for Evers's death on a host of shoulders. It was the "southern political system," he asserted, "lily-white southern governments, local and state, senators, governors, state legislators, mayors, judges, sheriffs, chiefs of police, commissioners and so forth. . . .

"In faraway Washington," he continued, "the southern system has its outpost in the Congress of the United States and by their deals and maneuvers they helped to put the man behind that deadly rifle. . . . The killer must have felt that he had, if not immunity, then certainly a protection for whatever he chose to do, no matter how dastardly."

On June 19, four days after the near riot in Jackson, Medgar Evers was buried in Arlington National Cemetery, an honor due him because of his service in World War II. The crowd of two thousand mourners sang "We Shall Overcome." That same day Kennedy sent a package of civil rights legislation to Congress, this time asking for provisions that guaranteed blacks access to the services and facilities of any hotels, restaurants, amusement parks, and retail establishments involved in interstate commerce—so-called public accommodations; the package allowed federal programs to be cut off if they were administered in a discriminatory fashion, toughened employment discrimination laws, and established a Community Relations Service to help resolve racial disputes at the local level.

Thurmond had an instant evaluation of the proposals: "unconstitutional, unnecessary, unwise, and extend[ing] beyond the realm of reason." He reminded the administration of the legislative armaments southerners had at their disposal—"extended debate . . . committee chairmanships . . . and votes." And he vowed "to completely stymie [Kennedy's] legislative program unless he withdraws his so-called civil rights program. Our backs are to the wall," Thurmond conceded, "but we are not without weapons with which we can fight back."

The day after Kennedy's presentation, Thurmond was paired once again with Javits and two representatives—John Bell Williams of Mississippi and Richard Bolling of Missouri—for a discussion of the legislation on NBC's *Today* show. Perhaps neither the more senior Russell nor Eastland, who was chairman of the Judiciary Committee, was available, or perhaps they chose not to come. More than likely they found something positive in Thurmond's brash resistance. The fact that he was so out front in opposition gave them the opportunity to seek compromises behind the scenes, as Russell had done in 1957.

Network newsman Frank Blair opened the discussion by observing that a civil rights bill that incorporated most of the president's requests had been introduced by the Senate Republican leader, Everett M. Dirksen, and the majority leader, Mike Mansfield. "Mr. Dirksen's action forecasts Republican support of the administration in breaking a southern filibuster," Blair pointed out. "If this is the right interpretation, the consensus is that a strong civil rights bill can be passed in this session of Congress."

The newsman was right conceptually and was wrong in his timing by only a few months.

After Javits spoke in favor of the legislation, agreeing that it had bipartisan support, Thurmond was given his turn. "The civil rights bills the president sent to Congress yesterday would burn down the house to put out the fire," he charged. "They are the most objectionable and obnoxious civil rights bills that any president has ever sent to Capitol Hill. They would deprive business people of selling to whom they please and serving to whom they please."

Though Williams was also there to represent the South, he presented his case with less fury than Thurmond. "It seems to me that there has already been too much bloodshed and violence as a result of this political agitation for civil rights," Williams said. "Instead of pouring gasoline on the flames of racial hatred, I think the time has come for us to stop and think and reflect."

Several minutes later, when Javits was trying to point out differences between the North and South, Thurmond sought to make a point. "You're talking more than anybody else. Why not give the rest of us a chance?"

"May I just finish my sentence now?" Javits asked.

"Go ahead and finish if you want to finish," Thurmond replied. "You take most of the time anyway." But instead of letting Javits continue, Thurmond went on with a litany of questions, like a boxer pummeling his opponent into the ropes. "Isn't it a matter of fact that integrated housing in New York ends up as segregated housing? Hasn't that been the result? And don't you know that the white people of New York eventually move out when housing becomes integrated? In your neighborhood, you live in—you may call it an integrated neighborhood, but as a matter of fact it's segregated, isn't it?

"How many of your children go to integrated schools?" Thurmond asked. "As a matter of fact, the white people prefer to be with their own race; the colored people prefer to be with their own race. Now what the president has done is yield to the demands based on violence to send these bills up here. The president," Thurmond insisted, "is asking the Congress to submit to blackmail."

In a brief exchange between Thurmond and Bolling, the Missouri congressman pointed out that the cycle of violence had started with lynch mobs. "They were lynch mobs. They were made up of white people who lynched Negroes. The violence started on the side of the whites. As you know, I grew up in the South . . ."

"But you don't represent the southern viewpoint now," was all that Thurmond could answer.

The senator's mail, which continued to stream into his office, was proof to him that his message was the right one. "I want to thank you for the fight you are waging on behalf of the white people of this country," wrote one Columbia woman. "Goodness knows we need a friend."

In his reply, Thurmond said the Kennedys were "directly responsible for what has been happening lately. They encouraged these Negro groups and then the Negro groups took over. Now we are being told that we must completely capitulate or the Negroes will completely wipe us out. This is so much hogwash."

To another constituent, Thurmond conceded that "Negroes may have some problem in regard to getting accommodations at hotels and eating establishments." But, he said, "the decision to serve or not to serve should be discretionary with the owner of the business. If any owner wants to open his doors to everyone, I certainly have no objection. . . ."

While the letters from individuals encouraged Thurmond to keep up the resistance, equally important was support from business organizations. Especially welcome was a resolution from the state Chamber of Commerce opposing the civil rights bills. Sounding just like the senator himself, the resolution maintained that "Sensible and responsible action is producing solid answers to this problem at the state and local levels in South Carolina."

There were a smattering of letters—most from black Carolinians but a few from whites—criticizing Thurmond's position and urging him to support the legislation. To these constituents he had a stock states' rights answer: the bills were unconstitutional because they gave too much power to the federal government. He also defended his record. "I am not prejudiced against the Negro," he wrote. "When I was Governor, I did more to help the Negroes in our State than any previous Governor, and I think you can find Negro leaders in the State who will attest to this fact.''

The public accommodations bill was considered the ''symbolic heart'' of the civil rights package because exclusion of blacks from public facilities had been the focal point of their demonstrations. Expecting a good deal of trouble on that part of the package, the administration chose to introduce it as a separate measure and drafted it in a way that sent it to the Senate Commerce Committee instead of the Judiciary Committee, which was more hostile to civil rights measures.

The Commerce panel began hearings on the legislation July 1, starting off with Attorney General Kennedy, who noted that a number of states still had segregated public accommodations mandated by quite rigid laws. To help make his point he cited a section of the city code in Greenwood, South Carolina, that made it unlawful for any person operating a restaurant or soda fountain to serve blacks and whites with the same dishes and glasses.

Thurmond opened his round of questioning with a blunt assessment: ''I want to say I do not think your bill is going to pass this Congress.'' For the next two hours he peppered Kennedy with questions about the commerce clause of the Constitution—the brief section that gives the federal government authority to regulate matters ''affecting interstate commerce''—and about states' rights. Federal authority for a public accommodations bill was said to come from the commerce clause because enterprises open to the general public broadly affect commerce. Thurmond believed this was spurious reasoning and tried to get the attorney general to agree with him. He also doubted whether Kennedy had a good grasp of the Constitution, as Thurmond understood it. At one point he reached over the dais to give Kennedy a slim volume containing the Constitution with explanations next to each section, ''written in such an interesting way that anyone can understand it.''

''Thank you, Senator,'' Kennedy replied. ''I appreciate your kindness and your courtesy.''

Twenty-seven years after the exchange, Thurmond recalled the moment and pointed to a copy of the volume he still kept in his Senate office. He remained convinced that the young Kennedy could have learned something from the book.

When Secretary of State Dean Rusk came to testify July 10,

Thurmond questioned him about communist involvement in the civil rights movement. While Rusk acknowledged that the communists were probably using the racial turmoil to exploit their own aims, he said he had been "deeply impressed by the loyalty of the Negroes of the United States."

At the conclusion of Rusk's testimony, Senator John Pastore of Rhode Island said his comments had been an "exhilarating and satisfying experience" for the members of the committee. The immediate applause that followed Pastore's praise prompted Thurmond to growl, "I see, as usual, the audience is packed with civil righters and left wingers, and the outburst that just occurred is not only in violation of the rules, but indicates the pressure that is being brought to pass an unconstitutional civil rights bill."

Governors Barnett and Wallace also testified, blasting the administration for aiding communist subversives by failing to crack down on the civil rights unrest. In August, Thurmond added his voice to the chorus of white southern leaders who insisted the civil rights movement was riddled with communists. Three times between August 2 and August 13 he went to the Senate floor to speak about the alleged infiltration and to enter news articles on the subject into the *Record*. His August 13 presentation was aimed primarily at Bayard Rustin, a King lieutenant who was playing a leading role in the March on Washington set for August 28. A *Washington Post* article had called Rustin "Mr. March on Washington."

Rustin had been a member of the Young Communist League, had traveled to the Soviet Union in 1958 for a meeting on nuclear disarmament, and had pleaded guilty to a morals charge in San Francisco after being arrested with two other men. Thurmond was unhappy with how the paper had presented that information. "This article is a classic example of news reporting because the reporter took a series of ludicrous facts and directed them so that they literally came out smelling like a rose and looking like a gilded lily," Thurmond said.

Condemning what he called the attorney general's "whitewash" of communist involvement in demonstrations that "have been turning into race riots," the senator insisted there be a congressional investigation of the communist–civil rights link before any action was taken on the civil rights bills. He also had printed in the *Record* a full-page copy of the booking slip from Rustin's San Francisco arrest.

Two days later Thurmond made a television clip sharpening

his charge of communist infiltration. "The evidence in the hearings and the *Congressional Record* shows that the man most generally credited with inciting and organizing the riots, Dr. Martin Luther King, has had top assistants with questionable backgrounds." He then cited Rustin.

Speaking more directly of King, Thurmond said he "has been a lecturer at the Highlander Folk School (in Tennessee) with admitted communists and pro-communist characters." To make matters worse, the senator added, "this school has been closed by the State of Tennessee and cited as subversive by the Attorney General of Georgia."

Two weeks later the capital was awash in humanity. Two hundred thousand people streamed into the city on planes, trains, buses, and, in the case of one determined individual, on roller skates, where they gathered at the Lincoln Memorial to demonstrate their support for civil rights. King was the last of the day's speakers and the one who etched the moment into history. "I have a dream that one day on the red hills of Georgia, the sons of former slaves and the sons of former slave-owners will be able to sit together at the table of brotherhood," he told the attentive crowd. "I have a dream that one day even the state of Mississippi, a state sweltering in the heat of injustice, sweltering with the heat of oppression, will be transformed into an oasis of freedom and justice. I have a dream that my four little children will one day live in a nation where they will not be judged by the color of their skin but by the content of their character. I have a dream that one day every valley shall be exalted, every hill and mountain shall be made low, the rough places will be made plain and the crooked places will be made straight, and the glory of the Lord shall be revealed and all flesh shall see it together." The crowd returned to their home communities ready for the battle ahead.

Within three weeks the spiritual triumph of Washington had turned into numbing tragedy. September 15 was Youth Sunday at Birmingham's Sixteenth Street Baptist Church, where many youngsters who had been part of the demonstrations four months earlier would lead the congregation in song and participate as ushers. At 10:22 A.M. a bomb planted outside exploded with such force that it shook the entire church. Four girls who had been happily chatting in the ladies' lounge were killed instantly: Denise McNair, age eleven, and Addie Mae Collins, Carole Robertson, and Cynthia Wesley, all only fourteen.

By the time the chaos had subsided and the rubble was thoroughly searched, more than twenty people had been taken to the hospital with injuries. One of them was Sarah Collins, Addie Mae's sister, who had been blinded in one eye.

The FBI investigated immediately and determined that the bombing had been planned by Klansmen angered by a new school desegregation order. Although there was reported to be an eyewitness who had seen four men plant the bomb, no one was charged with the crime until fourteen years later, when Alabama attorney general William Baxley reopened the case. Robert Chambliss, by then seventy-three years old, was charged with first-degree murder and convicted. He was sent to prison and died there, the only one ever charged in the incident.

Hours after the bombing, Birmingham recorded another black death. Thirteen-year-old Virgil Ware, riding on the handlebars of his brother's bike, was shot to death by two sixteen-year-old white boys who passed by on a motor scooter decorated with Confederate stickers. The two were quickly identified and arrested for the shooting. Before the shooting they had attended a rally of an arch-conservative group that taught that blacks were less than human and did not belong in the United States. The two boys were tried not for murder but manslaughter. They were convicted and sentenced to seven months in prison. But the boy who pulled the trigger was released after only a few days with a warning from the judge not to have another "lapse."

The day after the killings, Charles Morgan, a white Birmingham lawyer who would go on to make the American Civil Liberties Union a force in Washington, cast a wide net of responsibility. "Who did it?" he asked his audience during a speech to the Young Men's Business Club. "We all did it. . . . Every person in this community who has in any way contributed to . . . the popularity of hatred is at least as guilty or more so than the demented fool who threw that bomb."

Morgan's message had rung the same notes as Roy Wilkins's two months earlier on the death of Medgar Evers, but it was a message alien to Thurmond, who felt no connection to either violent episode. He saw such incidents as unfortunate, even aberrational acts unrelated to his passionate resistance seven hundred miles north in Washington.

Through the summer and fall, Eastland worked to squelch the civil rights proposals sent to the Judiciary Committee, but the Commerce Committee October 8 approved a public accommodations measure. Almost as soon as the panel adjourned, Thurmond fired off a statement condemning the bill as "the most clearly unconstitutional, objectionable and impractical so-called 'civil rights' legislation ever approved by a committee of Congress." It went "even further in restricting the rights of individuals in the operation of their businesses and in their free choice of association than the Civil Rights Act of 1875, which the Supreme Court ruled unconstitutional in 1883."

Because the brunt of the measure's dictates would be borne by "the average American who cannot afford to establish or join private clubs and associations which are exempted from the coverage of the bill," those average Americans, Thurmond predicted, would "rise up in protest against this intrusion on [their] liberty, and I predict that Congress will not approve this abominable legislation."

Three weeks later, after intense negotiations between House Republicans and the administration, the House Judiciary Committee approved a broad civil rights bill after all. In the first week of November, Thurmond used his weekly broadcast and newsletter to belittle the negotiations in the House, saying that "The only compromise of significance is the addition of the Republican Party's name to share in the blame for foisting this 'civil rights' fraud on the American people."

John Kennedy's assassination in Dallas eighteen days later brought the nation to a wrenching halt. Like other politicians, Thurmond offered a public expression of sadness, put aside his general distaste for the man, and praised him as "one of the most personable and popular presidents ever to serve our nation." But woven into his comments was another attack on communism via mention of the communist background of the accused assassin, Lee Harvey Oswald. "To a communist the life of any individual is not worth much because it is society—the planned society—which counts most," Thurmond said.

Looking to the future, he spoke of Lyndon Johnson as "one of the most capable and experienced public officials I know," and described his relationship with the domineering Texan as "pleasant, even though we have not agreed on all issues." In what would prove to be enormous understatement, Thurmond predicted that he and the new president "will be in disagreement on more occasions." Before Johnson had completed a year as president, he would become the catalyst for Thurmond's exit from the Democratic Party.

Five days after Kennedy's death, Johnson returned to Capitol Hill to tell Congress that civil rights would be at the top of his agenda. "No memorial oration or eulogy could more eloquently honor President Kennedy's memory than the earliest possible passage of the civil rights bill for which he fought so long," Johnson said, skillfully tying his legislative goals to the memory of the slain president.

As a gesture of goodwill, Thurmond decided to put aside his antipathy toward Johnson in the early days of the new administration, telling his aide Stilwell, "I'm gonna give him a chance." The senator's attempt at cooperation was short-lived, however, after it became clear that the president was serious about moving the civil rights legislation.

On January 31 the House took up the package, which included the public accommodations section, authority for federal lawsuits to desegregate schools and public facilities, and an extension of the Civil Rights Commission. After disposing of 122 amendments over nine days of debate, the House passed the measure February 10 by a comfortable 290–130 margin.

Determined to avoid Eastland's graveyard in the Judiciary Committee, Senate supporters of the legislation successfully engineered a vote February 26 to place the House bill directly on the Senate calendar. On March 26, after sixteen days of debate, the senators voted to start work on the legislation after rejecting a delaying tactic that would have sent the bill to the Judiciary Committee for two weeks. Russell, as committed a southerner as Thurmond, knew in his heart that resistance was a lost cause. "You tell Lyndon that I've been expecting the rod for a long time," he confided to Johnson aide Bill Moyers. "I'm sorry that it's from his hand the rod must be wielded but I'd rather it be his hand than anybody else's. Tell him," Russell added, "to cry a little when he uses it."

On March 18 Thurmond and Hubert Humphrey had debated the public accommodations issue on the network program *CBS Reports.* The interchange was predictable. Humphrey said this section of the package, known as Title II, "has but one purpose, and that is to guarantee to every American citizen, regardless of his place of residence or his race, equal access to public places, and this is as old as common law itself—since the time of Chaucer, as a matter of fact." He pointed out that thirty-two states had already enacted similar laws.

Thurmond, in language honed by more than two dozen public statements against the legislation, called Title II "entirely a misnomer." In staccato fashion he spit out his points: "It's not public accommodation. It's invasion of private property. This will lead to integration of private life. The Constitution says that a man shall not be deprived of life, liberty or property. We should observe the Constitution. A man has a right to have his property protected."

Toward the end of the debate, Thurmond alluded to the heart of the matter—white control. "To persons in such a state as Minnesota, it may seem feasible to accomplish total integration of the races," he said. "In Minnesota there are only seven Negroes for 1,000 persons. It is an entirely different matter, however, where there are 250 to 400 Negroes for 1,000 persons.

"Now, no one should believe that he has learned all about the force bill before the Senate from this brief discussion," Thurmond added, returning to a term he had used in the 1948 presidential race. "No bill is a civil-rights bill if it takes away basic liberties and constitutional rights and guarantees and replaces them with arbitrary Government powers."

Once it was clear that the Senate was going to debate the civil rights bill, southerners ensured that the debate would be long. They were accustomed to filibustering, and in the past had been better organized and prepared than their opponents. But this time supporters of the legislation determined to match the southerners at their own game. With the help of Californian Thomas H. Kuchel, the assistant GOP leader, Humphrey made certain they always had enough senators on hand to keep the Senate going, and they sent out a newsletter to keep senators up to date on the debate. During previous civil rights filibusters, northerners had let many of the southerners' criticisms go unanswered. Now they stayed on the Senate floor to answer charges against the legislation.

As the debate wore on through April, it became obvious that, Johnson's wishes aside, some changes would have to be made in the bill in order to recruit enough Republicans to cut off debate. Early in May, Humphrey, Robert Kennedy, who had remained as attorney general, Dirksen, and a few other interested senators started negotiations on the package. By May 13 they reached agreement on a substitute. Although there were more than seventy changes, few were substantive. The most significant specified that in cases of alleged employment discrimination or discrimination in public accommodations, the federal government could bring a lawsuit only if it found a "pattern or practice" of discrimination. All other cases would go to local agencies established to handle discrimination complaints. If that failed, one of two newly created entities, the Community Relations Service or the Equal Employment Opportunities Commission, would try to find a solution. If that alternative also failed, then the aggrieved individual could bring a lawsuit and the Justice Department would be free to enter the case.

While the Senate negotiations were under way, there was also a concerted effort by civil rights groups, now aided by church and labor organizations, to pressure uncommitted senators into voting to end debate.

Finally on June 10 the Senate made history, voting for the first time since the initial civil rights filibuster in 1938 to cut off debate and actually work toward passage of civil rights legislation. Supporters had four votes to spare over the required sixty-seven, winning 71–29. A large part of the credit went to Republican leader Dirksen, whose persistent dealings with the Justice Department and with his own ranks led to legislation that enough of the GOP could accept. From this moment on, it was only a matter of time before the bill would pass. Each senator could speak for only an hour, and only those amendments that had been filed before the June 10 vote could be considered.

Thurmond called the southerners' defeat "a sad day for America when the United States Senate votes to foreclose debate on such a vicious, unreasonable, unconstitutional and impractical piece of so-called civil rights legislation. . . .Far from solving racial problems in this country, this legislation will only serve to increase tensions, disorders and racial difficulties."

Johnson saw it differently. Interrupting prepared remarks to a group of presidential scholars, the president observed that "today's action demonstrates that the national will manifests itself in congressional action." He, too, was publicly acclaimed, not for his legendary negotiating skills—he had stayed out of the bargaining—but for keeping the issue on the public agenda. Privately, he had helped choreograph the Senate action, telling Humphrey at one point in the spring, "Now you know this bill can't pass unless we get Ev Dirksen. . . . You've got to let him have a piece of the action. He's got to look good all the time."

Well aware of Senate rules, Thurmond had filed the last of seventy-three amendments to the bill just before the cloture vote and now insisted on offering thirty of them for consideration—more than any other senator. But there was a solid majority in favor of preventing dramatic change in the measure, and Thurmond's amendments, along with those of other southerners, were rejected by lopsided margins.

On June 19 the Senate finally passed the civil rights bill by a vote of 73–27. Six Republicans joined twenty-one Democrats—all of them southerners—in opposing the measure. One of the Republicans was Barry Goldwater, who was already the front-runner for the GOP presidential nomination. He asserted that the public accommodations and equal employment provisions "fly in the face of the Constitution and . . . require for their effective execution the creation of a police state."

Thurmond was harsher. "This is a tragic day for America, when Negro agitators, spurred on by communist enticements to promote racial strife, can cause the United States Senate to be steamrollered into passing the worst, most unreasonable and unconstitutional legislation that has ever been considered by the Congress. This legislation," Thurmond predicted, "will make a Czar of the President of the United States and a Rasputin of the Attorney General."

Before the House could consider the Senate's civil rights package, violence struck once again in Mississippi. On June 21, three civil rights workers—two white northerners, Andrew Goodman and Michael Schwerner, and James Chaney, a black Mississippian—were ambushed on a highway near Philadelphia by a group of Klansmen, shot at point-blank range, and then buried in a hastily dug grave in an earthen dam. Their disappearance in the midst of what had been dubbed "Freedom Summer" reverberated throughout the country. The Justice Department was notified immediately, and within a week one hundred FBI agents had been assigned to search for the missing men. It took an anonymous tip before federal agents located the earthen dam August 4 and found the three decomposed bodies buried under ten tons of dirt.

(Three years later, seven Klansmen were found guilty of federal civil rights violations in connection with the murders. They were sentenced to prison, the first time any Klansman had been convicted in Mississippi of killing a black or a civil rights worker.)

There was a painful symmetry to the events in Washington and Mississippi, as if every step forward exacted the ultimate human price. Two weeks after Chaney, Goodman, and Schwerner were shot, their bodies still unrecovered, the House gave final approval to the strongest civil rights bill the Congress had ever passed. Within hours of the 289–126 vote, President Johnson signed the bill into law while the nation watched the ceremony on television. Surrounded by members of Congress, cabinet officials, and civil rights leaders, the president acknowledged that "we have come now to a time of testing. We must not fail. . . . Let us close the springs of racial poison. Let us lay aside irrelevant differences and make our nation whole."

Picking up on the notion of "a time of testing," a short editorial in the Columbia *State* called "not for intemperate action but for deliberation and intelligent reserve. It is a time for the working of the mind, not the unbridling of emotion." In Charleston, *The News and Courier* preached much the same message, though it felt compelled to describe the new law as a "momentous departure from the Constitution." The testing Johnson spoke of, the paper added, would be for blacks and whites, as illustrated by "a picture of President Johnson and the Rev. Dr. King clasping hands."

Thurmond had continued to receive supportive letters from home during debate over the civil rights bills, some with petitions attached signed by fifty or sixty residents of a South Carolina town. Once the legislation had passed, people troubled about what the law might do to their businesses wrote to ask whether their establishments—laundries, barbershops, drugstores—were covered by the law and whether they had to accept black customers. One barber from Greer, not anxious to serve blacks but worried about any backlash, explained that he would be "caught in an embarrassing situation if forced to serve a negro in my chair. . . . There is a definite difference in the skill required to properly serve a negro as compared to a white man."

Thurmond wrote back that because the barbershop did not serve out-of-state customers, in his view it was not covered as a "public accommodation." If asked for service by a black, the senator advised, "I believe that you would be on sound grounds in refusing him service, stating that your establishment is not covered by the so-called 'civil rights' act and that you do not have the skill or experience to cut his hair."

Even with the bill now signed into law, Thurmond still found ways to register his resistance. Title X of the new law established the Community Relations Service to help mediate racial disputes at the local level. In the hope of easing the ongoing transition in the South, Johnson selected a white southerner, former Florida governor LeRoy Collins, to be the first director.

Collins had to be confirmed by the Senate, and it fell to the Commerce Committee, on which Thurmond served, to hold hearings on his nomination. Although Collins had once supported segregation, he had since had a change of mind. Thurmond reminded Collins of statements he had made in the mid-fifties and, though he stopped short of using the word, intimated that he was a traitor to the South.

An irritated Collins said he resented the implication of disloyalty and conceded only that he had evolved. He told the senator that "we all agree that we all change. We all adjust to new circumstances."

Thurmond was unmoved. He had been particularly upset by a speech Collins had made the previous December in which he criticized southern leaders for being "harsh and intemperate." Among other things, Collins had told the Columbia Chamber of Commerce, "We have allowed the extremists to speak for the South—the very ones against whom we in the South have had to struggle . . . for much of the progress we have made." It was understandable how Thurmond could have taken it personally when Collins likened southerners' speeches on the floor of Congress to "anti-American diatribes from some hostile foreign country. . . . And all the while," Collins admitted, "too many of the rest of us have remained cravenly silent or lamely defensive while Dixie battle cries have been employed to incite sick souls to violence—egged on by the rabble-rousers' call to stand up and fight."

After putting the speech into the committee record, Thurmond suggested, to Collins's rising indignation, that the Floridian had sought to blame southerners for Kennedy's assassination.

"I am absolutely and deeply shocked that you would do what you have just done," Collins protested, explaining that the Associated Press had made a mistake in transmitting his speech and had later corrected the errors.

On July 9, the committee was scheduled to take a final vote on the nomination. For two days in a row the panel had had trouble getting a quorum, so when Thurmond arrived with Stilwell and learned that the committee did not yet have a quorum that day either, the senator decided to wait out in the hall, hoping he might stall the panel yet again.

Soon Senator Yarborough of Texas, another member of the committee, came down the hallway and jokingly said, "Come on in, Strom, and help us get a quorum."

"Tell you what," Thurmond replied in an equally jocular manner. "If you can take me in, then I'll go in there, but if I can keep you out, then you don't go in." He was certain he could best the Texan. Yarborough and Thurmond both were army officers in the reserves, and although Yarborough was only a year younger than Thurmond, he was twenty pounds heavier and not in as good shape.

The horseplay began calmly enough, with the two senators grabbing each other's hands and tugging to and fro. After a minute or so they stopped and decided they should take their suit coats off, so they handed them to the bemused but slightly worried Stilwell, who was at that moment the only witness to this senatorial wrestling match.

The tussling continued, and it was soon clear that Yarborough was having the more difficult time of it. He was panting and out of breath as Thurmond handled him any way he wanted. Eventually Thurmond threw Yarborough to the floor, got down on top of him, and pinned his arms to the marble. He smilingly told Yarborough he would let him up if he asked, but the Texan refused. Several minutes into the fracas, Senator Lausche of Ohio came by and told the two senators they ought to quit before one of them had a heart attack. The warning did nothing to deter the men.

The high ceilings, hard walls, and marble floors made distant footsteps easy to hear; hearing someone approaching, Stilwell went down the hall and spied a reporter about to turn the corner for a full view of the fight. It would be to no one's advantage to have firsthand press accounts of Thurmond and Yarborough rolling around on the floor, so he quickly turned around and told the senators the press was on its way and that they really should get up.

About the same time, committee chairman Warren Magnuson, informed of what was going on in the hall, came out of the committee room and told the men to "Get up off that floor!"

This gave Yarborough the excuse he needed, telling Thurmond, "I have to yield to the order of my chairman."

The two entered the meeting room, where Collins's nomination was sent to the Senate on a 16–1 vote. Thurmond was the lone opponent.

Despite the lack of eyewitnesses, newspapers around the country carried stories about the wrestling, many of them accompanied by a picture of the smiling, aging combatants holding their clasped hands aloft.

When the Senate took up the nomination July 20, Thurmond used his brief remarks in opposition to deliver a compelling lesson on the sociology and psychology of southern resistance. "Mr. President," he said, "the enforcement of the recently enacted so-called 'Civil Rights' Act will mean the upheaval of social patterns and customs more than a century old in many communities, both in the South and in other areas of the nation as well. To force people to change their pattern of living overnight, to require them to forget how they have acted and reacted over the entire span of their lifetime, creates a potentially dangerous situation."

He advised civil rights groups "to discontinue their demands and their agitation." And he concluded with another verbal punch at Collins, telling the Senate, "I have little respect for turncoats who are willing to sacrifice their previous principles for political expediency."

Collins was confirmed with fifty-three votes. Only seven senators, all of them southerners, joined Thurmond in voting against the nominee.

Thurmond already had a history as a maverick, but his willingness to go it alone would be even more apparent by the fall.

In mid-July, between the committee debate on Collins and the full Senate vote, the Republicans had held their national convention in San Francisco. Barry Goldwater had come to California holding a commanding lead based on his gospel of conservatism and his dogged work in precinct after precinct across the country. Three years earlier, *The New York Times*'s James Reston had traveled to the heart of the Midwest, Appleton, Wisconsin, to write about America's interest in this tough Arizonan. With foresight, Reston had described the politician's attractiveness. Goldwater, he wrote, appealed to residents' "wistful longing for the past. He is offering simple solutions to complex problems at a time when the diversity of events increases the general desire for snappy and tidy answers. And he is encouraging the paradoxical belief that somehow it is possible to decrease the power of the Federal Government, cut the budget and be tougher on Communists all at the same time."

In a last-minute bid to derail Goldwater, Pennsylvania governor William Scranton had put himself forward as a moderate alternative, but support failed to materialize. Goldwater won easily on the first ballot. He subsequently picked the GOP national chairman, Representative William E. Miller of New York, to be his running mate.

Goldwater had won all of the southern delegations. Their support was symptomatic of the backlash among white voters distressed over the civil rights movement and over the response it was getting from Washington. George Wallace's strong showing in the Democratic primaries in Wisconsin and Maryland that spring had confirmed this trend. A bit prematurely, *The News and Courier* trumpeted the beginning of a new day after Goldwater was nominated. "No matter what happens in the November elections, the Republican Party and the nation turned a corner when the Eastern forces in the GOP went down to defeat in the national convention," the paper said. "What emerges from the struggle is a realignment of political power in this country, with the South, Middle West and the Far West joined together in a new alliance."

Thurmond had always felt ideologically compatible with Goldwater and liked him personally. He and his aides never forgot that Goldwater had lent a hand during the 1957 filibuster, taking some time on the floor for unrelated business to give Thurmond a breather during the night. Equally important, Thurmond was increasingly uncomfortable in the Democratic ranks, and so were the two men who had his ear most of the time, Dent and Buzhardt. When Johnson picked Hubert Humphrey to be his running mate, as obvious a symbol of liberalism as one could want, Thurmond's disaffection was at a peak. (He had missed this convention—the first time in decades—to represent the Senate at an international meeting in Europe. It was a fortuitous circumstance; Thurmond would have been like a fish out of water at this gathering.)

The senator had voted for Republicans before and intended to do so again, but this time he wanted to maximize support for Goldwater. The question was how to do it: stay aloof from the Democrats, as he had done in 1960; endorse Goldwater publicly but remain a Democrat; or endorse Goldwater, become a Republican, and campaign openly for him in the South.

Dent and Buzhardt quietly had been urging Thurmond to leave the Democratic Party and in fact had contemplated switching their own allegiance regardless of what the senator did. By Labor Day, Thurmond had pretty much agreed that their suggestion was the right one, but first he wanted to test the waters at home.

Over the Labor Day weekend, the senator and Dent went back to South Carolina for a series of appointments with businessmen, newspaper editors, and a few political friends whose advice Thurmond trusted. One of the first on the list was Walter Brown, the Spartanburg businessman who had been a longtime Thurmond supporter. He flatly told the senator he was crazy to change parties and even crazier to follow the advice of a young man like Dent "who is not even dry behind the ears."

By the time Dent and Thurmond had gotten to Greenville for a meeting with Roger Peace, a prominent businessman, Brown had already called ahead and warned Peace to try to dissuade Thurmond. At one point, Peace called Dent aside, shook his finger in Dent's face, and told him the word was spreading that "that young fella is gonna destroy Strom Thurmond."

When the two got to Columbia for a meeting with three editors at *The State,* they met with a less hostile reaction. The editors termed the notion an interesting one.

By this time, Dent had figured out the least incendiary way to make the presentation. He would advance the party switching as his idea, not the senator's, so that Thurmond could sit like a judge hearing one side presented and then wait for the rebuttal.

When Dent and Thurmond presented the idea to James F. Byrnes, the premier Democratic politician in the state, the former governor immediately called for his wife. "Maude," he shouted. "Bring me a drink." Byrnes agreed that a party switch would be an audacious move, but in the end he counseled Thurmond to support Goldwater openly but remain a Democrat, the better to preserve his own political career.

It was a somewhat chastened Thurmond who returned to Washington. "I think we've lost him," Dent told Buzhardt. But the two didn't want to give up. They believed that switching parties would serve Thurmond in Washington, where Dent had long felt the senator was "the unwelcome guest at every Democratic Party caucus." They also believed that there was untapped GOP strength back home. Newsman William D. Workman, a Republican, had challenged Olin Johnston in 1962, painting him as the "handmaiden" of the Kennedys. He lost, but he did get about 43 percent of the vote, a symbol of growing white backlash and in Dent's view "a pretty good poll."

There seemed to be a Republican future in South Carolina that Thurmond could help shape. Republican growth looked possible in other states as well. In the 1960 presidential election in Mississippi, an unpledged slate of electors supporting Governor Barnett and Democrats committed to segregation had won 39 percent of the vote. In Alabama two years later, Republican businessman James B. Martin nearly upset Lister Hill, who won with only 50.9 percent of the vote. It was the same year that Workman had given Johnston a scare.

Hoping to keep Thurmond focused on switching parties after their less-than-conclusive trip to South Carolina, Dent decided he should start "pumping air back into the tires." As he started into the senator's office shortly after their return, he had a pang of remorse at the memory of Jean Thurmond. He knew that, had she been alive, she would have argued against him with all her strength and might have turned the senator around. After all, she had come from a family of party loyalists, and it would have been anathema to her to abandon the Democrats.

Thurmond made Dent's job easy. He had already decided to stick by the plan, but first he wanted to make sure Goldwater liked the idea. He went to the senator's Washington home September 12 and got the answer he was looking for. "I very much want you to come out for me, and I want you to go all the way and change parties," Goldwater said.

Dent and Buzhardt now could put into place the plans they had been working on for weeks—preparing the senator's statement to constituents, finalizing press releases, booking airtime for his statewide address, which now was set for September 16. On the fourteenth, Thurmond left Washington to attend a funeral in Greenville for the late Charles Daniel, the businessman who had served a few months as a senator in 1954. That same day, press releases were to be sent out announcing the party switch.

Back in Washington, a nervous Dent told Buzhardt he was going to hold off on the releases because he was sure Thurmond would be talked out of the change by importuning friends at the funeral. But when the funeral was over, Thurmond called the office. "Have you put those things in the mail yet?" he asked.

"No, Senator, I didn't," Dent replied. "I knew they'd talk you out of it."

"Didn't I tell you to put 'em in the mail?"

"Yessir."

"Put 'em in the mail."

"But Senator—," Dent started to say.

"Oh, they all talked to me," Thurmond said. "Put 'em in the mail. We're still goin'."

CBS News broke the story of Thurmond's switch the evening of September 15. On September 16, Thurmond flew down to South Carolina to explain his decision on statewide television. Standing before a giant poster of Goldwater, Thurmond, still fit and trim, projected the vigorousness that would stay with him for another two decades. The strong jaw had not slackened, and despite the baldness he looked younger than his sixty-one years.

"It has been wisely said that 'For evil to triumph, it is only necessary that good men do nothing,' " he began. "Particularly is this true in time of crisis. Seldom before in the history of our nation have we faced so great a crisis."

From the "position of trust" in the national government in which the people of South Carolina had placed him, he had "observed at close hand," he said, "the conduct and factors which have brought about this crisis" and would be derelict in his duty were he to remain silent. "The Democratic Party has abandoned the people," he asserted, launching into a twenty-two-count indictment of his erstwhile colleagues. The Democrats had "forsaken the people to become the party of minority groups, power-hungry union leaders, political bosses, and businessmen looking for government contracts and favors," had "invaded the private lives of people by using the powers of government for coercion and intimidation of individuals, . . . encouraged lawlessness, civil unrest and mob actions," and had "nominated for vice president a key leader of the Americans for Democratic Action, the most influential Socialist group in our Nation."

If the Democrats are reelected, Thurmond warned, "freedom as we have known it in this country is doomed, and individuals will be destined to lives of regulation, control, coercion, intimidation and subservience to a power elite who shall rule from Washington."

The senator explained that he had remained a Democrat for years "because experience proves it necessary to work within the framework of one of the two national parties to be effective." But he had maintained independence on issues, he reminded the people, and always sought to "protect their rights and freedom. I shall always maintain my independent judgment and action and put the people of South Carolina first." But to do so he would now have to work "within the framework of the Goldwater Republican Party. For me there is no alternative. The future of freedom and constitutional government is at stake, and this requires that I do everything in my power to help Barry Goldwater return our Nation to constitutional government through his election to the Presidency."

Thurmond acknowledged that many of his supporters had counseled against the move. He realized the political risk involved and that his chances for reelection might "go down into oblivion. But in the final analysis," he said, "I can only follow the course which, in my heart and conscience, I believe to be in the best interest of our State, country and the freedom of our people."

The senator had given up one part of the past to preserve another. As *The News and Courier* pointed out, "Republican was once a dirty name in South Carolina"—a view once promoted by Thurmond's own father and by his boyhood mentor, Pitchfork Ben. "Though no longer a reminder of carpetbagger government of a century ago," the paper continued, "the GOP has not yet attained a winning formula in the Palmetto State. This year may be different." The editorial, like one in *The State,* also complimented Thurmond's courage and independence and added a brief but accurate description of the senator's style: "Never a machine politician, he has depended for his own support on direct appeal to the people."

A contrary view of the party switch came from *The Anderson Independent,* which felt that there wasn't really all that much new in Thurmond's formal announcement. Calling the senator a "synthetic model of Goldwater," the paper said Thurmond "has been the common law spouse of the Republican Party for many years."

Once the announcement had been made, Dent could see that Thurmond was almost immediately more comfortable. Gone was the tension of being the odd man out. His new Republican colleagues made him feel welcome. Having no committee chairmanship to lose, he'd had less at stake in switching parties than several of his more senior southern colleagues. (Russell had conceded as much in a letter to one constituent who had written to ask why he didn't switch parties, too.) Although no deal had been cut with Thurmond in advance, Republicans gave him the same rank on their side of the committees he worked on as he had had as a Democrat.

Not long after the announcement, Dent went down to South Carolina to run the "Thurmond Speaks for Goldwater" operation, which used privately raised money to send the senator throughout the South and into a few western states on behalf of the candidate.

A schedule of activities published September 24 shows twenty-nine appearances between September 24 and October 20 and then a full two weeks in South Carolina before election day. The entries for October 15 and 16 make clear that Thurmond would give Goldwater the same energetic effort he had put into his own campaign: Tallahassee, Florida, at noon; supper in Valdosta, Georgia; Waycross, Georgia, in the later evening; La Grange, Georgia, for breakfast on October 16; and then Gainesville, Florida, for the afternoon and evening.

One trip that required the senator to be in Alabama for a breakfast meeting had a ghoulish twist. In an effort to help Thurmond sleep during the journey, his handlers had commandeered an old hearse, thinking the senator would be more comfortable if he could lie down. He didn't get much rest, but that was the fault of the bumpy roads rather than any queasiness over his temporary accommodations.

While the thrust of his campaign speeches was to praise the Republican candidate—"My sole purpose in life until November 3 is to do everything possible to elect Barry Goldwater President of the United States," he told an audience in Greenville—Thurmond also found Humphrey to be a convenient foil. "A vote for Hubert Humphrey for Vice President is a vote which could make him President, and he is the choice of Socialists and all left-wingers for that job," Thurmond said at a campaign rally in Charleston. "When it comes to extremism," the senator added, attempting to reverse the "extremist" label that had been pasted on Goldwater, "the choice of Humphrey for Vice President is the ultimate."

Near the end of the campaign, Thurmond acknowledged that when he made his decision to switch parties, he knew that it could ruin his own chances for reelection and that the "odds at that time were against Barry Goldwater's election." But he knew Goldwater needed the South to have a chance, and he had "faith that the people of the South will support Barry Goldwater, not under any false illusions that he is a segregationist, but because he is a man of great integrity and ability, he stands for fiscal sanity, he believes in Constitutional government, and he knows and understands the communist enemy and how best to ensure that we retain our freedoms from both internal and external threats.

"I would not change my decision for a million dollars or a million votes."

On November 3 Johnson trounced Goldwater, carrying forty-four states and receiving 60 percent of the vote. But the Republican carried Alabama, Mississippi, Georgia, Louisiana, and South Carolina by handsome margins. Assisted by the credibility Thurmond had given him in the South, Goldwater brought seven new Republican candidates to Congress from districts in Alabama, Georgia, and Mississippi that had been Democratic since Reconstruction. A two-party South was emerging.

12.
THE CENTER CANNOT HOLD

1965–1970

THURGOOD MARSHALL WAS no stranger to South Carolina when Lyndon Johnson tapped him in 1965 to be solicitor general of the United States, the government's representative before the Supreme Court. He had won three major lawsuits in the state—two that won blacks the right to vote in primaries and a third that outlawed segregated schools. His name was synonymous with integration, and it was no secret that this new position was often a stepping-stone to a seat on the high court itself.

Editorials in South Carolina's two major papers greeted the appointment with barbed resignation. The Columbia *State* conceded that Marshall had the legal credentials for the job, but wondered in print whether he could "bring to the office that species of detachment which it ideally should enjoy—in the interest of *all* citizens." Johnson could have selected another qualified black attorney not so closely associated with the civil rights movement. "But that," the paper piously observed, "wouldn't have filled the political bill."

With a touch of self-pity, the Charleston *News and Courier* found Marshall's nomination "in keeping with administration policies'' but wished "white people who question the extent of current policies could have representation on such important posts." That view, the paper noted sarcastically, "is considered 'racism' by those in power."

Three months later, in a promotion the papers and Thurmond found easier to bless, Harry Dent became head of South Carolina's burgeoning Republican Party, wresting control from a handful of entrenched GOP stalwarts. As a condition of his election, Dent had to promise that he would work for all Republicans, not just Thurmond.

Dent and Marshall had very little in common beyond the fact that both were lawyers. But at this moment, their simultaneous career moves signaled a sea change in political life that would throw into disarray conventional wisdom about blacks, Republicans, and the South. This was the heyday of Earl Warren's Supreme Court and a theory of constitutional interpretation that found room in the majestic words of the charter to protect those who previously had been treated as afterthoughts. To white southern men who had controlled so much for so long, a distressing result of the court's forays into new territory was to diminish their power and disrupt their sense of order. Thurmond spoke for many when he blamed the justices for the "growing disintegration and chaos in the country."

That a black man could speak for the federal government before the country's most august tribunal was irrefutable evidence that the racial status quo was changing. Over the next five years it was going to change even more. Enactment of a new voting rights law in 1965 would bring thousands of blacks into the electorate and literally transform the face of "the people." But in the black community itself, factionalism over tactics began to disrupt the sense of common purpose, and the demand for "black power" turned some toward violence. Martin Luther King's assassination in the midst of the upheaval at once gave emotional urgency to the push for new antidiscrimination laws and triggered paroxysms of violence that inflamed already volatile domestic politics.

Through all of this Thurmond remained the defender of "constitutional government" and the voice of resistance on civil rights issues, whether new legislation or new federal appointees. Nothing in his public statements reflected an appreciation for black Americans' struggle to break with the past; he pressed his opposition with as much fervor as they pressed their case. He preached to the choir of white Carolina, unconcerned about how his remarks would play with the politically weak minority population. Less conservative politicians deplored the violence and hatemongering that marked these years, and Thurmond claimed to feel the same; but many of them spoke with a greater understanding of the ingrained inequities that had fostered the conflict, and they had greater faith in government to help find solutions.

The speculation that Marshall was headed for the Supreme Court proved true, and by the time that nomination came forward in 1967, Thurmond had joined soulmate Jim Eastland on the Judiciary Committee. Now he could rail at the nominee in committee as well as on the Senate floor. He would have the same opportunity to turn his ire on Abe Fortas, Johnson's nominee to succeed Chief Justice Warren.

A year later, Thurmond would help lead the South back into the front line of national politics by playing a critical role in Richard Nixon's election to the White House. For so long the voice of resistance, the senator could now be an agent of change—albeit not on racial matters. When Republicans gathered in Miami in August of 1968, Thurmond would emerge as Nixon's kingmaker. The "southern strategy" was born, and Harry Dent, its chief architect, would be rewarded with a desk at 1600 Pennsylvania Avenue. Fred Buzhardt, Dent's close ally and fellow tactician, was headed for a top job in the Defense Department, a perfect spot for a West Point graduate. With their customary hyperbole, pundits referred to the Nixon White House as Uncle Strom's Cabin. *Time* magazine singled out Dent as the "southern-fried Rasputin."

Dent rejected the witty put-down. He did not consider himself a devious insider but a "big-picture man," and once in the White House he realized the politics of resistance as practiced by Thurmond couldn't last forever. He told his old boss what he thought, and even though Thurmond never explicitly acknowledged Dent's advice, it would become clear that the senator had gotten the message.

Republican lawmakers in Washington wasted no time in making Thurmond feel at home when the Senate reconvened in January 1965. His new colleagues gave him a seat on the GOP policy-making committee, the first time a southerner had been represented in the group. But there were still some rough spots over the matter of committee assignments. In this new congressional session, where more civil rights legislation was expected, moderate-to-liberal Republicans weren't going to throw away their seniority in favor of Thurmond. After three days of internal skirmishing, party leaders agreed to let Thurmond keep his seat on the Armed Services Committee and take a spot on the Banking Committee, but he would have to give up his seat on Commerce, where he had been a subcommittee chairman. The Banking post was made available only after northerners blocked Thurmond from getting a position on three other committees, Commerce, Judiciary, and Labor.

While the Vietnam War was pushing its way into daily news reports, so too was a new initiative on civil rights in Dallas County, Alabama, fifty miles west of Montgomery. Before it was over the effort would galvanize the president, Congress, and the country and result in a law that would remake the southern electorate and require adjustment by the white politicians who served it.

Despite SNCC's extensive work in Dallas County, only 353 blacks—a paltry 2.1 percent of those eligible—had been able to register at the courthouse in Selma. King, who had just received the Nobel Peace Prize, had come to Selma to join the effort, observing dryly that at the current pace, "it would take about one hundred years" to register the area's blacks.

The county election board was open just two days each month, allowing only a fraction of the black applicants to be processed. Making matters even worse was a complicated literacy test that had been put in place the previous year. Among other requirements, an applicant had to write a dictated portion of the Constitution, answer four questions on the governmental process, read four passages on the Constitution and answer a question on each, and then sign an oath of loyalty to the United States and Alabama. Since 1961 the Justice Department had been involved in litigation to stop Dallas County registrars from discriminating, but even though a court order had been issued November 1, 1963, discrimination still persisted. On February 4, 1965, a federal judge ordered the Board of Registrars to speed up its voter registration processes and threatened to appoint a federal voting referee if all those eligible and wanting to vote were not enrolled by July 1.

The reason for the resistance was obvious. If all the eligible blacks voted, Dallas County sheriff James G. Clark, the nemesis of the civil rights workers, would, as one of them put it, "be out picking cotton within two years."

The court order did little to calm the frustrations of civil rights leaders, who had little confidence that it would do any good. Joined by sympathetic northern whites and representatives of the clergy from all parts of the country, blacks determined to take their protest to the streets. The goal was to force the voter registration office to remain open every day until all blacks who wanted to vote were registered.

Just as the behavior of Bull Connor and the thugs in Birmingham had won sympathy for the freedom riders four years earlier, Sheriff Clark's handling of the Selma protesters would bring them favorable publicity nationwide.

After six weeks of clashes with law officers—in one, eighteen-year-old Jimmie Lee Jackson was clubbed to death by state troopers in nearby Marion—the civil rights activists decided to march from Selma to Montgomery to confront Governor Wallace with their demands. Six blocks into their fifty-mile walk, the 525 demonstrators reached the Edmund Pettus Bridge, which spans the Alabama River near the edge of town. As they started across they were ordered to halt by Major John Cloud, who was leading a well-armed phalanx of state troopers. "This march you propose is not conducive to public safety," Cloud said. "This march will not continue. You have two minutes to disperse."

"May we have a word with you?" asked Hosea Williams, a King lieutenant.

"There is no word to be had," Cloud replied.

There were two more exchanges and then a second warning that the marchers had two minutes to turn around. The protesters remained silently in place. The next sound was Cloud's voice: "Troopers, advance."

Reporter Roy Reed of *The New York Times* gave readers a vivid account of the action: "The mounted possemen spurred their horses and rode at a run into the retreating mass. The Negroes cried out as they crowded together for protection, and the whites on the sideline whooped and cheered.

"The Negroes paused in their retreat for perhaps a minute," Reed went on, "still screaming and huddling together. Suddenly there was a report like a gunshot, and a gray cloud spewed over the troopers and the Negroes.

" 'Tear gas,' someone yelled.

"The cloud began covering the highway. . . . But before the cloud finally hid it all, there were several seconds of unobstructed view. Fifteen or twenty nightsticks could be seen through the gas flailing at the heads of the marchers."

Among the seventeen wounded blacks was John Lewis, who pulled himself together to speak to shell-shocked demonstrators before heading to the hospital. "I don't see how President Johnson can send troops to Vietnam," he told them. "I don't see how he can send troops to the Congo—I don't see how he can send troops to Africa and can't send troops to Selma."

Johnson deliberately had withheld a strong show of federal force, fearing it would only inflame tensions and damage efforts to pass the voting rights legislation already in the drafting stages. But "Bloody Sunday," as it became known, prompted Democrats and Republicans who had seen graphic accounts of the brutality to call for a new bill immediately. Many criticized the president for not getting the measure to Congress sooner.

On March 8, King announced that he was going to stage another demonstration the next day. At the same time, Governor Wallace told John Herbers, now a reporter for the *Times,* that Montgomery state troopers and sheriff's deputies had not used unnecessary force. "We saved lives by stopping that march," he contended. "There's a good possibility that death would have resulted to some of these people if we had not stopped them."

In Washington, President Johnson now knew that he had to do something—and quickly. He immediately sent LeRoy Collins—whose appointment as head of the Community Relations Service Thurmond had bitterly and unsuccessfully opposed—to Alabama to negotiate a peaceful approach to the proposed demonstration. A few hours before it was to begin Collins and John Doar arranged a scenario allowing King and his followers, now swelled by hundreds of sympathetic northerners, to cross the Pettus Bridge, pray in front of heavily armed state troopers, and then turn back.

The agreement held, and the day ended peacefully. But violence intruded in the night.

The Reverend James Reeb and two other Unitarian ministers were walking in downtown Selma after the march when they were savagely beaten. Reeb was so badly injured that he was taken to a hospital in Birmingham for immediate surgery. He died March 11 of a skull fracture and large blood clot.

Though Jimmie Lee Jackson's death was equally brutal, it had not received the attention that Reeb's did. Memorial marches for Reeb were held all over the country, the president called his widow, and Vice-President Humphrey attended his funeral. (Four white men were eventually arrested and indicted in Reeb's death, but a jury acquitted them in ninety minutes.)

On March 15, eight days after Bloody Sunday, Johnson, under growing pressure to protect the marchers, went to Capitol Hill to address a joint session of Congress and the entire nation about voting rights, and to prepare the legislators for his forthcoming bill. The speech, which was drafted from Johnson's outline by Kennedy holdover Richard Goodwin, was an eloquent blend of lofty principle and common sense. The words alone had power. Spoken by a son of the South, they rose to another plane.

"I speak tonight for the dignity of man and the destiny of democracy," the president began, standing in a House chamber jammed to capacity with members of Congress and the cabinet. "At times, history and fate meet at a single time in a single place to shape a turning point in man's unending search for freedom. So it was at Lexington and Concord. So it was a century ago at Appomattox. So it was last week in Selma, Alabama."

In an instant, the president had made the quest for equal opportunity the entire nation's business, putting Bloody Sunday on a par with two pivotal moments in the country's history.

In Selma, the president went on, "long-suffering men and women peacefully protested the denial of their rights as Americans. Many were brutally assaulted. One good man—a man of God—was killed. . . . Our mission," Johnson said, "is at once the oldest and the most basic of this country—to right wrong, to do justice, to serve man. . . .

"What happened in Selma is part of a far larger movement which reaches into every section and state of America," Johnson continued. "It is the effort of American Negroes to secure for themselves the full blessings of American life. Their cause must be our cause too. Because it's not just Negroes, but really it's all of us who must overcome the crippling legacy of bigotry and injustice."

He paused now and leaned forward ever so slightly, aware of the power of his next four words.

"And we shall overcome."

Three years earlier in Oxford, Ross Barnett had offered a

clenched fist and homage to Mississippi's traditions. Tonight, invoking the motto of the civil rights movement, Lyndon Johnson was promising with his heart and soul to undo them.

"As a man whose roots go deeply into Southern soil," the president said, "I know how agonizing racial feelings are. I know how difficult it is to reshape the attitudes and the structure of our society. But a century has passed—more than one hundred years since the Negro was freed. And he is not fully free tonight."

Johnson claimed that when he was teaching "poor, undernourished students" in Texas, it had never occurred to him that now, in 1965, "I might have the chance to help the sons and daughters of those students and to help people like them all over this country. But now I do have that chance. And I'll let you in on a secret. I mean to use it."

By the time the president was done he had been interrupted thirty-six times for applause and had received two standing ovations that were nearly unanimous. Those sitting on their hands were the irritated southerners, including Thurmond, who had been unhappy about possible new voting rights legislation well before the president spoke to Congress.

Aware that some kind of bill was in the drafting stages, Thurmond had said in a radio broadcast three weeks earlier that the legislation would result in voting by illiterates and criminals.

Reminding listeners that each civil rights bill of the past was supposed to have been the final one, he'd said, "This proves that Martin Luther King and his kind will never be satisfied. This also shows that King must always have an agitation objective lest he end up in the street one day without a drum to beat or a headline to make."

Immediately after Johnson's televised address the senator put out a statement supporting "without reservation the right of all those qualified to vote" and insisting that in South Carolina that right was "available to all persons from both a legal standpoint and a practical standpoint." In his view, the real issue was whether alleged instances of discrimination would be investigated "by the orderly means of prescribed legal process" or whether "mass public demonstrations shall be condoned as alternative means of seeking political redress. . . . This is, in the final analysis, a choice between law and anarchy. So far, regrettably, anarchy is winning." And the real purpose of the "agitation," he charged in radio spots the following week, was not to secure the right to vote but "to induce violence, which would in turn provide headlines and money-raising potential across the country." After all, there was already a court order in Selma making it possible—as Thurmond saw it—for blacks who could read and write to register.

Despite Johnson's well-received speech and his promise of new legislation, civil rights leaders were determined to make the Selma-to-Montgomery march. In a court order issued March 17, U.S. District Judge Frank Johnson, Jr., authorized the march and ordered Wallace and other Alabama officials to refrain from "harassing or threatening" the marchers. That same day the president sent his voting rights bill to Congress. The heart of the legislation authorized the attorney general to appoint federal registrars in those states in which literacy or other voter qualification tests had been used and less than 50 percent of the eligible adults had voted in 1964. The legislation also barred literacy tests in the future.

The next day the Senate, in a vote that forecast eventual passage of the new bill, easily rejected a procedural effort to delay its consideration.

Meanwhile in Montgomery, Wallace gave Johnson the opening he needed for federal action. Saying Alabama did not have enough state and local lawmen to protect "the colossal demonstration," the governor asked the president to send U.S. marshals to the state to protect the marchers on their five-day journey. Johnson subsequently called up nearly four thousand troops.

On March 21 civil rights activists, their ranks now swelled beyond three thousand, moved out of Selma on their way to Montgomery—for the third time in two weeks. They arrived in the capital March 25 along with another twenty-two thousand who had streamed into the state for the final day. The marchers brought with them a petition challenging Governor Wallace to end discrimination. King tried to deliver it, but state troopers barred him from entering the capitol building even though Wallace had said he would meet with a delegation of protesters. The rebuff aside, the marchers were jubilant that they had reached Montgomery.

Later in the day violence once again erased triumph.

Viola Liuzzo, a white, thirty-six-year-old mother of five, had come from Detroit to join the protest, moved by the graphic reports she had seen on television. Her task had been to ferry participants back and forth between Montgomery and Selma. On a trip back to the capital in the evening of March 25, she was shot at close range in Lowndes County by a group of Klansmen who had followed her out of Selma.

Three Klan members were indicted for her murder. A fourth who was in the car, Gary Thomas Rowe, Jr., was later revealed to be an FBI informant who had been on the agency's payroll since 1959. Rowe had been arrested right after the shooting, but he was not indicted. Later he testified about the Liuzzo killing. The first state murder trial ended in a hung jury. The second all-white jury acquitted the defendants in less than two hours. But this time the Justice Department decided to bring federal charges against the three men for conspiring to violate Mrs. Liuzzo's civil rights. A federal jury found them guilty, and Judge Johnson gave each the maximum ten-year sentence—a milestone in this era of civil rights violence.

Back in Washington, the voting rights legislation was on a fast track. A majority of the Senate—over the strenuous objection of Chairman Eastland, who called it "an unheard-of thing"—had voted to require that the Judiciary Committee send the bill back within fifteen days. Eastland, famous for his ubiquitous cigar and his fondness for Chivas Regal, had only himself to blame for this special procedure. In his nine years as chairman, the Mississippian had allowed only one civil rights bill to come out of his committee, and that had been under orders from the Senate. He had blocked 121 others, claiming that he was protecting "the interests of people in Mississippi." He bragged that he had special pockets put in his pants to carry around all the other civil rights bills he had buried.

Like Thurmond, Eastland was born into a prosperous family. His grandfather, a Civil War veteran who had fought under one of the eventual founders of the Klan, bought a plantation in Doddsville, where both Eastland and his father were born. Woods Eastland was a successful businessman-lawyer whose acumen helped increase the holdings by the time his son, Jim, arrived in November 1904. The elder Eastland was steeped in Mississippi politics but preferred the backroom to public office. It would soon be clear that the lessons of the father had been passed on to the son.

At the University of Mississippi, young Jim showed that he, too, had an affinity for behind-the-scenes maneuvering. Recalling his college days, he admitted that once "I had to arrange for a whole board to get elected in order to elect myself business manager of the paper." Another time, he confessed, in a campus contest, he broke open a ballot box to fix the election of a friend as the prettiest young woman and to steal ballots naming him the biggest liar.

Eastland transferred to Vanderbilt after three years at Ole Miss but spent only one semester there before leaving to attend the University of Alabama. Before graduating, however, he passed the Mississippi bar, dropped out of school, and at age twenty-four was elected to the Mississippi House. Theodore Bilbo was governor, and Eastland became one of his loyalists. When Bilbo left office in 1932 beset by financial troubles, Eastland also left and went back to the Delta to practice law. For nine years he stayed out of public life, but in 1941, after U.S. Senator Pat Harrison died unexpectedly, Governor Paul Johnson first offered the post to Woods Eastland, then named the thirty-seven-year-old James when his father turned it down. There was a condition, however. Eastland was to serve only the eighty-eight days until a special election could be held, and he had to promise not to run for the seat.

Eastland kept his promise, but a year later he won a full Senate term. He had endeared himself to Mississippians in his short stint in Washington by denouncing a proposed plan to put a price ceiling on cottonseed oil. The plan eventually was abandoned, and the young interim senator returned home boasting that he had put $50 million in the pockets of southern cotton growers.

In 1956, Eastland became chairman of the Judiciary Committee. *Time* magazine put him on its March 26 cover, calling him "the spiritual leader of segregation" and citing as proof of this appellation his declarations from the Senate that "the Negro race is an inferior race" and that Mississippi would "maintain white supremacy throughout an eternity." He had been a strong supporter of Thurmond's states' rights effort and was one of only two senators—Stennis was the other—who had gone to Birmingham for the Dixiecrats' gathering.

By the time Johnson's voting rights bill was ready for consideration, Eastland's reputation as an obstructionist was secure.

(*Time* had also called him "tactiturn and humorless"; to some, he was plain nasty.) "Once in a position, he has proved almost impossible to move," said Majority Leader Mike Mansfield of Montana, "and indeed it requires nearly the entire Senate to budge him."

Such an effort already was under way, to the irritation of

Thurmond, who used his radio broadcasts and newsletter that week to accuse the attorney general of forcing the South to do "penance" by allowing blacks to vote, literate or not.

The Judiciary Committee got to work on the legislation immediately and fought over amendments right up until midnight April 9, the deadline for returning the measure to the full Senate. The bill that emerged included some new, tougher provisions, including a ban on poll taxes in state and local elections. (The constitutional amendment ratified a year earlier covered only federal elections.)

Between April 1 and April 5, while the panel was still working, the voltage of Thurmond's criticism went up a notch. Going after Johnson on radio and television, he called it "amazing" how much a man's view of the Constitution could change between his time "serving as a United States senator from the State of Texas and then later when he is serving as President of the United States under pressure from Martin Luther King." In 1949, promising to oppose a Truman bill that would set federal voting standards, Johnson had argued in favor of a state's right to set voter qualifications. "The issue on his voting rights bill today is the same as it was then," Thurmond told viewers, "and his bill violates the Constitution as much or more than did President Truman's 1949 legislation."

Thurmond was most disgruntled about the elimination of literacy tests and said that the answer was to require all voters, white and black, to reregister and be subject to the same test, impartially administered. He scoffed at the Justice Department's argument that blacks would be disadvantaged because they had been "systematically denied educational opportunity."

"Denial of the privilege of voting on account of race or color is unconstitutional, discriminatory and wrong," Thurmond concluded. "So is this bill. Two wrongs do not make a right; but for the President, the Attorney General and the sponsors of the 'Voting Rights Act of 1965,' two unconstitutional, discriminatory wrongs make 'civil rights.' "

As his radio broadcasts played in South Carolina April 5, the senator took his case directly to the Judiciary Committee, going over to the panel's hearing room, as other southern senators had done, to express his opposition in person. Compared with some of his previous broadsides on civil rights, this presentation was restrained, merely pointing out the particular flaws he saw in the legislation.

Thurmond conceded that the Fifteenth Amendment to the Constitution, which protects the right to vote, also authorized Congress to enforce the amendment by appropriate legislation. "In my judgment," the senator said, "the pending bill is not appropriate legislation." The assumption that the Fifteenth Amendment had been violated in a state simply because fewer than 50 percent of the voting-age residents were registered or had voted in the 1964 presidential election was, he said, "a presumption which has no logical or legal connection with the facts." The only voting discrimination barred by the Constitution was that based on race, color, or "previous condition of servitude." This legislation went beyond those strictures and imposed an unfair burden on the South, Thurmond argued. An illiterate would now be able to vote in six southern states and in thirty-four counties of a seventh, he contended, and yet that same person could not register in any of the other states that might still require a literacy test, simply because they were not covered by the bill. "It is grossly unfair to the people of these six southern states to have such rank discrimination imposed upon them." (Ultimately parts of other states outside the South would be affected by the law.)

Despite his own work and that of others to get out the vote for Goldwater in 1964, less than half of the eligible population of South Carolina had voted in that election—even though, he pointed out, the total had exceeded any previous mark by at least one hundred thousand votes. Thurmond drew the "inescapable conclusion that freedom necessarily includes the right *not to vote* as well as *the right to vote* as each individual decides."

The senator was particularly angry that South Carolina would be covered under the law; the attorney general, Nicholas Katzenbach, had already said there was little evidence of specific voting abuses in the state. But he had also said that "other forms of racial discrimination are suggestive of voting discrimination" and could be taken into account. Thurmond called this "guilt by association in its worst form."

The Senate started debate on the voting rights bill April 22. Instead of immediately mounting a traditional filibuster, southerners tried to amend the bill into pap. But this tactic failed to work. Most of the amendments—the majority offered by Judiciary member Sam Ervin—were rejected by margins of better than two to one.

Though he was as vocal as any other southerner, Thurmond played a secondary role in this fight. He confined himself to Senate floor speeches opposing the bill and supporting amendments to weaken its impact.

By mid-May the debate was still droning on despite efforts by Majority Leader Mansfield to bring discussions voluntarily to a close. Finally on May 25 senators voted 70–30 to cut off debate and move toward final passage. It was only the second time the Senate had ended a filibuster on a civil rights bill, but it was the second time in two years the chamber had done so—as good a sign as any that public perceptions about civil rights, or at least the right to vote, were changing. The bill passed the next day by a vote of 77–19. All the opponents were southerners.

Just before the vote was taken Thurmond got up to speak once again, criticizing the Senate for a debate that had been "signally unproductive. Few if any votes have been influenced by it," he said. "In fact, from all appearances little attention has been paid to the debate," which he characterized as "a rather one-sided contest between power on the one hand and argument of constitutional issues on the other." He wound up with a flourish, accusing the Senate of turning into the "final resting place of the Constitution and the rule of law; for it is here that they will have been buried with shovels of emotion under piles of expediency."

Like his earlier pronouncements, this was a passionate but skewed reading of the past and present in defense of a cherished way of life. Left out was any allusion to white America's legacy of harassment, intimidation, and brutality visited upon blacks who had tried over the years to claim the franchise. Had this not been the case, George Lee could have turned on his television in Belzoni, Mississippi, and heard for himself Lyndon Johnson's stirring words. The senator could bemoan the loss of constitutional prerogatives of the states, but missing was any lament for the rights of George Lee and others who had perished in the cause. There was, likewise, not a hint of South Carolina's particular story, where it had taken two federal lawsuits to enable blacks to vote in primaries, the only election that mattered. With the weeds of history grown so tall around him, the senator still saw only magnolias.

The House passed its version of the voting bill July 9. A conference committee of House and Senate members completed work July 29 after the House agreed to remove a flat ban on the poll tax. The final provision was similar to the Senate-passed language, which declared the poll tax to be an abridgment of the right to vote and directed the attorney general to bring lawsuits to block enforcement of the tax.

The House approved the conference report August 3 by an overwhelming 328–74 vote, and the Senate followed suit the next day, 79–18. The "nay" votes were again cast by southerners.

The critical section of the bill remained as originally proposed: authorization for federal examiners to supervise voter registration in states and cities or counties that had used some kind of voter qualification test before the November 1964 elections and where fewer than 50 percent of the voting-age residents had participated in the presidential election that year. The new law also suspended the use of literacy tests in selected southern states and in scattered counties elsewhere, and it required approval from the Justice Department before these states and counties could change election procedures or laws. The process came to be known as "preclearance."

At a nationally televised signing ceremony August 6, broadcast from the imposing second-floor rotunda of the Capitol, President Johnson referred to the history embodied in the legislation. Blacks had come to America "in darkness and they came in chains," he said. "And today, we strike away the last major shackle of those fierce ancient bonds." After his remarks the president went into a small office near the Senate chamber to sign the bill. It was the same room where Abraham Lincoln, 104 years earlier to the day, had signed the Emancipation Proclamation.

Thurmond and the other members of the South Carolina delegation boycotted the event. Later, with obvious sarcasm, the senator said it would have been "most fitting if precedent could be ignored so that civil rights leaders could co-sign the bill into law with the president. After all," he added, "Dr. King initiated the legislation and the president reacted to King's acts of disobedience and the attorney general felt it necessary to get King's OK" on the final bill.

The State prophetically observed in an editorial August 8 that as of this moment, "the South has a new electorate."

(South Carolina officials immediately challenged the law in federal court. On March 7, 1966, the Supreme Court upheld the statute, ruling that Congress had properly exercised its authority to enforce the Fifteenth Amendment.)

The Justice Department wasted no time making use of its new legal tool. On August 7 government lawyers filed a suit to eliminate Mississippi's poll tax. Similar actions were filed August 10 against Alabama, Texas, and Virginia. The same day, the department suspended literacy tests and similar qualification devices in Alabama, Alaska, Georgia, Louisiana, Mississippi, South Carolina, and Virginia, as well as in twenty-seven counties in North Carolina and one in Arizona.

On August 9, Attorney General Katzenbach named the first group of southern counties and parishes where federal examiners would process blacks' voting applications and order their registration. In a television interview, Katzenbach pointed out that white illiterates had been registered for decades "and now this same standard must be applied to Negroes." Thurmond fired off a statement of his own saying this showed "just how unreasonable this administration is going to be in administering this law for the purpose of trying to get complete control over the southern states, especially those which voted for Goldwater in the presidential election."

By August 25, Johnson announced that in the first nineteen days under the law, 27,385 blacks in three southern states had been registered by federal registrars. The impact of the law was particularly striking in Selma. On August 14, 381 blacks, more than all those who had been able to register in the previous sixty-five years, were put on the rolls by a federal examiner. By November that number had risen to nearly 8,000. Other southern states were posting similar numbers, and the implications of a larger black electorate would not be lost for long on a politician who paid as much attention to "the people" as Thurmond did.

As the voting rights bill was making its way through Congress, Johnson had selected Thurgood Marshall to be the next solicitor general. He made the announcement July 13. Two days later, *The New York Times* ran a front-page story confirming the speculation of many insiders that Marshall was in training for a Supreme Court appointment.

Unlike his stormy confirmation to the appeals court, Marshall's passage through the Judiciary Committee was painless. His nomination was sent to the full Senate August 10 along with one other: the appointment of Johnson confidant Abe Fortas as an associate justice to replace Arthur Goldberg, who had agreed to become ambassador to the United Nations.

Both were confirmed by the Senate August 11. Hinting at future troubles for the justice, Thurmond opposed Fortas, telling colleagues that his nomination "is, in my opinion, most unfortunate." The senator said that after studying all the available information about the lawyer, "I am convinced that he is totally lacking in judicial temperament."

The sense of triumph in the black community over passage of the Voting Rights Act and Marshall's appointment came crashing to earth abruptly. On August 11 rioting erupted in Watts, a predominantly black section of Los Angeles, touched off when a white California highway patrolman stopped a weaving car and gave the black driver a sobriety test. The rioting lasted six days and left thirty-four dead, more than eighteen hundred injured, and $200 million in property damage. Some thirty-one thousand individuals were arrested. It took a combined force of sixteen thousand national guardsmen and other lawmen to restore order.

Violence broke out in Chicago at the same time, where for two days blacks battled police after an out-of-control fire engine killed a black woman bystander in a predominantly black neighborhood. Eighty persons were injured and more than one hundred twenty were arrested.

This was the beginning of several more big-city riots that rocked the country over the next three years, prompting the president to appoint a special commission to investigate the causes of the turmoil.

Thurmond didn't need any blue-ribbon panel to tell him what the trouble was. While rioting was still gripping the streets of Watts, he blamed the violence on "the policies of our national leadership over the last few years. The seeds of the insurrections in Los Angeles and Chicago were planted across the nation by the protection, tolerance, and encouragement of law-breaking racial demonstrations," he charged. "A nation cannot condone the deliberate mass defiance of laws in a particular section of the country without undermining respect for law and order throughout the country. As long as national policies prevail which establish a precedent that one race is exempted from particular laws and punishment for mob crimes, we should expect repetitions of the Los Angeles and Chicago phenomena."

The senator could also have included in his litany of violence the murders of civil rights workers in Jackson and Philadelphia, Mississippi, or in Lowndes County, Alabama. Racial demonstrators were hardly the only ones whose "defiance of the laws" was condoned. The argument could be made with just as much force that Chicago and Los Angeles and the riots that were to come in Detroit and other cities were the poison fruits of 150 years of discrimination.

In September, Thurmond learned that Drake Edens, head of South Carolina's GOP, was resigning as head of the party. This created an opportunity for Dent to go back home and put his two-party-South ideas to work. Thurmond gave him his blessing in a formal statement September 15, calling Dent "the best possible man for the job" and adding that he had "performed magnificently" on behalf of Barry Goldwater in 1964.

When Dent got back home he found himself in a contest for party chief with Arthur Ravenel, Jr., a Charleston businessman who headed the party in the southeastern part of the state and who had been a Republican for longer than Dent or Thurmond. The party hierarchy was backing Ravenel to block what they feared was a takeover by Thurmond.

Ravenel and Dent started out on a debate tour before Carolina Republicans, but after the second one Ravenel dropped out of the race, telling a group of reporters that the debates were creating too much dissension and threatened party unity. He also said he was now convinced that Dent would expand his horizons beyond Thurmond's career.

After his election October 2, Dent confirmed Ravenel's assurances. "As chairman I realize I must be a leader but not a dictator. My boss until the March state convention will be the executive committee. . . . My job is to elect candidates."

President Johnson hoped to pick up in 1966 where he'd left off the previous year. In his State of the Union address January 12, he said he wanted passage of a law barring discrimination in the sale and rental of housing and new protections for civil rights workers. But success was to elude him. Even though the House passed a bill in August, the Senate refused to go along. Opponents, Thurmond among them, made clear they were ready to talk indefinitely about the measure, and when Majority Leader Mansfield tried to summon two-thirds of his colleagues to cut off debate, he failed by ten votes. After an unsuccessful second attempt September 19, the legislation died.

Throughout the spring and summer Thurmond used Senate floor speeches, weekly radio broadcasts, and his newsletters to criticize the civil rights bill. On July 4, he wrote that the new legislation represented "an astonishingly bold grab for power" by the national government. Major portions of the bill, he claimed, embodied "a new departure in the field of so-called 'civil rights.' " The next week, in a report called "Foot in the Door," he attacked the fair-housing provision, accusing sponsors of asking for "a more harsh measure than most thought possible to pass" so they could then " 'compromise' the harshest provisions. In each case, however, the 'compromise' establishes a new precedent for power, which once established can be expanded to the harshest extremes in subsequent bills."

When the measure was debated in the Senate in September, Thurmond bellowed that it was "one of the most vicious, vindictive, politically inspired measures to be forced upon Congress since the founding of the Republic." The senator's office promptly put out a statement trumpeting that he had "stood in the front line" to prevent the bill from being passed.

There were other setbacks for the administration as well. Congress, in order to signal its unease with the speed of racial change and the form that it was taking, restricted the right of federal education officials to withhold funds from school districts charged with failing to desegregate. Lawmakers also barred dispensing antipoverty funds to anyone convicted of promoting a riot or activities that resulted in property damage.

There was plenty of that during the summer of 1966, much of it the result of black crowds roaming the streets, hurling debris and taunting police. Between July 12 and 20, rioting broke out in the black sections of Chicago, Cleveland, Jacksonville, Florida, New York City, and South Bend, Indiana. The worst was in Chicago and Cleveland, where the National Guard had to be called out and two people were killed in each city.

This was the summer when the vocabulary of the civil rights movement started to change. "Negro" was moving out of the lexicon; "black" was moving in, and with it the new slogan of "black power." SNCC chairman Stokely Carmichael (who later changed his name to Kwame Toure) was credited with coining the phrase during a June voter registration drive in Mississippi. A march through the state to register blacks had been started by James Meredith, but he was wounded June 6 by hidden snipers as he walked along a state highway. Carmichael, along with other SNCC workers, came to carry on the effort. "Black power," which became the marchers' chant, first appeared in press reports on June 17. The day before in Greenwood, Carmichael had roused a crowd of one thousand blacks, telling them, "We want black power. We want black power." King, who was also in Mississippi, embellished the thought twenty-four hours later when he told a voter registration rally, "Do you know what power is? Power is the ability to make the power structure say 'yes' even when it wants to say 'no.' The way to do this is to be voters."

King had one view of black power, but others had a more militant interpretation, and the differences were creating strains among the leading civil rights groups. While CORE gave its blessing to "black power" at its July convention, a day later the NAACP refused to follow suit after a dramatic speech by Roy Wilkins. He likened the concept to black racism that could lead only to "black death."

Despite the hostilities, the Mississippi march was emblematic of a peaceful surge all across the South. Blacks were registering to vote by the tens of thousands in anticipation of the November election. The statistics for the four Deep South states tell the story. Between 1964 and 1966, black registration in Alabama jumped from 19.3 percent to 51.2 percent; Georgia rose from 27.4 percent to 47.2 percent; Mississippi from 6.7 percent to 32.9 percent; and South Carolina from 37.3 percent to 51.4 percent of eligible blacks.

In addition to the established civil rights groups, some of the credit went to a special program run out of Atlanta, the Voter Education Project, which provided voter registration help to several states, among them South Carolina, where registration efforts had been under way before 1965. The Voting Rights Act only intensified activity in the state. Within days of the law's passage, Richard Miles, the field director for the South Carolina project, prepared a sample registration application to help prepare would-be voters, bluntly reminding them that "VOTELESS People Are Hopeless People."

Increased black registration, while dramatic, was not all that easy to accomplish; "voter education" proved to be more than simply showing individuals how to enroll at the courthouse. After years of living in the shadows, black citizens had to develop a new mind-set that let them step forward and demand the franchise. Two weeks after the new law went into effect, a frustrated Miles, who was based in Columbia, wrote colleagues out in rural areas that he wanted a more aggressive posture. "I am tired of hearing our county leaders say that they do not really need federal registrars in their county because 'they always give us as many days as we want [to enroll] and we just can't get the people out,' " Miles wrote. "If you *can't* get the people out, then you are *not* using the Field Director whose salary you are paying. The squeaking wheel gets the grease, so I would suggest that county chairmen start sounding off. It does not do us much good if we register a thousand Negroes in one county and none in a county right next to it, and this happens over and over again."

By mid-1966, as a result of these efforts, many more blacks had registered and would play a part in the upcoming election. At stake were two Senate seats, Thurmond's and the one vacated by the death of Olin D. Johnston on April 18, 1965. Donald Russell had stepped down as governor to take the Senate seat in the interim, but Hollings had trounced him in the spring primary. Now Hollings was running for the remaining two years of Johnston's term. He was opposed by Republican Marshall Parker, a state senator from northwestern Oconee County. It was the first time in the twentieth century that the GOP—now under Dent's direction—was mounting an organized effort to elect state and federal officials.

Thurmond announced for reelection March 25, reminding constituents that he would be running this year as a Republican. "I chose the Republican Party because of its basic orientation to the Constitution and to sound government," Thurmond said, "and in order to more effectively represent the beliefs of South Carolinians. The Democratic Party has proved to be immune to ideas and principles which conflict with, or even moderate, its headlong plunge toward socialism and authoritarian government."

Greenville attorney P. Bradley Morrah, who was also a state senator, announced April 12 that he was running against Thurmond. (Nineteen years earlier he had gained a little notoriety as a defense attorney in the Willie Earle lynching.) Morrah cast himself as a South Carolina Democrat but disdained being classified as "an ultraconservative." He criticized the senator for switching parties, contended Thurmond had "lost effectiveness to negotiate and give forceful representation to South Carolina in Washington," and said the incumbent had "taken a negative attitude on everything."

Thurmond's own campaign was the customary boosterism adorned with some homey touches. His reelection committee paid for "The Thurmond Story," a multipage insert in *The News and Courier* charting his career and extolling his virtues. For that down-home flavor, the campaign printed up recipe cards for pecan pie, pecan cookies, and "two-o'clock dinner shrimp" that included what might be called "The Sayings of Strom." Paired with the pecan pie was a brief ode to free enterprise, "the mainspring of the spectacular progress this country has made in a relatively short time." The cookies came with a nugget about individual liberty, an ideal that had "held ascendancy in the minds of those who framed our government." With the dinner shrimp, the senator offered an oblique criticism of government: "To ears attentively tuned for reassurances, the voices of government leaders sound like the council of Babel; and to eyes strained for acts of recoupment, the response of government appears to be indecision half-implemented."

Although he was now sixty-four years old, Thurmond campaigned with the same gusto he had twenty years earlier. A Columbia *State* reporter who accompanied him on one trip described a day on the hustings. "His campaign car, a medium-priced 1966 sedan, is crammed with circulars, cards, posters and clothes. Improvised litter bags quickly overflow with wrappings of hamburgers, apple cores and boiled peanut hulls. Lunch stops follow a set routine: an assistant orders several hamburgers 'to go,' with cartons of milk. While the food is cooking, Thurmond literally sprints between downtown stores shaking hands with clerks and customers. Lunch and sometimes supper is eaten en route in the car, laced with conversation about people and the history of the areas traveled through, usually recited for the benefit of the young campaign workers who travel with him.

"When he meets an acquaintance or a campaign supporter," the reporter added, "he invariably asks two questions: 'How does it look for us here?' and 'Can you make any suggestions on what I ought to be doing . . . ?' "

The reporter noted that Thurmond's reception by voters was "usually polite and often enthusiastic."

Race, muted in the early going, became a more public issue in the later months. Under Dent's tutelage, the GOP put out a regular newsletter that combined party information with partisan appeals under the headline HAD ENUF? What particularly irritated the Democrats in one issue was a picture of Governor Robert E. McNair shaking hands with a black lawyer in the town of Cheraw. Dent defended the picture, noting that it had run in the Cheraw paper, whose editor was a well-known Democrat.

Much more incendiary were the brochures offered by a group called "The S.C. Independents," sporting pictures of riot-torn streets and blacks congregating in front of storefronts. The brochures asked: "Black Revolution—Who Is to Blame? Democrat Leaders Endorse Black Revolution," and then offered what it said were "actual quotes" that proved their case from Lyndon Johnson, Hubert Humphrey, and Robert F. Kennedy. Another flyer said, "It's as simple as 2 + 2 = 4. The Negro Bloc Vote + Democratic Machine = Black Power. . . . It's your vote, use it. Support those men who will support you." Then it listed Thurmond, Congressman Albert Watson, Jr, a conservative Democrat who had switched parties, and Joseph O. Rogers, the GOP candidate for governor.

In an October 23 editorial, the *Florence Morning News* condemned the Independents and the GOP, contending that "Some of the partisan political literature now circulating is deeply revolting. It is directed to bigotry and demagoguery of the rankest sort." Singling out the Independents' literature, the paper chastized, "It is gutter politics at the worst, without any apparent regard for truth and appealing only to the worst instincts in man."

Two weeks later, just prior to the November 8 vote, *The State* talked about the "racial factor" in the campaigns, observing that "South Carolinians are caught up in an acknowledged nationwide reaction against the Johnson administration's compulsive (and compulsory) insistence on racial integration in schools, housing, hospitals, business and industry."

The paper also observed that state Republicans, "realistically but perhaps unwisely, have given public notice that they expect to get little or none of the Negro vote." Pointing a finger at the Independents for "fanning the flames of racial discord," *The State* added, "Not only does it tend to harden racial animosities, but it is likely to push the Negroes even deeper into the Democratic bag."

On paper, Thurmond looked beatable. The conventional wisdom was that he couldn't get the black vote—that would be about 18 to 20 percent—and he would lose the sheriffs, court clerks, and others who had benefitted by a one-party system.

The returns proved the conventional wisdom wrong. Thurmond not only whipped Morrah with 62 percent of the vote but he was also the largest vote-getter in the state, outpolling Governor McNair by 15,400 votes.

Parker came up 11,500 votes short of defeating Hollings. *The State* reported that "solid support from Negroes estimated at roughly 75,000 to 80,000 provided the margin of victory."

Republicans failed to pick up any new congressional seats, but they significantly increased their representation in the state legislature, winning seventeen seats in the House and six in the Senate. It was the first time since Reconstruction that more than two Republicans had been in the legislature, a credit to Dent's leadership and a sign that the two-party South Carolina Thurmond believed possible could be a reality. If Ben Tillman was spinning in his grave, it was not because the hated Republicans were ascending but because his Democrats had broken faith with white supremacy.

Back in Washington for the start of a new Congress, Thurmond shifted his committee assignments, giving up the Banking Committee post to take a seat on the Judiciary Committee. He was now in a position to work on civil rights bills at ground level and to grill federal judicial nominees in person instead of flailing away at them only on the Senate floor. The power of this committee assignment, however, would not be fully realized for another fourteen years.

From a legislative standpoint, 1967 was a year of debate and dissension that yielded no new legislation, often the case in the first year of the two-year congressional cycles. On February 15, President Johnson sent Congress a repackaged version of civil rights bills from the previous year, but no attention was given to the omnibus proposal. Instead, advocates divided the package into separate measures dealing with protections for civil rights workers, fair housing, and selection of federal juries.

The rioting that had erupted in 1966 continued into 1967, but this time in addition to violence in the cities—sixty-seven experienced turmoil—there was a wave of protests on predominantly black campuses. These were triggered by arrests of black students by white law officers. Thurmond capitalized on these events to continue his message of resistance.

One such incident at Fisk University in Nashville occurred shortly after black-power advocate Stokely Carmichael addressed students at nearby Vanderbilt University. Thurmond immediately went to the Senate floor April 18 to tell colleagues that Carmichael's presence "must be regarded as part of the worldwide communist strategy to incite insurrection and revolution throughout the free world." He said that Carmichael had signed a joint manifesto with Puerto Rican communists and that he had "integrated his organization into the communist plan for world revolution." Citing a Carmichael speech that described American blacks as "a colony within the United States" and that linked blacks with "the struggles of the peoples of Asia, Africa and Latin America against foreign oppression," Thurmond accused him of preaching "rhetoric deliberately designed to stir hatred and incite violence."

The senator also found a new reason to attack King—the minister's entry into the movement against the Vietnam War. In another of his Senate floor speeches, Thurmond said he was shocked not only by King's arguments against the war but also by his attempt to introduce racism into the debate. "In attempting to link the war in Vietnam with the civil rights movement, King demeans his race and retards the advancement of his people."

He thought King should be more like Senator Edward Brooke of Massachusetts. Brooke, a black Republican, had been elected to the Senate the previous November, the first black to serve in the Senate since Reconstruction. "Even though Brooke is a Negro," Thurmond lectured, "he has spurned all inducements to make race an issue in his policies." Brooke had been leaning toward opposing the U.S. presence in Vietnam, but he changed his mind after visiting the country and seeing conditions firsthand, Thurmond said. "In my opinion, Senator Brooke grew in statesmanlike stature by his decision to take the hard way."

King, by contrast, "would split Americans into white and black, and urge Negroes to feel put upon because so many of them have volunteered to fight with zeal and bravery for their country. In so doing he creates resentment and counter-resentment. In so doing he assists communist purposes."

On June 13, President Johnson nominated Marshall to succeed Justice Tom Clark on the Supreme Court, telling reporters at a news conference that "I believe it is the right thing to do, the right time to do it, the right man and the right place."

Thurmond didn't think so. He immediately said he would oppose Marshall because he would be another liberal on a court already filled with too many leftists.

The State offered no comment on this latest Marshall elevation. *The News and Courier* was restrained. "Perhaps when Thurgood Marshall takes the oath of office he will be able to put aside the role of advocate, which he has enacted with such success, and assume the impartiality which the robe of justice is supposed to symbolize."

Marshall's confirmation was never in doubt. The only question was how long it would take. The Judiciary Committee held five days of hearings on his nomination between July 13 and July 24. Thurmond got his chance to ask questions July 19, grilling Marshall, among other things, on some obscure points of constitutional history. During one particularly convoluted question, it was not clear that the senator understood the inquiry himself. Marshall and Senator Edward M. Kennedy, Democrat from Massachusetts, both said they were lost, and Kennedy asked Thurmond to rephrase the question. Thurmond curtly refused.

In a trenchant analysis after the hearings, Fred Graham, *The New York Times*'s legal affairs reporter and a lawyer himself, suggested that the hearing record would raise more questions about committee nomination procedures than it would about Marshall. "For the solicitor general's ordeal by committee provided little beyond some embarrassing moments for a future Justice, a release of senatorial steam over defendant-oriented Court decisions and an opportunity for three Southern Senators to publicize for home consumption their opposition to the nomination of the first Negro to the Supreme Court."

The Senate confirmed Marshall August 30 by a vote of 69–11. Ten of the opponents were southerners. The eleventh was border-state Democrat Robert C. Byrd of West Virginia.

Thurmond took an hour of Senate time to level his criticisms of Marshall, repeating for the full body his constitutional quiz and disparaging the nominee for "a surprising lack of knowledge" about the amendments passed after the Civil War. The senator added that he was unimpressed by Marshall's many successes as a lawyer before the high court. "We all know that the U.S. Supreme Court in recent years has decided cases based on factors other than the law as laid down by the framers when the Constitution was written," he fumed. "All that can be said is that a majority of the Supreme Court was prepared to go along and accept the position he advocated, for reasons which probably had nothing to do with his competency as counsel. I think that it is a fair observation to say that a majority of the members of the Court would have so ruled regardless of who had been the attorney in the case."

Even though several civil rights bills were pending in Congress, at year's end only a five-year extension of the Civil Rights Commission was sent to the president for his signature. There were just four dissenting votes in the Senate on this legislation: Eastland, Ervin, McClellan, and Thurmond.

It would have been hard to predict at the beginning of 1968 how the year would end, for confrontation engulfed the country in the spring and summer and ushered in yet another cycle of change. The departures from public life of Lyndon Johnson and Earl Warren, who had been the agents of so much readjustment in American life, signaled that one hand had finally been played for all it was worth. Judge Waring's death early in the year symbolized closure of one era and the beginning of another, one whose makeup and direction would unfold step by step as a new president and a new chief justice assumed power. Thurmond was going to play a role in the selection of each.

Johnson started off the year renewing his push for a fair-housing bill. The previous August the House had passed a measure barring discrimination in the sale or rental of housing, and the Senate Judiciary Committee had sent one to the full Senate in November.

Debate on the legislation started in January and continued until March 4, when sixty-five senators voted to cut off the discussion. Thurmond, who had spoken on the Senate floor against the bill and had devoted a radio address and a weekly newsletter to the issue, was among the thirty-two senators who wanted to keep talking. After the defeat, he issued the now customary statement deploring the action. It was one of his more lively expressions of discontent.

"I am grievously disappointed at senators on both sides of the aisle who succumbed to the obvious arm twisting by the Johnson Administration," he said. "The arm twisters induced, seduced and cajoled enough votes to limit debate on this extreme and tyrannical civil rights bill."

Noting that a special commission investigating the 1967 riots had just released its report, Thurmond accused the administration of deliberately leaking the document "in a brazen move by the executive branch of our government. The result was that the Senate invoked cloture at pistol point, one weapon in the hands of the President and the other in the hands of the rioters."

Thurmond successfully added an antiriot provision to the bill to clarify that there were federal penalties for traveling interstate with intent to incite a riot or to take part in one. He wanted to make sure that such activities were not considered to be "civil rights" work and thus protected under federal law.

The Senate passed the housing bill March 11 by a vote of 71–20. All but two of the opponents were southerners. By 1970 it would cover about 80 percent of all housing. Exempted from the law's regulations were private homes sold or rented by an owner without the services of a real estate agent. In the necessary compromises to get the bill through, however, the Department of Housing and Urban Development, which was to administer the act, was not given any enforcement power. This issue would be revisited twice more by the Congress when it became clear that the law had failed to live up to its promise.

The same day the bill passed, Thurmond sent out a newsletter castigating the riot commission's report and accusing its members of "fighting fire with gasoline. The commission's conclusions could not have been better calculated to foster a deepening division between the races in this country." He was particularly incensed by the report's claim that "white racism is essentially responsible for the explosive mixture which has been accumulated in our cities since the end of World War II." The commission, he charged, "oversimplifies the mysteries of the human heart. Its report builds up stereotypes of hatred, and falsely accuses a whole people of vices they do not practice."

These words would be a hollow echo twenty-four years later, when angry blacks rioted in Los Angeles after four white policemen were found not guilty of assaulting a black man who had led them on a car chase. The police beating had been captured on a home videotape and shown on television throughout the country.

During the postverdict violence, much of the commentary invoked the warnings of the riot commission that Thurmond had so caustically dismissed.

Before the House could consider the Senate's housing bill, President Johnson, his moral authority sapped by Vietnam, stunned the nation March 31 when he went on television to announce that he would not seek reelection. His words made an indelible imprint on anyone who had tuned in: "I shall not seek, and I will not accept, the nomination of my party for another term as your president."

Overnight the lid had come off presidential politics. Potential candidates in both parties were initially flabbergasted and a moment later thrown into a frenzy of reassessment. This was sufficient upheaval to require weeks of sorting out, but before Johnson's news could settle, the country was jolted yet again by the assassination of Martin Luther King. The minister, who had gone to Memphis in support of striking garbage collectors, was shot down April 4 on his hotel balcony by James Earl Ray. His death set off a wave of rioting and looting all over the country—125 cities in twenty-eight states. Forty-five people were killed, more than half of them in Washington, D.C., all but five of them black. In the capital alone there were more than seven hundred fires.

Johnson went on national television that night to express his grief and that of the nation. He assured black leaders that he intended to continue the civil rights fight and that the absence of King would not signal any retrenchment. Thurmond issued a curt, unsympathetic statement the day after the murder: "I was shocked to learn of the death of Martin Luther King, and unless all types of violence to achieve political goals are condemned the safety of every citizen will be jeopardized."

As King was being buried in Atlanta April 9, the House Rules Committee was debating whether to accept the Senate's fair-housing bill or to go into conference with the Senate. The next day the House accepted the Senate bill, and Johnson signed it April 11.

Thurmond fired off another volley against the legislation, contending that "Congress has allowed the death of Martin Luther King to replace reason with emotion. . . . We are told that passing so-called 'civil rights' bills will halt the terrorism sweeping America," the senator continued. "The very opposite is true. Each new invasion of state, local and individual rights has been accompanied by a further breakdown in America's ability to govern itself peacefully."

Echoing his extemporaneous remarks from Birmingham twenty years earlier, Thurmond said Americans of all races had made greater progress than the people of any other country and that this progress "has been due to the character, hard work and determination of the individual citizen who has respected and abided by the law. Government cannot change the individual by decree or legislation," he cautioned, "only the individual, through effort and preparation, can accomplish this for himself." It was Thurmond's version of the white southern credo that you can't legislate morality.

There was a certain truth in this, although a superficial one. Decrees and legislation may not directly "change the individual"; but they can change behavior. Over time, the new behavior becomes habit and finally is internalized as acceptance. There would be no better illustration of this evolutionary process than what eventually happened to Thurmond himself.

On June 13 Earl Warren privately submitted his resignation to Johnson, but it was not made public until a week later, at which time the president said he would accept it as soon as a new chief justice was named. But Republican senators Robert Griffin of Michigan and John Tower of Texas immediately promised to block any appointment by a president who was on his way out of office. Ignoring the threat, Johnson moved to promote his friend and adviser, Associate Justice Abe Fortas. This was not a popular choice among southerners, who were not that happy to have him on the bench, let alone as chief justice. Fortas had advised Johnson on civil rights legislation since 1957, and no fewer than five bills had been enacted. What's more, he had aligned himself with the Warren forces and in 1966 had been part of the five-justice majority in the controversial *Miranda* decision requiring that criminal defendants be notified of their rights—a case whose name almost immediately became part of the country's legal and political vocabulary.

Late in June, Thurmond wove all of these issues together in the opening volley of his opposition. Fortas was unacceptable for three reasons, the senator said: "his long reputation as a fixer and his involvement with many questionable figures," his alignment with "the radical wing of the Court," and finally, decisions he supported that have "extended the power of the federal government and invaded the rights of the states, turned criminals loose on technicalities," and aided communists.

Identifying a particular source of irritation to Republicans, Thurmond charged that there had been "collusion between President Johnson and Chief Justice Warren to prevent the next president from appointing the next chief justice." Five days later, Thurmond told like-minded colleagues it was now in their power to change things. "Oftentimes my opposition vote stood alone" as liberal appointees "moved to lifetime positions on the high court," the senator scolded. "Those who have wailed about the damage the Supreme Court has done the country now have a chance to let the people speak through their new president regarding the court leadership for possibly the next twenty years."

The Senate Judiciary Committee began hearings on the nomination July 16, with Fortas making the first appearance ever by a nominee for chief justice. He dropped something of a bombshell when he testified that while on the court, he had attended meetings with the president on the Vietnam War and urban riots. But he insisted he never advised Johnson on issues that could reach the Supreme Court.

When Thurmond took his turn to question the justice July 18, hammering away at the nominee for two hours, it was the senator who did most of the talking. He persisted in asking questions about already decided cases and the justice continually refused to answer—approximately fifty times. In response, Thurmond developed his own refrain, reeling off question after question about recent Supreme Court rulings on voting rights and the rights of criminal suspects, ending each one with, "And you refuse to answer that?"

"Yes," the justice answered.

At one point Fortas offered Thurmond a careful if windy explanation for his reticence: "Senator, with the greatest deference and the greatest respect I assure you, my answer must stand. I cannot address myself to the question that you have phrased because I could not possibly address myself to it without discussing theory and principle. And the theory and principle I would discuss would most certainly be involved in situations that we have to face."

An irritated Thurmond said he couldn't understand why Fortas could write books and give law school lectures about these legal issues but couldn't answer his questions now. The senator said the public would also have a hard time understanding this.

"Senator," Fortas replied, "all I can say is that I hope and trust that the American people will realize that I am acting out of a sense of constitutional duty and responsibility."

"Well," Thurmond replied, "I am disappointed, even more so, in you, Mr. Justice Fortas."

"I am sorry to hear that, Senator."

The justice was unflappable during these interchanges, but he had a hard time remaining calm when Thurmond pressed him about a 1967 decision, *Mallory v. United States,* in which a confessed rapist's conviction had been overturned because his arraignment was delayed to permit an interrogation.

"Mallory!" the senator shouted. "I want that word to ring in your ears. Mallory! . . . Mallory! A man who raped a woman, admitted his guilt and the Supreme Court turned him loose on a technicality free to commit other crimes. . . . As a justice of the Supreme Court, can you condone this?"

Fortas visibly flushed and sat silent for a few moments before he gathered himself to reply in measured tones: "Senator, because of my respect for you and this body and my respect for the Constitution of the United States and my position as Associate Justice of the Supreme Court of the United States, I will adhere to the limitations I believe the Constitution places upon me and will not reply to your question as you phrase it."

"Can you suggest any way that I can phrase it differently so you can answer it?" Thurmond pressed.

"That would be presumptuous," Fortas answered. "I would not attempt to do so."

Thurmond's performance earned him newspaper headlines. But James Lucier, one of his aides (later to work for Jesse Helms of North Carolina), wrote a blisteringly candid memo afterward. "In my judgment," he said, "our strategy in the Fortas hearings has been a disastrous mistake. . . . [T]he line of questioning did not appear to be a sincere attempt to investigate his views; rather, it appeared to be an irrational attempt to delay and harass."

The strategy should have been to illustrate that Fortas "is a radical and a revolutionary dedicated to remaking society," Lucier explained. "He is a legal and moral relativist and thereby temperamentally unfit for the judiciary. He is a political animal who does not possess the necessary independence and integrity to break off the connections and habits of a political past." There is no evidence that the memo, which got tucked away in Thurmond's files, ever influenced the senator.

(In the midst of the hearings, Thurmond unveiled a paperback book he had written criticizing the high court. The slender volume, called *The Faith We Have Not Kept,* charged that the government had not kept faith with the Constitution and blamed the high court for leading "the assault" against it.)

On a less lofty subject Thurmond used a newsletter and a radio broadcast to accuse the justice of fostering pornography. Calling this one "Fortas on Filth," he charged that the justice had been the swing vote in ruling that materials determined by lower courts to be "hard-core pornography were protected by the U.S. Constitution. Since Fortas has been on the Court," the senator charged, "state restrictions on filthy books and pictures have been virtually swept away. . . . The effect of the Fortas decisions has been to unleash a floodtide of pornography across the country. . . . This is not a question simply of girlie magazines and salacious literature. The new era of pornography features photographs which leave nothing to the imagination and which appeal to the most perverted interests of mankind."

To make sure his colleagues didn't miss the point, he showed them several of the movies and magazines in question. This tactic drew a scathing criticism from Attorney General Ramsey Clark, who called the committee inquiry "itself obscene. To show dirty movies, books and magazines . . . as if they were in any way relevant to the qualifications of this nominee . . . [is] outrageous," Clark said. It also prompted a sarcastic cartoon in *The Washington Post* that showed "Obscenator" Thurmond in a doorway clutching a film and inviting a straitlaced man to come inside: "Psst—Want to see some dirty pictures?"

On the tenth of September, after a break for the political conventions, Eastland sent the justice a telegram asking him to return to the committee to be questioned about obscenity issues "and on other matters relative to your confirmation." On September 13, Fortas "respectfully" declined. The committee went ahead with the hearing anyway, and at Thurmond's request heard testimony that Fortas had been paid fifteen thousand dollars for teaching at the American University Law School in Washington, the funds having been raised by his former law partner. The dean of the school defended Fortas's appearance at the summer session, but Thurmond questioned the propriety of a justice accepting compensation for work outside the court.

Four days later, on September 17, the committee recommended Fortas to the full Senate by a vote of 11–6. When the nomination was considered in the Senate, Griffin, who had opposed Fortas from the beginning, launched into a filibuster. He was immediately joined by Thurmond and other opponents. On October 1 the administration pressed for a decision on the matter but came up fourteen votes short of cutting off the debate. The next day Fortas asked that his name be withdrawn.

"In my judgment, this is the wisest decision Justice Fortas has made since he has been on the Supreme Court," Thurmond said after hearing the news. "I suggest that Mr. Fortas now go a step further and resign from the court for the sake of good government."

During the August recess, Thurmond had put aside judicial politics for presidential ones, heading to Miami August 4 for the Republican convention.

Earlier in the spring Dent had been instrumental in urging southern GOP chairmen to "hang loose but hang together"—a cute way of saying that every state should keep its options open on a nominee. He also had persuaded the other chairmen to have meetings with the top three contenders, Richard Nixon, California governor Ronald Reagan, and New York governor Nelson Rockefeller, to see which one they might back.

While Dent had always liked Reagan, he believed Nixon would ultimately be the better candidate. It was tough to sell Thurmond on the proposition, however, for Thurmond was as enamored of the former movie actor as anyone. "I love that man," he once said. "He's the best hope we've got." (Reagan had given a magnificent performance the previous year at a South Carolina GOP fund-raising rally in Columbia, stirring Republican hearts and erasing the party's debt in one evening's work.) But when Reagan met with GOP leaders May 19, he was unwilling to go on record as a candidate, clearing the path for Dent to lead Thurmond toward Nixon.

Nixon's meeting with the southern Republicans began May 31

in Atlanta. Dent asked Thurmond to come down the next day for the group's second meeting. As the session went on, the senator was particularly pleased to hear Nixon talk about the Supreme Court, promising that if elected he would appoint only "strict constructionists"—a euphemism for anyone whose interpretation of the Constitution was not considered as liberal as the Warren court's. On the sensitive issue of school integration, Nixon stood by the 1954 *Brown* decision but opposed busing to achieve racial balance. Of particular interest to the southern camp was Nixon's unwillingness to "balance" the ticket either ideologically or geographically. He said he would look for a vice-presidential candidate who shared his philosophy. This calmed worried southern hearts who feared an alliance with some northern liberal of the Rockefeller stripe. What finally put Thurmond solidly into the Nixon camp was the candidate's support for a strong military in the fight against communism.

After the meeting, as the two men and their aides were standing in the hotel lobby ready to leave, Nixon asked Thurmond to accompany him to the airport. The senator accepted, and the ride immediately took on larger significance. When reporters saw the candidate welcome the symbol of a new Republican South into his car, they assumed the two men were in the midst of brokering a political deal to enhance Nixon's standing in the region. But Dent, who was intimately involved in the episode, has insisted that no such thing occurred. The airport ride was icing on the cake, a final thank-you. While that may have been true, the picture of these new allies huddled together in the car nonetheless sent a much louder message about political alignments.

Thurmond was now ready to throw his support to Nixon—exactly what Dent believed was necessary to blunt a third-party challenge from George Wallace. Who better to throw a body block against this rabid southerner than an equally forceful southerner who had once been a third-party candidate himself?

When the South Carolina delegation met in Columbia June 22, Thurmond and Albert Watson were committed to Nixon. The hope was that the other convention delegates would go along—no sure thing since almost all of them were backing Reagan. But the senator was at his best in situations that required energy, determination, and feistiness. With rhetorical help from Dent, he found a mantra that would resurface six weeks later in Miami, when he would be called upon again to keep southern delegates in line. "A vote for Reagan is a vote for Rockefeller . . . ," he told his fellow Republicans, who would agree to follow his lead. "We have no choice, if we want to win, except to vote for Nixon. . . . We must quit using our hearts and start using our heads. I have been down this road, so I know. I am laying my prestige, my record of forty years in public life, I'm laying it all on the line this time. . . . Believe me, I love Reagan. But Nixon's the one."

In a formal statement later, the senator, who would be a favorite-son candidate, explained why he was backing Nixon: "He offers the best hope of recovering from domestic lawlessness; a bloody no-win war in Asia; runaway spending and rising costs of living; strategic military inferiority; loss of influence in world affairs; and a power-grasping Supreme Court."

Thurmond added that while he did not agree with Nixon on all issues, he believed that he was the "best of the candidates of either party for America and the cause of freedom." The first important piece of the southern strategy was now in place.

When the delegates finally gathered in Miami August 4, Nixon was clearly the front-runner, but both Rockefeller and Reagan (who hadn't declared but was now acting more like a candidate) were trying to come up with strategies to stop a first-ballot nomination and throw the voting wide open. One of the first worrisome signals for Dent and Buzhardt, who had been in town for a week assessing the atmosphere for Thurmond, was the rumor that Nixon was indeed going to balance the ticket with a liberal from either the North or the West—a rumor that was untrue.

Thurmond was doing his best at preventive medicine, making phone calls and sending telegrams. In his phone calls he repeated the June mantra that "A vote for Reagan is a vote for Rockefeller." The threat was that if Nixon failed on the first ballot, then the New Yorker would win the nomination.

Despite a last-minute plea from Reagan forces, South Carolina's delegates held tight, reaffirming their support for Nixon just before the official opening of the convention. But it was clear that Reagan was still a threat.

On the afternoon of Monday, August 5, Reagan made it official that he was a candidate. Earlier in the day, Dent and two other southerners had spent an hour and a half trying to talk him out of it, but to no avail. Thurmond by now was immovable, but Reagan's announcement shook the southern GOP leaders who were backing Nixon, so Dent stepped up what he called his "dog and pony show'' for the southern delegations. Everywhere Reagan operatives went, Dent brought in Thurmond—he called him his "big cannon"—right behind him. Dent would warm up the group, reminding them of the senator's stellar conservative credentials, his loyalty to the South, and his willingness to put it all on the line for Nixon. Then Thurmond would speak for a few minutes, extolling Nixon's virtues. After the senator left, Dent followed up with last-minute exhortations.

It was a reflection of how far Thurmond had come from the detail-minded young man who had gone county to county in 1937 running his own judicial campaign. Now he had almost nothing to do with strategy and everything to do with ephemeral notions of prestige and credibility. He had become a symbol. The combination of Dent the workhorse and Thurmond the show horse meshed so well because Dent could give effect to the senator's broadest concerns. There was no need to twist Thurmond's arm to do anything. Dent just had to show him the way, turning the senator's unerring political instinct into specific action.

The dog and pony shows worked. Nixon won the nomination on the first ballot, and Thurmond was widely credited with playing a major role in the nominee's victory. Political analysts dubbed him Nixon's "kingmaker." *The State* told the story through an interview with Dent, who said, "Richard Nixon can thank a man named Strom Thurmond for the nomination. I know what he did. Richard Nixon knows what he did. Nelson Rockefeller knows what he did and Ronald Reagan knows what he did." As part of its convention coverage, *Newsweek* told of delegates who ended up "eyeball to eyeball with Strom" as he raced from delegation to delegation on Nixon's behalf.

Proof of Thurmond's importance was the fact that before the balloting was even over, he and Dent had left the convention floor to attend a meeting at Nixon headquarters about picking a running mate—a fact Dent made sure news reporters understood.

Ten days after Miami, Thurmond was questioned about his role on the NBC news program *Meet the Press,* particularly about whether he'd had veto power over a vice-presidential selection. (Nixon had selected Maryland governor Spiro T. Agnew.) "I didn't veto anybody," Thurmond said. "I did not have the right to veto anyone. I did express the opinion that certain candidates were too liberal in their philosophy. . . ."

Asked why he, as a former third-party candidate, was now

opposing George Wallace, Thurmond replied that the circumstances of the two elections were different. The people had had "no real true choice" between Dewey and Truman, and at that time the South had only one party. Now it was a two-party region, where "the Democrats will vote for their man, the Republicans will vote for their man, [and] I think the third-party candidate will be left out."

Thurmond added that he had received no commitment from Nixon on whom he would name as attorney general or appoint to the Supreme Court. He repeated a standard refrain: "All that the South can ask and all that we do ask is to be treated fairly and equitably and justly like the rest of the states in the Union, which has not always been the case in the past."

With the presidential campaign now in full swing, Thurmond worked just as hard for Nixon as he had back in Miami. Where there had been "Thurmond Speaks for Goldwater" in 1964, now there was "Thurmond Speaks for Nixon-Agnew." The Democrats, in a boisterous, hostile convention in Chicago, had nominated Vice-President Humphrey, and Thurmond modified the Miami mantra slightly, telling southerners now that "A vote for Wallace is a vote for Humphrey." He campaigned all over the South on behalf of the GOP ticket, working to blunt the effect of the Alabama governor. In October, *The New York Times* featured him in a long magazine piece with a title evocative of the senator's political odyssey: "Ex-Democrat, Ex-Dixiecrat, Today's 'Nixiecrat.' "

Nixon eked out a slim victory over the vice-president, carrying South Carolina and five other southern states. *The News and Courier* wrote after the election that "few would dispute that [Thurmond] had carried the brunt of the battles that also gave Nixon victories in Virginia, North Carolina, Tennessee, Florida, and Kentucky. Either by personal appearances or providing campaign material from 'Thurmond Speaks' headquarters, the senator had used his prestige and influence to blunt the Wallace appeal." *The Atlanta Constitution* ran a postelection cartoon showing Nixon with his arms being held up in victory by Dent on the right side and Thurmond on the left. And the president-elect himself had told the senator, "You did a fabulous job."

As he traveled the state during the campaign, Dent had heard a persistent rumor that the senator, now sixty-five, was "seeing"

Miss South Carolina of 1966, Nancy Moore. They had met when she came to work as an intern in his office, and news that he might be going out with such a young woman distressed a number of his admirers. Dent and Buzhardt had what they termed a "sons-to-father" talk with the senator, expressing their deep concern about a courtship or possible marriage during the campaign. They warned him that an alliance with someone young enough to be his granddaughter could ruin his career, and they kept him away from her during the height of the electioneering. Their hope was that the budding romance would end.

A few days after the election, Thurmond called Dent to tell him about his trip to New York to see the victorious Nixon. "Harry, now that the election is over, guess what I'm going to do," he said.

"Rest, Senator, get plenty of rest. You deserve it and more."

"I plan to do that, Harry, when Nancy and I get married."

"Oh, Senator, you can't do that," Dent blurted out.

"But you and Fred said if we waited until after the election it would be okay."

Dent tried again, telling the senator that he would ruin his career and that he'd better not plan on running again in 1972. "In fact," Dent continued, "you might as well resign now like King Edward and get public sympathy to offset all the public wrath that'll follow."

Dent immediately called Buzhardt to commiserate about the senator's decision. They agreed to meet with him one more time to go at him with every argument they could think of. When they were done, a chastened Thurmond told them to speak with Nancy and "tell her everything you've told me, and if you can talk her out of it, it'll be all right with me."

The two did just that, going to see her four times in a two-week period and painting every horrible consequence they could think of, including the possibility of abnormal children. "If you really love the man, for goodness' sake, leave him alone," Dent urged.

"But I love him," Nancy insisted, tears streaming down her face. Dent and Buzhardt gave up.

The Thurmond-Moore engagement was announced in the press December 8. *The State* captured everything in four words and two pictures. THURMOND TO WED BEAUTY was the headline on the front-page story. On one side was a picture of Thurmond, still strong of jaw but now completely bald. On the other was Nancy in a light bathing suit, high heels, and a "Miss South Carolina" streamer diagonally across her front.

The senator was incensed by the picture. Nancy's parents had sent over a traditional head shot for the announcement, but instead the paper had run the beauty-queen photo. Thurmond fumed that it was "outrageous, uncouth and uncalled for."

Thurmond insisted on a private wedding in Aiken, where the couple was married December 22 before about seventy family members and close friends, including Dent and Buzhardt. (It was a good day for Republican unions. Julie Nixon, the president-elect's daughter, and David Eisenhower, the former president's grandson, were also married on the twenty-second.)

A new administration, particularly when the party in power changes, always heralds wide-ranging readjustments in Washington. And when an outgoing president has deeply identified himself with a cause, as Lyndon Johnson had with civil rights, the change is even more marked. Under Richard Nixon, there would be no clarion calls to action on behalf of the dispossessed. But that wouldn't prevent one pressing legislative matter from coming before the Ninety-First Congress. The key enforcement section of the Voting Rights Act of 1965 was scheduled to terminate in 1970, and civil rights advocates wanted to start work right away on a five-year renewal with no changes.

The Nixon administration was willing to accept an extension, but with amendments that would make it cover every state, not just those with a particular history of discrimination. Civil rights lawyers contended that this would dilute the bill's effectiveness because it would take resources away from places where voting rights abuses were still prevalent. After several months of jockeying in the House, a bill finally went to the House floor. There the administration prevailed in its wish for nationwide coverage, moving the fight to preserve the original bill over to the Senate—a fight that would not take place until the following year.

In the meantime, the Senate found itself once again caught up in the politics of the Supreme Court. Earl Warren was still chief justice because no successor had been appointed. The new president was working on the matter, however. On May 21 he nominated federal appeals court judge Warren E. Burger, who had been serving on the District of Columbia bench, considered by many the most prestigious of the appellate circuits.

Before Burger could be confirmed, however, Fortas became front-page news again. On May 4 *Life* magazine reported that in his first year on the court, Fortas had received and later returned twenty thousand dollars from the family foundation of Louis Wolfson, a wealthy industrialist convicted of violating federal securities laws. Demands for his resignation were instant, with Thurmond among the leaders.

"Members of the Supreme Court should be, like Caesar's wife, above suspicion," Thurmond said. He called the acceptance of the fee unwise and was unmoved by the fact that Fortas had returned the money. "It brings to mind the questionable arrangement which Justice Fortas had with the American University Law School," he said, "and certainly raises questions about the proper conduct for a member of the nation's highest court." The senator acknowledged that he did not know all the facts, "but Justice Fortas does. I hope he will search his conscience to determine if the faith of the people in the integrity of the Supreme Court would be better served by his resignation."

Thurmond's wish was granted May 15, when Fortas resigned from the court to quiet the controversy. In a letter to the chief justice, he said he wanted the court to "proceed with its vital work free from extraneous stress." He insisted "there has been no wrongdoing on my part."

In his next newsletter, "The Fortas Affair," the senator told constituents that the justice "has betrayed the public trust and resignation is the appropriate response. Nothing so befits his tenure on the court as his leaving it."

He then turned his attention to Justice William O. Douglas, who he said had been accepting twelve thousand dollars annually from the Albert Parvin Foundation, an entity, the senator told readers, whose assets "are based upon stock in gambling casinos. It must not pass without notice that the tax lawyer who advised the Parvin Foundation was none other than Justice Fortas's wife, Carolyn Agger Fortas."

Several times over the next three weeks Thurmond called on Douglas to resign, saying in one newsletter that "the most distressing aspect of the Douglas case, as in the Fortas case, is the conviction of the principal participants that there was no impropriety in their actions. Their continued defiance of common standards of decency does not speak well for the judgment of men sitting on the highest court in the land."

(There would be an effort in the House to bring articles of

impeachment against Douglas—the equivalent of a criminal indictment—to force him out of office, but the attempt failed.)

On a happier note for Thurmond, the nomination of Warren Burger was moving along nicely. The Judiciary Committee had unanimously recommended his nomination to the Senate, and on June 9 the senator went to the Senate floor to praise the nominee. (He recycled the speech into his regular newsletter and his weekly radio broadcast.)

"It is evident that Judge Burger has a record which is one of integrity and character," the senator said. "A judge should be 'Mr. Integrity,' and Judge Burger satisfied the Committee on this score." Striking themes that were going to be played out repeatedly over the next twenty years, the senator said the committee had been pleased to find that Burger was a strict constructionist of the Constitution, interpreting the law but not writing it. Thurmond praised Burger for his belief in "strong enforcement of the law, and in equal treatment—with favoritism towards none. It is a long time since such qualities have been evident in a sitting Chief Justice."

The senator was particularly impressed with Burger's hard line on criminal defendants, citing the nominee's observation that "the seeming anxiety of judges to protect every accused person from every consequence of his voluntary utterances" gave rise to "myriad rules, sub-rules, variations and exceptions which even the most able and sophisticated lawyers and judges are taxed to follow."

Thurmond found such positions to be "like a fresh breeze rustling across the courtroom. They indicate an expansive mind of wise and true humanity." Others would come to have a harsher view of Burger, finding in those same passages evidence of a crabbed and sterile view of the law.

The Warren court finally came to an end June 23, when the retiring chief justice, with Richard Nixon looking on, swore in his successor. Thurmond could not let the occasion pass without comment, and as before, his remarks were clearly those of someone whose world had been involuntarily rearranged by the forces of change. Where many had seen welcome—if turbulent—movement, Thurmond saw "growing social disintegration and chaos." If many liberals hailed Warren's reign as a model of progress, the senator argued that "one only has to look at the social reality to see that the court decisions over which he presided are milestones on the retreat from civilized order. Great civilizations are marked by reverence toward God, respect for learning, public decency, social harmony, a high regard for the safety of life and property, solidarity in the face of the common enemy, and a fine restraint in the overturning of traditions and precedent. Any civilization, however it is constituted, cannot ignore such goals without beclouding its future."

Meanwhile there was still Fortas's vacancy to fill. On August 18 Nixon nominated Clement F. Haynsworth, Jr., a federal appeals court judge from Greenville, South Carolina. Haynsworth had been a successful lawyer, taking over a firm his father and grandfather had led. Though for years he was a registered Democrat, he, like Thurmond, supported Eisenhower in 1952 and 1956, and then finally became a Republican in 1964. Eisenhower had appointed him to the bench in 1957.

While the senator thought highly of Haynsworth, he had favored Donald Russell, the former governor who was now a district court judge. Russell was equally conservative, Thurmond thought, but as a Democrat stood a better chance of being confirmed because he would not trigger the same opposition from organized labor. Thurmond had made his pitch to Attorney General John Mitchell, but Mitchell felt more comfortable with Haynsworth because he had more experience on the bench.

Democrats still festering over the Fortas defeat contended that Haynsworth, while not necessarily guilty of corruption, was not sensitive enough to the need to avoid even the appearance of impropriety. Labor and civil rights lobbyists, who had announced their opposition the day Haynsworth was nominated, pressed that point, arguing that the Senate should not use one standard for Fortas and another for Haynsworth. He was the first nominee organized labor had opposed in thirty years.

The ethics issue arose from charges that as a judge, Haynsworth had participated in decisions indirectly affecting the welfare of companies in which he had a small financial interest. The principal case involved a dispute between a textile mill and the Textile Workers Union. The head of the union testified before the Judiciary Committee that Haynsworth should have disqualified himself from the case. But William H. Rehnquist, who was then a senior Justice Department official, said Haynsworth had been "under a duty to take part in that decision." He found no conflict, nor did other experts on judicial disqualification.

In his defense, Haynsworth pointed out that the total profit he received from the transaction was $390. He told the committee that "while I am concerned about myself and my reputation, I much more am concerned about my country and the Supreme Court as an institution, and if there is substantial doubt about the propriety of what I did and my fitness to sit on the Supreme Court, then I hope the Senate will resolve the doubt against me. If there is no substantial doubt, I hope the thing will be laid aside so that the Supreme Court can serve with me on it."

Right in the middle of the Haynsworth struggle, Thurmond received some unwanted publicity. On September 19, *Life* magazine published a long article—"Strom's Little Acres"—claiming that the senator and his old law partner, Charles Simons, now a federal judge, had made an unusually large profit in a real estate transaction involving land he and Simons had bought in Aiken in 1953.

The article also said that Thurmond had recently purchased land near Columbia that turned out to be in the path of a proposed bridge. While acknowledging that "it cannot be stated that Thurmond had foreknowledge or control over" decisions about the bridge, the article did say he would stand to make three times his investment if the bridge were built.

When interviewed for the story, Thurmond had insisted that he had assiduously tried to avoid any conflict of interest. "I resigned every connection that I had of any kind of any business nature," he told a reporter. "I don't have any connection of any kind where there is any influence to bear." The Aiken land had been purchased just before he went to the Senate, he said, and Simons had handled all subsequent transactions.

The day the story came out Thurmond blasted South Carolina Democratic Party leader Donald Fowler for helping the magazine publish "the false, malicious, defamatory and libelous story. It makes my blood run cold to think that a South Carolinian would be involved in helping these anti-South northern liberals in their effort to stop the voice of the South being heard in Washington and to stop Judge Haynsworth from being placed on the Supreme Court." Fowler denied that he had played a role in the article, and Denny Walsh, the reporter, said that while he had talked to Fowler, the Democrat was not the prime source for the story.

The article turned out to be but a momentary irritation that did not affect the senator's career nor that of Judge Simons. Haynsworth's career didn't fare as well, though the article could not be blamed for that.

On October 9, the Judiciary Committee voted 10–7 to send Haynsworth's nomination to the Senate. Two Republicans joined five northern Democrats in opposing the nomination. And there were other signs of trouble ahead. The previous week Senator Brooke had sent Nixon a letter asking him to withdraw the nomination, but the president said he was sticking by Haynsworth.

The normally vocal Thurmond had deliberately taken a quieter role than usual in helping the judge, staying out of the limelight and off of television so that the effort, the senator explained, would not "look like a South Carolina fight." Instead, he was working nonstop in the background to line up support.

On November 20, the day before the Senate vote, prospects for Haynsworth looked bleak. Three senators, two of them Republicans, said they would vote against him, bringing him ever closer to losing a majority. Thurmond went to the Senate floor to criticize his colleagues for their shoddy treatment of his fellow Carolinian. Harsher words were reserved for the interest groups that sought to influence the Senate's decision. "Let us not get ourselves in the situation where the president's nominees shall be sent through a clearinghouse of labor and minorities," he said. "We need no unofficial 'second Senate.' "

The next day the Senate rejected Haynsworth by a vote of 45–55. Seventeen Republicans deserted the president to oppose his nominee.

In his December 1 newsletter, Thurmond let loose his anger, charging that the judge had been rejected because he was "born and bred to a more exacting tradition of law and history than the liberals would accept. The false charges that the judge violated ethical standards hits a new low in the ethical standards of politics. The charges were nothing but a smokescreen to hide the frenzied activity of organized labor and other pressure groups." Thurmond closed by reassuring his constituents that "knowledgeable people" were confident that the president would pick another southerner as his next nominee.

While that would be true, the Senate would be in for another wrenching fight.

In his December 22 newsletter Thurmond praised the Nixon administration for the accomplishments of its first year—chiefly Burger's appointment to the Supreme Court and a victory in the House on the weakened voting rights bill. "When a nation has slipped off course, it is not easy to bring it back into the mainstream of political thinking," the senator said. "Yet the president has struggled long and hard to overcome the obstacles set up by the liberals and the minority groups who have long exercised a disproportionate share of political power."

It was a remarkable assessment of minority power considering the white majorities in Congress, the legislatures, local governments, and the judicial systems of every state—particularly those, like South Carolina, with sizable minority populations. But Thurmond's assessment was no surprise. He had opposed two Supreme Court decisions—one in 1962, the other in 1964—that were designed to make legislatures more representative, accusing the court of meddling in political matters. After the second case, he had claimed that the justices "didn't ignore the Constitution. They tore it up and threw it out the window."

Nixon moved early in January to fill the Fortas seat on the Supreme Court, selecting G. Harrold Carswell, a little-known federal appeals judge from Florida. Thurmond immediately announced his support. "I understand that he is a conservative, sound thinker, and a competent jurist and one who will give a strict construction to the Constitution," the senator said. With an optimism that proved to be unwarranted, Thurmond added, "Judge Carswell . . . should be on the court for a long time."

By the time the Judiciary Committee started its hearings on the nomination January 27, there were already rumblings of opposition. During a campaign for public office in 1948, Carswell had said that he would always be governed by the "principles of white supremacy." Like so many other southern politicians of the time, Carswell had also defended the social order: "Segregation of the races is proper and the only practical and correct way of life in our states. I have always so believed and I will always so act."

When the speech came to light, Carswell went on television to say that "specifically, categorically I renounce and reject the words themselves and the thought they represent. They are abhorrent." And in his first day of testimony before the Judiciary Committee, Carswell said the remarks were "like something out of the disembodied past." He also told senators, "I do not harbor racial supremacy notions."

Beyond Carswell's own words, some of his judicial decisions on civil rights cases also proved troubling. Fred Graham noted in the *Times* that Carswell's penchant for restraint had allowed "dilatory school officials to delay desegregation."

Unruffled by the criticism swirling about the nominee, Thurmond told Carswell at the January 28 committee session that "nothing shows that you do not believe in equal and fair treatment for all."

Despite the brewing opposition, on February 16 the Judiciary Committee approved the nomination by a vote of 13–4. Although it was ready for Senate consideration by the beginning of March, Majority Leader Mansfield, determined to move the voting rights bill, said the nomination would not be voted on until after the Senate had finished work on the legislation.

Once again the Senate had insisted on giving the Judiciary Committee a timetable for considering the measure, requiring that it be returned to the full chamber by March 1. The committee obliged, and the Senate began work on the bill, sifting its way through several amendments over the next eleven days. Most were efforts by southerners to weaken the existing law.

Those who opposed the controversial House version, with its proposal to cover the entire nation, ultimately substituted a simple five-year extension. But they did make three important changes: one lowered the voting age to eighteen, another suspended literacy tests nationwide for five years, and the third, rather than extending the law to the country as a whole, brought specific counties in six northern and western states under its strictures.

The Senate passed the bill March 13 by a vote of 64–12. Once again, southerners cast all the "nay" votes.

(The House passed the bill June 17 after weeks of wrangling over whether the voting-age provisions should be considered separately as a constitutional amendment. Nixon signed it five days later. In December, the Supreme Court ruled that Congress had overstepped its authority in lowering the voting age for state and local elections.)

With the voting rights bill out of the way, the Senate returned to the Carswell nomination. Opposition by civil rights groups remained an important factor, but an equally damaging development was the crescendo of opposition from lawyers across the country. A statement signed by 457 attorneys said Carswell lacked "minimum qualifications" for the court, and more than two hundred former law clerks said they considered Carswell to be of "mediocre ability."

This prompted an infamous defense from Nebraska senator Roman L. Hruska, the senior Republican on the Judiciary Committee, who said that "even if he was mediocre, there are a lot of mediocre judges and people and lawyers. They are entitled to a little representation, aren't they, and a little chance?" he asked. Hruska aides said the senator had been jesting, but his comments were repeated over and over again by Carswell's detractors.

Opposition senators thought they had found a way to kill the nomination short of outright rejection—sending it back to the Judiciary Committee for a quiet burial. But that effort failed on April 6 when fifty-two senators opposed the move. Two days later, the Senate rejected Carswell by a vote of forty-five "yeas" to fifty-one "nays." Applause broke out in the Senate gallery, drowning out a smattering of boos. Such outbursts are normally silenced in an instant by Senate officials, but this one went on for two full minutes despite demands for order from Vice-President Agnew, who was presiding.

Thurmond blamed the "liberal element" for defeating "a sound thinker, a competent lawyer and a conservative and objective judge."

Finally, Nixon nominated Harry A. Blackmun, a federal appeals court judge from Minnesota. He was confirmed April 14 by a Senate relieved to avoid another controversy.

Still critical of "the labor lobby and the civil rights zealots" who had derailed Haynsworth and Carswell, Thurmond said that this "group of militants" had declined to go after Blackmun because he was a northerner. By contrast, the senator said in a fit of pique, "any southerner proposed for national office is immediately attacked by northern liberals unless he casts off his heritage and principles."

Back home in South Carolina there were important state political matters to consider. Robert McNair's term as governor was up, and John West, the Democratic lieutenant governor, was seeking to replace him. But when Representative Watson announced that he was giving up his congressional seat to enter the race, Republicans believed they had a realistic chance of taking the statehouse.

The state's electorate, though, was not the same as it had been even four years before. Now more than half of South Carolina's eligible black voters—54.6 percent—were registered to vote, up nearly 17 percent from 1964. As important, census figures showed that white registration had slipped from 75.7 percent in 1964 to 71.5 percent in 1969.

There was no hiding from racial issues in this campaign. School integration was squarely in front of the candidates. Already fifteen school districts in South Carolina had faced federal fund terminations because of failure to desegregate their systems adequately. By midsummer, federal officials would be preparing to bring new sanctions to desegregate South Carolina colleges.

While Democrat West defended South Carolina and made sure he did not embrace integration, Watson staked himself out more sharply as a defender of the old order. His campaign painted West as a compatriot of Hubert Humphrey who had also publicly praised the NAACP's Roy Wilkins. A campaign circular blamed the NAACP for Haynsworth's defeat and for "destruction of freedom of choice in our public schools," and it castigated West for using "the prestige of his high office to dignify the aims and activities of this organization."

The campaign was set on edge in March when a group of whites, angered by a federal court order to desegregate, overturned two school buses in Lamar, a small town sixty miles east of Columbia. The young riders had just gotten out under the watchful eyes of state troopers, but several black youngsters suffered cuts and bruises and at least two highway patrolmen were injured by the angry crowd.

Watson's critics charged him with helping to incite the fracas, a charge he denied. A week earlier he had praised white parents for demanding "freedom of choice" for their children and had commended them for ignoring critics "who call you racist, bigot and hard-core redneck." In fact, he had promised to "stand with them" in their fight. Watson refused to repudiate his comments. In Washington, Thurmond rushed to Watson's defense, contending that those who blamed him failed to realize "an important element of human psychology": that people are less likely to resort to violence if they think their leaders—whoever they may be—are standing up for them through "every legal resource." The implication was that Democratic leaders had fallen short of the task.

The Lamar incident was a useful rallying cry for Democrats,

who used it to link Watson to the extremist elements in the state. West, by contrast, was portrayed as the voice of moderation.

Both Thurmond and Hollings put their prestige on the line in the contest, each crisscrossing the state for his candidate. Thurmond even persuaded Nixon and Agnew to campaign on Watson's behalf. In a preelection analysis, *The State* said Watson's campaign staff was "counting on Thurmond's power and influence to carry their man to victory." It was not to be. West was elected with 51.7 percent of the vote, outpolling Watson by just over 29,000 votes. At the same time, three blacks were elected to the state House, two from Columbia, the other from Charleston.

The result, according to *The State,* meant that voters "prefer identification with the moderation and progress of the upper South instead of with the emotional negativism of the lower South." Watson's focus on school integration "undoubtedly spurred the substantial turnout in critical areas where solid black support of West turned the tide in the Democrat's favor."

One bit of folklore that grew out of this election was Thurmond's supposed postmortem to Watson on election night. According to West, a confidant who was at Watson headquarters saw the senator put his arm around the defeated candidate and say, "Well, Albert, this proves we can't win elections any more by cussin' Nigras." Told of the story twenty years later, Thurmond hotly denied it. "I said no such thing."

The Voter Education Project, headed in South Carolina by Thomas Moss, could claim a great deal of credit for the black turnout that was so helpful to West.

Since taking over the office in 1969, Moss had tried to keep the program bipartisan, and over the past few years he had gotten to know Harry Dent. They developed a bond that was to last a lifetime. When Dent summoned a White House car in late November and rode over to see his old boss, Thurmond, it was Moss who was on Dent's mind. After some pleasantries and some general political talk, Dent got to the reason for his visit. It was time, he told Thurmond, to think about making a move toward the black community. One way to do it would be to hire a black on his staff, and Dent thought he had just the person.

Thurmond listened politely and made no commitments. But just as he had an instinct for politics, the senator had an instinct for good advice. Not long after, ignoring the objections of his own aides, Thurmond had one of them get Moss on the phone.

"I'm Strom Thurmond," the senator said. "Mr. Moss, I'm thinking of making a black appointment—a major position on my staff. I'd like for you to consider it. You know the state. You know the people. You know the needs."

"I appreciate your considering me," a surprised Moss responded, adding that he surely would think about it but that he would also make recommendations of other black Carolinians who might do the job.

"I'd rather you consider it," the senator replied. "You think about it. Talk it over. You're not going to have any trouble out of the white people and very little out of the blacks," Thurmond added, never shy about handicapping a political situation.

A few weeks later Moss accepted the position.

Hollings, who was considered much more of a civil rights supporter than Thurmond, had been known to be searching for a black aide, too. The headline in *The State* nicely summed up what had happened: THURMOND STEALS HOLLINGS' THUNDER.

Mired so long in custom and tradition, the senator was inching himself free.

13. READADJUSTMENT

1971–1979

IN THE SPRING of 1971, four major newspapers, three of them northern, the other from Florida, predicted the end of Thurmond's political career. The headline on the *New York Times* story declared, SERIES OF REVERSALS BACK HOME IN SOUTH CAROLINA PUTS THURMOND'S CAREER IN JEOPARDY.

All the stories wove together quotations and information to support their pessimistic conclusions, which at the time seemed plausible. The South was changing rapidly, prompted by the rush of blacks into the electorate and the social readjustments required by the new civil rights laws. Still caught up in the romance of states' rights and unwilling to let go of "custom and tradition," Thurmond looked like a relic of the past.

But these speculative obituaries were premature. Though he never acknowledged publicly the need to do so, the senator was accommodating himself to this new era. If he voted against civil rights bills in Washington, he paid attention to black concerns at home. Always a hands-on politician who thrived on the human touch, he now turned that considerable skill toward the black community. It wasn't just that he did favors for constituents; it was the way he got things done, turning routine political business into personal gestures that individuals long remembered. Chatting with a constituent he would reminisce about the voter's grandfather or mother; he'd make phone calls in honor of milestone events. When it came time for reelection, Thurmond might not get much black support, but he was not going to excite much black opposition, either.

In the words of Ike Williams, who had worked his way out of a Charleston housing project, through college, and into the top position of the state NAACP, the black community had no permanent friends, no permanent enemies, only permanent interests. Thurmond saw to it that he tended those interests.

The senator successfully faced the voters in 1972, the same year as Richard Nixon's fateful reelection, and then again in 1978, when he ran against his most formidable opponent in twenty-four years, Charles "Pug" Ravenel. Articulate, young, successful, and handsome, Ravenel looked like a good bet against Thurmond. But the senator, by now the father of four, won easily.

The changes in political life were manifest throughout the region. By 1978 more than 960 blacks would hold elected office in South Carolina, Mississippi, Alabama, and Georgia. Two years earlier a southern Democrat who made an obvious pitch to black America had been elected president. At the same time, Republicans were becoming a force in the region for the first time since Reconstruction. Helped by internecine clashes in the state Democratic parties, South Carolina would elect a Republican governor and Mississippi would send a GOP senator to Washington for the first time in nearly a century.

The Republican gains in Mississippi came at the expense of Thurmond's kindred spirit, Jim Eastland. Rather than fight off younger opponents in 1978, he chose not to run again. Thad Cochran, an amiable forty-year-old congressman from Jackson, took his seat, giving the state GOP a new foothold in Washington. This changing of the guard in Mississippi stood in contrast to Thurmond's career and at the same time honored it. Eastland retired, while Thurmond showed his durability; Republican Cochran's election was the legacy of Thurmond's groundbreaking switch to the GOP.

Making room for blacks in political life was proving easier than the day-to-day adjustments required to meld southern society into a single whole from its regimented parts. That the promise of

Brown v. Board of Education was unfulfilled after fifteen years was evidence of the country's deep racial cleavage, and the continued opposition to integration showed that many whites shared Thurmond's states' rights ideology, now expanded to embrace the rights of counties and cities. The school bus would be the focus of the conflict in the first half of the seventies as local communities in the South and then the North struggled to merge the all-white and all-black neighborhood schools. To fulfill *Brown*'s mandate that entire school systems had to be desegregated, it was no longer enough to move one or two black students into a white school. The school bus became the means for redrawing district boundaries.

Opposition to busing arose swiftly in white communities all over the country. The immediate complaint may have been about the bus ride itself, but underlying the fury was concern about what lay at the other end of the ride. Parents' unspoken fear was that their children would inherit the legacy of separate but equal: now white children would have to attend an inferior school and, even worse, might be in danger. Black parents also worried about the safety of their children in hostile territory, but they couldn't help a rueful smile at the loud complaints from whites about long bus trips. These blacks recalled from years past the miles they'd had to travel beyond whites-only schools to attend the ones set aside for them.

More than a dozen desegregation cases over the previous fifteen years had turned the Supreme Court into a nine-member national school board. Across the street, Congress was keeping a vigilant and increasingly disapproving eye on the justices, and by 1975, after five years of debate, a majority of the House and Senate went on record in support of restrictions on busing.

White America's defenses against racial change clearly were not all of a piece. The barriers to integration in the public arena—the right to vote, to use public facilities, to equal protection of the laws—were coming down more easily than the barriers protecting more private concerns—the education of one's children and one's own personal associations in the workplace and in leisure time. While racial animosity to this day keeps the breach unhealed, the growth of the black electorate continues to influence the body politic. Thurmond's accommodations once again would be living proof.

On April 4, 1971, *The Miami Herald* predicted a bleak future for the senator in a spirited and occasionally catty piece. (It described Thurmond's clothes as a mesh of electric blues and sherbert pink and his face as having "the bushy brows and fixed jawline of some of the more amiable small primates.") "In 1968, he held the Deep South for Nixon—but will he do the same in '72?" the paper wondered.

Five weeks later *The Washington Post* reported that "OLE STROM" GIRDS FOR HIS TOUGHEST CAMPAIGN. Then *The New York Times* and *The Washington Star* offered their pessimistic assessments. The *Star* said the senator "is no longer unbeatable." The headline reported TROUBLE FOR THURMOND.

Both the *Times* and *Post* said internal bickering among South Carolina Republicans could spill over into the election year and hurt Thurmond, and all four articles mentioned the growing black vote—now about 25 percent of the electorate—that was sure to go against him.

The *Herald* concluded that most black Carolinians viewed the senator as a "moist-fanged racist."

In his own way, Thurmond was trying to temper his segregationist image, more by altering his actions than by words. His explanation to the *Herald* of his standing in the black community was as unpolished as it was sincere. "The pity of it is that they have so misunderstood or have been so misled about my position," he said. "Now, if I was a racist, I would expect that, I wouldn't be disappointed. I'm disappointed because the Nigras let their leaders vote 'em like a bunch o' sheep, more or less. My newsletters go out. I send 'em to everybody who wants 'em. In fact, if you gave the impression you were *catering* to 'em, why some of the other people might not understand—in other words I try to be nice to everybody."

Three months later, writing in the black monthly *Ebony,* Thurmond addressed his relationship with the black community more thoughtfully. He told the story of a black South Carolinian asked to support him for reelection. "Let me think about it," the man had answered. "Senator Thurmond has never stabbed us in the back; he might stab us in the front, but never in the back."

Thurmond reacted to the story with "mixed emotions," he wrote. "I was naturally pleased that someone thought me innocent of the charge of being two-faced," but it was "quite disturbing" to realize that blacks might consider him "strongly opposed to their interests. The truth is that I believe in promoting the best interests of all of our citizens, both black and white, and in most instances, I am confident that we have more in common as southerners than we have reason to oppose each other because of race."

He pointed out that he had hired Tom Moss "in order to facilitate my service to the black people of South Carolina." From his work with Moss, the senator said, "it is apparent that blacks in South Carolina today are interested in performance, not promises; in practical accomplishment, not political theory; in actual progress for the black community, not pacifying showmanship." Whites wanted the same thing, he said.

"It would be naive to assume a complete identity of interests, a complete harmony, in the years ahead," the senator concluded. "Political differences will probably continue, and some of these may be of deep concern to members of both races. Nevertheless, we are all in the same boat; we have both common and complementary resources to call on, and I, for one, am optimistic."

Earlier in the year, one of the stellar figures of the political Old South had died before having to adjust to the New. As *The State* observed, the death of Senator Richard Russell of Georgia had particular meaning for South Carolina because it had twice championed him for the presidency. "But Richard Brevard Russell," an editorial pointedly contended, "came from the wrong part of the nation to become the nominee of a national political party." (Within five years, *The State* would be proved wrong in its lament that a southerner couldn't be elected president.)

Thurmond's homage to Russell was as much a statement of his own beliefs as it was a tribute to the Georgian. He praised him as a man who "stood firm as a champion of constitutional government" against "the so-called civil rights bills of recent years. His opposition to these legislative proposals was soundly based on his conviction that they were contrary to the Constitution and politically inspired."

Almost three months to the day after Russell's death, the Supreme Court announced a decision that would have disappointed him greatly. On April 20, 1971, the justices upheld the legality of busing, setting off a new round of litigation and bringing Congress, Thurmond included, into the debate over the specifics of civil rights enforcement. To those, like Thurmond, who had railed against the high court for years, *Swann v. Mecklenburg* was another in a long list of insults. But these critics overlooked the fact that the judiciary had become involved in civil rights only after voluntary desegregation efforts had failed.

It had been a long journey from *Brown* to *Swann,* encompassing four administrations with differing civil rights policies, recalcitrant school officials, hostile politicians, and the judicial progeny of *Brown:* case after Supreme Court case interpreting the 1954 ruling. In 1963, nine years after the original decision, the justices had signaled their impatience with plans that made only cosmetic moves toward unified school systems; they struck a Tennessee proposal because it was "readily apparent" that it would perpetuate separate schools.

Between the Tennessee litigation and 1969, when the Nixon administration scaled back the aggressive desegregation plans of the Department of Health, Education and Welfare, the justices had addressed school desegregation in seven other cases. In a 1968 case they finally used a lawsuit from New Kent County, Virginia, to crack down on obdurate school officials. There, a "freedom-of-choice" plan had been put into effect three years earlier as a means to integrate, allowing blacks and whites to attend the school of their choice within their district. A unanimous court determined that such plans did not fulfill the obligation to desegregate schools. Justice Brennan sternly lectured local officials, noting that eleven years after *Brown* the county was just beginning to desegregate. "The deliberate perpetuation of the unconstitutional dual system can only have compounded the harm of such a system," he wrote. "The burden on a school board today is to come forward with a plan that promises realistically to work, and promises to work *now.*"

The court did not specify what kind of desegregation plan might work better than another; that was up to each school district. It would be another three years before the justices would directly address busing as a remedy.

Nixon had issued his first policy statement on school desegregation barely seven months into his first term, and opinions differed about what the president intended. On the one hand, the statement declared the administration "unequivocally committed to the goal of finally ending racial discrimination in schools steadily and speedily." But on the other it said, "Setting, breaking and resetting unrealistic 'deadlines' may give the appearance of great federal activity, but in too many cases it has actually impeded progress."

The most immediate compliance problems were in the more than four thousand school districts in seventeen southern and border states that had maintained racial segregation as official policy. The statement said it was "not our purpose to lay down a single arbitrary date by which the desegregation process should be completed or to lay down a single arbitrary system by which it should be achieved. A policy of requiring all school districts, regardless of the difficulties they face, to complete desegregation by the same terminal date is too rigid to be either workable or equitable."

Despite Nixon's claimed dedication to ending school discrimination, civil rights leaders, congressional liberals in both parties, and the National Education Association saw the statement as an invitation to more dilatory tactics by southern school boards. To them it seemed a retreat in the face of pressure from southern politicians who had been so instrumental in Nixon's victory.

The administration's litigation strategy also sent a mixed message. While officials had started proceedings in the summer of 1969 against segregated Georgia school districts, at the same time government lawyers had gone into a federal appeals court to allow thirty-three Mississippi school districts more time to desegregate. It was an ominous sign, for if the administration prevailed on behalf of one of the most obstinate states, then the federal courts would be flooded with requests from other southern districts.

The appeals court granted the delay August 28, 1969, but the Supreme Court reversed the decision two months later. In a brief, unsigned opinion, the court said that "all deliberate speed" was "no longer constitutionally permissible" and ordered the school districts involved to begin immediate operation of unified school systems. The justices defined these as "systems within which no person is to be effectively excluded from any school because of race or color."

Early in 1970 differences within the administration erupted into the open, forcing the resignation of Leon Panetta, the aggressive head of HEW's Office of Civil Rights and the focus of southern politicians' unhappiness. Thurmond was so delighted that he immediately sought out the ailing Russell to tell him. "Dick, did you hear the good news? They just booted Panetta." (Panetta subsequently returned to his native California, switched parties, and later was elected to the House as a Democrat.)

Already angry at HEW, Thurmond soon found another enemy in the administration: the Internal Revenue Service. In July of 1970 the agency announced it would no longer grant what had been routine tax exemptions to private schools if they practiced racial discrimination. An angry Thurmond went immediately to the Senate floor to protest. "I condemn these actions; I strongly condemn them; without end I condemn them," he thundered. "They are wrong as social policy, and they are wrong as law. This is the sort of program which we would expect to get from a Democratic administration."

Worse, he said, the government had committed "a breach of faith with the people of the South, who are making many sacrifices to comply with the law."

It was no secret, he acknowledged, that private schools were thriving in the South because "white people wish to have the freedom of choice to send their children to school with those of their own cultural group." This was not discrimination but rather "the natural and wholesome desire" on the part of "people of either race . . . to educate their children among their own kind." Nor was the phenomenon confined to the South. Wherever integration was instituted, whites either moved to a new neighborhood or sent their children to private schools, he pointed out, resulting in the resegregation that already had taken place in Charleston, Atlanta, Richmond, and Washington, D.C., "not to speak of nearly every Northern city."

Having worked so hard for Nixon's election, Thurmond believed he could make a credible political threat to the president. "I am warning the Nixon administration—I repeat, I am warning the Nixon administration today—that the people of the South and the people of the nation will not support unreasonable policies. I remind the chief executive that the presidency is an elective office, and that what the people give, the people also can take away."

The major flaw in Thurmond's reverence for freedom of choice was evident in his own remarks—the policy would in reality perpetuate segregation because whites would never willingly send their children to schools with large numbers of black children. Furthermore, because of generally better economic circumstances, white parents would be able to send their children to private schools, while blacks would not have that option. Laws and court orders might not erase the prejudice that lay behind opposition to integration, but they could require a halt to the discriminatory behavior.

That was part of what lay behind the Supreme Court's decision in the *Swann* case nine months later. Chief Justice Burger, who wrote the opinion, observed at the outset that the federal judiciary involved itself in remedies only when local authorities failed to end dual school systems. If school officials did default on their responsibilities, as the district court judge had already determined in this case, then the judge had "broad power" to find ways to desegregate the schools.

Swann v. Mecklenburg had a complicated history. During the 1969–70 academic year, there were eighty-four thousand students—71 percent white and 29 percent black—in the school system of Mecklenburg County, North Carolina. Most of the black students lived within the city limits of Charlotte and attended all-black schools. Three out of every four white students in the system attended schools that were primarily white. To desegregate the schools nearly a third of the students—twenty-nine thousand—were bused.

In February 1970 a federal district judge ordered thirteen thousand additional students bused. More than nine thousand of them were elementary school children. No school remained all black, and an effort was made to reach a black–white ratio that reflected the racial breakdown of the system.

Three months later a federal appeals court reversed the elementary school part of the plan, asserting that it imposed an unreasonable burden on the school board. The NAACP Legal Defense Fund, which represented black parents, appealed to the Supreme Court, arguing that the entire plan should have been left intact. The school board argued that even *more* of the order should have been modified.

In the decision rendered April 20, 1971, the justices basically upheld the district court plan. To overcome segregated residential patterns, the court endorsed redrawing attendance lines and grouping schools together, even though their neighborhoods were not necessarily geographically contiguous. "As an interim corrective measure, this cannot be said to be beyond the broad remedial powers of a court," said Burger's opinion.

Turning to busing, the chief justice noted that bus transportation had been an "integral part of the public education system for years" and was an acceptable technique to overcome segregation. The justices acknowledged that there could be valid objections to busing "when the time or distance of travel is so great as to either risk the health of children or significantly impinge on the educational process." The limits on busing, he added, would vary with many factors, particularly with the age of the children involved. Burger acknowledged that there would be difficulties in working out desegregation plans, but "all awkwardness and inconvenience cannot be avoided in the interim period when remedial adjustments are being made to eliminate the dual school systems."

The court took pains to note that the decision covered only segregation resulting from state law. Segregation as a result of de facto separation of the races was not being addressed.

Civil rights lawyers hailed the decision as a continuation on the road to integration. Governor Wallace, reflecting a prominent strain in southern reaction, said, "The people in Alabama insane institutions could have written a better decision."

The State and *The News and Courier* took resigned, philosophical approaches, each pointing out the anomaly, in their view, of Congress's refusal to pass a law mandating nationwide desegregation, including in those areas with de facto separation. *The State* expressed confidence that "the South will live with—and through—this latest punitive decree of the federal courts. . . . Whether other parts of the nation could do as well is highly questionable—so questionable, in fact, that all branches of the federal government shy away from any meaningful attempt to make the non-South abide by rules imposed upon the Southern states."

Thurmond's opposition to busing was by this time well known. During the August congressional recess he told a convention of Optimist Club members in Columbia, "It does not make sense that little children can be put on buses and hauled several hours each day to schools in other neighborhoods merely to achieve a racial balance." Schools were no longer being used for education, he charged, but for "sociological experiments and as a means for playing politics." HEW, he charged, had been "overzealous on this subject and went entirely too far, but the Supreme Court has gone even further." The only solution was a constitutional amendment to stop this "unjustified and impractical course," Thurmond said, noting that he had already introduced such a proposal to end busing. Nothing would come of it, however—a reflection both of the procedural difficulties in passing a constitutional amendment (a two-thirds majority of Congress is required) and of the fact that Thurmond's solution was too radical.

Five months later, a federal judge in Richmond delivered another jolt. On January 10, 1972, U.S. District Judge Robert Merhige, Jr., ordered busing across city and county lines, merging a largely black city school system with two white county systems.

The *Richmond Times-Dispatch* assailed the decision as "a nauseating mixture of vacuous sociological theories and legal contradictions." The paper accused Merhige of being "more interested in manipulating human attitudes than in promoting excellent public education." As proof, it cited his endorsement of "the pernicious gibberish of those social engineers who argue, in effect, that a school system's primary function is to promote racial togetherness, not to give children the best academic education."

In Columbia, *The State* derisively said the judge had "dug into the seemingly inexhaustible Constitution and turned up yet another nugget that previous diggers had overlooked." Integration "was on its last leg," the paper asserted. "No sooner was it pushed to extremes than whites got up and moved out of the district. Now Judge Merhige has authorized pursuit. If this precedent stands, a man ultimately may need a passport to escape."

President Nixon seemed to agree. On March 16 he made a nationally broadcast statement on school desegregation, asserting that some federal courts "have gone too far." He asked Congress to halt all new busing orders and to approve his plan for spending more than $2 billion to upgrade impoverished neighborhood schools. "The great majority of Americans, black and white, feel strongly that the busing of schoolchildren away from their own neighborhoods for the purpose of achieving racial balance is wrong," he told the nation. "What we need now is not just speaking out against more busing but action to stop it."

The News and Courier was quick to praise the president's statement as an accurate reading of public sentiment. "President Nixon has sounded what we believe to be a popular note," said one editorial. "Opponents will contest it at their peril." The not-so-subtle reference was to the upcoming presidential election and Nixon's effort to draw a line that would separate Republicans from Democrats, particularly in the South.

As winter turned to spring, politicians' thoughts turned to the elections. Thurmond had his own race to prepare for, and once again—despite his warnings on the Senate floor—he would be working for Nixon. He had actually started in November of 1971, speaking at a dinner in Charlotte in the president's honor. While applauding Nixon's accomplishments—particularly his help for textile industries in North and South Carolina—the speech was as noteworthy for its sarcastic appraisals of the potential Democratic nominees, an edge not seen in Thurmond since the nasty exchanges with Olin Johnston during the 1950 Senate race. Thurmond said Senator George McGovern of South Dakota, who would eventually capture the nomination, described himself as a "dove" on the Vietnam War but was "the only bird I have seen with two left wings. Some candidates go down the campaign trail. Senator McGovern is the only one who goes down the Ho Chi Minh Trail."

Senator Fred Harris of Oklahoma had described himself as a populist who wanted to share the wealth. "As possessor of one of the largest oil fortunes in Oklahoma," Thurmond said, "we might suggest that he start with his own."

He called Hubert Humphrey "one of the conservative Democrats. The liberals in the Democratic Party don't like him. I have never figured out whether it was because he helped LBJ send all those troops to Vietnam or because Hubert Humphrey's troops were so successful in the street fighting the battle of Chicago in 1968."

The most acerbic comment was reserved for Senator Edward Kennedy: "He is for peace. He wants to get us out of the war in South Vietnam and into the war in Northern Ireland. But he hasn't even learned to drive a car yet." This last remark, a reference to the Chappaquiddick affair two years earlier in which a young woman lost her life when Kennedy's car went off a bridge, had been written into the text by the senator himself.

But Thurmond reserved sarcasm for the presidential scene. For his own reelection effort his style would be much different—benign and statesmanlike. The strategy was to portray himself as nonpartisan and indispensable. The previous December *The Columbia Record* had helped set the tone, telling readers that Thurmond was "counting the rewards" for having worked so hard for Nixon. "Numerous federal grants for South Carolina and high government posts for dozens of Thurmond's constituents"—including, of course, Dent and Buzhardt—were cited as examples of Nixon's gratitude "and of the senator's influence on the White House."

(The same article reported the complaint by a Hollings aide that Thurmond's ability to get advance notice of grants made it look as though his office had done all the work, when in truth Hollings's staff had done more than its share. "We don't even get word on construction of an outhouse," the aide lamented.)

Thurmond's reputation for such good works had been well known in the white community for years. Now the word was seeping out to black Carolinians with the help of Tom Moss and activists like Victoria DeLee, one of the state's most outspoken black voters.

DeLee was born in 1924 in rural Dorchester County, some sixty miles north of Charleston, to a black woman and a Native American man DeLee never knew. Like most other black children across the South, she had little formal schooling and was forced to work beside her mother, grandmother, and sisters picking cotton on white-owned farms. The hard early life left her a bitter teenager with an abiding hatred of whites and a willingness to defy the system.

By the time DeLee was twenty-two she had already been married for six years, had two children, and was pregnant with the third. The hatred that once drove her had by now evolved into a fearless determination to change the status quo, whatever the risk. Six months before the NAACP's 1947 challenge to the white primary, DeLee was staging her own one-woman voter registration drive in St. George, the Dorchester County seat. Undeterred by the white male registrar who told her she was not on the informal list of blacks approved for enrollment, DeLee refused to leave his courthouse office until she had gotten her certificate. Such was the climate of intimidation that when she came out to the waiting room and proudly announced her victory, no other black stepped forward, not even her husband. S. B. DeLee's main concern was to hustle his wife out of St. George and back home to Ridgeville before any trouble started.

Like George Lee in Mississippi, DeLee believed that voter registration was the first step toward improving the lives of southern blacks. Though she had no official relationship with the Voter Education Project in the early sixties, she founded the Dorchester County Voters' League in 1960 and after passage of the Voting Rights Act five years later immediately helped secure federal registrars for the county.

DeLee's activism was not without cost. In 1966, as voter registration efforts intensified, the family house was burned to the ground. Authorities said the fire was the result of arson.

During these turbulent years, DeLee considered Thurmond to be the enemy. She thought he was a racist who only took care of his white constituents. But she changed her mind after she asked him to help her get a federal grant for a day-care center she was operating. He got the money and delivered it personally.

At the start of Thurmond's 1972 campaign, DeLee went to Charleston to pay her respects at a "Strom Thurmond Appreciation Day" rally put on by area Democrats. Newspaper reporters writing about the event noted the nonpartisan atmosphere and the presence of this civil rights activist. Her testimonial to the senator, which wove its way into state political lore, couldn't have been better if Thurmond had written it himself. "I'm for whoever gets the job done, and Strom is getting the job done," she said. Later she told reporters, "What a man was yesterday doesn't matter. It's what he is today that counts."

(DeLee's day-care project soured within five years. In 1976, probably more as a result of incompetence than dishonesty, she and three of her children faced federal fraud charges involving the funds sent to the day-care center. All pleaded guilty and were sent to prison, and she served four months before being paroled. But DeLee forever remained grateful to Thurmond for his help.)

By 1972 the senator's Washington office was a fountain of press releases announcing grants to communities around the state: funds for housing, preschool programs, new water and sewer lines. Thurmond was hardly the only politician sending money back home to his state, but he had a special knack for making what was essentially pork-barrel politics look like a personal mission. Sometimes he would come back home to announce a grant himself, or he would attend the dedication of a new building put up with federal help. It made an impression on local residents that the senator took time out from his schedule to be with them, and he could draw on that memory when election day came. He could—and did—ask more of local officials, seeking expressions of appreciation for his good works to put in campaign ads. Most were more than happy to give their public thanks.

Now more aware of his black constituents, Thurmond took particular care to point out his assistance to their communities. In a press release he made public a summary of these boons, citing among other things new housing and water and sewer facilities in predominantly black rural areas; funds for day-care centers run by blacks, including Victoria DeLee; the appointment of Tom Moss; the appointment of a black deputy federal marshal; financial assistance to black students through the Strom Thurmond Foundation (by 1991, $750,000 had been dispensed); and assistance to local blacks serving in the armed forces who had problems with assignments, hardship discharges, and the like. One of the more unusual items the senator listed—an apparent effort to touch the symbolic as well as practical bases—was his attention to heavyweight boxing champion Joe Frazier. He noted that he had presented a plaque to the fighter, appeared with him on a radio show, and had inserted complimentary remarks about him into the *Congressional Record.*

Thurmond's opponent this time around was fifty-year-old state senator Nick Zeigler of Florence, a World War II veteran and a graduate of Harvard Law School. Although Zeigler was nineteen years younger than the sixty-nine-year-old Thurmond, the senator's personal news at the start of the campaign helped deflect arguments that he might be too old to serve again. On March 21 the Thurmonds announced that their second child would be born shortly before the November election. Their first one, Nancy Moore, would be a year old March 30.

A poll early in the year showed Zeigler what he would be up against in challenging Strom Thurmond. The senator, naturally, would sweep the Republican vote, but the survey also showed Thurmond preferred by 65 percent of those who considered themselves independent. Even worse, 27 percent of the Democrats said they expected to cross party lines and vote for the senator.

At the start of the campaign, *The Charlotte Observer,* which paid close attention to neighboring South Carolina, thoughtfully summarized the upcoming contest. Conceding that Zeigler was the underdog, the paper said he was nonetheless the strongest challenger Thurmond had yet faced. He represented the "new face of the South Carolina Democratic Party and that new party face has been regularly winning the approval of the voters. 'Moderate-progressive' is the best description for it, and those words are suitable for Sen. Zeigler."

The editorial went on to describe the changes in South Carolina politics, singling out Governor West, Senator Hollings, and several state legislators as illustrative of this new era.

"In abiding contrast," the *Observer* wrote, "Sen. Thurmond is the last representative at the state level of the old-style politics of hard-line conservatism." While his image may have changed, the paper said, his views had not. "He artfully plays porkbarrel politics for South Carolina in Washington; but at the same time he continues to vote often against the deeper interests of most of its people, opposing federal programs that address themselves to the kind of problems which the chief Democrats in the Columbia capital concern themselves with." This was an apt description of the senator's record, although Thurmond did not believe that he was voting "against the deeper interests" of the people. If he still opposed federal solutions to almost all domestic problems, it was because in his view federal involvement remained a greater danger to freedom than the deprivations the government programs sought to redress.

Zeigler tried to tarnish Thurmond's image as the man who gets things done, labeling the senator a naysayer who voted against everything that was important to South Carolinians. (The one thing that wasn't an issue was busing. Zeigler opposed it as much as Thurmond did.)

To buttress his argument, Zeigler printed up a list of thirty-eight federal programs Thurmond opposed. Included on the list were Medicare, child nutrition programs, urban renewal, school breakfast and lunch programs, environmental protection, the Peace Corps, manpower training and employment, and the minimum wage. Zeigler summed up his view of the senator with a catchy barb: "He wants to be Scrooge in Washington and Santa Claus at home."

Thurmond's campaign countered with literature that sought to deepen the image of the senator as doer. One pamphlet featured a photographic collage of the senator in different settings with blacks and whites. The caption read: "close to the people . . . working for South Carolina."

A brochure aimed at young voters said, "Strom Thurmond . . . In Step with the Times." The words framed a picture of the senator, ramrod straight, striding forward with nine young people. "Want a good listener?" the flyer asked. "Drop a line to your Senior Senator. Speaking on high school and college campuses throughout the country, he studies student opinion and listens to their ideas, problems and aspirations. Strom Thurmond, a man of deep convictions, welcomes new ideas and constantly looks ahead." The flyer also noted that every year, the senator had a number of young South Carolinians work in his office as interns, giving them "the opportunity to learn firsthand the operations of their government."

The Clemson University paper, *The Tiger*, suggested that these internships were not as valuable as the campaign portrayed them. One intern complained anonymously to *The Tiger* that his job consisted of opening mail, grocery shopping for Mrs. Thurmond, cutting the senator's grass, and other menial chores. The assertions were no doubt true—such tasks were not uncommon in Senate offices—but the real value of an internship was the opportunity to see the inside of a Senate office and absorb the atmosphere of the legislative process, however lowly the intern's daily responsibilities.

Three weeks before the election, the Thurmonds announced the arrival of James Strom Thurmond. Commenting on her son's name, Mrs. Thurmond said she hoped the baby would grow up to be "as kind and helpful to people as his father."

Despite Zeigler's spirited campaign, like previous challengers he came up short. Thurmond prevailed November 7 with 63.3 percent of the vote. *The State* called it "a sweet victory for the conservative solon whose political fate was thought to be a question mark because of changing attitudes on Vietnam, segregation and more liberal social concepts."

Nationally, President Nixon trounced George McGovern, winning 520 electoral votes to McGovern's 17 and carrying every state except Massachusetts. Within a year, however, Nixon's victory would prove to be flawed.

A tragic sidelight earlier in the year was the shooting of George Wallace, a figure who, more than Thurmond, had played the race card in deeds as well as words. The bullet pierced the governor's spine, and while he survived, he would be confined to a wheelchair for the rest of his life. Wallace continued to be a presence in Alabama politics and a conservative voice nationally, but the injury diminished his ability to compete effectively again for the White House.

Thurmond and Wallace had never personally been close, even before the senator opposed his 1968 presidential race. But there was an ideological link between the two men that became apparent in 1964: Thurmond took his energy and state's rights philosophy out of the Democratic Party and into the GOP; Wallace stayed behind but entered three primaries that year talking the same line.

Wallace won an estimable 43 percent of the Democratic vote in Maryland, 34 percent in Wisconsin, and 30 percent in Indiana. (He did not, however, mount a formal challenge to Johnson at the Democratic convention.) By 1972, when Wallace narrowly won the Michigan primary the day after he was shot, the battling governor had proved the truth of Thurmond's 1948 contention—that a message about the perils of a powerful central government, particularly when racial issues were involved, had appeal outside the South.

But even if that bullet had never found its mark, Wallace's own history almost surely would have turned out to be an insurmountable barrier. Unlike Thurmond, Eastland, Ervin, and Russell, he *had been* a frontline politician during the height of the civil rights movement. He had called out state troopers in Selma and had personally blocked the doorway to black students at the University of Alabama. This made him an even starker embodiment of white resistance than Thurmond. As the entire country continued to adjust to a surging black electorate, it would have been harder and harder for a man with Wallace's record to be considered a credible presidential candidate. Although he would ultimately make his peace with Alabama's black community, that was an adjustment on home territory, where he, like Thurmond in South Carolina, well understood the pulse of his constituency.

By the middle of 1973, Nixon's presidency was beginning to unravel. What had appeared to be a second-rate break-in and bugging of Democratic headquarters in the Watergate apartment-office complex had mushroomed into a scandal that was leading to the Oval Office. Added to charges of political subterfuge were more serious allegations of obstruction of justice in an attempt to cover up the crime.

Five years earlier, Thurmond had to be persuaded to support Nixon, but once he had made his choice the senator was as loyal a partisan as any president could want. When Watergate, as the imbroglio was quickly dubbed, first became an issue, Thurmond took Nixon at his word that he'd had no knowledge of the original crime or attempted cover-up. And he continued defending Nixon right up until his resignation, giving no quarter to the liberal critics Thurmond believed were hounding him from office.

At first the senator applauded the appointment of special prosecutor Archibald Cox and the creation of a special investigating committee in the Senate (headed by fellow southerner Sam Ervin). But by September he had lost patience with the inquiry and considered the break-in to be the folly of overzealous political operatives. "A few men chose to break the law and then attempted to cover up their actions," he told a group of constituents during a trip back home. "They committed a crime against the American people and the president. They lied to us and they lied to him. They caused his administration great trouble and caused our president to suffer. They embarrassed the United States. The men responsible should be punished. They should be brought to justice."

That said, the senator announced he was "sick and tired of the Watergate sideshow, better known as the Ervin committee. . . . Instead of being a fair and unbiased investigation, it has become an inquisition with the target being the president of the United States."

On November 6, asked on NBC's *Today* show whether Nixon should resign, Thurmond defended the president even more resolutely. He acknowledged that there had been some loss of confidence in the president, but he blamed it on opposition from "the big labor bosses," consumer advocate Ralph Nader "and his crowd," the American Civil Liberties Union, and "certain others that are just against him, it seems."

The senator conceded that Nixon should have supervised his staff more closely, but added, "I think some of those people have betrayed his trust. I think they went beyond their responsibilities and their authority."

A week later, the senator cited with approval an editorial critical of the "chorus of voices" demanding Nixon's resignation. "As we read the mood of the people," the editorial said, "they are puzzled and saddened, but not disposed to cast down their president. History will be his judge. Today's enemies are not necessarily qualified historians. As we see them they are taking on the cruel emotions of a mob."

In his own travels around the state and the country, Thurmond added, "I have found tremendous grass-roots support for President Nixon and for the preservation of due process of the law. The orchestrated voices against the president are not serving the interests of our country."

At the beginning of 1974 Thurmond was still defending the president with his usual vigor, claiming that his mail was running eleven to one in favor of Nixon. By the spring, however, the president's troubles were mounting. The previous October, after he had abruptly fired Cox, the House had directed the Judiciary Committee to begin an exploration of impeachment proceedings, the equivalent of preparing an indictment of charges for trial in a court of law.

In February, the committee was given authority to investigate the president and subpoena power to gather information. A special staff was assembled to undertake the inquiry. Starting in May, House Judiciary members began working their way through the information the committee lawyers had gathered, sparring early in the summer with Nixon's lawyers over procedures and the substance of the possible charges against him. On July 24 final deliberations began on articles of impeachment drawn up to remove the president from office. For three days the thirty-eight members explained their views in nationally televised sessions that culminated in approval of the first article of impeachment the evening of July 27. It charged that the president had obstructed justice in the Watergate case. The next day the committee approved a second article of impeachment, this one charging the president with failure to uphold the country's laws. The final article, charging the president with unconstitutional defiance of the committee's subpoenas, was approved July 30.

The same day the committee had started its debate, the president had lost a critical fight in the Supreme Court. The justices ruled unanimously that Nixon must turn over to the special prosecutor tape recordings of sixty-four White House conversations.

Three critical tapes recorded shortly after the 1972 break-in were released August 5, six days after the final article of impeachment was approved. They showed that despite previous declarations to the contrary, the president had participated in the cover-up. Reaction at the Capitol was strong and immediate. Key Republicans in the House and Senate said the president's support was rapidly dwindling. Senator Griffin of Michigan, the second-ranking Republican, called on Nixon to resign. By the next day that was the prevailing opinion among GOP senators, who would have to join their Democratic colleagues in trying the president should the impeachment articles be approved by the House. On August 8, eleven days before the full House was to begin debating the charges, Nixon announced his resignation, telling the nation that it had "become evident to me that I no longer have a strong enough political base in Congress" to fight to remain in office. He made no specific mention of the impeachment proceedings.

Thurmond had remained quietly in the background during the tense days immediately after the tapes were released. His reaction to the resignation was a mixture of relief that the Watergate turmoil could now end, disappointment at the troubling revelations that had forced the president out of office, and a loyalist's defense of the administration's record. While conceding that the resignation was "probably best for the nation," he praised Nixon's presidency as "one of great accomplishment," citing the end of the Vietnam War, his overtures to China and the Soviet Union, the building of a strong national defense, and "sound appointments to the Supreme Court already resulting in decisions better protecting the safety and well-being of our citizens."

When President Ford granted a full pardon to Nixon a month later, the senator pronounced the action "proper and in the interest of the country."

Dent and Buzhardt, who had been rewarded by Nixon for their work in 1968, had their own connections to Watergate. Buzhardt was one of the four men in Nixon's inner circle in the last tumultuous days, acting as special counsel for Watergate. So intense was his work schedule—Buzhardt had to be helicoptered from the White House to his son's wedding—that he suffered a heart attack early in 1974. He returned to work just in time to handle many details of the beleaguered Nixon's final weeks in office.

Although Dent had left the White House in 1972, the special prosecutor charged him with violating an old campaign-practices law because he had helped dispense funds in 1970 from an illegally organized political committee. On December 11, 1974, Dent pleaded guilty to a misdemeanor and was sentenced by a federal judge to one month's unsupervised probation, hardly more than a slap on the wrist. It had seemed to the judge that "Mr. Dent was more the victim than the perpetrator" in the campaign scheme. Dent made light of his punishment, comparing it to a speeding ticket: "That's what you call a high-class moving violation."

By the end of the year, Thurmond was already thinking about two civil rights issues that would be on the congressional agenda in 1975, voting rights and busing—the subject of even more federal court decisions in the previous two years.

In a year-end newsletter, the senator wrote that the "so-called voting rights act," which was up for renewal in 1975, "should be allowed to expire unceremoniously." He called it "unfortunate that the Congress ever enacted such an unconstitutional piece of legislation" and repeated his charge that supporters "were guilty of discrimination, which they claimed to oppose by this act."

But however much they may have detested the law, Thurmond and every other southern politician knew how effective it had been. The next presidential election would be proof positive.

As had been the case with the past two voting bills, the House acted first on the legislation, in the spring of 1975, easily staving off Republican-backed proposals to weaken the law. The main provisions of the measure, which passed the chamber June 4, renewed the act for another ten years and extended the antidiscrimination sections to cover Spanish-speaking voters. This brought Texas and counties in several other states under the act's provisions.

After several weeks of maneuvering, Senate supporters saw their chamber's version of the bill pass July 24 by a vote of 72–12. In opposing the legislation for the third time, Thurmond repeated that "I want to see everybody vote, but to have this bill reenacted here is completely unreasonable." What particularly galled him was that South Carolina, like the other covered states, had to "come to Washington and request preclearance from the Attorney General for every little piece of legislation that is passed, even the day of an election in a city or community, or the time of voting or the place of a polling precinct, any little thing pertaining to an election. . . .

"When this bill was passed, we had more than fifty percent of the people registered," he went on, "but fewer than fifty percent voted. No one can make the people vote. Why should the state of South Carolina be insulted and embarrassed and intimidated when it is one of the sovereign states of the nation?"

By this time Thurmond had defended the South in public office for more than twenty-five years, and throughout he had refused to concede that his state or any other in the region was responsible for what he perceived as federal punishment. The belief would remain through the rest of his career, but as time moved on, the rhetoric softened and actions belied the words.

House sponsors, concerned that Senate opponents would try to block any conference agreement between the House and Senate, persuaded the chamber to accept the Senate bill. The measure was passed July 28, ten days before the law was set to expire.

Thurmond was among the handful of southerners who still opposed the legislation—James Allen and John Sparkman of Alabama, Stennis of Mississippi, Talmadge of Georgia, and Jesse Helms of North Carolina. Now, however, there were some southern senators willing to support a voting rights bill—Sam Nunn, the new Democratic senator from Georgia; Hollings, Thurmond's South Carolina colleague; and the senators from Florida, Kentucky, Louisiana, and Tennessee.

The relative ease with which the act was extended reflected the effectiveness of the 1965 law and the nation's general acceptance of political participation by blacks and other minority groups. By contrast, school desegregation—busing in particular—was becoming a lesson in the boundaries of acceptable change in more private arenas, south and north. The growing opposition to government-mandated change was a vindication of Thurmond's long-held states' rights views. Only now it was not just states' rights that mattered, but the rights of counties and cities, too.

Judge Merhige's much-maligned decision ordering busing across city and country lines had been overturned by a federal appeals court in June of 1972, and nearly a year later, on May 23, 1973, the Supreme Court had deadlocked 4–4 on whether to let that decision stand. Justice Lewis F. Powell, who had joined the court in 1971, had been a school board member in Virginia and did not participate. The tie automatically upheld the appeals court decision, but there was no written opinion in the case and it carried no weight as precedent. Fourteen months later—July 25, 1974, in the midst of the impeachment debate—the Supreme Court spoke once again on desegregation, this time using a case from Detroit to put limits on busing plans. In this ruling, the court said that busing students among fifty-four school districts in three counties was not appropriate unless *all* of the districts were responsible for segregation.

For their part, members of Congress opposed to busing had been trying to restrict the practice through legislation almost since the first school bus rolled out of the garage to further a desegregation plan. They were unsuccessful until the fall of 1975, when the defection of several northern Democratic senators to the antibusing side meant that there would finally be a majority in both chambers of Congress who favored restricting the remedy.

Thurmond had entered the debate a year earlier, criticizing HEW secretary Caspar Weinberger for not enforcing desegregation orders in the North and West with as much vigor as in the South. He devoted a weekly newsletter and one of his radio broadcasts to the subject, noting that federal funds were being withheld from some South Carolina school systems "because of their alleged failure to technically comply with complex percentage and quota regulations" for desegregation. "I find it incredible that Secretary Weinberger would announce that federal funds will not be similarly denied to Northern school systems. All Americans pay taxes, and it is intolerable for one section of our country to be singled out and denied benefits of federal expenditures for education."

Violence had erupted in Boston over desegregation orders, and "although it may be unkind to rub it in," Thurmond said, "the Boston violence further dispels the notion, held in some parts of this country, that the citizens of Massachusetts have a 'higher morality' than the citizens of the Southern states." The real issue, he insisted, was "fundamental opposition to unreasonable federal coercion—the same thing the citizens of the South have opposed all these years."

The 1975 debate was begun in September when Senator Jesse Helms of North Carolina tried to amend HEW's annual appropriations. The agency had the power to coerce school districts into assigning teachers and students to specific schools or classes according to their race or national origin: the mechanism was the withholding of federal funds. The Helms proposal barred HEW from using that tactic and also from requiring a school district to keep records on its students' race or national origin. The House had approved an almost identical amendment in 1974, but senators had not been willing to accept such a broad prohibition on the federal agency.

The Helms amendment was rejected by five votes, but Senator Joseph R. Biden, Jr., a young Democrat from Delaware, offered a more limited version of the Helms amendment. The senator contended that his amendment would not prevent a federal court from ordering busing, but he pointed out that it would bar HEW from acting as if it were a court.

Senator Brooke, the chamber's only black member, argued that Biden's proposal barred HEW from using other remedies, such as school closings or consolidations, to bring integration. But the amendment was adopted by a vote of 50–43, with fourteen northern Democrats supporting it. This was a dramatic change from the previous year, when ten of the fourteen senators, including Biden, had voted against antibusing efforts. He gave this explanation to colleagues: "I firmly believe that we have got to . . . declare that busing does not work. It is a counterproductive concept that is causing more harm to equal education than any benefit from it."

Thurmond had been a cosponsor of Biden's proposal, and after it was added to the appropriations measure he pronounced himself delighted.

On September 23, amid a flurry of chessboard moves, the Senate eventually adopted an amendment offered by Senator Byrd that barred HEW from requiring the busing of students beyond the closest school offering the courses the students wanted. The House eventually accepted the West Virginian's amendment, and the appropriations measure finally was sent to President Ford, who vetoed it because it was one billion dollars above his budget request. The veto was overridden, and the legislation became law at the end of January 1976 with the Byrd language still in it.

The amendment had minimal practical effect because virtually all busing was the result of federal court orders, not HEW directives, but it represented the first congressional stance against busing and sent an unmistakable message of disapproval to officials responsible for desegregation.

(Twenty-one years after the *Swann* decision, almost to the day, Charlotte-Mecklenburg school officials voted to drop the busing plan that had been in effect for two decades. While asserting their commitment to integrated schools, school board members said they would use other techniques to bring black and white students together.)

The busing debate continued into 1976 but with no new successful initiatives, and by the time of the political conventions in the summer, legislative matters had taken a backseat to presidential politics. The Democratic "moderate-progressives" that *The Charlotte Observer* had spoken of four years earlier were coming into their glory in the person of Jimmy Carter, the forty-six-year-old governor of Georgia. It looked as if the South might rise again, but not the way Thurmond would have chosen.

An unsuccessful gubernatorial candidate in 1966, Carter had run again in 1970, this time sharing a ticket with the much more conservative governor, Lester Maddox, who was running for lieutenant governor because he could not succeed himself. Maddox had risen to fame as an ardent segregationist committed to staving off civil rights advances. He had built up a successful restaurant in Atlanta, the Pickrick, and in 1964 had symbolized white defiance by brandishing an ax handle and a pistol to show how he would prevent blacks from coming in to be served. In one newspaper ad he declared: "Just in case some of you Communists, Socialists and other Integrationists have any doubt—THE PICKRICK WILL NEVER BE INTEGRATED! If you want some fried chicken, it will have to be something other than Pickrick chicken." Rather than obey a federal court order to integrate, he closed the restaurant in 1965.

Carter, whose campaign did not echo the racism of Maddox's career, won in 1970, and his twelve-minute inaugural address the following January declared that a new day had dawned in Georgia—one that mirrored changes in other southern states. "I say to you quite frankly that the time for racial discrimination is over. . . . No poor, rural, weak or black person should ever have to bear the additional burden of being deprived of the opportunity of an education, a job, or simple justice." Adding to the moment was a stirring rendition of the "Battle Hymn of the Republic" sung by the all-black chorus from Atlanta's Morris Brown College.

Once in office, Carter moved on a substantive and symbolic level to include black Georgia in his plans for the state. He set up a biracial commission to deal with black-white problems, appointed blacks to important positions, and hung a portrait of Martin Luther King, Jr., in the capitol. Lieutenant Governor Maddox was quick to retort that the slain civil rights leader and Nobel laureat "did more to spread the cause of communism and socialism than any Georgian ever to live."

Carter was one of several New South moderates elected that year, including South Carolina's John West, Reuben Askew in Florida, and Dale Bumpers in Arkansas. *Time* magazine put Carter on a May cover, blessing him as the leader of these moderate southern Democrats. (Thurmond's nascent evolution was used in the article as evidence of a New South, citing his hiring of Tom Moss and quoting one South Carolina wag who said, "Next to having that baby at sixty-eight, it's the best thing Strom has done.")

Six years later the Democrats nominated Carter for president, giving the South another chance at the White House. But *The News and Courier*'s cool reception to his nomination showed that regional loyalty couldn't be taken for granted. Carter, the paper said, had described himself as "an American and a Southerner." "The question is due to be rephrased many times and asked again. Which comes first, the South or the Democratic Party? Viewing Jimmy Carter's remarkable ascendancy in national politics Southerners cannot help but remember a time when it was presumptuous to ask such a question of any respectable Democrat."

The State, in the midst of a broader historical analysis, raised a similar caution: "A new South emerged during the 1960's in the terrible turmoil of the civil rights struggle and in the quiet economic resurgence of new industrial development," the paper wrote. "As the South moved into the 1970's toward the mainstream of America, it brought new, young and progressive governors forward for the nation to see. Mr. Carter is one of them. . . . The Carter candidacy by no means assures that his fellow Southerners will automatically fall in line as a matter of pride," however. The Democratic Party had made Southerners "demonstrate their independence. Mr. Carter will have to woo them along with voters in the rest of the nation."

Although the Republicans had a sitting president who wanted to remain in office, Gerald Ford's nomination was not a foregone conclusion. Ronald Reagan had declared himself a candidate, precipitating a boisterous fight in Kansas City. Three weeks before the convention, Thurmond had announced that he was supporting Reagan this time, a commitment he claimed to have made right after the 1972 election.

Careful to cover his bases, Thurmond added, "I think highly of President Ford," and promised to support "whichever of these two outstanding men receives the Republican nomination at the convention next month." That turned out to be Ford, who chose Senator Robert Dole of Kansas as his running mate.

A few weeks after the GOP convention, Thurmond showed up on the cover of the magazine *Family Weekly* alongside George McGovern and Hubert Humphrey. "What's it like to run for the White House?" the article wanted to know. Each of the three men, along with Barry Goldwater and George Wallace, was asked about his losing efforts.

Thurmond voiced no regrets. "I can say with satisfaction that my campaign called national attention to the problem of growing federal encroachment in areas where it had no constitutional authority," he told the magazine. "I also helped break the grip of one-party domination in the South." (In this he was taking credit too early. Though he may have made a difference in 1964 by switching parties and campaigning for Goldwater, he'd had no such effect running for president. In 1948 Thurmond had in fact been *helped* by the Democratic Party apparatus in the four states that he carried.) "If I had been elected president in 1948, history would be vastly different," Thurmond went on. "I believe we would have stemmed the growth of Big Government, which had begun with the New Deal and culminated with the Great Society."

Rarely the sort of person who admits to failure, the senator came close by adding that he wasn't sure he would have run in 1948 if current conditions had existed then. "Today the federal giant is a reality. In 1948 we were at a crossroads where our national direction needed to be challenged." His comment suggests that the challenge had been lost.

During the fall campaign, Thurmond made sure South Carolinians knew how he felt about Carter. In one radio and television spot just prior to the nominee's visit to the state, the senator asserted that "once you get past the smile and the Georgia accent, Jimmy Carter talks and acts like a northern liberal—not a southern conservative."

In another television spot, Thurmond said he wanted a southerner for president, "but not just somebody who's *from* the South, somebody who is *for* the South. . . . Jimmy Carter is not *for* the South when he comes out for gun registration, or for programs that mean more federal control over our businesses, our schools, and our lives. He is not *for* the South on busing, on welfare, on taxes, on any issue I can name.

"President Ford may not have a southern accent," Thurmond argued. "But when he talks about the issues, he sure sounds *more* like a southerner than Jimmy Carter."

Carter won a slim victory in November, edging Ford with just over 50 percent of the vote.

Although Thurmond's own reelection was nearly two years away, he was already preparing for it by 1976. He assumed his opponent was going to be "Pug" Ravenel, a rising Democratic star and someone the senator's aides had kept their eye on since he ran for governor in 1974. One of Thurmond's more clairvoyant assistants had got hold of a fund-raising brochure by Ravenel, called it to the senator's attention, and then put it in the file for his reelection four years hence.

Ravenel seemed to be the ideal candidate, blessed with good looks, intelligence, and an appealing background. Born in Charleston to a family of modest means, with scholarship money and part-time jobs he managed to spend a year at the Philips Exeter Academy in New Hampshire, then earned both a bachelor's and master's degree in business administration at Harvard University, where he was elected the equivalent of class president.

To add to the luster, Ravenel was also a fine athlete. In high school he was named the most valuable player in an all-star football game, and at Harvard, where he played quarterback, he was named the school's most outstanding athlete. The honors continued after graduate school: first a fellowship allowing him to travel through twenty-seven countries to study politics and economics, and then in 1966 a White House fellowship to work with the secretary of the treasury. After spending a few years with a New York investment firm, he moved back to Charleston in 1973 to start his own company.

The next year Ravenel won a stunning victory in the Democratic primary contest for governor. But the South Carolina Supreme Court ruled that he didn't meet the state's residency rule because he had been absent from South Carolina for several years. His name was stripped from the November ballot, and Democrats then nominated his primary opponent, Representative William Jennings Bryan Dorn, to be the party standard-bearer. Ravenel declined to give him full support, contending that his credibility would have been damaged had he turned around and embraced Dorn. James Edwards, a GOP activist from Charleston, became the state's first Republican governor since Reconstruction. Many Democrats grumbled that Ravenel's pique had hurt Dorn's chances and cost them the statehouse, and while Ravenel considered the episode ancient history by 1978, party stalwarts had much longer memories.

By the middle of 1976, Thurmond was already getting reports that Ravenel was seeking political and financial support for a Senate race. One informant reminded Thurmond that though the senator was "an awfully strong candidate," any politician could be defeated.

On July 25, 1977, after thirteen months of deliberating, Ravenel announced he was seeking the Democratic nomination for the Senate. "Almost four years ago, I ran for elective office because I wanted to serve, to make a difference," he told supporters. "I believed then, as I do now, that someone fresh, someone unencumbered by political obligations, could most truly represent and offer leadership to the people of our state."

He would not be seeking the governorship again, he explained, because there were other Democratic candidates who shared his political philosophy. But there was one statewide officeholder with whom he differed drastically. Without naming Thurmond, he said that "even a preliminary review of his recent record suggests that he reflects neither the judgment, the will nor, the heart of the people he has been elected to serve." He then listed several matters where "our senior senator" had voted "wrong" according to the National Education Association, the Consumer Federation of America, the National Farmers Union, and the Leadership Conference on Civil Rights, an umbrella organization for a variety of civil rights groups—hardly the most popular checklist for many white Carolinians.

Ravenel's main pitch was that South Carolina could do better. "I think our United States senator should take a leadership position *for* education, *for* civil rights, *for* consumer protection, *for* farmers and other working people . . . ," he said. "Consequently, I think that in 1978 the statewide office in which I can make the greatest difference, the most distinctive contribution to the people of South Carolina, is the office of United States senator."

Immediately a *State* editorial observed that, because of the Charlestonian's decision, "this summer's heat may be surpassed by next summer's politics." The paper also pointed out the irony that the list of organizations "that have down-graded the Thurmond voting record may serve to emphasize the senior senator's strengths." The editorial found it unlikely that anyone else would enter the race, "for potential candidates have shown little enthusiasm for tangling with Senator Thurmond. The fact that 'Pug' Ravenel has entered the list gives promise of a lively race between two aggressive individuals widely separated in age, background, experience and political philosophy."

Two months before Ravenel's announcement, Thurmond had

been soliciting support from businessmen, military officials, doctors, and dentists. In special campaign pitches aimed at each audience he explained that he was running for office again, talked about his support of matters important to them, and asked for their help, monetary and political.

Five years ahead of a famous telephone company commercial, he was also engaging in his own reach-out-and-touch-someone campaign. It knew no bounds. According to one senior Ravenel aide, on Christmas eve he had received a call at home from the Thurmonds. "This is Senator Strom Thurmond," he said. "Nancy and I were here sitting by the fire thinking about you, and we want to wish you a Merry Christmas."

Thurmond knew the gesture wouldn't bring support, but he had a reason for making calls to opposing forces. "Even though I knew they were against me," the senator later explained, "we would call people to temper 'em so they wouldn't be active. You never make a mistake showing people attention and being kind to them. People like to be acknowledged."

Ravenel also felt the power of Thurmond's reaching hand when he tried putting together fund-raising parties. "I can talk to somebody on Monday about having a fundraiser in his home later in the week, and by Wednesday Strom will be on the phone to the man's business partner talking about it," Ravenel lamented to a *Washington Post* reporter. He quickly realized, as he put it, that "Asking someone to vote against Strom Thurmond is like asking him to cut down a Palmetto tree," a reference to South Carolina's symbol.

In Thurmond's formal announcement of his candidacy April 5—which some mistakenly thought would be his last campaign—he focused on what would become his major theme: that his time and experience in Washington had placed him in "the top ranks of the Senate, and in leadership positions on three key Senate committees—Judiciary, Armed Services and Veterans Affairs." As a result, he told the television audience, "I am now in a better position to serve you and to deal more effectively with the important problems confronting our state and nation."

Serving the people, he said, has "always been my primary goal—service with an open door and a helping hand for everyone." He deftly reminded viewers of the largesse that had flowed from Washington. "As I travel around South Carolina, a great satisfaction for me is the sight of so many public facilities for which I have worked with your local leaders to secure federal funds: projects of lasting value, such as state, county and municipal buildings; housing developments; education and health facilities; law enforcement, civic and recreation centers; water and sewer systems; flood control and soil conservation projects; and numerous others. It has been a particular pleasure to help you and your local officials cut through the red tape, so South Carolina could receive its fair share of federal services."

He closed by inviting viewers to come by the family's home in Columbia for a reception two days later. Nearly six thousand Carolinians took him up on the offer, streaming through the family's eight-room house during a three-hour open house.

To help voters understand just how good Thurmond had been for South Carolina the senator's office put together an inch-thick booklet listing the projects that had come into the state between 1968 and 1978. The grand total was an impressive number: four billion, four hundred ninety-eight million dollars, or approximately four hundred fifty million dollars every year. (According to one survey, though, South Carolina ranked twenty-eighth among the states in terms of the federal money it received.)

As *The State* had pointed out, the Thurmond-Ravenel race was a contest between generations, a difference that showed itself not only in age but in campaigning styles as well. The senator was an acknowledged master at one-to-one politics, a process that required time, energy, and a capacity for endless small talk on the telephone, at street corners, at plant gates, and at civic club luncheons.

Ravenel had shown in 1974 that South Carolinians were receptive to another kind of campaigning: well-crafted television messages that featured the candidate's handsome face. He could reach five thousand voters in one TV spot, perhaps only fifty at a Kiwanis Club gathering. But Donald Fowler, head of the state Democratic Party, conceded to a visiting reporter that it would still be an uphill battle, even with a successful media campaign. "If Pug wins, it will be on the basis of the television," he said early in the campaign. "Strom has got everything else."

The major responsibility for keeping the campaign on Thurmond's terms, making sure he could use "everything else," fell to field director Lee Atwater, a young GOP activist who had come to the senator through Harry Dent. His work on this campaign later catapulted Atwater into the top echelon of the national Republican Party. Both jobs required a keen understanding of the opposition's strengths and how to deflect them.

In 1972 Thurmond had ducked Zeigler's challenge to debate in all forty-six counties. Now it became even more important to avoid a face-to-face debate with Ravenel, something the Democrat requested after he easily beat his opponents in the June 13 primary. Two days later, aware of the advantage the younger man would have, Thurmond issued an acerbic response to Ravenel's suggestion that televised debates would help cut campaign expenses. The senator had originally suggested that they agree to a limit on advertising, but Ravenel's counterproposal, he charged, was just a ruse for pushing the debates. "My position on debates has been clear for months. I will appear before any group of South Carolinians to discuss the campaign and the issues," the senator said. "However, I will do my own campaigning and trust that my opponent will do the same."

Ravenel took the direct approach in late July, reminding the senator in a personal letter that he had debated Olin Johnston in 1950, debated foreign policy with another senator in 1977, offered to debate President Carter, and had wanted to debate Truman on civil rights in 1948. "I commend your tradition of a strong stand on debates and your willingness to participate in them. Now I am writing to ask that you continue that tradition by joining with me to debate the critical issues which affect the people of South Carolina."

A Thurmond campaign official wrote back that the senator "prefers to carry his campaign to the people in his own way. I am sure you are capable of doing the same." When Ravenel's goading started to get under Thurmond's skin—he had chastised the senator for "patent arrogance"—Thurmond almost gave in. Atwater had to ask Harry Dent to talk the senator out of it.

With the youth-age issue so prominent in the contest, Thurmond had decided to alter his image. He was still in remarkable physical condition, but now hair transplants covered the bald head, and dye had turned the gray into an eye-catching shade of red-brown. Adding to Thurmond's image of youthful vigor was the senator's growing family. Baby Paul had arrived two years earlier, so now there were four children under seven.

To make the best use of this natural asset, the campaign came up with *Strom Trek*—a red-white-and-blue camper that served as rolling campaign headquarters for Nancy Thurmond and the four children, each sporting a T-shirt that read, "Vote for My Daddy." It was the children's idea, Mrs. Thurmond explained, to name the camper after the popular science-fiction TV show. "Just as *Star Trek* on television brought good will throughout the galaxies, we hope to bring good will to the people of South Carolina," she told reporters at *Strom Trek*'s July kickoff.

Ravenel sought to tarnish this homey touch by noting that *his* three young children were spending a normal summer at home. Mrs. Thurmond retorted that she wouldn't think of leaving the children behind. "We just wanted to keep the family together. Besides," she admitted, "because of the difference in Strom's and my age, people are interested in our children. If I didn't bring them along, people would wonder where they were."

Thurmond, too, was unapologetic. "It showed the family was human," he later explained. "Some families wouldn't have paid that price. (Mine) didn't sit back in air-conditioned houses. They got out and sweated in the sun."

To enhance his reputation for vigor, the senator slid down the pole at a fire station in Columbia where Strom junior was celebrating his sixth birthday. Concerned that photographers might miss a good shot, he repeated the slide twice more. One reporter who watched the performance aptly observed in his story that Thurmond was "no shrinking violet or stickler for dignity."

Thurmond sought to make money an issue in the race, portraying Ravenel as a big-spending liberal whose campaign was bankrolled by northern investors. The tactic seemed to work. When old-time political foe Solomon Blatt announced his support for Thurmond, he said he was proud to back the incumbent and opposed a man who "would make a good third senator from New York"—a jab that haunted Ravenel throughout the campaign. It was true that he had made fund-raising excursions outside of South Carolina and drew on his contacts from his days at Harvard. One of the more obvious moves, a fund-raising letter from "Harvard Business School Friends of Charles 'Pug' Ravenel," appears, wisely, to have been circulated only in the New York City area. It was the sort of campaign pitch that would have been poorly received back home.

But if Ravenel received out-of-state money, so did Thurmond. *The Columbia Record* reported in September that the senator had raised two-thirds of his nearly one million dollars from out-of-state sources. Most of it, the paper said, came from small contributors reached by direct-mail specialist Richard Viguerie, who had raised money for Ronald Reagan and Senator Jesse Helms. Ravenel had raised about the same percentage of funds out of state, but had gathered only half of what Thurmond had taken in. The sources of each man's funding offer telling signs of their relative strengths. Notably absent from the Ravenel coffers were contributions from state Democratic officials who would have been expected to support him. Also missing were contributions from prominent Democratic businessmen and bankers, a reflection of Ravenel's support of a labor reform bill that was unpopular with local industry. Ravenel did receive large contributions from organized labor.

Thurmond, on the other hand, logged in hefty amounts from the textile industry, oil and gas interests, and from defense contractors who wanted to show their appreciation for the senator's support of military spending.

With good reason, Ravenel was counting on solid support from the black community, which now made up 26 percent of the state electorate. *A Black Voter's Guide to the 1978 Elections* listed Thurmond as one of twenty-four people in Congress hostile to black interests. In its introductory piece on the senator, the guide cited his votes against the 1965 Voting Rights Act, its 1970 and 1975 extensions, his opposition to Thurgood Marshall's Supreme Court nomination, and his support for G. Harrold Carswell. And it reminded black voters of his 1948 campaign: "There are not enough troops in the army to force southern people to admit Negroes into our theaters, swimming pools and homes."

The pamphlet's recommendation was blunt: "Thurmond has been trying to shed his racist image by wooing black support," the guide said, "but the black electorate must not be fooled by these gestures. Thurmond's voting record on issues important to blacks remains dismal. The Ravenel campaign must work to produce a large black turnout in the general election and so ensure Thurmond's defeat."

That task was more difficult than it appeared from afar. David Broder, *The Washington Post*'s highly regarded political reporter, got a flavor of the racial dynamics of the campaign when he came to South Carolina in its closing days. During a stop at the state fair, a black woman saw Thurmond and rushed up to introduce herself. "Senator, I'm Darley Cochran from Clarendon County. You sent that newsletter saying to let you know if you could help, and I want to tell you you've helped." Turning to Broder, she explained that the senator had helped in getting funds for a park and sewage treatment plant in her predominantly black community. Broder asked her if she planned to vote for a man who had walked out of the Democratic Party over civil rights and joined the "Goldwater Republican Party."

Sounding like a later version of Victoria DeLee, Cochran said, "I'm forgetting about the party. I'm for the man that's getting the job done."

Columnists Rowland Evans and Robert Novak heard a similar story when they visited the state. A black clergyman from McCormick (the town a few miles from Thurmond's Edgefield roots, where the senator had taught school) explained why he was going to vote for the senator: "My boy got burned real bad eleven years ago, and Senator Thurmond had him carried to a hospital in Cincinnati. It saved his life." The senator had gotten a special U.S. Air Force plane to transfer the boy north. Evans and Novak noted that it was "a constituent service not available to every senator but well within the gift of Thurmond," who by then was a senior member of the Armed Services Committee.

Thurmond also won the endorsement of the state's black mayors, a sign of their appreciation for the federal money that was reaching municipal coffers. And he had gotten additional help from William T. Coleman, Jr., secretary of transportation under Gerald Ford and one of the most prominent black Republicans. Coleman and the Thurmonds had become friends in Washington, so when the senator asked him to campaign in South Carolina, the former secretary was happy to oblige. Coleman, however, sensitive to southern mores, asked one of Thurmond's aides before leaving Washington whether he should keep a respectful distance from Mrs. Thurmond when she met him at the airport. He was used to greeting her with a friendly hug. Flustered for a moment, the young aide excused himself to make further inquiry. The word from the senator's office was to greet Nancy Thurmond as he always had.

Countering these voices of black support was some highly vocal opposition. The caucus of black state legislators endorsed Ravenel and used their announcement to excoriate Thurmond. Representative Robert Woods of Charleston called him a "radical who has refused to compromise on issues that dealt with race. He is the kind of person who is forced to have placed upon him the kinds of principles that this great nation accepted long before his birth. In his attempt to prevent others from living up to those principles he became an embarrassment to South Carolina."

Such harsh judgments were possible because, for all his attention to the black community, Thurmond neither appreciated the deprivations white society forced upon blacks nor committed himself to their alleviation. Questioned about his record by a black student at the University of South Carolina, the senator gave his usual answer: "When I was governor, the laws said the races should be separated. But now the law is different, customs are different, public opinion has changed, and it's an entirely different situation." As if to underscore the point, he noted that he had pushed a black civil rights lawyer for the federal bench in South Carolina and had voted in favor of granting voting representation in Congress to the heavily black District of Columbia.

The senator's stock reply was both artful and superficial, consonant with a man who spoke of himself as a neutral participant in government, one who had no responsibility to question whether the old laws were good ones, even after blacks had challenged them. There was, as well, no hint of his fierce resistance to the federal mandates requiring an end to segregation. Custom and tradition had changed in spite of him, not because of him. It was a tribute to his political skills that he could, without apology, ignore the past like some bothersome gnat.

One Republican strategist told Broder that the senator had "made his way with the black folks, and they are not mad at him anymore. He's anesthetized them." Dent embellished the notion. "Thurmond these last few years, instead of being the shrill negative voice, has been Mr. Deliveryman—for blacks as well as whites. The state has changed and he's changed with it. He's an ideologue who ain't crazy."

The State's endorsement of Thurmond November 2 reflected his hold on South Carolina. During his long career, the paper observed, "Mr. Thurmond had been guided by personal integrity and conviction rather than by political affiliation. His detractors, of whom there are an appreciable number, point to his break with the national Democratic Party in 1948 to lead the States' Rights Democrats and to his switch, in 1964, to the Republican Party. But in each instance, as was also the case when he won election to the U.S. Senate as a write-in candidate, he has reflected the prevailing sentiment of a majority of his fellow Carolinians—

standing firm for his (their) convictions while adapting to changed circumstances and attitudes."

The State praised Ravenel for turning his "energy, ambition and resources toward public service" but said that because of his "record of personal service to his county, state and nation—and to his conscience—Sen. Strom Thurmond deserves reelection."

Thurmond prevailed November 7 by 70,500 votes—55.6 percent of the electorate. It was the closest race of his career. Tossing a barb at Ravenel, several Thurmond workers came into headquarters election night with handmade badges declaring, "The debate is over."

Shortly after the election Thurmond made a special point of sending certificates of appreciation to the ten black mayors who had endorsed him. (There were no statewide estimates of how many blacks had voted for Thurmond. *The News and Courier* reported that in Charleston's twenty-three predominantly black precincts he won only 17 percent of the vote.)

Over in Mississippi, the Eastland years were coming to a close, and a much younger man, a Republican, was on the rise. Thad Cochran's eventual victories on election day could be traced to the partisan realignment Thurmond had fostered.

Cochran had had no thoughts of a political career when he finished law school at Ole Miss in 1965. His goal was to have a lucrative practice in Jackson, and he was well on his way when Nixon's 1968 presidential campaign drew his eye. What he particularly liked was the candidate's desire to moderate the upheaval the South had experienced under Lyndon Johnson. Like many other white Mississippians, Cochran was chagrined by his state's violent reaction to the push for civil rights, and he shared their distress at Ross Barnett's clumsy handling of the Meredith affair in Oxford. But now he wanted to slow things down and let Mississippi catch its breath.

Cochran believed Nixon was committed to civil rights, and he felt comfortable that going to work for this Republican was not a coded message for holding on to segregation. Cochran joined the nonpartisan "Citizens for Nixon," but despite the committee's hard work—and the visible support of Thurmond—Mississippians in 1968 voted overwhelmingly for George Wallace.

Four years later, when a vacancy opened up in the congressional district that included Jackson, Cochran decided to run for the seat as a Republican. But he warned state party officials that he intended to campaign for black votes and to present himself as supportive of civil rights. He won the seat easily, but by his third term Cochran was growing restless.

More than a year in advance of 1978's senatorial election, rumors abounded that Senator Eastland, now seventy-three years old, had lost his zest for the job and was ready to come home for good. He had told Cochran as much and also informed some of his close associates, but several of them persuaded Eastland that he should run again, partly on the promise that he would face no Democratic primary challenges.

By March those reassurances had evaporated, and Eastland announced his retirement. Cochran, who in deference to Eastland had decided not to pursue the seat, now threw his hat into the ring. He won election with a plurality of 45 percent, beating Democrat Maurice Dantin and independent Charles Evers, brother of the slain Medgar Evers. (Evers had siphoned off nearly 23 percent of the vote, most of it coming from blacks, that might otherwise have gone to Dantin.)

The link between Cochran's victory and Thurmond's 1964 party switch is neither obvious nor direct, but it does exist. The label "Republican" had been anathema to white southerners since the time of Reconstruction, but Goldwater redefined the party's ideology in a way that comforted white southern segregationists. Thurmond first lent his credibility to the Goldwater cause and then four years later to Richard Nixon's quest for the White House. By the time Cochran wanted to run for the House in 1972 in Nixon's embrace, the GOP had become a credible force in southern politics. By 1978, many white southerners considered it the party to protect their interests, and while Cochran might not have exploited this usually unspoken message (he was not the doctrinaire conservative many Mississippi Republicans were), he was, by his own admission, a beneficiary.

Although Eastland and Thurmond shared the same ideology, they were very different politicians. Thurmond thrived on contact with constituents; Eastland was never comfortable with personal appearances, preferring to let Mississippi's power brokers line up support. This was heresy to Thurmond, who could never have been described as Eastland was by one Mississippi newspaper: "Nothing is more incongruous than to see Senator Eastland with a baseball cap on his balding head, a dollar cigar held like a baby clutching a teething ring, listening to the plight of an economically wounded little farmer."

Their responses to a changing constituency also illuminated their differences. Thurmond hired Tom Moss in 1971. It took Eastland another six and a half years before he put a black on his staff.

Eastland's retirement meant that Senator Edward Kennedy of Massachusetts, as liberal as Eastland was conservative, would take over the Judiciary Committee. And because three other Republicans had left the Senate, the very moderate Charles Mathias, Jr., of Maryland was in line to be Judiciary's GOP leader. But Thurmond had other ideas.

Senate custom is to allow an individual senator to hold the position of ranking minority member on only one committee at a time, and Thurmond was already senior Republican on Armed Services. Confident that John Tower, who was next in line, could protect Republican interests there, and concerned about having such a moderate party member representing the GOP on Judiciary, Thurmond exercised his seniority and stepped in front of Mathias to take the ranking position on that committee. As the senior Republican it would now be his duty to work out a relationship with Kennedy on behalf of his GOP colleagues. Neither Kennedy nor Thurmond knew just how short Kennedy's tenure would be.

14. BACK OVER THE RUBICON: A MAN REDEEMED, A LIFE REMEMBERED

1980–1992

WHEN THURMOND WOKE up in Aiken the morning of November 5, 1980, control of the Senate Judiciary Committee was his for the asking. What had happened overnight was more than a presidential election of landslide dimensions. It was the end of a half-century of looking to Washington to solve every problem. To pull the country out of the Depression, Roosevelt had concentrated power in the capital, and in the intervening decades this notion of a strong and beneficent central government had been sustained by Truman, protected by Eisenhower, mined to the core by Johnson, preserved by Nixon, and inadvertently buried by Jimmy Carter when a wave of discontent with his leadership swept Ronald Reagan into the White House. Although he had campaigned for the presidency as an outsider, Carter shared the overall philosophy of Roosevelt and Johnson, and it was ironic that opposition to a southerner's administration had pushed the country back toward the limited government so long advocated by others from the South.

Happy as Thurmond was to see Reagan in the White House—though he had initially backed John Connally—more important for the senator was the electoral disaffection that had spilled over to the Senate races. Republicans picked up twelve new seats, and for the first time in twenty-eight years the GOP would be in control of the chamber. For the first time in his twenty-six years in Washington, Thurmond would be in a majority party whose views he shared.

There is no better way to gauge the upheaval than by what happened in the Senate Judiciary Committee. Ted Kennedy, the embodiment of northern liberalism, had been at the helm for two years. Overnight, the reins of the committee were moving into the hands of a man who had left the Democratic Party over civil rights—this at a time when the all-important Voting Rights Act would be up for renewal again. It looked as though Kennedy's tenure had been but a brief intermission between two acts of southern obstructionism, one from Mississippi, the other from South Carolina.

Thurmond played right into that script in his first press interviews after the election and at a news conference when he returned to Washington. Reporters and Senate aides, crowded into the committee's hearing room in the building named for Everett Dirksen, heard the senator talk about gutting the Voting Rights Act and getting the federal government out of education altogether. Civil rights lobbyists shook their heads in distress, and reporters smiled in near disbelief that Thurmond was giving them such a good story.

In the back of the room—"226 Dirksen" was the informal address—Dennis Shedd, a lawyer on Thurmond's staff, shook his own head in disappointment that verged on disgust. The senator had done himself a disservice, he thought, acting like a stereotypical southern segregationist instead of a thoughtful, if conservative, legislator. Shedd had been hired by Thurmond in August of 1978 at the recommendation of Harry Dent. His first job was handling constituent problems, but he had moved on to Judiciary work by the next year. By the middle of 1981 he would have a senior position with responsibility for the most sensitive legislative issues on the senator's agenda. Shedd's goal would be reasoned moderation.

At the suggestion of Lee Atwater, who was now working in the White House, Thurmond hired Mark Goodin, a young reporter from Anderson, to handle the press. There was instant rapport between Shedd and Goodin—in fact Shedd had paid for Goodin's plane ticket to Washington for his interview and had put him up in his apartment for the night. For nearly six years, the two would be the 1980s version of Dent and Buzhardt, advising the senator at a time in his career when he had more visibility than ever before. Each of the young men—young enough to be his grandsons—well understood that Thurmond assumed the committee dais with a reputation that would be a silent partner to every move he made.

Only one of the senator's contemporaries from the days of opposition remained, Stennis of Mississippi. While he was a reliably conservative southerner, he had devoted most of his time in the Senate to defense issues and had never opposed civil rights as vocally as Thurmond. So of all the southern senators who had dug in their heels for states' rights, it was Thurmond who would have the greatest challenge in revisiting these issues in a new world not at all of his making. That he would succeed with his rough-hewn charm was proof once again of his intuitive political skill. Nor had he lost the equally important ability to recognize good advice when he heard it. In this sixth decade of his career Thurmond would win easy reelection in 1984 and then completely dominate the opposition six years later, a month before his eighty-eighth birthday.

Beyond the accommodations he had made with the black electorate, Thurmond's image had been helped by the type of Republicans swept into the Senate in 1980—a group whose brand of conservatism, like that of Jesse Helms, was much more rigid than his. It was ideology with a hard edge, resistant to the diversity in American society. Compared to these newcomers, Thurmond would look like an elder statesman, and the very legislative business before his committee—abortion, busing, school prayer—was going to prove that the touted "Reagan revolution" had its limits. The less astute foot soldiers in the philosophical war would find themselves out of office after one term in the Senate. Their successors, who followed a more moderate line, would play a critical role in another battle royal over a Supreme Court nominee, this time with the Senate back in Democratic control. A byproduct of the occasionally rough confirmation proceedings would be a national consensus that the civil rights advances that had begun in 1954 were now an accepted part of American life.

Thurmond could live with this even if he never wanted to take back 1948, never recanted the daylong filibuster, nor lost his distaste for civil rights "agitators" and "so-called emancipators." But his six-year stewardship of the Judiciary Committee provided some balance to a career that otherwise would have been remembered only for obstructionism. It was as much what he didn't do when he had the power as what he did.

When Thurmond began his political career, there was one political party in the South, the Democrats, and all of them were white. His switch to the Republican Party at first looked like a gamble in a region so steeped in the Democratic Party tradition, but Thurmond had struck a chord of unease in the white community, and many white southerners followed him out of the Democratic column in droves. Today there are two parties in the South, and by 1990 the GOP in South Carolina was nearly dominant and virtually all white. The Democrats were struggling to hold together a coalition of black Carolinians and moderate-to-liberal whites.

By the way he had framed the issues in the fifties and sixties, Thurmond ultimately helped turn the Republican Party into one that spoke largely to white interests. The 1988 presidential campaign was further evidence of this political transformation. Lee Atwater, the senator's tough, glib protégé, was a high-technology version of Ben Tillman, putting together a strategy for George Bush that exploited racial fears. Bush was portrayed in the 1988 contest as the white protector, his opponent, Michael Dukakis, as the modern-day equivalent of a Radical Reconstructionist.

But by the time he became Judiciary chairman, Thurmond symbolized more than the resistance of the sixties and partisan realignment in the South. He had also shown that accommodation and adjustment were possible. The senator always believed he was "standing with the people," and his great strength in a half-century of public life was determining who and where the people were and finding a way to reach them. His continued reelections were proof of his success. The whole of his career became not only the story of a gifted politician, but an illustration of how the franchise can bring change—just as George Lee had argued twenty-five years earlier in Belzoni, Mississippi.

The transition period after the 1980 elections was busy but sweet, a time to plan and to savor the Republicans' victory. As soon as the results were certain, Thurmond called Dent to tease him that he had been "wrong again" about politics. In their discussions over switching parties sixteen years earlier, Dent had listed all the possible negatives, and one of them was that Thurmond would never get to be a committee chairman because, for the foreseeable future, the Democrats would maintain their hold on the Senate.

As was his custom after election day, Thurmond headed back to Washington so that he could meet with his staff and begin planning for the next Senate session. The office was ebullient, but the senator was all seriousness, lecturing his aides about their added responsibilities now that they were the majority party.

Thurmond's decision to take over the Judiciary Committee instead of Armed Services, where he could have been chairman, was a perfect fit for Shedd, an honors graduate of Wofford College in Spartanburg (Olin Johnston's alma mater) and an honors graduate of the University of South Carolina law school.

Thurmond didn't mind that Shedd and some other close aides were disappointed with his postelection comments on civil rights. What mattered to him was making clear that the Kennedy era was over. When he was asked during this transition period whether he would treat Kennedy fairly, Thurmond replied with a straight face that he would treat him "just as fairly as he treated me."

The senator's remarks on civil rights had caught Dent's attention, and he, like Shedd, was disconcerted by their tone. He called the senator to offer an updated version of the advice he had given ten years earlier, before Tom Moss was hired. "You've got to move," Dent told him. "It's time to go with the flow."

In his own way, the senator was making accommodations. The rhetoric of his statements might have been Old South, but many of his actions recognized modern-day realities. At the end of November he invited a group of black Reagan supporters from South Carolina to meet with him in Washington to "discuss matters of mutual concern." Eager that constituents know of his overture, Thurmond's staff put out a press release describing the event.

But Thurmond was first and foremost a conservative. When the new Senate convened in January, he made good on his promise to move the Judiciary Committee to the right of center by recruiting three new conservative Republicans. Two of them were southerners like himself: John East of North Carolina, who with Helms's backing had come from nowhere to knock off one-term senator Robert Morgan; and Alabama's Jeremiah Denton, a Vietnam hero who had been a longtime prisoner of war. The other conservative Republican was Charles Grassley of Iowa, a former state legislator. Neither Denton nor Grassley was a lawyer—a break with committee tradition—but their conservative credentials were good. Pressed by reporters about his choices, Thurmond waved off their queries with dispatch: "You don't have to be a lawyer to know the law." The fourth new Republican was Arlen Specter of Pennsylvania, who had been a prosecutor in Philadelphia and was more moderate than many of his party colleagues.

In addition to adding conservative voices to the committee, Thurmond also rearranged the subcommittee structure, abolishing the one on antitrust so that he could keep control of these matters—the only ones in Judiciary's jurisdiction that involved big business and big money. Chairmanship of the Constitution Subcommittee, which would get first crack at voting rights legislation, went to Utah Republican Orrin Hatch, who had made a name for himself two years earlier leading the successful opposition to changes in the labor laws sought by big unions.

Always frugal with money, Thurmond also immediately cut about one million dollars from the committee budget, resulting in a reduction in the number of committee staff, which had grown considerably in Kennedy's two years. The old Constitution Subcommittee alone had had thirty-five staff members.

As the senior senator in the majority party, Thurmond also became president *pro tempore* of the Senate, a ceremonial post that made him fourth in line for the presidency, after the vice-president and Speaker of the House. Although the position had no power, Thurmond took his role seriously, interrupting committee business, if necessary, to open the Senate every day for official business. He also had special key chains made that were decorated with his signature and the "president pro tempore" legend. He passed them out to visitors who came by to see him.

Voting rights, the main civil rights issue that would confront Thurmond as Judiciary chairman, would not come before the committee for nearly a year, but by the summer of 1981 the spotlight fell on the panel when Reagan executed his own bold stroke and nominated Sandra Day O'Connor, an Arizona state judge and former legislator, to be the first woman on the Supreme Court. She was picked to succeed Potter Stewart, who had retired when the court term ended July 3.

O'Connor's nomination was the first in what was to be a

continual struggle between Republicans and Democrats over filling federal judicial vacancies. Jimmy Carter had made an obvious and concerted attempt to change the demographics of the bench by appointing women, blacks, and other minorities to seats that had been held for nearly two centuries by white men. But diversity on the federal bench was not high on the new administration's list of priorities. The Reagan administration made clear that it intended to change the course of federal law by seeking out judges who shared conservative GOP ideology. The younger the better so that they could stay in their life-tenured positions for decades.

Thurmond would demonstrate his loyalty to the president by playing hardball politics to get Reagan's nominees on the bench. He would also demonstrate the power that comes with controlling the committee schedule, forcing Democrats onto his timetable for processing nominations and short-circuiting what he believed were obstructionist delays—a tactic he knew well.

The selection of a woman for the Supreme Court gave the O'Connor confirmation proceedings a different cast. Archconservatives worried about whether she would support their efforts to restrict the right of women to obtain abortions, and they feared she might be a secret feminist who would be biased in favor of women when they came before her as litigants.

The hearings, which Thurmond set for the first week in September, would be a test for him, too. Though not quite the sophisticated southern gentleman, he had been imbued with traditional southern male sensibilities, which came into play almost automatically around women. He had already raised eyebrows and earned himself some public jabs back in January when a group of women testified about William French Smith's membership in a club that excluded women. He had been nominated to be attorney general.

As the women—all of them professionals—sat down at the witness table in the committee hearing room, Thurmond observed, "These are the prettiest witnesses we have had in a long time. I imagine you are all married. If not, you could be if you wanted to be."

Titters ran through the audience. The witnesses were surprised and irritated. Thurmond had meant no harm. He thought he was paying them a compliment and was oblivious to the element of chauvinism in his comments.

Later Thurmond told the women that while he favored equal opportunity for women "in every way," there had to be limits.

"Suppose a group of men got together and had a men's exercise club? One of the exercisers wore nothing but an athletic belt. Would it be appropriate for a woman to be there with them?" he asked.

"We came here today to address the question of a public servant and his responsibilities," one of the witnesses frostily replied, "not to argue the merits or demerits of male clubs versus female clubs."

By the time of the O'Connor hearings, Dennis Shedd had moved into a more senior position and was making his presence felt with the senator. He wanted to make sure that there would be no "prettiest witnesses" comments and no gaffs about appropriate dress in the gym. He tried to impress upon the senator that while chivalry might still be alive, some things had changed. He urged him to treat any woman who came before the committee, including the nominee herself, exactly as he would treat a male nominee and male lawyers coming before the committee.

In addition to watching out for the senator's short-term interests, Shedd, along with Goodin, was also looking ahead to the senator's next reelection. Admittedly it was three years away, but there had already been speculation that Richard Riley, the popular Democratic governor, was thinking about mounting a challenge. It was important that the senator avoid mistakes that would give Riley an opening to seize.

Shedd reminded the senator that the hearings would provide opportunities for good television footage that could be used during the campaign. He told other aides that he wanted no whispering in the senator's ear during the proceedings. That might be all right for a senator in his forties or fifties, but for one who was almost seventy-nine, it took on a completely different meaning.

With television cameras ever more present in congressional hearings, the senator's wardrobe was revamped to give him a better image. Instead of plaids and checks, he now wore tasteful dark suits. Occasionally, he was reminded on his daily schedule card to "wear the blue suit, with a white shirt and red tie"—the standard for the Senate's ninety-eight men when the cameras were to be present.

Thurmond presided over the O'Connor sessions like a gracious host. To accommodate the great interest in the proceedings, he and the Democrats agreed to move them out of the committee's hearing room to a cavernous room on the first floor of the

Dirksen Building that could hold several hundred people. At the opening session, the senator escorted O'Connor down the center aisle as though she were a bride and he were giving her away. He left her at the witness table and then made his way to the dais to gavel the proceedings to order. Throughout the three days of testimony he treated all the witnesses, men and women, in a respectful manner. (Old habits die hard, however. At a hearing a few years later, the senator told a well-regarded woman law professor that when he was in school, he never had such a pretty teacher. Likewise, he was fond of referring to his sons as fine athletes and his daughters as great beauties.)

Thurmond had known ahead of time that Denton, an avowed opponent of abortion, wanted to grill O'Connor on the subject. And as the hearing went on it became clear that the new senator was unhappy that the nominee would not state whether she opposed *Roe v. Wade,* the landmark 1973 decision that made abortion legal nationwide. To help deflect Denton's possible opposition, Thurmond gave him extra time, letting him question O'Connor repeatedly on the subject. Thurmond's patience paid off. O'Connor was unanimously confirmed by the Senate on September 25.

The O'Connor proceedings had been Thurmond's first test of leadership, but the measure of how much he and the South he represented had changed would be his handling of the voting rights legislation.

The senator's opposition to the original 1965 law and the two extensions in 1970 and 1975, and his apparent lack of enthusiasm now for any new extension, mirrored white Carolina's hostile relationship with black voters. The *Elmore* and *Brown* decisions of 1947 and 1948, which in theory allowed blacks to vote in the Democratic Party primary, had not ended the problems. In subsequent years, even after the 1965 law, blacks seeking to vote had encountered continued resistance, particularly in areas where they outnumbered whites or came close to it. In 1959 the Civil Rights Commission had investigated McCormick County, where Thurmond first taught, and uncovered telling information. Although blacks made up nearly 63 percent of the population, not a single one was registered to vote. The first black subsequently registered in August 1959 followed by three more early in May of 1960. After the attorney general announced later in the month that county records were going to be inspected, another forty-five blacks registered, but the commission reported in a subsequent study that some of them soon lost their jobs. As a result, only one of the forty-nine registered blacks voted in the June primary, and none voted in the November election. "Fear of reprisals was the principal reason why Negroes had not registered until May 1960, and the same fear has deterred any further registration or voting," the commission said.

When northern senators in 1964 cited the report as evidence of why that year's civil rights bill was needed, Thurmond jumped to his state's defense and pilloried the commission for stretching to reach "preordained conclusions." The agency itself, he noted, had acknowledged receiving no sworn complaints from South Carolina. "It is difficult for me to imagine any group of men possessing intuitive powers sufficient to reveal a pattern of discrimination when there are absolutely no facts to substantiate such a claim," Thurmond bellowed. "Their conclusion that voting rights were being denied was reached in spite of, rather than because of, the fact that . . . no suits had been filed by the attorney general."

Thurmond's home county of Edgefield had its own special history, going back to Ben Tillman and the Hamburg killings of 1876. Even after the Voting Rights Act of 1965, blacks, who made up more than half the population, were only 39.6 percent of the registered voters. No black had ever been elected to the county council or the county school board. That was because these panels were chosen by an "at-large" election, which permitted every voter to vote on every vacancy; there was no geographic representation. White candidates, therefore, could always outpoll a black, who would have to reach across racial lines to win support—an unlikely prospect.

Tom McCain, born in McCormick but a resident of Edgefield for thirty years, wanted to change that. A product of the county's black-only schools—the Bettis Academy that Thurmond had tried to help as a young lawyer in 1935, and Edgefield County Colored High School—McCain earned a bachelor's degree at Paine College in nearby Augusta and then earned a master's degree in mathematics from the University of Georgia. After registering to vote in 1967, he noticed that despite the large black population in the county, no blacks were involved in precinct work and not one had been elected to any office since Reconstruction.

By 1970, McCain had decided that the black community

should move to become part of the process, and after gathering like-minded neighbors he showed up at a precinct meeting, where he and his group outnumbered the white organizers. The session was hastily put off until enough white residents could get to the building to keep control of the precinct, but McCain's sister was elected an alternate delegate to Democratic Party gatherings. A short time later McCain received a phone call telling him he had been assigned to the wrong precinct. He was instructed to report to one that was nearly 80 percent black but with only a handful of the blacks registered to vote. McCain quickly undertook a registration drive, and within months he was elected to the precinct's executive committee.

By 1974 McCain wanted to run for the county council. He paid the filing fee, but the Democratic Party refused to put his name on the ballot. Party officials put his fifty-dollar check in a safety-deposit box while he pursued a complaint through the Justice Department.

By this time white Edgefield had been aware of McCain's activism for four years. In 1970 he had fought to give blacks a voice in planning the integration of Strom Thurmond High School. Although school opened on schedule that year, by the middle of September black members of the football team, band, and cheerleading squad were boycotting games to protest the high school's official name, its nickname—"the Rebels"—and the waving of the Confederate flag at school functions. McCain and others filed a lawsuit claiming the nickname and flag amounted to the "badges and indicia of slavery and second-class citizenship of Negroes." In October, seventy-five students staged a walkout, and a local judge issued an order to stop the protests. Finally, the two sides reached a compromise. They would still be the Rebels of Strom Thurmond High, but the playing of "Dixie" and displays of the Confederate flag would no longer be allowed at school events.

McCain had also been the prime mover behind lawsuits that successfully challenged the exclusion of blacks from grand juries as well as the separation of prisoners on chain gangs by race. So when he found himself unable to run for the council in 1974, he decided it was time to challenge the county's at-large election plan. With help from the American Civil Liberties Union office in Atlanta, McCain filed a lawsuit charging that the election procedure unconstitutionally weakened the voting strength of Edgefield's blacks.

Judge Robert F. Chapman, a Spartanburg lawyer who had been appointed to the bench by Nixon, heard the case at the end of November 1975, but procedural complications delayed his ruling four and a half years, until April 1980. Chapman sided with the plaintiffs, using the starkest language to conclude that the county's at-large election system had kept blacks from government positions. "The court's overall finding," he wrote, "is that blacks were virtually totally excluded up to 1970 and since that time they have progressed to minimal tokenism."

Some barriers to black participation had been removed before the lawsuit, but he found that "there is still a long history of racial discrimination in all areas of life, with bloc voting by whites on a scale that this court has never before witnessed."

To those who argued that the only legal requirement was the right to cast a ballot, Chapman offered a sharp rebuttal. "Participation in the election process does not mean simply the elimination of legal, formal or official barriers," he said. "The standard is whether the electoral system . . . tends to make it more difficult for blacks to participate with full effectiveness in the election process and to have their votes fully effective and equal to those of whites. Blacks have no right to elect any particular candidate or number of candidates," Chapman added, "but the law requires that black voters and candidates have a fair chance of being successful in elections."

Although by that time a black had been appointed to the county school board and was subsequently allowed to run unopposed, Chapman concluded that the black member "obviously serves as a token and at the pleasure of the white power structure."

The district court victory was short-lived. Not long after the decision was announced, the Supreme Court ruled in an Alabama case that an at-large method of election that had been challenged under Section Two of the 1965 law wasn't unconstitutional unless the process had been created for the *purpose* of racial discrimination. Unlike the Section Five preclearance provision, which covered only selected southern states and counties, Section Two applied to the entire country. It barred states and political subdivisions from adopting election laws or procedures that denied or hampered the right to vote. Edgefield blacks had laboriously proved the effect of the county electoral system, but they had not shown that the process was part of a deliberate plan to disfranchise them. Chapman withdrew his order, and the Supreme Court had created a new issue to be fought out in the struggle to renew the 1965 law.

It was true that Thurmond had not lived in Edgefield County since early 1947, when he moved into the governor's mansion. But to advocates of a strong voting rights law, he would always be a son of Edgefield. (A statue of him in the pose of a country lawyer stands at the center of the square facing the courthouse.) To them he remained the adversary—and nothing about that changed when they heard his harsh words after assuming chairmanship of the Judiciary Committee.

Between November 1980 and early summer of 1981 Thurmond tempered his remarks on voting rights, saying that he could support an extension of the law if the enforcement provisions were expanded to cover the entire nation. But critics considered this the same as gutting the law because valuable resources would have to be spent in areas that had no history of discrimination.

On June 28, in reaction to Thurmond's position on the Voting Rights Act, hundreds of protesters gathered at a rally in Edgefield sponsored by the local NAACP and Jesse Jackson's Chicago-based Operation PUSH. Jackson, a native of Greenville, made reference to the county's charged history when he encouraged the crowd to be disciplined and "send a clear message of what is on our minds. We didn't come as Pitchfork Ben," he said, "but we come as citizens asking to share in our government. We don't want to dominate, we want to participate."

Two days later in Washington, Jackson, flanked by McCain and other civil rights activists from South Carolina, delivered the message to Thurmond in person. Seeking to avoid the circus atmosphere of a press event, the senator saw the group in his private office in the Capitol and then later declined to discuss it with reporters.

Even before the 1980 elections gave Republicans control of the Senate, civil rights lobbyists had been preparing a strategy for the voting rights bill that called for action in the House first. The wisdom of that decision was only reinforced by the need to face an unsympathetic White House and a less receptive Senate. In the House, by contrast, advocates could start the all-important hearings in friendly surroundings, before the House Judiciary Committee's Subcommittee on Civil and Constitutional Rights. Chairman

Don Edwards of California was a committed liberal, much more moderate even than his own district, and if he wasn't the most dynamic speaker, he was a careful legislator who believed that planning and meticulous vote counting were the essentials to victory.

On May 6, 1981, Edwards's subcommittee began several days of hearings in Washington and in the South to build the case for renewing the principal enforcement mechanism, the Section Five preclearance. One key Republican, Henry Hyde of Illinois, the senior GOP member on Edwards's panel, had not been so sure that the Voting Rights Act should continue, but during a hearing June 12 in Montgomery, he said he now could see that voting rights abuses still existed and that federal protections were still required. In an instant, the terms of the debate had shifted. The question no longer was whether the Voting Rights Act should be extended but what the extension should look like.

Edwards and Hyde and their staffs negotiated through much of June and July without making substantial progress, but to move the legislation forward, the subcommittee approved a simple ten-year extension, leaving the more serious dickering to the full committee. The eventual compromise made the Section Five preclearance permanent but added a section that allowed states that had substantially curbed voting rights abuses to get out from under the preclearance requirement. This became known as the "bailout" section.

Hyde considered the compromise unworkable because the requirements for a bailout were too stringent. He tried to amend the bill when the full House debated it in the fall, but he and his supporters—southerners and conservative northerners—were no match for the intense lobbying campaign the civil rights community had been mounting since spring. A coalition of black, Hispanic, religious, and labor groups had made countless lobbying visits emphasizing the need for strong legislation. Their personal entreaties were backed up by grass-roots pressure at home. As the amendments were voted on October 5, the proposals were crushed by huge margins, some better than three to one. The final vote on the bill was 389–24. Although South Carolina's six congressmen had voted in favor of amendments to water down the bill, each of them voted to pass the final measure, including the four Republicans—a fact that Thurmond would be reminded of many times in the coming months.

The House legislation overturned the troublesome Supreme

Court decision requiring proof of intentional discrimination. New Section Two language said a voting rights violation could be proved by showing that an election procedure had been imposed "in a manner which results" in voting discrimination. The section had caused barely a ripple in the House, but it would produce a flood of debate in the Senate.

In contrast to previous civil rights measures going back nearly twenty years, this legislation had been put together without participation by the administration. Although the specter of White House opposition had loomed overhead, all President Reagan did was request that Attorney General Smith make a thorough study of the act and give him a recommendation by the first of October. On that day, Reagan said he supported the Voting Rights Act in principle, but he declined to endorse the House bill.

Over in the Senate there had already been negotiations over a timetable for action on the bill. But when no agreement had been reached by October 14, nine days after the House bill was passed, Democratic senators reached back to one of their old protective tactics and placed the House bill directly on the Senate calendar. It was insurance against a burial in the Judiciary Committee if Thurmond tried to run things the way Eastland had.

The new chairman was not happy, calling it "a mistake" to try to bypass his panel and promising that "hearings will be held by the Judiciary Committee whether the bill is referred to it or not."

Civil rights lobbyists were eager to set a schedule. The law expired in mid-August 1982, and they worried that opponents could delay until time ran out.

There had been pressure from archconservatives to do just that. Quentin Crommelin, a Thurmond aide from Alabama who had been hired before Thurmond became committee chairman, had approved of the senator's hard line on civil rights. He argued that Republicans could tie up the bill in committee until it expired. Shedd told Crommelin that was unrealistic and that whether he thought so or not, the bill was going to come before the Senate. (Crommelin left Thurmond's staff not long after.) At a subsequent meeting of Republican Senate staff, an aide to Jesse Helms, the most visible right-wing senator, contended that it was good strategy for the GOP senators to fight the bill to the end.

"Maybe it will help in your state," Shedd retorted, "but I can't believe it would help any Republican anywhere else."

Shedd was thinking of his own boss's political future. Thurmond was never going to get more than a fraction of the black vote. He had a solid lock on the white conservative vote, but neither one alone was enough to win an election. The key was the middle ground, that group of largely white younger voters, many of them newcomers to the state, who hardly knew Thurmond. If they knew anything at all about him, they knew the caricature, not the character. The important thing was to avoid alienating these voters, to show that despite his age—he would be nearly eighty-two for this reelection—he was a man of the times in all senses. To appear once again as the old segregationist would not do him any good where he most needed support.

Civil rights lobbyists, of course, were not privy to these discussions. All they had to go on were Thurmond's attacks on the voting rights law in years past, from which they assumed they could predict his behavior now.

As further insurance against delay, in December Kennedy and Mathias introduced a Senate version of the House bill with just enough Senate cosponsors to break a filibuster. (The rule for cloture had been changed from two-thirds of the senators voting to a flat sixty votes.)

"They must not have read the bill," Thurmond sputtered to a reporter after he learned how many cosponsors were on it.

By now, the Judiciary Committee had agreed to a hearing schedule. Because he was a member of the Constitution Subcommittee, where the hearings would be held, Thurmond would be at the sessions, and civil rights lobbyists wondered what it would be like to face this symbol of the Old South now that he wielded more power than he ever had before. His own staff wondered, too. Lawyers armed with their stories of abuse would be eager to remind everyone that some of the most flagrant had come right from Edgefield County. Shedd assumed they'd be laying for the senator, and several times he reminded Thurmond, "Don't let 'em bait you. Don't let 'em bait you."

As chairman of the full committee, Thurmond had the privilege of opening the hearings. "I want to make one point emphatically clear," he said. "I support, have supported and will continue to support the right of every eligible voter in this country to have free, equal and unhindered access to the ballot box, to cast his or her vote in all local, state and national elections." His past opposition to the voting rights law had been based on the mechanics of the statute, he added, a position that "must not be interpreted as opposition to the right to vote itself.'' It was a statement he would repeat several times over the next five months.

The leadoff witness was Attorney General Smith, who supported a ten-year extension of the key enforcement provision—the preclearance requirement—but not a permanent extension. The Justice Department also supported requiring bilingual election materials, but Smith said the administration strongly opposed any language that would weaken the effect of the Alabama decision that had required proof of intentional discrimination.

The House bill was not acceptable, he said, because it focused on the results of an action, not on why the action was taken. If the House bill were enacted, he told the senators, at-large election plans like that in Edgefield County would be challenged and ''the only ultimate logical result'' would be federally mandated proportional representation.

The issue over Section Two had now been joined, and over the next six weeks Orrin Hatch would hammer away at it, spending much less time on the issue that mattered most to Thurmond and other southerners, the bailout provision.

On the second day Laughlin McDonald, the ACLU lawyer who was representing the Edgefield litigants, came to the committee room to testify. No one knew what to expect when Thurmond faced the man who had drawn up the papers challenging his ancestral home. So when the senator put the first question to McDonald, people expected anything but what they heard.

''Mr. McDonald,'' Thurmond asked, ''do you live in Atlanta?''

''Yes, I do, Senator.''

''I know the McDonald family in South Carolina,'' Thurmond continued. ''They originally came from Winnsboro. Some moved to Chester, some to Greenwood, some to Columbia. Haywood McDonald is a state senator down there now.''

''Yes sir, he's my cousin,'' McDonald said.

''Who was your father?''

''Tom McDonald from Winnsboro.''

''Tom is your father?''

''Yes sir.''

Thurmond told him that Tom McDonald had been a good friend.

''I know he was, Senator.''

''We've tried cases together. And I had the pleasure of appointing your mother to the state hospital board. She is a very lovely woman.''

"And nothing has ever pleased her any more in her life, I might add, Senator, than that appointment. She speaks about it often to me."

"I just wondered if you were connected with the McDonalds there," Thurmond said, "because they are all very fine people and friends of mine."

"Well, I appreciate that, Senator Thurmond."

"I have no questions," Thurmond added. "Thank you."

Hatch quickly switched on his microphone. "I knew Senator Thurmond was a legend in his own time," he said, "but I didn't realize he knew everyone in the South." The audience broke into laughter that only increased when McDonald observed, "I think he just got my vote when I move back to South Carolina."

Those in the hearing room, all of them much younger than the chairman, had just seen vintage Thurmond politics and its disarming effect. For an instant the senator had wiped away any memory of his segregationist past.

On February 11, when Tom McCain came to testify, Thurmond decided to address the Edgefield lawsuit directly. Shedd had drafted the remarks for him earlier but so far had persuaded the senator to hold off, arguing that a speech wasn't going to do much good in the face of Chapman's decision. But now Thurmond insisted. "I have repeatedly heard Edgefield County referred to as 'the home of Senator Thurmond,' " he told those in the hearing room. "While it is true that I was born in Edgefield, I have not lived there in thirty-five years. My home is Aiken, South Carolina, and has been for almost four decades. Of course I make this point as a matter of clarification for the record," he added, "and not to cast aspersions in any way on the people who live in Edgefield."

He said he was concerned that the House and Senate hearings might have given people the wrong impression of Edgefield. "I feel that it is unfair to those who live in Edgefield County to allow the record to reflect anything less than a full and accurate picture." To restore the balance he read a long passage about Edgefield written by newspaper editor William Watts Ball, whose disaffection with the Democratic Party had predated Thurmond's.

"Edgefield," Ball wrote, "should have a book of its own. It has had more dashing, brilliant, romantic figures, statesmen, orators, soldiers, adventurers, daredevils, than any county of South Carolina, if not of any rural county in America." Ball then listed stellar Edgefield citizens, including James Bonham and William Travis, the men who had helped defend the Alamo, and several others.

To this list Shedd had added several new names, deliberately including two black leaders in education, Alexander Bettis and Alfred W. Nicholson, whom Thurmond had helped with school funding almost fifty years earlier. Shedd, anticipating that someone might criticize the senator for including only whites, saw to it that Thurmond was prepared.

Compared to Ball's paean, McCain's testimony was a much darker description of Edgefield life. He called the county's at-large election system textbook proof of why the Voting Rights Act was still needed and why there had to be some easing of the Supreme Court's stringent intent test. The 1965 law might have permitted blacks to register and vote, but because of the at-large system and Edgefield's tendency to vote along racial lines, "voting by black people simply is not worth as much and not counted as much as the votes of white people."

He made it clear that he was not insisting on proportional representation on the county council. All he was seeking was a plan that gave blacks "a chance of electing someone. At present blacks do not have a chance of electing anyone."

Hearings on the bill ended March 1, and on March 24 the Constitution Subcommittee approved a ten-year extension of Section Five, the enforcement provision. Republicans, however, refused to add the House language that incorporated the "results" test in Section Two of law. It left in place the requirement of intentional discrimination as decided by the Supreme Court.

The full Judiciary Committee was not yet ready to send the bill forward. The disagreements over Section Two that had surfaced during the subcommittee hearings had hardened. Nine members supported the House version of the legislation and seven, including Thurmond—all of them Republicans—opposed it. Republican Robert Dole of Kansas and Democrat Howell Heflin of Alabama held the balance of power. If they sided with opponents, any bill would fail on a 9–9 tie vote. If either one of them joined with backers of the House bill, then the measure could be sent to the full Senate.

Although Thurmond's position was clear, he let it be known through his chief Judiciary counsel, Dee Lide, that he wanted to get a bill reported out of the committee and that he would not obstruct efforts to reach a compromise. He had made the same promise a few months earlier to the NAACP's Ike Williams. The senator was far from endorsing the bill, but it was still a major change from the obstructionist politics of the past.

Bob Dole, who had been pressed by lobbyists in Washington and civic groups back home, stepped in to try to put together a package that would command a majority of the committee regardless of Thurmond's support. The deal had not quite jelled when the committee gathered April 28 to begin consideration of the legislation, but the proceedings started anyway. Thurmond made a short speech saying he recognized that "there are strong convictions held by every member" and promising members that each would have time to express his views.

The committee reconvened the afternoon of the twenty-eighth but was unable to get a quorum. "Where are the proponents of the voting rights bill?" Thurmond asked, a jab at the absent senators who were still trying to wire their deal together. "Those who want the voting rights bill, where are you?"

After thirty minutes, the panel adjourned until the next morning, when it met only briefly for a few general remarks. Out of view, the talks were continuing among Dole, Kennedy, Mathias, their aides, and a half-dozen civil rights lawyers. Late on the twenty-ninth, when an agreement was all but final, Dole asked Ralph Neas, the head of a Washington civil rights coalition, to meet with Grassley and Thurmond and Nevada Republican Paul Laxalt, a committee member who was also Reagan's good friend. These meetings were a courtesy; the negotiators knew they had enough votes to get their proposal to the full Senate, with or without the three Republicans' backing.

Around ten o'clock on Saturday morning, May 1, a delegation of civil rights activists went to Thurmond's personal office to make their case. Joining Neas were Benjamin Hooks, head of the NAACP, Althea Simmons, head of its Washington office, and Bill Taylor, a veteran civil rights lawyer. It was not the first time Hooks and Thurmond had met and not the first time Hooks had asked for help. In a previous meeting, the civil rights leader had told the senator one of his favorite stories illustrating that political support could be offered at different levels. It involved a chicken and a pig who lived on a farm in the rural South. The time was the sixties, and the two animals were out in the yard one day watching a group of civil rights marchers head down the road. The chicken remarked that they looked tired and hungry and that perhaps they should offer them some breakfast. The pig agreed.

"How about some ham and eggs?" the chicken suggested.

"For you that's just a contribution," the pig soberly replied. "For me it's total commitment."

On this day, Thurmond gave neither a contribution nor a commitment. He happened to mention that the state's black mayors had not taken a position on the bill either, and added that he was going to meet with them within the next few days. This was just the kind of tip Neas wanted to get. Now he had a new idea about how to apply pressure to the chairman. As soon as the meeting broke up, Neas headed straight for a public telephone to call Armand Derfner, a civil rights lawyer from Charleston. He asked Derfner to contact the black mayors so that when the senator did see them they could tell him they supported the bill. While the pressure wouldn't affect Thurmond's committee vote, the payoff would come on the Senate floor.

On May 3, Dole announced that he had reached a compromise agreement and had gotten backing for it from the administration. He had held off his news conference until returning from the White House with a presidential okay.

The compromise package had two main provisions, the most controversial being the resolution of the intent issue. The proposal retained the House "results" test but added language from a 1973 Supreme Court decision specifying the guidelines a judge should use in weighing a voting discrimination case. To take the steam out of the opposition argument that proportional representation was inevitable, the compromise stated directly that nothing in the bill created a right for minority group members to be elected to public office in numbers equal to their proportion in the population.

A second part of the package extended the preclearance enforcement section for twenty-five years, a compromise between the House bill's permanent extension and the ten years approved by Hatch's subcommittee. On bailout, the compromise required that Congress reexamine the proposed criteria within fifteen years, although Congress could look at it sooner if it wished. A third, less contested provision extended protections for non-English-speaking voters until 1992.

When the committee met the following day, May 4, Hatch charged that the compromise was "little more than cosmetics" and would turn every political decision into a debate about race.

Ten years earlier this kind of comment would have been made by Thurmond. But now he was letting Hatch, thirty-one years younger and a more polished debater, carry the ideological ball. He would vote with the Utah Republican, but he wouldn't be a cheerleader. The committee adopted the compromise by a 14-to-4 vote, but not with Thurmond's support. He opposed it along with East, Denton, and Hatch. But then Thurmond agreed to send the bill to the full Senate, voting with sixteen other colleagues to move the legislation along. East was the lone opponent.

Thurmond explained his opposition to the compromise in separate remarks that were made part of the committee's report. Once again he reaffirmed his support for the right to vote and asserted that his vote to send legislation to the Senate "reflects my commitment to this ideal." He said he was still concerned that the compromise on Section Two would not prevent proportional representation in elections, but he devoted most of his remarks to repeating the criticisms the Republican members of the subcommittee had leveled at the new bailout provisions—that they would be too difficult to administer and would lead to a "generation of massive litigation."

On June 9 the bill went to the Senate floor, and Helms, joined by East, Denton, and Harry Byrd, immediately started a filibuster. Six days later the Senate cut them off and started to work on the measure. The most compelling interchange of the debate began the next day when Hollings came to the Senate floor to challenge East's claim that the law was no longer needed. Hollings's passionate speech set off an exchange with Thurmond that would show the distance between the two men. It would also show—considering Thurmond's final vote—the distance Thurmond had traveled.

The remarks by East, who was not a native southerner, "completely disregard the historical practice and experience of his backyard and my backyard over the many years," Hollings said. When he talked with his children about "certain things that occurred back in those days—and those days are not so long ago," he reminded East—his children had "a difficult time believing it." Back then, he pointed out, neither blacks nor women could serve on juries. Hollings recalled fighting alongside blacks during the war only to realize that when they got back home, they could not drink from the same water fountains as their white neighbors. And he told East of a chance breakfast meeting with Thurgood Marshall before the 1954 *Brown* cases were argued. Hollings, who was then a young lawyer helping South Carolina on its lawsuit, had to ask Marshall to keep their breakfast meeting a secret because "If you say you had breakfast with me, I am ruined." He also told East about the oath of office he'd had to take to be a

South Carolina Democrat, before it was struck down by Waties Waring. The oath, Hollings said, was "nothing more than a ruse and a scheme to make sure that blacks did not vote."

Turning now from the South's past to its present, Hollings cited the Edgefield case, pointing out Judge Chapman's indictment of white bloc voting that prevented black candidates from being considered on their merits. What's more, he reminded southerners, Chapman was a "Republican judge . . . a pedigree Republican, not a white-flight Republican," a man who was as deeply a part of South Carolina as Waties Waring had been. It was "not easy or a happy thing to get up and tell of this particular history, but unless we can speak honestly and realistically and objectively of what we have learned from our experiences, then we are not going to be able to vote intelligently on this particular matter."

The day before, East had claimed never to have seen legislation come before the Senate that was "so ill-conceived and so badly flawed." "On the contrary," Hollings retorted, "it is well-conceived, well-adjusted not for the academic but for reality. . . .

"We are not trying to expose ourselves on the floor of the U.S. Senate," he added. "But if this debate is going to continue on as though a bunch of technical nuts got together in the Judiciary Committee and reported an ill-conceived and so badly flawed law, someone has to give the hard, bitter experience of the past thirty years, and even years before that, where the official policy, practices, conspiracies, societal habits, customs, mores and what-have-you said, 'No, you're not going to come in the door.' "

When he disputed East's charge that the law treated one state differently from another, he could have been talking to Thurmond. It's not that the law treats the states differently, he lectured his colleague. "The states treated the people differently. That is where you cannot understand and see what I see."

Finally, Hollings noted that both South Carolina's attorney general and governor supported the House bill. Governor Riley had written Judiciary Committee members about the great change in the state's black electorate, pointing out that between Reconstruction and 1965, only one black had held elective office. In 1982 there were fifteen blacks in the legislature and fifty-eight "in significant county offices." He saw that as proof that the Voting Rights Act had worked. "Should we now abandon this landmark of liberty?" Riley asked. "Should we pat ourselves on the back for a job well done? I think not. That we have achieved great strides is without question; that we have met the task of eradicating the blight of discrimination from our election process is just not true."

The next day in the Senate Thurmond rose to answer Hollings. "Yesterday's statement by my distinguished colleague from South Carolina, regrettably, focused almost entirely on negative aspects of our state and its citizens in the past and failed to present positive aspects of South Carolina today," he said.

He pointed out proudly that almost 62 percent of the state's blacks had registered to vote compared with only 50 percent of the white, and he noted as Riley had that many blacks were now serving in state offices and serving "with distinction."

No one had challenged this record of progress during the hearings, he reminded Hollings, nor had anyone presented evidence "that anyone in my state is being denied the right to register or vote. I have repeatedly stated that if anyone gives me the name of a person who has been denied this right, I would immediately send that information to the Department of Justice for investigation." This was typical Thurmond. He understood the retail issue—the plight of a specific person—but he didn't grasp the wholesale problem, the election procedures themselves, which were overlaid on a history of discrimination.

Trying to contain his irritation, Thurmond added, "The implication that we in South Carolina are dealing with the issue of voting rights in any way other than a proper manner is simply inaccurate and without foundation. It ignores the efforts of thousands of our citizens to achieve a peaceful and harmonious society in which citizens of all races can participate in our democratic society. It is irresponsible to overlook these efforts and must be frustrating to our citizens who have worked so hard for good relations between the races."

He criticized Hollings—though in keeping with Senate traditions he didn't mention him by name—for singling out Edgefield without mentioning "the positive and decent character of its citizens." He repeated his contention that even if the allegations in the lawsuit were proved true, "that certainly is no indictment of all the people of Edgefield County any more than a school discrimination case in Boston or Detroit or Cleveland or Baltimore is a comment on all the citizens who live in these cities."

In comments to a reporter Thurmond was even harsher,

charging that Hollings "is running for president. Otherwise, it would be an unheard-of thing for a senator to speak against his own state and his own people."

Hollings could not let that go by. He returned to the Senate floor, and now two generations of Carolina politicians were debating one another. The men not only reflected different eras in the state's history, but in demeanor and style also represented South Carolina's distinct regions. The urbane, elegant Hollings, with his shock of snow-white hair, epitomized Charleston and the aristocratic Lowcountry that Tillman so despised. (Ironically, Hollings had not come from great wealth. His family had been devastated by the Depression, and he'd had to borrow money to go to college.) The plainspoken Thurmond, less elegantly tailored than his colleague, was the salt-of-the-earth politician who embodied the Upcountry.

Their differences, to be sure, were more than skin-deep. In 1954, when Thurmond was entrenched in resistance, Hollings was but a young lawyer on the fringes of South Carolina's fight against integration. By the time Hollings became governor he knew that segregation was nearing its end, and at an off-the-record press briefing in January 1962, the year before Harvey Gantt was admitted to Clemson, Hollings told reporters that in the coming year, "South Carolina's legal defenses will fall like a house of cards. You might as well start preparing your readers for the inevitable. We are not going to secede." Only four and a half years earlier, in the aftermath of Little Rock, Thurmond had insisted, "We in the South are not about to surrender, not now or in the future."

On the Senate floor, Hollings disputed Thurmond's charge that he had demeaned South Carolina. His remarks, he insisted, were "in pride of what we have done in equal justice under the law." The senator said his purpose in speaking was "to try to fill a vacuum." No one else had come forward to describe "what voting conditions were, what they have been over the several years, what they are today, and what we hope will continue under the Voting Rights Act extension. It is something that really in a way I get impatient with, and I get a feeling of frustration as to why we are even debating it."

Thurmond, in turn, thanked Hollings for explaining his earlier remarks, but he offered no apology for his jab about the presidency. He insisted again that South Carolina had been brought under the law in the first place because of technicalities, not bias.

In his mind, "It was not on account of discrimination. It was not because anybody had been deprived of the right to vote. It was simply the fact that enough citizens did not register to vote or those who registered did not actually vote." He refused to make the connection between low registration and the spoken and unspoken barriers to the ballot box.

On June 18 the senators went back to work, defeating by large margins fifteen amendments that sponsors said would weaken the bill. Thurmond supported all but one of the amendments and even authored one himself: an extension of the enforcement section for fifteen years instead of twenty-five.

As the day's work began, the senator addressed his colleagues, telling them yet again that he supported the right to vote and reminding them that "Over thirty-five years ago as governor, I personally led the fight in South Carolina to eliminate the poll tax," a task his state had accomplished seventeen years before the federal government. He also supported a constitutional amendment giving the District of Columbia voting representation in Congress because he believed "that all people in this nation should be treated equally and fairly, especially when voting is at issue."

Alluding, albeit obliquely, to his obstructionist past, Thurmond continued that his previous opposition to voting rights legislation "must not be interpreted as opposition to the right to vote itself. At the time the act was proposed and later modified, I felt that some of the mechanisms incorporated in the legislation were unconstitutional. I considered it my responsibility to point out those deficiencies to my colleagues in the Senate and the American people."

In fact he still had problems with the legislation and was unhappy that they had not been dealt with adequately in the compromise before the Senate. "The explanation for this situation is painful, but obvious," Thurmond said, in a muted version of his past attacks. "The emotional nature of these issues has severely limited reasoned analysis, and the deliberative process has been seriously marred by rhetoric. The understandable willingness of many of my colleagues to support a voting rights act has been, for some, transformed into a willingness to support practically any voting rights act." Tossing a barb at the civil rights community, he added that "this unfortunate tendency has been encouraged by the activities of a single powerful interest group, which has seemed to exercise a veto over the provisions of the bill."

Several hours later, as the debate was drawing to a close, Thurmond took the floor for the last time. His biggest concern, he said, was how he could be most effective—by opposing a bill he still had concerns about or by supporting it now and trying to change it at a later date. "I must take into account the common perception that a vote against the bill indicates opposition to the right to vote and, indeed, opposition to the group of citizens who are protected under the Voting Rights Act," he said. To safeguard against having such a misperception laid against him, which in turn might affect his ability to "secure full satisfaction of my concerns about this legislation," the senator made his choice. "I have decided to support final passage of [the bill], while at the same time committing myself to securing necessary relief through future legislative action. In this way I can make clear once and for all my resolute commitment to the right to vote and at the same time gain support for future improvements in this legislation."

What made this speech different from all those that had come before it was the conclusion the senator reached. The others had always ended in a flourish of opposition. This was quiet, if grudging, support.

When Mathias finally called for a vote on the legislation and Thurmond answered, "Aye," his first vote in favor of a civil rights bill was official. It would not be the last.

Five days later the House accepted the Senate version of the bill, and President Reagan signed it into law June 29.

Thurmond's vote reflected his acceptance of a political reality that overrode his fealty to state supremacy. It still stuck in his craw that the federal government could dictate behavior from Washington, and his response to Hollings was evidence that he still gave no quarter to anyone, even another southerner, who thought the South had brought some of this regulation on itself. But because his views came from political philosophy and not racial animus, Thurmond rejected the notion that his defense of his homeland made him a racist. And even though his philosophy remained constant, the fact that he had made adjustments was evident in the ease with which he moved in a new order where blacks, once without power, were his political equals and, in the eyes of the law, his social peers. If he failed to appreciate the deprivations that white society had imposed upon its black neighbors, if he still disdained broad-gauge government solutions to meet these systemic problems, he now recognized black interests and was receptive to black Carolina's concerns.

Many older black Carolinians who remembered 1948, the 1957 filibuster, and the unstinting opposition to the civil rights bills of the sixties could not reconcile themselves to his accommodations. (William James, a black Sumter lawyer, wrote the local newspaper in January 1982 criticizing a young black professor for praising Thurmond's help to a black college. James said the tribute "embarrasses a large segment of us who know and have lived through the oppression placed upon us by the man the lady would have us be 'proud' of." Because of the laws Thurmond had helped make and enforce, James had been unable to attend the law school of the university "for which my father was taxed.") But younger blacks, and a few older ones of a more pragmatic and forgiving heart—Victoria DeLee was the epitome—accepted what he was offering. They came to regard him with bemused affection. He certainly was a character, but now he was partly theirs.

If blacks' attitude toward Thurmond had modulated, there was one piece of lore that refused to go away completely. Legend in the black community had it that in Thurmond's bachelor days he had fathered a child with a black woman. The story was passed through three generations of black Carolinians, embellished at each telling with details of what the girl looked like. But no one could produce a specific name or whereabouts for the alleged offspring or mother. One northern reporter who journeyed south in the sixties to write about Thurmond commented that, while he hadn't found anyone who had seen the girl, "she certainly lived in their minds." She was a personal embodiment of "custom and tradition" as blacks understood it: powerful white men were assumed to have their way with black women.

Thurmond always scoffed at the notion that he had an out-of-wedlock child.

He denied the allegation once again, in the summer of 1992, when there was another flurry of publicity about his reputed black daughter. Stories identified a black woman whom Thurmond had befriended decades earlier as his alleged child, but she denied that Thurmond was her father. He called this latest assertion of fatherhood "absolutely not true."

When the Senate took up legislation in 1983 creating a legal holiday honoring Martin Luther King, Thurmond's accommodations to the black community became strikingly apparent. The bill was not at all of the political magnitude of the voting rights legislation, but Thurmond's willingness to pay tribute to the slain leader was in a way far more dramatic. The man he had once so viciously attacked he now found himself able to praise.

Bills honoring King had been introduced repeatedly since his assassination in April 1968, and in 1979 the House had come close to passing one. That same year the Senate Judiciary Committee had approved its own bill by a vote of 10 to 6. Among the six opponents was Thurmond. No American "should be singled out during his own lifetime or in the contemporary years following his death for an official holiday of national recognition," he argued. That honor was a "test of history." Only two individuals had thus far been honored, he pointed out, Christopher Columbus and George Washington. "No one else in our history—not Thomas Jefferson, not Benjamin Franklin, not Abraham Lincoln, not Booker T. Washington, not George Washington Carver, not Dwight Eisenhower, not John Kennedy to name a few—has ever been honored with a national holiday." In the text of his speech, the names of Booker T. Washington and Carver had been added in Thurmond's own hand.

The senator also managed to find a states' rights angle to the debate. Noting that several states and communities had already recognized King's birthday, he said the establishment of legal public holidays, "except in rare instances, should be the primary prerogative of the states. In fact the birthday of Dr. King is an optional holiday now in my home state of South Carolina."

Thurmond spoke up at another hearing in June, contending that a legal public holiday for King could cost taxpayers $200 million and such a price was "just *not* reasonable."

In the intervening four years, Thurmond had changed his mind. The visceral reactions of constituents could make a visceral politician like him understand what previously he had not. As the King debate resurfaced in 1983, Thurmond personally telephoned several black leaders, including the presidents of the state's black colleges. Telling them he was now ready to support a holiday to honor a black American ("to show this country is not discriminating"), he asked them whom they wanted to honor. He suggested Carver or Washington, and mentioned that when he was a child, his father had taken him to hear Washington when the black leader came to Edgefield to speak.

To a person, the leaders told him they preferred King.

At around the same time, the senator spoke at Voorhees College, a predominantly black school in Denmark. During his speech he talked about different blacks who had made significant contributions. Once again he mentioned Carver and Washington, but when he mentioned King, the students broke out into applause.

When he returned to Washington, he told Shedd that now he realized how important King was to twentieth-century black America.

Thurmond had always zealously defended his committee's jurisdiction, but when the House bill on the King holiday came over to the Senate in the fall of 1983, Thurmond agreed to let the measure stay at the Senate desk and forgo committee consideration. While it would have been his prerogative to manage the debate in the Senate (a chore he handled on most crime legislation), he delegated the duty to Dole and Mathias—two GOP supporters of the bill.

He took no part in the proceedings, which repeatedly turned ugly when Helms charged that King had been linked to the Communist Party. (Outside the Senate, Helms had tried unsuccessfully to persuade a federal judge to unseal raw FBI tapes about King's alleged conduct. They had been ordered sealed until the year 2077.) Fifteen years earlier Thurmond might have done the same thing. His attacks on Bayard Rustin and Abe Fortas were of the same ilk. But the senator had mellowed. There were still issues that could send him into a tirade—crime and the need for a death penalty were two—but in this particular case, Thurmond had made his own internal reconciliation with King and his legend.

On October 3, the same day he yielded Judiciary's jurisdiction, Thurmond explained his apparent change of position to his colleagues. Actually, he had "never opposed a day of recognition for Dr. King," he said, "provided the cost problem could be adequately addressed." Colleagues had provided the traditional fig leaf, promising future legislation to handle the cost problem.

More to the point, Thurmond said, "I fully recognize and appreciate the many substantial contributions of black Americans and other minorities to the creation and preservation and development of our great nation." He now was ready to express that recognition through a federal holiday, and said that his own personal survey had shown that "the overwhelming preference among our minority citizens is for a holiday honoring Dr. King, and I respect these views."

During the height of King's influence Thurmond had spoken about him and his cause with venom. King was as far from inclusion in the senator's pantheon of heros as anyone could be. But in typical fashion the senator now ignored the past, finding it unnecessary to reconcile the harsh words of twenty years earlier with the benign remarks of today. What's more, his black constituents didn't demand explanations, either. His support was enough.

In conservative circles, Thurmond's position was not well received. One movement magazine pronounced him "scalawag of the year" for his vote to honor King.

A month later Thurmond received two awards that would have been unlikely a decade earlier. In the same week, Morris College, a black school in Sumter, gave him an honorary degree (its president thanking him for "Your tireless efforts to serve the good people of our state and nation"), and South Carolina's fourteen black mayors named him legislator of the year. Shedd considered this another important signal to Riley or any other Democrat thinking of taking on Thurmond. It showed that he could compete for votes in the Democratic base and would not write off any constituent group.

By the time Thurmond announced he was running for reelection in March of 1984, Riley and other well-known Democrats had decided not to run. (Riley had been elected to a second term in 1982, the first governor to be able by law to succeed himself, and he was immersed in administering a new education improvement program.) As important, Thurmond supporters, led by influential banker W. W. "Hootie" Johnson, had raised over one million dollars for the senator's campaign, and if that wasn't enough to dissuade high-profile opponents, members of the party establishment had already announced they were backing the incumbent.

At his press conferences around the state to announce his candidacy, an enthusiastic Thurmond, flanked by Nancy and the four children, told audiences, "I'm eighty-one, and I feel like a million dollars." To those who wanted to know how he stayed so fit, he described his regimen. "I take forty-five minutes of exercise every morning, weight-lifting, jogging, riding the stationary bike. I take forty-five minutes of exercise at night. I try to watch my diet. I don't think it's a question of age as much as it's a question of what kind of shape you're in."

The senator's Democratic opponent turned out to be Melvin Purvis, Jr., a nondenominational minister from Florence. His father was the FBI agent who had tracked down John Dillinger. Thurmond beat him with 66.8 percent of the vote, his highest winning percentage since becoming a Republican.

It was another landslide victory for Reagan, too, who trounced Walter Mondale by winning 525 electoral votes to Mondale's 13. The Republicans kept their hold on the Senate, but their margin slipped by two. Democrats had won three new seats but had lost a fourth to the Republicans in Kentucky.

Closer to home, there was very significant news in Edgefield. Three blacks had been elected to the county council, giving them a one-vote majority on the five-member board. It had taken another lawsuit, this one arguing that a previous election change had been made without the mandatory preclearance, to force the county to abandon the at-large system. Now there were five single-member districts. One of the first things the new county council did was to appoint Tom McCain as county administrator. It was a 3–2 vote along racial lines.

In his fifth and sixth years as Judiciary chairman, Thurmond would find himself enmeshed in civil rights matters in a slightly different way from past legislative campaigns. Now they were surfacing in the context of nominees put forward by Reagan for the federal bench. The judiciary had been the one place where black Americans felt their concerns could be heard, and as South Carolina history had shown, their first important triumphs had come in the courts.

Carter's deliberate effort to appoint more women, blacks, and Hispanics to the bench—he'd had 150 newly created judgeships to fill in addition to the usual replacements—had allowed him to exert a palpable influence on the trial and appellate courts. Though the generalization was not always true, his nominees were considered to be liberals—conservatives scornfully called them "judicial activists" in the mold of Earl Warren—who went beyond their prescribed authority and encroached on legislators' terrain. They were too kind to criminal defendants, put too many restrictions on government, and sided too often with poor plaintiffs suing wealthier defendants. It was criticism Thurmond shared, but like most other politicians of the time he was willing to defer to a president's wishes and had supported most of Carter's nominees—in fact he helped get the first black on South Carolina's federal bench. But the federal courts were still suspect in Thurmond's eyes because they had stepped in too often and with too heavy a hand to redress grievances he believed were best settled in legislative bodies. The senator refused to concede that Congress and state legislatures were still run by white men and therefore not necessarily representative of "the people."

The Reagan administration was intent on reversing Carter's influence, and Thurmond was a big help in achieving this goal. In his first four years as chairman, the senator had moved the president's nominees through the committee with dispatch, helping Reagan put 167 new judges on the bench by the end of 1984. (All but 27 were white men.) By the summer of 1986, two new Supreme Court nominations would allow Thurmond to demonstrate anew the power that comes with controlling the committee agenda, though the next year he would see it turned back on him and his GOP colleagues.

On June 17, Reagan made a surprise announcement. Chief Justice Burger, now seventy-eight, was retiring. William Rehnquist, who had served on the court since 1971, would replace him as chief justice, and Rehnquist's seat would be filled by Antonin Scalia, a feisty, voluble conservative who was serving on the federal appellate court in Washington, D.C. Neither man gave the civil rights community much to cheer about, and it was going to be particularly difficult to handle two nominees at once. Civil rights lawyers met with Thurmond in person to ask for separate proceedings so that they could research one nominee and finish with him before going on to the next one. But Neas knew going into the session that the chairman "obviously had all the cards."

Thurmond enjoyed being thought of as fair, and he knew that if he tried to railroad the nominations through the committee, there would be a publicity blitz accusing him of being just the opposite. This gave the other side a sliver of negotiating room, but the most they could buy was a couple of extra weeks in exchange for promising the chairman a vote on the nominees on a date certain. Thurmond put off the start of the hearings until the end of July—forty-four days after Reagan's announcement, but still in enough time to ensure that the court could be at full strength when it reconvened the first Monday in October.

When Rehnquist came before the committee July 30 and 31, Biden, Kennedy, and Howard Metzenbaum, a liberal Democrat from Ohio, grilled him about matters that touched on civil rights. They first wanted to know his overall views, and then they raised allegations that in the 1960s he had harassed minority voters in Phoenix, where he was a lawyer active in politics. They also pointed out that there were restrictive covenants on his two homes barring their sale to nonwhites and people "of the Hebrew race."

Rehnquist strenuously denied that he had a bias against minorities, disputed the charges of voter harassment (though later five witnesses came to Washington to contradict the nominee), and said that he had been unaware of the covenants. In any event, he reminded the senators, they were unenforceable.

Scalia came before the committee for only one day of questioning, on August 5, and senators' biggest complaint was his evasiveness in answering questions. He repeatedly told them that the issues they wanted to know about either were pending before the appeals court on which he served or were likely to come to the Supreme Court.

On August 14 the committee sent Rehnquist forward with a favorable recommendation by a vote of 13–5; Scalia's recommendation was unanimous.

Both men were confirmed September 17. The civil rights community had put together a full-scale effort to defeat Rehnquist, and Democrats tried to block the nomination. Rehnquist's tally was 65–33, the largest number of opponents to date for a successful Supreme Court nominee. Scalia, with everyone's attention focused on Rehnquist, won a unanimous confirmation, but shortly after being sworn in he would draw criticism from civil rights groups who believed that he, too, was insensitive to minority rights.

Despite the large vote against Rehnquist, Thurmond had done his job. He had moved him out of the committee with dispatch and he had defended him in the Senate against Democrats' attacks, particularly the charge that he was not vigilant enough on civil rights. "I simply say that Justice Rehnquist in all his testimony said he was opposed to discrimination, that he believes in equal rights for all," Thurmond told colleagues, as if the nominee's declaration alone would end the matter. "If this committee felt that he was in favor of discrimination in any way, shape or form," he continued, "I do not believe they would have confirmed him."

Although Thurmond was not up for reelection that November, the 1986 Senate races would be important to him and the rest of the Republicans. The tide that had swept the GOP into the White House and into power in the Senate was now on its way out. Nowhere would that be more evident than in the South. Four states that had elected Republicans in 1980—Alabama, Florida, Georgia, and North Carolina—would turn around and send Democrats back in their place. In Louisiana, the venerable Russell Long had chosen not to seek reelection, and Representative John Breaux beat out Henson Moore, a former congressman who had spearheaded an antibusing effort in 1982. Each of the southern Democrats had put together winning coalitions that were the opposite of Thurmond's, earning a huge majority of the black vote but still carrying nearly 40 percent of the white vote. These new southerners were going to be of critical importance in the next Supreme Court fight, whose intensity and bitterness would dwarf those that came before it.

Overall, the Democrats had picked up eight Senate seats, taking back control of the Senate with a fifty-five-to-forty-five majority. Overnight, Thurmond had gone back to being in the minority. And Joe Biden, forty years his junior, would now be chairman of the Judiciary Committee.

The two senators had adjacent offices in the Russell Building, Biden having taken over a suite that had belonged to John Stennis. What came with the Stennis rooms was a beautifully finished oval wood table that had once belonged to Richard Russell. Around that table, Stennis explained to the younger Democrat, strategies had been set for blocking civil rights legislation. It was appropriate, the Mississippian added, that the table now pass to a new generation.

In the previous six years Biden had developed a genuine fondness for Thurmond. The young Democrat appreciated Thurmond's political skill—he realized he was sitting next to a living piece of history—and he respected the straight-up way they could deal with one another. When Biden became Judiciary's senior Democrat, he had promised Thurmond he would never do anything to undercut him. Thurmond had always reciprocated. To repay Thurmond's courtesies, Biden now held off announcing his committee reorganization plans until he could track down Thurmond and tell him first. The search took him all the way to a small town in South Carolina, where he found the senator on a reviewing stand awaiting a parade.

When the Supreme Court's 1986–87 term ended, Lewis Powell retired. Because he was widely perceived to have been the swing vote that kept the court from veering sharply to the right, his successor was of critical importance both to the administration and to the traditionally liberal community of civil rights, labor, and mainstream religious organizations. Robert Bork, now a federal appeals court judge, was rumored to be in line for the high court. Among his other credentials—antitrust specialist, Yale law professor, prolific writer—he had been the one to execute Nixon's order to fire Watergate special prosecutor Archibald Cox after Attorney General Richardson and his assistant, William Ruckelshaus, refused.

If he had often been mentioned for the Supreme Court, his detractors believed it was because he had campaigned for it in his provocative writings. Those made him anything but a blank slate, and where conservatives saw a shining intellect who would hew strictly to the Constitution, liberals saw a threat to their hard-won gains on civil rights and the related issue of privacy, which was at the heart of the abortion controversy.

As Reagan was considering his options, Neas called up Duke Short, a tough but congenial former FBI agent who had been an aide to Thurmond since 1974 and another moderating force in the senator's office. Knowing Short would listen, Neas told him that if the president nominated Bork, he would see a confirmation fight the likes of which he had never seen before. Neas intended that Short pass the message on to Thurmond, which he did. Neas made a similar call to one of his contacts in the White House.

On July 1 Reagan announced that Bork was his choice. Less than an hour later Kennedy went to the Senate to lay down the opposition line. He portrayed Bork's past record in the harshest possible terms, setting the tone for the next three months. Just as songwriters build "hooks" into their music and lyrics, Kennedy found a hook for his speech: life in "Robert Bork's America" (based on Kennedy's partisan interpretation of Bork's writings over the years). Critics accused Kennedy of the worst sort of distortion, but he wanted to leave no doubt about the high stakes in this fight.

"Robert Bork's America," Kennedy charged, "is a land in

which women would be forced into back-alley abortions, blacks would sit at segregated lunch counters, rogue police could break down citizens' doors in midnight raids, schoolchildren could not be taught about evolution, writers and artists would be censored at the whim of government, and the doors of the federal courts would be shut on the fingers of millions of citizens for whom the judiciary is often the only protector of the individual rights that are the heart of our democracy." Because Bork had already been approved by the Senate for the appeals court—Biden had even said then that he could support him for the high court—lobbyists feared a bandwagon of senators endorsing him now based on his previous confirmation and his impressive credentials. As Kennedy was speaking, Neas was already making phone calls from Kennedy's subcommittee office, urging Senate staffers to tell their bosses to remain uncommitted until after Judiciary Committee hearings.

Inside the committee, once again the main issue was timing, but now that Thurmond was in the minority he had no power to set the agenda. All he could do was press for prompt consideration of the nomination so that the court would not start its new term one justice short. But this time the Democrats were in no rush, feeling the pressure from galvanized civil rights organizations who wanted enough time to pore over Bork's extensive "paper trail." Late in July Biden told Thurmond that he was going to put off the hearings until September. Thurmond acceded without a fuss, but then when he was criticized by hard-line Bork supporters, he backed off the agreement. Biden chose not to defend himself publicly. He let Thurmond have his say and quietly kept to his own schedule.

By the time the hearings started September 15, the committee—which had been reduced to fourteen members—was already polarized. Even before Bork had uttered his first word of testimony, six Democrats were all but certain to vote against him and five Republicans were sure to support him. The three undecided votes were Republican Specter of Pennsylvania and Democrats Heflin of Alabama and Dennis DeConcini of Arizona.

That the debate was shaping up over judicial philosophy put Thurmond in a difficult position. He could hardly argue that such inquiry was inappropriate; nineteen years earlier he had opposed Fortas on the grounds that his ideology was abhorrent.

Thurmond's opening remarks were direct but tempered.

"Some have said that philosophy should not be considered at all in the confirmation process. In fact, I have been incorrectly aligned with that position," he said. "Others say that philosophy should be the sole criterion. I reject both of these positions. I believe that a candidate's philosophy may properly be considered, but philosophy should not be the sole criterion for rejecting a nominee with one notable exception. The one exception is when the nominee clearly does not support the basic, long-standing consensus principles of our nation." He added that the committee had to be careful "not to confuse core, fundamental principles with evolving and debatable applications of those principles."

Thurmond said that Bork's record showed he was "well within the mainstream of legal debate and discussion within this country." It was a point to which opponents took strong exception.

When Neas ran into Shedd after the hearing, he complimented Shedd on having helped the senator walk a careful line in his remarks. Civil rights groups, Neas explained, had been ready to use Thurmond's own past words against him if he had objected to exploring judicial philosophy. Shedd nodded that he knew very well what was in the record.

Bork's five days of testimony—covered gavel to gavel by television networks—were unlike any previous confirmation proceeding. Nominees might be grilled about their personal finances or asked questions bearing on their fitness for office, but what was on the table here was the Constitution of the United States and theories of how it should properly be interpreted to resolve the problems of everyday modern life. At the center of the debate were principles most Americans had come to regard as the ones that made their society unique in the world—freedom of speech, equal protection of the law, due process, a right to privacy. The main opposition strategy was to persuade the Senate that with Bork on the court, these cherished concepts would be in danger in the very forum that had given them meaning.

By the time the Judiciary Committee got ready to vote on Bork, the fight was all but over. Specter had declared his opposition, and on October 1 and 2 several southern senators went to the Senate floor to announce that they, too, would vote against him. All said they were troubled by Bork's views on civil rights and wanted to avoid any perception that the country might reverse course to refight the unsettling, painful battles that had already been won.

The civil rights organizations and their Senate allies had succeeded in making the debate about American values; Bork had been painted as a constitutional bogeyman who would put those values under threat. His five days of testimony had not erased that image.

The Judiciary Committee met October 6 and voted 9 to 5 to send Bork's nomination to the Senate with an unfavorable recommendation. Heflin and DeConcini had joined Specter in opposing him. Three days later, after an emotional meeting with Republican supporters, Bork decided that even though defeat was certain, he would not withdraw his name.

The final vote came on October 23. Before the roll was called, Thurmond had the last word: "Mr. President," he said, addressing the chair, "I would like for the presiding officer to admonish the audience in the galleries that there will be no outburst when the outcome is announced." The final tally was 42–58. Six Republicans joined fifty-two Democrats in opposing Bork. Two Democrats, Hollings and David Boren of Oklahoma, sided with his Republican supporters.

(After Bork, Reagan nominated federal appeals court judge Douglas Ginsberg, who had been head of the antitrust division of the Justice Department. But he was forced to withdraw after allegations surfaced that he had used marijuana once as a law student and then while he was a law professor at Harvard. Reagan then selected federal appeals court judge Anthony M. Kennedy, who was confirmed February 3, 1988.

(Bork resigned from the federal appeals court January 7, 1988, writing President Reagan that "I wish to speak, write and teach about law and other issues of public policy more extensively than is possible in my present position." In his book *The Tempting of America,* he assailed his critics in unemotional but blunt language for dissembling and disingenuousness, for using the "guise of protecting our civil rights" as a means of forcing the courts to adopt positions that "in fact divide public opinion and are nowhere to be found in the Constitution or the statutes of the United States—and which, in fact, the American people will not allow their legislators to enact.")

As a loyal Republican, Thurmond did not like to see the president's nominee lose, but his heart had not been in the fight to save Bork. He had wanted Powell to be replaced by another southerner, favoring Billy Wilkins, a former aide, for the post, but he could not persuade Biden to help him make the case to the administration.

As important, Thurmond's zealotry of the fifties and sixties had waned. Where twenty years earlier he might have made a daily speech haranguing the committee about the schedule or the way it made up a witness list, now Thurmond was silent. During the hearings he dutifully asked Bork questions designed to put him in the best possible light, but he did not go on the attack against Bork's opponents. That was left to his younger, more strident colleagues.

The odds were good that in the summer of 1988 Vice-President George Bush would win the GOP nomination and then succeed Ronald Reagan, but other Republicans believed that they, too, were credible candidates. Among the early contenders were television evangelist Pat Robertson and Senator Dole of Kansas. By this time Mark Goodin had become part of the Bush operation, and Dent was supporting him as well, having kept up contacts with the White House even though he had left politics and law and had started a lay ministry in Columbia with his wife.

Dent and Goodin thought Thurmond's best course was to stay neutral, arguing that he had nothing to gain by endorsing either Bush or Dole, but the senator wanted to back the Kansan. He liked his toughness and he believed he was more conservative than Bush. Besides, Nancy liked Elizabeth Dole, the senator's wife, and she was working on her husband to support him. Goodin argued that, skilled as Dole was, he was no match for the Bush operation. Early in the primary season, Goodin even suggested that Duke Short call directory assistance in Florida cities and ask for Dole campaign headquarters. "You can't find it," an exasperated Goodin said. It did no good. Thurmond endorsed Dole.

When the balloting was over in South Carolina's March 5 primary, Bush had beaten Dole by a margin of more than two to one. Thurmond's backing had not been enough, and Lee Atwater, Bush's campaign strategist, who was initially annoyed that his mentor had crossed him, turned the senator's endorsement into a plus for Bush. Even with backing by the legendary Strom Thurmond, he pointed out, Dole couldn't come close.

The Democrats nominated Massachusetts governor Michael Dukakis to go against Bush, and once again the GOP administered a drubbing to its opponent. Bush carried forty states and amassed 426 electoral votes to Dukakis's 111.

The once-Democratic South without exception had gone Republican. The southern strategy that Thurmond had helped put in place was now more than a strategy. It was an accomplished fact. The Senate race in Mississippi that year confirmed it.

Trent Lott, who had been second in command of House Republicans, faced Representative Wayne Dowdy, a scrappy Democratic congressman from Macomb. Lott was a more conservative Republican than Cochran; most recently he had opposed the 1982 voting rights bill and the Martin Luther King holiday. But he was glib and telegenic, with a shock of dark hair that was never out of place even when the wind blew.

When Dowdy tried to paint Lott as a chauffeur-driven elitist who was out of touch with Mississippi, Lott struck back by tying Dowdy to the national Democratic Party, which he said was out of step with the South. Though he didn't say it directly, everyone knew he meant the white South.

There was another facet to Lott's campaign, however, and this one was a leaf out of Thurmond's book of adjustment. Just like Thurmond, Lott wanted to keep his white base solid, but at the same time he wanted to make enough appeals to the black community to avoid creating backlash against him. He knew that the Mississippi of 1988 was not the Mississippi of 1958 or 1968. One of Lott's campaign points was his willingness to create a minority business committee in the state to advise him in the Senate, and "Blacks for Lott" was set up to help him.

Lott beat his opponent by four percentage points.

Two years later, a month shy of Thurmond's eighty-eighth birthday, South Carolinians would be voting on whether to return him to the Senate for a seventh term. By the spring of the year it was clear that he would have only token opposition, and on November 6 he was elected with 64.2 percent of the vote. This would be the last campaign that featured the entire Thurmond family. Four months after the election, Nancy Thurmond announced that the couple was separating.

Thurmond's neighbor in North Carolina, Jesse Helms, did not have it so easy. If Lott's 1988 election, with its modest approach to the black community, represented Thurmond's legacy of accommodation, Helms's ideologically driven campaigns epitomized the legacy of division—a legacy that grew out of the way Thurmond and other opponents of civil rights legislation had framed the debate three decades earlier. Railing against President Kennedy's proposals in the spring of 1963, Thurmond had accused the government of placing "greater stress on equality than on personal liberty" and had argued that the legislation forced Congress to choose between "liberty or equality."

It was just the kind of dichotomy Helms was able to exploit in his tough and occasionally ugly 1990 campaign against Harvey Gantt, the man who had integrated Clemson and had gone on to be mayor of Charlotte. (Helms had had a similarly rough contest against former governor Jim Hunt in 1984, winning the most expensive Senate campaign ever by less than four percentage points.) In the contest with Gantt, Helms found the latest civil rights legislation before Congress to be a perfect tool. The bill was an effort to roll back several Supreme Court decisions that detractors said made it almost impossible to prove employment discrimination. The technical issues involved burdens of proof and methods of evidence, but the Bush administration and many Republicans called the measure a "quota bill." (Thurmond sided with his party colleagues and opposed it.) Their underlying message was that blacks and other minorities would get a leg up at the expense of whites. One of Helms's most searing television ads, rolled out at the end of the campaign, showed a pair of frustrated white hands crumpling up a job rejection letter while a voice-over explained that this would be the result of the "Ted Kennedy quota bill" pushed by the Democrats.

At various points in the campaign, polls showed Helms trailing Gantt, but in the end a blitz of ads that focused on the quota matter, and others raising allegations about one of Gantt's business transactions, gave Helms a victory with just under 53 percent of the vote.

This kind of campaigning was not Thurmond's style—nor had he ever had such a close election. The one time race had overtly been an issue in South Carolina—in the 1950 campaign against Olin Johnston—it was Johnston who had tossed around "nigger" and had criticized Thurmond for putting a black doctor on a medical board. But when he switched parties in 1964 in the embrace of Goldwater's conservative philosophy, Thurmond had set in motion the factors that transformed the white South from a Democratic stronghold to a bastion of Republicanism. Helms's ability to play on the fears of white North Carolinians—to update Thurmond's choice of "liberty or equality"—was both the legacy of resistance and continuing proof that race was still the same powerful force Ben Tillman had exploited a century earlier.

Helms's attacks on the civil rights bill showed that the gloried notion of equal opportunity became less appealing and more divisive when it appeared that whites, particularly white men, might be hurt by efforts to redress past discrimination.

Vetoed by Bush in 1990, the legislation was reintroduced in 1991. After six months of bruising negotiations, Congress and the president finally reached a compromise that was enacted in the fall. The Senate vote on the measure was 93–5. As senators were leaving the chamber to head back to their offices, Thurmond, who had supported this latest version, stopped to talk to a group of civil rights lobbyists. "A good vote," he told them. "Ninety-three to five—and I wasn't one of the five."

There was a double edge to Thurmond's comment. He was proud of the fact that he was in the majority, but at the same time he was defensive. He knew that, because of his past, some people might have expected him to vote with the archconservatives now serving in Congress.

The compromise was the byproduct of a changed political atmosphere in the Senate—a change that had come in the aftermath of the fight over the nomination of Clarence Thomas to the Supreme Court. Senators and key members of the administration wanted to try to heal the deep wounds opened during that imbroglio. Thomas, a forty-three-year-old black conservative and federal appeals court judge, was opposed by several civil rights groups, starting with the NAACP. Based on his past record, these organizations argued that Thomas would seek to weaken, even destroy, the very civil rights laws that had helped him and so many other black Americans. It was particularly galling to them that he had been picked to replace the retiring Thurgood Marshall. But what nearly derailed the nomination were allegations of sexual harassment brought against him by Anita Hill, a black law professor who had worked for Thomas when he headed the Equal Employment Opportunity Commission.

The Judiciary Committee, where Thurmond was still the senior Republican, held hearings on the nomination, including Hill's explosive charges. Thurmond played almost no role in this phase of the hearings, and that was no accident. One former aide astutely observed that "a man of his age, with his background, cannot question a thirty-five-year-old black woman about sex."

But the senator was an enthusiastic Thomas supporter—one more measure of how much he had changed. In 1948, Thurmond had stood before a cheering crowd in Birmingham and promised that there were "not enough troops in the army to force the southern people to . . . admit the Negro race into our theaters, into our swimming pools, into our homes, and into our churches." Now he was doing all he could to help a member of "the Negro race" onto the Supreme Court.

After Thomas was confirmed by the Senate, Thurmond went out to the new justice's suburban Virginia home to congratulate him. A crowd of supporters had already gathered outside on this rainy evening, hoping to see the victorious nominee. Thomas wanted to stay in the house, but at the senator's urging he finally went out to greet his friends, Strom Thurmond smiling at his side. It was a scene Ben Tillman could never have imagined.

But this tableau illustrated the political transformation that had taken place over the previous twenty years, even if racial cleavages still wracked the nation. Federal laws, backed up when necessary by federal court orders, had brought blacks into public life and had given them the power both to influence the decisions that affected their communities and to influence the white politicians who would help make them. Thurmond's career proved the case. At the beginning of his public life, his constituency and his fellow politicians were almost exclusively white men. In the twilight of his career, he courted black voters and worked with black public officials as though it were second nature. (Tom McCain, who now met regularly with the senator to talk about Edgefield problems, prominently displayed Thurmond's autographed picture in his private office behind the county's historic courthouse.)

"You've got to meet the challenges as they come," the senator observed three months after his 1990 reelection. "If you can't change with the times when it's proper to change, you'd be lost in the shuffle. I don't think I've sacrificed any principle throughout my career, but times change. When I grew up the black people were just all servants," he explained. "Now they've developed and developed and come up and we've got to acknowledge people when they deserve to be acknowledged, and the black people deserve to be acknowledged."

Thurmond still spoke of the past as though it had been ordained by a law of nature. And after sixty years in public life, he still presented himself as a neutral player on the political stage, as if he had no responsibility for the rules that white society had imposed upon blacks, even when deprivations were brought to light with unmistakable clarity. But if he never rose up in indignation and vowed to help change the rules, his long career had shown that few knew better how to adapt once the rules were changed.

From the time he ran his first campaign for Edgefield County superintendent of education, Thurmond's public life had always come first. Even as a child the events that made the deepest imprint were in some way connected to politics—his father's talk around the dinner table, Ben Tillman's lesson in shaking hands, the thrill and the inspiration of seeing his first candidates' debate at the age of nine.

"May success ever be yours," the cadets at Clemson had wished their graduating classmate, and Thurmond had found plenty. Winning elections became a habit. Other than his symbolic presidential race in 1948, he had lost only one. And he bounced back from that defeat to become the only U.S. senator ever to be elected by a write-in vote. For more than a half-century the political terrain had shifted constantly under Thurmond's feet, but he never lost his footing.

On November 24, 1989, current and former staff gathered in Columbia for a dinner in the senator's honor. It was an event that took place every two years, and as in the past, several generations of aides were present. A few got up to tell stories about working for Thurmond and to talk about his long career. The guests at the buffet dinner were almost all white. Tom Moss, who was still on the senator's staff, had business elsewhere but had sent his good wishes in a message delivered from the podium. The young men and women serving the meal were Columbia area blacks.

After the program was over and the crowd had emptied out of the hall, a few of the last guests stood around visiting, when they realized the senator was not with them. They turned to look for him and found him in the back of the room shaking hands with the kitchen staff, thanking each of them for helping to serve the dinner.

Once he had seen servants. Now he saw constituents.

Abbreviations Used in Source Notes

CQ: Congressional Quarterly, used to identify yearly *Almanacs*, *Weekly Reports*, and special books on government.
CQCN: Congressional Quarterly's *Congress and the Nation.*
DNCR: Democratic National Committee Records, Proceedings of Conventions and Meetings, Harry S. Truman Library, Independence, Missouri.
EBP: Edgar Brown Papers, Clemson University, Special Collections.
JCTP: Jean Crouch Thurmond Papers, Clemson University, Special Collections.
JMP: John McCray Papers, University of South Carolina, Caroliniana Library.
JWWP: J. Waties Waring Papers, Moorland-Spingarn Research Center, Howard University.
NAACP: Papers of the National Association for the Advancement of Colored People, Library of Congress.
ODJP: Olin D. Johnston Papers, University of South Carolina, Caroliniana Library.
RFP: Robert McC. Figg Papers, University of South Carolina, Caroliniana Library.
ST: Strom Thurmond, identifies him as speaker, letter writer, recipient of correspondence.
STC: Strom Thurmond Collection, Clemson University, Special Collections.*
STG: Strom Thurmond Gubernatorial Papers, researched at the University of South Carolina, Caroliniana Library; papers transferred to Clemson University Special Collections, fall 1990.
STHR: Strom Thurmond Historical Records, Clemson University, Special Collections.
WBS: William Baskin Scrapbook, University of South Carolina, Caroliniana Library.
W/CUOH: Reminiscences of J. Waties Waring, Columbia University Oral History Project, Columbia University Library.

WWBP: William Watts Ball Papers, Manuscript Department, Duke University Library.
WWP: William Workman Papers, University of South Carolina, Caroliniana Library.

*In some instances two citations are given for Strom Thurmond's speeches or statements, the box number from the Strom Thurmond Collection and the page number for the *Congressional Record* in which Thurmond's remarks in the United States Senate were recorded.

Newspapers
AC: *The Atlanta Constitution,* Atlanta, Georgia.
JCL: *The Clarion Ledger,* Jackson, Mississippi.
LCJ: *The Courier-Journal,* Louisville, Kentucky.
NC: *The News and Courier,* Charleston, South Carolina.
NYT: *The New York Times,* New York, New York.
POST: *The Washington Post,* Washington, D.C.
RECORD: *The Columbia Record,* Columbia, South Carolina.
STATE: *The State,* Columbia, South Carolina.

Notes

CHAPTER 1: Standing with the People

Page

14 "I never thought": int., Ike Williams, Jan. 15, 1991.
14 "shaking hands": undated article, *The Timmonsville Times*, STHR.
15 "a master politician": int., Harry S. Dent, Sept. 20, 1989.
16 "you kinda get a feelin' ": ints., Mark Goodin, Apr. 10, 1989, Apr. 15, 1991.
17 called one of his drivers: int., Althea T. L. Simmons, Mar. 9, 1989.

CHAPTER 2: The Legacy of Pitchfork Ben

Page

18 "the harlot slavery": *Encyclopedia Americana, International Edition,* s. v. Sumner, vol. 26, p. 8; see also Simkins, *A History of the South,* p. 200.
19 redbrick courthouse: Ransford, Central Business Revitalization Study, Edgefield, S.C., p. 6; see also pp. 1–7.
19 twelve lawyers: ibid., p. 5.
19 intimidation, harassment: Simkins, *Pitchfork Ben Tillman,* p. 57.
20 Sweetwater Sabre Club: ibid., p. 58.
20 White League . . . White Line: Simkins, *A History of the South,* p. 291.
21 "waved the bloody shirt": Simkins, *Tillman,* pp. 62–64; Tillman, *The Struggles of 1876: How South Carolina Was Delivered of Carpetbag and Negro Rule,* pp. 35, 38–39.
21 "out of the ordinary": Simkins, *Tillman,* p. 92.
21 "hoodwinked by demagogues": ibid., pp. 92–93.
21 "pent-up indignation": ibid., p. 100.
22 Alexander C. Haskell: ibid., p. 164.
22 "beyond the capacity": ibid., p. 171.
22 five lynchings: ibid., pp. 224–25.
22 elected to the United States Senate: ibid., p. 272.
22 "old bag of beef": ibid., p. 315.
23 any male South Carolinian: ibid., p. 297; see also Aba-Mecha, "Black Woman Activist in South Carolina: Modjeska Monteith Simkins," p. 158.

23 forbade any mixing: Simkins, *Tillman,* p. 303.
23 the constitution went into effect: ibid., p. 307.
24 "a virtility": Holmes, *The White Chief,* p. 86.
24 whipping crowds to a frenzy: White, "Anti-Racial Agitation in Politics: James Kimble Vardaman in the Mississippi Gubernatorial Campaign of 1903," p. 10.
24 "coon-flavored miscegenationist," "chinch bug": Holmes, *White Chief,* p. 105.
24 "White Chief": ibid., p. 108.
24 "no more decency": ibid., p. 99.
24 "rancid 'coons' ": ibid., p. 99.
24 Mrs. Cox: ibid., p. 100; see also White, "Anti-Racial Agitation," p. 50.
25 "an obvious nigger postmaster": House Document 422, 57th Cong., 2d sess., Resignation of the Postmaster of Indianola, p. 21.
25 "negro domination": Holmes, *White Chief,* p. 100.
25 "race antagonism": *The Commonwealth,* Greenwood, Mississippi, Dec. 5, 1902.
25 "neck broken": Gatewood, "Theodore Roosevelt and the Indianola Affair," p. 61.
26 "kill more negroes": White, "Anti-Racial Agitation," p. 105; see also Holmes, *White Chief,* pp. 105–11.
26 end of the political careers . . . black elected officials: I. A. Newby, *Black Carolinians: A History of Blacks in South Carolina from 1895 to 1968,* p. 43. State assemblyman John W. Bolts was defeated for reelection, as was George W. Harriot, who had been superintendent of schools in the eastern shore town of Georgetown.
27 "encourage them . . . religious creed": Dubose, Louise Jones, "James Strom Thurmond: First South Carolina Presidential Candidate Since 1931," *South Carolina Magazine,* Nov. 1948, pp. 14–17.
27 cut down another ham: ints., Mary Thurmond Tompkins, Apr. 30, 1989; Martha Thurmond Bishop, May 1, 1989; Mary Thurmond Tompkins, Allen George Thurmond, May 24, 1989.
28 barrel of apples: int., Mary Thurmond Tompkins, Allen George Thurmond, May 24, 1989.
28 a running account: int., Mary Thurmond Tompkins, Apr. 30, 1989.
28 carrying Gertrude's books: int., Mary Thurmond Tompkins, Apr. 30, 1989.
29 named U.S. attorney: Simkins, *Tillman,* p. 531.
29 killed a man: ibid., p. 531; see also Banks, "Strom Thurmond and the Revolt Against Modernity," p. 37.
29 "Why in hell won't you shake": int., ST, Feb. 15, 1989.
30 Edgefield blacks . . . suffered reversals: Burton, *In My Father's House Are Many Mansions,* p. 311.

30 Railway coaches: Newby, *Black Carolinians,* p. 47.
30 "he will smell": Michie and Ryhlick, *Dixie Demagogues,* p. 271.
31 "Coley": Wallace, *The History of South Carolina,* p. 425.
31 "absolutely a child": Simkins, *Tillman,* p. 495.
31 "You people": Burnside, "The Governorship of Coleman Livingston Blease of South Carolina," p. 154.
31 silent vow: int., ST, Mar. 21, 1989.
31 "drastic action": int., ST, June 9, 1989.
32 murder, arson, robbery: Burnside, "Coleman Livingston Blease," p. 97. Between 1889 and 1918, 120 individuals were lynched in South Carolina, fewer than in any neighboring southern state. Georgia was the highest with 386, followed by Mississippi with 373 and then Alabama with 276.
32 Richard Carroll: Newby, *Black Carolinians,* p. 179.
32 Capital City Civic League: Aba-Mecha, "Modjeska Simkins," pp. 154–57.
32 sprawling to the ground: int., ST, June 9, 1989.
32 Albert Covar: int., Mary Thurmond Tompkins, Apr. 29, 1989.
33 running the seventeen miles: int., ST, Feb. 15, 1989.
33 "always be a man": *Taps,* Clemson College 1923 yearbook, p. 83.
33 "tremendous push and drive": *Saturday Evening Post,* Oct. 8, 1955, p. 32.
33 Harley Davidson: int., ST, Apr. 18, 1991.
34 "half-trained fool": Newby, *Black Carolinians,* p. 83.
34 William K. Tate: Burnside, "Coleman Livingston Blease," pp. 208–10.
34 By 1920, expenditures for black students: Newby, *Black Carolinians,* p. 86.
34 promotes "clean living . . .": article, Nov. 29, 1921, STHR.
35 "I shall be glad": undated article, STHR.
35 *The Coontown Aristocrats:* program of April 4, 1924, event, STHR.
35 "zealous instructors": *The Augusta Herald,* Aug. 25, 1927.
36 too much time hunting: int., ST, Feb. 15, 1989.
36 free health examinations: ibid.
36 "the country people": ibid.

CHAPTER 3: *On the Move*

Page
37 Fewer than 2,000: Hayes, "South Carolina and the New Deal 1932–1938," pp. 36–37.
37 two blacks died of starvation: ibid., p. 5.
38 "My sweetheart": Michie and Ryhlick, *Dixie Demagogues,* p. 266.
39 "big burly": ibid., p. 275.
39 a thriving practice: ints., ST, Feb. 15, 1989; June 6, 1989.
39 examine the schoolchildren: undated article, STHR.

40 cutting expenses by $33,000: article, Oct. 3, 1932, STHR.
40 finish in eighteen months: int., ST, Feb. 15, 1989.
40 illegitimate siblings: *In re Johnson's Estate. Carroll v. Sheppard et al.,* 154 S.C. 359.
41 best bar exam score that year: int., ST, Feb. 15, 1989.
41 YOU UNANIMOUSLY: Jan. 14, 1931, telegram, STHR.
41 unpaved and unlit: Hoffman, "The Genesis of the Modern Movement for Equal Rights in South Carolina, 1930–39," p. 349.
42 B. R. Tillman: int., ST, Feb. 15, 1989.
42 educational reforms: *The People,* Oct. 20, 1932, STHR.
42 no guaranteed term: Newby, *Black Carolinians,* p. 221.
42 2,350–538 margin: chart of election returns, Aug. 31, 1932, STHR.
42 twin duties: ST letter, Jan. 10, 1933, STHR.
43 "make up our minds to cut appropriations": *State,* Jan. 12, 1935, letter to the editor, STHR.
43 "your foolish questions": ibid., undated article, STHR.
43 "worth the service": undated article, STHR.
44 twenty-seven bills: *Journal of the South Carolina Senate, 1933,* p. 1986.
44 exemption for the Ku Klux Klan: *State,* Mar. 2, 1933, p. 2.
44 Thurmond was not recorded: *Journal of the S.C. Senate, 1933,* pp. 643–45.
44 "attachés, helpers": ibid., p. 1986.
44 "I never pushed it": int., ST, July 6, 1989.
44 seven of his ten bills: *Journal of S. C. Senate, 1934,* pp. 1554–55.
45 joined a handful of: *State,* May 19, 1935, p. 15A; see also *Journal of S. C. Senate, 1935,* pp. 1716–17.
45 "true Americans": *State,* Apr. 21, 1935, p. 15B.
45 "limit freedom of speech": ibid., p. 11B.
46 "a constant worker": *South Carolina Education,* vol. 17, no. 5, Jan. 1936, p. 153.
47 "mongrel meeting": Michie and Ryhlick, *Dixie Demagogues,* p. 266.
47 "Political equality": *State,* June 25, 1936, p. 1.
47 "another dose": ibid., June 26, 1936, p. 1; *NYT,* June 26, 1936, p. 15.
47 "saved them from starvation": Hoffman, "The Genesis of the Modern Movement," p. 364.
47 Four other Carolinians: Bouknight, "The Senatorial Campaigns of Ellison Durant ('Cotton Ed') Smith of South Carolina," p. 135.
47 "virtue of a woman": *Newsweek,* May 4, 1935, p. 10.
48 "social hell": Newby, *Black Carolinians,* pp. 229–30.
49 allocation of funds: *Journal of S. C. Senate, 1937,* pp. 1198, 1565.
49 seat on the Winthrop Board: Banks, "Strom Thurmond," p. 44.
49 nurses came to lobby: int., ST, Feb. 15, 1989.

49 "romance of the courtroom": int., ST, June 6, 1989.
50 Bettis Academy: ST letter to Jackson Davis, Nov. 12, 1935, STC Legal Series, Box 17, Folder D.
50 "in terrible shape": ST letter to Guy B. Foster, Dec. 3, 1935, STC Legal Series, Box 17, Folder F.
51 "We are anxious": ST letter to Rep. John C. Taylor, undated, STC Legal Series, Box 17, Folder T.
51 left work for his secretary: int., Rebecca Strom Morgan, May 24, 1989.
51 "I saved your life": ST letter to Andrew Taylor, Oct. 10, 1935, STC Legal Series, Box 17, Folder T.

CHAPTER *4: Insulation Against the Turmoil*

Page
53 August 10, 1937: *Record,* Aug. 17, 1937, STHR.
54 George Bell Timmerman: *Lexington Dispatch News,* Aug. 19, 1937, STHR.
54 "letting you know my decision": George Bell Timmerman letter to ST, Aug. 12, 1937, STC Legal Series, Box 18, Folder T–Z.
55 Speaker Solomon Blatt and Senator Edgar Brown: letters from ST to Solomon Blatt and Edgar Brown and from Blatt and Brown to ST, Aug. 10–28, 1937, STC Legal Series, Box 18, Folder A–B.
56 "leave no stone unturned": ST letter to Hon. Joseph H. Bryson, Aug. 10, 1937, STC Legal Series, Box 18, Folder A–B.
56 "encourage them as much as possible": ibid.
56 T. B. Greneker: T. B. Greneker letter to Sen. James Pruitt, Aug. 10, 1937, STC Legal Series, Box 18, Folder F–H.
57 "You have lots of friends": ST letter to C. Kenneth Grimsley, Aug. 16, 1937, STC Legal Series, Box 18, Folder F–H.
57 "get your Mother and Father": ST letter to Katherine Anderson, Aug. 23, 1937, STC Legal Series, Box 18, Folder A–B.
57 "I expect to vote for you": Q. Britt letter to ST, Aug. 25, 1937, STC Legal Series, Box 18, Folder A–B.
57 four-door Chevrolet: int., ST, June 9, 1989.
57 "Everything appears bright": ST letter to Hon. and Mrs. W. P. Baskin, Jr., Aug. 30, 1937, STC Legal Series, Box 18, Folder A–B.
57 "about two-thirds of the Senate": ST letter to Hon. Joseph H. Bryson, Sept. 2, 1937, STC Legal Series, Box 18, Folder A–B.
57 "Everything is looking fine": ST letter to Hon. William P. Baskin, Jr., Sept. 6, 1937, STC Legal Series, Box 18, Folder A–B.
58 "amounts to nothing": ST letter to Hon. W. L. DePass, Jr., Sept. 13, 1937, STC Legal Series, Box 18, Folder C–E.
58 "If you will say a word": ST letter to W. T. C. Bates, Dec. 7, 1937, STC Legal Series, Box 18, Folder A–B.
58 got up as usual: int., ST, Aug. 22, 1989.

58 took out a pad: ibid.
59 "high honor": articles from several South Carolina papers, Jan. 13–14, 1938, STHR.
59 highway commission: *The Anderson Independent,* Jan. 16, 1938, STHR.
59 "two-to-one": int., ST, June 9, 1989.
59 "a political upset": *The Anderson Independent,* Jan. 16, 1938, STHR.
59 "a great admirer": Solomon Blatt letter to ST, Jan. 15, 1938, STC Legal Series, Box 18, Folder A–B.
60 "When I go after a thing": int., ST, June 9, 1989.
60 sworn into office: *State,* Jan. 21, 1938, STHR.
60 majority white: historical statistics from the U.S. Department of Commerce, Bureau of the Census.
60 penitentiary . . . filled by blacks: Newby, *Black Carolinians,* p. 65.
60 more than half of all criminal defendants: compiled from a report of the board of directors of the penitentiary and the attorney general's annual report to the South Carolina legislature.
60 called the trial a farce: Aba-Mecha, "Modjeska Simkins," pp. 272–74.
61 "passed life sentences": undated article, STHR.
61 disposed of twenty-nine cases: Banks, "Strom Thurmond," p. 45.
62 decried the rising crime rate: *NC,* Dec. 10, 1938, STHR.
62 "good reports": L. D. Lide letter to ST, July 1, 1983, STC Legal Series, Box 19, Folder G–O.
62 "taking into consideration": ST letter to Laneau D. Lide, July 5, 1938, STC Legal Series, Box 19, Folder G–O.
63 "a pert little monster": Percy, *Lanterns on the Levee: Recollections of a Planter's Son,* p. 148.
63 first name was Bilbo: Michie and Ryhlick, *Dixie Demagogues,* p. 90.
63 "treat the negro fairly": Doler, "Theodore G. Bilbo's Rhetoric of Racial Relations," p. 69.
64 "God created": Michie and Ryhlick, *Dixie Demagogues,* p. 105.
64 "the quadroon, the octaroon": *Congressional Record,* 1938, pp. 873–94; see also Doler, "Theodore Bilbo's Rhetoric of Racial Relations," p. 160.
64 failed twice to cut off debate: CQCN, vol. 1, p. 1637.
64 "on a cotton bale": Bouknight, "The Senatorial Campaigns," p. 140; see also *State,* June 25, 1938, p. 7.
65 "horrid days of Reconstruction": Bouknight, "The Senatorial Campaigns," p. 131.
65 "going to make it highbrow": ibid., p. 137.
65 enduring themes: ibid., pp. 139–43.
66 "Bacon Brown": ibid., p. 145.

66 "unnecessary, hackneyed": Aba-Mecha, "Modjeska Simkins," pp. 275–76.
66 another Red Shirt victory: Bouknight, "The Senatorial Campaigns," p. 167.
67 J. C. Hann: *State,* Feb. 24, 1940, STHR; *State v. Hann,* 196 S.C. 211 (1940).
67 convicted a second time: *Post,* Apr. 26, 1981, article by David Bruck, Outlook section, p. 1.; int., Billy Coleman, July 27, 1989.
68 a machine gun was mounted: *Post,* Apr. 26, 1981, article by David Bruck, Outlook section, p. 1.
68 Joseph Murray: Joseph Murray letter to ST, Jan. 18, 1941, STC Legal Series, Box 20, Folder H–Z.
69 J. Reuben Long: transcript of the record, *State v. Thomas,* pp. 57–62; see also *Georgetown Times,* Jan. 31, 1941, STHR.
70 denied the request: transcript of the record, *State v. Thomas,* pp. 57–62.
71 Isaac Gibson: *State,* Feb. 1, 1941, STHR.
71 "say something about the Klan": Stephen Nettles letter to ST, Jan. 3, 1940, STC Legal Series, Box 20, Folder N–Z.
72 "masked riders": *NC,* Jan. 8, 1940, STHR.
72 "Religious training": ST letter to Gwendolyn Anderson, Nov. 1, 1941; Gwendolyn Anderson letter to ST, Oct. 24, 1941, STC Legal Series, Box 20, Folder A–C.
72 "to the chain gang": *The Anderson Independent,* Mar. 13, 1940, STHR.
73 suspend their sentences if they enlisted: military officers' letters to ST, ST reply, Jan. 27, Jan. 29, and Feb. 3, 1940, respectively, STC Legal Series, Box 20, Folder A–F.
73 the Timmermans and the Logues: Lachicotte, *Rebel Senator,* pp. 6–8; *The Augusta Herald,* Nov. 18, 1941; *The Greenville Piedmont,* Nov. 20, 1941, STHR.
74 enter the army: Spartanburg *Herald,* Apr. 11, 1942; *The Sumter Daily Item,* Apr. 11, 1941; *The Greenville News,* Apr. 2, 1941, STHR.
75 "cheaply printed prayer books": Hoffman, "The Genesis of the Modern Movement," pp. 354–55.
75 "come of age": ibid., pp. 353–54.
75 Levi S. Byrd: ibid., pp. 368–69.
76 none was successful: CQCN, vol. 1, p. 1637.
77 a concerted drive: Kesselman, *The Social Politics of the FEPC: A Study in Reform Pressure Movements,* pp. ix–x.
77 "like a rising wind": Aba-Mecha, "Modjeska Simkins," pp. 301–303.
78 "an agency of the state": *Smith v. Allwright,* 321 U.S. 649 (1944).
78 "so long as I am governor": Farmer, "The End of the White Primary

in South Carolina: A Southern State's Fight to Keep its Politics White," p. 11.

78 "If whites stick": ibid., p. 22.

79 Southern Democratic Party: ibid., pp. 22–23.

79 "seeking the amalgamation": *NYT,* Mar. 1, 1944, p. 13.

79 "Your resolution . . . is astonishing": *NYT,* Mar. 2, 1944, p. 34.

79 harass the NAACP: int., Modjeska Simkins, May 23, 1989.

80 "uninhabitable by decent white people": *NC,* Apr. 4, 1944, p. 1.

80 "why I made white supremacy": Farmer, "The End of the White Primary," p. 26.

80 "We'll fight him": *State,* Apr. 14, 1944, p. 1.

80 "keep our white Democratic primaries pure": *NC,* Apr. 15, 1944, p. 1.

80 "where you now sit": *NC,* Apr. 15–21, 1944, p. 1; *State,* Apr. 15–21, 1944, p. 1; Huss, *Senator for the South: A Biography of Olin D. Johnston,* pp. 123–25.

81 "I am utterly ashamed": *State,* Apr. 21, 1944, p. 5.

81 "at a time when all soldiers": *State,* Apr. 16, 1944, p. 1.

81 "Killbillies": *Newsweek,* May 1, 1944, p. 33.

81 ended Cotton Ed's: *State,* July 26, 1944, p. 1.

81 Eighty-nine dissident delegates: CQ, *National Party Conventions,* 1831–1984 p. 93.

82 Progressive Democratic Party: JMP, May 17, 1944, letter.

82 Osceola McKaine: Aba-Mecha, "Modjeska Simkins," p. 203.

82 "My, my": Greenwood *Index-Journal,* Sept. 14, 1944; undated article, STHR.

83 promptly resumed his judicial duties: undated article, STHR.

83 On the fifteenth he officially resigned . . . and announced: STC Legal Series, Box 21, Folder 1946A, May 15, 1946.

83 twenty-three years of public service: STC Speeches, Box 1, Folder 7, May 15, 1946.

83 legislature was all-powerful: Key, *Southern Politics,* pp. 150–51.

83 "felt so good when I came downtown": Burnside, "Coleman Livingston Blease," p. 184.

84 "We dare not": STC Speeches, Box 1, Folder 7, May 15, 1946, announcement.

84 basic localism: Key, *Southern Politics,* pp. 131–32.

85 The ten candidates who joined Thurmond: Banks, "Strom Thurmond," pp. 57–58; article, June 14, 1946, STHR; int., ST, Aug. 22, 1989.

85 "purest form": Banks, "Strom Thurmond," p. 59.

86 "political acrobats": article, June 14, 1946, STHR.

86 "Barnwell ring": ibid., see also Workman, *The Bishop from Barnwell: The Political Life and Times of Senator Edgar A. Brown,*

pp. 107–15; *NC*, June 12, 1946; *The Greenville News*, June 20, 1946, STHR.
86 a certain cohesion to the group: Key, *Southern Politics*, p. 153.
86 "somewhat synthetic issue": Banks, "Strom Thurmond," p. 65.
86 "the leading henchmen": undated article, *NC*, STHR.
87 "dominate South Carolina": *NC*, June 26, 1946, pp. 1, 11.
87 Stone . . . accepted: Banks, "Strom Thurmond," p. 66.
87 Simultaneously he released letters: Workman, *The Bishop from Barnwell*, pp. 109–14.
89 "scheming, conniving": undated speech, 1946, STC Speeches, Box 1.
90 "never favor mixing the races": *NC*, July 24, 1946, p. 1.
90 "so much a part of the thinking": Banks, "Strom Thurmond," p. 76.
90 candidate of the CIO: ibid., p. 77.
91 THURMOND FOR A PROGRESSIVE: Spartanburg *Herald*, Aug. 31, 1946, STHR.
91 September 3 vote: *State*, Sept. 4, 1946, p. 1.
91 "in bad shape": *State*, Sept. 8, 1946, STHR.
91 "a triumph": *State*, Sept. 4, 1946, p. 1.
91 three blacks had voted in Spartanburg: undated article, STHR.

CHAPTER 5: *Making Choices*

Page
95 "capitol belonged to the people": int., ST, Nov. 13, 1989.
96 Eleanor Thurmond looking on: *Record*, Jan. 21, 1947, STHR.
96 data processors: int., Robert McC. Figg, Nov. 25, 1989.
96 "carried her cross": Jan. 21, 1947, STC Speeches, Box 1.
97 "an earnest message": *Record*, Jan. 22, 1947, STHR.
98 until one in the morning: int., ST, Nov. 13, 1989.
98 forty commitments: Littlejohn, *Littlejohn's Half-Century at the Bench and Bar* (1936–86), p. 37.
98 a certain debt to him: int., Bruce Littlejohn, Dec. 6, 1989.
98 "cooperate with me": int., ST, Nov. 13, 1989.
99 "build up his own group": undated article, *The Timmonsville Times*, STHR.
99 "except for Thurmond": int., Bruce Littlejohn, Dec. 6, 1989.
99 so badly mutilated: *State*, Feb. 18, 1947, p. 1.
99 "a blot on the state": ST speech, Feb. 18, 1947, STC Speeches, Box 1.
99 "To my knowledge": ibid., Mar. 1, 1947.
100 "earned the enmity": *NYT*, May 18, 1947, p. 7E.
100 "outside interests": R. B. Herbert letter, Feb. 22, 1947, STG, Willie Earle file.
100 "prompt and aggressive action": C. Lamar Black letter to ST, Feb. 25, 1947, STG.

100 "immediate and principal reason": Osceola McKaine letter to ST, March 12, 1947, STG.
101 "ready for a progressive government": James McBride Dabbs letter to ST, Feb. 22, 1947, STG.
101 John H. McCray: Aba-Mecha, "Modjeska Simkins," pp. 172–75; McCray vita, JMP.
101 "burning, most important": John McCray speech, Jan. 25, 1947, JMP.
102 "concentrate on one": ibid., Mar. 16, 1947.
102 fair-skinned black: int., Modjeska Simkins, Nov. 12, 1989; Aba-Mecha, "Modjeska Simkins," p. 205; Harold Boulware letter to Frank H. Williams, Jan. 31, 1947, NAACP II-B, Legal File 1940–55, Box 214.
102 Law students at Columbia: January 1947 letters between Thurgood Marshall and Justice Department officials, NAACP II-B, Legal File 1940–55, Box 214.
103 "awaiting the Georgia move": John McCray letter to Oliver W. Harrington, Jan. 18, 1947, ibid.
103 "To make a long story short": Thurgood Marshall letter to John McCray, Jan. 22, 1947, ibid.
103 *Elmore v. Rice:* Civil Docket #1702, District Court of the United States, Eastern District of South Carolina, Feb. 21, 1947, ibid.
104 medium-length story: *State,* Feb. 22, 1947, p. 10.
104 John Wrighten: Yarbrough, *A Passion for Justice,* p. 58.
105 So Timmerman asked Waring: ibid., p. 60.
106 Waring was born July 27: ibid., pp. 3–11; W/CUOH, p. 12.
106 "a good deal of a demagogue": ibid., pp. 130a–131a.
106 "excellent character": Yarbrough, *A Passion for Justice,* pp. 18–22.
107 "mouth hanging open": ibid., p. 43.
107 second teacher pay case: ibid., pp. 44–45.
107 more dramatic racial case: ibid., pp. 48–53.
109 "atmosphere of respectability": ibid., p. 52.
109 "baptism in racial prejudice": ibid., p. 53.
110 "a good deal of power": W/CUOH, pp. 24–45; Yarbrough, *A Passion for Justice,* pp. 53–54.
110 "a chance to be elected": int., ST, Nov. 13, 1989.
111 trial of the thirty-one men: *State,* May 15–23, 1947, p. 1 stories; West, Rebecca, "Opera in Greenville," *The New Yorker,* June 14, 1947, p. 37.
111 "an insult to decency": *The Atlanta Journal,* May 23, 1947, STHR.
111 "new and stronger emphasis": *The Greenville News,* May 23, 1947, p. 4.

112 "a very firm stand": June 9, 1947, letter, STC, Box 1, Willie Earle file.
112 *Missouri ex rel. Gaines v. Canada:* 305 U.S. 337 (1938).
112 Robert L. Carter . . . T. C. Callison: *Record,* June 6, 1947, STHR.
113 "only fair and just": *Wrighten v. Board of Trustees of the University of South Carolina,* 72 F. Supp. 948, 953 (1947).
114 "almost impossible": Yarbrough, *A Passion for Justice,* pp. 59–60.
114 "we should win the suit": William P. Baskin letter to Herman Talmadge, May 16, 1947, NAACP II-B, Legal File 1940–55, Box 214.
115 *United States v. Classic:* 313 U.S. 299, 318 (1941).
115 took most of June 3 and 4: *State,* June 4, 5, 6, 1947, p. 1 stories.
116 answers to the judge: Yarbrough, *A Passion for Justice,* p. 63.
116 sided with the NAACP: *Elmore v. Rice,* 72 F. Supp. 516 (1947).
116 "a pretty heavy penalty": W/CUOH, pp. 256–57.
117 make "provisions immediately": *The Augusta Herald,* July 13, 1947, STHR.
117 "It would have been edifying": Charleston *Evening Post,* July 16, 1947, STHR.
117 "for our part": *Sumter Daily Item,* undated editorial, STHR.
117 "nothing left for South Carolina": *NC,* July 13, 1947, p. 4.
118 "South Carolina negroes": *Greenville News,* Aug. 14, 1947, STHR.
119 "a lovely ash-blonde": undated article, STHR.
119 He first saw Jean Crouch: int., ST, Mar. 21, 1989.
120 "What are you hunting": Lachicotte, *Rebel Senator,* pp. 13–20.
120 "plowboy from Edgefield": int., Robert McC. Figg, Nov. 25, 1989.
121 football season: undated picture, STHR.
121 "We've thought about it": Lachicotte, *Rebel Senator,* pp. 18–19.
121 "Darling Jean": JCTP, Box 2.
122 "My dearest Strom": ibid.
122 a cartoon: ibid.
122 "This acknowledges receipt": ibid.
122 "VIRILE GOVERNOR": *Life* magazine, Nov. 17, 1947, pp. 44–46.
122 did a handstand: undated picture (inscription refers to summer vacation), STHR.
122 private family wedding: *Record,* Nov. 7, 1947, p. 1, STHR.
123 massage a cramp: Lachicotte, *Rebel Senator,* p. 31.
123 his legislative program: ST speech, Dec. 23, 1947, STC Speeches, Box 1.
123 "Let's Look at '48": Oct. 2, 1947, STC Speeches, Box 1.
124 "the most sensational": President's Committee on Civil Rights, "To Secure These Rights: Report of the President's Committee on Civil Rights," pp. x, 99–101; recommendations, pp. 156–67.

125 "the denial to the Negro": *Elmore v. Rice,* 162 F.2 387, 392 (1947).

CHAPTER 6: *Irreversible Course*

Page

126 "As a lifelong Democrat": *States' Rights Information and Speakers Handbook,* STC Speeches, Box 3.
128 praise the legislators: ST address, Jan. 14, 1948, STC Speeches, Box 3.
128 "advocating ideas": *State,* Jan. 30, 1948, p. 1.
129 "It is inconceivable": Borsos, "Support for the National Democratic Party in South Carolina During the Dixiecrat Revolt of 1948," p. 7.
129 "the duty of every government": Harry S. Truman, Special Message to the Congress, Feb. 2, 1948, Public Papers of the President.
129 Swainsboro, Georgia: *JCL,* Feb. 4, 1948, p. 1; see also *NYT,* Feb. 4, 1948, p. 6.
130 "organized mongrel minorities": *Time,* Feb. 16, 1948, p. 25; *JCL,* Feb. 4, 1948, p. 1.
130 withdraw from the national party: Borsos, "Support for the National Democratic Party," pp. 10–11.
130 "a vicious and unconstitutional program": *JCL,* Feb. 5, 1948, p. 6.
130 "it does seem that Mr. Truman": *State,* Feb. 4, 1948, p. 4A.
131 "Gestapo": *The Atlanta Journal,* Feb. 7, 1948, STHR.
131 Fourth Circuit denied a request: *NC,* Feb. 7, 1948, STHR.
131 "spread like wildfire": *JCL,* Feb. 6, 1948, pp. 1, 2.
131 "join any movement": *The Atlanta Journal,* Feb. 8, 1948, STHR.
132 gone to the meeting well prepared: int., Robert McC. Figg, Dec. 18, 1989.
132 "shocked by the spectacle": ST motion to governors' conference, Feb. 7, 1948, STC Speeches, Box 2.
133 argued for a coalition: Collins, *Whither Solid South: A Study in Politics and Race Relations,* pp. 258–62.
133 Thurmond was named to head: *The Charlotte News,* Feb. 9, 1948, STHR.
134 "keen disappointment": *State,* Feb. 9, 1948, p. 1.
134 "White Mississippians": *JCL,* Feb. 13, 1948, p. 1.
134 note of caution: *The Charlotte News,* Feb. 13, 1948, STHR; see also Chesteen, "Mississippi Is Gone Home," p. 50.
134 pledged $61,500 to spread the word: Chesteen, "Mississippi Is Gone Home," p. 52.
134 "un-American": Greenwood *Index-Journal,* Feb. 13, 1948, STHR.
134 very public snub: *State,* Feb. 19, 20, 1948, p. 1; see also Borsos, "Support for the National Democratic Party," p. 12.

135 "applications for Ku Klux Klan": *State,* Feb. 20, 1948, p. 11B.
135 "Do you as Chairman": transcript of ST questions to J. Howard McGrath, Feb. 23, 1948, STG.
135 refused to agree to block: *State,* Feb. 24, 1948, p. 1.
135 "would not yield": *NYT,* Feb. 24, 1948, p. 1.
136 "no longer 'in the bag' ": *State,* Feb. 24, 1948, p. 1.
136 "gone too far": *State,* Mar. 2, 1948, p. 1.
136 "political fraud": ibid., Mar. 5, 1948, p. 1.
136 "Let's give the government": Chesteen, "Mississippi Is Gone Home," p. 53.
137 "brief period of pouting": *The New Republic,* Mar. 8, 1948, p. 10.
137 "all had laws": int., ST, June 9, 1989.
137 "the unavoidable conclusion": report of southern governors' committee, STC Speeches, March 13, 1948 Box 2.
138 "practical help on economic lines": ST speech, Mar. 17, 1948, STG; see also *NC,* Mar. 18, 1948, STHR.
139 "disastrous loss of personal liberties": McLaurin, "The Role of Dixiecrats in the 1948 Election," p. 59.
139 Dixon . . . McCorvey: Ness, "The States' Rights Movement of 1948," pp. 77–80; see also Burns, "The Alabama Dixiecrat Revolt of 1948," generally pp. 100–142.
139 "Nobody in this room": *The Montgomery Advertiser,* Apr. 5, 6, 1948, p. 1.
140 Editorial opinion was diverse: Burns, "The Alabama Dixiecrat Revolt," pp. 141–42.
140 "Defeat Truman's": ibid., p. 134.
140 "paradoxical political picture": *NYT,* May 2, 1948, p. 63.
140 E. D. Rivers: Ness, "The States' Rights Movement," p. 84.
141 PETITION: telegram, Apr. 19, 1948, NAACP II-B, Legal File 1940–55, Box 214.
141 "It is the wish": undated article, WBS.
141 "I was shocked": ST speech, Apr. 21, 1948, STC Speeches, Box 2.
142 "sober consideration": *Record,* Apr. 26, 1948, WBS.
142 "No Cause for Shock": *State,* May 21, 1948, WBS.
142 "Dixiecrats": *William Safire's Political Dictionary,* p. 176.
143 "stirring up of prejudices": Fielding Wright speech, Mississippi Department of Archives and History. The speech is on the end of a roll of microfilm that contains *The States' Righter,* the newspaper of the 1948 states' rights movement; see also *JCL,* Feb. 9, 10, 1948, p. 1.
144 covenants to bar blacks: *Shelley v. Kraemer,* 334 U.S. 1 (1948).
144 "Welcome States' Rights Democrats": *JCL,* May 19, 1948, p. 1; McLaurin, "The Role of Dixiecrats," pp. 128–30; int., Robert McC. Figg, Nov. 25, 1989.

144 "We have gathered here": ST speech, May 10, 1948, STC Speeches, Box 2.
147 dozens of delegates swarmed: *State,* May 11, 1948, WBS.
147 extreme heat: *JCL,* May 11, 1948, p. 1; *NYT,* May 11, 1948, p. 1.
148 "like a religion": *NYT,* May 11, 1948, pp. 1, 22.
148 "In no sense": Ness, "The States' Rights Movement," p. 107; see also *The States' Righter* of April 1948 at the Mississippi Department of Archives and History.
148 "fight to the last ditch": *Record,* May 19, 1948, WBS.
148 refrain from voting for Truman: Borsos, "Support for the National Democratic Party," pp. 16–17.
148 first time since 1877: *State,* May 20, 1948, WBS.
149 "first step was taken": *State,* May 20, 1948, WBS.
149 key part of the oath: *State,* May 21, 1948, WBS; see also JWWP, Folder 827.
149 "Down with half-citizenship": *State,* May 27, 1948, WBS.
150 good tactical move: Borsos, "Support for the National Democratic Party," pp. 25–26.
150 statewide radio address: ST speech, May 26, 1948, STG.
150 "only a member of the Nazi": *Record,* May 28, 1948, WBS.
151 public disapproval was intense: *State,* May 30, 31, 1948; *The Anderson Independent,* May 30, 1948, WBS.
151 such narrow instructions: *State,* June 3, 1948, WBS.
151 "grass-roots movement": Borsos, "Support for the National Democratic Party," p. 28.
151 "defiance of orders": *The Anderson Independent,* June 6, 1948; *State,* June 8, 1948, WBS.
151 half of them women: *State,* June 9, 1948, WBS.
152 small milestone: *State,* June 8, 1948, WBS.
152 openly defying Baskin: *NC,* June 19, 1948; *The Anderson Independent,* June 8, 1948; *The Greenville News,* June 20, 1948, WBS.
152 another closed-door meeting: *NC,* June 18, 1948; *State,* June 18, 1948.
152 E. H. McClenney: undated article, WBS; see also Borsos, "Support for the National Democratic Party," p. 31.
153 "The party belongs": ST letter to William Baskin, *State,* June 27, 1948, WBS.
153 On July 8, David Brown: *State,* July 9, 1948, p. 1.

CHAPTER 7: *Candidate by Default*

Page

154 "sodden gloom": Ross, *The Loneliest Campaign,* p. 111.
155 the party's savior: ibid., p. 112.

155 "politics just doesn't work that way": int., ST, Jan. 11, 1990.
155 "federal invasion": *State,* July 10, 1948, p. 1.
156 "I would refuse": *NYT,* July 10, 1948, p. 1.
157 "most experienced": *NYT,* July 11, 1948, pp. 1, 4.
157 "We have been betrayed": *NC,* July 12, 1948, p. 1.
157 "collapsed utterly": *NYT,* July 12, 1948, p. 1.
158 hunting for a candidate: *AC,* July 12, 1948, p. 1.
158 "I have told": *NC,* July 13, 1948, p. 1.
158 "Business Ben": *Arkansas Gazette,* Jan. 23, 1977, p. 1.
158 "Where is the courage": *NYT,* July 13, 1948, pp. 1, 2.
159 "the scheming": *AC,* July 13, 1948, p. 6.
159 "homebred conscience": *AC,* Feb. 14, 1969, p. 1.
160 "That is the first I heard of it": July 10, 1948, Democratic National Committee proceeding, pp. 19–22, DNCR, Box 3.
160 Although McCray was scheduled: *State,* July 10, 1948, p. 1; see also Borsos, "Support for the National Democratic Party," p. 38.
161 "there was not a Negro vote": July 13, 1948, Credentials Committee proceeding, p. 15; entire S.C. credentials debate, pp. 15–69, DNCR, Box 3.
162 "I will answer you nothing": ibid., p. 58.
164 controversial voice vote: *NYT,* July 14, 1948, pp. 1, 4.
165 delegates supporting a stronger civil rights plank: Ross, *The Loneliest Campaign,* pp. 120–21.
165 "splitting the party wide open": Griffith, *Humphrey: A Candid Biography,* pp. 152–54.
165 "That's it. I'll do it": ibid., p. 154.
166 conciliatory reassurances: Brown, *Democracy at Work: Being the Official Report of the Democratic National Convention (1948),* p. 182. The debate and final vote on the platform continue through p. 211.
167 mixture of cheers and boos: Ross, *The Loneliest Campaign,* pp. 125–26.
167 "never to cast their vote": ibid., p. 127; *NYT,* July 15, 1948, pp. 1, 3.
167 "I don't want to run": *State,* July 15, 1948, WBS.
167 boy wonder of Georgia politics: *AC,* Jan. 22, 1971, p. 1; *NYT,* Jan. 22, 1971, pp. 1, 43.
168 "we . . . are not bolters": Brown, *Democracy at Work,* p. 230.
168 "It is medicine": ibid., pp. 263–64; ST speech, July 14, 1948, STG.
169 "Mississippi is gone home": Chesteen, "Mississippi Is Gone Home," p. 59.
169 "it had no friends here": *AC,* July 15, 1948, p. 10.
169 had to leave Philadelphia: *State,* July 13, 1948, WBS.

169 "I feel quite ashamed": Yarbrough, *A Passion for Justice,* pp. 70–71.
170 black citizens in Beaufort: memo from Harold Boulware to Thurgood Marshall, NAACP II-B, Legal File 1940–55, Box 213.
171 is it "objectionable": Yarbrough, *A Passion for Justice,* pp. 72–73.
171 Waring bristled and took the bait: ibid., pp. 73–74.
173 "not a private party": *Brown v. Baskin,* 78 F. Supp. 933, 941 (1948).
173 HOW TO STOP: *NC,* July 17, 1948, p. 1; Yarbrough, *A Passion for Justice,* p. 76.
173 White Charlestonians shunned: Yarbrough, *A Passion for Justice,* p. 76.
174 "Only the thoughtless": *AC,* July 16, 1948, pp. 1, 15.
174 "Concerted Southern action": *State,* July 17, 1948, p. 4.
174 Birmingham was full of enthusiasm: Barnard, *Dixiecrats and Democrats: Alabama Politics, 1942–50,* p. 113; Burns, "The Alabama Dixiecrat Revolt," pp. 165–67; Starr, "Birmingham and the Dixiecrat Convention of 1948," pp. 23–50.
175 rearrange his schedule: *State,* July 17, 1948, p. 1.
175 approached by Frank Dixon: ints., ST, Oct. 12, 1989, Jan. 11, 1990; see also Lachicotte, *Rebel Senator,* p. 92.
176 Beulah Waller: Starr, "Birmingham and the Dixiecrat Convention of 1948," p. 41.
177 "totalitarian, centralized": *States' Rights Information and Speakers Handbook,* STC Speeches, Box 3, p. 4.
177 "I want to tell you": Twentieth Century–Fox Movietone News footage of States' Rights Democrats convention, July 17, 1948, Birmingham, Alabama.
177 "I couldn't believe": confidential interview.
177 "word it differently": int., ST, June 9, 1989.
178 "We do not invite": *State,* July 20, 1948, WBS.
178 "a respectful hearing": Washington *Evening Star,* July 21, 1948, p. 10A.
178 "I came here . . . recommended for President": *NYT,* July 19, 1948, pp. 1, 8.
179 "sideshow drums": *AC,* July 18, 1948, p. 2A.
179 "Claghornesque goings-on": Ashley, "Selected Southern Liberal Editors and the States' Rights Movement of 1948," pp. 305–6.
179 "destruction of the Democratic Party": ibid., p. 307.
179 using his candidacy to bolster: *The News and Observer,* July 18, 1948, p. 1; int., Robert McC. Figg, Nov. 25, 1989.
180 "hoarse blasphemies": McLaurin, "The Role of Dixiecrats," p. 185.
180 "true Southerner": *AC,* July 19, 1948, p. 6.

180 "Thurmond for President": *NC,* July 18, 1948, p. 1.
180 "particularly gratifying": ST letter to William Watts Ball, July 21, 1948, WWBP.
180 "rest on firmer ground": *State,* July 19, 1948, p. 4.
181 "fight to the limit": *NYT,* July 28, 1948, p. 1; special session generally, Ross, *The Loneliest Campaign,* pp. 137–39; *NYT,* Aug. 8, 1948, p. 1.
181 "suicidal": Ness, "The States' Rights Movement of 1948," p. 178.
181 on the North Carolina ballot at all: The States' Rights Democrats filed a petition to get on the ballot within the deadline, but signers weren't checked. The states' righters promised to pay a ten-cents-per-name fee for checking the names and also protested the claim that the signers had to be those citizens who had not voted in the recent primary party primaries. A judge ruled for the States' Rights Democrats, and the Supreme Court upheld the decision, allowing the states' righters to get on the ballot. *States' Rights Democratic Party v. Board of Elections,* 229 N.C. 179 (1948).
182 Truman's name: Schlesinger, *History of American Presidential Elections, 1789–1968,* p. 3140.
182 "solemn agreement": *The Dallas Morning News,* Aug. 5, 1948, STHR.
182 "I insist": *NYT,* Sept. 26, 1948, p. 48.
183 every little "pigtrail": McLaurin, "The Role of Dixiecrats," p. 224.
183 Thurmond had to rely: int., ST, Oct. 12, 1989.
183 "again with photographers!": Lachicotte, *Rebel Senator,* pp. 53–54.
184 "close to the people": ST speech, July 21, 1948, STG.
184 "Thurmond's harp": *LCJ,* Oct. 17, 1948, p. 2A.
185 "misnamed civil rights program": ST speech, Aug. 11, 1948, STG.
185 Radio commentators: NBC Radio Collection, RWB 7849-A1-A4, Library of Congress.
186 "forced to work, side by side": ST speech, Sept. 7, 1948, STG.
186 "This is no fight": ST speech, Sept. 8, 1948, STG.
186 "The real issue": *LCJ,* Oct. 16, 1948, p. 17.
187 IS THE ISSUE BLACK AND WHITE: *Time,* Oct. 11, 1948, cover, pp. 24–27.
188 "ridiculous to invite him": *Newsweek,* Oct. 25, 1948, p. 37.
188 Governor William M. Tuck: Ashley, "Selected Liberal Editors," p. 370.
188 "What's the sense of jumping": Ness, "The States' Rights Movement," p. 227.
188 "most astounding presidential": ST speech, Nov. 1, 1948, STG.
189 placed third: CQ, *Guide to U.S. Elections,* pp. 304, 357.
189 Eric Sevareid: Ralph McGill telegram to Eric Sevareid, Nov. 4,

1948. Papers of Arnold Eric Sevareid, Fan Mail, B-2, Library of Congress.

189 "the greatest service": int., ST, Feb. 15, 1989. He repeated this observation in several other interviews.

189 The lion's share: Heard, *A Two Party South?*, pp. 251–55; see also pp. 20–33.

190 major papers were hostile: int., ST, Jan. 11, 1990.

190 "did his best": J. Melville Broughton letter to John Sanford Martin, July 25, 1948, John Sanford Martin Papers, Manuscript Department, Duke University Library.

190 "whole South had been Democratic": int., ST, Jan. 11, 1990.

191 "The Dixiecrat Mind": *AC,* July 30, 1948, p. 8.

191 "You can rest assured": ST telegram to Harry Truman, Nov. 3, 1948, STG.

191 "my sincere appreciation": ST letter to William Watts Ball, Nov. 8, 1948, WWBP.

192 "honestly in my heart": int., ST, Jan. 11, 1990.

192 a special moment for Waring: Yarbrough, *A Passion for Justice,* p. 93.

192 "The last citadel": *The New Republic,* Aug. 14, 1948, p. 187.

193 "an absurdity": *Brown v. Baskin,* 80 F. Supp. 1017 (1948).

CHAPTER 8: *In the Shadow of the Court*

Page

194 "an old country town": South Carolina Writers Project, *South Carolina: A Guide to the Palmetto State,* p. 313.

194 a rudimentary shack: Kluger, *Simple Justice,* pp. 6–7; see also *County and City Data Book,* 1952, U.S. GPO, 1953.

196 "white Democrats": newspaper ad, ODJP, 1950 campaign file.

197 "every turn": STC Speeches, Jan. 12, 1949, Box 4.

198 a movement, not a separate national party: Grover Hall letter to ST, Jan. 23, 1949; ST response, undated, RFP, Strom Thurmond folder.

198 take a hard line: *The Greenville News,* Feb. 26, 1948, STHR.

198 "work together in harmony": undated article, STHR.

198 "existing laws and traditions": ST speech, Apr. 7, 1949, RFP; *The Sumter Daily Item,* Apr. 14, 18, 1949, STHR.

199 "The governor missed": John McCray column, *The Lighthouse and Informer,* Apr. 19, 1949, JWWP, Box 42, Folder 1257.

200 progressive but controversial: *The Anderson Independent,* Apr. 25, 1949, STHR.

200 Dr. T. C. McFall: *The Lighthouse and Informer,* undated article, STHR.

201 "The names of J. Strom Thurmond": *The Greenville Piedmont,* undated article, STHR.

201 "would know nothing": *Record,* Feb. 13, 1950, STHR.
202 "It must be obvious now": Greenwood *Index-Journal,* Aug. 26, 1949, STHR; see also news stories from several South Carolina papers, Aug. 22–26, 1949, STHR.
202 Jonathan Daniels: *The Augusta Chronicle,* Jan. 10, 1950, STHR.
202 "she does not understand": *Record,* Feb. 13, 1950, STHR.
203 "I am glad": ST statement, Apr. 13, 1950, STC Speeches, Box 6.
203 "every outside influence": ST speech, Apr. 29, 1950, STC Speeches, Box 6; see also *State, NC,* Apr. 30, 1950, both p. 1.
204 Johnston grew up: *State, NC,* April 1, 19, 1965, both p. 1; see also generally, Huss, *Senator for the South.*
206 Before each meeting: int., Harry S. Dent, Sept. 20, 1989.
207 "he'll do anything": int., Rep. Elizabeth Patterson, Mar. 14, 1990.
207 "I do not intend": ST speech, May 23, 1950, STC Speeches, Box 5.
207 "begged" General Eisenhower: *The Charlotte Observer,* May 30, 1950, STHR.
207 "repudiated his oath": *State,* June 8, 1950, STHR.
207 "wobbles in": ST speech, May 25, 1950, STC Speeches, Box 6.
208 *Sweatt v. Texas:* 339 U.S. 629 (1950); see also *NYT, State, NC,* June 6, 1950, p. 1.
208 *McLaurin v. Oklahoma State Regents:* 339 U.S. 737 (1950); see also *Henderson v. U.S.,* 339 U.S. 963 (1950).
208 "a share of responsibility": *State,* June 7, 1950, p. 1.
209 "relief . . . from any federal judge": review of ST career, WWP, 1950 Senate campaign file.
209 FIRES HIS MUD GUN: *The Anderson Independent,* June 8, 1950, STHR.
210 "let 'em heckle": *The Charlotte News,* June 29, 1950, ODJP, 1950 campaign file.
210 "Did you pardon him?": int., ST, Feb. 26, 1990.
210 "seven campaigns": *The Greenville News,* June 8, 1950, STHR.
210 "five-week-old personal attack": ODJP, 1950 campaign file.
210 "you can get addled": *State,* June 24, 1950, p. 1.
211 "silent as a tomb": int., Harry S. Dent, Mar. 29, 1990; reference to near fight, Greenwood *Index-Journal,* June 27, 1950, STHR; see also *Post,* June 27, 1950.
211 "I'm for segregation": *Florence Morning News,* June 22, 1950, p. 1.
211 "I have done more": ibid.
212 "whose every point": John McCray column, *The Lighthouse and Informer,* July 15, 1950, ODJP, 1950 campaign file.
212 "a sordid mess of pottage": undated speech, ODJP, 1950 campaign file.
212 "THURMOND APPOINTS A NEGRO": undated ad, STHR.
213 "Make those niggers": *NC,* July 7, 1951, p. 1.

213 cite with *pride:* int., ST, Feb. 11, 1990.
213 Johnston-McGrath picture: ODJP, 1950 campaign file.
213 "valiant soldiers": ibid.
214 "The orders have come down": ibid.
214 "a definite victory": ST statement, May 3, 1950, STC Speeches, Box 6.
214 "a damned nigger lover": *The News and Observer,* July 1985, special edition on North Carolina, "Into the Mainstream," pp. 11, 14.
214 "MENACE TO DEMOCRACY": ST election ad, WWP, 1950 campaign file.
214 "Don't desert": ibid.
215 60,000 black votes . . . "made the difference": *The Lighthouse and Informer,* July 15, 1950, pp. 1, 4; *NC,* July 13, 1950, p. 10A.
215 "negro bigwigs": WWP, memo in 1950 campaign file.
216 "develop into a statesman": John McCray column, *The Lighthouse and Informer,* July 15, 1950, p. 4.
216 The better strategy: int., ST, Feb. 26, 1990.
216 "dead horse's rear end": int., Harry S. Dent, Sept. 20, 1989.
216 "I didn't worry over it": int., ST, Feb. 26, 1990.
216 Preelection statistics: WWP, 1950 campaign file; ODJP, 1950 campaign file.
217 glaring evidence of the inequality: Yarbrough, *A Passion for Justice,* p. 173.
217 "awful little wooden shacks": W/CUOH, p. 341.
217 Parents had to: int., Billie Fleming, Mar. 27, 1990; Kluger, *Simple Justice,* p. 14.
217 lit the fire: Kluger, *Simple Justice,* pp. 14–17.
219 *Pearson v. County Board of Education:* Kluger, *Simple Justice,* pp. 14–26; Yarbrough, *A Passion for Justice,* pp. 172–74.
219 an ill-considered move: Kluger, *Simple Justice,* pp. 19–20; pamphlet on Clarendon County case; private papers of Billie Fleming.
220 "fire here": Kluger, *Simple Justice,* p. 23.
220 Harry Briggs: ibid.
220 "Is this the price": ibid., p. 24.
221 "sly reign": JWWP, Folder 85.
221 "a sick, confused": Yarbrough, *A Passion for Justice,* p. 130.
221 "the professional agitator": *NC,* Jan. 17, 1950, p. 8; Jan. 19, 1950, p. 12A.
222 "stubborn, savage": *NC,* Oct. 11, 1950, p. 1.
222 "carries himself": Kluger, *Simple Justice,* pp. 222–23.
223 " 'Nigguh' ": *Time,* Sept. 19, 1954, pp. 23–27.
223 "was never political": int., Robert McC. Figg, Nov. 25, 1989, Dec. 18, 1989, Mar. 29, 1990; Kluger, *Simple Justice,* pp. 340–41.

224 "a brand new suit": *NC,* Nov. 18, 1950, p. 1.; W/CUOH, pp. 345–46.
224 "magnolias instead": Waring interview with Carl Rowan, newspaper tear sheet, JWWP.
225 "embarrassingly unequal": ints., Robert McC. Figg, Nov. 25, 1989, Mar. 29, 1990; Yarbrough, *A Passion for Justice,* p. 180; Kluger, *Simple Justice,* chapters 14–15, generally.
225 "we will abandon": Yarbrough, *A Passion for Justice,* p. 177.
225 "Whites and Negroes": *NC,* Mar. 19, 1951, p. 2A.
226 "defaulting": ST letter to Robert McC. Figg, May 28, 1951, STC, unprocessed personal correspondence, 1950s.
226 "a little whiff of freedom": W/CUOH, p. 358.
226 "I wanted to make a statement": Yarbrough, *A Passion for Justice,* p. 180.
227 "The defendants do not oppose": *NC, State,* May 29, May 30, 1951, p. 1 for newspaper coverage of hearing.
228 Their only visual aids: Yarbrough, *A Passion for Justice,* p. 181.
228 "disreputable": *NC,* Oct. 7, 1951, p. 1.
229 "His numbers were small": Kluger, *Simple Justice,* pp. 354–55.
229 E. R. Crow: transcript of *Briggs v. Elliott,* JWWP, Folders 760–61; Kluger, *Simple Justice,* pp. 359–61.
230 "admitted inferiority": Kluger, *Simple Justice,* p. 363.
231 "a rigid segregationist": W/CUOH, pp. 358–60.
231 " 'Thank God for Mississippi' ": Yarbrough, *A Passion for Justice,* p. 90.
232 The 2–1 decision: *NC,* June 24, 1951, p. 1.
232 stinging dissent: *Briggs v. Elliott,* 98 F. Supp. 529, 538 (1951).
233 "To my precious": JWWP, Folder 741.
234 "with no regrets whatever": Yarbrough, *A Passion for Justice,* p. 212.
234 "most of his promises": *NC,* Jan. 8, 1951, STHR.
235 "four years of tireless service": *State,* Jan. 16, 1951, STHR.
235 Thurmond, Lybrand and Simons: int., U.S. District Judge Charles Simons, Mar. 28, 1990.
236 a new Cadillac: *Record,* Jan. 15, 1951, STHR; Leon Moore letter to Robert McC. Figg, Nov. 1, 1950, RFP.
236 "When Strom came to town": int., U.S. District Judge Charles Simons, Mar. 28, 1990.
236 ante up seventy-five thousand dollars: int., ST, Feb. 26, 1990.
237 weeping Margie Kennedy: *The Augusta Herald,* Oct. 18, 1951, STHR; int., ST, Feb. 26, 1990.
237 "I have not publicly": ST letter to James Byrnes, Nov. 1, 1952, RFP. Figg file also contains five letters to ST urging him to back Eisenhower; all are dated Aug. 16, 1952.
237 intention to vote for Eisenhower: *NC,* Nov. 3, 1952, STHR.

237 "The $64 question": *The Augusta Chronicle,* Oct. 30, 1953, STHR.
237 STROM THURMOND IS ENIGMA: *AC,* Nov. 1, 1953, STHR.

CHAPTER 9: The Year of Precedents

Page

239 "You know": int., Harry S. Dent, Mar. 29, 1990.
241 research alternatives: NAACP II-B, Series B, Container 140.
241 John W. Davis: Kluger, *Simple Justice,* p. 529.
241 "a liberal system": *State,* Jan. 9, 1952, p. 1.
241 two-to-one margin: *State,* Nov. 5, 1952, p. 1. The actual vote on the constitutional amendment was 187,435–91,823.
242 "wholly irrelevant": *Briggs v. Elliott,* 342 U.S. 350, 352 (1952); see also Kluger, *Simple Justice,* pp. 531–32.
242 "show beyond question": *Briggs v. Elliott,* 103 F. Supp. 920, 921 (1952).
243 "never sat on a bench": New York *Daily News,* Sept. 30, 1953, p. 4.
243 "If the Japs are released": Kluger, *Simple Justice,* pp. 659–64; see also Warren, *Memoirs,* p. 149.
243 "a sweeping civil rights program": Pittsburgh *Courier,* Apr. 19, 1952, p. 28.
244 "Segregation with the sanction": *Brown v. Board of Education,* 98 F. Supp. 797 (1951).
245 "puts the Supreme Court": Kluger, *Simple Justice,* p. 424.
245 Huxman would acknowledge: ibid.; see chapter 17 generally.
245 eighty-five years after: The first black lawyer was Macon B. Allen. From *The Negro Handbook,* Johnson Publishing Co., 1966.
246 "he is entitled to": *Belton v. Gebhart,* 87 A2d 862 (1952); see also *Wilmington Journal,* Oct. 22–25, 1951; Kluger, *Simple Justice,* chapter 18 generally.
246 decision was affirmed: *Belton v. Gebhart,* 91 A2d 137 (1952).
247 State Literary Fund . . . April 23, 1951: Kluger, *Simple Justice,* pp. 459–60, 466–71.
248 "due diligence and dispatch": *Davis v. County School Board of Prince Edward County,* 103 F. Supp. 337, 341 (1952).
249 segregation in the Washington schools: Kluger, *Simple Justice,* pp. 521–23.
249 "a comparatively simple case": Kluger, *Simple Justice,* p. 678.
249 drove Black to court: int., David Vann, May 30, 1990.
250 "I immediately said": ibid.
250 "I think you boys": Kluger, *Simple Justice,* p. 701.
252 " 'separate but equal' has no place": *Brown v. Board of Education,* 347 U.S. 483, 495 (1954).

252 "getting pretty sticky": int., David Vann, May 30, 1990.
252 "You've got to decide": Kluger, *Simple Justice,* p. 698.
253 "real credit": Warren, *Memoirs,* p. 4.
253 "wide applicability": *Brown v. Board of Education,* 347 U.S. at 495 (1954); Kluger, *Simple Justice,* p. 707.
253 "it would be unthinkable": *Bolling v. Sharpe,* 347 U.S. 497 (1954).
254 "shocked to learn": *State,* May 18, 1954, p. 1.
254 "go slow": *JCL,* May 18, 1954, p. 1.
254 "reduced our Constitution": *AC,* May 18, 1954, p. 1.
254 "will not abide": *Post,* May 18, 1954, p. 1.
254 "pliant tool": *AC,* May 18, 1954, p. 1.
255 "We receive the decision": *NC,* May 18, 1954, p. 1.
255 "create many problems": *State,* May 18, 1954, p. 4A.
255 "a black day of tragedy": *JCL,* May 18, 1954, p. 6.
255 "gigantic social revolution": *Florence Morning News,* May 18, 1954, p. 4.
256 Rembert Dennis: *NC, State,* Sept. 4, 1954, p. 1.
256 "the most powerful man": Key, *Southern Politics,* p. 152.
257 "a handful of men dictating": *NC,* Sept. 4, 1954, p. 1.
257 "People Weren't Consulted": ibid.
257 "resent it rightfully": ibid.
257 not complied with . . . regulations: *State,* Sept. 5, 1954, p. 1.
257 "denies the people": *Florence Morning News,* Sept. 6, 1954, STHR.
258 "sharpen their pencils": *NC,* Sept. 7, 1954, p. 8B.
258 "the fast deal": *NC,* Sept. 7, 1954, p. 1.
258 "DON'T LET BROWN": Herman W. Shelley telegram to ST, Sept. 4, 1954, STC Campaigns, 1954.
258 "announce your candidacy at once": L. R. Corbin letter to ST, Sept. 4, 1954, STC Campaigns, 1954.
258 "political maneuvering": *NC,* Sept. 8, 1954, p. 1.
259 "Thurmond Is the Man": ibid.
259 "a spectacular fight": *State,* Sept. 8, 1954, p. 1.
259 sixteen dailies: Banks, "Strom Thurmond," p. 241.
259 "SIC'IM": postcard signed "A Voting Democrat" to ST, undated, STC Campaigns, 1954.
259 "greatest upsurge": *The Augusta Chronicle,* Sept. 8, 1954, STHR.
260 "The people must determine": *Florence Morning News,* Sept. 9, 1954, STHR.
260 "quiet, orderly and thoughtful": Neville Bennett statement, Sept. 13, 1954 EBP Campaigns, 1954.
260 "deliberate falsehoods": *NC,* Oct. 2, 1954, p. 9.
261 "unfalteringly served": *State,* Sept. 14, 1954, p. 1.

261 "justifiably angered": *State,* Sept. 15, 1954, p. 12A.
262 "rescind the previous action": *State,* Sept. 15, 1954, p. 1.
262 "no selfish ambition": *State,* Sept. 19, 1954, pp. 1, 2A.
262 "Don't be fooled": *NC,* Oct. 2, 1954, p. 9.
263 "I am a Democrat": *State,* Sept. 21, 1954, p. 1.
263 "On voting day": *State,* Oct. 6, 1954, p. 1.
263 "marking an 'X' ": ibid.
263 "this Chicago lawyer": *State,* Oct. 7, 1954, p. 1.
263 "step down and submit": *NC,* Oct. 5, 1954, p. 1.
264 "misleading, untrue": Workman, *Bishop from Barnwell,* p. 265.
264 letters and brochures: campaign materials for 1954 campaign, STC Campaigns, 1954.
264 "100 percent expediency": Banks, "Strom Thurmond," p. 239.
265 "Upside Down Again!": Edgar Brown campaign letter, EBP Campaigns, 1954.
265 "stood on the State House steps": ibid.
265 "I shall write in": *State,* Oct. 24, 1954, p. 1.
266 "has turned his back": *NC,* Oct. 28, 1954, p. 1.
266 telephoning influential people: int., John West, May 23, 1990.
266 "intent of the voter": *State,* Oct. 29, 1954, p. 10A.
266 "everybody was coming by": int., John West, May 23, 1990.
266 Thurmond had won: *State,* Nov. 3, 1954, p. 1.
266 "ruthless machine": ibid.
267 "I was sixty-six": Workman, *Bishop from Barnwell,* p. 256; int., John West, May 23, 1990.
267 the first time since Reconstruction: *State,* Nov. 3, 1954, p. 1.

CHAPTER *10: Resistance and Resolve*

Page

269 "all the bordering counties": Bullard et al., *Free at Last, A History of the Civil Rights Movement and Those Who Died in the Struggle,* p. 36; int., Rosebud Lee Henson, Aug. 28, 1990.
269 "in a plain envelope": Gus Courts letter to NAACP, 1954, NAACP II-A, Administrative File 1940–55, Box 422.
269 Half of his face: *JCL,* May 9, 1955, p. 16; *JCL,* May 12, 1955, p. 1. See also Dr. A. H. McCoy letter to Attorney General Herbert Brownell, May 11, 1955, and memo of Ruby Hurley on Lee investigation, May 13, 1955, NAACP II-A, Administrative File 1940–55, Box 422.
271 two likely promoters: Bartley, *The Rise of Massive Resistance,* pp. 92–93, chapter 6 generally. See also Quint, *Profile in Black and White,* pp. 46–51; Southern Regional Council, *Pro-Segregation Groups in the South;* Atkinson, "Citizens' Councils of South Carolina: 1955–61."

271 "Manicured Kluxism": Southern Regional Council and Fleming, *Resistance Movements and Racial Desegregation,* p. 5.
271 "restore decency": ibid.
271 "to preserve and maintain": Quint, *Profile in Black and White,* p. 47.
273 "They spent money": int., ST, Aug. 20, 1990.
273 "closely attentive to his duties": *NC,* Nov. 7, 1954, WWP.
273 "gets good results": *The Greenville News,* Sept. 12, 1955, WWP; information on building of hospital comes from interview with staff at Fort Jackson, July 31, 1990.
273 "Don't you worry about Harry Dent": int., Harry S. Dent, Aug. 7, 1990; see also *State,* Oct. 28, 1957, WWP.
274 Harvard University: see ST speech, Dec. 6, 1957, STC Speeches, Box 7.
274 fond of both men: int., Harry S. Dent, Aug. 7, 1990.
274 "serious implications": *NC,* Dec. 16, 1954, WWP.
275 Jackson . . . Harlan: *NYT,* Oct. 10, 1954, p. 1 (Jackson obituary); *NYT,* Dec. 30, 1971, p. 1 (Harlan obituary).
275 one of the eleven senators: *Congressional Record,* Mar. 16, 1955, p. 3036.
275 testy exchange: Warren, *Memoirs,* pp. 113–14; Kluger, *Simple Justice,* pp. 730–32.
276 "eating food that has been prepared": Kluger, *Simple Justice,* p. 734.
276 "practical flexibility": Brown II, 359 U.S. 294 (1955).
277 "a long way off": *JCL,* June 1, 1955, p. 1.
277 "The people of Georgia": *AC,* June 1, 1955, p. 1.
277 "unhappiest public servants": *The Montgomery Advertiser,* June 1, 1955, p. 1.
277 "the great bulk of pupils": *NC,* June 1, 1955, p. 1.
278 "communist conspiracy": *State,* June 1, 1955, p. 1, 7A.
278 new groups sprouting: Atkinson, "Citizens' Councils of South Carolina," pp. 109–13; see also Quint, *Profile in Black and White,* pp. 46–48.
278 "It does not forbid": *Briggs v. Elliott,* 132 F. Supp. 776, 777 (1955).
279 "Should one race": Martin, *The Deep South Says "Never,"* pp. 64–67.
279 "destroy everything you believed": ibid.
279 "A brief review": *The Washington Star,* July 16, 1955, STHR.
280 Lamar Smith: *JCL,* Aug. 14–20, 1955; Bullard et al., *Free at Last,* pp. 38–39.
280 Emmett Till: *NYT,* Sept. 18, 1955, sec. 4, p. 7; *JCL,* Sept. 1–3, 1955; *NYT,* Sept. 24, 1955, p. 1; *NYT,* Nov. 10, 1955, p. 31; Bullard et al., *Free at Last,* pp. 40–41.

281 "interposition": Bartley, *The Rise of Massive Resistance,* pp. 126–31.
281 biggest boost: ibid.
282 "not worthy to wear the robes": *State,* Jan. 27, 1956, p. 1.
282 "unwarranted economic pressure": CQCN, vol. 1, p. 1620.
282 "Such a resolution": *ST Reports to the People,* Jan. 1956.
283 "any advantage": *State,* Mar. 4, 1956, pp. 1, 6A, 12A; *ST Reports to the People,* Mar. 3, 1956, STC Speeches, Box 7; see also *State,* Mar. 5, 1956, p. 4A.
283 "None of them": int., Harry S. Dent, Sept. 20, 1989.
283 "modern-day sociologists and psychologists": first draft of the Southern Manifesto, STC Originals, Box 4. The file contains a chronology of developments and the various versions before the final product.
284 "wasn't just a senator from Texas": Miller, *Lyndon,* p. 188.
285 "opposing propagandists": *Congressional Record,* Mar. 12, 1952, p. 4459.
286 "Calhoun was walking": ibid., p. 4462.
286 "three-year practical armistice": *NYT,* Mar. 13, 1956, pp. 1, 14.
287 Kefauver won: CQ, *National Party Conventions,* p. 103.
287 turned aside a plank: *State,* Aug. 17, 1956, p. 1.
287 "true progress": CQ, *National Party Conventions,* p. 104.
288 "an almighty board of education": *South,* July 2, 1956, STHR.
288 ending the segregation: *The Montgomery Advertiser,* Nov. 14, 1956, p. 1; Dec. 16, 1956, p. 1; see also *Browder v. Gayle,* 142 F. Supp. 707 (1956).
288 "digging their own graves": Anderson, *Eisenhower, Brownell and the Congress*: The Tangled Origins of the Civil Rights Bill of 1956–57, p. 139.
289 black registration: Southern Regional Council, *The Negro Voter in the South: A Report of a Survey by the Southern Regional Council.*
289 "Bars against Negro voting": ibid., p. 3 of first essay, "Negro Registration—Present and Prospective."
290 "vigorously resisted": CQ, *1957 Almanac,* p. 556.
290 "meddle with private business": ST testimony, Feb. 26, 1957, STC Speeches, Box 7; see also House Judiciary Committee hearings, 85th Cong., 1st sess., Feb. 26, 1957.
291 "the whole might": CQ, *1957 Almanac,* pp. 559–69; see also Miller, *Lyndon,* pp. 304–12.
292 picked up seventeen new allies: Lawson, *Voting Rights in the South, 1944–69,* p. 167.
292 William Knowland: *NC,* July 9, 10, 14, 1957, p. 1; *Congressional Record,* July 16, 1957, pp. 11829–32.

292 "vicious weapon": ST speech, July 11, 1957, STC Speeches, Box 7; see also *Congressional Record,* July 11, 1957, p. 11367.
293 "common sense of America": *NC,* July 18, 1957, p. 1.
293 kill . . . Title III: *NYT,* July 25, 1957, p. 1; see also CQ, *1957 Almanac,* p. 564. The Senate vote was 52–38.
293 jury trials in a host of cases: *State, NC,* Aug. 2, 1957, p. 1; see also McPherson, *A Political Education,* pp. 144–48; Branch, *Parting the Waters,* pp. 220–21; CQ, *1957 Almanac,* p. 558.
294 made a surprise move: *State,* Aug. 28, 1957, p. 1. The Senate vote was 66–18.
294 cooked him a sirloin steak: news articles from South Carolina papers, *Baltimore Sun, Post,* Aug. 29–30, 1957, JCTP, scrapbook.
294 "I rise to speak against": *Congressional Record,* Aug. 29, 1957, p. 16263.
296 "You tell him to get off": int., Harry S. Dent, Aug. 7, 1990.
297 "Strong Thurmond": article, Aug. 30, 1957, JCTP, scrapbook.
297 "Snoozes Serenely": *Post,* Mar. 17, 1957, STHR.
298 "nothing to gain": *AC,* Aug. 31, 1957, p. 1.
299 "we've got to be reasonable": McPherson, *A Political Education,* p. 145; see also Miller, *Lyndon,* p. 187; Branch, *Parting the Waters,* pp. 220–21.
299 "get so many odd fellows together": *NYT,* Aug. 3, 1957, pp. 1, 6.
299 refused to concede: int., ST, Aug. 20, 1990.
300 "your courage and wisdom": Mrs. J. P. Marshall letter to ST, Mar. 12, 1956, STC Subject Correspondence, Segregation 1956, Box 12, March folder.
300 "the dastardly attempt": J. P. Marvin telegram to ST, Aug. 24, 1957, STC Subject Correspondence, Segregation, Box 13, Aug. 12–Sept. 26, 1957 folder.
300 "more Christian": Mrs. Harry A. Orr letter to ST, Nov. 19, 1957; ST reply, Nov. 27, 1957, STC Subject Correspondence, Box 34, Segregation and States' Rights folder.
300 Faubus called out: *Arkansas Gazette, NYT,* Sept. 4–25, 1957; Ashmore, *Hearts and Minds: The Anatomy of Racism from Roosevelt to Reagan,* pp. 253–67; Huckaby, *Crisis at Central High: Little Rock, 1957–58,* pp. 14–24; Bartley, *The Rise of Massive Resistance,* pp. 266–67.
301 "storm troopers": *AC,* Sept. 25, 1967, p. 1.
302 "The folly of forced": *Congressional Record,* Feb. 21, 1958, p. 2562; see also *Arkansas Gazette,* Feb. 21, 1958, pp. 1–2A.
302 "will bring a flush": ST speech, May 22, 1958, STC Speeches, Box 8; see also *Congressional Record,* May 22, 1958, p. 9291.
303 "made by closed minds": *State,* Sept. 13, 1958, pp. 1, 2A.

303 "nine puppets of the NAACP": ST speech, Oct. 14, 1958, STC Speeches, Box 8.
303 "not about to surrender": *State,* Nov. 8, 1958, p. 1.
304 "the outstanding judicial blunder": ST speech, Jan. 29, 1959, STC Speeches, Box 9.
304 "in contrast to previous years": *The Greenville News,* Jan. 20, 1959, JCTP, scrapbook; int., ST, Aug. 20, 1990.
305 "viciously anti-Southern": ST testimony, Mar. 18, 1959, STC Speeches, Box 8; see also Senate Judiciary Committee hearings, 86th Cong., 1st sess., Mar. 18, 1959, p. 42.
305 Mack Charles Parker: *JCL,* Apr. 26–31, 1959, generally; Bullard et al., *Free at Last,* pp. 46–47.
306 Senate floor to denounce a report: *Congressional Record,* Sept. 14, 1959, pp. 19483–84.
306 "policy of 'no cooperation' ": Ernest F. Hollings statement, RFP.
307 brain tumor: Lachicotte, *Rebel Senator,* pp. 144–56.
307 "sleep with Jean": int., Harry S. Dent, Aug. 7, 1990.
307 offering . . . to resign: ST letter to Jean Thurmond, Oct. 27, 1959, JCTP, Box 2.
307 couldn't remember the names: int., Betty Dent, Aug. 7, 1990.
308 "he got what he came for": int., Harry S. Dent, Aug. 13, 1990.
308 "most outright defiance": *ST Reports to the People,* Jan. 25, 1960, STC Speeches, Box 10.
308 "pledge my utmost efforts": *ST Reports to the People,* Mar. 7, 1960, STC Speeches, Box 10.
309 "weak, lame": *NC,* Mar. 31, 1960, WWP.
309 89.5 percent: CQ, *Guide to U. S. Elections,* p. 1098.
309 really a southern triumph: *NYT,* Apr. 9, 1960, pp. 1, 15.
310 "gold reserves in Fort Knox": Lawson, *Voting Rights in the South,* pp. 247–48.
310 "anti-South attitudes": ST speech, Apr. 1, 1960, STC Speeches, Box 9; see also *Congressional Record,* April 1, 1960, p. 7146.
311 "Not All Black": *ST Reports to the People,* Apr. 1, 1960, STC Speeches, Box 10.
311 "best friend of the South": *NC,* July 12, 1960, p. 1.; see also *NYT,* July 14, 1960, p. 14.
312 offered a minority report: CQ, *National Party Conventions,* pp. 105–8.
312 "Lynching at Los Angeles": *NC,* July 14, 1960, p. 6A.
312 "a juicy lure of political pap": analysis of 1960 Democratic platform, July 24, 1960, STC Speeches, Box 10.
313 "any accusing fingers": *The Washington Star,* Aug. 9, 1960, p. 8A.
313 " 'Rastus' McGill": *State,* Aug. 10, 1960, WWP.
314 "only humiliation and harassment": *NC,* Nov. 8, 1960, WWP.

314 electoral vote: CQ, *Guide to U.S. Elections,* pp. 307, 315, 360.
314 "offset by the Negro support": *NYT,* Nov. 9, 1960, p. 1; Branch, *Parting the Waters,* pp. 364–66.
314 "A man would be foolish": *NC,* Nov. 17, 1960, WWP.

CHAPTER *11: Breakthrough*

Page

315 hatless: *NYT,* Jan. 21, 1961, pp. 1, 8, 9.
316 well-dressed black students: Morris, *Origins of the Civil Rights Movement,* p. 195; *NYT,* Feb. 3, 1960, p. 22; see also Branch, *Parting the Waters,* pp. 271–311.
317 "against the government": int., H. Samuel Stilwell, July 10, 1990.
317 "out-segged": Bass and DeVries, *The Transformation of Southern Politics,* p. 62.
318 "fought the ticket": ST letter to Joseph Clark, Jan. 8, 1961, STC Speeches, Box 11; see also *Post,* Jan. 15, 1961, p. A2.
319 alienate southern supporters: CQCN, vol. 1, p. 1630.
319 "horrendus absurdum": *NC,* May 10, 1961, pp. 1, 2A.
319 "It is my belief": transcript of March 25, 1961, NBC news program, STC Speeches, Box 12.
320 looked stiff and uncomfortable: int., H. Samuel Stilwell, July 10, 1990.
320 "sit-in and kneel-in": transcript of ST radio spot, April 1 and 2, 1961, STC Speeches, Box 12.
321 rolled into Anniston: Peck, *Freedom Ride,* pp. 124–26; see also Branch, *Parting the Waters,* pp. 416–20; *The Birmingham News,* May 15, 1961, pp. 1, 4, 10, 24; *NYT,* May 15, 1961, pp. 1, 22.
322 "Where were the police?": *The Birmingham News,* May 15, 16, 1961, p. 1.
322 baseball bats, bottles: Raines, *My Soul Is Rested,* p. 120; Branch, *Parting the Waters,* pp. 445–50.
323 two hundred more federal marshals: *NYT,* May 21–23, 1961, p. 1, generally.
323 jailed in Jackson: Raines, *My Soul Is Rested,* pp. 126–29; Branch, *Parting the Waters,* pp. 451–91.
324 "hands of the agitators": ST speech, May 23, 1961, STC Speeches, Box 11.
324 "Red pawns": ST speech, May 27, 1961, STC Speeches, Box 11.
325 "use your influence": letter from Ettie Barber to Richard Russell, Dec. 1, 1961, Series X, Box 155, Folder "Negro Correspondence, June 1952–April 1962," Richard B. Russell Memorial Library, University of Georgia.
325 Edwin Walker: *NYT,* July 13, 1961, pp. 1, 15.

326 no remedial action . . . was required: hearings before the Special Preparedness Subcommittee of the Senate Committee on Armed Services, 87th Cong., 2d sess., January–May 1962.

326 160-page report: unnumbered document, Report of the Senate Armed Services Subcommittee, 87th Cong., 2d sess., serial no. S 1705.

326 "fed information": ints., Harry S. Dent, Oct. 18, 1990, June 5, 1991.

327 "an act of wisdom": ST speech, Aug. 29, 1961, ST Speeches, Box 12; see also *Congressional Record,* Aug. 29, 1961, p. 17332.

327 Herbert Lee: *JCL,* Sept. 26, 1961, p. 1; Bullard et al., *Free at Last,* pp. 48–49; Branch, *Parting the Waters,* pp. 509–15.

328 Louis Allen: *Meridian Star,* Feb. 2, 1964, p. 1.; see also *JCL,* Feb. 2, 1964; Bullard et al., *Free at Last,* pp. 48–49.

328 "a popular sport": *ST Reports to the People,* Apr. 30, 1962, STC Speeches, Box 15.

328 poll tax had a long congressional history: CQCN, vol. 1, p. 1632.

329 "no significant effect": ST speech, Mar. 19, 1962, STC Speeches, Box 14.

329 Thurgood Marshall: *NYT,* Sept. 8, 1962, pp. 1, 11; *NYT,* Sept. 2, 1962, pp. 1, 23.

329 "the entirety of his legal profession": ST speech, Sept. 11, 1962, STC Speeches, Box 15; see also *Congressional Record,* Sept. 11, 1962, p. 19021.

330 James Meredith: *NYT,* Sept. 21–Oct. 2, 1962, generally.

330 "I love Mississippi": *NYT,* Sept. 30, 1962, p. 66.

332 "decontaminating Cuba": ST statement, Sept. 27, 1962, STC Speeches, Box 15.

332 "shocking and disturbing": ibid., Sept. 30, 1962.

333 "We are thankful to God": letter from Mr. and Mrs. William C. Johnson to ST, Sept. 15, 1962, STC Subject Correspondence 1962, Civil Rights (Race Relations), Box 3, Folder I.

333 "a military heel pressed down": *Congressional Record,* Oct. 9, 1962, pp. 22886–87.

333 Harvey Gantt: *NYT,* July 10, 1962, p. 24; *NYT,* Nov. 20, 1962, p. 26; *NYT,* Nov. 21, 1962, p. 33; *NC,* Dec. 31, 1962, p. 1.

334 "I am opposed to Gantt's": *NC,* Dec. 31, 1962, pp. 1, 2A.

334 "Concerned Clemson Alumni": letter from Concerned Clemson Alumni to President Robert C. Edwards, Nov. 30, 1962, Series II, Office of the President Robert C. Edwards Correspondence, 1959–65, Folder 197, Clemson University Special Collections.

334 "running out of courts": *State,* Jan. 9, 1963, pp. 1, 2A.

334 "mockery": *NC,* Jan. 23, 1963, p. 8A.

335 "would not be embarrassed": int., Judge Donald S. Russell, U.S.

Court of Appeals for the Fourth Circuit, July 10, 1990; see also *NC*, Jan. 25, 1963, p. 1; *State*, Jan. 25, 1963, p. 1.

335 FORCED ACCOMMODATION: *NC*, Jan. 29, 1963, p. 8A.

335 "my purpose in Washington": ST letter to E. C. Collins, Feb. 5, 1963, STC Subject Correspondence 1963, Civil Rights (Race Relations), Folder I.

336 "Segregation now": *The Birmingham News*, Jan. 15, 1963, p. 12.

336 "a strong odor": ST statement, Feb. 28, 1963, STC Speeches, Box 18.

337 made him "sick": Branch, *Parting the Waters*, p. 764; see also *NYT*, May 4–14, 1963, generally.

337 "centralizers": *ST Reports to the People*, May 20, 1963, STC Speeches, Box 18.

337 "most vigorous opposition": transcript of television spot, May 23, 1963, STC Speeches, Box 18.

337 "dictatorship over American business": transcript of radio broadcast, June 8–9, 1963, STC Speeches, Box 18.

338 "we are confronted": *NYT*, June 12, 1963, p. 1.

338 Medgar Evers: *NYT*, June 13, 1963, p. 1.

339 John Doar: *NYT*, June 16, 1963, pp. 1, 58.

340 "lily-white southern governments": ibid.

340 package of civil rights legislation: *NYT*, Jan. 20, 1963, pp. 1, 17; see also CQCN, vol. 1., p. 1633.

340 "unnecessary, unwise": ST statement, June 19, 1963, STC Speeches, Box 18.

340 NBC's *Today* show: transcript of NBC's *Today* show, June 20, 1963, STC Speeches, Box 18.

342 "I want to thank you": letter from Mrs. Arthur Gray Davis to ST, June 14, 1963 and ST response, STC Subject Correspondence 1963, Civil Rights (Race Relations), Box 5, Folder IV.

342 "Negroes may have": ST letter to Fred E. Dabney, July 20, 1963, STC Subject Correspondence 1963, Civil Rights (Race Relations), Box 3, Folder IV.

342 "Sensible and responsible": Chamber of Commerce letter to ST, July 16, 1963, STC Subject Correspondence 1963, Civil Rights (Race Relations), Box 3, Folder IV.

342 "I am not prejudiced": ST letter to Veronica A. Roland, July 11, 1963, STC Subject Correspondence 1963, Civil Rights (Race Relations), Box 3, Folder III.

343 "I want to say": Senate Commerce Committee hearings on a bill to eliminate discrimination in public accommodations affecting interstate commerce, 88th Cong., 1st sess., July 1, 1963, p. 84.

344 "civil righters and left wingers": ibid., July 10, 1963, p. 319.

344 aiding communist subversives: *NYT,* July 13, 1963, p. 1; *NYT,* July 16, 1963, p. 1.
344 Bayard Rustin: *Congressional Record,* Aug. 13, 1963, p. 14838.
345 "questionable backgrounds": ST statement, Aug. 15, 1963, STC Speeches, Box 18.
345 "I have a dream": *NYT,* Aug. 29, 1963, pp. 1, 16.
345 Sixteenth Street Baptist Church: *The Birmingham News,* Sept. 16, 1963, pp. 1, 4; Bullard et al., *Free at Last,* pp. 58–59; Robert Chambliss convicted, *NYT,* Nov. 19, 1977, p. 1.
346 Virgil Ware: Bullard et al., *Free at Last,* p. 60.
346 "Who did it?": *NYT,* Sept. 17, 1963, p. 24; see also *The Birmingham News,* Sept. 17, 1963, generally.
347 "objectionable and impractical": ST statement, Oct. 8, 1963, STC Speeches, Box 17.
347 "The only compromise": *ST Reports to the People,* Nov. 4, 1963, STC Speeches, Box 18.
347 "most personable and popular": transcript of ST radio broadcasts, Dec. 1–2, 1963, STC Speeches, Box 19.
348 "No memorial": *NYT,* Nov. 28, 1963, pp. 1, 20.
348 "give him a chance": int., H. Samuel Stilwell, July 10, 1990.
348 "You tell Lyndon": Miller, *Lyndon,* p. 369. The Senate vote was 67–17; see also CQCN, vol. 1, pp. 1635–41 for discussion of legislation.
348 *CBS Reports:* Transcript of *CBS Reports* of Mar. 18, 1964, from *U.S. News & World Report,* Mar. 30, 1964, pp. 102–4, STC Speeches, Box 21.
350 a concerted effort by civil rights groups: Miller, *Lyndon,* p. 369.
350 "a sad day": ST statement, June 10, 1964, STC Speeches, Box 22.
351 "unless we get Ev": Miller, *Lyndon,* p. 368.
351 offering thirty: CQ, *1964 Almanac,* pp. 674–96 for Senate votes; see pp. 338–78 for discussion of legislation.
351 "fly in the face": CQCN, vol. 1, p. 1637.
351 "a tragic day": ST statement, June 19, 1964, STC Speeches, Box 22.
351 three civil rights workers: *NYT,* June 23, 1964, p. 1; *NYT,* Aug. 5, 1964, p. 1; Bullard et al., *Free at Last,* pp. 66–69; conviction of defendants, *NYT,* Oct. 21, 1967, pp. 1, 18.
352 "a time of testing": *NYT,* July 3, 1964, pp. 1, 9.
352 "intemperate action": *State,* July 4, 1964, editorial page.
352 "momentous departure": *NC,* July 4, 1964, p. 6A.
352 "embarrassing situation": Dortcha Smith, Sr., letter to ST, July 8, 1964, and ST response, July 11, 1964, STC Subject Correspondence 1964, Civil Rights Legislation, Box 6, Folder XXIV.
353 LeRoy Collins: Senate Commerce Committee hearings on the nomi-

nation of LeRoy Collins to be director of the Community Relations Service, 88th Cong., 1st sess., July 7, 1964, p. 36.

354 "Tell you what": *NC,* July 10, 1964, p. 1; *NYT,* July 10, 1964, p. 1; see also assorted articles, STHR; int., H. Samuel Stilwell, July 10, 1990.

355 "little respect for turncoats": ST speech, July 20, 1964, STC Speeches, Box 22.

355 "wistful longing": *NYT,* May 5, 1961, p. 28.

356 "No matter what happens": *NC,* July 16, 1964, p. 15A.

356 Thurmond's disaffection: int., Harry S. Dent, Oct. 6, 1990.

357 "dry behind the ears": ibid.; also ints., Sept. 20, 1989 and Aug. 6, 1990.

357 "Bring me a drink": int., Harry S. Dent, Aug. 6, 1990; see also Dent, *The Prodigal South Returns to Power,* p. 66.

358 "a pretty good poll": int., Harry S. Dent, Oct. 25, 1990.

358 presidential election in Mississippi: Lamis, *The Two-Party South,* pp. 45, 47.

358 "in the mail yet?": int., Harry S. Dent, Sept. 20, 1989; see also Dent, *The Prodigal South Returns to Power,* pp. 64–66.

359 "It has been wisely said": ST speech, STC Speeches, Box 20; see also *State,* Sept. 17, 1964, p. 1, and *U.S. News & World Report,* Sept. 24, 1964, pp. 83–84 for text of speech.

360 "once a dirty name": *NC,* Sept. 17, 1964, p. 1.

360 "synthetic model": *The Anderson Independent,* Sept. 17, 1964, STHR.

360 Russell had conceded: Richard Russell letter to W. O. Johnson, Oct. 13, 1964, Richard B. Russell Papers, Series VI, Box 118, Richard B. Russell Memorial Library, University of Georgia.

361 an old hearse: int., ST, Aug. 20, 1990.

361 "My sole purpose": ST speech, Oct. 24, 1964, STC Speeches, Box 21.

361 "A vote for Hubert Humphrey": *NC,* Oct. 27, 1964, pp. 1–2A.

362 "false illusions": undated ST speech, STC Campaigns, 1964.

362 seven new Republican: *NYT,* Nov. 4, 1964, p. 1.

CHAPTER *12: The Center Cannot Hold*

Page

363 "bring to the office": *State,* July 15, 1965, p. 10A.

364 "white people who question": *NC,* July 16, 1965, p. 10A.

366 northerners blocked: *Post,* Jan. 15, 1965, p. 2A; see also ST statement, Jan. 11, 1965, STC Speeches, Box 24.

366 "about one hundred years": Lawson, *Voting Rights in the South,* p. 308.

366 Since 1961: CQCN, vol. 1, p. 357.

367 "out picking cotton": Lawson, *Voting Rights in the South,* p. 308.
367 Jimmie Lee Jackson: Bullard et al., *Free at Last,* pp. 72–73.
367 "not conducive to public safety": *Post,* Mar. 8, 1965, pp. 1, 3.
367 "mounted possemen": *NYT,* Mar. 8, 1965, p. 1.
368 "Bloody Sunday": Lawson, *Voting Rights in the South,* p. 310; Miller, *Lyndon,* pp. 430–31; for congressional reaction, *NYT,* Mar. 9, 1965.
368 "We saved lives": *NYT,* Mar. 9, 1965, pp. 1, 23.
368 arranged a scenario: *NYT,* Mar. 10, 1965, pp. 1, 22; Lawson, *Voting Rights in the South,* p. 311.
368 Reverend James Reeb: Bullard et al., *Free at Last,* pp. 72–75; Lawson, *Voting Rights in the South,* p. 311; *NYT,* Mar. 12, 1965, p. 1.
369 "I speak tonight": *NYT,* Mar. 16, 1965, pp. 1, 30; see also Miller, *Lyndon,* pp. 431–32.
370 "never be satisfied": transcript of ST radio broadcasts, Feb. 21–22, 1965, STC Speeches, Box 25.
370 "without reservation": ST statement, Mar. 18, 1965, STC Speeches, Box 18.
370 "agitation": transcript of ST radio broadcasts, March 21–22, 1965, STC Speeches, Box 25.
371 Frank Johnson, Jr.: *NYT,* Mar. 18, 1965, p. 1.
371 forecast eventual passage: *NYT,* Mar. 19, 1965, p. 1; vote tally was 67–13.
371 "colossal demonstration": *NYT,* Mar. 21, 1965, pp. 1, 71.
371 barred him from entering: *NYT,* Mar. 26, 1965, pp. 1, 22.
371 Viola Liuzzo: *NYT,* Mar. 26, 1965, pp. 1, 23; see also Bullard et al., *Free at Last,* pp. 76–77.
372 "an unheard-of thing": *NYT,* Mar. 19, 1965, pp. 1, 21.
372 born into a prosperous family: *Time,* Mar. 26, 1956, pp. 26–29; see also *JCL,* Feb. 20, 1986, pp. 1, 15A; "Mississippi's Senator James O. Eastland," 1972 campaign brochure.
374 "penance": transcript of ST radio broadcasts, Mar. 28–29, 1965, STC Speeches, Box 25.
374 "amazing": transcript of ST television spot, Apr. 1, 1965, STC Speeches, Box 25.
374 "Denial of the privilege": transcript of ST radio broadcasts, Apr. 4–5, 1965, STC Speeches, Box 25.
375 "In my judgment": ST Senate Judiciary Committee testimony, Apr. 5, 1965, STC Speeches, Box 25.
375 The Senate started debate: CQ, *1965 Almanac,* pp. 533–64, 1042.
376 "signally unproductive": *Congressional Record,* May 26, 1965, p. 11730.
376 A conference committee: CQ, *1965 Almanac,* pp. 562–64.

377 "the last major shackle": *NYT,* Aug. 7, 1965, pp. 1, 8.
377 "most fitting": *State,* Aug. 7, 1965, p. 1.
377 "new electorate": *State,* Aug. 8, 1965, p. 14A.
377 upheld the statute: *South Carolina v. Katzenbach,* 383 U.S. 301 (1966).
378 "same standard": *State,* Aug. 9, 1965, p. 1.
378 "complete control": ST statement, Aug. 9, 1965, STC Speeches, Box 25.
378 381 blacks: CQCN, vol. 2, p. 362; Lawson, *Voting Rights in the South,* pp. 329–30.
378 next solicitor general: *NYT,* July 14, 1965, p. 1.
379 "totally lacking": ST speech, Aug. 11, 1965, STC Speeches, Box 26.
379 rioting erupted: CQCN, vol. 2, pp. 354–55.
379 "seeds of the insurrections": ST statement, Aug. 16, 1965, STC Speeches, Box 26.
380 "best possible man": ST statement, Sept. 15, 1965, STC Speeches, Box 25.
380 "not a dictator": *State,* Oct. 3, 1965, p. 1B; *NC,* Oct. 3, 1965, p. 1; ints., Harry S. Dent, Nov. 10, 1990, Dec. 2, 1990.
381 "astonishingly bold grab": *ST Reports to the People,* July 4, 1966, STC Speeches, Box 27.
381 "Foot in the Door": *ST Reports to the People,* July 11, 1966, STC Speeches, Box 27.
381 "vicious, vindictive": *Congressional Record,* Sept. 8, 1966, p. 22130.
381 "in the front line": ST statement, Sept. 8, 1966, STC Speeches, Box 27.
381 Congress . . . restricted the right: CQCN, vol. 2, p. 366.
381 black crowds roaming: ibid.
381 "black power": *JCL,* June 18, 1966, pp. 1, 10.
382 black racism: CQCN, vol. 2, p. 367; see also the *Negro Almanac,* 4th ed., 1983, p. 43; *NYT,* July 5, 1966, pp. 1, 16; *NYT,* July 6, 1966, pp. 1, 14.
382 Blacks were registering: Lawson, *Voting Rights in the South,* p. 331; see also Voter Education Project (VEP) materials, South Carolina Council on Human Relations file, Caroliniana Library, University of South Carolina.
382 "VOTELESS People": sample registration form from Voter Education Project materials, Caroliniana Library, University of South Carolina.
383 "tired of hearing": ibid., Richard Miles letter to VEP workers in South Carolina, Aug. 24, 1965.
383 "I chose the Republican Party": ST statement, Mar. 25, 1966, STC Speeches, Box 28.

383 P. Bradley Morrah: article, Apr. 12, 1966, STHR.
384 pecan pie: campaign cards, STC Campaigns, 1966.
384 "His campaign car": *State,* Nov. 3, 1966, p. 1.
385 HAD ENUF?: *State,* Oct. 25, 1966, p. 1B.
385 "Black Revolution": campaign ads, STHR; see also WWP.
385 "deeply revolting": *Florence Morning News,* Oct. 23, 1966, WWP.
385 "fanning the flames": *State,* Nov. 5, 1966, WWP.
386 whipped Morrah: CQ, *Guide to U.S. Elections,* p. 630; see also *State,* Nov. 9, 1966, p. 1. Thurmond's vote total was 271,297; McNair's was 255,854.
386 winning seventeen seats: *State,* Jan. 9, 1967, p. 1B.
387 "incite insurrection": *Congressional Record,* Apr. 18, 1967, p. 9934.
387 "demeans his race": *Congressional Record,* Apr. 6, 1967 p. 8526.
388 "right thing to do": *NYT,* June 14, 1967, p. 1.
388 "assume the impartiality": *NC,* June 15, 1967, p. 12A.
388 grilling Marshall: Senate Judiciary Committee hearings on the nomination of Thurgood Marshall to be associate justice of the Supreme Court, 90th Cong., 1st sess., July 19, 1967, p. 161.
388 "ordeal by committee": *NYT,* July 30, 1967, p. 10E.
388 "surprising lack of knowledge": *Congressional Record,* Aug. 30, 1967, pp. 24650–54.
389 only a five-year extension: CQCN, vol. 2, pp. 374–77.
390 "seduced and cajoled": ST statement, Mar. 4, 1968, STC Speeches, Box 32.
390 antiriot provision: CQ, *1968 Almanac,* p. 5S.
390 passed the housing bill: CQCN, vol. 2, pp. 578–82.
390 "fighting fire with gasoline": *ST Reports to the People,* Mar. 11, 1968, STC Speeches, Box 33.
391 wave of rioting: Miller, *Lyndon,* p. 514.
391 "I was shocked": ST statement, Apr. 5, 1968, STC Speeches, Box 32.
391 "replace reason": ST statement, Apr. 10, 1968, STC Speeches, Box 32.
392 "a fixer": ST statement, June 28, 1968, STC Speeches, Box 34.
393 "wailed about the damage": ST statement, July 3, 1968, STC Speeches, Box 34.
393 "And you refuse": Senate Judiciary Committee hearings on the nomination of Abe Fortas to be chief justice of the Supreme Court of the United States, 90th Cong., 2d sess., pp. 180–93.
394 "a disastrous mistake": memo from "LA" to ST, July 19, 1968, STC Legislative Assistants, Box 44; int., James Lucier, winter 1990.
395 unveiled a paperback: *NC,* July 19, 1968, STHR.

395 "Fortas on Filth": *ST Reports to the People,* Aug. 5, 1968, STC Speeches, Box 33.
395 "To show dirty movies": *Post,* Sept. 14, 1968; cartoon, *Post,* Sept. 8, 1968; STHR.
395 "respectfully" declined: Abe Fortas letter to James O. Eastland, Sept. 13, 1968, STC Legislative Assistants, Box 44.
396 "wisest decision": ST statement, Oct. 2, 1968, STC Speeches, Box 35.
396 "I love that man": Chester, Hodgson, Page, *An American Melodrama: The Presidential Campaign of 1968,* pp. 438–39; see also Dent, *Prodigal South Returns to Power,* pp. 78–80.
397 calmed worried southern hearts: int., Harry S. Dent, June 5, 1991; Chester et al., *An American Melodrama,* p. 447.
397 icing on the cake: int., Harry S. Dent, June 5, 1991; see also Dent, *Prodigal South Returns to Power,* p. 82.
398 "quit using our hearts": Chester et al., *An American Melodrama,* p. 447.
398 "the best hope": *State,* June 23, 1968, p. 1.
398 "A vote for Reagan": Dent, *Prodigal South Returns to Power,* pp. 86–87.
398 reaffirming their support: *NC,* Aug. 5, 1968, p. 1.
398 "dog and pony show": int., Harry S. Dent, spring 1990; *State,* Aug. 6, 1968, p. 8A; Dent, *Prodigal South Returns to Power,* pp. 89–90; int., ST, Dec. 17, 1990.
399 "eyeball to eyeball": *Newsweek,* Aug. 19, 1968, p. 26.
399 a meeting at Nixon headquarters: *State,* Aug. 8, 1968, p. 1.
399 "didn't veto anybody": transcript of NBC's *Meet the Press,* Aug. 18, 1968, STC Speeches, Box 34.
400 "Ex-Democrat": *NYT Magazine,* Oct. 6, 1968, p. 36.
400 "few would dispute": *NC,* Nov. 7, 1968, p. 12A; for cartoon see Dent, *Prodigal South Returns to Power.*
400 "fabulous job": *NC,* Nov. 7, 1968, p. 2B.
401 "you can't do that": int., ST, Dec. 17, 1990; Dent, *Prodigal South Returns to Power,* pp. 116–17.
401 THURMOND TO WED: *State,* Dec. 8, 1968, p. 1.
402 "outrageous": int., ST, Dec. 17, 1990.
403 Fortas had received: *NYT,* May 6, 1969, pp. 1, 27.
403 "like Caesar's wife": ST statement, May 5, 1969, STC Speeches, Box 37.
403 Fortas resigned: *NYT,* May 16, 1969, pp. 1, 20, 21.
403 William O. Douglas: *ST Reports to the People,* May 19, 1969, STC Speeches, Box 37.
403 "the most distressing": *ST Reports to the People,* June 2, 1969, STC Speeches, Box 37.

404 "integrity and character": *ST Reports to the People,* June 9, 1969, STC Speeches, Box 37.

404 "growing social disintegration": *ST Reports to the People,* June 30, 1969, STC Speeches, Box 37.

405 Haynsworth . . . Russell: int., ST, Dec. 20, 1990; int., Harry S. Dent, Dec. 21, 1990.

406 "while I am concerned": Senate Judiciary Committee hearings on the nomination of Clement F. Haynsworth to be an associate justice of the Supreme Court of the United States, 91st Cong., 1st sess., Sept. 17, 1969, p. 105.

406 "Strom's Little Acres": *Life,* Sept. 19, 1969, p. 41; see also *State,* Sept. 20, 1969, p. 1.

407 staying out of the limelight: *State,* Nov. 16, 1969, p. 1; int., ST, Dec. 17, 1990.

407 "Let us not": *Congressional Record,* Nov. 21, 1969, pp. 35378–92.

407 rejected Haynsworth: *NYT,* Nov. 22, 1969, p. 1.

407 "born and bred": *ST Reports to the People,* Dec. 1, 1969, STC Speeches, Box 37.

408 "a disproportionate share": *ST Reports to the People,* Dec. 22, 1969, STC Speeches, Box 37.

408 "tore it up": ST statement, June 15, 1964, STC Speeches, Box 22; *Baker v. Carr,* 369 U.S. 186 (1962); *Reynolds v. Sims,* 377 U.S. 533 (1964).

408 "understand that he is a conservative": ST statement, Jan. 19, 1970, STC Speeches, Box 39.

408 "principles of white supremacy": *NYT,* Jan. 22, 1970, pp. 1, 22.

408 "I renounce and reject": Senate Judiciary Committee hearings on the nomination of G. Harrold Carswell to be associate justice of the Supreme Court of the United States, 91st Cong., 2d sess., Jan. 27, 1970, p. 10.

409 "dilatory school officials": *NYT,* Jan. 20, 1970, p. 44.

409 "nothing shows": ST statement, Jan. 28, 1970, STC Speeches, Box 39; see also Carswell hearings, Jan. 28, 1970, p. 57.

409 voting rights bill: CQ, *1970 Almanac,* pp. 192–98.

410 "a lot of mediocre judges": CQCN, vol. 3, p. 296.

410 "civil rights zealots": *ST Reports to the People,* May 11, 1970, STC Speeches, Box 42.

411 more than half of South Carolina's: Lawson, *Voting Rights in the South,* p. 331.

411 overturned two school buses: *State,* March 4–6, 1970, generally.

411 "human psychology": *State,* Mar. 6, 1970, p. 8A.

412 "counting on Thurmond's": *State,* Nov. 3, 1970, p. 1.

412 "undoubtedly spurred": *State,* Nov. 5, 1970, p. 20A.

413 "Mr. Moss, I'm thinking": int., Tom Moss, Nov. 30, 1990.
413 THURMOND STEALS: *State,* Feb. 21, 1971, p. 6B.

CHAPTER *13: Readjustment*

Page

414 SERIES OF REVERSALS: *NYT,* May 30, 1971, p. 25.
415 960 blacks: *Black Elected Officials in the U.S.,* Joint Center for Political and Economic Studies, Washington, D.C., 1976.
417 electric blues: *The Miami Herald,* Apr. 4, 1971, p. 6.
417 "OLE STROM" GIRDS: *Post,* May 16, 1971, p. 2B.
417 "no longer unbeatable": *The Washington Star,* May 30, 1971, p. 8A; see also *NYT,* May 30, 1971, p. 25.
417 "moist-fanged racist": *The Miami Herald,* Apr. 4, 1971, p. 10.
417 "The pity of it": ibid.
417 "stabbed us": *Ebony,* July 1971, p. 165.
418 "the wrong part": *State,* Jan. 23, 1971, p. 10A.
418 "stood firm": ST statement, Jan. 25, 1971, STC Speeches, Box 46.
419 "readily apparent": *Goss v. Board of Education of Knoxville,* 373 U.S. 683 (1963).
419 "deliberate perpetuation": *Green v. County School Board of New Kent County, Va.,* 391 U.S. 430, 437–38 (1968); see generally, CQ, *Guide to the U.S. Supreme Court* for discussion of school desegregation cases, pp. 591–97.
419 "unequivocally committed": *NYT,* July 4, 1969, pp. 1, 7; see also Bardolph, *The Civil Rights Record: Black Americans and the Law, 1849–1970,* p. 464.
420 a retreat in the face of pressure: *NYT,* July 5, 1969, pp. 1, 23.
420 "no longer constitutionally permissible": *Alexander v. Holmes County Board of Education,* 396 U.S. 19 (1969).
420 "booted Panetta": Panetta and Gall, *Bring Us Together,* p. 365; see also *NYT,* Feb. 18, 1971, p. 1.
421 "I condemn": ST speech, July 17, 1970, STC Speeches, Box 46.
422 "As an interim": *Swann v. Mecklenburg,* 402 U.S. 1, 7, 27, 29 (1971); see also CQ, *Guide to the U.S. Supreme Court,* pp. 592–94.
423 "insane institutions": *State,* Apr. 21, 1971, p. 1.
423 "punitive decree": *State,* Apr. 25, 1971, p. 2B.
423 "does not make sense": ST speech, Aug. 14, 1971, STC Speeches, Box 45.
424 "a nauseating mixture": *Richmond Times-Dispatch,* Jan. 11, 1972, p. 16A; see also *Bradley v. School Board of the City of Richmond,* 338 F. Supp. 67 (1972).
424 "yet another nugget": *State,* Jan. 14, 1972, p. 20A; see also *NC,* Jan. 13, 1972, p. 4A.

424 "a popular note": *NC,* March 18, 1972, p. 10A.
425 "the only bird": ST speech, Nov. 9, 1971, STC Speeches, Box 48.
425 "counting the rewards": *Record,* Dec. 23, 1971, STHR.
426 one-woman voter registration: int., Victoria DeLee, Jan. 16, 1991.
427 burned to the ground: DeLee for Congress campaign flyer, *State* Victoria DeLee file.
427 He got the money: int., Victoria DeLee, Jan. 16, 1991; int., ST, Feb. 13, 1991.
427 "I'm for whoever": *The Charlotte Observer,* Feb. 22, 1972, p. 38.
427 day-care project soured: *State,* Dec. 21, 1976, Sept. 20, 21, 1977, DeLee file.
428 Joe Frazier: *The Charlotte Observer,* Mar. 30, 1972, p. 4A.
428 poll early in the year: South Carolina election poll by Central Surveys Inc., of Shendoah, Iowa, p. 22, STC Campaigns, 1972.
428 "new face": *The Charlotte Observer,* Sept. 1, 1972, p. 14A.
429 "Scrooge in Washington": Zeigler news release, STC Campaigns, 1972.
429 "close to the people": ST campaign flyer, STC Campaigns, 1972.
429 "a good listener?": ibid.
430 opening mail: ibid.
430 "as kind and helpful": Nancy Thurmond statement, Oct. 19, 1972, STC Speeches, Box 51.
430 "a sweet victory": *State,* Nov. 8, 1972, p. 1.
430 entered three primaries: CQ, *Guide to U.S. Elections,* pp. 414–16.
432 "A few men": ST speech, Sept. 29, 1973, STC Speeches, Box 55.
432 "big labor bosses": transcript of NBC's *Today* show, Nov. 6, 1973, STC Speeches, Box 57.
432 "chorus of voices": ST statement, Nov. 13, 1973, STC Speeches, Box 57.
434 "great accomplishment": ST statement, Aug. 8, 1974, STC Speeches, Box 59; transcript of Nixon resignation speech, *NYT,* Aug. 9, 1974, p. 2.
434 "a high-class moving violation": *NYT,* Dec. 12, 1974, p. 43.
435 "expire unceremoniously": *ST Reports to the People,* Dec. 2, 1974, STC Speeches, Box 59.
435 renewed the act: CQ, *1975 Almanac,* pp. 529–33.
435 "completely unreasonable": *Congressional Record,* July 21, 1975, p. 23756.
436 handful of southerners: CQ, *1975 Almanac,* p. 49S.
436 deadlocked 4–4: *Richmond School Board v. Virginia Board of Education,* 412 U.S. 92 (1973).
436 Detroit: *Miliken v. Bradley,* 418 U.S. 717 (1974).
437 "I find it incredible": *ST Reports to the People,* Oct. 1, 1974, STC Speeches, Box 59.

437 HEW's annual appropriations: *Congressional Record,* Sept. 17, 1975, p. 29113; CQCN, vol. 4, pp. 663–69.
438 pronounced himself delighted: ST statement, Sept. 17, 1975, STC Speeches, Box 65.
438 the *Swann* decision: *NYT,* Apr. 15, 1992, p. 11B.
439 Lester Maddox: Henderson and Roberts, *Georgia Governors in an Age of Change, from Ellis Arnall to George Busbee,* p. 196; *NYT Magazine,* Nov. 6, 1966, p. 27.
439 "No poor, rural": Henderson and Roberts, *Georgia Governors in an Age of Change,* p. 233; see also *Newsweek,* Jan. 25, 1971, p. 51.
439 on a May cover: *Time,* May 31, 1971, p. 14.
440 "an American and a Southerner": *NC,* July 17, 1976, p. 10A. For details of Carter's nomination see CQ, *National Party Conventions,* pp. 125–33; *AC,* July 15, 1976, p. 3A.
440 "A new South": *State,* July 15, 1976, p. 24A.
440 supporting Reagan this time: ST statement, July 20, 1976, STC Speeches, Box 68.
441 "say with satisfaction": *Family Weekly,* Sept. 5, 1976, STHR.
441 "once you get past the smile": transcript of radio and television spot, undated, STC Speeches, Box 66.
441 "not just somebody": transcript of TV spot, Oct. 18, 1976, STC Speeches, Box 66.
442 put it in the file: "AA" letter to ST, July 31, 1974, STC Campaigns, 1978.
442 ideal candidate: Ravenel 1974 campaign brochure, STC Campaigns, 1978; int., Charles D. Ravenel, Feb. 6, 1991.
443 "an awfully strong candidate": John Bolt Culbertson letter to ST, June 25, 1976, STC Campaigns, 1978.
443 "someone fresh": Ravenel statement, July 25, 1977, STC Campaigns, 1978.
443 "this summer's heat": *State,* July 27, 1977, p. 22A.
444 campaign pitches: ST letters, May 6, 1977, May 9, 1977, undated 1977, STC Campaigns, 1978.
444 "thinking about you": int., Charles D. Ravenel, Feb. 6, 1991.
444 "temper 'em": int., ST, Feb. 13, 1991.
444 "I can talk": *State,* March 2, 1978, p. 9C.
444 "Asking someone": int., Charles D. Ravenel, Feb. 6, 1991.
444 "the top ranks": ST reelection announcement, April 5, 1978 STC Speeches, Box 76.
445 inch-thick booklet: brochure on federal money in South Carolina, STC Campaigns, 1978.
445 ranked twenty-eighth: *Record,* Oct. 31, 1978, p. 11.
445 "If Pug wins": *State,* Mar. 2, 1978, p. 9C.

446 easily beat his opponents: *State,* June 14, 1978, pp. 1, 11A.
446 "My position on debates": ST statement, June 15, 1978, STC Campaigns, 1978.
446 "I commend your tradition": Charles D. Ravenel letter to ST, July 26, 1978, STC Campaigns, 1978.
446 "prefers to carry": Allison Dalton letter to Charles D. Ravenel, July 28, 1978, STC Campaigns, 1978; ints., Harry S. Dent, Jan., Feb., 1991.
446 "patent arrogance": *Record,* Oct. 20, 1978, p. 1B.
447 *Strom Trek: Record,* July 10, 1978, p. 1B.
447 "keep the family together": *Record,* Sept. 5, 1978, p. 1B.
447 "the family was human": int., ST, Feb. 13, 1991.
447 "no shrinking violet": *State,* Oct. 26, 1978, p. 10A.
447 "third senator from New York": Solomon Blatt letter to David Benjamin Gohagan, Oct. 16, 1978, STC Campaigns, 1978.
447 "Harvard Business School": Harvard Business School Friends of Charles "Pug" Ravenel letter to Albert F. Gordon, March 27, 1978, STC Campaigns, 1978.
447 out-of-state sources: *Record,* Aug. 18, 1978, p. 1C.
448 "shed his racist image": Cross and Slater, *A Black Voter's Guide to the 1978 Elections,* pp. 17–20, STC Campaigns, 1978.
448 "Darley Cochran": *State,* Oct. 26, 1978, p. 10A.
449 "My boy got burned": ibid.
449 keep a respectful distance: int., William T. Coleman, Jr., Apr. 5, 1991.
450 "an embarrassment": *State,* Nov. 4, 1978, p. 17A; see also *State,* Oct. 11, 1978, p. 10A.
450 "an entirely different situation": *State,* Oct. 26, 1978, p. 10A.
450 "Mr. Deliveryman": ibid.
450 "integrity and conviction": *State,* Nov. 2, 1978, p. 16A.
451 "The debate is over": *NC,* Nov. 8, 1978, p. 1.
451 17 percent: *NC,* Nov. 9, 1978, p. 1.
451 "Citizens for Nixon": int., Thad Cochran, Feb. 8, 1991; see also *Post,* Oct. 10, 1978, p. 1.
452 "Nothing is more incongruous": *NYT,* March 21, 1978, pp. 1, 25.

CHAPTER *14: Back over the Rubicon*

Page

455 twelve new seats: CQ, *1980 Almanac,* pp. 7B–10B. Republican gains were in Alabama, Alaska, Florida, Georgia, Idaho, Indiana, Iowa, New Hampshire, North Carolina, South Dakota, Washington, and Wisconsin. In addition, Republicans held on to their ten seats that were contested.
455 shook his own head: int., Dennis Shedd, Mar. 16, 1991.

455 hired Mark Goodin: ibid.; also int., Mark Goodin, Mar. 19, 1991.
457 "wrong again": int., Harry S. Dent, Jan. 27, 1991.
458 take over the Judiciary Committee: int., ST, Mar. 26, 1991.
458 "just as fairly": int., Dennis Shedd, Mar. 16, 1991.
458 "You've got to move": int., Harry S. Dent, Mar. 18, 1991.
458 "mutual concern": ST statement, Nov. 25, 1980, STC Speeches, Box 83.
459 "You don't have to be a lawyer": CQ, *Weekly Report,* Jan. 24, 1981, pp. 184–85.
459 Always frugal: ibid.
460 "prettiest witnesses": Senate Judiciary Committee confirmation hearings on William French Smith to be attorney general of the United States, 97th Cong., 1st sess., Jan. 15, 1981, p. 99.
461 "an athletic belt": ibid., p. 106.
462 question O'Connor repeatedly: CQ, *1981 Almanac,* p. 409.
463 "Fear of reprisals": *Congressional Record,* Mar. 31, 1964, p. 6651.
463 "preordained conclusions": ibid., pp. 6645–46.
464 received a phone call: int., Tom McCain, Apr. 30, 1989; see also Edds, *Free at Last,* pp. 28–50; *State,* June 18, 1989, p. 1D.
465 "minimal tokenism": Civil Order No. 74–281, U.S. District Court for the District of South Carolina, Greenwood Division.
465 an Alabama case: *City of Mobile v. Bolden,* 446 U.S. 55 (1980).
466 "send a clear message": *State,* June 29, 1981, p. 1B.
467 abuses still existed: House Judiciary Subcommittee on Civil and Constitutional Rights, hearings on extension of the Voting Rights Act of 1965, 97th Cong., 1st sess., June 12, 1981, p. 1584; pp. 1511–1750 generally.
467 The final vote: CQ, *1981 Almanac,* pp. 415–18.
468 "a mistake": *Congressional Record,* Oct. 14, 1981, p. 23915.
468 "Maybe it will help": ints., Dennis Shedd, Mar. 16, Mar. 30, 1991; int., Quentin Crommelin, Apr. 18, 1991; int., Scott Wilson, Mar. 28, 1991.
469 "must not have read": int., Ralph Neas, Apr. 3, 1991; int., Burt Wides, Mar. 19, 1991.
469 "Don't let 'em bait you": int., Dennis Shedd, Mar. 16, 1991.
469 "I want to make": ST testimony, Jan. 27, 1982, Senate Judiciary Subcommittee on the Constitution, hearings on bills to amend the Voting Rights Act of 1965, 97th Cong., 2d Sess., p. 59.
470 "ultimate logical result": ibid., William French Smith testimony, pp. 66–75.

470 "Mr. McDonald": ibid., Laughlin McDonald testimony, Jan. 28, 1982, pp. 372–73.
472 To this list: int., Dennis Shedd, Apr. 6, 1991.
472 McCain's testimony: Senate Judiciary Constitution Subcommittee hearings, Feb. 11, 1982, pp. 1130–33.
472 approved a ten-year extension: CQ *1982 Almanac,* pp. 373–77 generally.
472 the same promise: int., Ike Williams, Jan. 15, 1991.
473 "strong convictions": transcript of Apr. 28, 1982, Senate Judiciary Committee meeting, p. 16.
473 "where are you?": ibid., p. 39.
473 Dole asked Ralph Neas: int., Ralph Neas, Apr. 3, 1991.
473 chicken and a pig: int., Dennis Shedd, Mar. 16, 1991.
474 call Armand Derfner: int., Ralph Neas, Apr. 3, 1991; int., Armand Derfner, Apr. 10, 1991.
474 "results" test: int., Sheila Bair, Apr. 2, 1991; int., Ralph Neas, Apr. 3, 1991; int., Burt Wides, Mar. 19, 1991; int., Armand Derfner, Apr. 10, 1991.
474 "little more than cosmetics": transcript of May 4, 1982, Senate Judiciary Committee meeting, pp. 69–75.
475 "reflects my commitment": Senate Report 97–417, pp. 88–93.
475 Hollings . . . East: *Congressional Record,* June 16, 1982, pp. 13789–97.
477 "negative aspects of our state": ST speech, June 17, 1982, STC Speeches, Box 98.
478 "We are not going to secede": *Saturday Evening Post,* Mar. 16, 1963, pp. 15–21.
478 "in pride of": *Congressional Record,* June 17, 1982, p. 14119.
479 "not on account of discrimination": *Congressional Record,* June 17, 1982, p. 14126.
479 "I personally led the fight": *Congressional Record,* June 17, 1982, p. 14115; see also June 18, 1982, pp. 14315–16.
481 "embarrasses a large segment": William B. James letter to *The Sumter Daily Item,* Jan. 19, 1982, William James Collection, Caroliniana Library, University of South Carolina.
481 Thurmond's bachelor days: The story of Thurmond's alleged black child was repeated in interviews in 1989 and 1990 with Modjeska Simkins and Tom McCain; see also Sherrill, *Gothic Politics in the Deep South,* pp. 244–45.
481 He denied: *Penthouse,* Aug. 1992, p. 40; *Post,* Aug. 4, 1992, p. 1E; ints., Harry Dent, Aug. 10, 1992, Sept. 4, 1992.
482 "test of history": ST statement, Mar. 27, 1979, STC Speeches, Box 79.
482 "just *not* reasonable": ST statement, June 21, 1979, STC Speeches, Box 79.

482 personally telephoned: int., ST, Mar. 26, 1991; int., Dennis Shedd, Mar. 29, 1991.
483 "I fully recognize": *Congressional Record,* Oct. 3, 1983, p. 13462.
484 "scalawag of the year": int., Dennis Shedd, Apr. 18, 1991.
484 received two awards: int., Dennis Shedd, Mar. 30, 1991; Luns Richardson letter to ST, Nov. 9, 1983, STC Press Assistants, Box 25.
484 Riley . . . decided: int., Richard Riley, Apr. 10, 1991; int., Dwight Drake, Apr. 8, 1991.
484 W. W. "Hootie" Johnson: *The Charlotte Observer,* Mar. 20, 1984, pp. 1C, 2C.
484 "like a million dollars": ibid., p. 1C.
485 taken another lawsuit: *McCain v. Lybrand,* 465 U.S. 236 (1984); see also Edds, *Free at Last,* pp. 29–50.
486 167 new judges: CQ, *1984 Almanac,* pp. 243–45.
486 "all the cards": int., Ralph Neas, Apr. 3, 1991; see also CQ, *1986 Weekly Report,* p. 1580.
487 Rehnquist came before the committee: CQ, *1986 Almanac,* pp. 67–72.
487 Scalia came before the committee: ibid.
487 "I simply say": *Congressional Record,* Sept. 12, 1986, p. 23071; see also Sept. 17, 1986, pp. 23736–39.
488 a genuine fondness: int., Joseph R. Biden, Jr., Apr. 16, 1991; int., Mark Gitenstein, Apr. 11, 1991.
489 called up Duke Short: int., Ralph Neas, Apr. 3, 1991.
489 "Robert Bork's America": *Congressional Record,* July 1, 1987, pp. 18518–19.
491 "a candidate's philosophy": Senate Judiciary Committee, hearings on the nomination of Robert Bork to be associate justice of the Supreme Court of the United States, 100th Cong., 1st Sess., Sept. 15, 1987, pp. 29–32.
491 walk a careful line: int., Ralph Neas, Apr. 3, 1991; int., Dennis Shedd, Apr. 6, 1991.
492 voted 9 to 5: CQ, *1987 Almanac,* p. 273; see also pp. 271–74 on Bork nomination generally.
492 "admonish the audience": *Congressional Record,* Oct. 23, 1987, p. 29121.
492 "guise of protecting": Bork, *The Tempting of America,* p. 323.
492 favoring Billy Wilkins: int., Joseph R. Biden, Jr., Apr. 16, 1991; int., Mark Gitenstein, Apr. 11, 1991.
493 stay neutral: int., Harry S. Dent, Mar. 1991; int., Mark Goodin, Mar. 20, 1991.
494 Lott . . . Dowdy: CQ, *Weekly Report,* Oct. 15, 1988, pp. 2912–13.
494 the couple was separating: statements of ST and Nancy Thurmond, Mar. 28, 1991, from ST Senate office.

495 Helms . . . Gantt: *The News and Observer,* Nov. 1, 1990, pp. 1, 4A; Nov. 2, 1990, pp. 1, 12A; Nov. 7, 1990, pp. 1, 6A; int., Ferrell Guillory, Apr. 4, 1991.

496 "A good vote": int., W. Henderson, Nov. 1991; see also CQ, *1991 Weekly Report,* pp. 3200–3202, 8284–85.

496 "a man of his age": confidential interview.

497 "meet the challenges": int., ST, Feb. 13, 1991.

Bibliography

BOOKS

Anderson, J. W. *Eisenhower, Brownell and the Congress: The Tangled Origins of the Civil Rights Bill of 1956–57.* University of Alabama Press, 1964.

Ashmore, Harry. *Hearts and Minds: The Anatomy of Racism from Roosevelt to Reagan.* McGraw-Hill, 1982.

Ball, William Watts. *The State That Forgot.* Bobbs-Merrill Co., 1932.

Bardolph, Richard. *The Civil Rights Record: Black Americans and the Law, 1849–1970.* Thomas Y. Crowell Co., 1970.

Barnard, William D. *Dixiecrats and Democrats: Alabama Politics, 1942–50.* University of Alabama Press, 1974.

Bartley, Numan V. *The Rise of Massive Resistance.* Louisiana State University Press, 1969.

Bass, Jack, and DeVries, Walter. *The Transformation of Southern Politics.* Basic Books, 1974.

Bass, Jack, and Nelson, Jack. *The Orangeburg Massacre.* Mercer University Press, 1984.

Bernstein, Barton J., ed. *Politics and Policies of the Truman Administration.* Quadrangle, 1970.

Bilbo, Theodore. *Take Your Choice—Separation or Mongrelization.* Dream House Publishing Co., 1947.

Black, Earl, and Black, Merle. *Southern Governors and Civil Rights.* Harvard University, 1976.

—. *Politics and Society in the South.* Harvard University, 1987.

Bork, Robert. *The Tempting of America.* Free Press, 1990.

Branch, Taylor. *Parting the Waters.* Simon & Schuster, 1988.

Bronner, Ethan. *Battle for Justice.* Anchor Books, 1990.

Brown, C. Edgar, comp. *Democracy at Work: Being the Official Report of the Democratic National Convention (1948).* The Local Democratic Political Committee of Pennsylvania.

Burton, Oliver Vernon. *In My Father's House Are Many Mansions.* University of North Carolina Press, 1985.

Carter, Hodding, III. *The South Strikes Back.* Negro Universities Press, 1970.

Cash, W. J. *The Mind of the South.* Vintage Books, 1969.

Chester, Lewis; Hodgson, Godfrey; and Page, Bruce. *An American Melodrama: The Presidential Campaign of 1968.* The Viking Press, 1969.

Collins, Charles Wallace. *Whither Solid South: A Study in Politics and Race Relations.* Pelican, 1947.
Congressional Quarterly. *Almanacs, 1957–89.* Congressional Quarterly Inc.
———. *Congress and the Nation,* vols. 1–4. Congressional Quarterly Inc.
———. *Guide to U.S. Elections.* Congressional Quarterly Inc.
———. *National Party Conventions, 1831–1984.* Congressional Quarterly Inc.
———. *Weekly Reports.* Congressional Quarterly Inc.
Dabbs, James McBride. *Southern Heritage.* Alfred A. Knopf, 1958.
———. *Who Speaks for the South.* Funk & Wagnalls, 1964.
Dent, Harry. *The Prodigal South Returns to Power.* John Wiley & Sons, 1978.
Edds, Margaret. *Free at Last.* Adler & Adler, 1987.
Grantham, Dewey W., Jr. *Hoke Smith and the Politics of the New South.* Louisiana State University Press, 1958.
Green, Adam Wigfall. *The Man Bilbo.* Louisiana State University Press, 1963.
Greenhaw, Wayne. *Elephants in the Cottonfields: Ronald Reagan and the New Republican South.* Macmillan Publishing Co., 1982.
Griffith, Winthrop. *Humphrey: A Candid Biography.* Morrow, 1965.
Gunther, John. *Inside U.S.A.* Harper, 1946.
Hamilton, Virginia Van der Veer. *Lister Hill.* University of North Carolina Press, 1987.
Heard, Alexander. *A Two-Party South?* University of North Carolina Press, 1952.
Henderson, Gerald P., and Roberts, Gary L. *Georgia Governors in an Age of Change, from Ellis Arnall to George Busbee.* University of Georgia Press, 1988.
Holmes, William F. *The White Chief.* Louisiana State University Press, 1970.
Huckaby, Elizabeth. *Crisis at Central High: Little Rock, 1957–58.* Louisiana State University Press, 1980.
Huss, John. *Senator for the South: A Biography of Olin D. Johnston.* Doubleday, 1961.
Kesselman, Louis Coleridge. *The Social Politics of the FEPC: A Study in Reform Pressure Movements.* University of North Carolina Press, 1948.
Key, V. O., Jr. *Southern Politics.* Alfred A. Knopf, 1949.
Kluger, Richard. *Simple Justice.* Alfred A. Knopf, 1976.
Lachicotte, Alberta. *Rebel Senator.* Devon-Adair, 1966.
Lamis, Alexander P. *The Two-Party South.* Oxford University Press (paperback), 1984.

Lauder, Ernest McPherson, Jr. *A History of South Carolina, 1865–1960.* University of North Carolina Press, 1960.

Lawson, Steven F. *Voting Rights in the South, 1944–69.* Columbia University Press, 1976.

Littlejohn, Bruce. *Littlejohn's Half-Century at the Bench and Bar (1936–86).* South Carolina Bar Foundation, 1987.

———. *Political Memoirs (1934–88).* South Carolina Bar Foundation, 1989.

Logue, Cal M. *Eugene Talmage.* Greenwood Press, 1989.

Logue, Cal M., and Dorgan, Howard, eds. *The Oratory of Southern Demagogues.* Louisiana State University Press, 1981.

Martin, John Bartlow. *The Deep South Says "Never."* Ballantine Books, 1957.

McGill, Ralph. *The South and the Southerner.* Atlantic Monthly Press, 1959.

McPherson, Harry. *A Political Education.* Houghton Mifflin (paperback), 1988.

Michie, Allan A., and Ryhlick, Frank. *Dixie Demagogues.* The Vanguard Press, 1939.

Miller, Merle. *Lyndon.* G. P. Putnam's Sons, 1980.

Morgan, Chester M. *Redneck Liberal: Theodore G. Bilbo and the New Deal.* Louisiana State University Press, 1985.

Morris, Aldon D. *Origins of the Civil Rights Movement.* Free Press, 1984.

Newby, I. A. *Black Carolinians: A History of Blacks in South Carolina from 1895 to 1968.* University of South Carolina Press, 1973.

Panetta, Leon, and Gall, Peter. *Bring Us Together.* J. B. Lippincott Co., 1971.

Peck, James. *Freedom Ride.* Simon & Schuster, 1962.

Percy, William Alexander. *Lanterns on the Levee: Recollections of a Planter's Son.* Alfred A. Knopf, 1941.

President's Committee on Civil Rights. *To Secure These Rights: Report of the President's Committee on Civil Rights.* Simon & Schuster, 1947.

Quint, Howard. *Profile in Black and White.* Greenwood Press, 1958.

Raines, Howell. *My Soul Is Rested.* G. P. Putnam's Sons, 1977.

Ross, Irwin. *The Loneliest Campaign.* New American Library, 1968.

Safire, William. Safire's Political Dictionary, Ballantine Books, 1980.

Salter, John Thomas, ed. *Public Men In and Out of Office.* University of North Carolina Press, 1946.

Schlesinger, Arthur M., ed. *History of American Presidential Elections, 1789–1968.* Chelsea House Publishers, 1971.

Sherrill, Robert. *Gothic Politics in the Deep South.* Grossman, 1968.

Simkins, Frances Butler. *Pitchfork Ben Tillman.* Louisiana State University Press, 1944.

———. *A History of the South.* Alfred A. Knopf, 1961.

Sosna, Martin. *In Search of the Silent South: Southern Liberals and the Race Issue.* Columbia University Press, 1977.

South Carolina Writers Project. *South Carolina: A Guide to the Palmetto State.* Oxford University Press, 1941.

Wallace, David Duncan. *The History of South Carolina,* vol. 3. The American Historical Society Inc., 1943.

Warren, Earl. *The Memoirs of Earl Warren.* Doubleday, 1977.

Wolfe, Albert Benedict. *Readings in Social Problems.* Ginn & Co., 1916.

Woodward, C. Vann. *The Strange Career of Jim Crow.* Oxford University Press, 1966.

———. *Origins of the New South.* Louisiana State University Press, 1961.

———. *Tom Watson: Agrarian Rebel.* The Beehive Press, 1938.

Workman, William. *The Bishop from Barnwell: The Political Life and Times of Senator Edgar A. Brown.* R. L. Bryan Co., 1963.

Yarbrough, Tinsley. *A Passion for Justice.* Oxford University Press, 1987.

PAMPHLETS

Ader, Emile B. *The Dixiecrat Movement—Its Role in Third Party Politics,* vol. 32. Public Affairs Press, 1955.

Bullard, Sara et al., eds. *Free At Last, A History of the Civil Rights Movement and Those Who Died in the Struggle.* Southern Poverty Law Center, 1989.

Cross, Theodore and Slater, Robert B. *A Black Voter's Guide to the 1978 Elections.* Business and Society Review, 1978.

Southern Regional Council. *The South and the Supreme Court's School Decisions: A Chronology, May 17, 1954–December 31, 1956.*

———*Pro-Segregation Groups in the South.* November 19, 1956.

Southern Regional Council and Fleming, Harold C., *Resistance Movements and Racial Desegregation.* March 1956.

———. *The Negro Voter in the South: A Report of a Survey by the Southern Regional Council.* July 18, 1957.

Tillman, Benjamin Ryan. *The Struggles of 1876: How South Carolina Was Delivered of Carpetbag and Negro Rule,* 1909.

ARTICLES

Chesteen, Richard D., "Mississippi Is Gone Home." *Journal of Mississippi History* (February 1970), pp. 43–59.

Gatewood, Willard B. "Theodore Roosevelt and the Indianola Affair." *Journal of Negro History* 53 (January 1968), pp. 48–69.

Halberstam, David. "The White Citizens' " Councils: Respectable Means for Unrespectable Ends." *Commentary,* October 1956, pp. 293–302.

Hoffman, Edwin D. "The Genesis of the Modern Movement for Equal Rights in South Carolina, 1930–39." *Journal of Negro History* 44 (October 1959), pp. 346–69.

Hofstadter, Richard. "From Calhoun to the Dixiecrats." *Social Research* 16 (June 1949), pp. 135–50.

Holmes, William F. "Whitecapping: Agrarian Violence in Mississippi, 1902–1906." *Journal of Southern History* 35 (May 1969), pp. 165–85.

Sitkoff, Harvard. "Harry Truman and the Election of 1948: The Coming Age of Civil Rights in American Politics." *Journal of Southern History* 36 (November 4, 1971), pp. 597–616.

Starr, J. Barton. "Birmingham and the Dixiecrat Convention of 1948." *Alabama Historical Quarterly,* spring and summer 1970, pp. 23–50.

White, Eugene, "Anti-Racial Agitation in Politics: James Kimble Vardaman in the Mississippi Gubernatorial Campaign of 1903." *Journal of Mississippi History* 7 (April 1945), pp. 91–110.

UNPUBLISHED WORKS

Dissertations

Aba-Mecha, Barbara Woods. "Black Woman Activist in South Carolina: Modjeska Monteith Simkins." Emory University, 1978.

Ashley, Frank Watts. "Selected Southern Liberal Editors and the States' Rights Movement of 1948." University of South Carolina, 1959.

Banks, James G. "Strom Thurmond and the Revolt Against Modernity." Kent State University, 1970.

Burnside, Ronald Dantan. "The Governorship of Coleman Livingston Blease of South Carolina." University of South Carolina, 1963.

Doler, Thurston Ermon. "Theodore Bilbo's Rhetoric of Racial Relations." University of Oregon, 1968.

Hayes, Jack Irby. "South Carolina and the New Deal, 1932–38." University of South Carolina, 1972.

Hemmingway, Theodore. "Beneath the Yoke of Bondage: A History of Black Folks in South Carolina." University of South Carolina, 1976.

McLaurin, Anne Mathison. "The Role of Dixiecrats in the 1948 Election." University of Oklahoma, 1972.

Ness, Gary Clifford. "The States' Rights Movement of 1948." Duke University, 1972.

Terry, Robert Lewis. "J. Waties Waring: Spokesman for Racial Justice in the New South." University of Utah, 1970.

Master's Theses

Borsos, John. "Support for the National Democratic Party in South Carolina During the Dixiecrat Revolt of 1948." University of South Carolina, 1987.

Bouknight, Martha Nelle. "The Senatorial Campaigns of Ellison Durant ('Cotton Ed') Smith of South Carolina." Florida State University, 1961.

Burns, Gladys King. "The Alabama Dixiecrat Revolt of 1948." Auburn University, 1965.

Farmer, James O., Jr. "The End of the White Primary in South Carolina: A Southern State's Fight to Keep its Politics White." East Carolina University, 1965.

Hilliard, Elbert Riley. "A Biography of Fielding Wright: Mississippi's Mr. States' Rights." Mississippi State University, 1959.

Honor's Thesis

Atkinson, James L. "Citizens' Councils of South Carolina: 1955–61." Honor's Thesis. University of South Carolina, 1987.

NEWSPAPERS

The State, Columbia, South Carolina.
The News and Courier, Charleston, South Carolina.
The Columbia Record, Columbia, South Carolina.
The New York Times, New York, New York.
The Atlanta Constitution, Atlanta, Georgia.
The Birmingham News, Birmingham, Alabama.
The Montgomery Advertiser, Montgomery, Alabama.
The Clarion Ledger, Jackson, Mississippi.
The Meridian Star, Meridian, Mississippi.
The Courier-Journal, Louisville, Kentucky
The Washington Post, Washington, D.C.

OTHER SOURCES

Papers of Strom Thurmond, Clemson University.
Papers of William Watts Ball, Duke University.
Papers of Edgar Brown, Clemson University.
Papers of Robert C. Edwards, Clemson University.
Papers of Robert McC. Figg, University of South Carolina.
Papers of Olin D. Johnston, University of South Carolina.
Papers of John Sanford Martin, Duke University.

Papers of John McCray, University of South Carolina.
Papers of the NAACP, Library of Congress.
Papers of Richard Russell, University of Georgia.
Papers of South Carolina Human Relations Commission, University of South Carolina.
Papers of Jean Crouch Thurmond, Clemson University.
Papers of J. Waties Waring, Howard University.
Papers of William D. Workman, University of South Carolina.
Political Scrapbook of William Baskin, University of South Carolina.

Acknowledgments

The great temptation in writing a first book is to thank everyone who ever said a kind word during the writing process. I will try to restrain myself, but symbolic of all those nice people is one of the Avis rental agents at the Birmingham, Alabama, airport, who innocently asked what brought me to her city and then got an earful about Strom Thurmond. She listened politely, told me the book sounded interesting and said she'd look for it in the bookstores. God bless her. She sent me smiling on my way to Tuscaloosa for my afternoon interview.

Much had happened before that trip to Alabama, and there were several people who helped get this book going and who provided encouragement, suggestions, and advice.

My thanks to Nancy Lisagor, who took time out from a book-signing party in Washington to encourage me to turn my thoughts about the senator into a book proposal and then pointed me in the right direction. And thanks to David Rapp, who offered support and suggestions through the entire writing of this book. Chapter by chapter, he was an invaluable sounding board. Thanks, too, to Mark Gitenstein for his help in the early going.

To my agent Philippa Brophy, my thanks for seeing the story in Strom Thurmond's career and for taking a chance on it—and perhaps most important, for being a voice of reassurance.

Allan Mayer was my first editor at Simon & Schuster. Though he left well before the manuscript was finished, he helped make the writing of it easier by making me think hard about the proposal. He told me from the beginning that he could "see the book." By the time I started the research, so could I.

Marie Arana-Ward took over the project, and my thanks for her support and encouragement every step of the way. To Ed Sedarbaum, appreciation for his thoughtful attention to detail in reading the manuscript. He made this a better book and me a better writer.

To my "landlord," The Alan Guttmacher Institute, thanks for providing me, to borrow from Virginia Woolf, a room of my own to write in and for making me feel so welcome during this entire adventure. My thanks to all for listening good-naturedly when I wandered the halls telling Strom Thurmond stories.

After doing research at eight libraries in five southern states and work by phone at a ninth, my respect for librarians has only increased. Those I met not only provided the materials I had known about in advance but also made suggestions that were helpful. My special thanks to Jim Cross, the archivist for Senator Thurmond's papers at Clemson University, and to the Special Collections staff: Michael Kohl, Laurie Varenhorst, Karen Bates, and Dennis Taylor for so promptly gathering the mounds of material I asked for. I'm sure that singlehandedly I helped Clemson pay for one of the very nice chairs researchers use in the work area. Thanks also to June Fitzgerald and Ove Anderson for their assistance.

At the Caroliniana Library at the University of South Carolina many thanks to Tom Johnson, Herb Hartsook, Henry Fullmer, Laura Costello, and James Hill, and to Dargan Richards at the Columbia *State.*

The library staff at Congressional Quarterly—my professional home for nearly ten years—was helpful beyond words. My great thanks to Kathleen Walton, Michael Williams, and Cary Schneider. I am, to be sure, prejudiced when it comes to CQ, but during the writing of this book, I gained a new appreciation for the value of the publication's attention to the federal legislative process.

This book would have been so much harder to write without the cooperation of individuals close to Senator Thurmond—aides and former aides and members of his family. My special thanks to the senator's twin sisters, Mary Thurmond Tompkins and Martha Thurmond Bishop, for welcoming me into their homes and for sharing their stories, and to Allen George Thurmond, the senator's brother, for his observations.

To Harry Dent and Dennis Shedd my thanks for the hours of enlightening conversations. Thanks to Mark Goodin and Duke Short for their insights. I must also thank Senator Thurmond first for being such a colorful politician and then for his willingness to talk—and argue—with me about his career. I appreciate that he never once asked to see any portion of the manuscript.

Ferrell Guillory and Bill Barnard read the first draft of the book, and each made many thoughtful suggestions that helped improve it.

Mike LeTorneau of Wide World Photos was patient, generous, and good-humored in helping me search for pictures.

Of the many books I read, two stand out as particularly helpful: Richard Kluger's *Simple Justice,* the lucid and dramatic account of the *Brown v. Board of Education* litigation, and Tinsley Yarbrough's *A Passion for Justice,* a biography of South Carolina federal judge J. Waties Waring, whose life offers such illuminating contrast to Thurmond's.

Closer to home, thanks to Jane Abbott, my friend of many years, for listening and learning along with me.

Finally, thanks to my brother for his advice and counsel along the way and to my mother for her generosity and for always providing a safe haven. The joy of writing this book was diminished by the fact that my father died before I began work on it. He was in my thoughts constantly. His generosity to me in his life and in his death makes so much possible, and it is with appreciation and respect for the example my parents set that I dedicate this book to his memory and to my mother.

Index

Abernathy, Ralph D., 323
abortion, 456, 460, 462, 489, 490
Acheson, Dean, 325
Agnew, Spiro T., 399, 400, 410, 412
Agriculture Department, U.S., 273
Aiken County, S.C., 235, 236, 287, 406, 471
Alabama:
  civil rights movement in, 139, 277
  Democratic Party in, 139–40, 167, 169
  Dixiecrat movement in, 139, 174–80, 181, 189–90
  freedom riders in, 320–23, 324
  segregation in, 277, 346
  violence in, 316, 320–23, 324, 345–46, 366–69, 371–72
  White Citizens' Councils in, 271
Allen, Fred, 179
Allen, James, 436
Allen, Louis, 328
Allen University, 75, 218
Almond, J. Lindsay, 188
American Civil Liberties Union (ACLU), 100, 346, 432, 464
Americans for Democratic Action (ADA), 164, 165, 166, 167, 313, 337, 359
Anderson, Eugenie, 165
Anderson Independent, 59, 209, 360
Arbor, J. Edward, 75
Arkansas:
  civil rights movement in, 270, 300–303
  Dixiecrat movement in, 158, 159, 183–84
  White Citizens' Council in, 302
Arnall, Ellis B., 78, 103, 118
Askew, Reuben, 439
Atlanta Constitution, 158, 159, 169, 191, 237–38, 277, 301, 313, 400
Atwater, Lee, 445–46, 455, 457
Avery Institute, 104, 105

Bagnall, Robert W., 48, 75
Baker, David, 161
Baker, D. Gordon, 96
Ball, William Watts, 78–79, 80, 117, 191–92, 471–72
Barkley, Alben, 164, 179
Barnett, Ross, 312, 323, 330–31, 344, 358, 369–70, 451
"Barnwell ring," 86–90, 93, 96, 98–99, 207, 231, 240
Bartlett, E. L., 326
Baskin, W. P., 57, 114–15, 116, 128, 151, 152, 153, 169, 170–71
Bastian, Walter, 249
Baxley, William, 346
Beattie, A. J., 85
Belser, Irving, 150
Belton, Ethel, 245
Belton v. Gebhart, 245, 246
Benet, Christie, 115, 150
Bennett, Neville, 260, 262
Benson, S. I., 220, 221
Bettis, Alexander, 472
Bettis Academy, 50, 463
Biden, Joseph R., Jr., 437, 438, 487, 488–89, 490, 492
Biemiller, Andrew J., 165, 166
Bilbo, Theodore (The Man), 13, 63–64, 77, 134, 373
Bill of Rights, 135, 296
Birmingham, Ala., 174–80, 184, 336–37
Black, Hugo, 242, 249–50, 253
Blackmun, Harry A., 410
"black power," 364, 381–82, 385
blacks:
  citizenship of, 25, 48, 76, 338
  civil rights demanded by, 64, 132, 136, 143, 155, 156, 178, 196, 200, 226, 288, 335–40
  constitutional rights of, 32, 108, 129, 141, 164, 177, 333, 337, 338, 349, 351, 352, 369, 489–91
  Democratic Party supported by, 46–47, 64, 132, 136, 152, 159, 161, 288, 314, 317
  disfranchisement of, 23, 54, 289, 376

blacks: *(cont.)*
education for, 25, 33–34, 40, 42, 49, 50, 97, 101–2, 112–14, 118–19, 150, 195–97, 198, 199, 200, 204, 216–34, 251–52
emancipation of, 177, 312
medical care for, 39–40
in North, 47, 310–11, 319, 320, 341–42, 437
in political factions, 364, 382
political participation by, 12, 19–26, 32, 48, 54, 78, 79, 91, 101–2, 116–18, 124, 129, 130, 141–42, 147, 189–90, 270, 272, 288–89, 298, 314, 327, 377–78, 381–83, 414–16, 436, 457
poverty of, 37, 194, 217, 292
as "pressure group," 64, 132, 136, 196, 203, 213–14, 310–11, 337, 385, 407
property owned by, 144, 219
quotas for, 495
rioting by, 379–80, 381, 386–87, 390–91, 393
in rural areas, 50, 194–95
taxation of, 219, 229, 481
Thurmond's views on, 29–30, 177, 198–200, 203–4
trials of, 60–61, 62, 67–71, 108–9, 111–12
white intimidation of, 19–26, 66, 279, 351–52, 376
Blair, Frank, 341
Blatt, Solomon, 55, 59, 86–90, 98, 282, 447
Blease, Cole, 30–31, 34, 36, 38, 83, 195, 205
Bloch, Charles, 168
"Bloody Sunday," 367–68, 369
Bolling, Richard, 340, 342
Bolling, Spottswood Thomas, Jr., 249
Bolling v. Sharpe, 253
boll weevils, 35, 50
Bonham, James, 18, 185, 471
Booker, Simeon, 321
Boren, David, 492
Bork, Robert, 489–93
Boston, Mass., busing in, 437
Boulware, Harold, 105, 107, 115, 192, 218, 219
Breaux, John, 487
Brennan, William J., 419
Briggs, Harry, 220
Briggs, Liza, 220
Briggs v. Elliott, 196–97, 220–34, 238, 241–42, 243, 248, 253–54, 275
Britt, Quince, 57
Broder, David, 448–49, 450
Brooke, Edward, 387, 407, 437
Brooks, Preston S., 18
Broughton, J. Melville, 190
Brown, David, 153, 169, 170, 172, 193, 204, 218
Brown, Edgar, 59, 81
in "Barnwell ring," 86–90, 98, 231, 240
gubernatorial campaign of (1946), 86–90, 98, 231
senatorial campaign of (1938), 64, 65, 66
senatorial campaign of (1954), 240, 255–67
Thurmond and, 55–56, 86–90, 231
Brown, Oliver, 243–44
Brown, Thomas W., 99
Brown, Walter, 96, 132, 144, 178, 207, 216, 357
Brownell, Herbert, 269, 301
Brown II, 270, 275–79, 281, 287, 288, 475
Brown v. Board of Education, 238, 243–45, 250–55, 475
political impact of, 250–55, 265, 287, 397, 462
Southern reaction to, 254–55, 270, 271,282,283,316,415–16,419
Thurmond's views on, 282, 283, 288, 304, 311, 329–30
Bruorton, H. B., 67–68, 69
Bryant, Roy, 280–81
Bryson, Joseph H., 56, 57
Bulah v. Gebhart, 246
Bumpers, Dale, 439
Burger, Warren E., 402–3, 404, 408, 422–23, 486
Bush, George, 457, 493, 495, 496
busing, 13, 102, 195–97, 218–19, 223, 245, 247, 270, 288, 320–24
congressional opposition to, 436–38
Supreme Court rulings on, 418–24, 436
Thurmond's opposition to, 423, 429, 436–38, 456
Butler, Andrew P., 18
Butler, Mary, 28
Butler, Matthew C., 19
Butler, Pierce Mason, 18
Buzhardt, J. Fred, Jr., 273–74, 307, 308, 312, 326, 356, 357–58, 365, 398, 401, 402, 425, 434, 456
Byrd, Harry, 90, 283, 284, 318, 319, 475
Byrd, Levi S., 75–76
Byrd, Robert C., 388, 438
Byrnes, James F., 81, 206, 282
as governor, 201, 225, 227, 231, 234, 241, 254, 258

senatorial race of (1954), 258, 262, 265–66
Thurmond and, 234, 237, 265, 357

Caldwell, Millard E., 131
Calhoun, John C., 38, 65, 127, 281
Callison, T. C., 113, 266
Carmichael, Stokely, 381, 382, 387
"carpetbaggers," 203, 212, 265, 360
Carroll, Richard, 32
Carswell, G. Harrold, 408, 448
Carter, Jimmy, 438–41, 446, 454, 460, 485–86
Carter, Robert L., 112, 223
Case, Francis, 254
Celler, Emanuel, 319
Chambliss, Robert, 346
Chaney, James, 351–52
Chapman, Robert F., 465, 471, 476
Chappaquiddick affair, 425
Charleston, S.C., 40, 75, 106, 107, 478
Charleston Interracial Committee, 75
Charleston Lions Club, 61–62
Charleston *News and Courier,* 80, 106, 117–18, 173, 180, 191–92, 215, 221, 228, 232, 237, 255, 257, 258, 259, 273, 274, 277, 278, 312, 324, 333–35, 352, 356, 360, 363–64, 384, 388, 400, 423, 424, 440, 451
Charlotte, N.C., 422, 438
Charlotte Observer, 428–29, 438
Cherry, R. Gregg, 181, 190
Chicago riots, 379
church bombings, 304, 310, 316, 345
CIO, 90, 211
Citizens Democratic Party, 151, 152, 159, 160–61, 162
Citizens for Nixon, 451
Civilian Conservation Corps (CCC), 51, 73
civil rights:
black demands for, 64, 132, 136, 143, 155, 156, 178, 196, 200, 226, 288, 335–40
communism and, 130, 199, 272, 282, 288, 324–25, 330, 334, 337–38, 344–45, 351, 387, 483
compromises on, 292, 293, 297–98, 317, 340, 381, 472, 473–74, 475
federal enforcement of, 293, 337, 350, 371, 419–20
legislation on, 11, 124–25, 274–75, 289–306, 316, 335–36, 340, 342, 348–51, 386, 391–92, 402
"outside agitators" and, 80, 111, 145, 199, 200, 203, 221, 272, 285–86, 323, 324, 457
political impact of, 93–94, 110–11, 114, 128–48, 494–96
press coverage of, 117–18, 130, 140, 180, 274, 333, 336, 367
Southern opposition to, 280–81, 305–6, 317–18, 332–33, 351–53, 355, 375, 376, 377
states' rights vs., 76, 94, 153, 155, 166, 290, 305–6, 342–43
student activism and, 316, 327, 387
Thurmond's views on, 132–33, 137, 144–47, 184, 188, 241, 274, 285–86, 292–97, 300, 301–2, 309, 312–14, 342–43, 349, 352–53, 364–65, 370, 381, 388–92, 414, 418, 455–58, 473, 481, 497–98
Civil Rights Act (1875), 347
Civil Rights Act (1957), 289–300
Civil Rights Act (1960), 304–6, 309, 310–11
Civil Rights Act (1964), 316, 317, 348–51, 355
Civil Rights Act (1991), 495–96
Civil Rights Commission, 289–90, 305, 306, 308, 310, 312, 319, 326–27, 336, 337, 348, 462
Civil War, U.S., 12, 18, 19, 20, 96, 106, 109, 132, 144, 176, 255, 311
Clarendon County, S.C., 118, 150, 194–97, 216–34, 238, 277–79, 286
Clark, James G., 367
Clark, Joseph, 318, 319
Clark, Kenneth, 228–29
Clark, Ramsey, 395
Clark, Tom, 250, 253, 388
Clayton, Faith, 200, 201
Clement, Arthur, Jr., 150, 161, 162, 217
Clemson College, 32–33, 49, 74, 205, 333–35, 430, 478, 495, 498
Cleveland, Grover, 22, 234
Clifford, Clark, 129, 133
Cloud, John, 367
Clyburn, Lewis M., 260
Cochran, Darley, 448–49
Cochran, Thad, 16, 415, 451–52, 494
Cold War, 326, 334
Coleman, Francis P., 257
Coleman, William T., Jr., 449
Collier, Bryan, 228
Collins, Addie Mae, 345
Collins, Charles Wallace, 133
Collins, LeRoy, 353, 355, 368
Collins, Sarah, 346
Colored Normal Industrial Agricultural and Mechanical College, 49, 104

Columbia Record, 142, 150, 425, 447–48
Columbia *State,* 43, 45, 47, 60, 61, 66, 81, 82, 97, 104, 109, 115, 130, 136, 142, 160, 174, 180, 235, 255, 257, 259, 263, 267, 301, 352, 357, 360, 363, 377, 384, 385, 386, 388, 399, 401–2, 411, 413, 418, 423, 424, 430, 440, 443, 450–51
Columbia University, 102, 155, 223
"Committee of 52," 281
Committee on Fair Employment Practices, 76–77
Commonwealth, 24, 25
communism:
  civil rights and, 130, 199, 272, 282, 288, 324–25, 330, 334, 337–38, 344–45, 351, 387, 483
  Thurmond's opposition to, 45–46, 324–25, 326, 332, 337–38, 347, 387, 393, 397
Community Relations Service, 340, 350, 353, 368
Confederate flag, 144, 174, 176, 191, 464
Congressional Record, 168, 283, 284, 297, 302, 310, 333, 344, 345, 428
Congress of Racial Equality (CORE), 320, 324, 382
Connally, John, 454
Connor, Eugene (Bull), 167, 322, 367
Constitution, U.S.:
  amendments to, 25, 94, 107, 208, 281, 285, 286, 328, 329, 374, 388, 409, 423
  constructionist interpretation of, 397, 404, 408
  electoral provisions of, 133, 161, 180
  freedoms guaranteed by, 11, 135, 165, 491
  individual rights protected by, 32, 108, 129, 141, 164, 177, 333, 337, 338, 349, 351, 352, 369, 489–91
  Thurmond's views on, 96, 144–45, 178, 191, 192, 214, 274, 278, 283–84, 302, 303, 317, 319, 332, 337, 340, 343, 360, 362, 364, 374–76, 383, 388, 389, 394, 395, 408, 418, 435
  see also specific amendments
Cooke, H. Kemper, 43
cotton, 35, 38–39, 44, 50, 64, 195, 273, 373
Courts, Gus, 268–69
Covar, Albert, 32
Cox, Archibald, 431, 433, 489
Cox, Gene, 130
Cox, Minnie M., 24–25, 26, 271
Crommelin, Quentin, 468
Crouch, Horace, 119
Crow, E. R., 229–30

Dabbs, James McBride, 81, 100–101, 151
Dabney, Virginius, 179, 191
Daniel, Charles E., 258, 272, 358
Daniels, Jonathan, 179, 190, 202
Dantin, Maurice, 452
Davis, Benjamin, 325
Davis, Dorothy E., 248
Davis, John W., 241, 275
Davis v. County School Board of Prince Edward County, 248
day-care centers, 427, 428
death penalty, 60–61, 67, 70
"Declaration of Constitutional Principles," 283–87, 300
Declaration of Independence, 124, 296
DeConcini, Dennis, 490, 492
de la Beckwith, Byron, 339
DeLaine, J. A., 218, 219, 220
DeLaine, Mattie, 220–21
Delaware, 245–46
DeLee, S. B., 426
DeLee, Victoria, 426–27, 428, 449, 481
Democratic National Committee, 135, 160, 183, 198, 201
Democratic National Conventions:
  of 1936, 46–47, 65, 66, 80
  of 1942, 81–82
  of 1948, 118, 131, 134, 154–69, 180, 286
  of 1956, 287
  of 1960, 311–13
  of 1968, 400
Democratic Party:
  black support for, 46–47, 64, 132, 136, 152, 159, 161, 288, 314, 317
  civil rights issue in, 157, 158, 163, 164–67, 188, 202, 287, 312–14, 368
  Credentials Committee of, 159–64
  membership of, 115, 116, 170, 172
  party loyalty and, 256–59, 260, 261, 262, 263–64, 318, 358
  primaries of, 77–81, 82, 91, 94, 96–97, 102–4, 114–18, 141–42, 151, 152, 161, 162–63, 172, 192–93, 196, 203, 204, 206, 363, 376, 462
  Southern influence of, 12, 47, 149, 166, 176, 202, 265, 267, 318,

362, 424, 439, 440, 441, 457, 493, 495
Southern revolt in, 128–48, 154–69, 174, 178–79, 181
Southern wing of, 46–47, 78–79, 126, 127, 128–48, 154–69, 312–14, 316, 318
states' rights issue in, 147–48, 156, 157, 166, 168–69; *see also* Dixiecrats
Thurmond's break with, 11–12, 90, 124, 154–69, 261, 266–67, 272–73, 313–14, 318, 348, 356–62, 450, 454
Thurmond's support for, 39, 47, 48, 90, 123, 132, 176, 191, 202, 207, 287, 318–19, 356
Dennis, Rembert, 256
Dent, Betty, 307
Dent, Harry, 239, 263, 455
as Republican Party leader, 364, 365, 380, 383, 385, 386, 396, 397, 398, 399, 400, 446, 493
Thurmond as viewed by, 283, 314, 401, 402, 450
as Thurmond's aide, 15, 206, 216, 273, 274, 307, 308, 313, 319, 326, 356, 357–59, 361, 412, 425, 445, 456, 457–58
Thurmond's filibuster and, 294, 295, 296
Watergate scandal and, 434
Denton, Jeremiah, 458, 459, 462, 475
Derfner, Armand, 474
desegregation:
federal enforcement of, 275–76, 277, 304, 419–20
schedule for, 277, 420
Southern resistance to, 271–72, 277–79, 281–82
Thurmond's opposition to, 278, 279, 282, 283–87
see also segregation
Dewey, Thomas E., 129, 154, 156, 179, 183, 189, 243, 400
Dillinger, John, 484
Dirksen, Everett M., 341, 349, 350, 351, 455
discrimination, 350, 421, 475–79
in education, 150, 195–97, 217, 224–25
intentional, 467–68, 470, 472, 474
pervasiveness of, 13–14, 203–4
in voting rights, 78, 94, 101–2, 104, 171–72, 173, 309–10, 366–69, 416, 463, 465, 467–68, 470, 472, 474, 476–77
"Dixie," 38, 134, 185, 191, 464
"Dixiecrat Mind, The" (McGill), 191
Dixiecrats:
conventions of, 141, 168, 174–80, 184, 185
defeat of, 188–92
political strategy of, 156, 181, 190–91, 313
racism of, 180, 185–88, 189, 191, 222
Southern revolt as basis of, 128–48, 154–69, 174, 178–79, 181
states' rights ideology of, 147–48, 156, 157, 166, 168–69
Thurmond as presidential candidate of, 11, 127, 148, 149–50, 156, 175–93, 198, 201, 212, 235, 349, 440–41, 448, 450, 456, 481, 498
Thurmond's address to, 142, 144–47
Dixon, Frank, 139, 142, 175, 176, 185
Doar, John, 327–28, 339, 368
Dobie, Armistead M., 242, 248
Dole, Elizabeth, 493
Dole, Robert, 440, 472–73, 474, 483, 493
Dorn, Fred, 73, 74
Dorn, William Jennings Bryan, 442
Douglas, Paul, 295–96, 299
Douglas, William O., 242, 250, 403–4
Dowdy, Wayne, 494
Du Bois, W.E.B., 32
Dukakis, Michael, 457, 493

Earle, Willie, 99–100, 111–12, 151, 204, 281, 383
East, John, 458, 475–76
Eastland, James O., 175, 307, 372–73, 415, 451, 452–53, 468
as chairman of Senate Judiciary Committee, 329, 340, 365, 372, 373
segregation supported by, 77, 130, 133, 254, 277, 278, 279, 282, 332, 373, 389, 395
Eastland, Woods, 372, 373
Edens, Drake, 380
Edgefield County, S.C.:
race relations in, 18–22
Thurmond as resident of, 26–32, 93, 185, 471–72
Thurmond as state senator for, 41–52
voter registration in, 463–66, 472, 476, 477, 485
education:
of blacks, 25, 33–34, 40, 42, 49, 50, 97, 101–2, 112–14, 118–19, 150, 195–97, 198, 199, 200, 204, 216–34, 251–52
constitutional rights for, 223–24,

education: *(cont.)*
227, 228, 230, 231–32, 241, 283–84, 303, 424
discrimination in, 150, 195–97, 217, 224–25
equal opportunity in, 94, 104–5, 112–14, 128, 207–9, 374
expenditures on, 34, 49, 62, 101–2, 112–14, 197, 217, 227, 230–31, 233, 242, 278
facilities for, 34, 40, 217, 224–25, 226, 228, 230–31, 232–33, 242, 247
federal involvement in, 209, 381, 455
"freedom of choice" in, 419, 421
integration in, 330–35, 397, 412, 416, 418–24, 436–38
legal, 39, 40–41, 112–14
segregation in, 23, 33–34, 128, 140, 151, 195, 207–9, 223, 231–32, 244–45, 250–55, 268, 270, 274, 275–79, 286, 288, 341–42, 348, 381, 416, 418–24
states' rights and, 283–84
taxation for, 219, 229, 437, 481
Thurmond's views on, 35, 39–40, 42, 45–46, 50, 61, 62, 84, 97, 118–19, 123, 128, 197, 204, 209, 218, 423, 437
of whites, 34, 49, 50, 217, 224–25, 229, 276
Educational Finance Commission, 229
Edwards, Don, 467
Edwards, James, 442
Edwards, Robert C., 334
Eisenhower, David, 402
Eisenhower, Dwight D., 454, 482
civil rights supported by, 254, 265, 269, 270, 274–75, 282, 289–90, 293, 295, 301, 304–6, 309, 310
judicial appointments by, 242, 279
presidential campaigns of, 287, 288, 405
as presidential candidate (1948), 155, 156–57, 207, 237
elections, *see specific candidates*
electoral college, 133, 139–40, 146, 181, 182, 189
Ellender, Allen J., 131
Elliot, Charles B., 115, 150
Elliot, Roderick W., 221
Ellis, Handy, 167
Elmore, George, 91–92, 94, 150, 215
Elmore v. Rice:
electoral laws challenged in, 102–4, 105, 107, 110–11, 218, 462
Supreme Court review of, 131, 141–42, 149
Thurmond's views on, 118, 125, 141–42, 204
Waring's ruling on, 114–18, 123, 125, 127, 141, 161, 163, 170, 171, 173, 193
Emancipation Proclamation, 312, 377
employment:
equal opportunity in, 76–77, 124, 165, 243, 340, 350, 496
workers' compensation and, 97, 205
Employment Security Commission, 200
Epps, Carl, 85
Equal Employment Opportunity Commission (EEOC), 350, 496
Ervin, Sam, 297, 299, 312, 329, 375, 389, 432
Evans, Rowland, 449
Evers, Charles, 452
Evers, Medgar, 280, 317, 338–40, 346, 452
Evers, Myrlie, 280, 338–39

Fair Employment Practice Commission (FEPC), 77, 129, 133, 135, 145, 149, 151, 185, 186, 312
Faith We Have Not Kept, The (Thurmond), 395
Faubus, Orval, 300, 301, 317
Federal Bureau of Investigation (FBI), 305, 324–25, 339, 346, 372, 483
Fifteenth Amendment, 25, 375, 377
Figg, Robert McC., 96, 132, 144, 146, 180
Briggs decision and, 223, 224, 225–27, 230, 275
Brown decision and, 170, 178
Fisk University, 387
Fitzgerald, Charles, 25
Fleming, Billie, 211
Fletcher, L. A., 160, 162
Florence Morning News, 173, 255, 257, 385
Florida, 131–34, 195–96, 214
Folsom, James E., 131–32, 139
Ford, Gerald R., 434, 438, 440, 441, 449
Fortas, Abe, 365, 378, 392–96, 403, 405, 408, 483, 490
Fortas, Carolyn Agger, 403
Fourteenth Amendment, 25, 107, 208, 219, 230, 232, 233, 250–51, 252, 275, 283, 285
Fowler, Donald, 406, 445
Frazier, Joe, 428
freedom riders, 13, 320–24, 367
Freedom Summer, 351–52
Freeman, G. W., Jr., 56

Freeman, Wayne, 118
Fulbright, J. William, 13
Fuller, W. W., 36
F. W. Woolworth stores, 316

Gadsden, Walter, 336
Gantt, Harvey, 333–35, 478, 495
Gathings, E. C., 330
Gebhart, Francis B., 246
George, Walter, 144, 284, 285
Georgia, 103, 114, 115, 116, 118, 277, 420, 439
  Democratic Party in, 140–41
  Dixiecrat movement in, 147–48, 158, 181, 182, 190, 191
Gibson, Isaac, 71
Gibson, Merritt, 183
Ginsberg, Douglas, 492
Goldberg, Arthur, 378–79
Goldwater, Barry, 351
  presidential campaign of (1964), 355–62, 440, 441, 449, 452
  Thurmond's support for, 11–12, 295, 356–62, 375, 378, 380, 400, 495
Gong Lum v. Rice, 244, 246
Goodin, Mark, 15–16, 455–56, 461, 493
Goodman, Andrew, 351–52
Goodwin, Richard, 369
Gore, Albert, 284, 293, 297, 309
Graham, Frank Porter, 214
Graham, Fred, 388, 409
Grassley, Charles, 459, 473
Gray, Martin W., 19
Great Society, 441
Greenville News, 111–12, 151, 173, 304
Greneker, T. B., 56
Griffin, Jean, 119
Griffin, Marvin, 277
Griffin, Robert, 396, 433
Guihard, Paul, 331
gun control, 441

Hamburg Riot (1876), 20–21, 463
Hamilton, Alexander, 338
Hammond, James H., 44
Hann, J. C., 67
Harlan, John Marshall, 275
Harrington, Oliver W., 103
Harris, Fred, 425
Harrison, Benjamin, 24
Harrison, Pat, 373
Haskell, Alexander C., 22
Hastie, William H., 187–88
Hatch, Orrin, 459, 470, 471, 474, 475
Haynsworth, Clement F., 405–7, 410, 411
Health, Education and Welfare Department (HEW), U.S., 419, 423
Heflin, Howell, 472, 490, 492
Helms, Jesse, 338, 436, 437–38, 448, 456, 468, 475, 483, 494–96
Henderson v. U.S., 208
Hennings, Thomas C., Jr., 290
Herbers, John, 368
Herbert, R. Beverly, 309
Hill, Anita, 496
Hill, Delmas C., 244
Hill, Lister, 13, 139, 140, 292, 358
Hill, Oliver, 247
Hinton, James M., 117, 118, 141, 150, 215, 217–18, 225
Hoey, Clyde R., 139
Hollings, Ernest F., 231–32, 307, 311, 383, 386, 412, 413, 426, 492
  segregation as viewed by, 271, 306, 334, 428, 436
  voting rights supported by, 428, 436, 475–79, 480
Hooks, Benjamin, 473
Hoover, Herbert, 37
Hoover, J. Edgar, 324–25
Hospital Advisory Council, 200, 213
House Judiciary Committee, 433, 434
House Rules Committee, 391
House Un-American Activities Committee (HUAC), 330
housing, 248, 381
  legislation for, 9–10, 380, 389, 390, 391
  segregation in, 275, 319, 320, 341, 380, 487
Housing and Urban Development Department (HUD), U.S., 390, 437–38
Houston, Charles, 222
Hruska, Roman L., 410
Hughes, Langston, 75
Humphrey, H. H., 163, 165, 166, 167
Humphrey, Hubert H., 164, 165, 288, 348–49, 385, 411, 425
  presidential campaign of (1968), 400, 440
  as vice president, 356, 359, 361, 369
Hunt, Jim, 495
Hurst, E. H., 328
Huxman, Walter, 244, 245
Hyde, Henry J., 467

Internal Revenue Service (IRS), 421
"interposition," 281–82, 286
interracial marriage, 47, 63–64, 202, 289
Interstate Commerce Act (1887), 208

Jackson, Jesse, 466
Jackson, Jimmie Lee, 367, 369
Jackson, Robert, 250, 275
Jackson *Clarion Ledger,* 130, 134, 143, 255, 328
James, William, 481
Japanese Americans, internment of, 243
Javits, Jacob, 319–20, 340–41
Jeffersonian Democrats, 134
Jester, Beauford, 158, 182
Jim Crow laws, 30
John Birch Society, 326
Johnson, Frank, Jr., 371
Johnson, Lyndon B., 393, 454
  civil rights program of, 291, 292, 297, 298, 299, 309, 317, 348, 350–51, 352, 353, 368, 369–70, 371, 373–78, 380–81, 385, 386, 390, 402, 451
  presidential campaign of (1964), 356, 359, 361, 362
  as presidential candidate (1960), 306, 311
  reelection decision of, 389, 391, 431
  as Senate majority leader, 284, 286, 291, 299
  Thurmond and, 294, 299, 304, 308, 347–48, 370, 374, 390
  as vice president, 311–12
Johnson, Olin, 40, 50
Johnson, Paul, 373
Johnson, W. W. (Hootie), 484
Johnston, Gladys, 135, 206
Johnston, Olin D., 204–6, 383, 458
  as governor, 45, 80, 81, 98, 209–10, 235
  segregation supported by, 117, 118, 130, 162–63, 254, 278, 279, 282
  as senator, 100, 117, 118, 130, 254, 329, 358
  senatorial campaign of (1938), 64, 65–66
  senatorial campaign of (1950), 179, 196, 200–216, 495
  states' rights supported by, 135, 160, 297
  Thurmond and, 13, 118, 148, 179, 215, 262, 263, 273, 425, 446
Johnston, Sallie, 207
Jones, Ira B., 31, 36
Justice Department, U.S., 125, 203, 289, 304–5, 332, 350, 377–78, 470

KAL 007 shootdown, 15–16
Kansas, segregation in, 243–45
Katzenbach, Nicholas deB., 375, 378
Kefauver, Estes, 284, 287, 293, 297, 309
Kennedy, Anthony M., 492
Kennedy, Edward M. (Ted), 388, 425, 453, 455, 458, 459, 469, 473, 487, 489–90, 495
Kennedy, John B., 236–37
Kennedy, John F., 287, 482
  assassination of, 317, 347, 348, 353
  civil rights program of, 314, 315–16, 319, 322–23, 328, 331, 332, 336–37, 338, 340, 348, 494–95
  freedom riders and, 322–23
  presidential campaign of (1960), 306, 311–14, 317, 319
  Thurmond's views on, 332, 342, 347
Kennedy, Margie Prescott, 236–37
Kennedy, Robert F., 314, 322, 323, 335, 343, 349, 385
Kentucky, 175, 190
King, Martin Luther, Jr., 270, 298, 314, 344, 439
  assassination of, 364, 391
  as civil rights leader, 325, 336, 345, 366, 368, 371, 382
  freedom riders and, 320–21, 323
  holiday named for, 481–84, 494
  Johnson and, 352
  Thurmond's views on, 326, 337, 370, 374, 377, 387, 481–84
Knowland, William, 292, 295, 296
Kuchel, Thomas H., 349
Ku Klux Klan (KKK), 16, 44, 71–72, 129, 135, 220, 271, 321, 346, 351–52, 372

Laney, Ben, 130, 144, 157, 158–59, 167, 168, 175, 178–79, 181, 193, 198
Langer, William, 296
Latimer, S. I., Jr., 238
Lausche, Frank, 297, 354
Laxalt, Paul, 473
Lee, George, 268–70, 272, 288, 376, 426, 457
Lee, Herbert, 327–28
Lee, Robert E., 176, 179
Legal Defense and Educational Fund, 330, 422
Lehman, Herbert, 302
"Let's Look at '48" (Thurmond), 123
Lewis, John, 368
Lide, L. D., 59, 60, 62
Life, 122, 210, 403, 406
Lighthouse and Informer, 101, 199, 211–12, 214, 215, 235, 265
Lincoln, Abraham, 47, 377, 482
Littlejohn, Bruce, 98–99
Little Rock, Ark., 270, 300–303

Liuzzo, Viola, 371–72
Lodge, Henry Cabot, 313
Logue, George, 73–74
Logue, Sue, 73–74
Long, John D., 79, 85
Long, J. Reuben, 69
Long, Russell, 488
Los Angeles riots (1965), 379–80
Los Angeles riots (1992), 9, 390–91
Lott, Trent, 494
Louisiana, 116, 181, 189, 190
loyalty oaths, 45–46, 62, 149–53, 161, 169–73, 174, 192–94, 325, 366, 475–76
Lucier, James, 394
Lybrand, Dorsey, 235
lynchings, 25, 39, 60–61, 67–68, 69, 70–71, 199, 342
  legislation against, 13, 47–48, 63, 64, 65, 76, 111, 124, 125, 129, 133, 135, 145, 168, 290, 305–6
  in South Carolina, 22, 30, 31–32, 99–100, 102, 111–12
  Thurmond's opposition to, 99–100, 111–12

McCain, Tom, 463–66, 472, 485, 497
McCarthy, Joseph, 326
McClellan, John, 308, 329, 389
McClenney, E. H., 152
McCord, James N., 131
McCormack, John W., 167
McCorvey, Gessner T., 139
McCray, John H., 101–2, 103, 117, 118, 150, 160, 161, 163, 199–200, 211–12, 215–16, 235
McDonald, Haywood, 470
McDonald, Larry, 15
McDonald, Laughlin, 470–71
McDonald, Tom, 470
McFall, T. C., 200, 201, 204, 212–13
McGill, Ralph, 159, 169, 174, 179, 180, 189, 313
McGovern, George S., 425, 430, 440
McGowan, Clelia, 75
McGrath, J. Howard, 135, 136, 142, 157, 160, 164, 176, 209, 213
McHale, Frank, 160
McKaine, Osceola, 82, 100
McLaurin, G. W., 208
McLaurin v. Oklahoma State Regents, 208, 244, 251
McLeod, James, 85, 90–91
McNair, Denise, 345
McNair, Robert E., 385, 386, 410
McNally, Harold J., 228
McNutt, Paul, 169
Maddox, Lester, 439
Magnuson, Warren, 354–55
Mallory v. U.S., 394
Manning Richard I., 194
Mansfield, Mike, 341, 373, 376, 380–81, 409
March on Washington, 344, 345
Marshall, Thurgood, 107, 310
  as federal judge, 329–30
  as NAACP lawyer, 102–3, 113, 115, 116, 141, 170, 192, 218, 219, 220, 222–30, 246, 268, 314, 330, 363, 475
  as solicitor general, 363–64, 378–79
  as Supreme Court justice, 365, 378, 388–89, 448, 496
Martin, James B., 358
Martin, J. Robert, 111
Maryland, University of, 222
Mathias, Charles, Jr., 453, 469, 473, 480, 483
Maybank, Burnet R., 80, 106, 117, 130, 139, 206, 213, 239, 240, 254, 255, 256, 258, 265
Meharry Medical College, 138
Mellott, Arthur J., 244
Meredith, James, 330–33, 382, 451
Merhige, Robert, Jr., 424, 436
Metzenbaum, Howard, 487
Mickum, George, 252
Milam, J. W., 280–81
Miles, Richard, 382, 383
Miller, William E., 356
Mims, M. H., 51, 58, 59
Misner, Charles, 163
Mississippi:
  black political participation in, 23–26, 289, 494
  civil rights movement in, 134, 139, 143, 255, 268–70, 327–28, 336–37, 345
  Democratic Party of, 142–43, 163–64, 167, 169
  Dixiecrat movement in, 139, 142–43, 158, 159, 181, 189
  integration in, 330–33, 336–37
  NAACP chapters in, 268–69, 270, 280
  poll tax in, 269, 377–78
  Republican Party of, 415
  segregation in, 244, 277, 330–33, 358, 420
  violence in, 255, 268–70, 280–81, 289, 305–6, 323–24, 327–28, 331–32, 336–37, 338–40, 345, 351–52
  voter registration in, 381–82
  White Citizens' Councils in, 271, 278, 339
Mississippi, University of, 330–33, 371–72

Mississippi State University, 331
Missouri ex rel. Gaines v. Canada, 112, 114
Mitchell, Arthur W., 47
Mitchell, Clarence, 294
Mitchell, John, 405
Mitchell, Stephen, 263
Mondale, Walter F., 485
Montgomery Advertiser, 180, 271, 277
Montgomery bus boycott, 270, 288
Moore, Henson, 487
Moore, Leon, 236
Morgan, Charles, 346
Morgan, Robert, 458
Morrah, P. Bradley, 383–84, 386
Morse, Wayne, 261, 286, 297
Morton, Thruston B., 314
Moses, Bob, 327, 328, 336
Moss, Cebrun, 69
Moss, Thomas, 412–13, 418, 426, 428, 439, 453, 458, 498
Moyers, Bill, 348
Murray, Joseph, 68–71

Nabrit, James, Jr., 248–49
Nader, Ralph, 432
National Association for the Advancement of Colored People (NAACP):
  "black power" and, 382
  lawsuits filed by, 102–4, 105, 107, 110–11, 112, 203, 218, 240, 241, 243–49, 278, 279, 363, 422
  Marshall as lawyer for, 102–3, 113, 115, 116, 141, 170, 192, 218, 219, 220, 223–30, 246, 268, 314, 330, 363, 475
  in Mississippi, 268–69, 270, 280
  primary laws investigated by, 82, 94, 102–11
  in South Carolina, 14, 32, 48, 75–76, 133–34, 279
  Thurmond's criticism of, 196, 203, 211, 286, 288, 303, 309, 311, 313, 330, 336
  white harassment of, 79, 411
National Education Association, 420, 443
National States' Rights Bureau, 198
Neas, Ralph, 473, 474, 486, 489, 490, 491
Nettles, Stephen, 71–72
New Deal, 65, 66, 441
Newsweek, 47, 81, 187, 399
New York Times, 100, 135, 157–58, 286, 336, 378, 400, 414, 417
Nicholson, Alfred W., 472
Nixon, Julie, 402
Nixon, Richard M., 412, 454
  civil rights as viewed by, 402, 409, 420, 421, 424
  presidential campaign of (1960), 313, 314, 317
  presidential campaign of (1968), 396–400, 401, 451, 452
  presidential campaign of (1972), 415, 425, 430
  resignation of, 431, 432, 433–34
  Supreme Court appointments of, 402–3, 404, 405–7, 408–10, 434
  Thurmond's support for, 365, 397–400, 408, 417, 421, 425, 431–34, 452
  as vice president, 287, 288, 296
  in Watergate scandal, 431–34, 489
North Carolina:
  civil rights movement in, 316
  Dixiecrat movement in, 175, 181, 184, 190
  senatorial races in, 195–96, 214, 494–96
Novak, Robert, 449
"nullification," 38, 281, 286
Nunn, Sam, 436

O'Connor, Sandra Day, 459–62
O'Donnell, John, 242–43
Oklahoma, University of, 208, 244
Old, William, 281
O'Neal, Del, 85
Operation PUSH, 466
Oswald, Lee Harvey, 347

Panetta, Leon, 420
Parker, John J., 224, 226, 227, 228, 230–31, 232, 234, 242, 278
Parker, Mack Charles, 305–6
Parker, Marshall, 383, 386
Parks, Rosa, 270, 288
Pastore, John, 344
Patterson, John, 317, 322, 323
Peace, Roger, 357
Pearce, John Ed, 186–87
Pearl Harbor attack, 243
Pearson, Drew, 201
Pearson, Levi, 195, 218–19
Pearson v. County Board of Education, 218–19
Pepper, Claude, 156–57, 214
Percy, William Alexander, 63
Peters, James S., 148
Pickens, Francis B., 18
Plessy v. Ferguson, 30, 208, 225, 232, 244, 245, 246, 249, 250, 251, 252, 275
"Politics of 1948, The" (Clifford), 129

poll tax, 13, 23, 76, 96, 102, 125, 129, 133, 145, 181, 199, 204, 269, 328–29, 374, 376–78, 479
Pope, Thomas, 98–99
Popham, John N., 140
Powell, Adam Clayton, Jr., 275
Powell, Lewis F., 436, 489, 492
Prettyman, E. Barrett, Jr., 250
Price, James H., 113
Prince Edward County, Va., 246–48, 278
Progressive Democratic Party, 82, 101, 117, 149–50, 159, 160, 161, 162, 163, 170, 172–73
Progressive Party, 102, 156
Prohibition, 146
Promised Land School, 231–32
Proxmire, William, 296
Public Works Administration (PWA), 247
Purvis, Melvin, Jr., 485

race relations, 12, 17, 46, 78, 230, 364
  "doll test" and, 228–29
  economic impact of, 132
  "separate but equal" doctrine and, 30, 33, 97, 114, 118, 150, 178, 208, 225, 228, 233, 234, 240, 244, 246, 250, 252, 253–54, 277, 285, 416
  terminology of, 381–82
  Thurmond's views on, 9–10, 48, 53–54, 63, 67, 74, 82, 90, 138, 150, 185, 198–99, 272, 497–98
Race Relations Committee, 279
racism:
  democratic ideals vs., 77, 81
  in political campaigns, 30–31, 39, 41, 63, 64–67, 385
  states' rights and, 186–87, 191, 192
  of Thurmond, 14, 29–30, 39, 41, 48, 147, 185–88, 191, 192, 211–12, 214–15, 265, 417, 427, 448, 449–50, 480
Raleigh *News and Observer,* 179, 190, 191
Ramage, C. J., 53, 56
Randolph, A. Philip, 76
rape, 31–32, 39, 67–68, 70
Rauh, Joseph L., 165
Ravenel, Arthur, Jr. (Pug), 380, 415, 441–51
Ray, James Earl, 391
Rayburn, Sam, 167, 286
Reagan, Ronald:
  civil rights legislation and, 454–55, 468, 480, 485
  as presidential candidate, 396, 397–99, 440, 448
  Supreme Court nominations of, 459–62, 486–93
Redding, Louis Lorenzo, 245, 246
"Red Shirt" campaign, 20–21, 135
Reeb, James, 368, 369
Reed, Roy, 367
Reed, Stanley, 250, 252, 253
Rehnquist, William H., 405, 486–87
Republican National Conventions:
  of 1948, 154
  of 1952, 243
  of 1956, 287
  of 1968, 396–400
Republican Party:
  black support for, 288, 314
  civil rights issue in, 181, 287, 288, 349, 350, 368, 468
  Southern influence of, 12, 25, 47, 138, 176, 265, 266, 318, 358, 362, 365, 386, 397, 415, 424, 452, 457, 493–94, 495
  "southern strategy" of, 365
  Thurmond and, 11–12, 313–14, 318, 356–62, 383, 450, 452, 455, 457–58, 485
Reston, James, 299, 355
Rice, Clay, 103
Rice, John I., 103, 151, 152
Richardson, Elliot, 489
Richmond News Leader, 281, 333
Richmond Times-Dispatch, 191, 424
Riley, Richard, 461, 476–77, 484
riots, race, 379–80, 381, 386–87, 390–91, 393
Rivers, E. D., 140–41
Rivers, L. Mendel, 217
Robertson, Carole, 345
Robertson, Pat, 493
Robinson, Spottswood, 247, 248
Rockefeller, Nelson, 396, 397–98, 399
Roe v. Wade, 462
Rogers, Joseph O., 385
Rogers, S. Emory, 223, 224, 271, 275–76, 279
Roosevelt, Eleanor, 130, 325
Roosevelt, Franklin D., 37, 38, 47, 54, 64, 65, 66, 76–79, 90, 130, 136, 225, 288, 454
Roosevelt, Theodore, 24, 25–26
Rowan, Carl, 224
Rowe, Gary Thomas, Jr., 372
Ruckelshaus, William, 489
Rusk, Dean, 343–44
Russell, Donald S., 335, 383, 405
Russell, Richard B., 294, 307, 340
  as presidential candidate (1948), 139, 159, 167–69
  segregation supported by, 131, 139, 181, 213, 254, 289–90, 291,

Russell *(cont.)*
297–98, 299, 301, 310, 325, 348, 360–61, 418, 420
Rustin, Bayard, 344, 345, 483

Sapp, Claude, 108
Scalia, Antonin, 486, 487
school prayer, 456
Schwerner, Michael, 351–52
S.C. Independents, The, 385
Scott, Roger W., 85, 86
Scott's Branch School, 217, 218–19, 228
Scranton, William, 356
Seals, J. W., 219
segregation, 60–61
busing and, 13, 270, 288, 320–24
constitutional rights violated by, 223–24, 227, 228, 230, 234, 242, 243, 245, 249, 253, 254, 276–77, 278, 284–85, 320, 420
demonstrations against, 335–40
economic impact of, 155–56
in education, 23, 33–34, 128, 140, 151, 195, 207–9, 223, 231–32, 244–45, 250–55, 268, 270, 274, 275–79, 286, 288, 341–42, 348, 381, 416, 418–24
"forced" integration vs., 76, 225, 277–78, 291, 302, 320, 334–35
in health care, 40
as ideology, 63–64, 130, 140, 151, 170–71, 177
inferior status conveyed by, 228–29, 230, 233, 239, 244–45, 251–52, 373
as institution, 196–97, 233, 339–40
legislation on, 129, 135, 137–38, 274–75, 289–306, 335–36, 348–51, 391–92
in North, 310–11, 319, 320, 341–42, 437
in public accommodations, 13, 124, 203, 208, 270, 316, 343, 347, 348, 349, 350, 352–53, 416, 490
states' rights and, 14, 147, 211–12, 279
Supreme Court rulings on, 12, 151, 195, 203, 207–9, 230, 238, 239–40, 241, 244, 249–55, 270, 275–79, 284, 285, 286, 302–3, 408–9
Thurmond's support for, 9, 12–14, 41, 48, 62, 90, 97, 128, 138, 145–47, 177, 184–87, 196, 198, 202–12, 265, 272, 285–86, 300, 302, 310–11, 317–18, 335–36, 341–42, 417, 450, 455, 469, 471, 497–98
in transportation, 13, 129, 270, 288, 320–24, 367
see also desegregation
Seigenthaler, John, 322
Seitz, Collins Jacques, 246
Selma-to-Montgomery march, 13, 367–69, 371–72, 431
Senate, U.S., 304, 366
cloture procedure in, 292, 351, 390
filibusters in, 13, 47–48, 64, 77, 168, 181, 291–92, 294–98, 299, 308, 328, 341, 349, 350, 351, 375, 376, 396, 469, 475
Southern faction in, 13–14, 64, 271–72, 275, 283–87, 293, 308, 341, 349, 350, 370, 375, 376, 377
Senate Armed Services Committee, 304, 326, 366, 444, 449, 453, 458
Senate Banking Committee, 366, 386
Senate Commerce Committee, 343, 347, 353–55, 366
Senate Judiciary Committee:
civil rights hearings of, 290–91, 294, 295, 309, 343, 347, 348, 372, 374, 389, 409
Constitution Subcommittee of, 305, 459, 466–67, 469, 474, 475
Eastland as head of, 329, 340, 365, 372, 373
Supreme Court nominations considered by, 392–96, 405–10, 456, 459–62, 486–93, 496–97
Thurmond as head of, 9, 454, 455, 456, 457, 458, 459–62, 466, 468, 469–74, 485, 487
Thurmond as member of, 386, 388, 393–96, 404, 444, 453, 488, 490–91, 496–97
Senate Veterans Affairs Committee, 444
Sevareid, Eric, 189, 325
sexual harassment, 496
Shand, Gadsden E., 151
sharecroppers, 26, 28
Sharpe, C. Melvin, 249
Shedd, Dennis, 455, 458, 461, 468, 469, 471, 472, 483, 484, 491
Short, Duke, 489, 493
Shull, Lynwood, 107–9
Simkins, Modjeska, 60–61, 66, 71, 77, 102
Simmons, Althea, 10, 16–17, 473
Simons, Charles, 235, 236, 406
Sims, Henry R., 120
Sitton, Claude, 314, 339
Sixteenth Street Baptist Church, 316, 345

slavery, 144–45, 333
Smathers, George, 214, 293
Smith, Ellison D. (Cotton Ed), 38–39, 41, 46–48, 64–67, 79, 80, 81, 106, 195, 206, 271
Smith, Farley, 271
Smith, Gerald L. K., 178
Smith, Lamar, 280
Smith, William French, 460, 468, 469
Smith, Willis, 214
Smith v. Allwright, 77–78, 80, 82, 103, 118
Sobeloff, Simon E., 279
socialism, 313, 317, 361
South:
  "black belt" of, 189–90, 293
  civil rights opposition in, 280–81, 305–6, 317–18, 332–33, 351–53, 355, 375, 376, 377
  "custom and tradition" in, 34, 41, 62, 67, 95, 106, 109, 127, 137, 144, 146, 147, 178, 186, 204, 240, 241, 242, 252, 276, 287, 292, 320, 321, 323, 355, 413, 414, 450, 481
  Democratic control of, 12, 47, 149, 166, 176, 202, 265, 267, 318, 362, 424, 439, 440, 441, 457, 493, 495
  economy of, 26, 35, 38–39, 44, 50, 64, 191
  New, 439, 440
  political change in, 16, 191, 239, 240, 254, 274, 275, 310–11, 353, 362, 377, 381, 414, 438, 439, 440, 457, 495
  political influence of, 133, 136, 139–41, 144, 146, 180, 189, 192, 313, 365
  Reconstruction period of, 19, 22, 80, 101, 108, 116, 138, 149, 176, 192, 203, 230, 255, 265, 267, 270, 313, 318, 362, 386, 415, 463, 476
  Republican influence in, 12, 25, 47, 138, 176, 265, 266, 318, 358, 362, 365, 386, 397, 415, 424, 452, 457, 493–94, 495
  Thurmond as representative of, 132, 144–45, 146–47, 187, 431, 435, 458, 462
  two-party system in, 12, 93, 142, 362, 380, 386, 400, 415, 457
  women in, 31–32, 47–48, 97, 151
  see also specific states
South Carolina:
  at-large elections in, 463, 464, 465, 470, 472, 485
  "Barnwell ring" in, 86–90, 93, 96, 98–99, 207, 231, 240
  black disfranchisement in, 20–23, 26, 29, 30, 32, 37, 77–81, 102–4, 110–11, 114–18, 141–42
  black education in, 33–34, 216–34, 241–42
  black mayors in, 451, 474
  black political participation in, 141–42, 149, 152, 159–63, 169–73, 192–93, 196, 199–200, 203–4, 213–17, 385, 386, 408, 410–11, 412, 462–66, 475–79, 480–81
  Chamber of Commerce of, 342
  civil rights movement in, 74–76, 134, 139, 478
  constitution of, 22–23, 30, 45, 78, 82, 96, 112, 114, 231–32, 241, 260
  Democratic Party of, 134, 136, 142, 148–53, 159–63, 167, 169–73, 198, 202, 203, 256–59, 260, 261, 262, 263–64, 383, 385, 411–12, 428, 442, 443, 448, 457, 464
  in Depression, 37–38, 40, 47
  Dixiecrat movement in, 139, 148, 158, 159, 180, 181, 189, 281
  economy of, 35, 37–39, 40, 44, 47, 50, 64, 84
  electoral procedures in, 96–97, 115, 117, 125, 257, 463, 464, 465, 470, 472, 477
  farmers in, 21–22, 42, 66, 84, 85, 195, 274
  federal funding in, 445
  General Assembly of, 54–59, 80, 98–99, 128, 148, 150, 197, 235, 241, 271, 334
  illiteracy in, 35, 97, 195, 231, 263
  legislature of, 41, 54–59, 78, 80, 83, 98–99, 114, 128, 148, 150, 197, 200, 206, 227, 235, 241, 271, 334, 386
  lynchings in, 22, 30, 31–32, 99–100, 102, 111–12
  NAACP chapters in, 14, 32, 48, 75–76, 133–34, 279
  National Guard of, 68, 70–71, 205
  party oath requirement in, 149–53, 161, 169–73, 174, 193–94, 366, 475–76
  political traditions of, 256–57, 258, 259, 260–61, 262, 263
  poll tax in, 23, 76, 96, 102, 199, 204, 479
  primaries in, 47, 256–60, 261, 262, 265, 442

South Carolina: *(cont.)*
  primary laws of, 77–81, 82, 91, 94, 96–97, 102–4, 114–18, 141–42, 151, 152, 161, 162–63, 172, 192–93, 196, 203, 204, 206, 363, 376, 462
  Republican Party in, 257, 266, 267, 364, 380, 383, 385, 410, 415, 417, 428, 457
  secession of, 109, 117, 255, 478
  segregation in, 30, 277–79, 333–35, 411
  Senate of, 41, 200, 334
  Supreme Court of, 67, 68, 71, 442
  voting rights in, 375, 462–66
  White Citizens' Councils in, 271, 278–79
South Carolina, University of, 49, 104, 105, 112, 205, 266, 450
South Carolina Association of Citizens' Councils, 282
South Carolina Citizens Committee, Inc., 79
South Carolina Industrial Commission, 200, 201, 206
Southern Christian Leadership Conference, 270, 298
Southern Democratic Party, 79
Southern Manifesto, 283–87, 300
Southern Regional Council, 151, 289
Sparkman, John, 13, 139, 140, 297, 436
Specter, Arlen, 459, 490, 491, 492
Stabler, John G., 60
State College, 113–14
States' Righter, 148
states' rights:
  civil rights vs., 76, 94, 153, 155, 166, 290, 305–6, 342–43
  education and, 283–84
  federal control vs., 38, 66, 109, 127, 129, 143, 178, 185, 198, 281–82, 301, 393
  law enforcement and, 64
  racism and, 186–87, 191, 192
  segregation and, 14, 147, 211–12, 279
  Thurmond's support for, 13, 14, 127, 138, 144–47, 168–69, 176, 178, 180, 183–87, 191, 192, 197–98, 203, 211–12, 214, 223, 256, 258, 274, 285, 299, 303, 317, 319, 332, 414, 416, 430, 436, 456, 480, 482
  voting rights vs., 115, 116, 374
  white supremacy and, 90, 222
  see also Dixiecrats
Stennis, John, 134, 136, 175, 273, 284, 307, 329, 436, 456, 488
Steptoe, E. W., 327–28
Stevenson, Adlai, 287
Stewart, Potter, 459
Stilwell, Sam, 317, 319, 348, 354
Stone, Marcus A., 85, 87, 88, 257, 266
"Strom's Little Acres," 406
Strom Thurmond Appreciation Day, 427
Strom Thurmond Foundation, 428
Strom Thurmond High School, 464
Strom Thurmond Pavilion, 14
Strom Thurmond Reports to the People, 273, 328
Strom Trek, 446–47
Student Nonviolent Coordinating Committee (SNCC), 327, 336, 366
Summerton, S.C., 217, 218, 219–20, 224, 279
Sumner, Charles, 18
Supreme Court, U.S.:
  busing supported by, 418–24, 436
  constructionists on, 397, 404, 408
  ethics issues and, 403, 405–7
  nominations for, 392–96, 402–10, 434, 456, 459–62, 486–93, 496–97
  segregation rulings of, 12, 151, 195, 203, 207–9, 230, 238, 239–40, 241, 244, 249–55, 270, 275–79, 284, 285, 286, 302–3, 408–9
  Thurmond's attacks on, 285–86, 287–88, 302–4, 364, 393–95, 398, 403, 404–5, 408, 423
  voting rights upheld by, 54, 74, 77, 114, 152, 377, 465–66, 467–68, 472, 474
  Watergate scandal and, 433
  see also specific rulings
Swann v. Mecklenburg, 418–19, 422, 438
Sweatt, Heman Marion, 208
Sweatt v. Texas, 208, 230, 244, 251

Taft, William Howard, 295
Talmadge, Gene, 140, 182
Talmadge, Herman, 103, 114, 140, 182, 190, 254, 292, 296, 307, 436
Tate, William K., 34
Taylor, Bill, 473
Taylor, John C., 51, 85
teachers, 34, 45–46, 62, 82, 84, 107, 123, 197, 217, 219, 222, 235, 247, 325
Tempting of America, The (Bork), 492
tenant farmers, 28, 195, 219
Tennessee, 175, 189, 419

Tenth Amendment, 94, 115, 127, 147, 164, 191, 281, 283
Texas, 77–78, 116, 144, 158–59, 181, 182, 185–86, 435
Texas, University of, 208, 244
Textile Industrial Institute, 204
Textile Workers Union, 405
Thomas, Calhoun, 55
Thomas, Clarence, 496
Thomas, George, 67–71
Thompson, M. E., 131, 140, 182
Thurmond, Allen George (brother), 26, 27, 28, 29
Thurmond, Eleanor Gertrude Strom (mother), 26, 27, 28, 95, 96
Thurmond, Gertrude (sister), 26, 60, 95, 120
Thurmond, James Strom:
- accommodation by, 177–78, 413, 414, 416, 456, 457, 458, 483, 496–98
- agricultural experience of, 26, 32, 33, 35, 48–49
- anticommunism of, 45–46, 324–25, 326, 332, 337–38, 347, 387, 393, 397
- as bachelor, 49, 119, 481
- "Barnwell ring" attacked by, 86–90, 93, 96, 98–99, 207, 231, 240
- black clients represented by, 40, 49–50
- black constituents of, 13, 14, 16, 50, 198–200, 378, 386, 412, 414, 417–18, 427–28, 453, 456, 458, 469, 480–81, 482–83, 497–98
- black opposition to, 199–200, 203, 211–12, 213–16, 235, 415, 448, 449–50, 481
- blacks appointed by, 200, 201, 204, 212–13, 412–13, 428, 439, 495
- black support for, 100–101, 133–34, 203–4, 415, 426, 448–49, 451, 481
- business support for, 283, 342, 448
- campaign style of, 54–59, 84–85, 91, 183–84, 204, 206–7, 209–11, 264, 361, 384, 429–30, 444–47
- childhood of, 26–32
- committee memberships of, 272–73, 274, 304, 360–61, 365–66, 386, 444, 449, 453, 458
- as conservative, 45, 274, 295, 326, 399, 428–29, 430, 455, 456, 458–59, 484, 495, 496
- constituency of, 13, 14–16, 44, 118, 262, 272, 283, 299–300, 306, 318, 335–36, 358, 383, 407, 414–15, 427, 431, 452, 469, 484
- "custom and tradition" upheld by, 34, 41, 62, 67, 95, 106, 127, 137, 146, 147, 178, 186, 204, 287, 292, 355, 413, 414, 450, 481
- in debates, 87, 88, 89, 262, 319–20, 348–49, 446, 451
- education of, 28, 32–33, 74
- federal government criticized by, 13, 384, 431, 441, 454, 481
- filibuster of (1957), 13, 294–98, 299, 300, 356, 456, 481
- fiscal reforms by, 42, 43–44
- as governor, 14, 53, 93–153, 197–200, 234–35, 260, 342–43, 450, 479
- gubernatorial campaign of (1946), 14, 83–92
- ideology of, 168, 176, 177–78, 187, 192, 272, 430, 452, 474, 480, 493, 497–98
- as judge, 53–74, 83, 88–89, 98, 150, 264
- labor support for, 90, 200, 407, 432, 448
- law practice of, 40–41, 49–50, 51, 58, 235–37, 238, 255
- legal education of, 39, 40–41
- legislation proposed by, 43–46, 99, 123, 125, 128, 150, 197, 303–4
- legislative record of, 90–91, 207, 235, 273, 383–84, 428, 429, 443
- loyalty of, 263–64, 318, 358, 431, 460
- lynchings opposed by, 99–100, 111–12
- male chauvinism of, 119, 460–62
- marriages of, *see* Thurmond, Jean Crouch; Thurmond, Nancy Moore
- military service of, 54, 74, 82–83, 89, 210, 234, 237, 301, 307
- newsletter of, 273, 308, 311, 328, 347, 374, 381, 395, 403, 404, 407, 417, 435, 437, 448–49
- physical appearance of, 33, 42, 95–96, 446
- popular support for, 89–90, 258, 259, 260–61, 297, 299–300, 314, 332–33, 342, 352, 360, 384
- presidential campaign of (1948), 11, 127, 148, 149–50, 156, 175–93, 198, 201, 212, 235, 349, 440–41, 448, 450, 456, 481, 498
- as president *pro tempore,* 459
- press coverage of, 35–36, 53, 61, 82,

Thurmond *(cont.)*
87, 97, 98–99, 122, 141–42, 178, 183, 184, 186–87, 190–91, 215–16, 234–38, 259, 266–67, 297, 355, 360, 384, 394, 399–401, 406, 413, 417, 428–29, 430
as progressive, 45, 97, 100–101, 123, 127, 128, 133–34, 178
racism of, 14, 29–30, 39, 41, 48, 147, 185–88, 191, 192, 211–12, 214–15, 265, 417, 427, 448, 449–50, 480
radio broadcasts of, 123, 150, 185, 320, 347, 370–71, 374, 381, 395, 404, 437
religious background of, 33, 72, 162, 187
reputation of, 35–36, 49, 53, 62, 74, 147, 175–76, 193, 215, 235, 299, 426, 447, 456, 469
resignation pledge of, 262, 267, 282–83, 287
rhetorical style of, 187, 206–7, 288, 302, 312, 397–98, 425, 435
as school superintendent, 36, 39–40, 41, 42–43, 50, 83, 498
senatorial campaign of (1950), 179, 196, 200–216, 235
senatorial campaign of (1954), 237, 240, 255–56, 257–67
senatorial campaign of (1960), 306, 308, 309
senatorial campaign of (1966), 360, 383–86
senatorial campaign of (1972), 401, 415, 424–31
senatorial campaign of (1978), 441–51
senatorial campaign of (1984), 456, 457, 461, 469, 484–85
senatorial campaign of (1990), 456, 457, 494
seniority of, 272, 283, 304, 366
Southern Manifesto and, 283–87, 300
South represented by, 132, 144–45, 146–47, 187, 431, 435, 458, 462
speeches of, 61–62, 96–97, 144–47, 177–78, 184–86, 236, 274, 283, 310–11, 312, 381, 477–80
as state senator, 41–52, 83, 88, 210
as teacher, 33–36, 83
television appearances of, 319–20, 340–42, 407, 432, 441, 445, 461
violence condemned by, 99–100, 111–12, 281, 324, 370–71
women appointed by, 200, 201
women's rights supported by, 97, 460–61
as write-in candidate, 257–67, 282, 450, 498
Thurmond, James Strom (son), 428, 430, 447
Thurmond, Jean Crouch (first wife), 119–23, 144, 155, 183–84, 188, 206, 216, 259, 274, 294, 295, 297, 306–8, 358
Thurmond, John William (brother), 26, 27, 28
Thurmond, John William (father), 26–29, 31, 39, 40–41, 49, 62, 498
Thurmond, Lybrand and Simons, 235
Thurmond, Martha (sister), 26
Thurmond, Mary (sister), 26, 28
Thurmond, Nancy Moore (daughter), 428
Thurmond, Nancy Moore (second wife), 400–402, 430, 444, 446–47, 449, 484, 493, 494
Thurmond, Paul (son), 446
"Thurmond Story, The," 384
Till, Emmett, 280–81
Tillman, Benjamin Ryan (Pitchfork Ben), 33, 96, 112, 335
as governor, 22–24, 30–31, 78, 85, 195
segregation supported by, 19–24, 335, 457, 463, 466, 495
Thurmond influenced by, 26, 28–30, 187, 260–61, 360, 386, 497, 498
Tillman, B. R., 42
Tillman, George, 20
Time, 183, 187, 373
Timmerman, Davis, 73
Timmerman, George Bell, 54–59, 98, 105–6, 107–8, 224, 231, 282, 307
Timmerman, George Bell, Jr., 105
Timmonsville Times, 14, 98–99
Tison, Sidney, 170, 171, 172
Tobias, Rowena W., 192–93
Today, 340–42, 432
"To Secure These Rights," 124–25, 127, 128, 138
Tower, John, 392, 453
Travis, William B., 18, 185, 471
Trout, Allan M., 184
Truman, Harry S., 234, 264, 279, 325, 454
civil rights program of, 94, 124–25, 127, 128–48, 149, 151, 158, 164, 181, 184, 185–86, 188, 208, 212, 316, 374

presidential campaign of (1948), 127, 154–69, 179, 181, 182, 183, 188–89, 400
South and, 128–48, 189, 198, 201–2
Thurmond's criticism of, 132–33, 136, 138, 144–47, 154–69, 177, 184, 185–86, 202–3, 207, 208, 213, 215, 223, 446
Thurmond's presidential challenge to, 11, 127, 148, 149–50, 156, 175–93, 198, 201, 212, 235, 349, 440–41, 448, 450, 456, 481, 498
Thurmond's support for, 123–24, 128, 130, 191
as vice president, 81
Tuck, William M., 188
Tuskegee Institute, 290

United Nations, 181
U.S. v. Classic, 115

Vann, David, 249–50, 252
Vardaman, James Kimble, 23–26, 30, 34, 38, 63, 195
Vaughn, George, 162, 163
Vietnam War, 366, 387, 391, 393, 425, 434
Viguerie, Richard, 448
Vinson, Fred, 242
Virginia, 54, 175, 179, 188, 281
segregation in, 246–48, 276, 278, 424
Voter Education Project, 382–83, 412, 426
voting rights:
"bailout" for, 467, 470, 474, 475
black support for, 268–69, 467
constitutional protection for, 115, 366, 374, 375, 376, 435, 465, 479
discrimination in, 78, 94, 101–2, 104, 171–72, 173, 309–10, 366–69, 416, 463, 465, 467–68, 470, 472, 474, 476–77
education on, 382–83, 470, 474
federal protection of, 293, 306, 308, 309–11, 377–78, 383, 402, 426, 467, 470
lawsuits on, 102–4, 114–18, 149, 151, 153, 156, 363, 376–77
legislation on, 364, 369–70, 372, 373–78, 409, 435–36, 462–81
literacy test for, 289, 328, 366, 375, 377, 378, 409
preclearance and, 377, 435, 465, 467, 470, 474, 485
record-keeping and, 304–5
registration drives for, 268–69, 272, 289, 306, 308, 327–28, 336, 377, 378, 381–82, 426, 462–64, 479
religious test for, 170, 172
requirements for, 23, 47, 116, 328, 366–67, 377
states' rights vs., 115, 116, 374
Supreme Court rulings on, 54, 74, 77, 114, 152, 377, 465–66, 467–68, 472, 474
Thurmond's views on, 13, 308–11, 327, 370–71, 373–78, 408, 434–36, 462, 466, 468, 469–81
violations of, 293–94, 467
white intimidation and, 72
Voting Rights Act (1965), 13, 373–78, 379, 382, 402, 409, 426, 434–36, 455
Voting Rights Act (1982), 11, 462, 463, 466, 472, 476–77, 480

Wakulla Springs conference, 130, 131–34, 137, 142, 175, 178
Walker, Edwin, 325–26
Wallace, George C., 317, 336, 344, 356, 367, 368, 371, 397, 400, 423, 430–31, 440, 451
Wallace, Henry A., 81, 127, 129, 130, 156, 189
Waller, Beulah, 176
Walsh, Denny, 406
Ware, Virgil, 346
Waring, Elizabeth Avery Mills Hoffman, 107, 109, 116, 173, 192, 202, 221–22, 233, 234
Waring, J. Waties, 203, 209, 389
black education as viewed by, 217
in *Briggs* decision, 196–97, 221–34, 253–54
Elmore decision of, 114–18, 123, 125, 127, 141, 161, 163, 170, 171, 173, 193
harassment of, 116, 172, 173, 221–22, 224, 234
"loyalty oath" ruling of, 169–73, 174, 192–93, 476
political transformation of, 94, 95, 105–7, 109–10, 240, 242
retirement of, 234, 242, 248
Thurmond compared with, 94–95, 105–6, 128, 155, 156, 174, 193, 234, 338
Wrighten decision of, 112–14, 123
Warren, Earl, 154, 242–43, 249, 250–54, 276, 302, 333, 364, 365, 389, 392, 393, 397, 402, 485
Washington, Booker T., 24, 482–83

Washington, D.C., 230, 242, 248–49, 253, 275, 391, 421, 450, 479
Washington Post, 297, 395, 417, 444
Watergate scandal, 431–34, 489
Watson, Albert, Jr., 385, 397, 410, 411–12
Weinberger, Caspar, 437
Weismer, William, 142
Welch, Robert H., 326
"We Shall Overcome," 340
Wesley, Cynthia, 345
West, John, 264, 266, 267, 410, 411, 412, 428, 439
White, Hugh, 254, 277
White, William S., 157–58, 286
White Citizens' Councils, 271–72, 278–79, 281, 302, 339
Whitehead, Matthew J., 228
white supremacy, 25–26, 63, 64–67, 79, 80, 81, 90, 107, 115, 117, 139, 147, 212, 222, 224, 233, 240, 386, 408
Whither Solid South (Collins), 133
Whittaker, M. F., 152
Wilkins, Billy, 492
Wilkins, Roy, 293, 310, 339–40, 346, 382, 411
Wilkinson, Horace, 176–77
Williams, Hosea, 367
Williams, Ike, 14, 415, 472
Williams, John Bell, 340–41
Williams, Ransome J., 85
Williams, Robert E., 179
Wirth, Gene, 134
Wolfson, Louis, 403
women:
  as political appointees, 200, 201
  rights of, 97, 460–61
  in South, 31–32, 47–48, 97, 151
  Thurmond's views on, 119, 460–62
Wood, A. L., 85
Woods, Robert, 449–50
Woodward, Isaac, Jr., 107–9
workers' compensation, 97, 205
Workman, William, 215, 233–34, 237, 257–58, 358
Works Progress Administration (WPA), 50
Wright, Fielding, 126, 131–32, 133, 134, 136, 143, 144, 175, 176, 181, 185, 188, 189, 193, 199, 202
Wrighten, John, 104–5, 112–14, 123
Wyche, C. Cecil, 105, 333

Yarborough, Ralph, 293, 297, 307, 354–55
Young Communist League, 344

Zeigler, Nick, 428, 429, 446

Picture Credits

1 Clemson University Library, Special Collections Unit
2 Clemson University Library, Special Collections Unit
3 University of South Carolina
4–14 Clemson University Library, Special Collections Unit
15 Ed Clark/*Life* Magazine/Time Warner Inc.
16 Clemson University Library, Special Collections Unit
17 *The New York Times*
18 UPI/Bettmann
19 University of South Carolina
20 University of South Carolina
21 AP/Wide World Photos
22 UPI/Bettmann
23 AP/Wide World Photos
24 Clemson University Library, Special Collections Unit
25 AP/Wide World Photos
26 AP/Wide World Photos
27 Clemson University Library—Special Collections Unit
28 Doug Gilmore—*The State,* Columbia, S.C.
29 AP/Wide World Photos
30 AP/Wide World Photos
31 UPI/Bettmann
32 Doug Gilmore/*The State,* Columbia, S.C.
33 Doug Gilmore/*The State,* Columbia, S.C.
34 Tom Reed